AF881082

ASCENT

CENTER FOR TECHNICAL KNOWLEDGE

3DEXPERIENCE CATIA 2022x Advanced Part Design

Learning Guide

1st Edition

ASCENT - Center for Technical Knowledge®
3DEXPERIENCE CATIA 2022x
Advanced Part Design
1st Edition

Prepared and produced by:

ASCENT Center for Technical Knowledge
630 Peter Jefferson Parkway, Suite 175
Charlottesville, VA 22911

866-527-2368
www.ASCENTed.com

Lead Contributor: Mark Potrzebowski

ASCENT - Center for Technical Knowledge (a division of Rand Worldwide Inc.) is a leading developer of professional learning materials and knowledge products for engineering software applications. ASCENT specializes in designing targeted content that facilitates application-based learning with hands-on software experience. For over 25 years, ASCENT has helped users become more productive through tailored custom learning solutions.

We welcome any comments you may have regarding this guide, or any of our products. To contact us please email: feedback@ASCENTed.com.

AS-3DE22-APD1-SG // RS-3DE22-APD1-SG

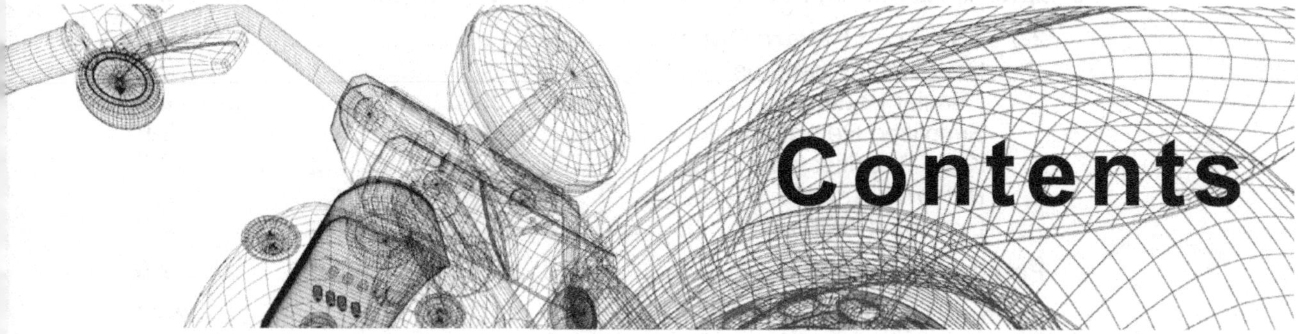

Contents

Preface

The *3D EXPERIENCE CATIA 2022x Advanced Part Design* learning guide is ideal for experienced CATIA users who want to extend their modeling abilities with advanced functionality and techniques. This extensive hands-on guide contains numerous projects focused on process-based exercises to give users practical experience while improving design productivity. Users will learn techniques for reusing data, tackling complex geometry, using wireframe, working through feature failure, and investigating the model with analysis tools.

Topics Covered

- Effective modeling practices and design methodology review
- Advanced multi-section solid and rib/slot operations
- Advanced draft and fillet creation and troubleshooting techniques
- Advanced patterning techniques and user patterns
- Power Copy creation and instantiation
- Design tables
- Catalog creation
- Creating and managing multi-model links
- Multi-body modeling techniques
- Performing Boolean operations
- Knowledge Templates
- Wireframe Lines and Curves
- Analysis Tools
- Feature Failure Resolution
- Thickness, Remove Face and Replace Face features
- Introduction to Automation

Prerequisites

- Access to the 3DEXPERIENCE CATIA 2022x version of the software, to ensure compatibility with this guide. Future software updates that are released by Dassault Systèmes may include changes that are not reflected in this guide. The practices and files included with this guide might not be compatible with prior versions (e.g., 3DEXPERIENCE CATIA 2021x).
- Completion of the 3DEXPERIENCE CATIA 2022x: Introduction to Modeling course and an additional 80 hours of CATIA experience are recommended.

Note on Software Setup

This guide assumes a standard installation of the software using the default preferences during installation. Lectures and practices use the standard software templates and default options for the Content Libraries.

Lead Contributor: Mark Potrzebowski

Mark Potrzebowski has been a trainer and curriculum developer in the PLM industry for over 14 years, with experience on multiple CAD systems, including Pro/ENGINEER, Creo Parametric, Inventor, and CATIA. Trained in Instructional Design, Mark uses his skills to develop instructor-led and web-based training products. Before joining ASCENT, Mark worked as a Technical Trainer with a focus on CATIA, Creo, and PLM systems. Mark holds a Bachelors degree in Computer Graphics Technology from Purdue University, West Lafayette, Indiana.

Mark has been the Lead Contributor for *3DEXPERIENCE CATIA: Advanced Part Design* since 2022.

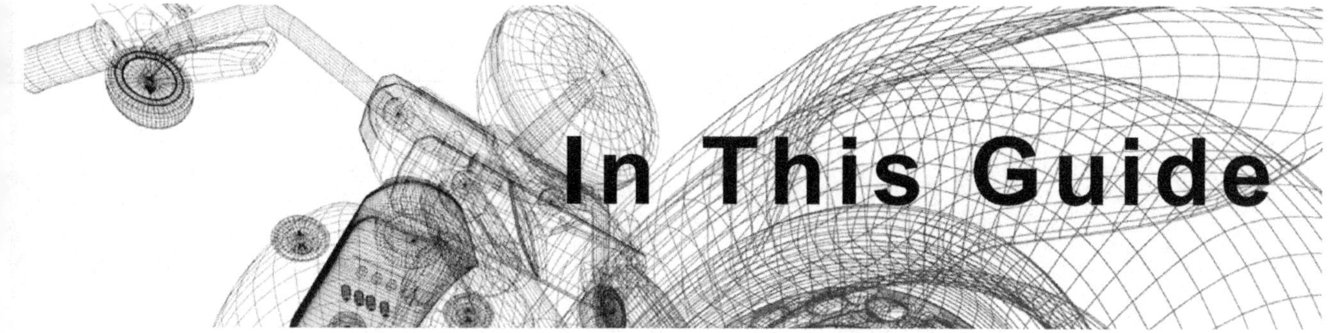

In This Guide

The following highlights the key features of this guide.

Feature	Description
Practice Files	The Practice Files page includes a link to the practice files and instructions on how to download and install them. The practice files are required to complete the practices in this guide.
Chapters	A chapter consists of the following: Learning Objectives, Instructional Content, and Practices. • **Learning Objectives** define the skills you can acquire by learning the content provided in the chapter. • **Instructional Content**, which begins right after Learning Objectives, refers to the descriptive and procedural information related to various topics. Each main topic introduces a product feature, discusses various aspects of that feature, and provides step-by-step procedures on how to use that feature. Where relevant, examples, figures, helpful hints, and notes are provided. • **Practice** for a topic follows the instructional content. Practices enable you to use the software to perform a hands-on review of a topic. It is required that you download the practice files (using the link found on the Practice Files page) prior to starting the first practice.
Appendices	Appendices provide additional information to the main course content. It could be in the form of instructional content, practices, tables, projects, or skills assessment.

Practice Files

To download the practice files for this guide, use the following steps:

1. Type the URL ***exactly as shown below*** into the address bar of your Internet browser to access the Course File Download page.

   Note: If you are using the ebook, you do not have to type the URL. Instead, you can access the page simply by clicking the URL below.

   https://www.ascented.com/getfile/id/dracaenaPF

2. On the Course File Download page, click the **DOWNLOAD NOW** button, as shown below, to download the .ZIP file that contains the practice files.

3. Once the download is complete, unzip the file and extract its contents.

   The recommended practice files folder location is:
   C:\3D EXPERIENCE CATIA Advanced Part Design Practice Files

   Note: It is recommended that you do not change the location of the practice files folder. Doing so may cause errors when completing the practices.

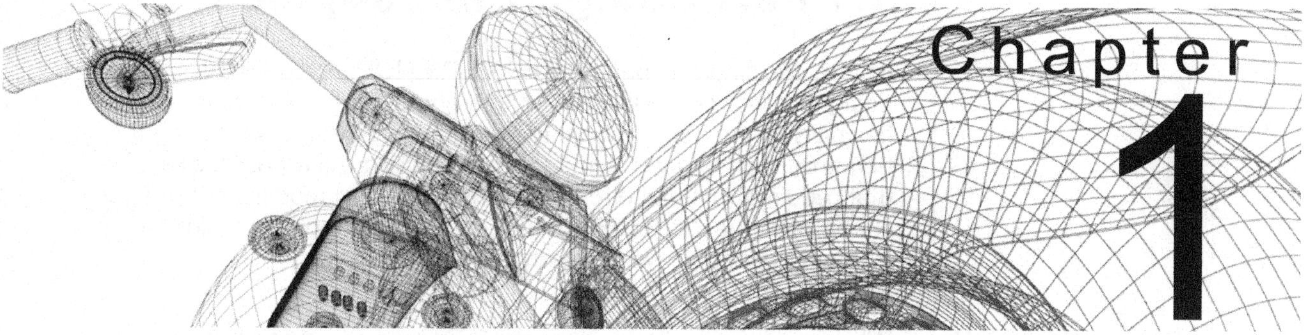

Part Design Overview

Starting with this chapter, you build on the fundamentals of modeling in 3DEXPERIENCE. You learn new techniques to help create and manage your part designs. These techniques help to ensure that a part design remains flexible and leads to the creation of robust models.

Learning Objectives in This Chapter

- Review the design intent items to consider when creating a new model.
- Review the tools available for manipulating a design.

1.1 Part Design Philosophies

Before creating any part in 3DEXPERIENCE, consider the design intent of the part. By doing so, you can maximize the flexibility of the design. Considering *what if* scenarios that might be introduced into the part helps you to create a robust model that requires minimal effort when incorporating modifications. Remember that 3DEXPERIENCE is a design tool. Consider the following questions when starting a new model:

Default Reference Planes

Why use default reference planes? Every part contains three default reference planes, as shown in Figure 1–1. They form a foundation for your model and cannot be deleted. Reference planes make an excellent selection as parents for subsequent features, thereby reducing the number of unwanted parent-child relationships.

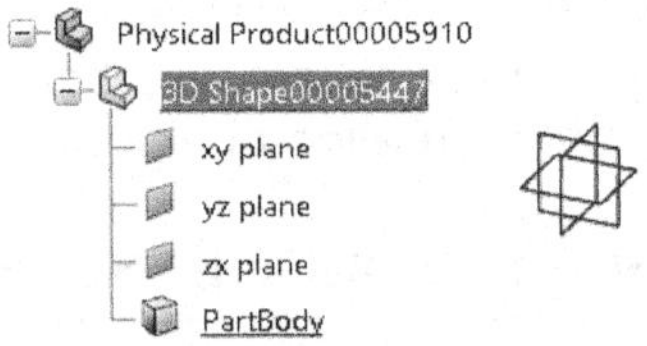

Figure 1–1

Base Feature

What is the best choice for the Base feature? The Base feature of the part is the first geometry feature added to the part (e.g., Pad, Spline, or Surface). Select a form that captures the fundamental shape of the model.

Active Body

Which body should be set to the active body in the model? As new features are created, they are added to the active body. These bodies can be used to perform boolean operations, group features, and separate model geometry. Features added to one body might not be accessible to other bodies in the same model. The active body is set by right-clicking it in the specification tree and selecting **Define in Work Object**.

Sketch Support

What is the best sketch support plane? It is important to carefully consider this reference, because it establishes parent-child relationships. Do not randomly select a sketch support simply because you think you must. This might create an unwanted parent-child relationship. Whenever possible, use a default reference plane to minimize the number of unwanted parent-child relationships. The selection of this reference also affects the default view of the model.

Sketcher References

Which entities should be selected as sketcher references? As you dimension and constrain your sketch, you select references that determine how the sketch reacts to modification. References can be removed and added as required in each sketch. Select references that incorporate your design intent.

Positioned Sketch

The use of a positioned sketch is highly recommended. It enables you to locate the origin of the sketch so that it updates correctly.

- Standard sketches are also called *Sliding* sketches. When the model is modified, it can reposition itself unexpectedly because its origin is not constrained.
- Positioned sketches enable you to develop the required parent-child relationships between features. For example, if the vertical axis of the sketch is constrained to a specific line or edge, the relationship is maintained throughout the design changes.
- If you need to translate, copy, or paste the sketch to another location, it can be done more easily with a positioned sketch.

Dimensions

Which dimensions are required to drive the design? CATIA is associative. You can take advantage of this with an intelligent dimensioning scheme. Place dimensions so that they enable modifications. The dimensions that are automatically added to the sketch by **Auto Constraint** are based on the references and sketched geometry that were originally selected. Additional dimensions can be added as required to capture the required design intent.

Which dimensions on the part would change? Always check that the dimensioning scheme works correctly by flexing the model. Test as many *what if* scenarios as possible.

Parent-Child Relationships

Which parent-child relationships work the best? Which parent-child relationships should be avoided? As mentioned earlier, parent-child relationships are established when selecting the sketch support, as well as all other references throughout the creation of a feature (e.g., dimensioning, using or offsetting edges, or the depth option).

Depth Options

Which limit type should be used to create features? The selection of the limit type affects the feature. Always consider the consequences if additional features are added or if other dimensions in the model are modified. Remember that some depth options result in parent-child relationships (e.g., **Up to next**, **Up to plane**, or **Up to surface**).

Formulas

Should any formulas be added? Formulas are user-defined mathematical equations used to capture and control design intent in a model. In 3DEXPERIENCE, you can use formulas in features, parts, and assemblies.

Feature Order

Which feature order best captures the design intent? The feature order of a model is important. For example, should a hole be placed before or after a Shell feature? Consider this type of question from the beginning to the end of the modeling process. Use the specification tree to easily review the feature order at any time during model creation.

Multi-body

Typically, all of the features that you create are added to the PartBody in the specification tree. This linear tree structure is acceptable for models with a low feature count or simple geometry. 3DEXPERIENCE enables you to create multiple bodies in a single 3D Part or a 3D Shape model. This enables you to structure your model based on your design intent. An important reason for creating multiple bodies is to be able to use the Boolean commands.

Using a multi-body approach to create a model provides the following advantages:

- Update times are reduced.
- Features are grouped by function or area, making the model easy to interpret.
- Bodies can be shown or hidden independent of each other.
- The creation of the part model becomes easier when the model is divided into smaller, functional areas.
- Features (such as a Shell or Fillet) can be restricted to a finite area of the model.

Boolean Operations

Boolean operations in 3DEXPERIENCE are a powerful design tool. The ability to combine feature-based modeling with boolean operations permits the creation of robust geometry. Working with various bodies in a single part file provides flexibility in design scenarios, promotes concurrent engineering, and enables the display and manipulation of multiple model states.

1.2 Maintaining Design Intent

*The **Feature Definition**, **Edit Parameters**, **Reorder**, and **Define in Work Object** options can also be accessed by selecting the geometry in the main window and right-clicking.*

Not all possibilities can be foreseen. 3DEXPERIENCE offers tools for manipulating the design when a change is required. They are described as follows:

Option	Description
Feature Definition	Attributes used to create a feature can be modified by double-clicking on the feature in the specification tree. The Feature Definition dialog box opens, enabling you to modify any aspect of the feature, including the sketch.
Sketch Definition	A section can be edited directly in the model. The Feature Definition dialog box does not need to be opened. Expand the feature in the specification tree and double-click on the sketch.
Edit Parameters	Dimensions that are associated with a specific feature can be modified.
Reorder	The feature order can be reordered for any number of features in the model.
Define in Work Object	Features can be inserted into the specification tree after the feature is selected.

Practice 1a

Capturing Design Intent in Sketcher

Practice Objective

- Use the sketcher tools to capture design intent.

The intent of this practice is to demonstrate how design intent can be captured using sketcher tools and techniques. As with every modeling process, you should use the simplest and most effective methods of capturing design intent. A proficient 3DEXPERIENCE user can create robust models that enable design changes to be made quickly and easily, resulting in predicable changes throughout the model.

Create the part using the following information:

- Figure 1–2 shows an isometric view of the completed pipe model.
- Figure 1–3 shows the design requirements that must be captured.
- Figure 1–4 shows the dimensioned drawing views.

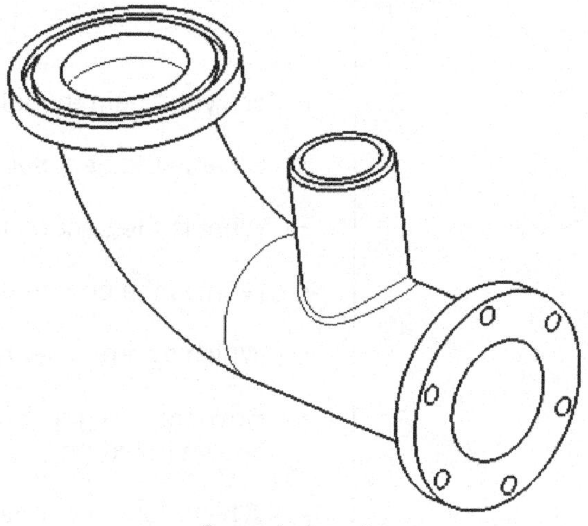

Figure 1–2

Design Considerations

Consider the following design requirements, as shown in Figure 1–3. Note that relations (formulas) cannot be used.

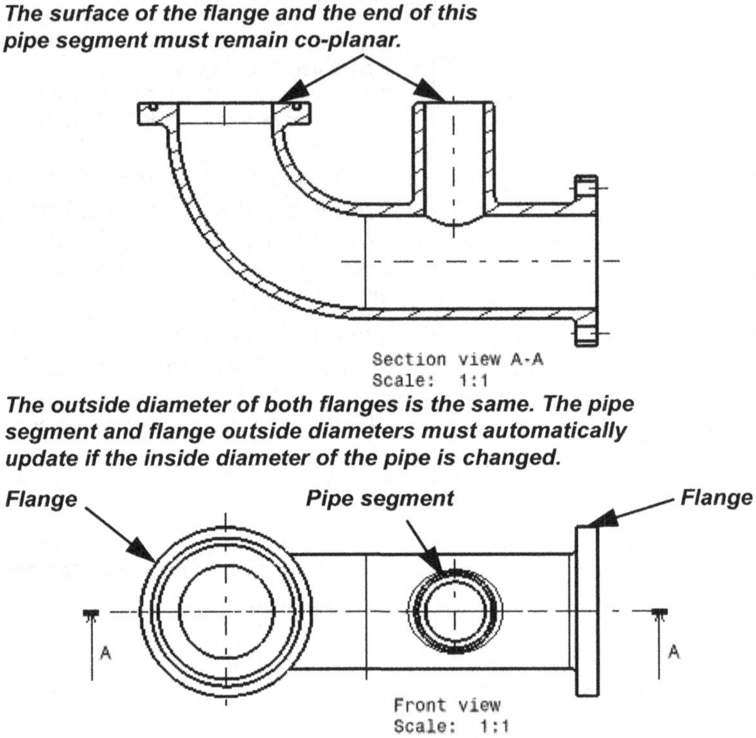

Figure 1–3

Before you begin modeling, ask the following questions:

- What is the best selection for a Base feature?
- What is the second feature going to be?
- What is the complete feature order going to be?
- Which references are going to be used in Sketcher?
- How are you going to incorporate the design requirements shown in Figure 1–4?
- Which depth options should be used?

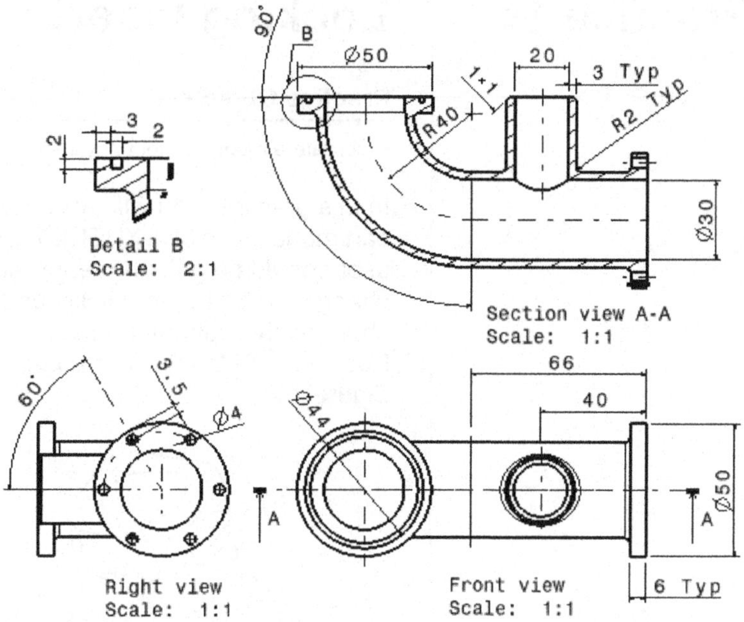

Figure 1–4

When you have completed the Pipe model, flex it by modifying the inside diameter of the pipe from *30* to **40**. The model updates, as shown in Figure 1–5.

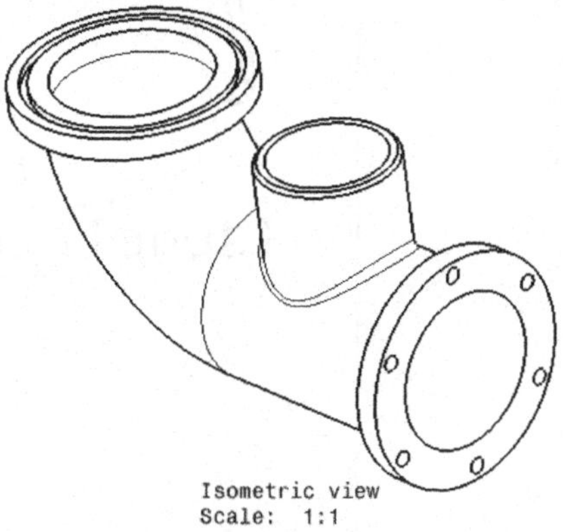

Figure 1–5

A step-by-step solution for this practice can be found in *Appendix C*.

Practice 1b Locking Insert

Practice Objective

- Create a model without any instructions.

In this practice, you will evaluate the level of your knowledge of part modeling in 3DEXPERIENCE. A proficient 3DEXPERIENCE user should be able to create robust models that enable design changes to be made quickly and easily, resulting in predictable changes throughout the model. You will create Pads, Holes, Pockets, and Drafts. The completed model is shown in Figure 1–6.

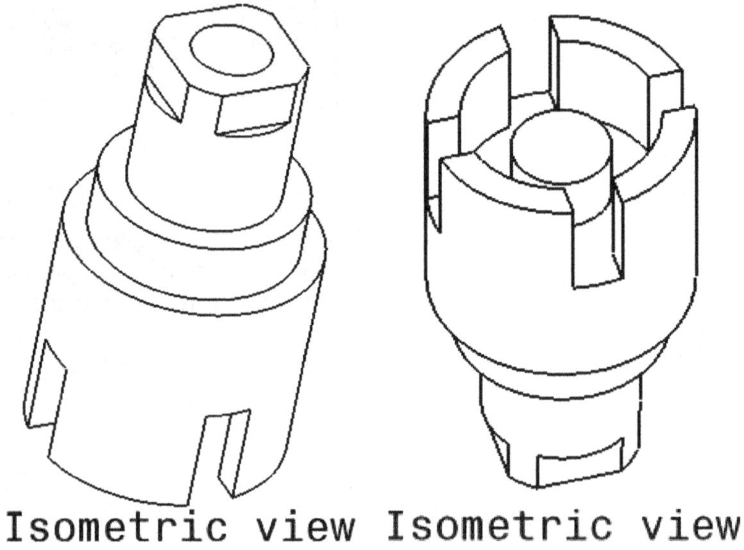

Figure 1–6

Use the drawing shown in Figure 1–7 to create the model.

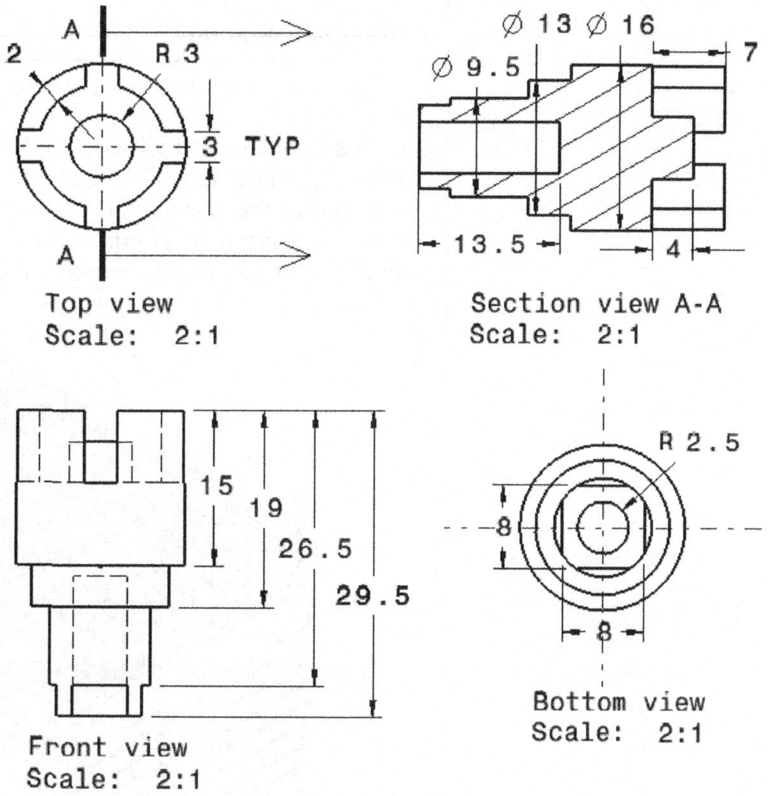

Figure 1–7

The part will be molded. To ease the process of removing the part from the mold, apply a **0.2deg** draft to the correct faces.

Practice 1c (Optional) Sketcher Analysis

Practice Objective

- Create a model with limited instructions.

In this practice, you will create the cooling fins for an aluminum heat sink extrusion. The base geometry has been created for you, as well as the sketch that defines the cooling fin geometry. Use the **Sketch Analysis** tool to solve the problem(s) with the sketch. The completed model displays as shown in Figure 1–8.

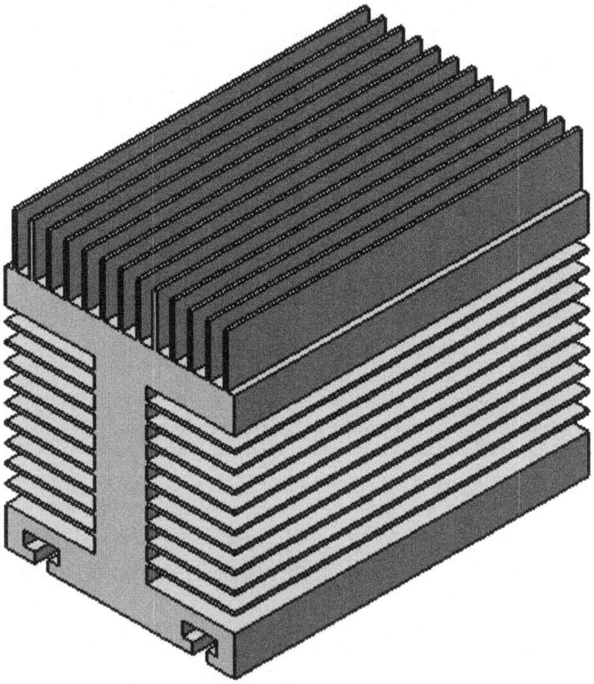

Figure 1–8

Task 1 - Open the part.

1. Import and open **HeatSinkExtrusion.3dxml** file for editing. When importing, type your initials followed by the dash symbol into the *Duplication string* field (e.g., **IA-**). The model displays as shown in Figure 1–9.

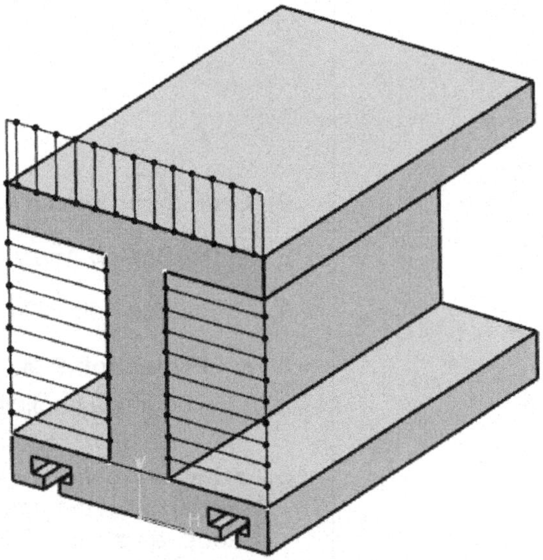

Figure 1–9

Task 2 - Create a pad.

1. Attempt to create a Pad feature using **Sketch.2**.

   The sketch cannot be used to create a Pad feature, as shown in the warning in Figure 1–10.

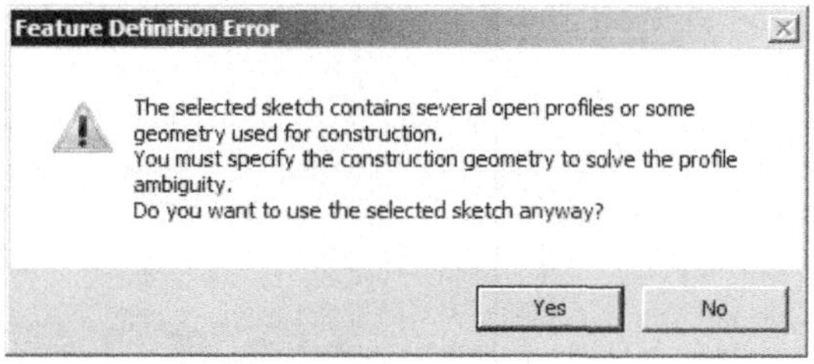

Figure 1–10

2. Click **No**.
3. Click **Cancel** to cancel the creation of the Pad feature.

Task 3 - Analyze the sketch.

1. Edit **Sketch.2** and click (Sketch Solving Status). The sketch status indicates that the sketch is fully constrained, as shown in Figure 1–11.

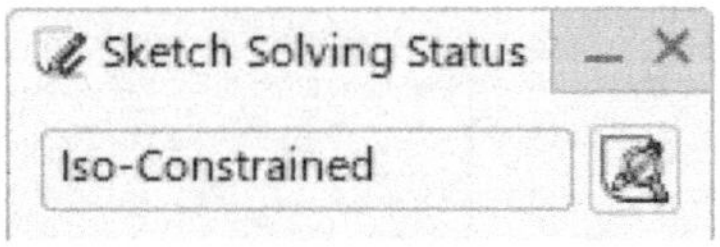

Figure 1–11

2. Click (Sketch Analysis).
3. In the Sketch Analysis dialog box, select the *Geometry* tab.
4. Press and hold <Ctrl> and select the following:
   - **Projection.9/Mark.1** and **Projection.13/Mark.1**.
   - The three Implicit Profiles at the end of the list.
5. In the *Corrective Actions* area, click (Set in Construction Mode) to set the appropriate sketch geometry in Construction mode, as shown in Figure 1–12.

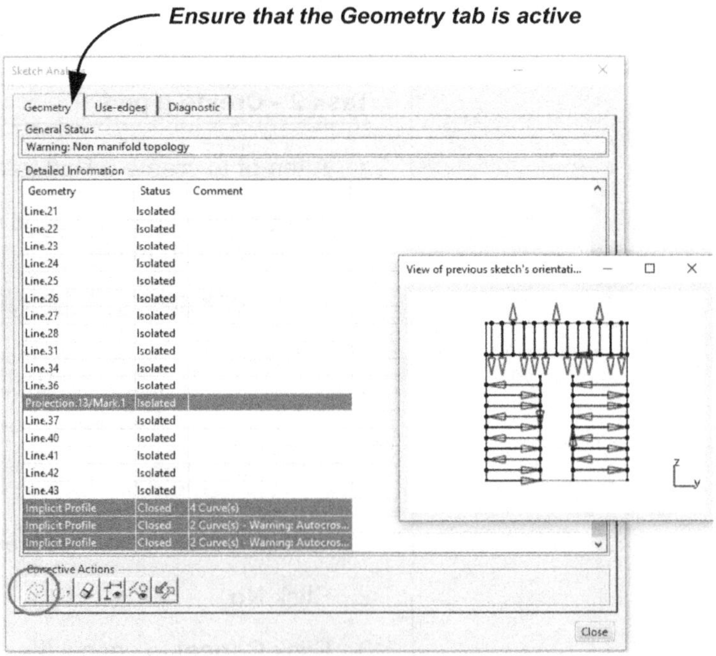

Figure 1–12

6. Verify that all of the geometry has a *Status* of **Isolated**, as shown in Figure 1–13.

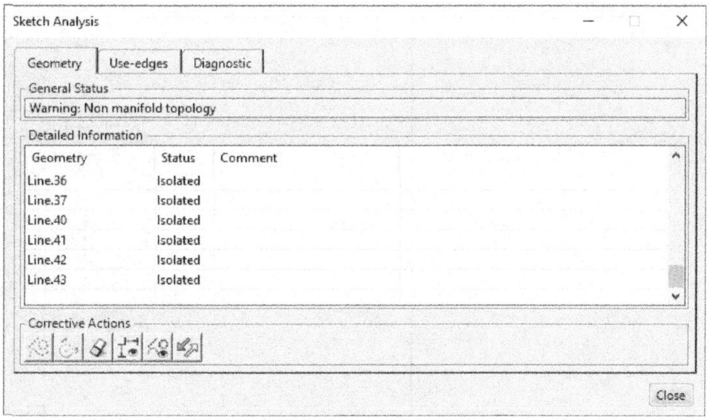

Figure 1–13

Once complete, the sketch displays as shown in Figure 1–14.

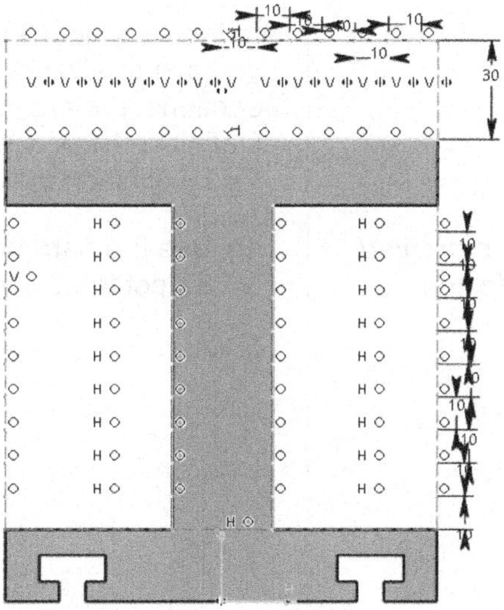

Figure 1–14

7. Click **Close**.

8. Exit the Sketcher app. The model displays as shown in Figure 1–15.

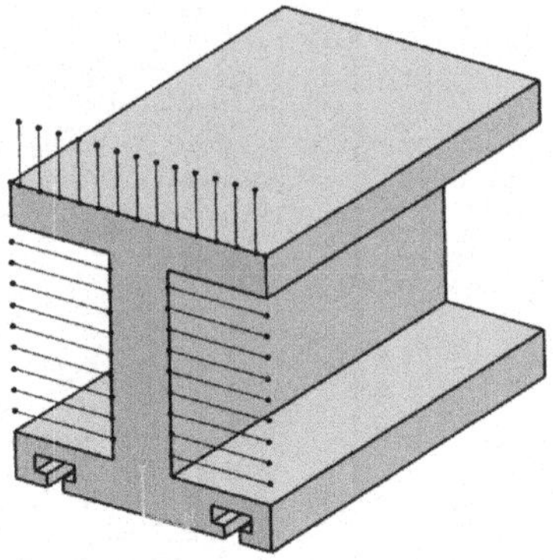

Figure 1–15

Task 4 - Create a Pad.

In this task, you will create a Pad feature using the sketch that you just analyzed. Because the sketch still contains open sections, the application continues to display the Feature Definition Error message until the **Thin** option is selected in the Pad Definition dialog box.

*Select **Yes**, if prompted to use the selected sketch.*

1. Use the parameters shown in Figure 1–16 to define **Pad.2**. Select the back face of the part for the up to plane reference.

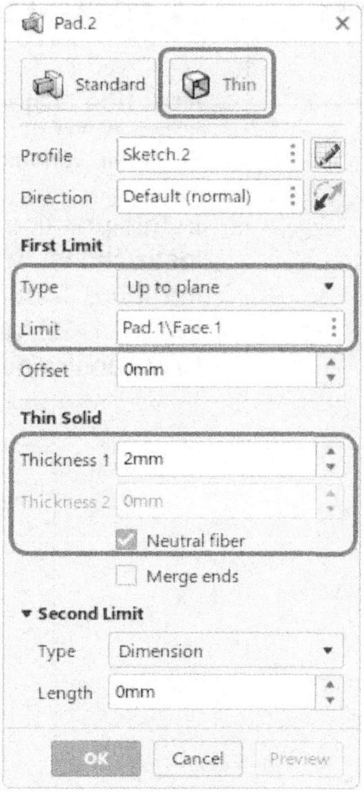

Figure 1–16

The completed model displays as shown in Figure 1–17.

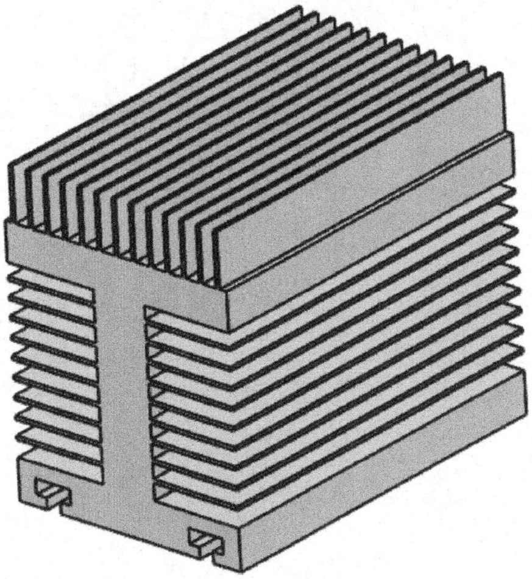

Figure 1–17

2. Save the model and close the file.

Practice 1d (Optional) Sketcher

Practice Objective

- Create various sketches.

In this practice, you will create several closed sketches without instructions. Try to complete at least three of the profiles shown in Figure 1–18, Figure 1–19, Figure 1–20, Figure 1–21, Figure 1–22, and Figure 1–23. Make sure all the sketches are fully constrained, and that no open profiles are in the sketches.

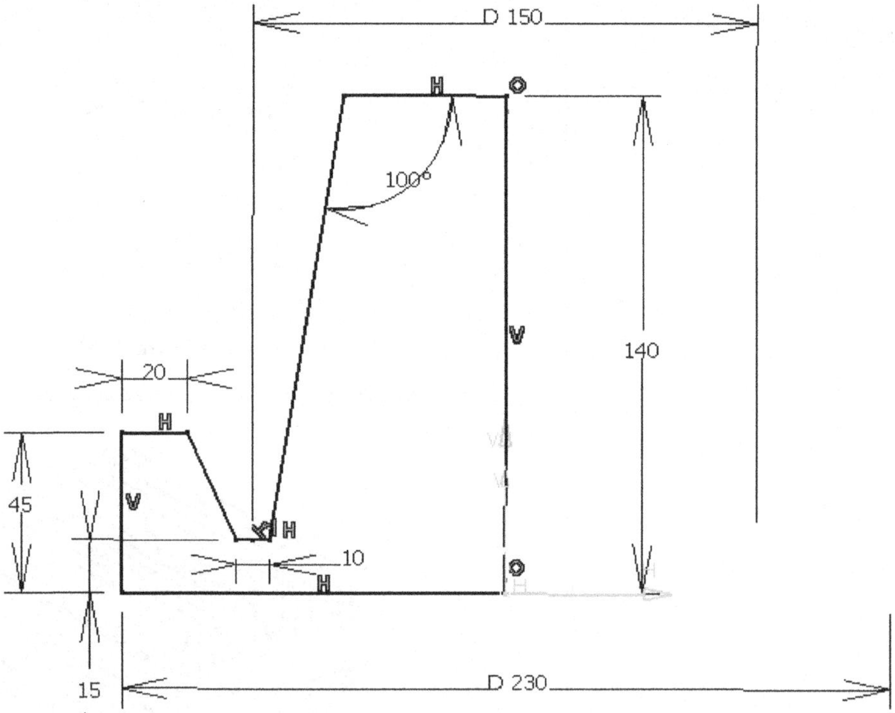

Figure 1–18

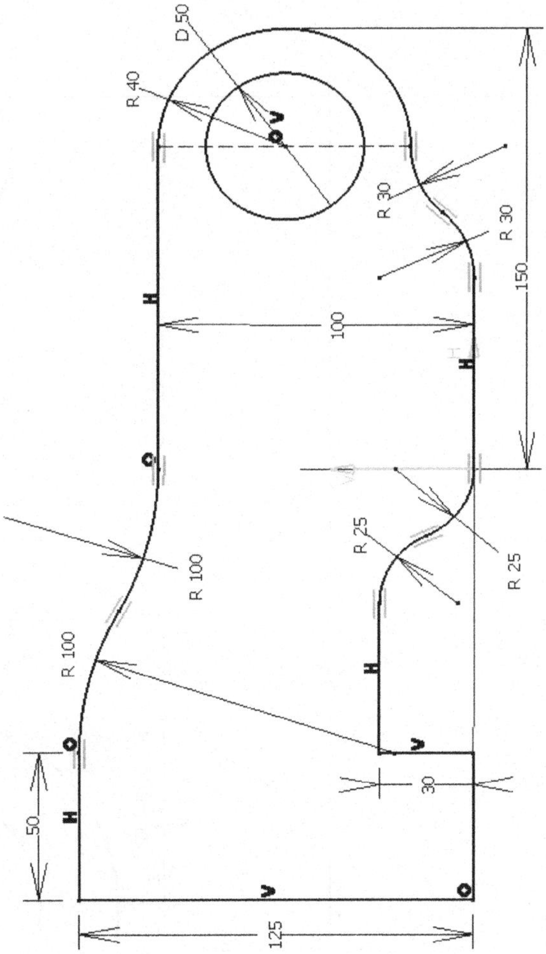

Figure 1–19

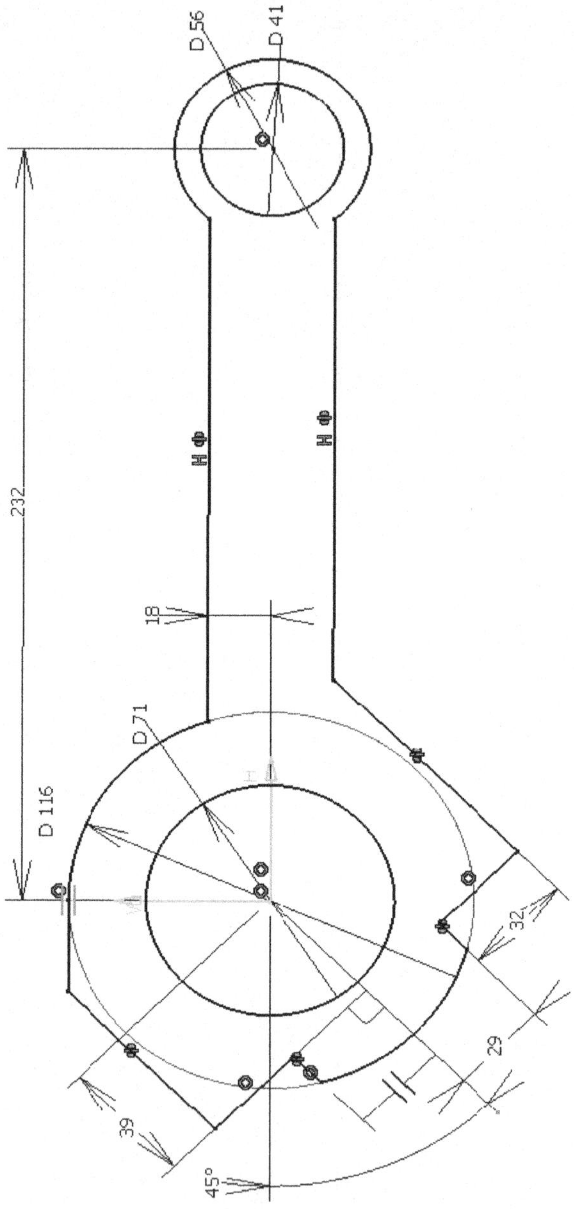

Figure 1–20

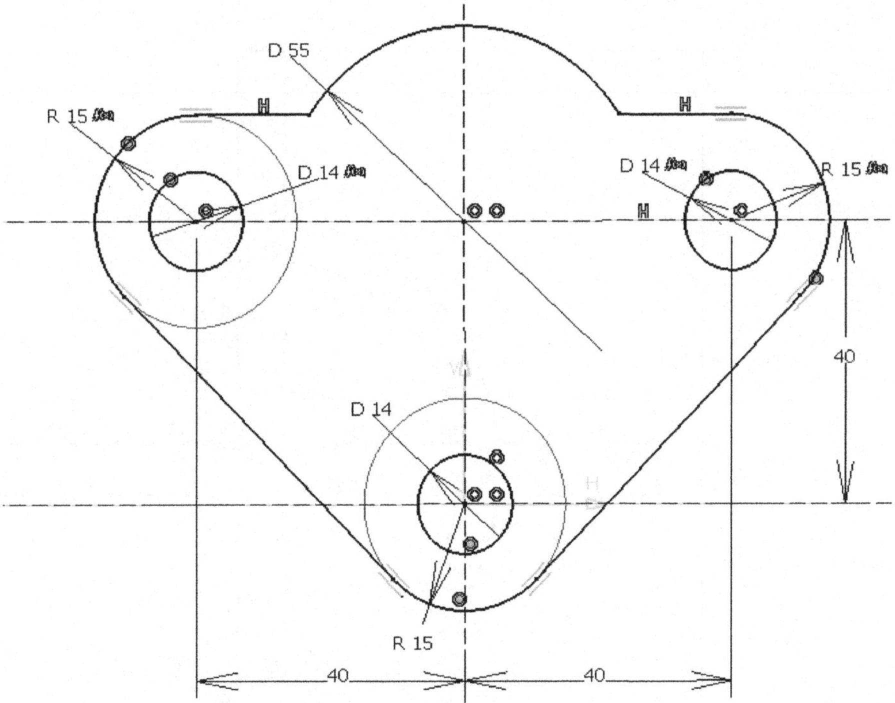

Figure 1–21

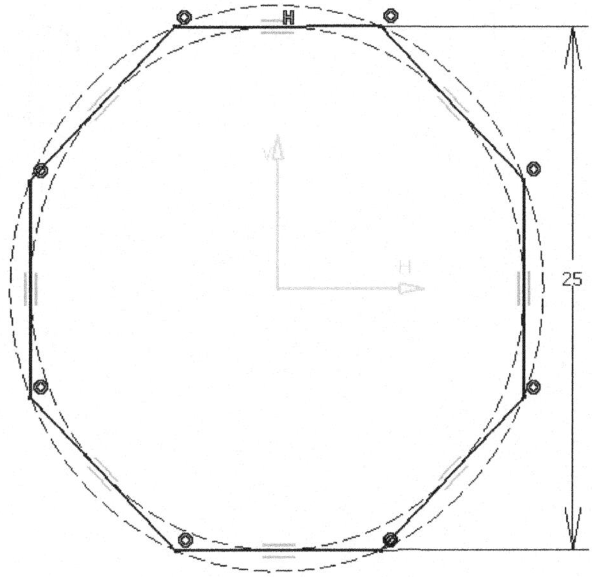

Figure 1–22

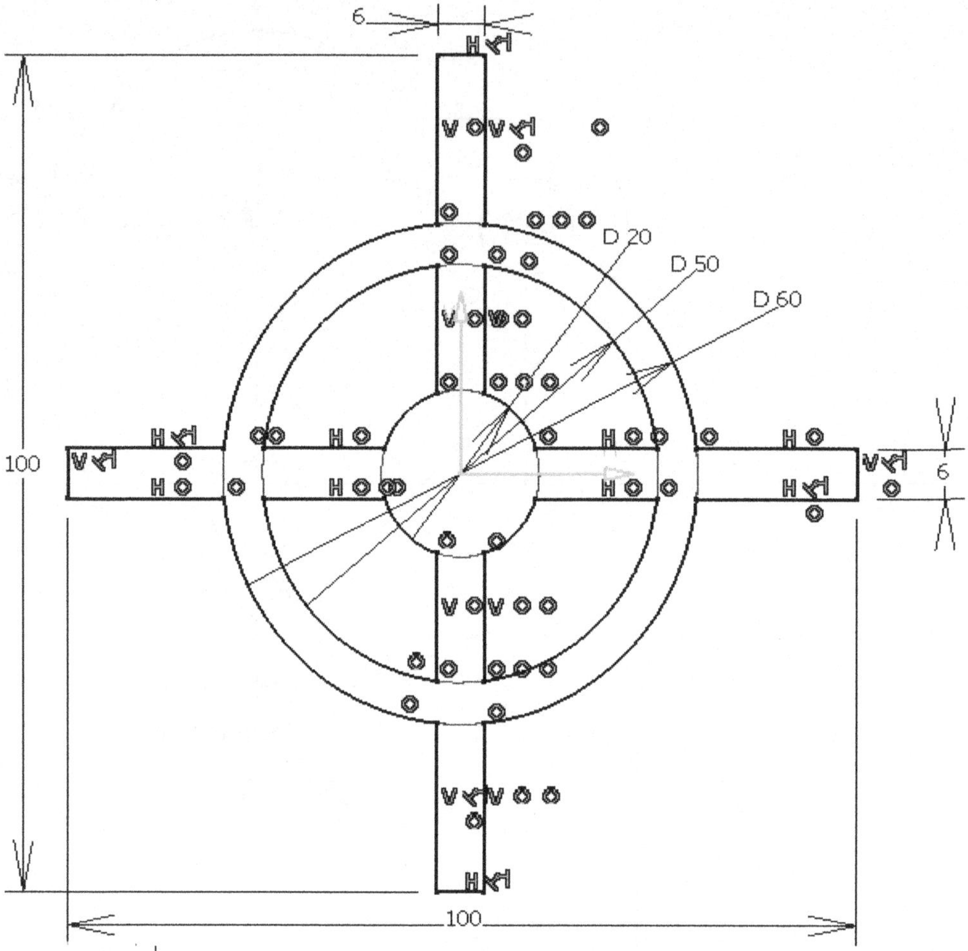

Figure 1–23

Chapter Review Questions

1. Why should you use the default reference planes?
    a. Every part contains three default reference planes, providing consistency from model to model.
    b. They form a foundation for your model and cannot be deleted.
    c. Referencing the default planes helps to reduce the number of parent/child relationships.
    d. All of the above.
2. One of the main problems with using a standard sketch is that when the model is modified, it can reposition itself unexpectedly because its origin is not constrained.
    a. True
    b. False
3. Why is it important to carefully select a sketch support?
    a. The selection of a sketch support dictates the type of feature being created.
    b. The selection of a sketch support creates a parent-child relationship.
    c. The selection of a sketch support dictates the dimensions and constraints that are available for sketching.
    d. All of the above.
4. What are the advantages of using a multi-body approach when modeling?
    a. Features are grouped by function or area, making the model easy to interpret.
    b. The creation of the part model becomes easier when the model is divided into smaller, functional areas.
    c. Features (such as a Shell or Fillet) can be restricted to a finite area of the model.
    d. All of the above.

5. To change the sequence in which features display in the specification tree, use _______.
   a. Resequence
   b. Regenerate
   c. Reorder
   d. None of the above.

Answers: 1d, 2a, 3b, 4d, 5c

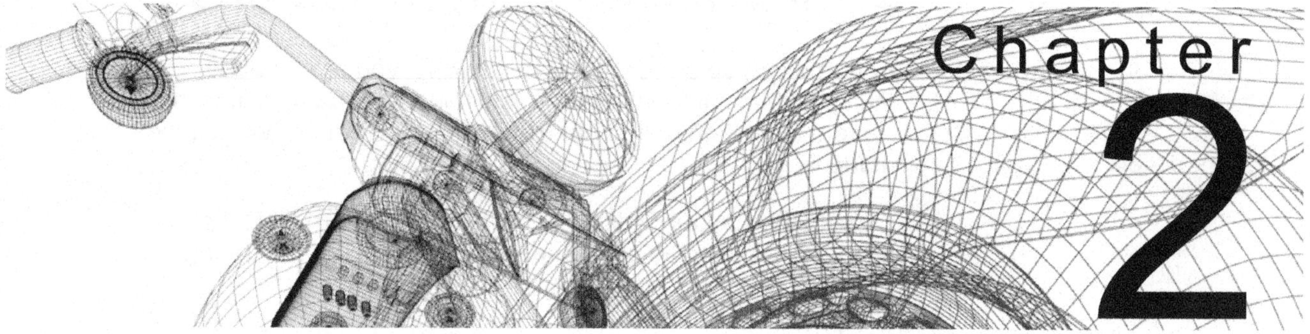

Advanced Pattern Options

Patterning provides options for creating efficiency and consistency in your part designs. The Advanced Pattern options introduced in this chapter aid in capturing design intent. Formulas and exploding patterns provide useful controls for meeting specific design requirements. User patterns enable you to create customized patterns by specifying pattern locations through the use of sketched points.

Learning Objectives in This Chapter

- Explore various pattern options.
- Use pattern formulas to automate changes to the model.
- Learn how to manage individual instances of a pattern using Explode Pattern.

2.1 Advanced Pattern Options

Patterns can be a great time-saver when you are creating multiple identical features. The additional options available in the Pattern Definition dialog box can help you create more complex models.

Expand the *Layout Options* section in the Pattern Definition dialog box to display all the additional options for patterning. These options help you to position the pattern.

Rectangular Patterns

Use the *Position* field in the Rectangular Pattern dialog box to change the position of the original feature in the pattern. For example, in Figure 2–1, the position of the original feature has been changed so that it is in the third column (First Direction) and in the second row (Second Direction) of the pattern.

Original Feature

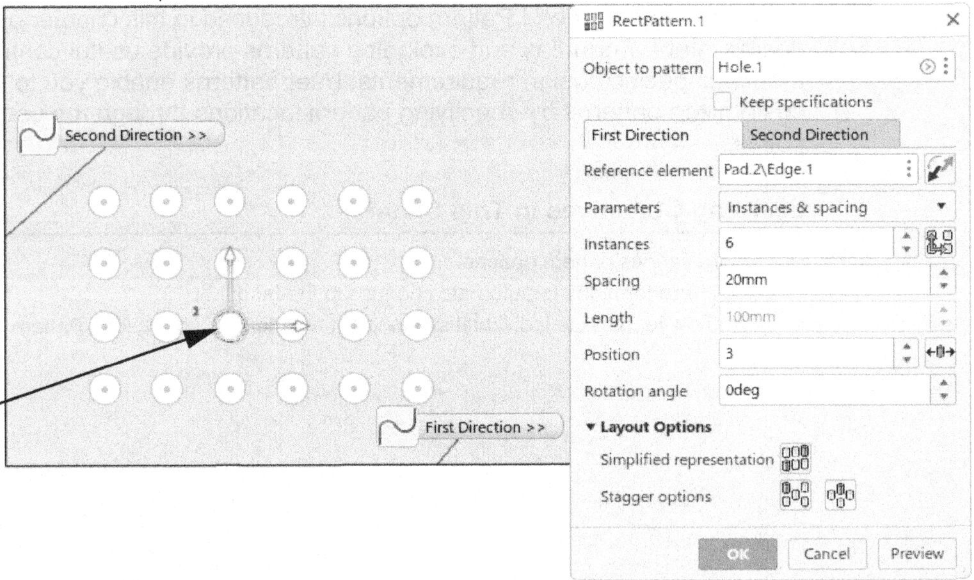

Figure 2–1

In Figure 2–2, a rotational angle of 35° has been added to the feature.

- Note that the position of the original feature has been changed so that it is in the first column (First Direction) and in the first row (Second Direction) of the pattern.

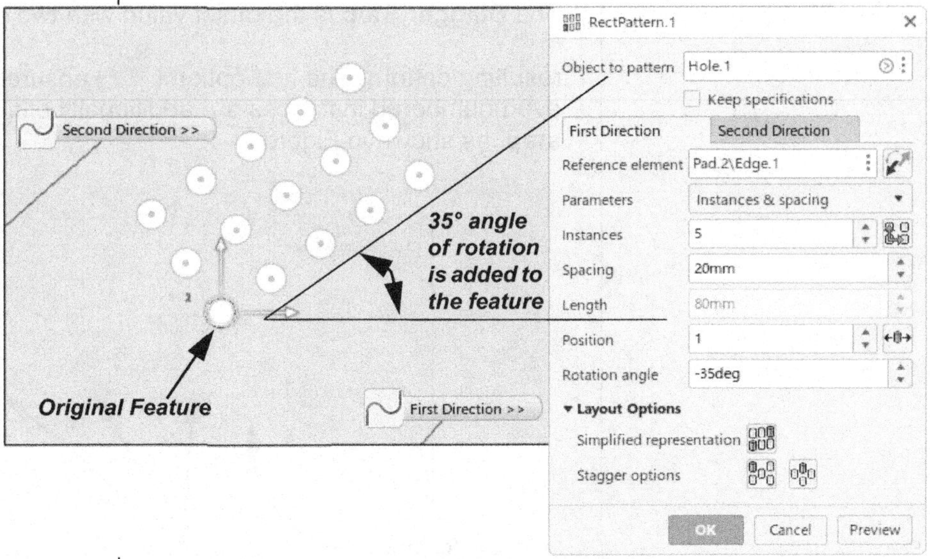

Figure 2–2

In a rectangular pattern, you can create a staggered pattern configuration in which alternate rows are offset by a specified value. To enable a staggered pattern, select required **Stagger options** in the *Layout Options* area, as shown in Figure 2–3.

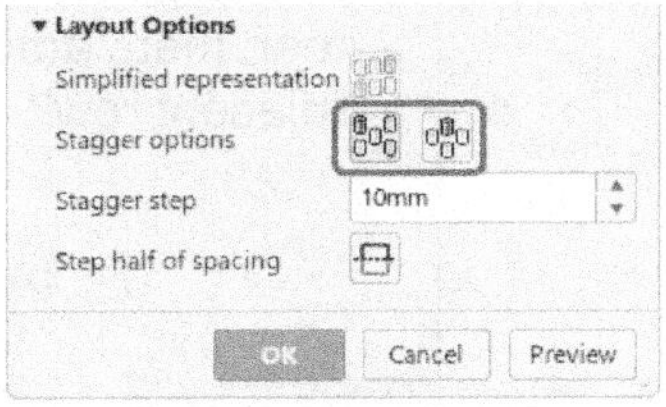

Figure 2–3

The **Stagger Step** is the offset value with two options for the resulting pattern. The first option () ensures that the even-numbered instances are additionally offset by the **Stagger step**, as shown in Figure 2–4.

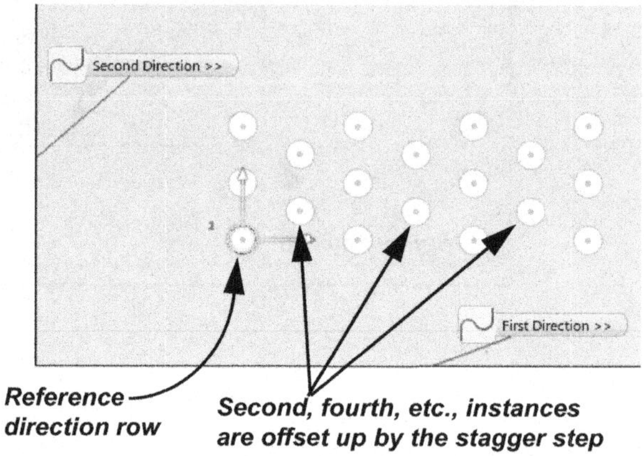

Figure 2–4

You can then use  to ensure that the even-numbered instances are additionally offset by the negative **Stagger step**, as shown in Figure 2–5. The **Set half of spacing** option will keep them auto-aligned in the middle of the instances of the adjacent row.

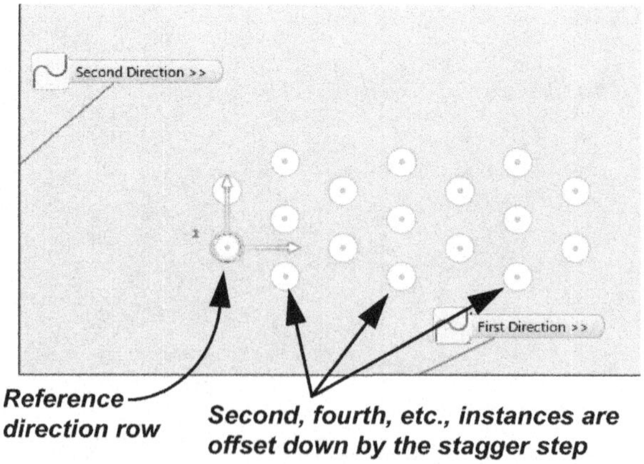

Figure 2–5

Circular Patterns

The Circular Pattern Definition dialog box has similar advanced options, except that the first direction is known as the *Angular direction*, and the second direction is known as the *Radial direction*.

A simple circular pattern rotated by 45° is shown in Figure 2–6.

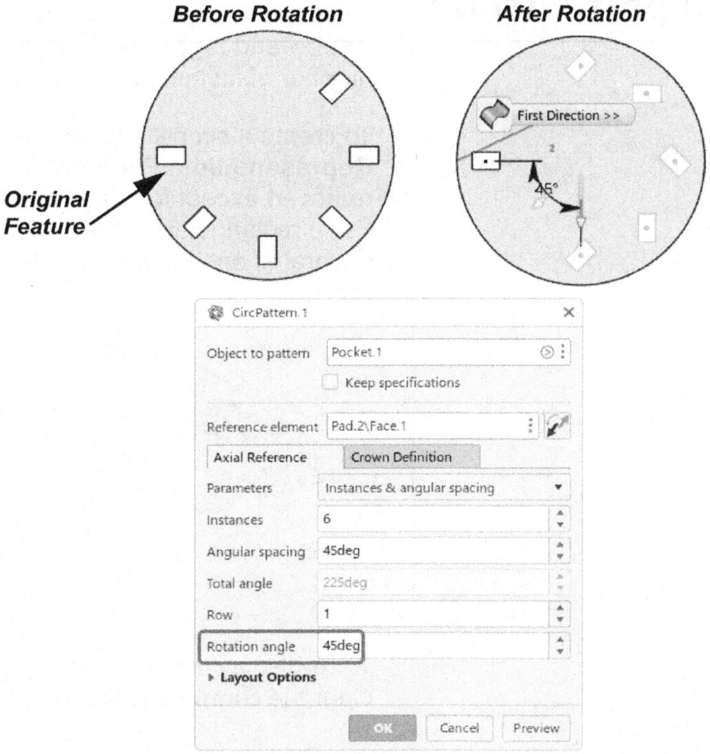

Figure 2–6

Additionally, you have the option of defining how to align the instances of a circular pattern. If the **Radial alignment** option in the *Layout Options* section is selected (default option), all instances remain tangent to the circle, as shown on the left in Figure 2–7. If this option is not selected, all of the instances remain in the same orientation as the original object, as shown on the right in Figure 2–7.

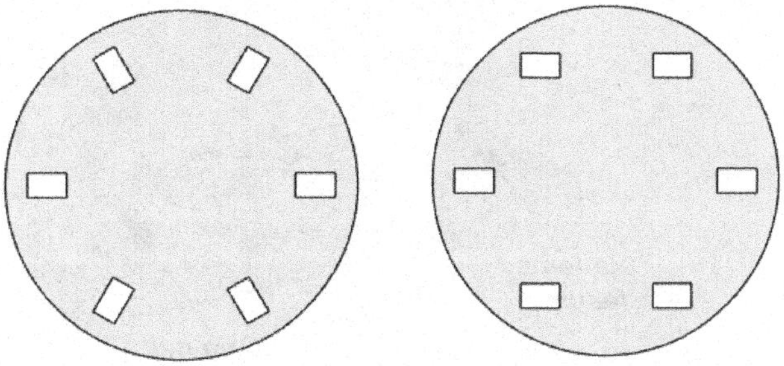

Figure 2–7

Simplified Representation

The **Simplified Representation** option for both rectangular and circular patterns enables you to display some of the pattern instances to represent the entire pattern. This option saves display and regeneration times if your pattern has a large number of instances and reduces the file size of the model.

To create a simplified representation, select **Simplified Representation**. For a circular pattern, all instances are removed except for the two innermost and two outermost rings. For a rectangular pattern, all instances are hidden except for several at each corner, as shown in Figure 2–8.

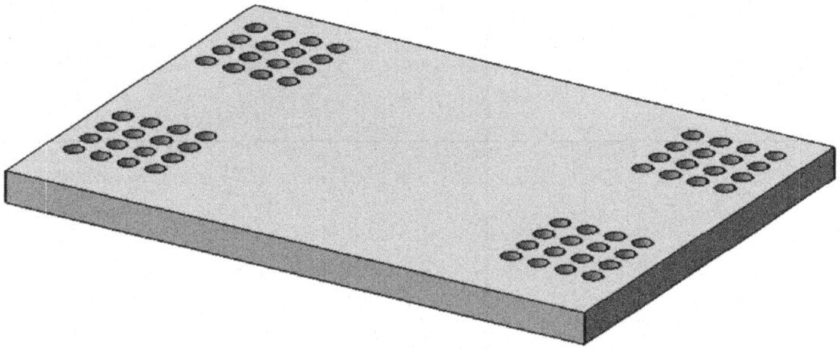

Figure 2–8

To re-display the full pattern, open the Pattern dialog box and clear the **Simplified Representation** option.

Keep Specifications

You can also keep the specifications of the original feature by selecting **Keep specifications**. For example, in Figure 2–9, the Pad feature is created using the **Up to surface** option. If the Pad feature is patterned without selecting **Keep specifications**, the patterned feature is identical to the original Pad feature.

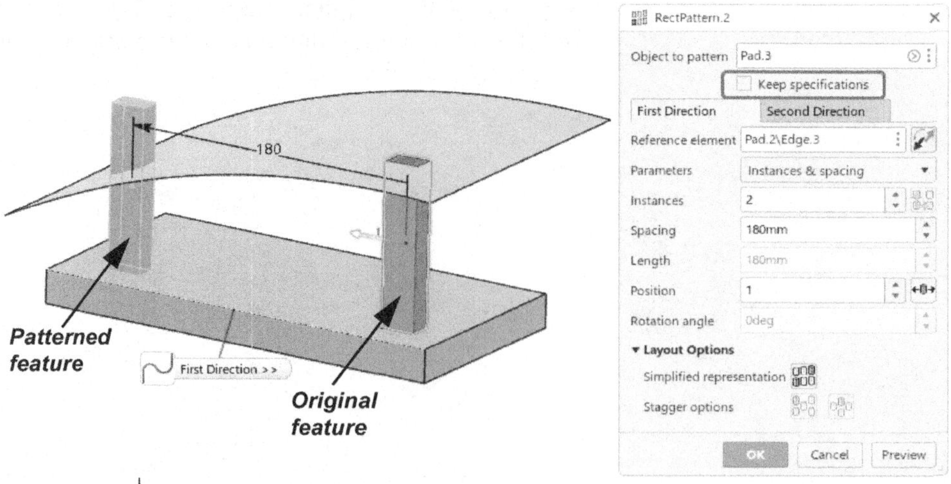

Figure 2–9

In Figure 2–10, the Pad feature is patterned with the **Keep specifications** option selected. The patterned feature is also created using the **Up to surface** option. The disadvantage of using this option is that it increases the update time.

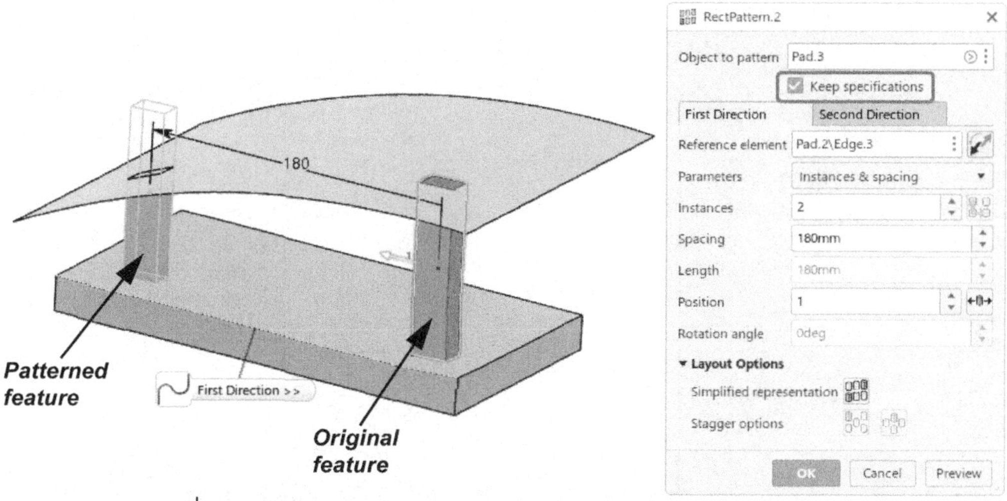

Figure 2–10

If the surface is modified, the patterned features update according to the changes. However, if the surface is modified so that the patterned features lose their references, the pattern fails. To avoid this, the original feature must be created using the Dimension type.

Pattern Formulas

Patterns can be controlled by formulas to automate changes in the model. For example, you might want to generate a relationship between the length of your geometry and the number of instances in a pattern. If the length of the geometry changes, the formula ensures that the number of pattern instances updates accordingly.

The need to generate a formula is often realized during the process of creating a pattern. A formula can be generated while creating a pattern by right-clicking in a field and selecting **Edit formula...**, as shown in Figure 2–11.

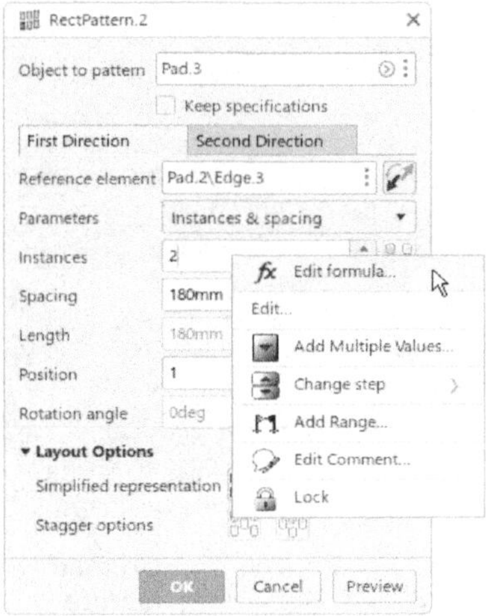

Figure 2–11

Exploding Patterns

After a pattern has been created, you might need to edit individual instances of a pattern. To do this, you need to explode the pattern. Once exploded, each instance of the pattern displays as a separate feature in the specification tree.

To explode a pattern, right-click on the pattern in the specification tree and select **<pattern name> object>Explode...**. Once you explode the pattern, the specification tree displays as shown on the right in Figure 2–12.

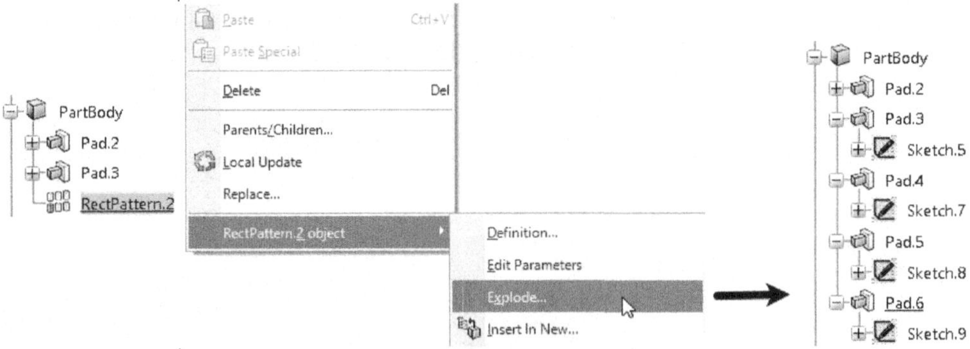

Figure 2–12

Practice 2a

Pattern Options

Practice Objectives

- Use Advanced Pattern options.
- Drive a pattern with a formula.

In this practice, you will create circular patterns of ventilation slots and drill holes in a brake Pad. You will use **Advanced Pattern** options to ensure that the drill holes penetrate the entire model and to ensure that the number of slots equal the number of drill hole groups. The model displays as shown in Figure 2–13.

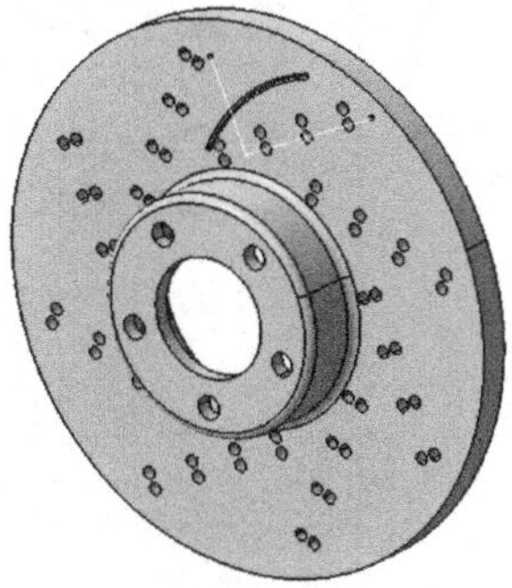

Figure 2–13

Task 1 - Open the part.

1. Import and open **BrakeRotor.3dxml** file for editing. When importing, type your initials followed by the dash symbol into the *Duplication string* field (e.g., **IA-**). The model displays as shown in Figure 2–14.

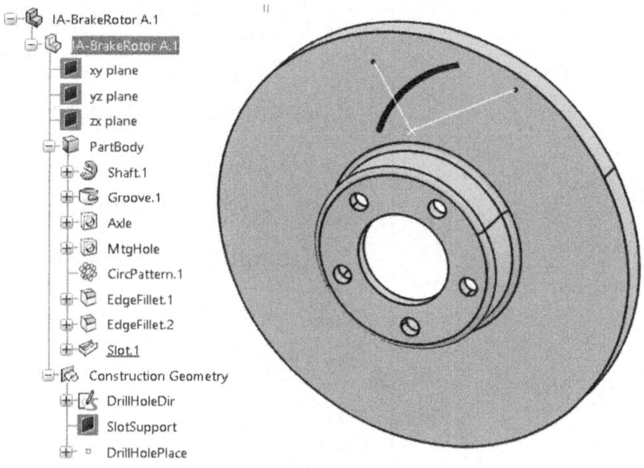

Figure 2–14

2. Investigate the features that have been created in the part model:

   - A Slot has been added to the face of the rotor that aids cooling.
   - In addition, a point (**DrillHolePlace**) and a sketch (**DrillHoleDir**) have been added to the **Construction Geometry** geometrical set. These features are used to create a drill hole pattern.

3. Measure the length of the longer line in the **DrillHoleDir** sketch. The line is approximately 100mm in length.

Task 1 - Create the drill hole.

1. Preselect the face of the rotor and the **DrillHolePlace** point element, as shown in Figure 2–15.

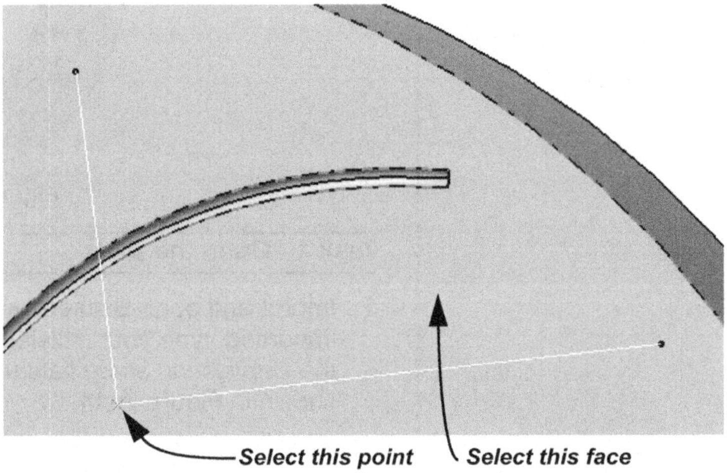

Figure 2–15

2. Create a Hole feature with the following parameters:

   - *Depth*: **Up To Last**
   - *Diameter:* **8mm**

3. Rename the feature as **DrillHole**.

Task 2 - Create a rectangular pattern.

1. Select **DrillHole** and click (Rectangular Pattern) to create a rectangular pattern. Make the following selections:
   - *Parameters:* **Instance(s) & Length**
   - *Instance(s):* **4**
   - *Length:* **100mm**
   - *Reference element:* **DrillHoleDir** (Select the long line of the sketch.)
   - Clear the **Keep specifications** option.

   The completed pattern displays as shown in Figure 2–16.

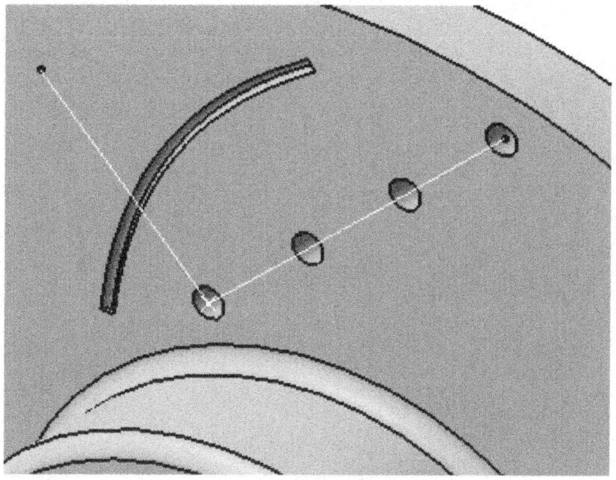

Figure 2–16

2. Rotate the model to display the back of the rotor. Note that the patterned holes do not go through the entire model, as shown in Figure 2–17.

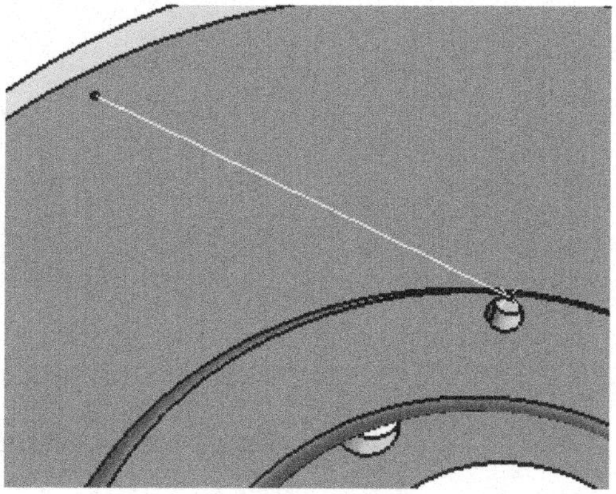

Figure 2–17

Design Considerations

By default, a patterned instance is an exact replica of the Lead Pattern feature. When the **Keep specifications** option is cleared, the patterned instances maintain the same depth as the original feature. In this case, the patterned features no longer cut through the entire model. To resolve this issue, the pattern must be forced to use the specifications of the original Hole feature.

3. Modify **RectPattern.1** and select **Keep specifications**, as shown in Figure 2–18.

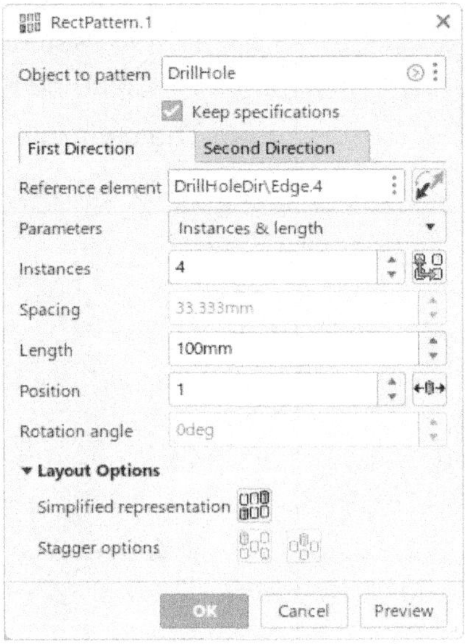

Figure 2–18

The completed pattern displays as shown in Figure 2–19.

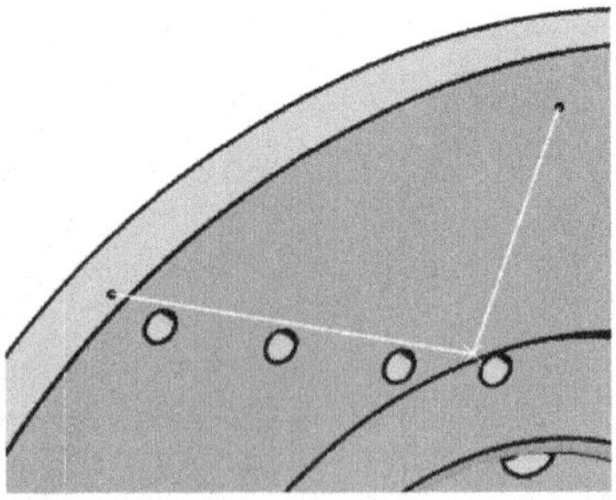

Figure 2–19

4. Rename the rectangular pattern as **DrillHoleRect**.

5. Apply the isometric saved view.

Task 3 - Investigate the staggered pattern options.

1. Edit the definition of **DrillHoleRect**.
2. In the DrillHoleRect dialog box, select the *Second Direction* tab.
3. Expand the Parameters drop-down list and select **Instance(s) & Spacing**.
4. Enter **2** for the number of instances.
5. Enter **10** for the spacing.
6. Select the *Reference element* field and then select the short arm of the **DrillHoleDir** sketch.

   The pattern updates as shown in Figure 2–20.

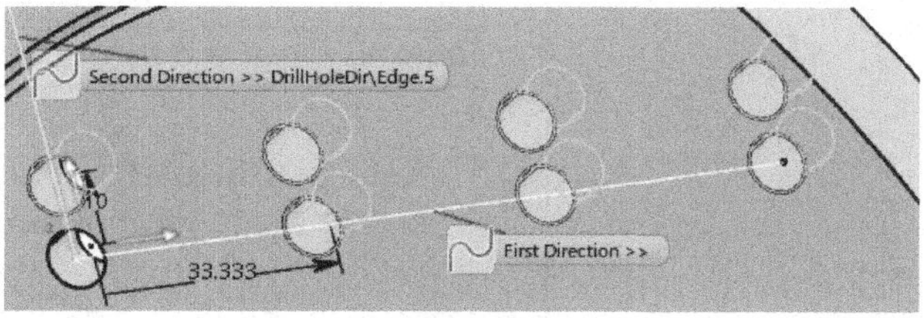

Figure 2–20

7. Expand the *Layout Options* section in the dialog box.
8. Click (Stagger).
9. Select **Step half of spacing**.
10. Reorient the model slightly and click **Preview** to display the result, as shown in Figure 2–21.

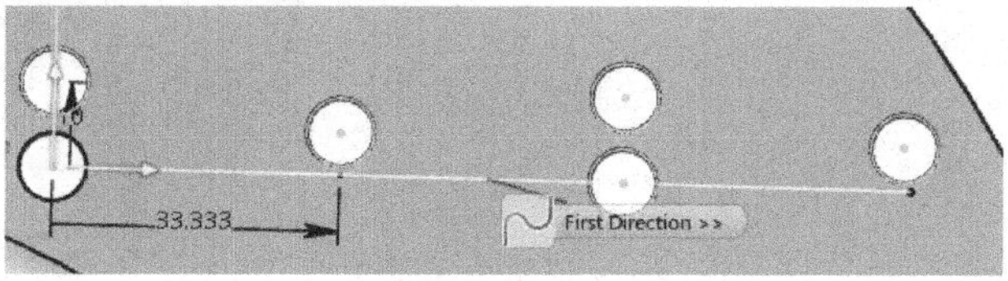

Figure 2–21

11. Click  and click **Preview** to change the stagger pattern, as shown in Figure 2–22.

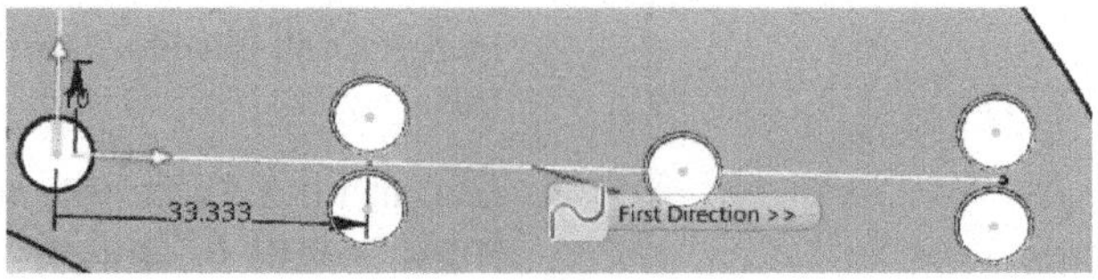

Figure 2–22

12. Click  to disable hole staggering.

13. Complete the pattern.

14. Apply the isometric saved view.

Task 4 - Create a circular pattern.

1. Select **DrillHoleRect** and click  (Circular pattern) to create a circular pattern. Make the following selections:
   - *Parameters:* **Complete crown**
   - *Instance(s):* **8**
   - *Reference element:* (Select the cylindrical face shown in Figure 2–23.)

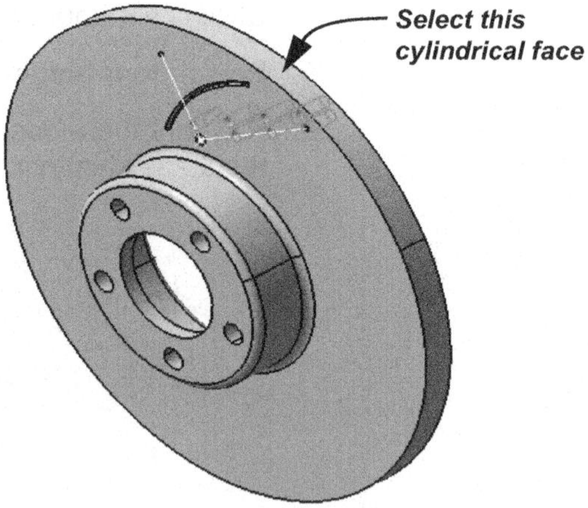

Figure 2–23

2. Rename the circular pattern as **DrillHoleCirc**. The resulting pattern is shown in Figure 2–24.

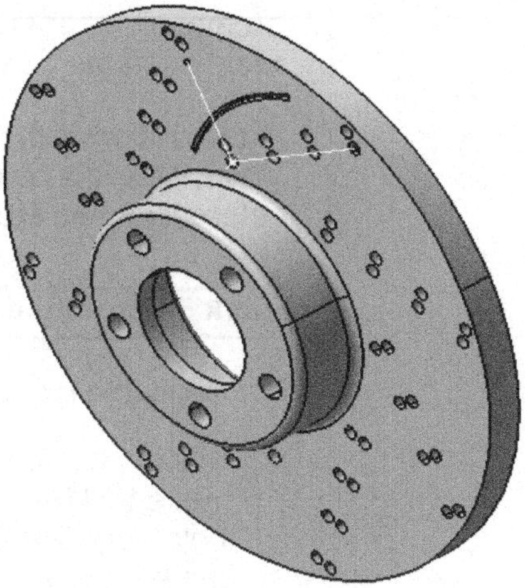

Figure 2–24

3. Rotate the model to display the back face of the rotor. The model displays as shown in Figure 2–25. Although the Lead Pattern feature cuts through the entire part, none of the circular pattern instances do so.

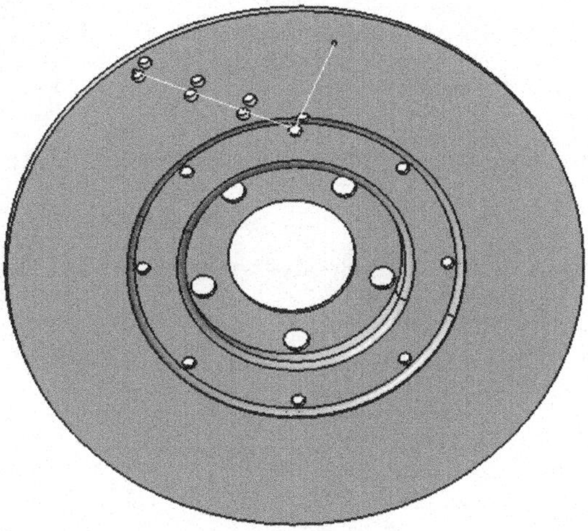

Figure 2–25

Design Considerations

When patterning a pattern, the **Keep Specification** option is not available. To resolve this issue, you must move the Lead Hole feature to an area on the rotor that has the maximum thickness so that all other instances cut through the entire part. The location of the Lead feature in the pattern can then be adjusted.

The position of the Hole is located using the **DrillHolePlace** point. This is a point created using the **On curve** option and referencing the **DrillHoleDir** linear sketch.

Task 5 - Modify the Lead Pattern feature.

1. Apply the isometric saved view.
2. Modify the **DrillHolePlace** point and change the *Length* value to **110mm**, as shown in Figure 2–26. This moves the hole approximately halfway up the longer line. It also pushes the patterned instances further up the line so that the last instance leaves the part model.

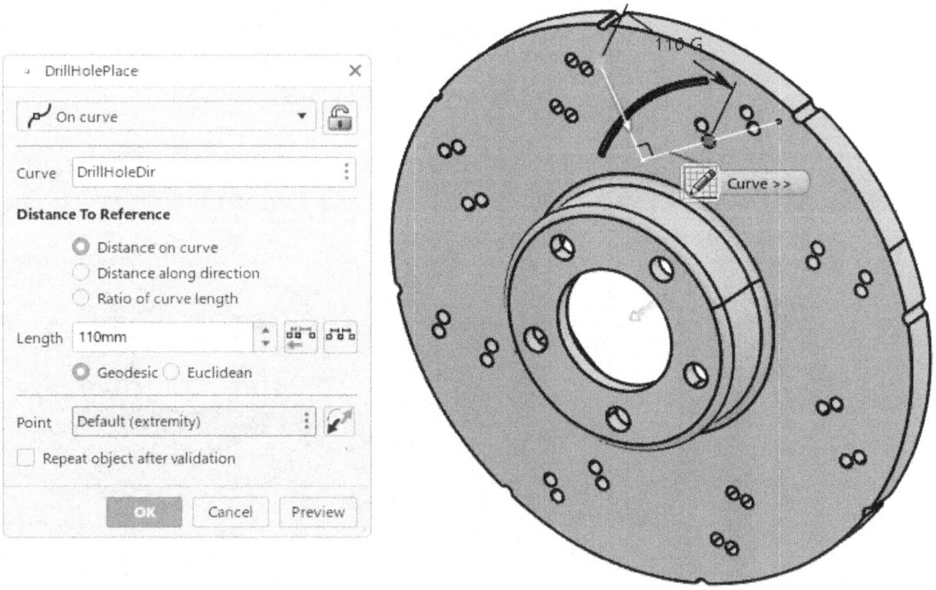

Figure 2–26

3. Click **OK**.

Task 6 - Modify the pattern.

To reposition the pattern instances, you will modify the rectangular pattern and make the Lead Pattern feature the third instance in the pattern.

1. Modify **DrillHoleRect**.

2. Note that the *Position* field displays a value of **1**, as shown in Figure 2–27. This is the position of the Lead feature along the *First Direction*.

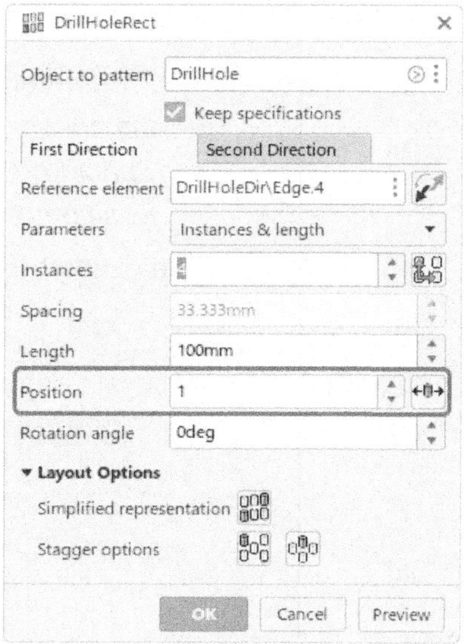

Figure 2–27

3. In the *Position* field, enter **3**. This places two instances before the Lead feature and one after the Lead feature. The model displays as shown in Figure 2–28.

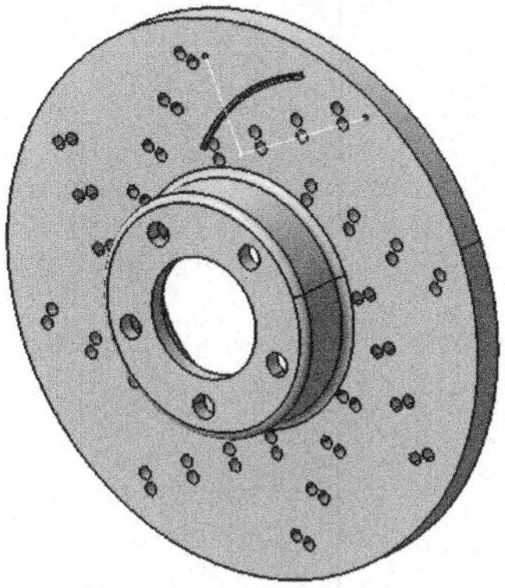

Figure 2–28

Task 7 - Modify the pattern by removing instances.

You have received a design change that requires you to change the spacing of the pattern to provide a greater cooling effect in the contact area between the brake pad and the rotor. This change requires an uneven spacing of the patterned instances. This uneven spacing is accomplished by modifying the rectangular pattern to correctly position the holes, then disabling the extra instances.

1. Edit the **DrillHoleRect** feature.

2. Modify the following pattern parameters:

   - *Parameters:* **Instances & spacing**
   - *Instances:* **6**
   - *Spacing:* **18mm**
   - *Position:* **4**

   The dialog box opens as shown in Figure 2–29.

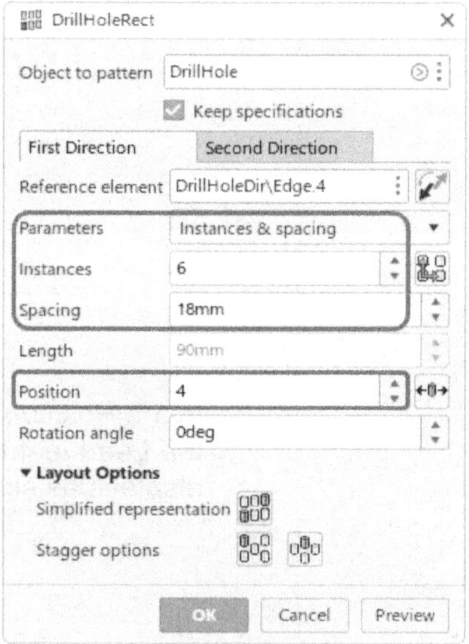

Figure 2–29

3. Zoom in on the pattern and disable the four pattern instances shown in Figure 2–30. This is done by selecting the dot at the center of the instances to be removed.

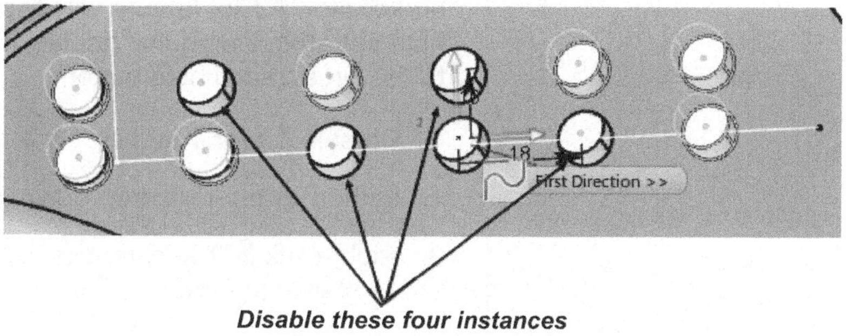

Figure 2–30

4. Complete the Pattern feature. The updated model displays as shown in Figure 2–31.

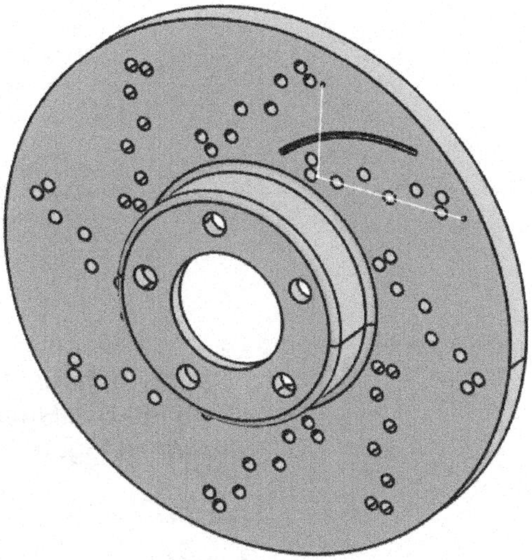

Figure 2–31

5. Hide **DrillHoleDir** and **DrillHolePlace**.

6. Save and close the model.

Task 8 - (Optional) Drive a pattern with a formula.

In this optional task, you will pattern the Slot feature around the brake rotor. A Slot feature will display between each of the drill hole patterns. Doing this enables the pattern values to be linked to the circular drill hole pattern.

1. Preselect **Slot.1** and create a circular pattern.
2. In the Parameters drop-down list, select **Complete crown**.
3. Right-click in the *Instances* field and select **Edit formula...**, as shown in Figure 2–32.

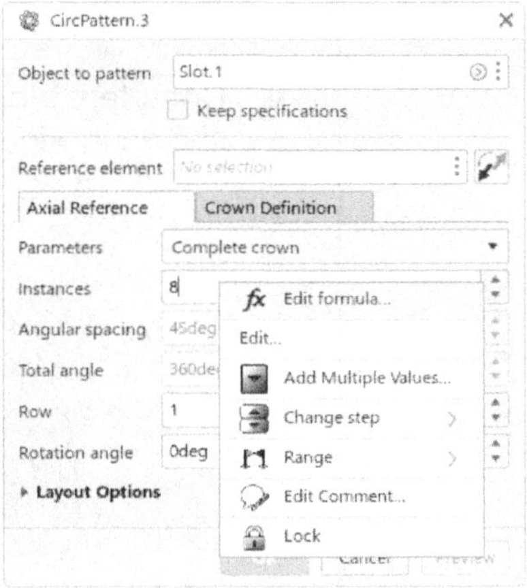

Figure 2–32

4. Set the number of instances equal to the number of instances from the **DrillHoleCirc** pattern. The formula will display as shown in Figure 2–33.

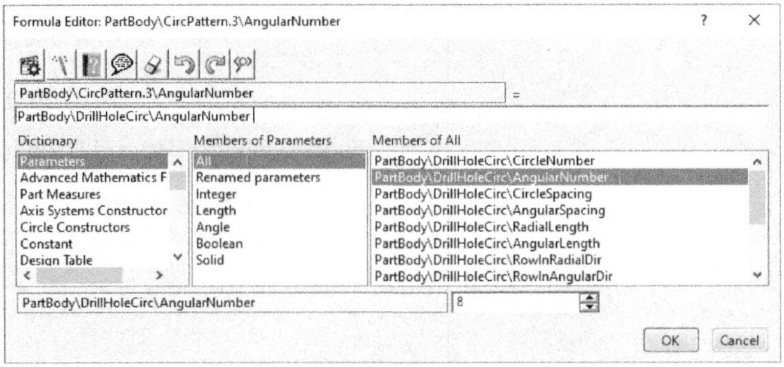

Figure 2–33

5. Select the outside cylindrical surface of the rotor as the reference element to drive the pattern. The completed pattern displays as shown in Figure 2–34.

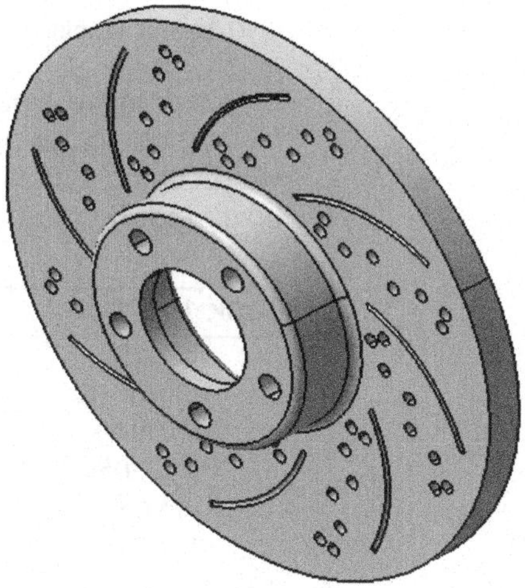

Figure 2–34

6. Rename the pattern as **SlotCirc**.

7. Modify the number of instances in the **DrillHoleCirc** pattern to **10** and update the model. The model displays as shown in Figure 2–35.

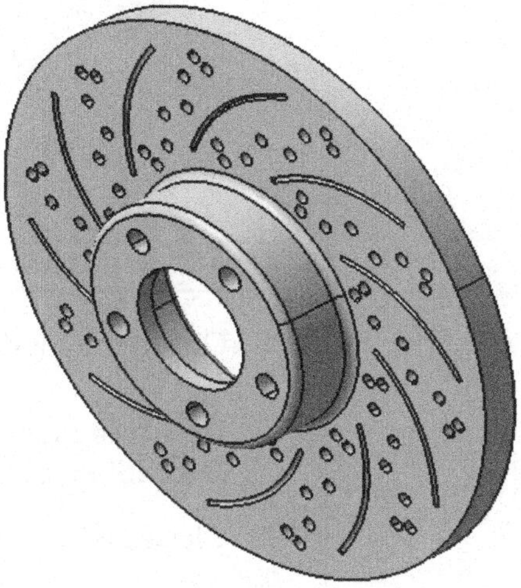

Figure 2–35

8. Save the model and close the window.

Practice 2b

Simplified Representations

Practice Objective

- Create a simplified representation of a pattern.

In this practice, you will create a simplified representation of a large rectangular pattern and examine the resulting geometry. When using simplified representations, the model display, file size, and moment of inertia of the part will change.

Task 1 - Open the part.

1. Import and open **SimRep.3dxml** file for editing. When importing, type your initials followed by the dash symbol into the *Duplication string* field (e.g., **IA-**). The model displays as shown in Figure 2–36.

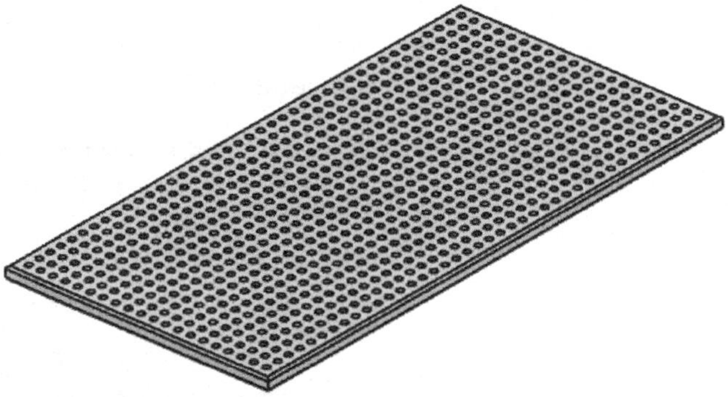

Figure 2–36

Task 2 - Measure the mass of the part.

1. Obtain the inertia properties of the PartBody by clicking  (Measure Inertia Data) in the Tools section of the Action Bar. Note that the mass of the part is 5.505 kg.
2. Close the Measure Inertia dialog box.

Task 3 - Create a simplified representation of the pattern.

1. Edit the rectangular pattern and expand the *Layout Options* section of the dialog box.
2. Select  (Simplified representation).
3. Click **OK**. The pattern is now represented by instances at each corner of the pattern, as shown in Figure 2–37.

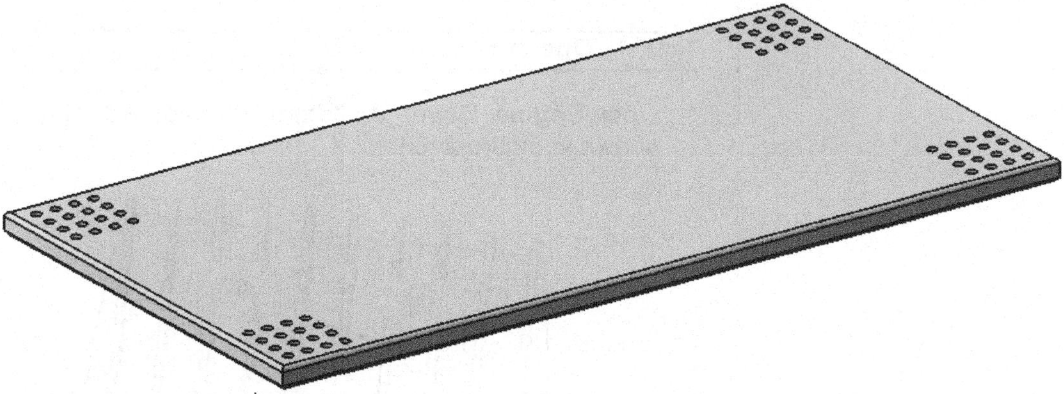

Figure 2–37

Task 4 - Measure the mass of the part with the simplified representation.

1. Obtain the inertia properties of the PartBody. Note that the mass of the part has increased to 6.641 kg. When using a simplified representation, the mass and inertia properties are not correct.
2. Close the Measure Inertia dialog box.
3. Close the part without saving.

Practice 2c Engine Cover

Practice Objective

- Use the Keep specifications option.

In this practice, you will clear the **Keep specifications** option for a rectangular pattern and examine the resulting geometry. You will then replace a reference surface for a Pad feature that is patterned.

Task 1 - Open the part.

1. Open **Engine_Cover_JY.3dxml**. The model displays as shown in Figure 2–38.

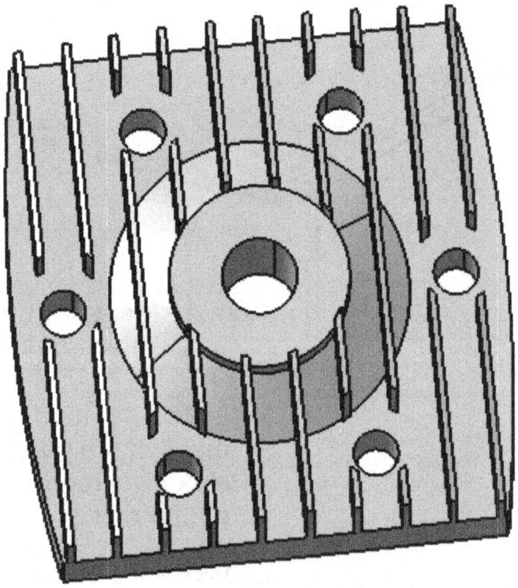

Figure 2–38

Task 2 - Modify the Rectangular pattern.

In this task, you will deactivate the **Keep specifications** option for the rectangular pattern.

Design Considerations

The rectangular pattern is created using a Pad feature. The **Up to surface** option is used to create the Pad feature, which uses an isolated surface as the limit.

1. In the **Surfaces** geometrical set, show **Surface.1**.

2. Orient the model, as shown in Figure 2–39.

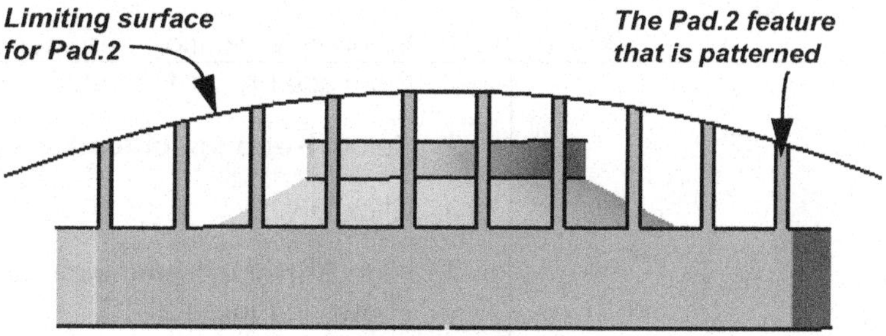

Figure 2–39

3. Double-click on **RectPattern.1**. The Rectangular Pattern dialog box opens as shown in Figure 2–40.

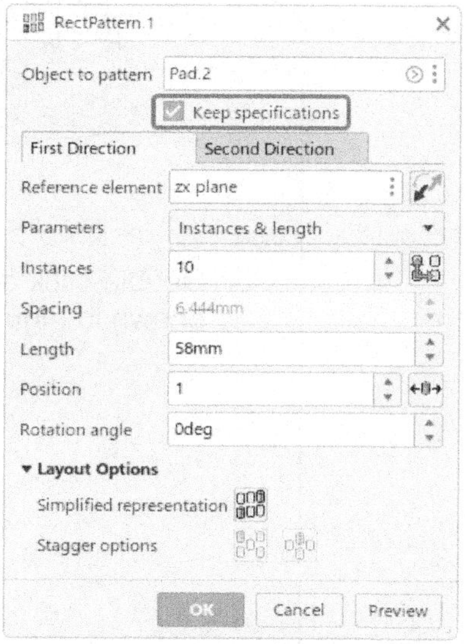

Figure 2–40

4. Clear the **Keep specifications** option.

5. Click **OK**. The model displays as shown in Figure 2–41. Note that the pattern is identical to the original Pad feature.

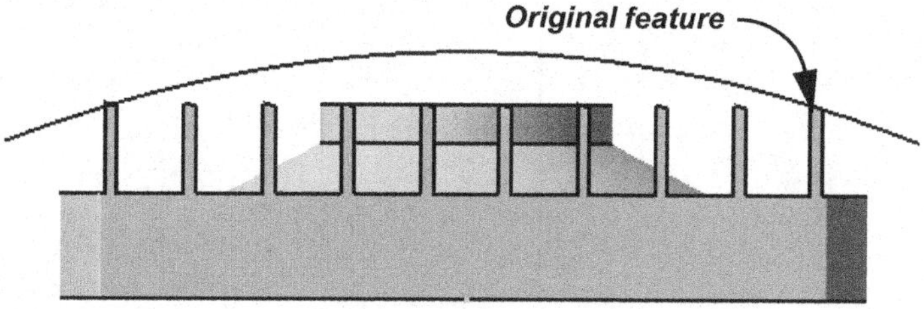

Figure 2–41

Task 3 - Replace the reference surface.

1. In the specification tree, double-click **RectPattern.1** to open the Rectangular Pattern Definition dialog box.
2. Select **Keep specifications** for the rectangular pattern.
3. Click **OK**.
4. Hide **Surface.1** and show **Surface.2**. The model displays as shown in Figure 2–42.

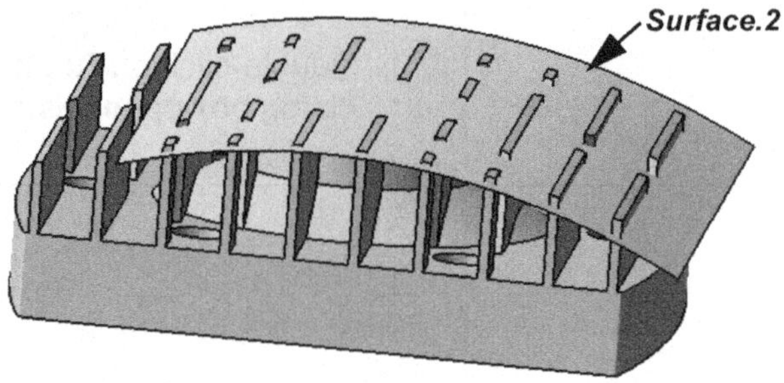

Figure 2–42

5. Double-click on **Pad.2** and select **Surface.2** as the *Limit*, as shown in Figure 2–43.

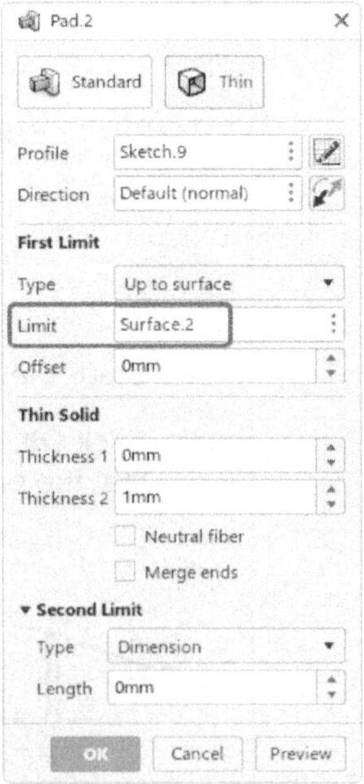

Figure 2–43

6. Click **OK**. The Update Diagnosis: Pad.2 dialog box opens as shown in Figure 2–44, indicating that some of the patterns are not intersecting the limiting element.

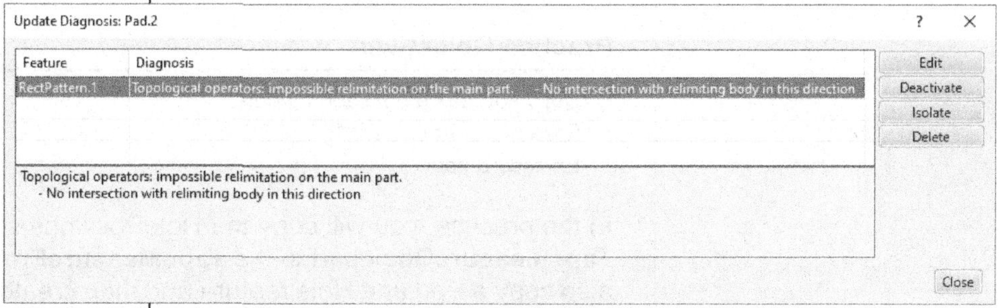

Figure 2–44

Design Considerations

If the surface does not intersect the patterned feature, the pattern loses its reference. This causes the pattern to fail.

7. Click **Close**.

8. Clear the **Keep specifications** option for the rectangular pattern. A warning message opens prompting you that the **Pocket.1** feature is unnecessary. Clearing the **Keep specifications** option results in the model not having any material for the **Pocket.1** feature to cut. This is why it is no longer required.

9. Close the warning. This time, the rectangular pattern updates successfully. However, the shape of the pattern does not match the design requirements.

There are a few possible solutions for this situation:

- Use the Generative Shape Design app to fix the surface.
- Create a new, more suitable surface.
- Create the Pad feature with a dimension that intersects the surface and then create a Pocket feature using the suitable surface.

10. Save and close the model.

Practice 2d Copying Features Between Models

Practice Objectives

- Copy and paste between models.
- Create a User Pattern.
- Explode a pattern.

In the practice, you will copy the HolePositions sketch from the **TapeMeasureBack** part to the **TapeMeasureFront** part. You will also copy a Pad and Hole feature and then create a User Pattern using the copied sketch and features. You will also explode the pattern. The completed model displays as shown in Figure 2–45.

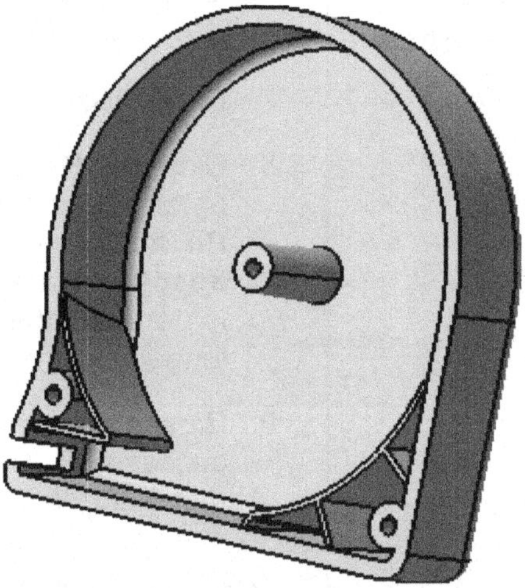

Figure 2–45

Task 1 - Open the part.

1. Import and open **TapeMeasureBack.3dxml** and **TapeMeasureBack.3dxml** files for editing. When importing, type your initials followed by the dash symbol into the *Duplication string* field (e.g., **IA-**). The TapeMeasureFront model displays as shown in Figure 2–46.

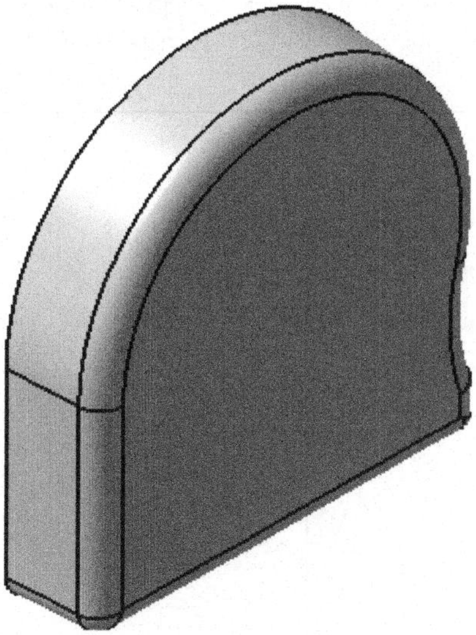

Figure 2–46

2. Activate the **TapeMeasureBack** window.

3. Right-click on the **HoleLocations** sketch and select **Copy**, as shown in Figure 2–47.

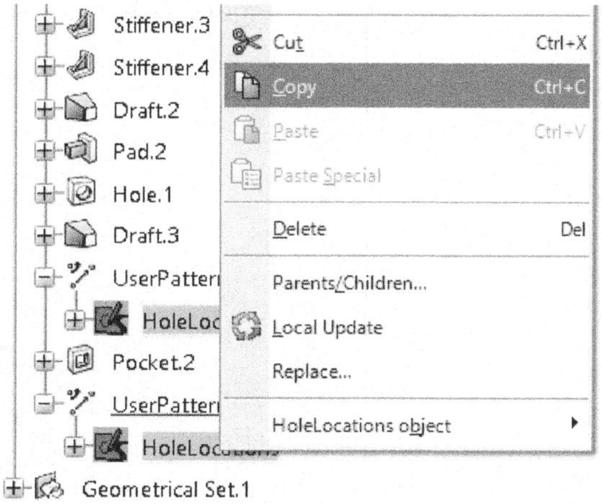

Figure 2–47

4. Activate the **TapeMeasureFront** window.

5. Right-click on the **PartBody** and select **Paste**, as shown in Figure 2–48.

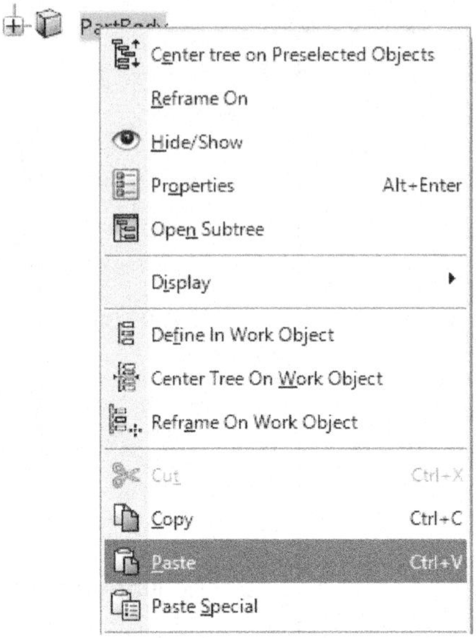

Figure 2–48

The **HoleLocations** sketch displays as shown in Figure 2–49.

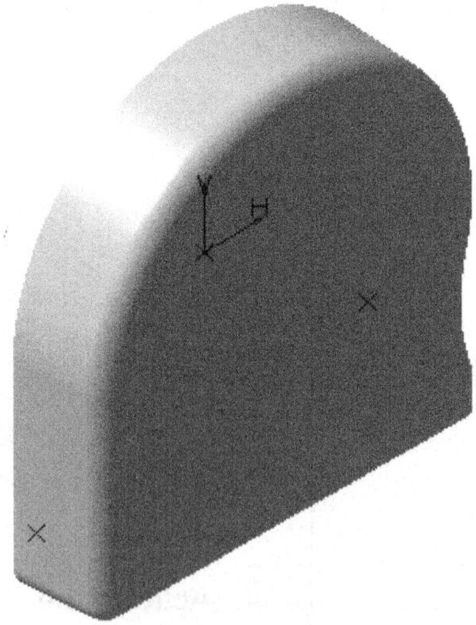

Figure 2–49

6. Copy and paste **Pad.2** from the **TapeMeasureBack** to the **TapeMeasureFront** model. The feature fails due to an incorrect direction of feature creation, as shown in Figure 2–50.

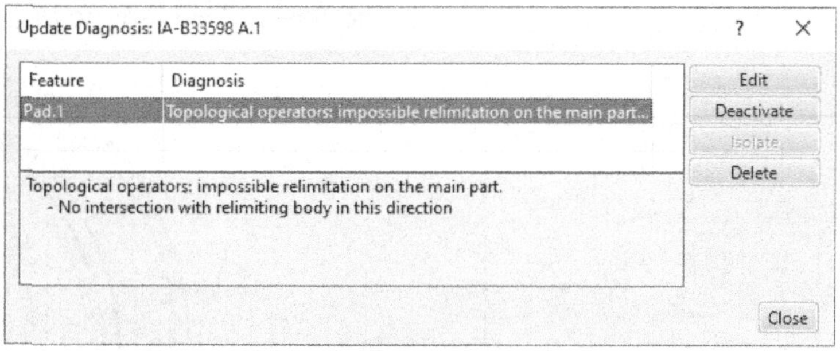

Figure 2–50

7. Click **Edit**. The Feature Definition Error dialog box opens.
8. Click **OK** in the Feature Definition Error dialog box.
9. Reverse the direction of feature creation. The correct direction for the Pad feature is shown in Figure 2–51.

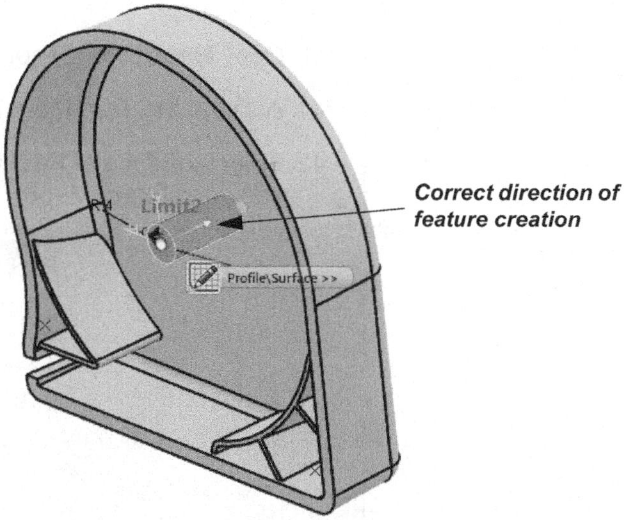

Figure 2–51

The pasted Pad feature displays as shown in Figure 2–52.

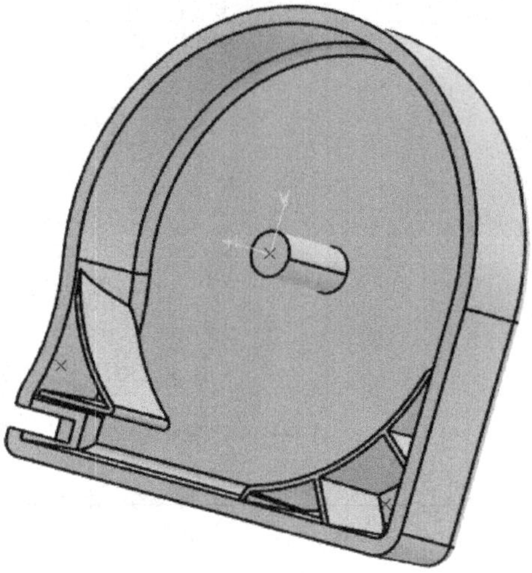

Figure 2–52

10. Copy **Hole.1** from **TapeMeasureBack**.
11. Activate the **TapeMeasureFront** window.
12. Select the face of **Pad.1**, right-click, and select **Paste**, as shown in Figure 2–53.

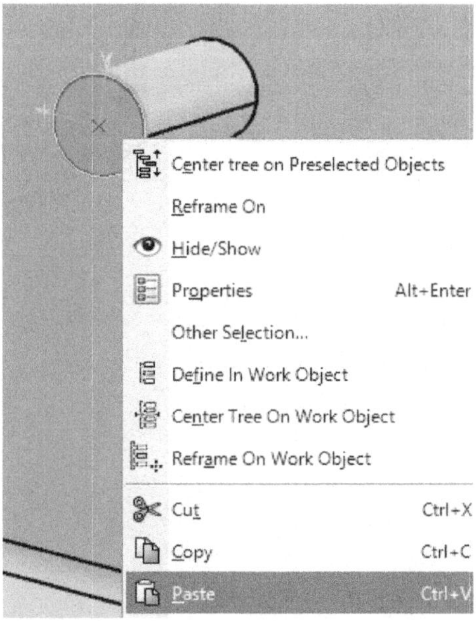

Figure 2–53

The result displays as shown in Figure 2–54.

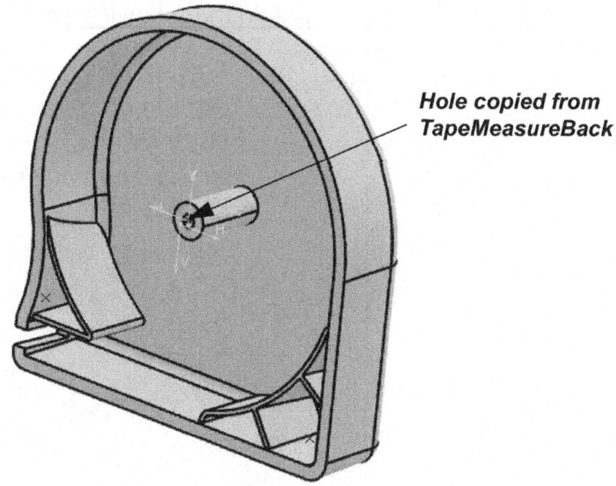

Figure 2–54

13. Make the following changes to the Hole feature, as shown in Figure 2–55:

- Verify that the Hole direction is pointing to the model.
- *Limit type:* **Blind**
- *Main depth:* **15mm**

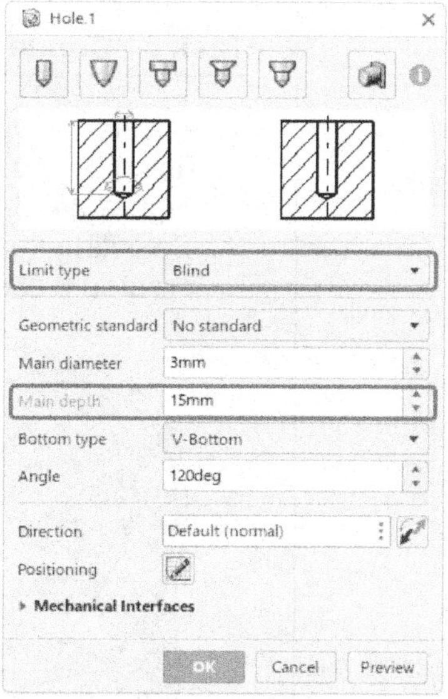

Figure 2–55

Task 2 - Create a Draft feature.

1. Add the following Draft to the cylindrical surface of the Pad:

   - *Angle:* **2**
   - *Faces to draft:* (cylindrical surface, as shown in Figure 2–56)
   - *Neutral elements:* (planar surface, as shown in Figure 2–56)

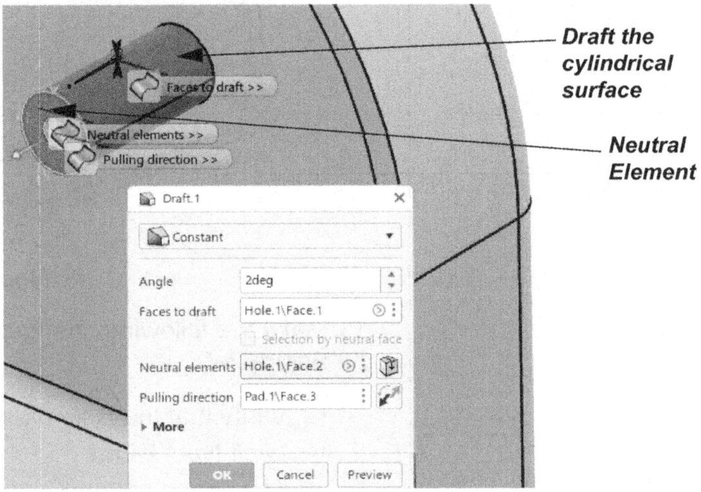

Figure 2–56

Task 3 - Create a User Pattern.

1. Create a user pattern of the Pad, Hole, and Draft features using the pasted **HoleLocations** sketch, as shown in Figure 2–57. Select the features in the specified order. Selecting the draft first will cause the User Pattern to be created incorrectly.

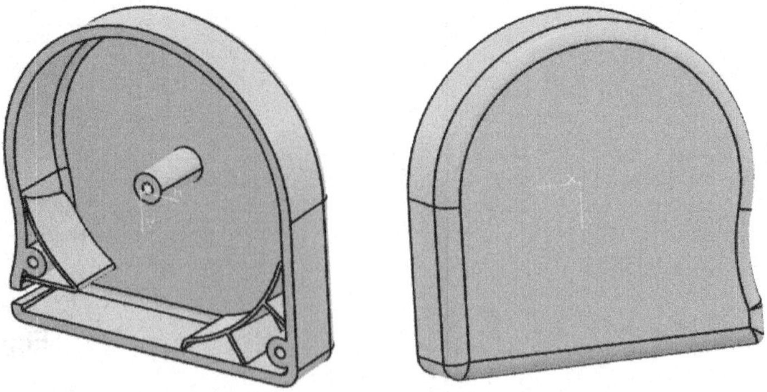

Figure 2–57

Design Considerations

Copying and pasting features is an effective method of duplicating features between part files. Remember that the pasted features are located in the same position as the source model. The pasted features are not associative using the **Paste** functionality.

Task 4 - Explode the pattern.

1. In the TapeMeasureFront model, right-click on **UserPattern.1** and select **UserPattern.1 object>Explode...**, as shown in Figure 2–58.

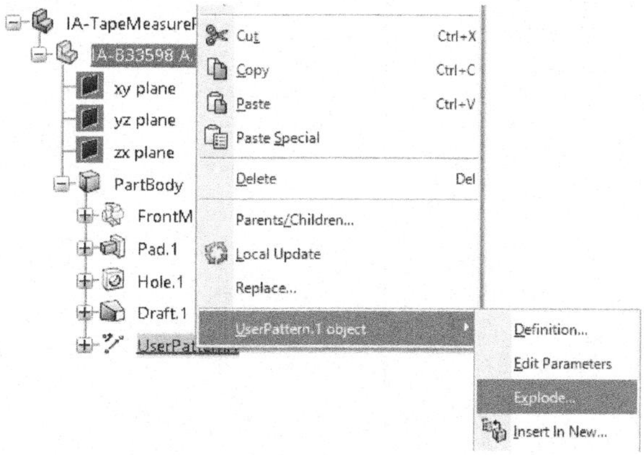

Figure 2–58

After the pattern has been exploded, the specification tree displays as shown in Figure 2–59.

Figure 2–59

2. Undo the explode with the **Undo** option.

3. Close **TapeMeasureFront** and TapeMeasureBack models without saving.

Design Considerations

Be cautious when using the **Explode** command. It cannot be undone once it no longer exists in the Undo history list. It is recommended that you save a backup of the model immediately before performing an explode.

Chapter Review Questions

1. When creating a rectangular pattern that extends in two directions, the original feature always displays in the first row and first column of the pattern.

   a. True

   b. False

2. To create a rectangular pattern in which alternate rows are offset by specified values, use the _____ option.

   a. Offset

   b. Alternating

   c. Pivot

   d. Stagger

3. To create a circular pattern, you need to define the _______ directions.

   a. First and Second.

   b. Angular and Radial.

   c. Rotation and Offset.

   d. None of the above.

4. You can use the **Simplified Representation** option to display some pattern instances instead of the full pattern.

   a. True

   b. False

5. Once a pattern has been created, you cannot break the pattern into separate features.

   a. True

   b. False

6. To create pattern instances that are identical to the original, disable the _______ option.

   a. .Keep specifications

   b. Maintain status

   c. Hold definition

   d. None of the above.

Answers: 1b, 2d, 3b, 4a, 5b, 6a

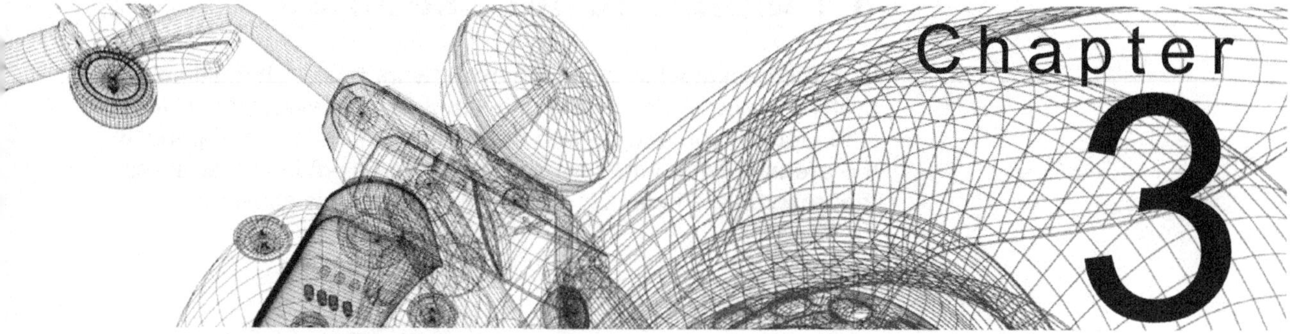

Working with Multi-Profile Sketches

A Multi-Profile sketch enables you to sketch multiple profiles in one sketch. In this chapter, you learn how to integrate Multi-Profile sketches with a variety of other features.

Learning Objectives in This Chapter

- Understand how sketches with multiple profiles can be used in a single pad feature.
- Select one or more sketch sub-elements to create a pad feature.
- Use Output features to make sketched elements independent of the sketch.
- Understand how to define a set of sketched elements as a single profile, using the Profile Feature.
- Learn the available propagation modes.
- Understand the domains in a multi-profile sketch.
- Understand multi-pad features that can have unique lengths for each domain.
- Learn about the available length options.

3.1 Multi-Profile Sketches

In some design situations, you might want to sketch multiple profiles in one sketch. If you use a multi-profile sketch to create a Pad feature, you end up with a solid feature that adds material in the areas between the profiles and leaves a void in other areas that resemble a hole or a pocket. An example is shown in Figure 3–1.

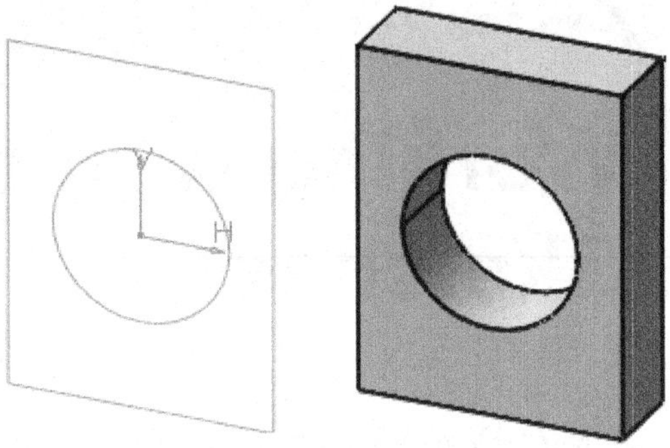

Figure 3–1

For a multi-profile sketch to work for a Pad feature, the profiles cannot intersect one another. This results in the error message shown in Figure 3–2.

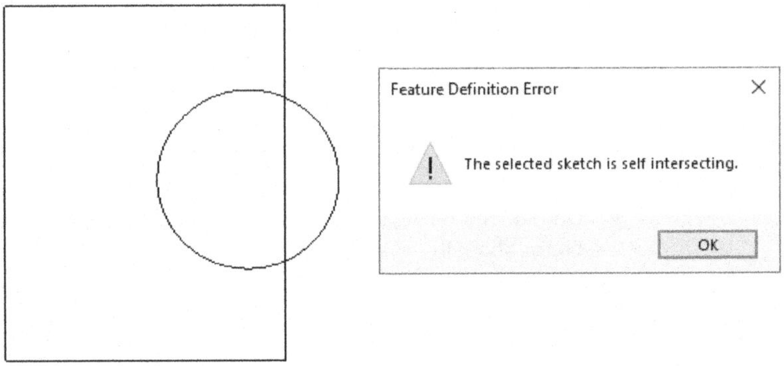

Figure 3–2

3.2 Creation of Sketch Sub-Elements

You can use multi-profile sketches to construct solid features by using a sub-element of the sketch for feature creation, instead of the entire sketch. The result of creating a Pad feature using each sub-element is shown in Figure 3–3.

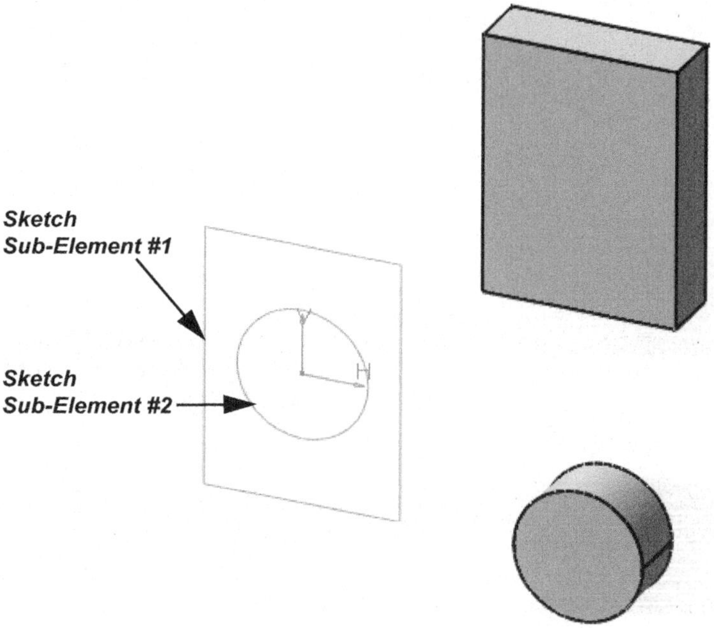

Figure 3–3

How To: Construct Solid Features Using a Sub-Element of a Sketch

1. Create a Pad feature without preselecting a sketch.
2. In the Pad Definition dialog box, place the cursor in the *Profile* field and right-click.

3. Select **Go to profile definition**, as shown in Figure 3–4. The Pad dialog box temporarily hides and the Profile Definition dialog box opens.

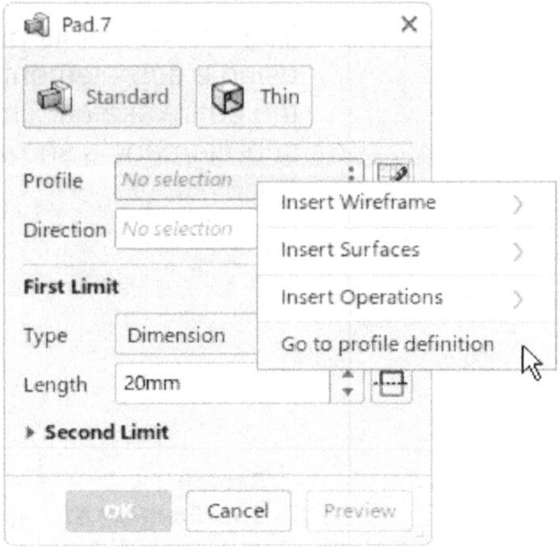

Figure 3–4

4. In the Profile Definition dialog box, select **Sub-elements**, select the required edge of the profile, and click **OK**, as shown in Figure 3–5.

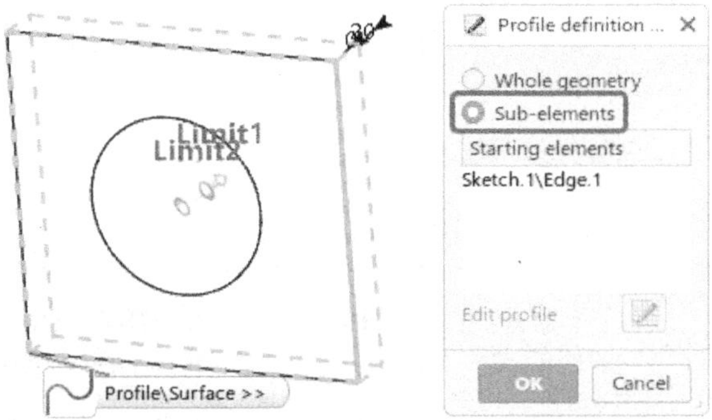

Figure 3–5

5. Continue to define the Pad feature as usual. Note that the *Profile* area lists **Complex**, instead of the name of the sketch, as shown in Figure 3–6.

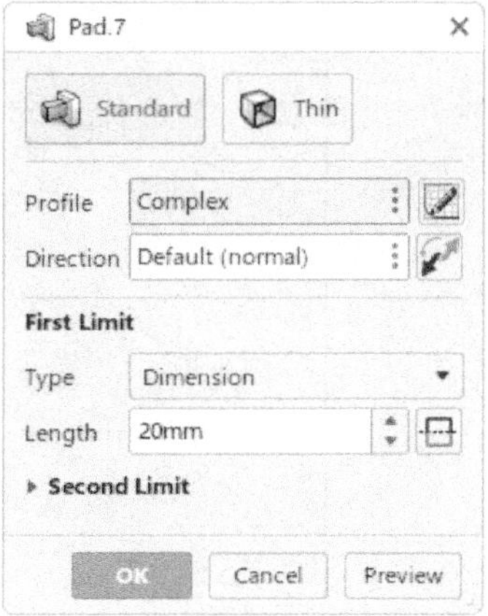

Figure 3–6

The sketch is not automatically hidden, as is the case when you use the entire sketch for a feature. The system assumes that you need to refer to the sketch again at a later time, and therefore, leaves it displayed, as shown in Figure 3–7. You must manually hide the sketch if you want to clean up the display.

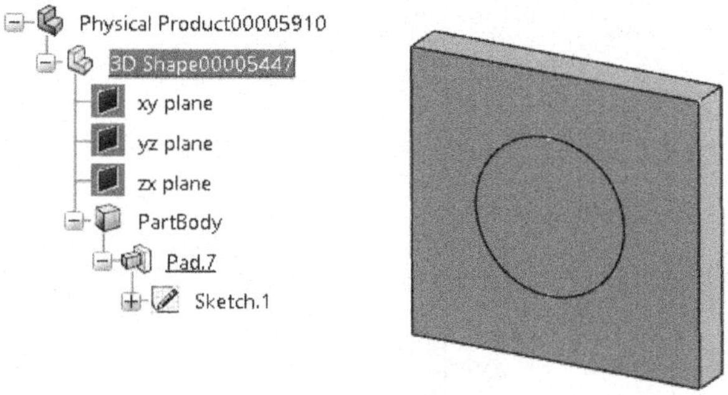

Figure 3–7

In some cases, creating a multi-profile sketch is more efficient than developing a series of separate sketches. Consider the sketch shown in Figure 3–8.

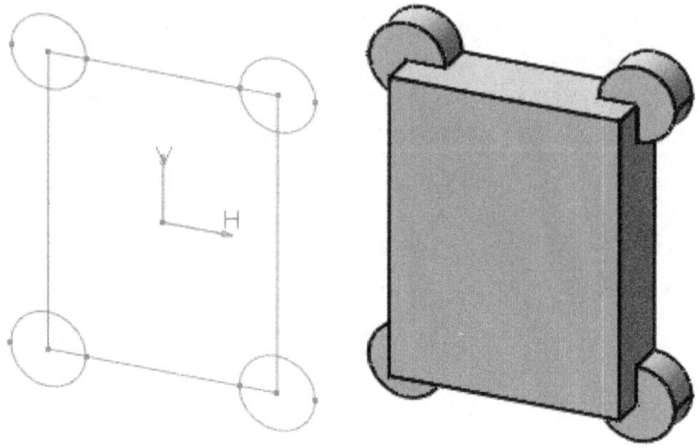

Figure 3–8

Five profiles are created in one sketch. With the rectangle sketched first, the centers of the four circles can be quickly constrained to the four corners of the rectangle. Construction geometry can also be added quickly to ensure that all four circles are the same size and controlled by a single diameter dimension.

3.3 Output Features

Output features enable you to make selected sketched elements independent of the sketch in which they were created. The independent elements can then be used independent to the rest of the sketch.

How To: Create an Output Feature

1. With the sketch active, click  (Output feature) in the Sketch section of the Action Bar, as shown in Figure 3–9.

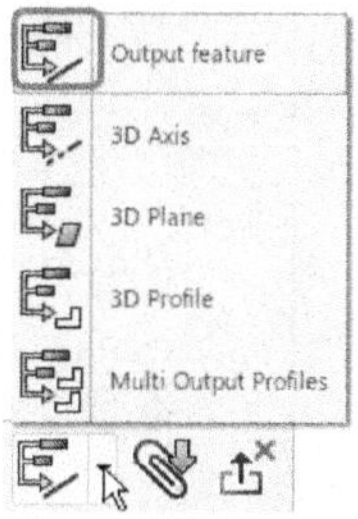

Figure 3–9

2. Select the sketched geometry that you want to make independent. In Figure 3–10, the spline entity is made independent from the rest of the sketched geometry.

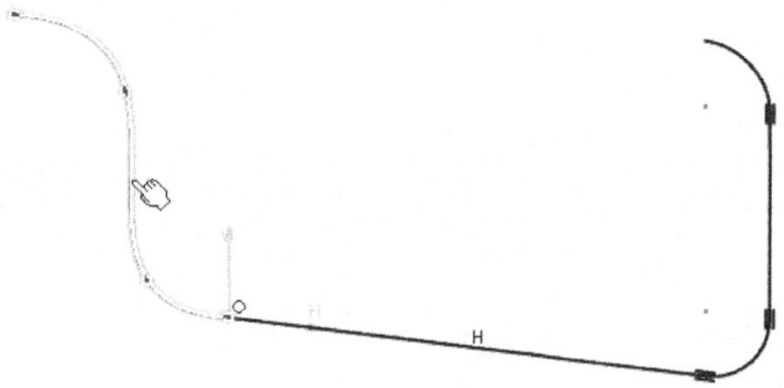

Figure 3–10

3. A completed output feature is listed under the **Outputs** node in the specification tree. It displays under the sketch in which it was created, as shown in Figure 3–11. The line thickness of the output feature is different from the rest of the sketched geometry to help visually distinguish it from the rest of the sketch.

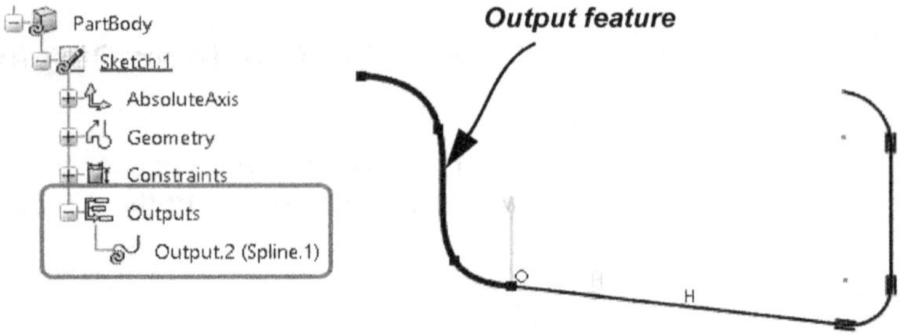

Figure 3–11

3.4 3D Outputs

3D axes and planes can be created by referencing sketcher entities, using (3D Axis) and (3D Plane) from the Sketch section of the Action Bar, as shown in Figure 3–12.

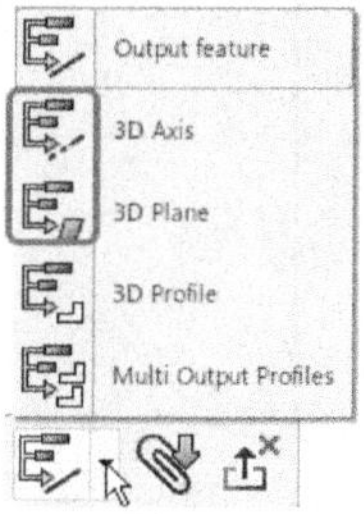

Figure 3–12

3D Axis

You can use sketch points to output 3D axes. In the Sketch section of the Action Bar, click (3D Axis) and select a point. The system generates an axis running through the point and perpendicular to the sketch support. The created output axis displays under the **Outputs** node in the specification tree, as shown in Figure 3–13.

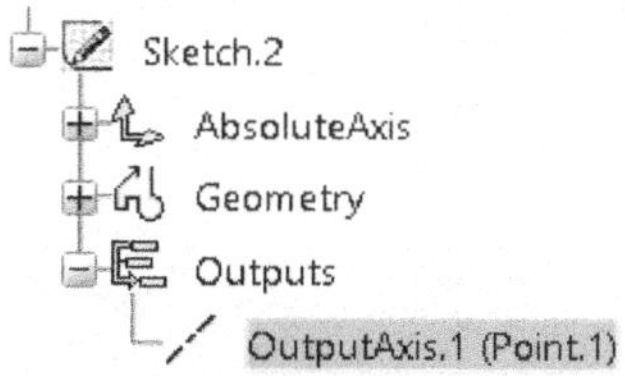

Figure 3–13

3D Plane

You can use a sketched line to output a 3D plane. In the Sketch section of the Action Bar, click  (3D Plane) and select a line. The system generates a plane running through the line and perpendicular to the sketch support. The created output plane displays under the **Outputs** node in the specification tree, as shown in Figure 3–14.

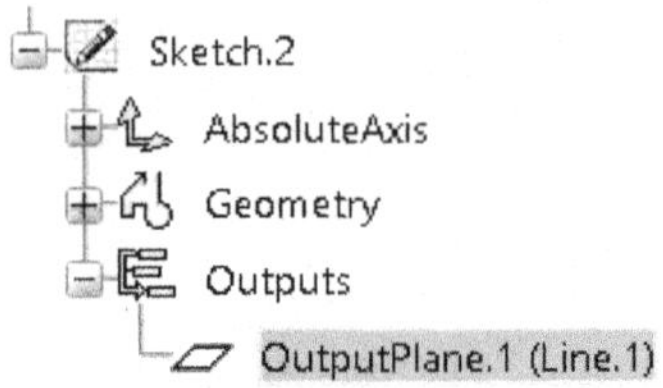

Figure 3–14

3.5 3D Profile

The **3D Profile** tool enables you to define a set of sketched elements as a single profile. As with output features, profile features become independent of the sketch in which they are created.

How To: Create a Profile of Sketched Elements

1. In the Sketch section of the Action Bar, click 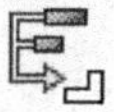 (3D Profile), as shown in Figure 3–15.

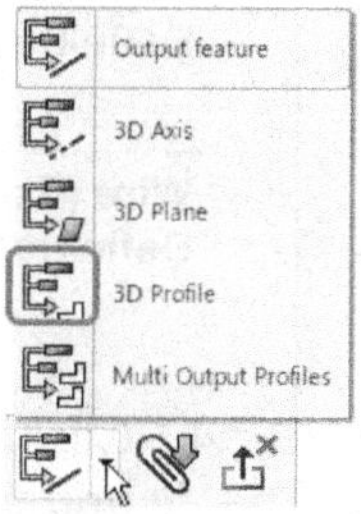

Figure 3–15

2. The Profile Definition dialog box opens as shown in Figure 3–16. You can enter a user-defined name for the profile and define a color.

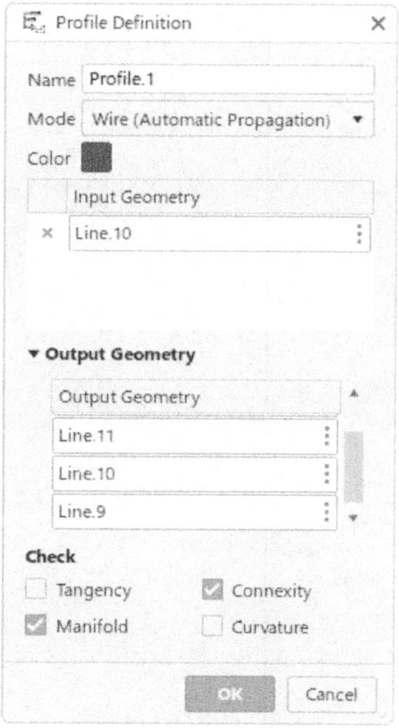

Figure 3–16

3. The *Input Geometry* field lists the items that have been selected to add to the profile. The *Output Geometry* field lists the items that are included in the profile. The type of geometry that you can select is dependent on the mode being used.

   Three different modes can be used for geometry selection. They are described as follows:

Mode	Description
Wire (Automatic Propagation)	The default mode. The system selects all of the point continuous entities, until a loop is selected or the system encounters a point that connects more than two entities.
Point (Explicit Definition)	Only points and vertices can be added to the profile. All entities must be explicitly selected. The *Input* and *Output Geometry* fields are the same.
Wire (Explicit Definition)	All sketched entities can be added to the profile. All entities must be explicitly selected. The *Input* and *Output Geometry* fields are the same.

4. Click **OK** to complete the profile. A completed profile is listed under the **Outputs** node in the specification tree, under the sketch in which it was created, as shown in Figure 3–17.

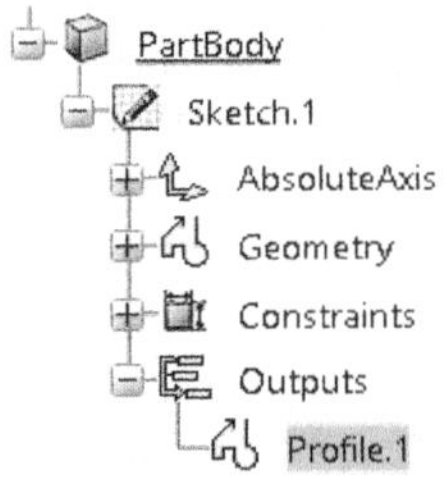

Figure 3–17

3.6 Creation of Multi-Pad Features

Multi-pad features enable you to specify a different length for each domain of the sketch, in which the domain is the space enclosed by each sub-element of the sketch. The domains cannot overlap. An example is shown in Figure 3–18.

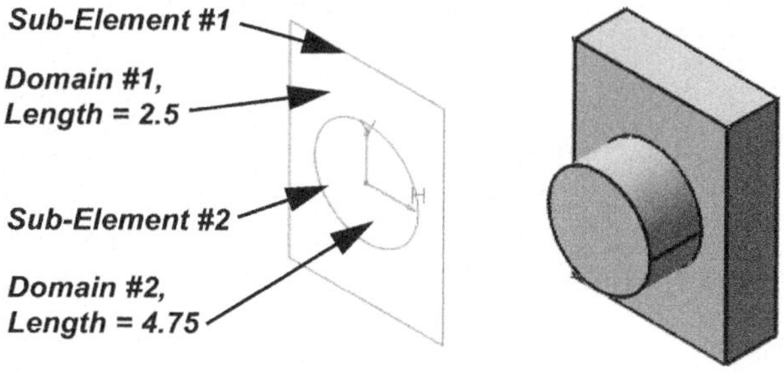

Figure 3–18

The system does not extrude the full area inside each profile to the length that you specify. It extrudes the domain, or the area **between** the profiles to the specified length. Note the results of different length values for each domain, as shown in Figure 3–19.

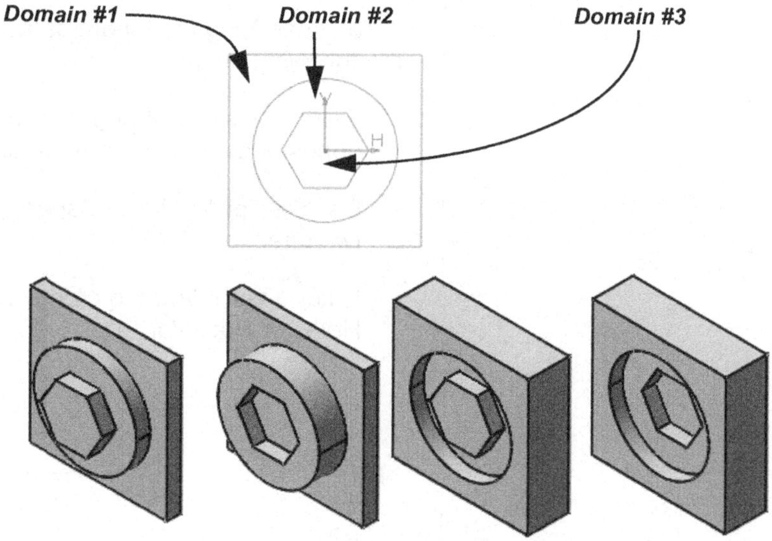

Figure 3–19

How To: Create a Multi-Pad Feature

1. Select a sketch with multiple profiles and click  (Multi-Pad). The Multi-Pad dialog box opens.
2. Select a domain from those listed in the dialog box.
3. In the *Limit 1 and Limit 2* fields, enter a value for the distance at which to extrude the selected domain.
4. Repeat this process for all domains, as shown in Figure 3–20.

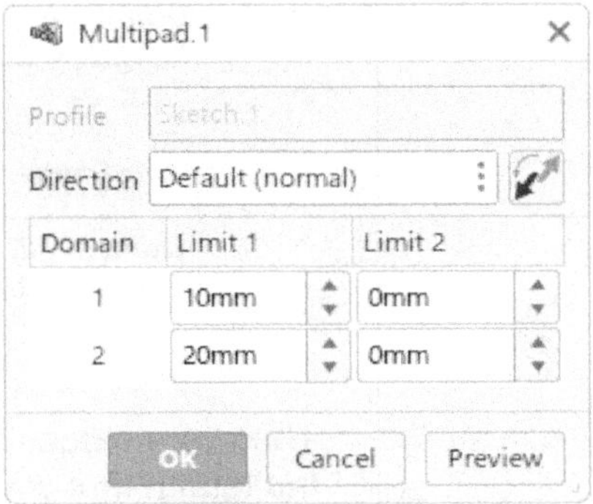

Figure 3–20

Length Options

When specifying the length of the domains, you can use one of the following options:

- Enter a positive or negative value to extrude the domain to opposite directions from the sketch.
- Use the second limit to specify the length of the domain in two directions.
- Enter a zero depth to create voids in the feature to resemble Holes or Pockets.

Practice 3a Creating a Multi-Pad Feature

Practice Objectives

- Use a sketch with multiple profiles to create a multi-pad feature.
- Add dress-up features to finish the part model.

In this practice, you will create the part shown in Figure 3–21. After creating a multi-profile sketch, you will use the multi-pad feature to create the Pad geometry. Later, you will modify the depths of the various profiles of the multi-pad feature using the Multi-Pad Definition dialog box.

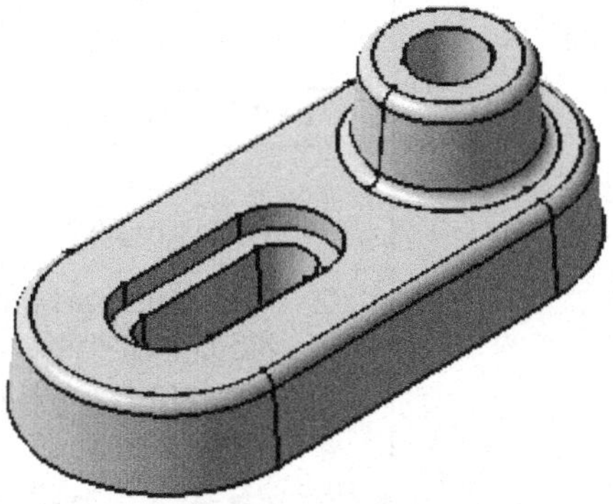

Figure 3–21

Task 1 - Create a new part.

1. Create a new 3D Part called **Sliding_Cam**. Ensure that the **Enable hybrid design** option is cleared.
2. Set model units to millimeters (mm).

Task 2 - Create a sketch with multiple profiles.

Design Considerations

A sketch with multiple profiles cannot be extruded to different heights using a single Pad feature. This multi-profile sketch will be used with a multi-pad feature to create a part that has surfaces of different heights.

1. Select the **xy Plane** and click  (Sketch).

2. Create the sketch shown in Figure 3–22. The geometric constraints are hidden to clarify the display.

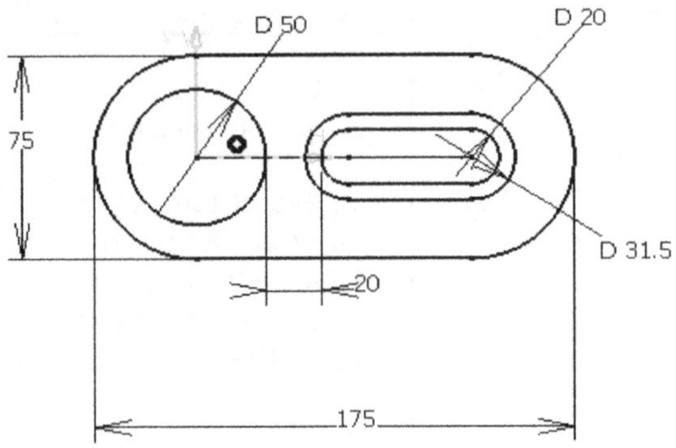

Figure 3–22

Task 3 - Create a multi-pad feature.

1. With the sketch still highlighted, click  (Multi-Pad).

2. The Multipad dialog box opens, as shown in Figure 3–23. Note that there are four domains in the sketch, indicated by the numbers 1 to 4 in the sketch graphics.

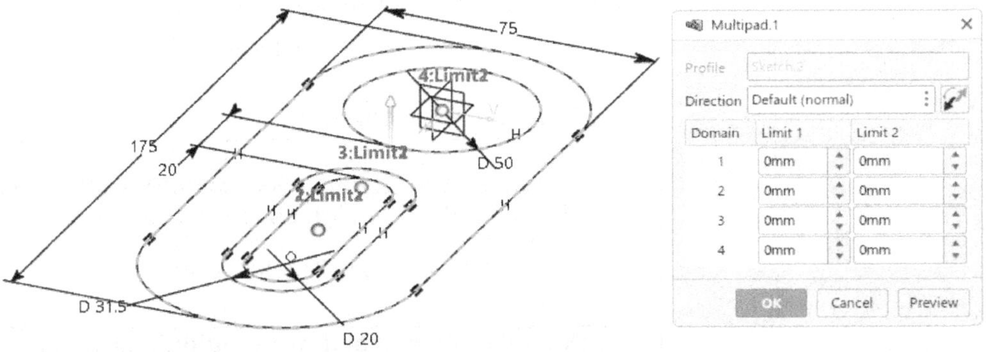

Figure 3–23

3. For the 4th domain (the circle), enter **50.0** in the *Limit 1* field and click **Preview**. The part displays as shown in Figure 3–24.

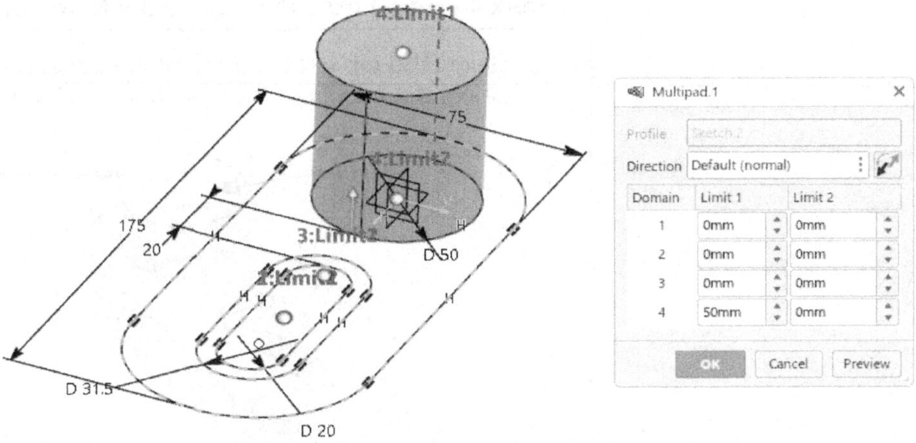

Figure 3–24

4. For the 2nd domain (area between the two elongated holes), enter **19.00** in the *Limit 1* field and click **Preview**. The part displays as shown in Figure 3–25.

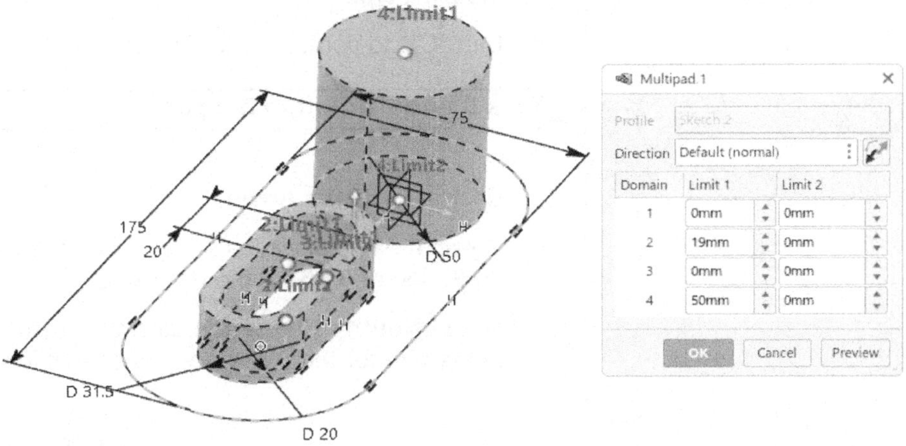

Figure 3–25

5. Select the domain for the large, outer elongated hole. Enter **25.0** in the *Limit 1* field and click **Preview**.

6. Leave the *Length* of the remaining domain at **0**.

7. Click **OK** to complete the feature.

8. Hide the three default planes.

Task 4 - Add a hole that is coaxial to the cylindrical boss.

1. Select the top circular face of the boss, hold <Ctrl>, and select the circular edge, as shown in Figure 3–26.

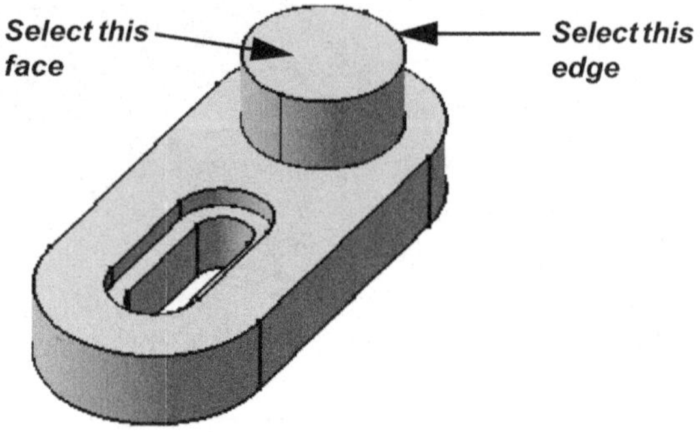

Figure 3–26

2. Click  (Hole) to create a hole.
3. Enter **19.00** for the *Main Diameter* and select **Up to last** for the *Limit type.*
4. Click **OK** to complete the feature.

Task 5 - Add a draft to the part.

1. Click  (Draft Angle).
2. Select the five surfaces shown in Figure 3–27 as the faces to draft, and enter **5** for the draft *Angle*.
3. Select **Neutral Element** to activate it and select the top face of the part for the reference, as shown in Figure 3–27.

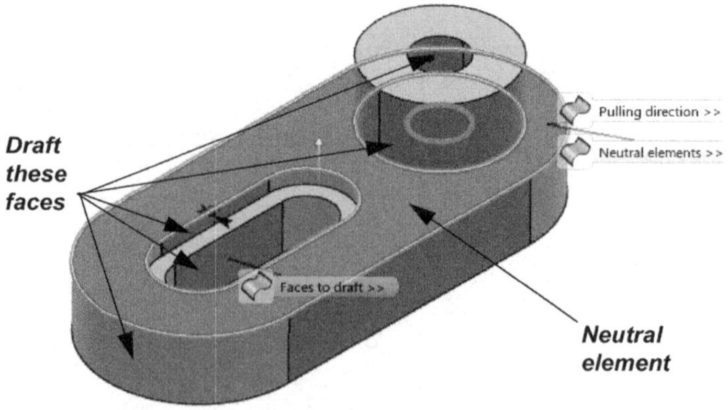

Figure 3–27

4. Click **OK** to complete the feature.
5. Go to the Back quick view and set the display to **Shading With Edges and Hidden Edges**. The model is now drafted, as shown in Figure 3–28.

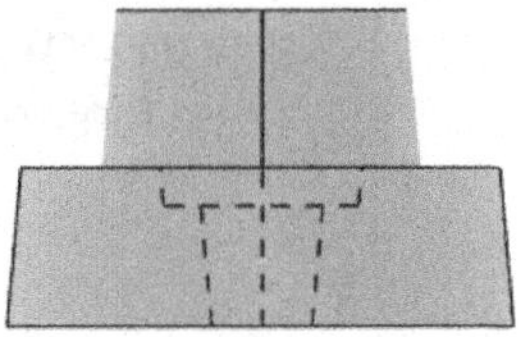

Figure 3–28

6. Set the display back to **Shading with sharp and smooth Edges**.

Task 6 - Add fillet features to the part.

1. Click  (Edge Fillet).
2. Enter **3.80** for the *Radius*.
3. Select the three edges shown in Figure 3–29 as the objects to fillet.

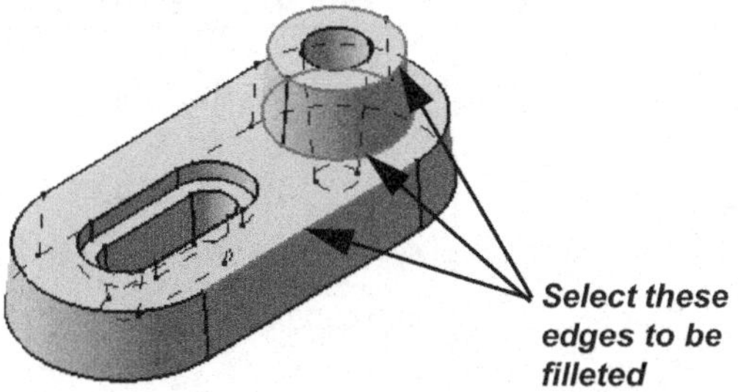

Figure 3–29

4. Click **OK** to complete the feature. The part displays as shown in Figure 3–30.

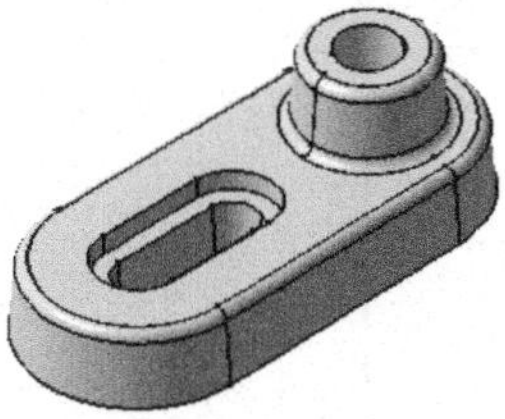

Figure 3–30

Task 7 - Change the depth of the multi-pad feature.

1. In the specification tree, double-click on **Multipad.1**.
2. Change the *Limit 1* of the large outer domain from *25.00* to **12.5**.
3. Click **OK** to complete the feature. The part displays as shown in Figure 3–31.

When working with multi-pad features, ensure that you make changes to all of the domains to maintain your design intent.

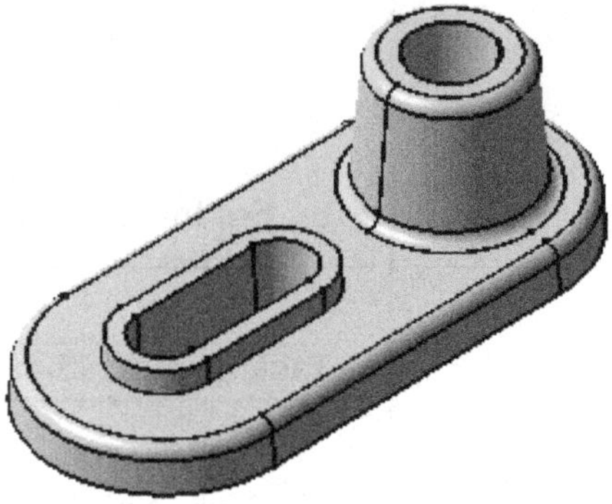

Figure 3–31

4. Click  to remove the last change.

Task 8 - Save the part and close the window.

1. Save the part and close the window.

Practice 3b Using Sketch Sub-Elements

Practice Objective

- Use portions of a multi-profile sketch to create several Pad features.

In this practice, you will create the part shown in Figure 3–32. You will begin by creating a self-intersecting multi-profile sketch. From this sketch, you will create Pad features using individual profiles from the sketch. You will also create Hole features on the cylindrical surface of one of the Pad features.

Figure 3–32

Task 1 - Create a new part.

1. Create a new 3D Part called ***<Your_Initials>*_Conn_Rod**. Ensure that the **Enable hybrid design** option is cleared.

Task 2 - Create a sketch with several intersecting profiles.

Design Considerations

When a sketch is created with intersecting profiles, it cannot be directly used as a profile for a Pad feature. However, you can select individual profiles to create Pad features (performed in the following task).

1. Select the **xy Plane** and click  (Sketch).

2. Create the sketch shown in Figure 3–33.

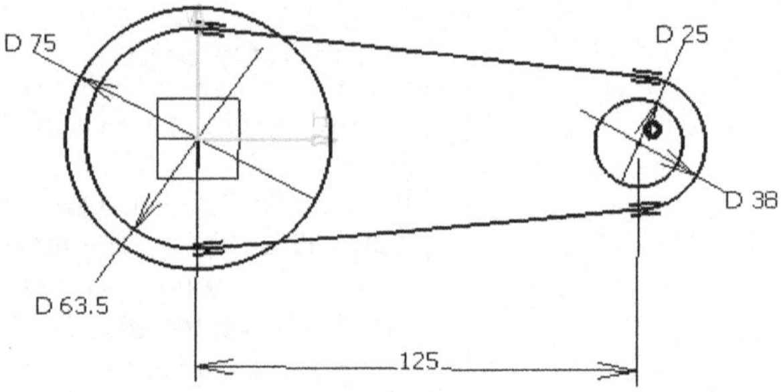

Figure 3–33

Task 3 - Create a Pad feature from a portion of the profile.

In this task, you will create a Pad feature using the sub-elements of a sketch.

1. With the sketch still highlighted, click  (Pad). An error message opens prompting you that the sketch is not valid. The sketch is invalid because the profiles intersect each other.
2. Click **OK** to continue using the selected profile.
3. Right-click in the *Profile* field and select **Go to profile definition**, as shown in Figure 3–34.

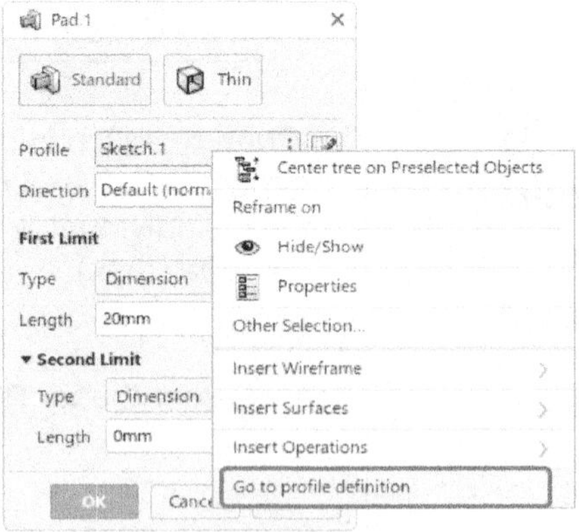

Figure 3–34

4. If required, select **Sketch.1** in the *Starting elements* field and click  to remove the sketch from the list.
5. In the Profile Definition dialog box, select **Sub-elements**.

6. Select one of the bi-tangent lines of the sketch to add the profile to the feature, as shown in Figure 3–35.

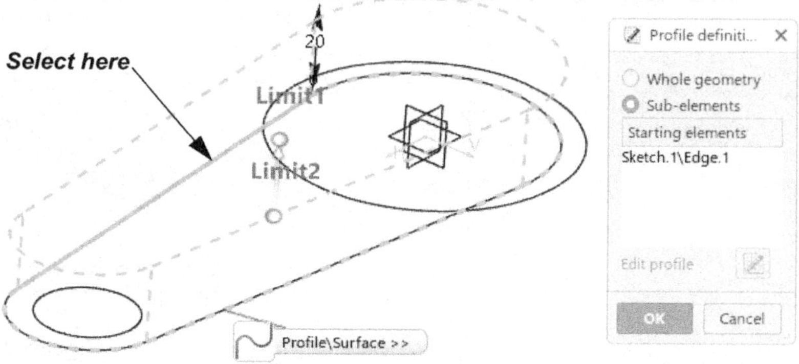

Figure 3–35

7. In the Profile dialog box, click **OK** to complete identification of the sub-element of the sketch.
8. In the Pad Definition dialog box, for the *Length*, enter **6.25**.

   Click (Mirrored extent).
9. Click **OK** to complete the feature. The part displays as shown in Figure 3–36.

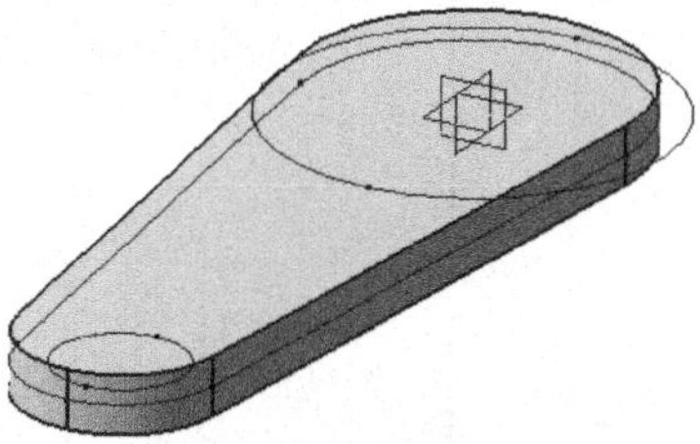

Figure 3–36

10. In the specification tree, select **Sketch.1** and repeat the process to create a second Pad feature, using the small circle sub-element. Set the *Length* to **12.50** and select **Mirrored extent**.
11. Repeat the process and create a third Pad feature, using the large circle sub-element. Set the *Length* to **16.00** and select **Mirrored extent**.

12. Hide the sketch and three datum planes. Two views of the model are shown in Figure 3–37.

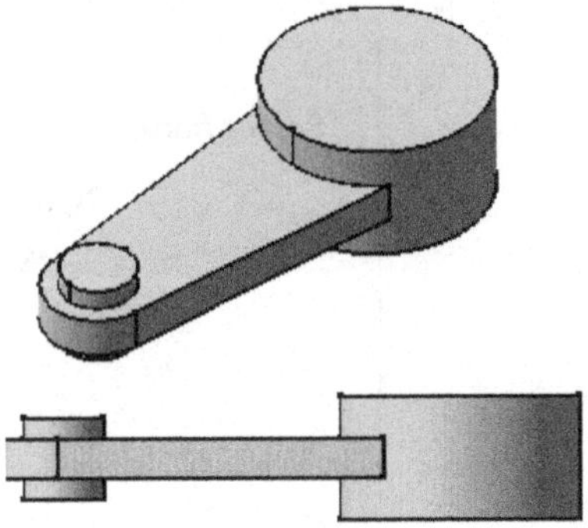

Figure 3–37

Task 4 - Create two holes that are coaxial to the bosses on the part.

1. Create a hole that is concentric to the large cylindrical boss, as shown in Figure 3–38, using the following values:
    - *Limit Type:* **Up To Last**
    - *Main Diameter:* **38.00**
2. Create a **12.50** diameter hole that is concentric to the smaller cylindrical boss.

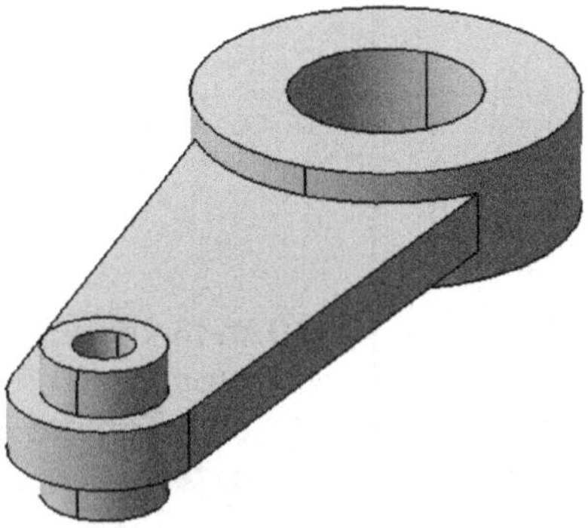

Figure 3–38

Task 5 - Create several holes on the large cylindrical boss.

1. Select the cylindrical surface of the large boss for the first hole, as shown in Figure 3–39, and click  (Hole).

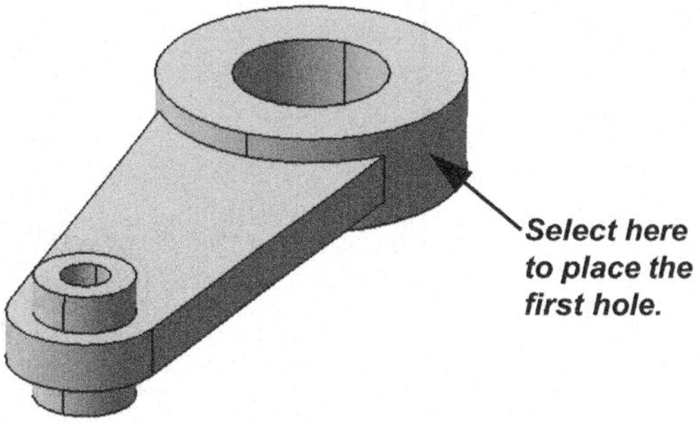

Figure 3–39

2. For the *Diameter*, enter **6.25**. The **Up to last** option remains selected from the previous feature.
3. To locate the hole around the cylinder, click .
4. Show the three datum planes.

*Go to the **Isometric** quick view and generate the geometric constraints.*

5. Constrain the asterisk to be coincident with the xy plane and the yz plane, as shown in Figure 3–40.

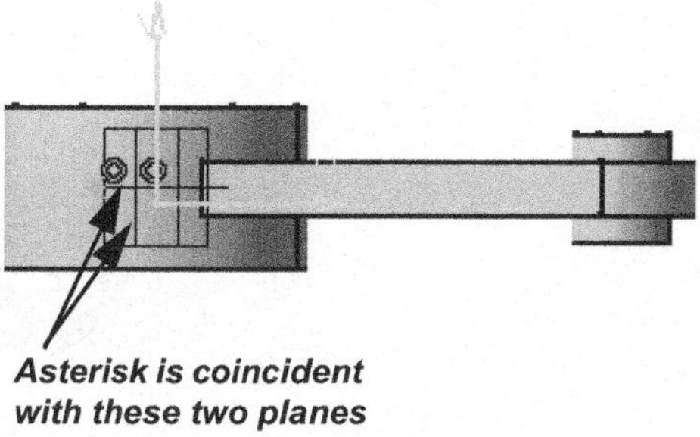

Figure 3–40

6. Click  (Exit app) to exit the sketch.
7. Click **OK** to complete the Hole feature.

8. Repeat the process to create a second **6.25** diameter hole. Select **Up To Next** for the extension and make the asterisk coincident with the xy plane and zx plane. The part displays as shown in Figure 3–41.

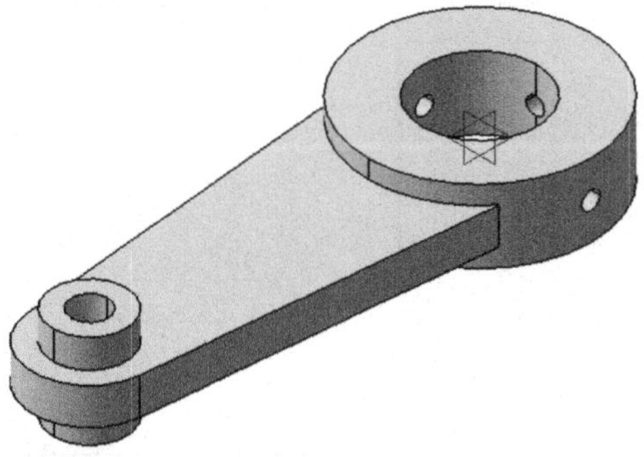

Figure 3–41

9. Hide the three datum planes.

Task 6 - Create several Fillet features to complete the part.

1. Complete the model by adding **2.50** radius edge fillets to the four faces shown in Figure 3–42.

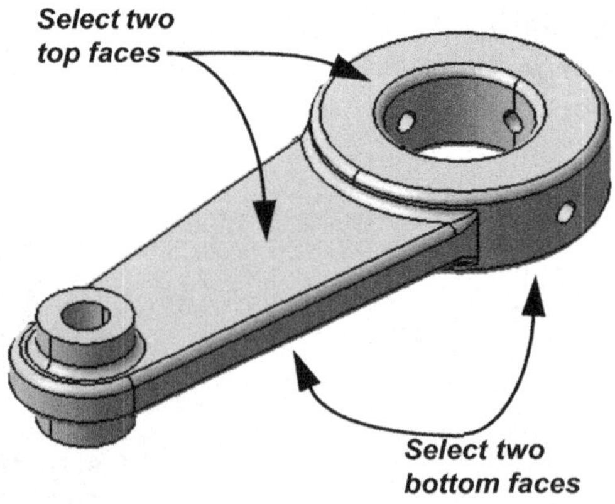

Figure 3–42

Task 7 - Save the part and close the window.

1. Save the part.
2. Close the window.

Practice 3c Engine Block

Practice Objectives

- Create profiles.
- Replace profiles.

In this practice, you will create an engine block, as shown in Figure 3–43. You will create the engine block using a .DXF file. The .DXF file contains all of the required 2D sections for the engine block. After creating the engine block, you will modify the model according to a set of design changes.

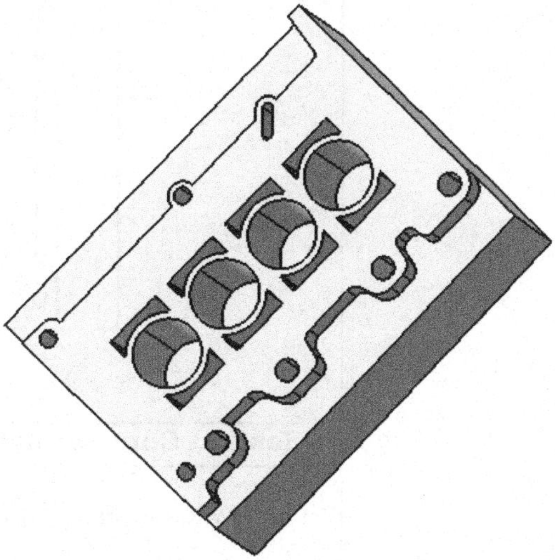

Figure 3–43

Task 1 - Create a new part.

1. Create a new 3D Part called ***<Your_initials>*_ Engine_ block**. Ensure that the **Enable hybrid design** option is cleared.

Task 2 - Open a part.

1. In the Top Bar, click (Add)>**Import**.
2. In the Format drop-down list, select **DXF2D (*.dxf)**.
3. Click on the **Open** icon in the *Filename* field.
4. Browse and select **Engine_block.dxf**.

5. Click **OK** to import the model. The file displays as shown in Figure 3–44.

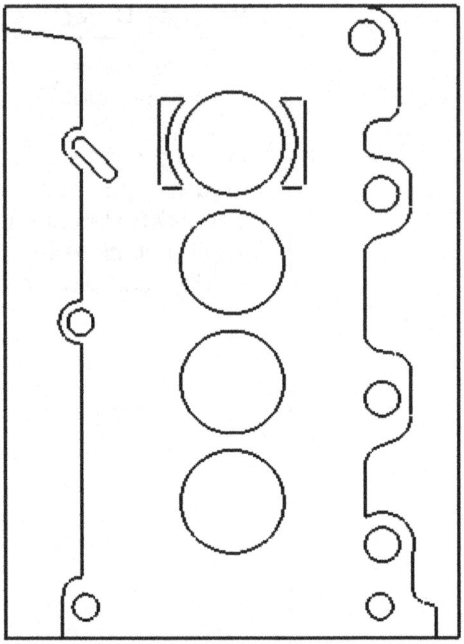

Figure 3–44

Task 3 - Copy the data to a 3D Part.

1. Switch to the new part window.
2. In the Essentials section of the Action Bar, click  (Geometrical Set) to insert a new geometrical set.
3. Leave the *Name* field empty and click **OK** to create a geometrical set with the default name.
4. Switch to the **Engine_block.dxf** window.
5. In the specification tree, right-click and copy the Main View. Switch to the new part window and paste it into **Geometrical Set.1**. The Main View sketch displays in the specification tree, as shown on the left in Figure 3–45, and in the drawing shown on the right.

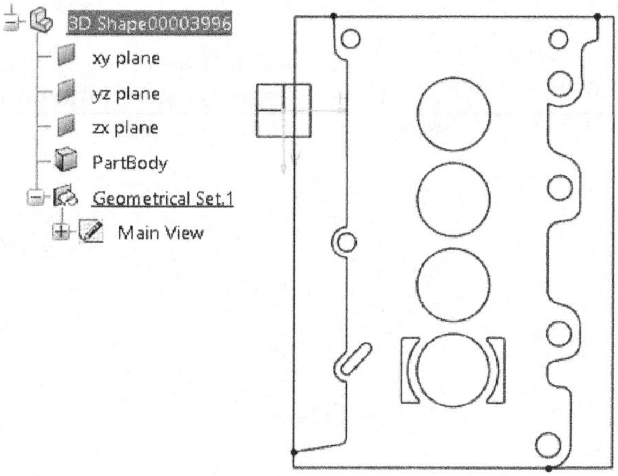

Figure 3–45

Task 4 - Create profiles.

In this task, you will create profiles from the Main View sketch. You will also create three lines, which are used to create one of the profiles.

1. Double-click on the Main View sketch to enter the Sketcher app.

2. Create the three lines shown in Figure 3–46.

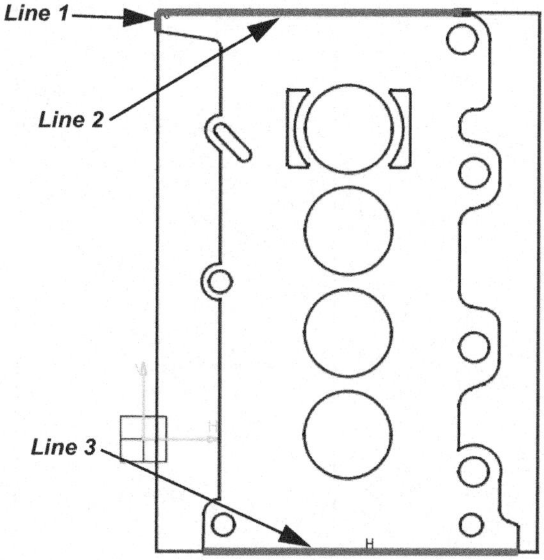

Figure 3–46

You might have to expand the Action Bar on the right side to find the icon.

3. In the Sketch section of the Action Bar, click (3D Profile). Select the line as shown in Figure 3–47. Change the *Color* to **Red**.

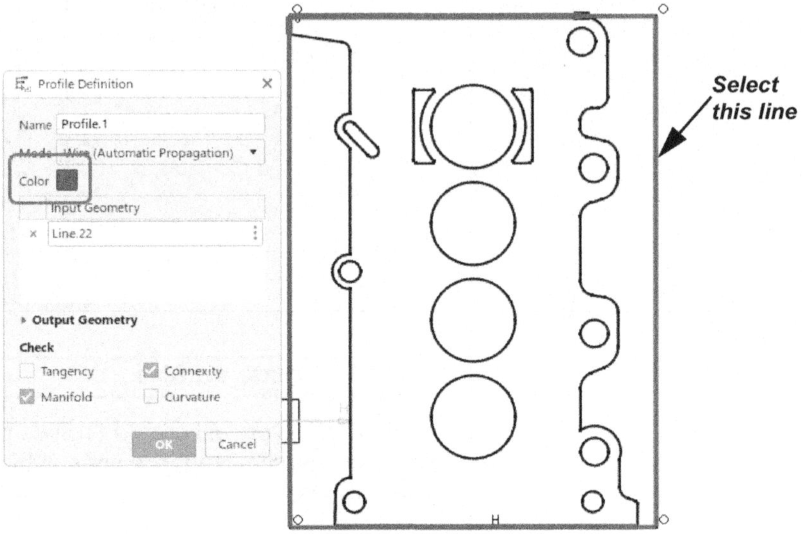

Figure 3–47

4. Click **OK** to complete the feature.

5. Click (3D Profile) again. Select the line, as shown in Figure 3–48. Change the *Color* to **Blue**.

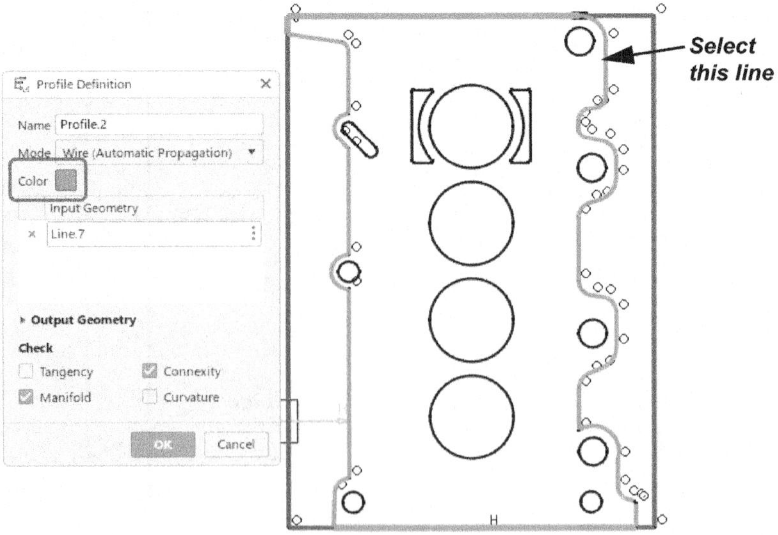

Figure 3–48

*The **Check connexity** option analyzes the profile for any gaps between the elements.*

6. Click **OK** to complete the feature.

7. Click  (3D Profile) again. Select the four large circles and change the *Color* to **Yellow**. Ensure that the **Check connexity** option is cleared.

8. Create the other profiles, as shown in Figure 3–49. Color the profiles as follows:

   - *Elongated hole:* **Orange**
   - *Seven small circles:* **Green** (one profile)
   - *Cooling channels:* **Brown** (one profile)

   Ensure that the **Check connexity** option is cleared for complex profiles (for the Green, Brown, and Yellow profiles).

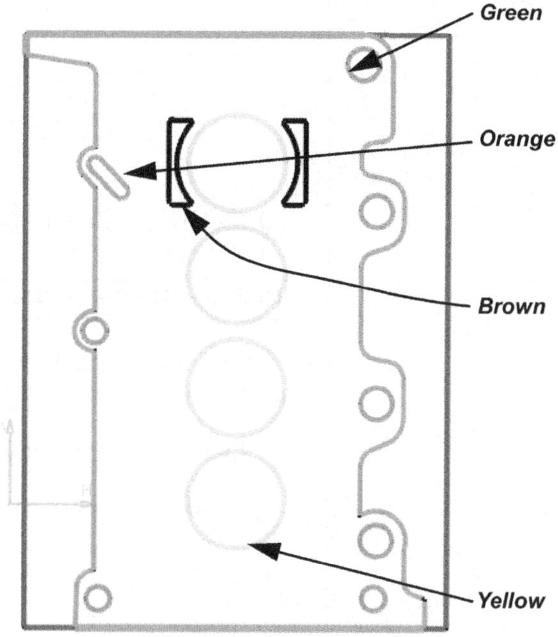

Figure 3–49

9. Create seven points that are concentric to the centers of the small green circles, as shown in Figure 3–50.

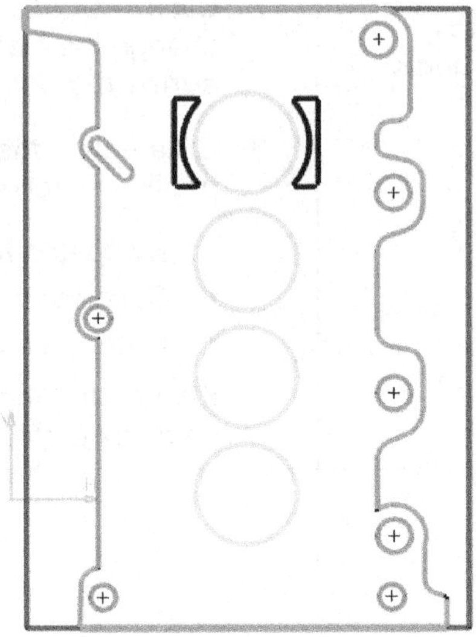

Figure 3–50

10. Exit the Sketcher app.

Task 5 - Create sketch-based features using the profiles.

In this task, you will create Pads, Pockets, and Holes using the profiles you have created.

1. Define the PartBody as the In Work Object.

2. Create a Pad with the red profile shown in Figure 3–51, as follows:

   - *Type:* **Dimension**
   - *Length:* **130mm**

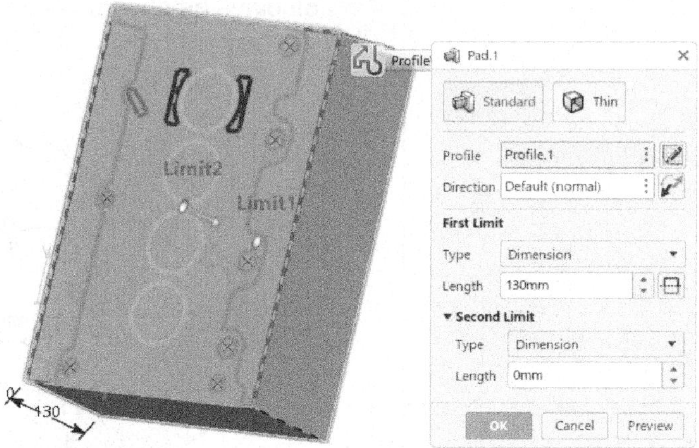

Figure 3–51

3. Create a Pad with the blue profile shown in Figure 3–52, as follows:

   - *Type:* **Dimension**
   - *Length:* **30mm**
   - *Direction:* (opposite to the 1st Pad)

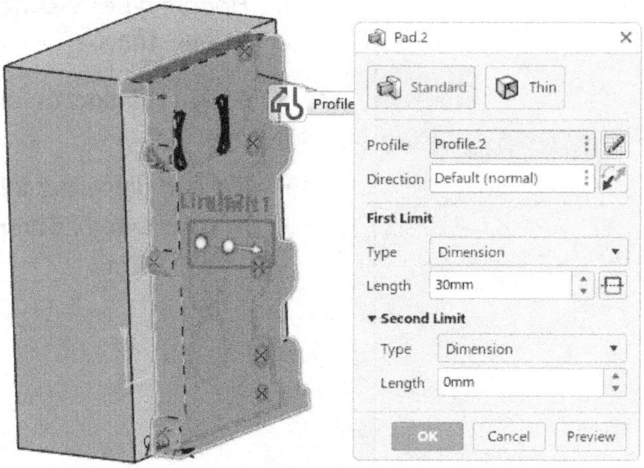

Figure 3–52

4. Create a Pocket with the yellow profile. The total length of the Pocket from the top surface is **110mm**.

5. Create two more Pockets with the brown and orange profiles. The total length of the Pockets from the top surface is 110mm. Hide **Profile.5** for the green circles. The model displays as shown in Figure 3–53.

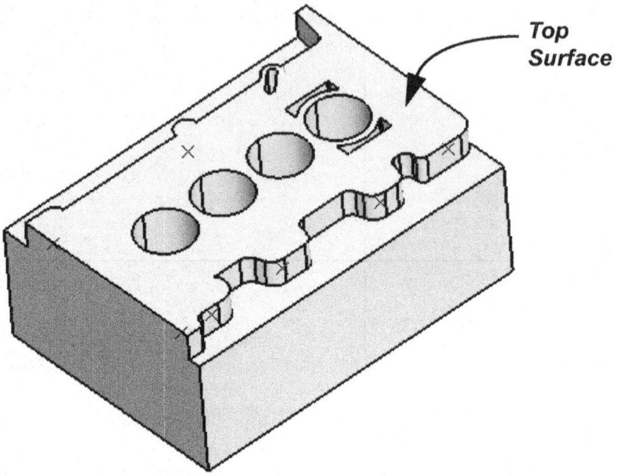

Figure 3–53

6. Create a threaded Hole as shown in Figure 3–54. Enter the following parameters:

   - *Main Diameter:* **20mm**
   - *Main Depth:* **60mm**
   - *Bottom type:* **V-Bottom**
   - *Angle:* **100deg**

7. In the *Thread* section of the dialog box, enter the following parameters:

   - *Thread diameter:* **22mm**
   - *Thread Depth:* **60mm**
   - *Pitch:* **1mm**

The model displays as shown in Figure 3–54.

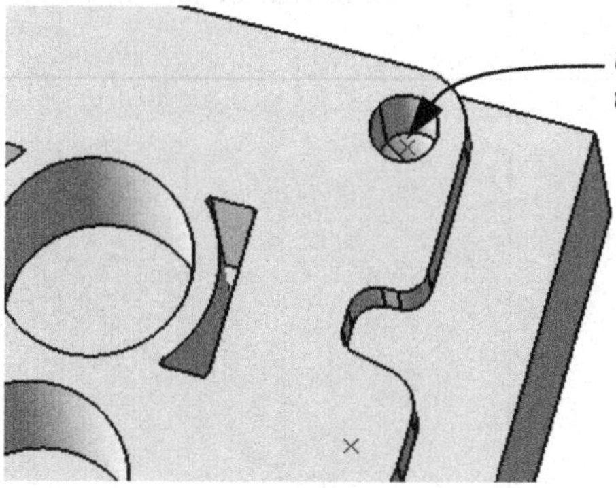

Figure 3–54

Task 6 - Create the patterns.

1. Create a rectangular pattern, as shown in Figure 3–55 with the following parameters:
   - *Parameters:* **Instance(s) & Spacing**
   - *Instances:* **4**
   - *Spacing:* **70mm**

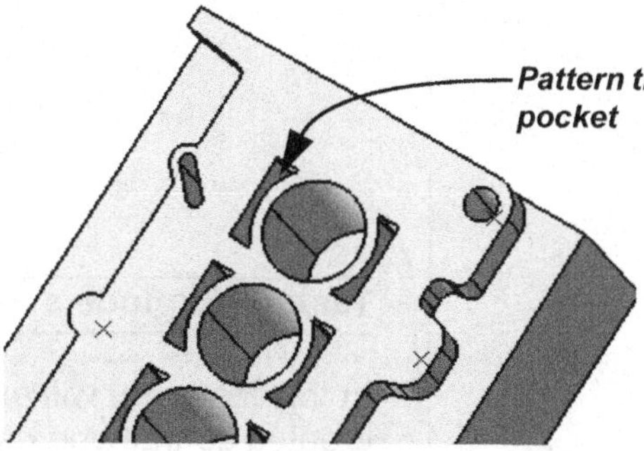

Figure 3–55

2. In the specification tree or the model, select the hole that you created in the previous task. Click  (User Pattern).

3. In the specification tree, select the **Main View** sketch. The User Pattern dialog box opens as shown in Figure 3–56.

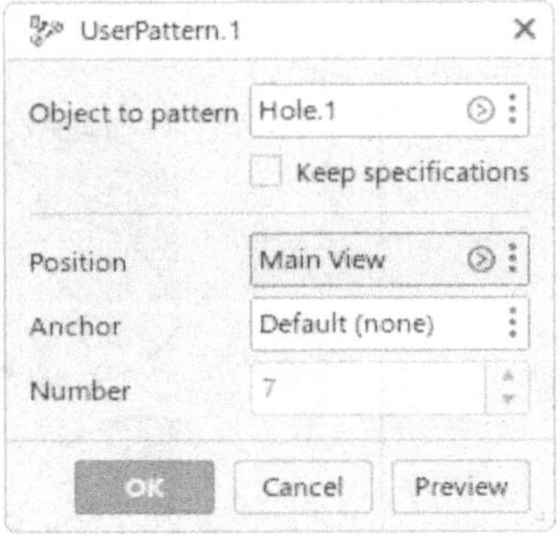

Figure 3–56

4. Click **OK** to complete the feature. The model displays as shown in Figure 3–57.

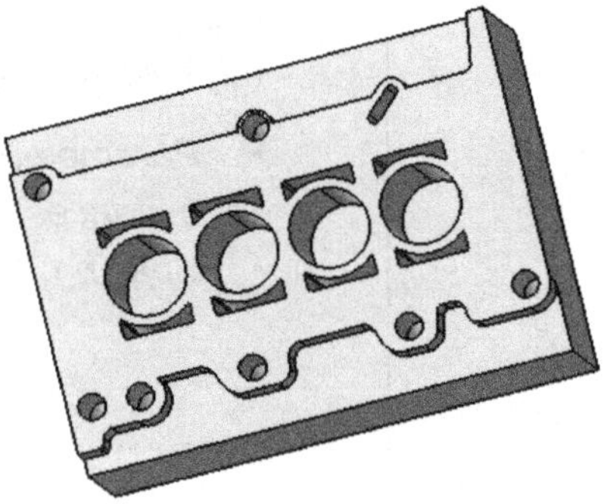

Figure 3–57

Task 7 - Explode a user pattern.

In this task, you will explode the user pattern that you have just created so that you can modify each hole separately.

1. In the specification tree, right-click on **UserPattern.1** and select **UserPattern.1 object>Explode...**, as shown in Figure 3–58.

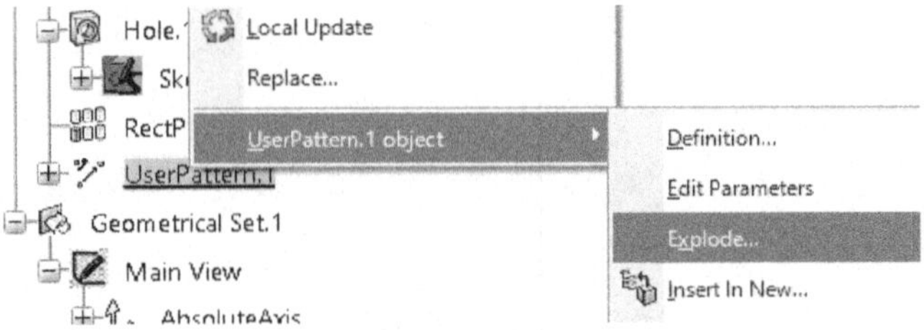

Figure 3–58

Note the change in the specification tree. **UserPattern.1** no longer displays and six new holes are added, as shown in Figure 3–59.

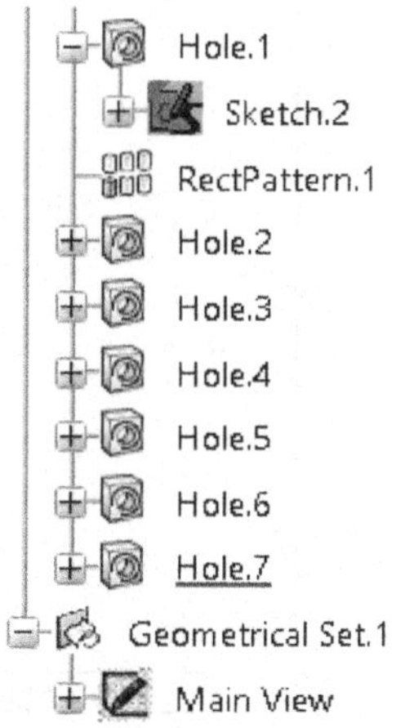

Figure 3–59

2. Show **Profile.5** for the green circles and then zoom in and inspect the diameter of the holes. Three holes need to be modified, as shown in Figure 3–60.

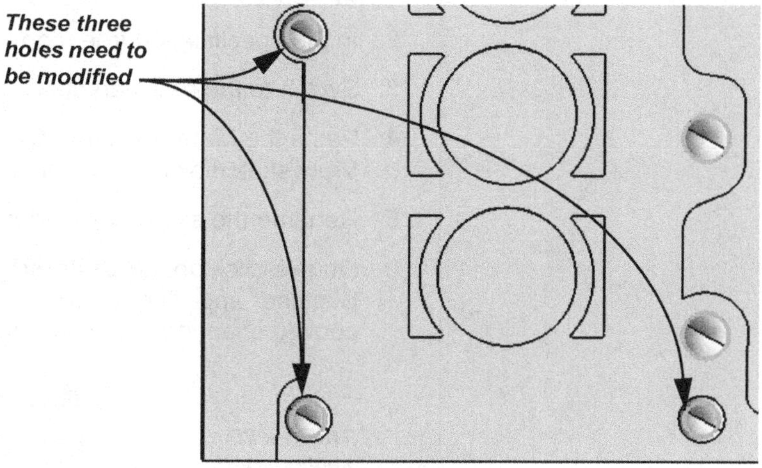

Figure 3–60

3. Change the hole diameters of the three holes to **15mm** and the thread diameters to **17mm**. The model displays as shown in Figure 3–61.

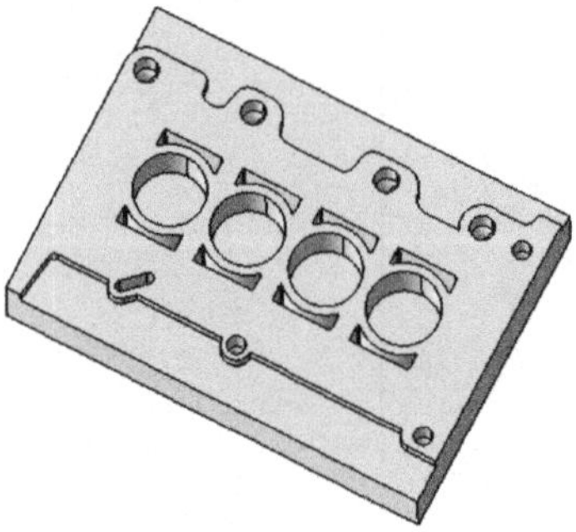

Figure 3–61

Task 8 - Replace a profile.

In this task, you will work with a revised 2D section .DXF file. According to the updated version, the cooling channels have changed and these changes need to be applied to the model.

1. Following the instruction in Task 2, open **Engine_block_ updated.dxf**.
2. In the specification tree, copy the **Main View**.
3. Switch to the new part file.
4. Paste the **Main View** into **Geometrical Set.1**. The **Main View** sketch displays in the specification tree and model.
5. Rename the sketch as **Updated_version**.
6. Double-click on the **Updated_version** sketch to enter the Sketcher app. The 2D section updates to the modified cooling channels, as shown in Figure 3–62.

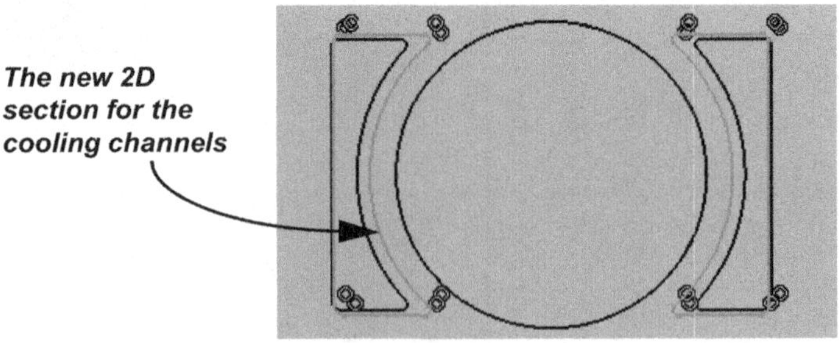

Figure 3–62

7. Click (3D Profile). Select the cooling channels and change the *Color* to **Dark Blue**. Ensure that the **Check connexity** option is cleared.

8. Click **OK** to complete the feature.

9. Exit the Sketcher app.

10. In the specification tree, locate the Pocket feature for the cooling channels and locate the brown profile. Right-click on the brown profile and select **Replace...,** as shown in Figure 3–63.

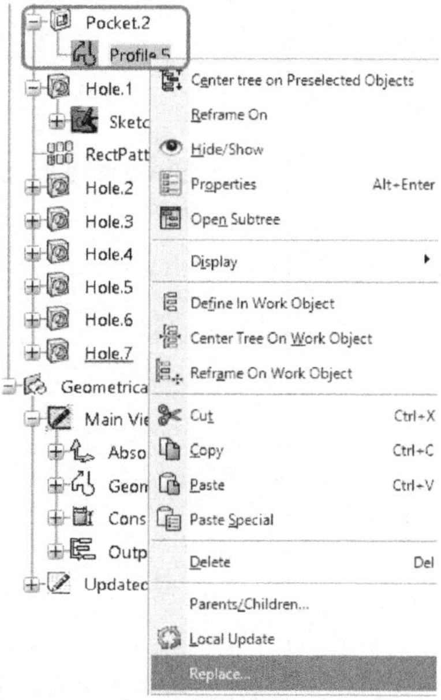

Figure 3–63

The Replace dialog box opens as shown in Figure 3–64.

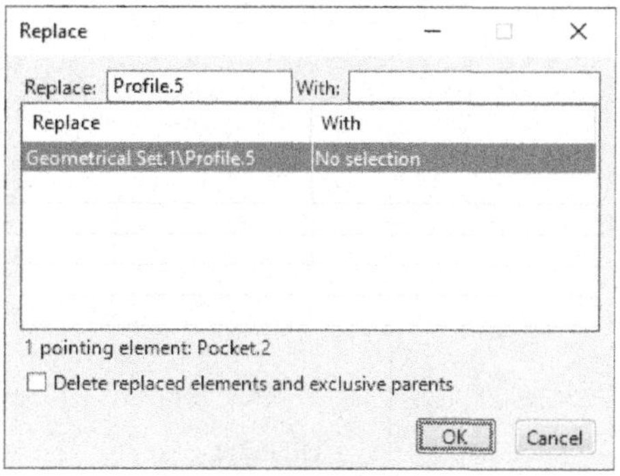

Figure 3–64

11. To replace the brown profile with the dark blue profile, select the dark blue profile in the specification tree or model.

12. Click **OK** to complete the feature. The model displays as shown in Figure 3–65.

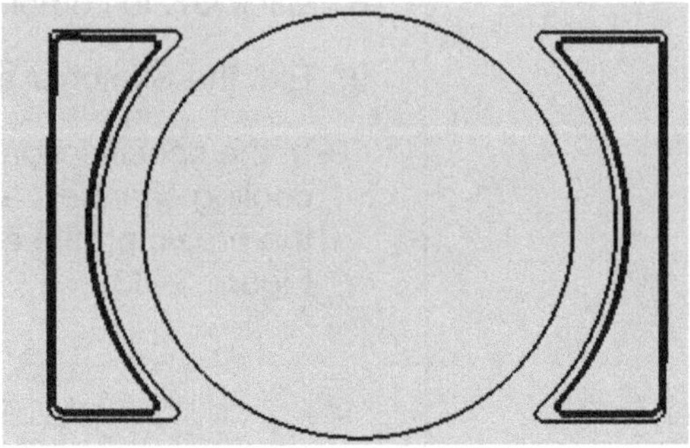

Figure 3–65

13. Save and close the part model. Close the two .DXF files as well.

Practice 3d Adjustable Bracket

Practice Objective

- Create a part without any instructions.

Create **AdjustableBracket** part from a single sketch, as shown in Figure 3–66.

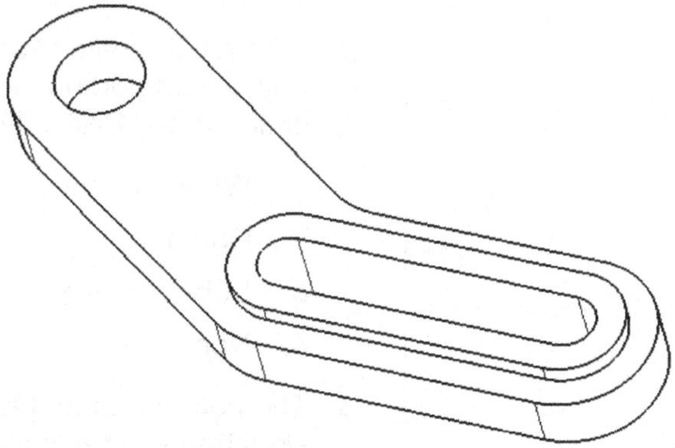

Figure 3–66

The drawing views are shown in Figure 3–67.

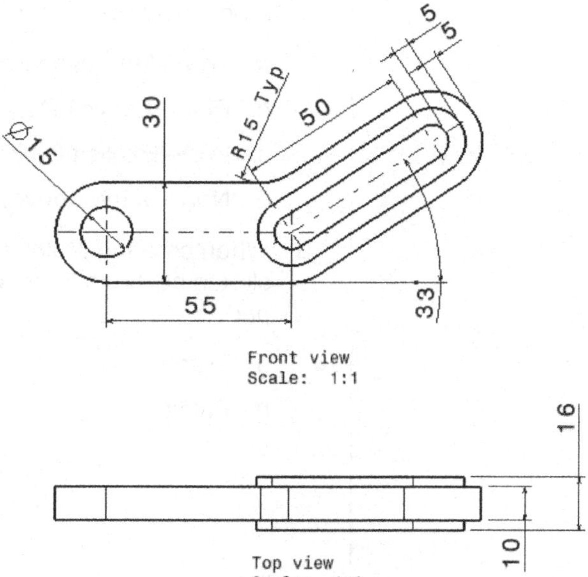

Figure 3–67

Chapter Review Questions

1. In a multi-profile sketch, if the two profiles intersect one another, 3DEXPERIENCE eliminates the intersecting parts of the profile, and creates the geometry.
   a. True
   b. False
2. With multi-profile sketches, you can create geometry from any closed portion of the profile by using the ________ option in the Profile Definition dialog box.
   a. Whole geometry
   b. Domain
   c. Sub-elements
   d. None of the above.
3. The purpose of an Output Feature is to make selected sketched elements independent of the sketch in which they were created.
   a. True
   b. False
4. When selecting the entities to include in a 3D Profile, which mode includes all of the point continuous entities?
   a. Wire (Automatic Propagation)
   b. Point (Explicit Definition)
   c. Wire (Explicit Definition)
   d. None of the above.
5. When creating Multi-Pad features, you can use the different sketch sections to define unique depths for each resulting pad.
   a. True
   b. False

6. The areas between each sketch section are called _____.
   a. Sub-sections
   b. Pad Areas
   c. Faces
   d. Domains

Answers: 1b, 2c, 3a, 4a, 5a, 6d

Advanced Part Design

Complex models often require more advanced options to create the required geometry. You might need to consider using advanced sketch-based features, such as Multi-sections Solids, Ribs, or Slots throughout the design cycle of complex parts. Multi-sections Solids have advanced options that control the transition surfaces using guides and spines. Ribs and Slots can be created using advanced options, which enable you to control the relationship between the profile and the center curve.

Learning Objectives in This Chapter

- Create a solid from the intersection of two profiles using a Solid Combine feature.
- Learn how to use Multi-sections Solids to create a solid between two or more sections.
- Understand the impact of closing points on resulting geometry.
- Understand the Rib feature and the Slot feature.
- Learn how to use the advanced options in the Shell Definition dialog box.

4.1 Solid Combine Feature

The Solid Combine feature enables you to create a solid from the intersection of two profiles that are projected perpendicular to their profile planes or along a specified direction. Think of it as creating a Pad feature from the profiles and then trimming everything except for the common volume between the solids. The sketch for each profile must consist of a single, closed chain of elements.

General Steps

Use the following general steps to create a solid combine:

1. Open the Solid Combine dialog box.
2. Select the two profiles.
3. Specify the direction (if required) and complete the feature.

Step 1 - Open the Solid Combine dialog box.

Click  (Solid Combine) in the Model section of the Action Bar, as shown in Figure 4–1.

Figure 4–1

The Combine dialog box opens as shown in Figure 4–2.

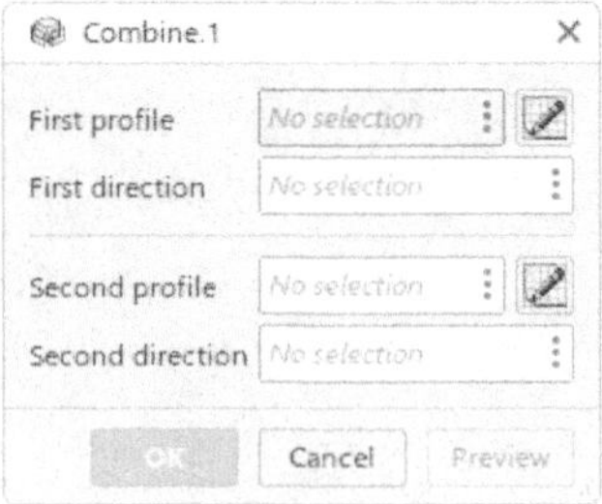

Figure 4–2

Step 2 - Select the two profiles.

Select the two sketches that define the profiles for the Solid Combine feature. In the example shown in Figure 4–3, two profiles have been developed to create the Base feature for an offset box end wrench.

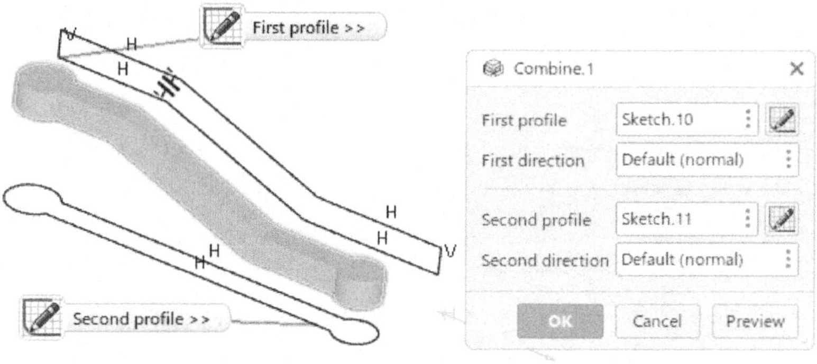

Figure 4–3

Step 3 - Specify the direction (if required) and complete the feature.

By default, normal to the profile directions are used. You can define a custom direction by specifying another direction. The direction can be defined by a line or plane or by right-clicking and selecting the X-, Y-, or Z-axis.

Click **OK** to complete the feature. The offset Wrench Base feature displays as shown in Figure 4–4.

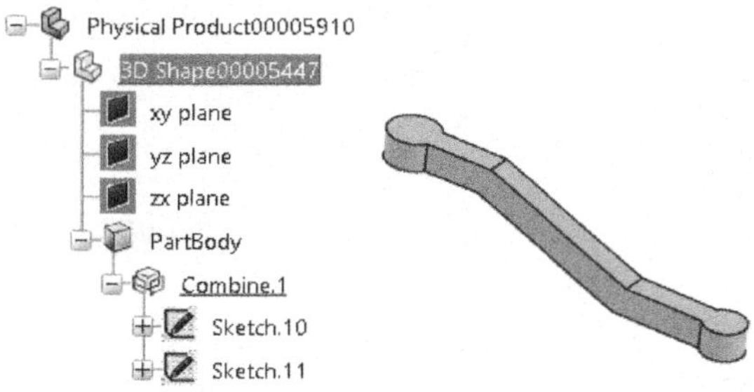

Figure 4–4

4.2 Creation of Multi-sections Solids

A Multi-sections Solid feature involves transitional surfaces being created between multiple selected sketches. The creation of a Multi-sections Solid between two sketched sections is shown in Figure 4–5.

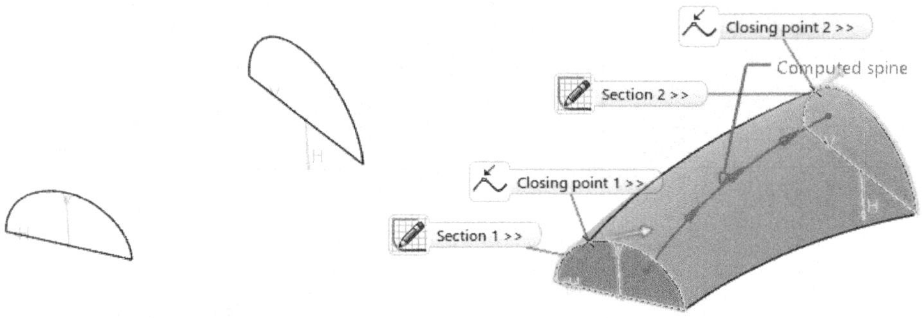

Figure 4–5

The transitional surfaces are created by connecting the vertices of the selected sketches with NURBS surfaces. The closing points indicate the first two vertices to connect. The system follows the sections in the direction indicated by the arrow.

The shape of a Multi-sections Solid feature is controlled using one or more of the parameters described in the table below. These parameters are defined using the Multi-sections Solid dialog box.

Parameter	Description
Sections	Any number of sections can be added to the feature to control its shape. A closed profile must be used to create the section.
Closing Points	Each section has a closing point that determines the starting point and direction of the Solid creation. The closing points must be located at the correct positions. The orientation arrows of the closing points must be pointing in the same direction.
Guides	A guide is a curve that defines the path that the Multi-sections Solid must follow as it transitions between sections. The guide must intersect each section. More than one guide can be specified.
Spine	A spine is a curve to which the cross-section of the Multi-sections Solid must remain perpendicular. There can only be one spine curve per Multi-sections Solid.
Coupling type	Determines the transition type between sections. Coupling curves can be specified to explicitly define the Solid creation. A coupling curve must intersect each section.
Relimitation	Enables a Multi-sections Solid to be extended beyond the first or last section, up to the shortest guide curve.
Area Law	You can define and control the shape of a Multi-sections Solid between its sections.

General Steps

Use the following general steps to create and control a Multi-sections Solid feature:

1. Start the creation of the Multi-sections Solid feature.
2. Control the profile geometry with guides and spines.
3. Set the **Coupling** and **Relimitation** options.

Step 1 - Start the creation of the Multi-sections Solid feature.

The techniques used to create sections for an advanced Multi-sections Solid are the same as those used to create sections for basic Multi-sections Solids.

To begin the creation of a Multi-sections Solid feature, click  (Multi-sections Solid) in the Model section of the Action Bar. The Multi-sections Solid Definition dialog box opens as shown in Figure 4–6.

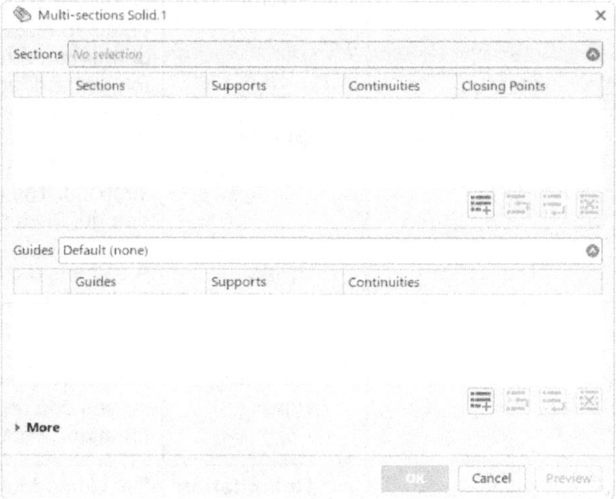

Figure 4–6

Sections for the feature are added by selecting curve geometry or sketches in the model or specification tree. The sections are added to the top of the dialog box, as shown in Figure 4–7.

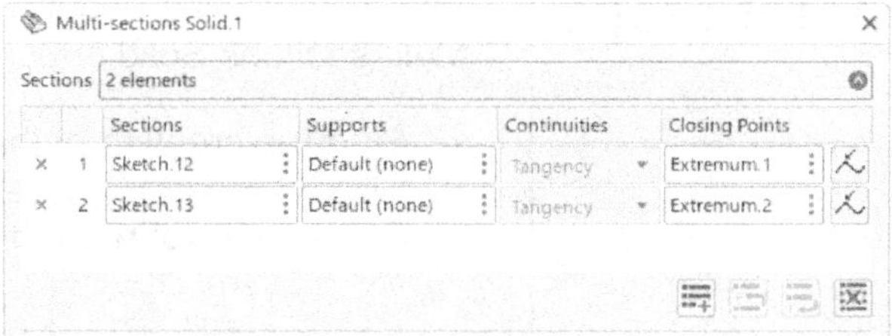

Figure 4–7

A section for a Multi-sections Solid can also be specified by selecting a face on the model that consists of a closed boundary. A Multi-sections Solid section requires the selection of curves. Therefore, 3DEXPERIENCE automatically adds a Boundary feature under the Multi-sections feature. The boundary of the surface is then used as the Multi-sections Solid section. An example is shown in Figure 4–8.

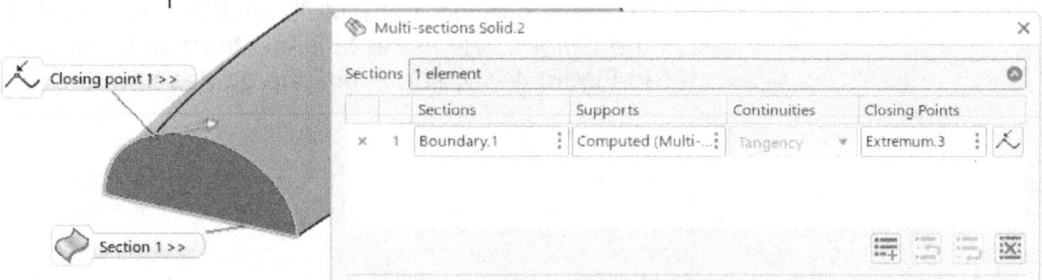

Figure 4–8

Step 2 - Control the profile geometry with guides and spines.

Once the sections have been selected, advanced options (such as guides and spines) can be added.

Guides

Guides provide an absolute path to blend the sections of the Multi-sections Solid together. The guide curve must intersect each section of the Solid feature. More than one guide can be used to control the Multi-sections Solid. The Multi-sections Solid only progresses as far as the last section, regardless of the length of the guide.

Although a guide can be created using a sketch, the curve is typically three-dimensional and created using wireframe features (e.g., Spline) in the Generative Shape Design app. In Figure 4–9, a splinar guide is created that connects the two sketches and extends past the end section.

The intersection of the guide and the Multi-sections Solid creates a vertex.

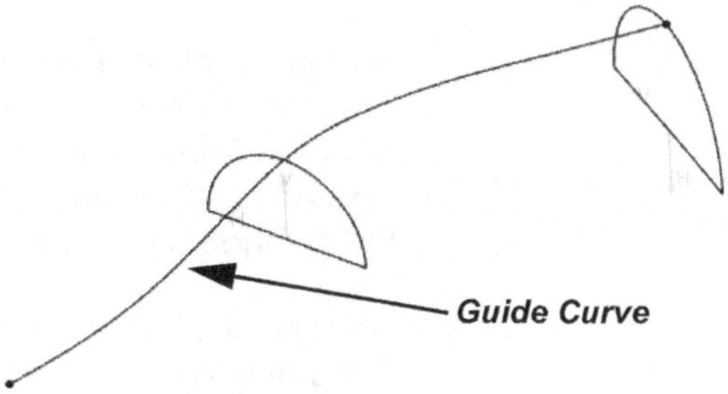

Figure 4–9

To use the guide in the Multi-sections Solid feature, select it in the *Guides* field in the Multi-sections Solid dialog box, as shown in Figure 4–10, and select the guides from the screen.

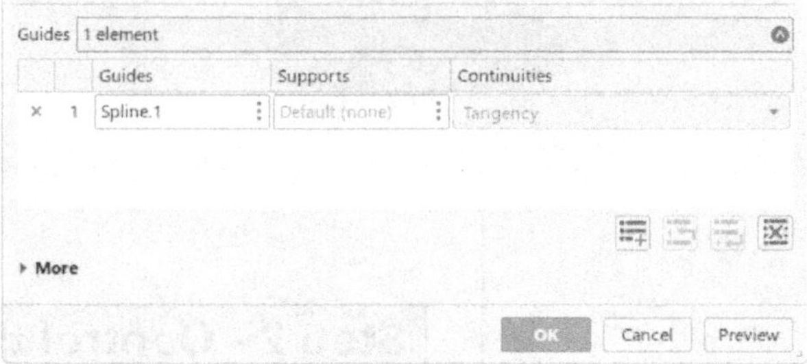

Figure 4–10

The Multi-sections Solid shown in Figure 4–11 is created with a guide to control the internal surface. Note the difference between this Multi-sections Solid and the Multi-sections Solid in Figure 4–5.

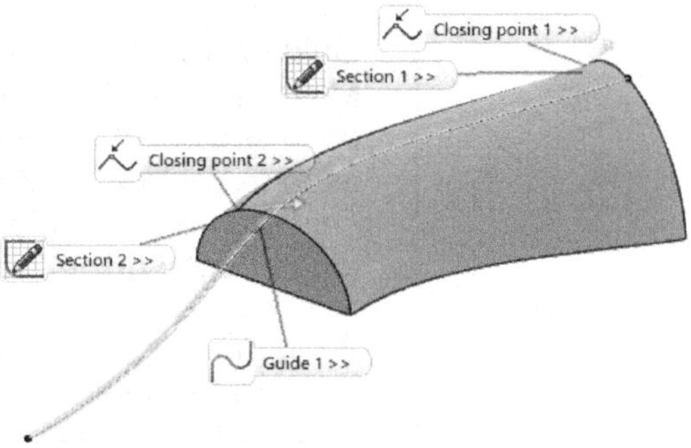

Figure 4–11

Spine

A spine controls the shape of the Multi-sections Solid as it progresses from one section to the next. The cross-section of the Multi-sections Solid must always be perpendicular to the spine. Therefore, only one spine can be selected for a Multi-sections Solid. The spine can be defined by a sketch, edge, or curve.

To specify a spine, select **More** to expand the Multi-sections Solid dialog box, as shown in Figure 4–12, and select the spine geometry to use.

If the Multi-sections feature cannot remain perpendicular to the spine while traveling through each section, then the feature might fail.

Figure 4–12

If a spine is not specified, 3DEXPERIENCE computes a default spine to control the shape of the Multi-sections Solid throughout its progression. To clear a spine and specify a system-default spine, right-click in the *Spine* field and select **Clear Selection**.

Step 3 - Set the Coupling and Relimitation options.

Coupling

The **Sections coupling type** option is used to define the transitions between the sections. These options are shown in Figure 4–13 and are as follows.

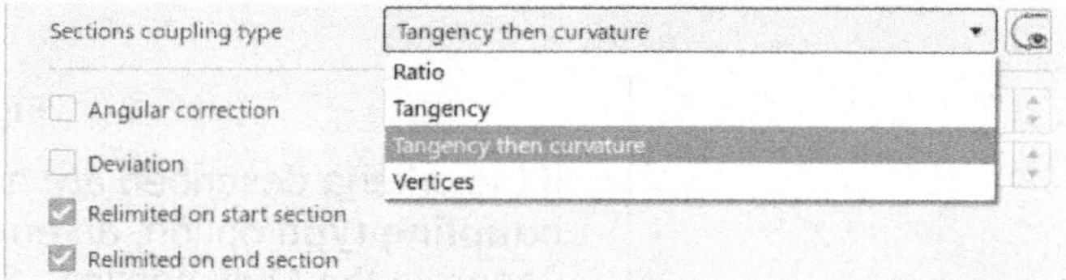

Figure 4–13

Coupling Option	Description
Ratio	If the sections are connected at positions, the ratio is computed by the percentage of the section profile length. This option is recommended when non-equal numbers of vertices are present in the sketch sections.
Tangency	If the sections have the same number of tangency discontinuity points, these points are coupled together between sections.
Tangency then curvature	If the sections have the same number of tangency and curvature discontinuity points, tangency discontinuity points are coupled together between sections, then curvature discontinuity points are coupled together between sections.
Vertices	If the sections have the same number of vertices, these points are coupled together between sections.
Couplings	You can create a coupling curve by selecting points on each section. After all of the coupling points have been selected, the coupling curve displays on the model.

An example of a model with couplings is shown in Figure 4–14.

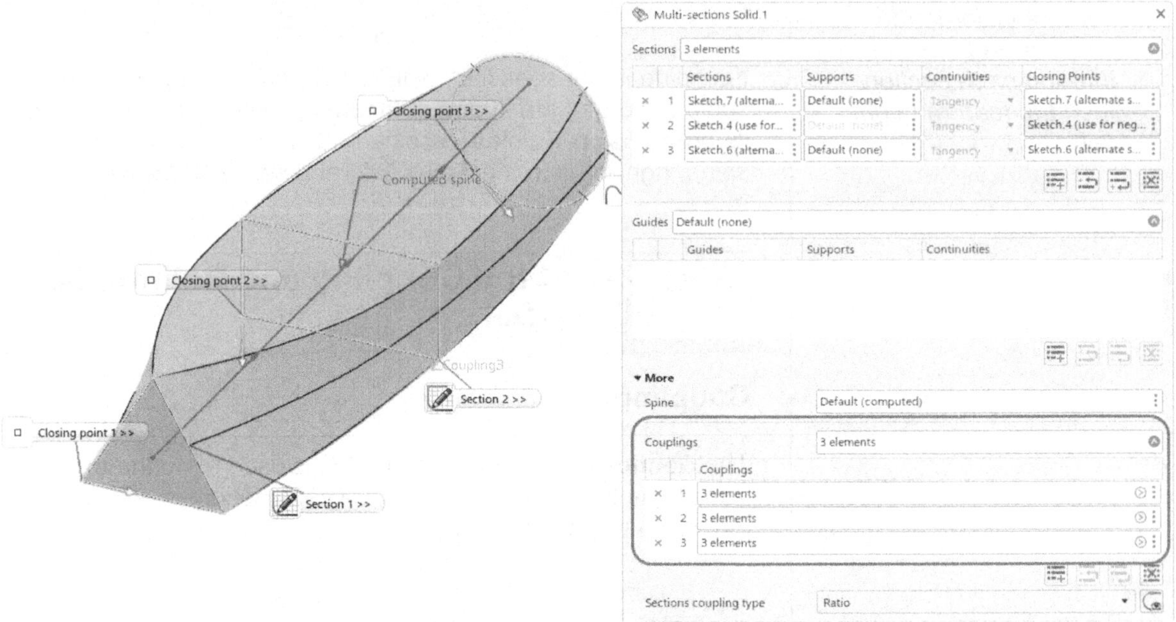

Figure 4–14

If the criteria described are not met for the selected **Sections coupling type** option, an error message opens when you try to generate the Multi-sections Solid feature. For example, setting the **Sections coupling type** option to **Vertices** results in an error message if you are trying to create transitions between a square and a circular section. This error occurs because the circular section does not have any vertices to couple with the square section.

Relimitation

Relimitation controls the progression of the Multi-sections Solid feature beyond the sections. By default, a Multi-sections Solid is relimited at both the start and end sections. CATIA only creates the transitional surfaces of the Multi-sections Solid between the first and last selected sections.

Disabling the Multi-sections Solid relimitation and using a guide, enables the geometry to extend as far as the shortest guide. Figure 4–15 shows the Multi-sections Solid shown in Step 2, except that the **Relimited on end section** option is not selected. Note that the Multi-sections Solid now extends past the last section. The shape of the Multi-sections Solid's cross-section in this area is controlled by the last section. The trajectory of the Multi-sections Solid is controlled by the guide.

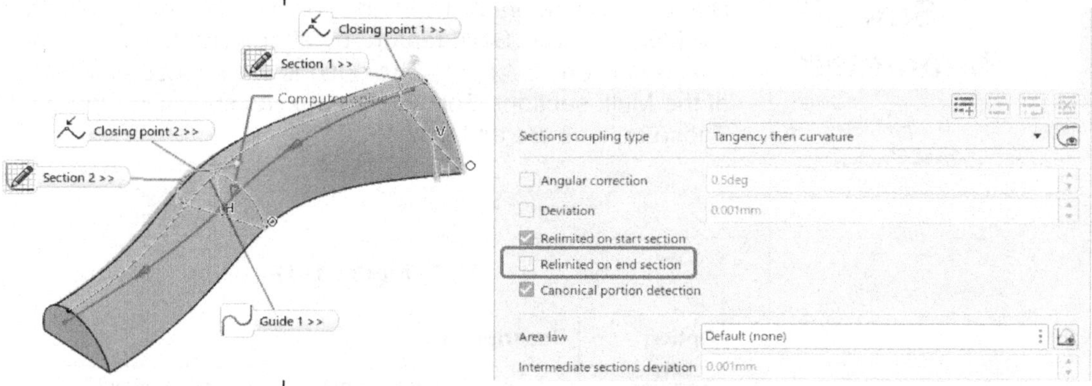

Figure 4–15

To specify Relimitation, clear the **Relimited on start section** or the **Relimited on end section** option.

A spine can also control the relimitation of a Multi-sections Solid. The two models shown in Figure 4–16 are created with the **Relimited on end section** option not selected.

- The Multi-sections Solid on the left in Figure 4–16 uses the system-defined spine and a guide. The cross-section at the end of the Multi-sections Solid is parallel to the last selected section.
- The Multi-sections Solid shown on the right in Figure 4–16 uses a selected spine. The cross-section at the end of the Multi-sections Solid feature is normal to the spine.

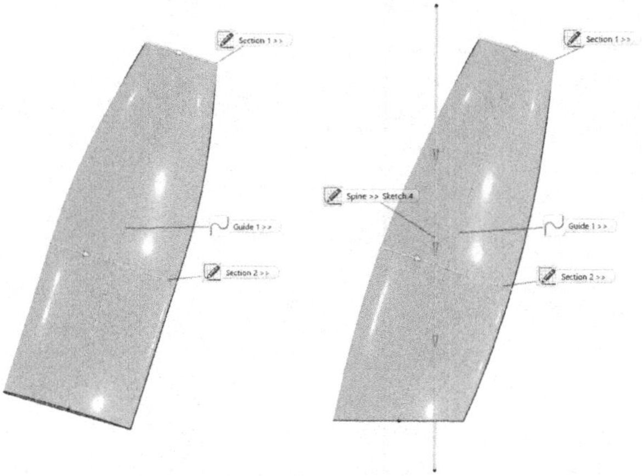

Figure 4–16

Smooth Parameters

Smooth parameters provide additional control over the shape of the Multi-sections Solid feature by attempting to smooth the shape between sections. The options are located at the bottom of the Multi-sections Solid dialog box, as shown in Figure 4–17. These options are as follows.

Figure 4–17

Option	Description
Angular Correction	Smooths any portion of the Multi-sections Solid feature with an angular deviation less than the value specified in degrees.
Deviation	Permits deviation from the guide curves by a specified distance to smooth the Multi-sections Solid feature.

4.3 Creation of Rib and Slot Features

The profile of a Rib feature is swept along a center curve that acts as the trajectory for the profile. It creates a feature that adds material. A Slot uses the same technique as a Rib, except that it removes material. Both Slots and Ribs are useful for creating features with non-linear trajectories, unlike Pads and Pockets. A part with Rib and Slot features displays as shown in Figure 4–18.

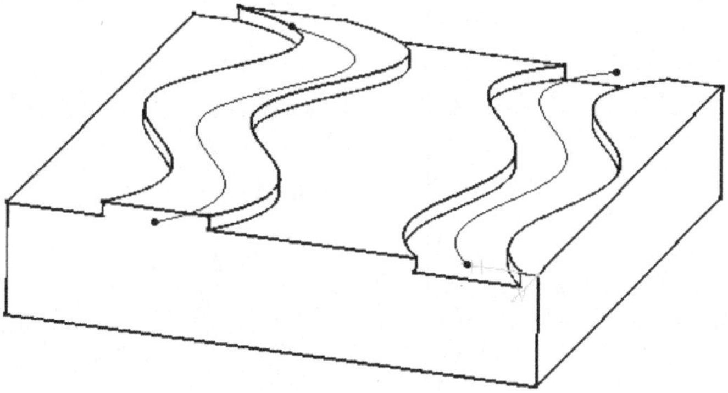

Figure 4–18

The profile of a Rib or Slot is the 2D geometry that is swept along a given center curve. The profile and the center curve can be created before clicking  (Rib) or  (Slot), or they can be created from the Rib or Slot definition dialog box.

- Click  to create a Rib feature.
- Click  to create a Slot feature.

General Steps

Use the following general steps to create a Rib or Slot feature:

1. Select or create a profile
2. Select or create a center curve.
3. Define the profile control.
4. Preview and complete the feature.

Step 1 - Select or create a profile.

Select an existing profile or sketch a new one. Click  next to the *Profile* field, as shown in Figure 4–19, to create a sketch to be used for the profile.

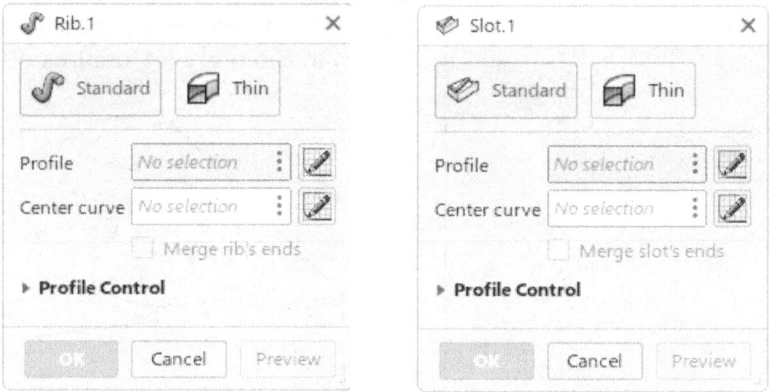

Figure 4–19

Step 2 - Select or create a center curve.

Select an existing center curve or click  to sketch a center curve. You can select a sketch, a 3D curve such as a spline, or edge for the center curve.

Step 3 - Define the profile control.

Define the **Profile Control** options, as shown in Figure 4–20.

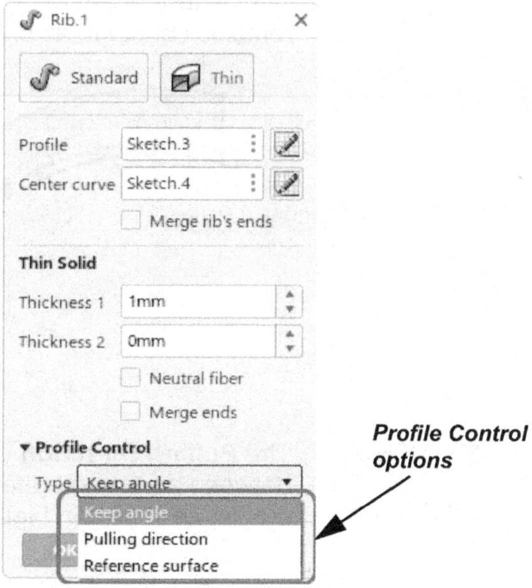

Figure 4–20

Keep Angle

The **Keep Angle** option is the default. This option keeps the angle constant between the support plane of the profile and the center curve along the length of the center curve. For example, if the support plane of the profile is normal to the center curve at the start point, the profile remains normal to the center curve as it is swept, as shown in Figure 4–21.

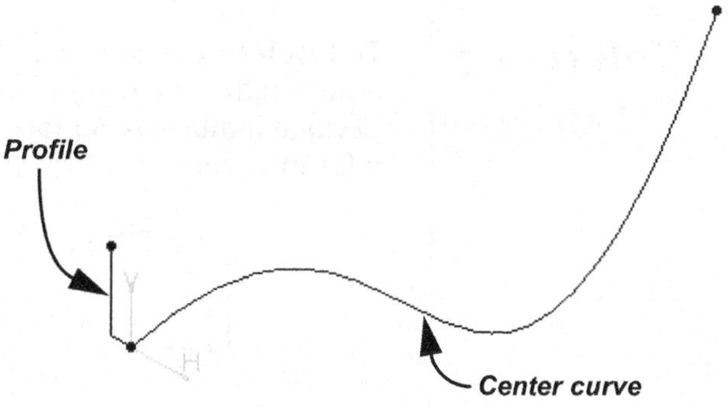

Figure 4–21

The relative angle between the profile and the center curve remains constant, as shown in Figure 4–22.

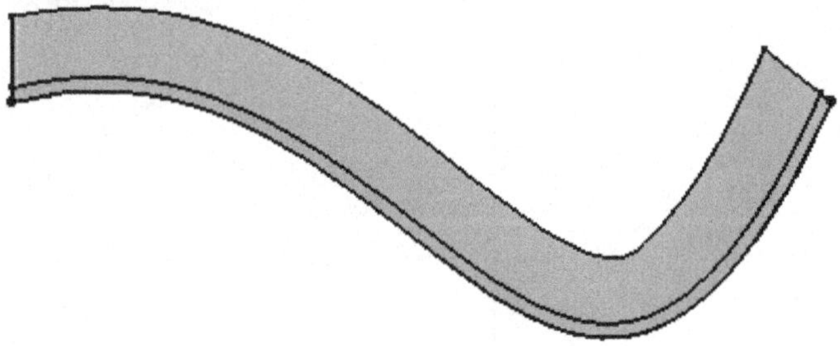

Figure 4–22

Pulling Direction

The **Pulling Direction** option maintains a constant angle between a selected reference plane or planar surface and the profile, as shown in Figure 4–23.

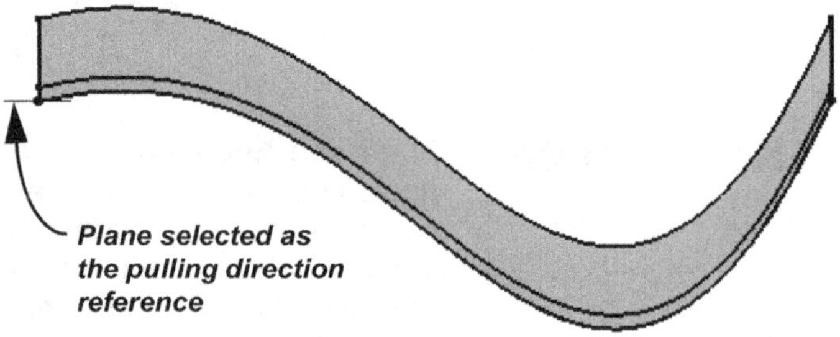

Figure 4–23

Reference Surface

The **Reference Surface** option maintains a constant angle between the H-axis of the profile sketch and the selected Surface feature. A Surface feature that has been selected as the reference surface is shown in Figure 4–24.

Figure 4–24

The Rib feature shown in Figure 4–25 follows the shape of the reference surface as it is swept along the center curve.

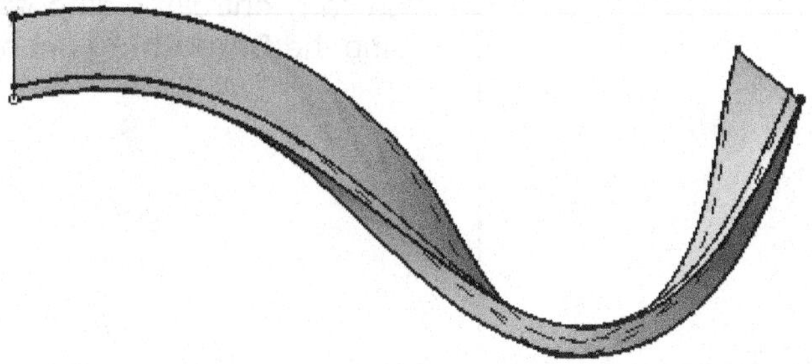

Figure 4–25

Step 4 - Preview and complete the feature.

Preview the feature before exiting the feature creation dialog box. This ensures that the geometry can be created. Click **OK** to complete the feature.

4.4 Advanced Shell Options

You can control the smoothness of the resulting shell surfaces using the **Smoothing** options, as shown in Figure 4–26.

Figure 4–26

Three options are available for the Smoothing mode:

- **None:** This is the default option in which no smoothing is applied.
- **Manual:** When selected you can apply a maximum deviation (the default is 0.1 mm) and can also apply a constant thickness, as shown in Figure 4–27.

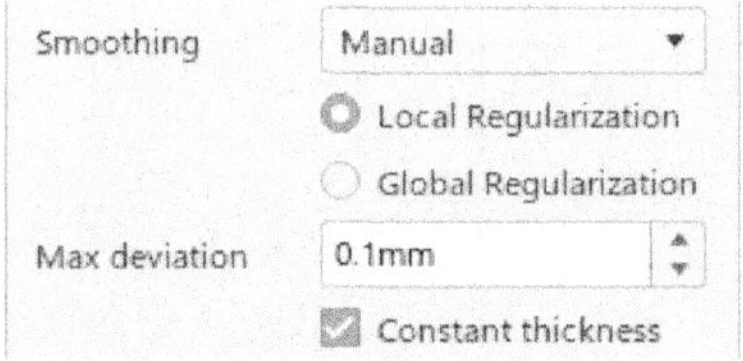

Figure 4–27

- **Automatic:** When selected, smoothing is automatically determined and applied. In this case, the **Max deviation** option is disabled, but the **Constant thickness** option is enabled, as shown in Figure 4–28.

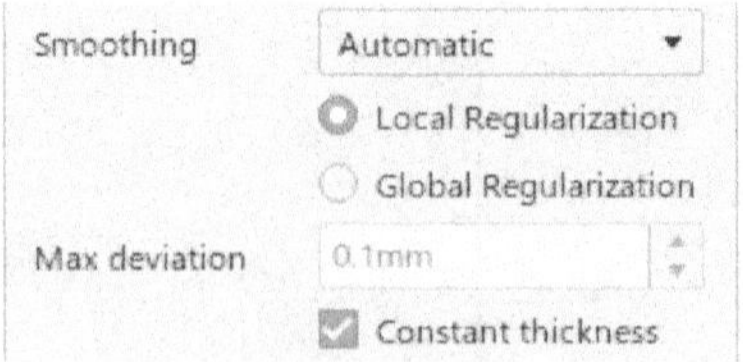

Figure 4–28

Note that the **Regularization** option is only available with **Automatic** and **Manual Smoothing** modes. It permits for the offset surfaces to be calculated either locally or globally and effects the accuracy of the wall thickness for each wall.

The Shell dialog box includes the **Tangency propagation for faces to remove** option, as shown in Figure 4–29.

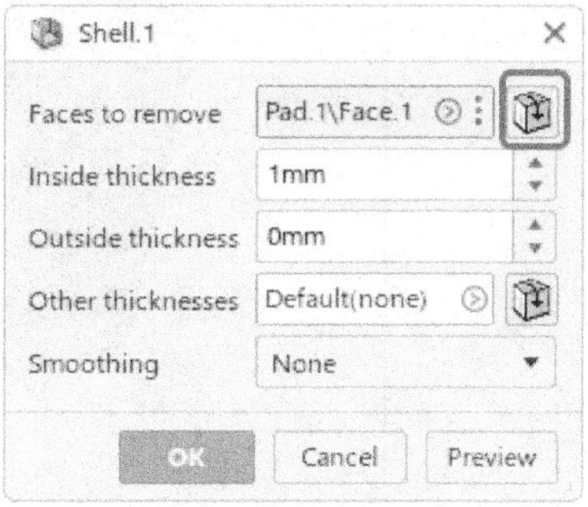

Figure 4–29

With this option selected (this is the default setting), the software removes any additional faces that are tangent continuous with the selected surface. For example, in the model shown in Figure 4–30, the highlighted surface has been selected for removal.

Figure 4–30

The resulting shell feature with **Tangency propagation for faces to remove** selected is shown on the left in Figure 4–31. All of the surfaces that are tangent continuous are removed. The resulting shell with the option toggled off is shown on the right. Only the selected surface is removed.

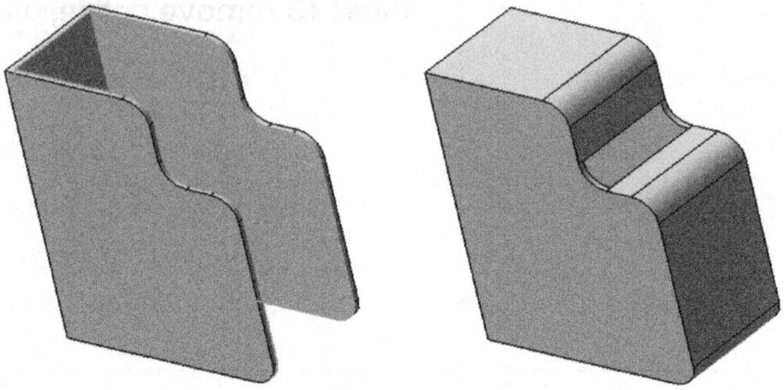

Figure 4–31

Practice 4a

Solid Combine

Practice Objective

- Create a Solid Combine feature.

In this practice, you will use the Solid Combine feature to create the part shown in Figure 4–32.

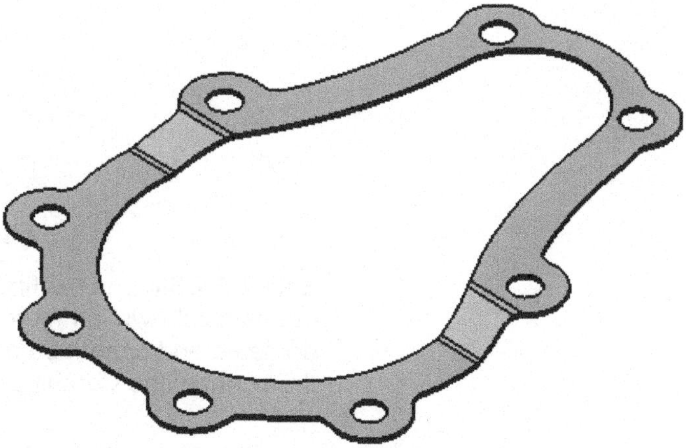

Figure 4–32

Task 1 - Open the part.

1. Import and open **Combine.3dxml** for editing, as shown in Figure 4–33. The part contains two sketches as the base of the Solid Combine feature.

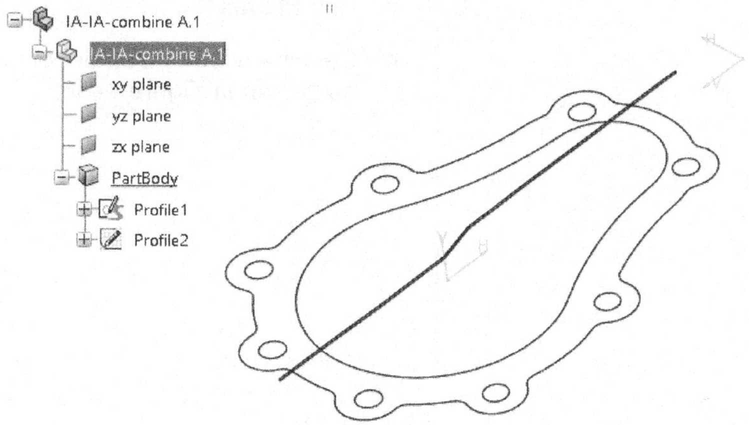

Figure 4–33

Task 2 - Create a Solid Combine feature.

1. Click (Solid Combine). The dialog box opens as shown in Figure 4–34.

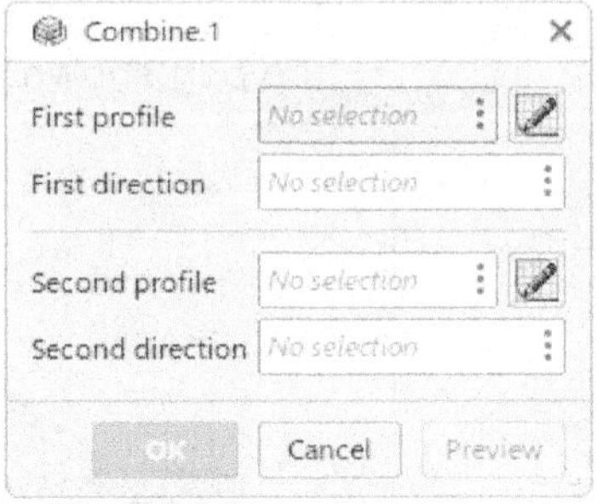

Figure 4–34

2. Select **Profile1** as the first component. An error message opens as shown in Figure 4–35. The sketch has too many domains and cannot be used as a component. Click **OK** and then cancel the Combine Definition.

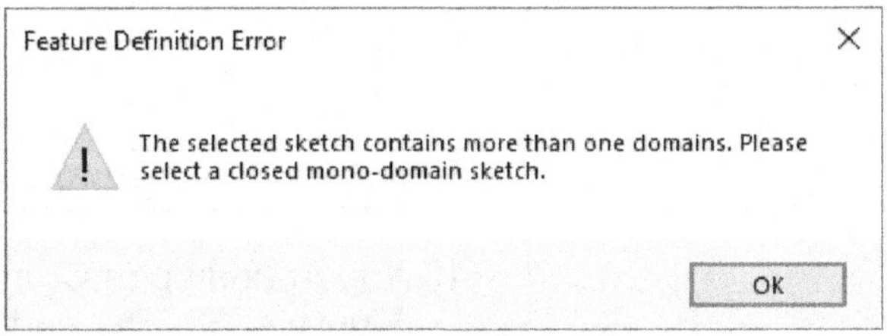

Figure 4–35

3. Edit **Profile1**.

4. Select any outer element of the sketch and use **Auto Search**, as shown in Figure 4–36.

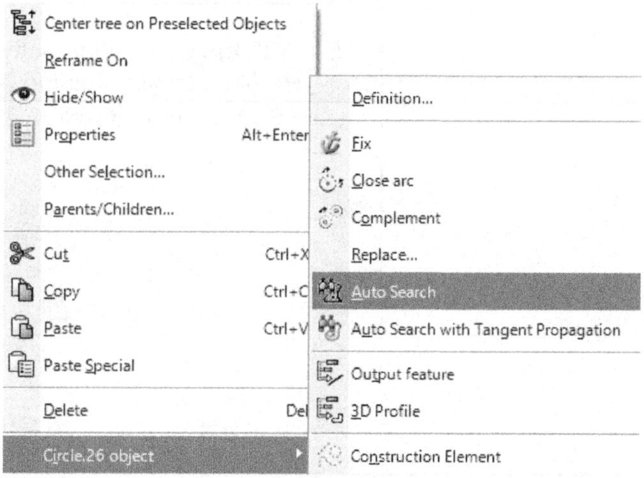

Figure 4–36

The sketch now displays as shown in Figure 4–37. Note how the entire outer edge is selected by the **Auto Search**.

The display of Profile1 has been modified to simplify the visualization.

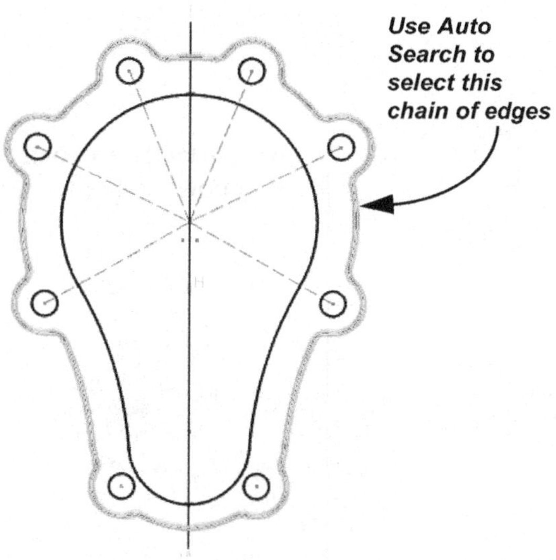

Figure 4–37

5. With the outer edge active, click  (3D Profile). The Profile Definition dialog box opens as shown in Figure 4–38. The selected elements are added.

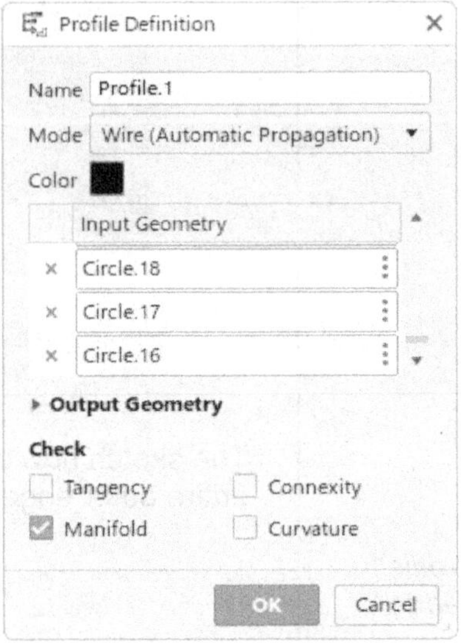

Figure 4–38

6. Click **OK** and exit Sketcher. The profile now displays as shown in Figure 4–39.

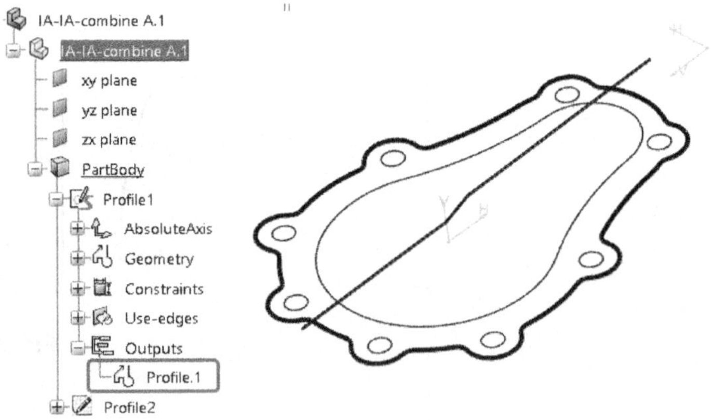

Figure 4–39

7. In the specification tree, locate the output profile under *Profile1* sketch and rename it as **OuterProfile**, as shown in Figure 4–40.

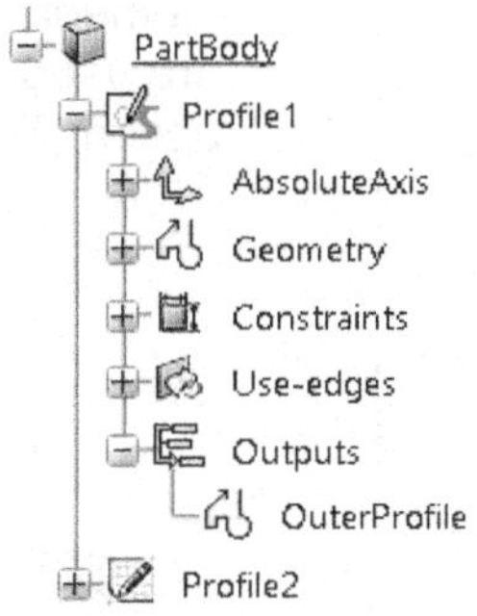

Figure 4–40

8. Click  (Solid Combine).

9. For the first component, select **OuterProfile** and for the second component, select **Profile2**.

10. Click **OK**. The result of the Solid Combine displays as shown in Figure 4–41.

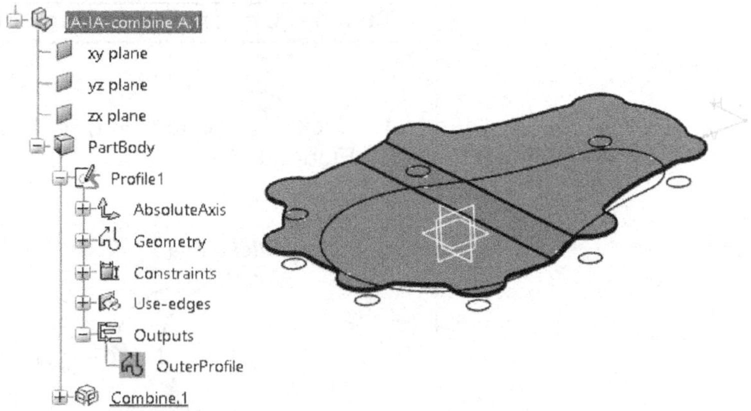

Figure 4–41

Task 3 - Create a Pocket.

1. Create a Pocket feature using Profile1. Note that all of the elements outside the 3D Profile feature created in Sketcher are used. Define the pocket using the **Up to last** depth option. The model displays as shown in Figure 4–42.

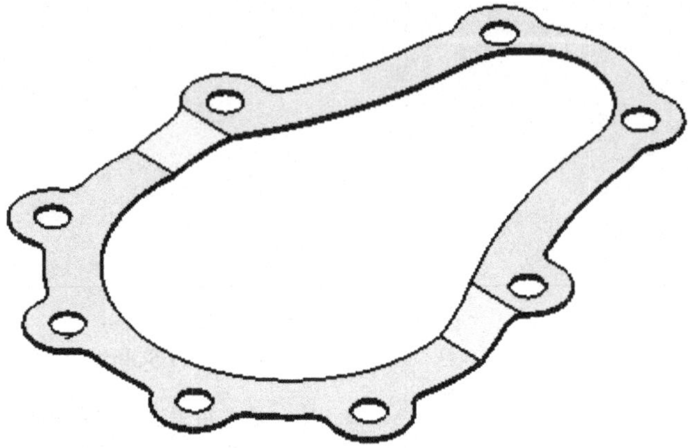

Figure 4–42

2. Save the model.

Task 4 - (Optional) Add Edge Fillets.

1. Click  (Edge fillet) and select the four edges shown in Figure 4–43.

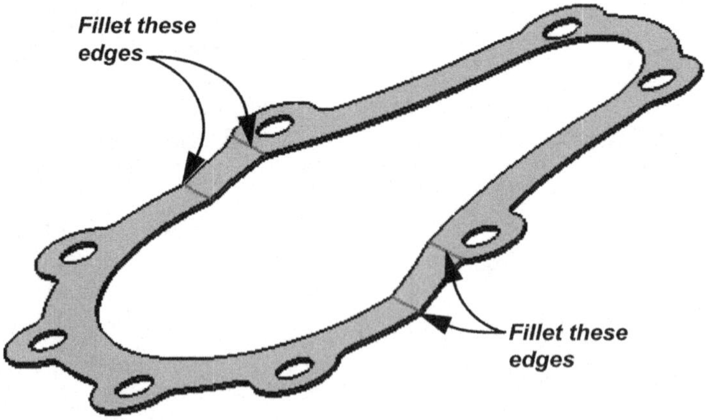

Figure 4–43

2. Enter **6** for the *Fillet radius* and click **OK**.

3. Fillet the 4 edges shown in Figure 4–44 with **6** radius.

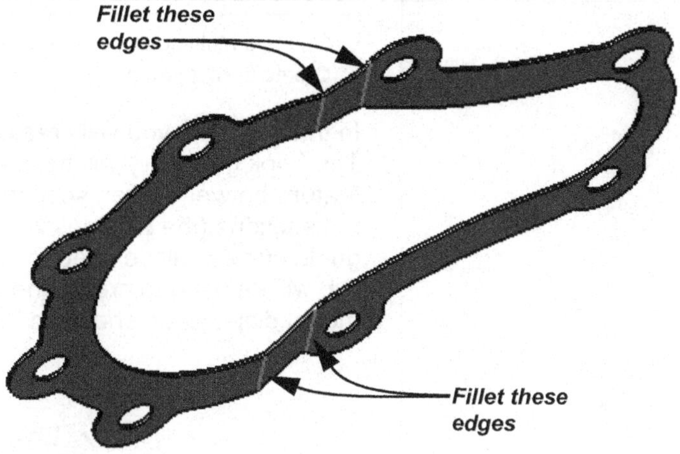

Figure 4–44

The completed model displays as shown in Figure 4–45.

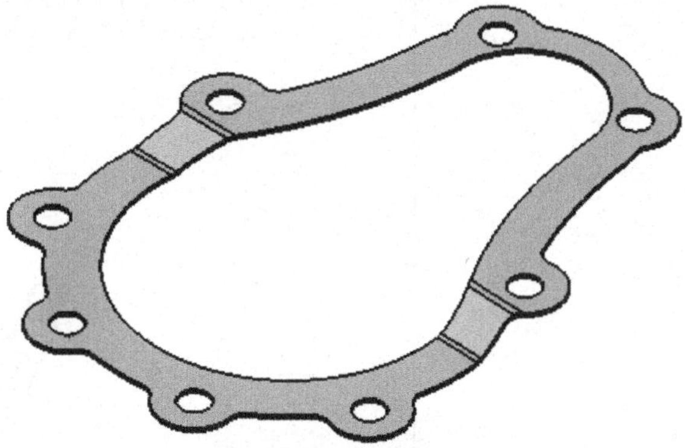

Figure 4–45

4. Save the model and close the window.

Practice 4b

Crane Hook

Practice Objectives

- Create a Multi-sections Solid using guide curves and a spine.
- Create a Rib feature.

In this practice, you will create a hook used by a crane or hoist. The hook geometry will be created using a Multi-sections Solid feature between three sections. A spine will be used to control the sections (the sections will stay normal to the spine) and guide curves will be used to control the size of the sections. A Rib will be used to create the eye of the hook. The completed model displays as shown in Figure 4–46.

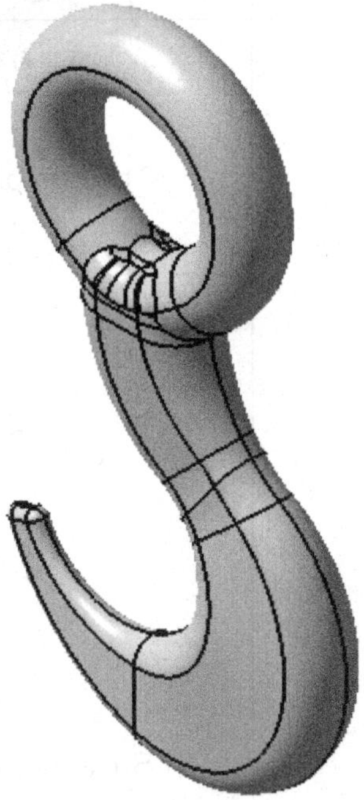

Figure 4–46

Task 1 - Open the part.

1. Import and open **CraneHook.3dsml** file for editing. When importing, type your initials followed by the dash symbol into the *Duplication string* field (e.g., **IA-**). The model displays as shown in Figure 4–47.

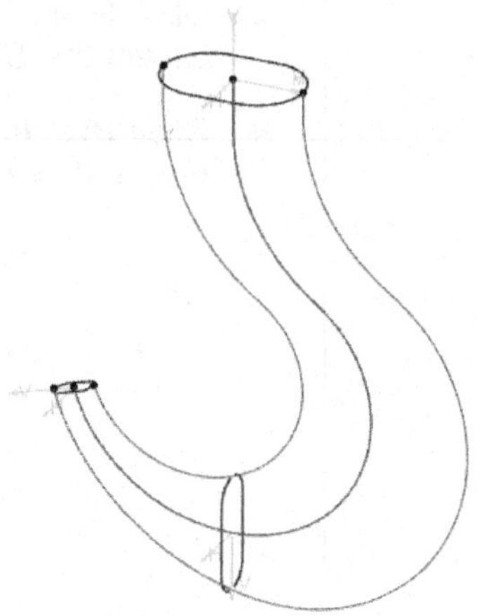

Figure 4–47

2. Click (Multi-sections Solid). Define the Multi-sections Solid feature by selecting the following sketches, as shown in Figure 4–48:

- **Sketch.1**
- **Sketch.2**
- **Sketch.3**

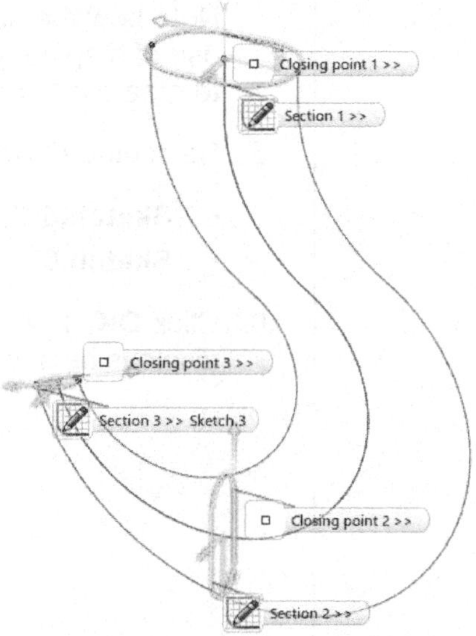

Figure 4–48

3. Click **More** to expand the Multi-sections Solid dialog box. Select the *Spine* field and select **Sketch.4**.

4. Click **Preview**. The preview displays as shown in Figure 4–49.

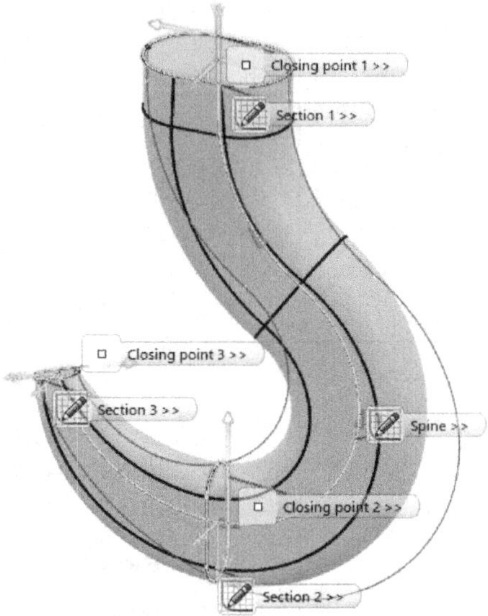

Figure 4–49

Note how the section stays normal to the spine. Without the use of a spine, you could not have used these three sections to create a Multi-sections Solid.

5. Select the *Guides* field and select the following:

- **Sketch.5**
- **Sketch.6**

6. Click **OK**. The completed Multi-sections Solid feature displays as shown in Figure 4–50.

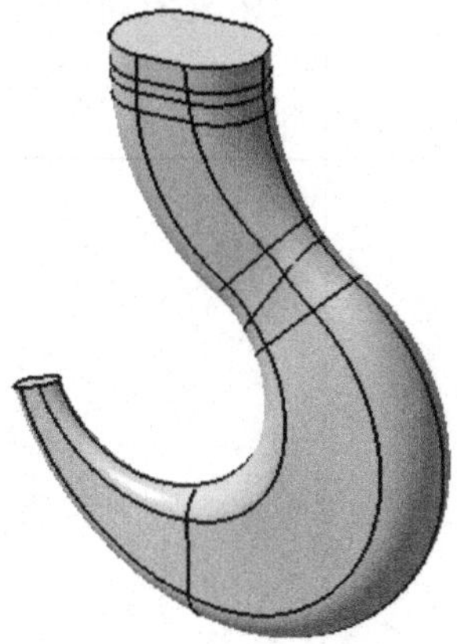

Figure 4–50

Task 2 - Create sketches for the eye of the hook.

1. Create the sketch shown in Figure 4–51 using the **yz plane** as the sketching plane.

Design Considerations

Click  (Intersect 3D Elements) and select the top planar surface of the hook to use as a reference for the sketched arc.

Use  (Construction/Standard Element) to convert the projection to a construction element. By referencing the projection, the sketch will be associative to the hook geometry.

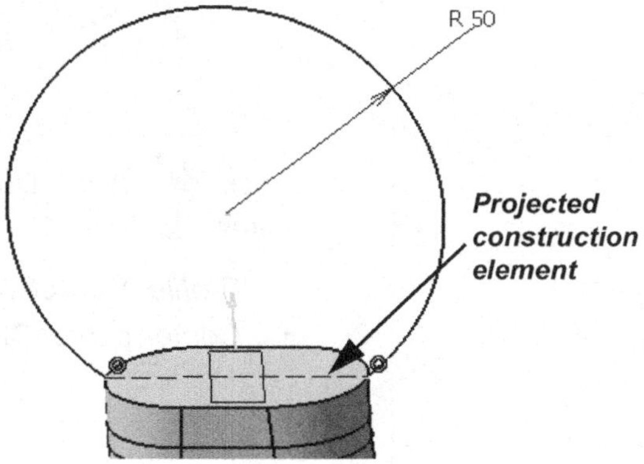

Figure 4–51

2. Create the reference plane shown in Figure 4–52.

   - *Plane type:* **Normal to curve**

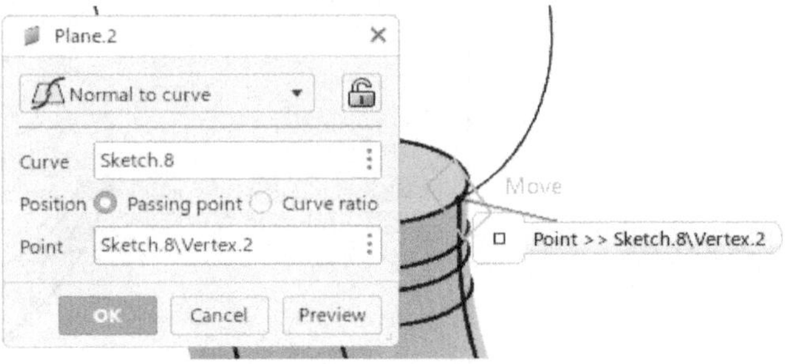

Figure 4–52

3. Create the sketch shown in Figure 4–53, using the plane you just created as the sketching plane.

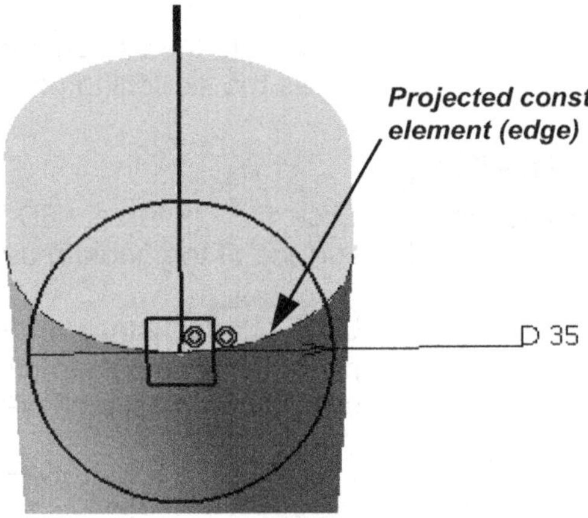

Figure 4–53

4. Click  (Rib). Define the Rib feature by selecting the following sketches:

   - *Profile:* **Sketch.9**
   - *Center curve:* **Sketch.8**

5. Preview the Rib. The feature displays as shown in Figure 4–54. Note that the Rib does not merge with the Multi-section Solid feature.

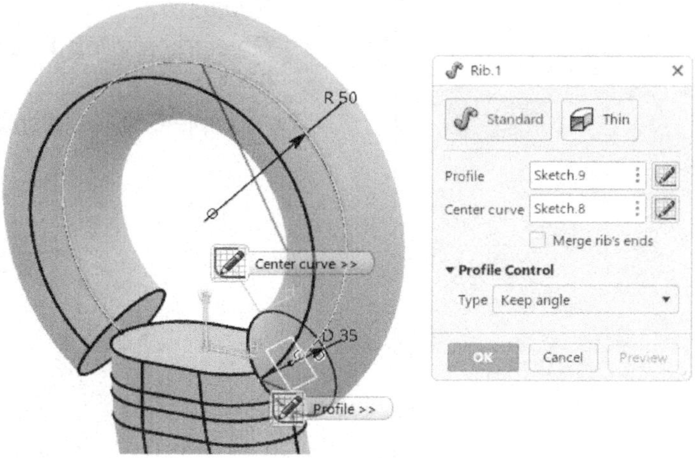

Figure 4–54

Design Considerations

Use the **Merge rib's ends** option to achieve the correct geometry. This option extrapolates the profile to meet the next solid surface.

6. Select **Merge rib's ends** and complete the feature. The model displays as shown in Figure 4–55.

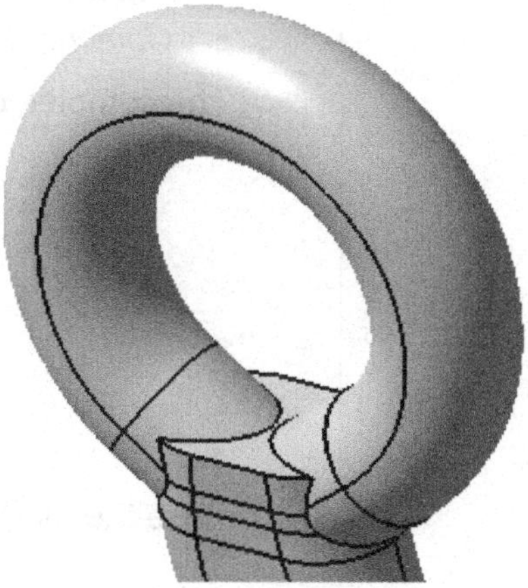

Figure 4–55

Task 3 - Create an Edge Fillet.

1. Create an Edge Fillet with the following parameters:
   - *Radius:* **12**
   - *Object(s) to fillet:* **1 Face** (the top planar surface of the hook)

   The completed Fillet displays as shown in Figure 4–56.

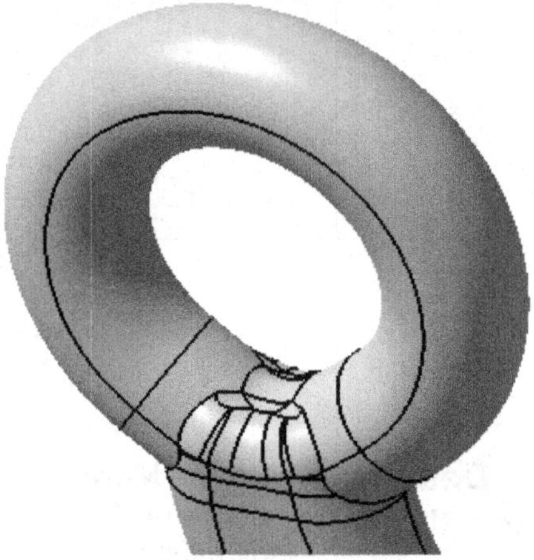

Figure 4–56

2. Create an edge Fillet with the following parameters:
   - *Radius:* **4**
   - *Object(s) to fillet:* **1 Face** (the planar surface at the tip)

   The completed Fillet displays as shown in Figure 4–57.

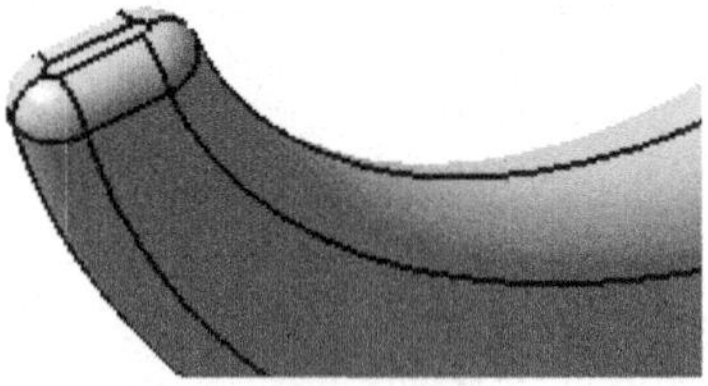

Figure 4–57

3. Save the model and close the window.

Practice 4c

Truck Bumper

Practice Objectives

- Create a Multi-sections Solid feature.
- Use a spine to control a Multi-sections Solid feature.
- Create an unrelimited Multi-sections Solid feature.
- Create a negative Multi-sections Solid feature.

In this practice, you will model the rear bumper for a truck. The bumper must fit the contours of the rear of the truck. Multi-sections Solid features are used to control the shape of the bumper, which will transition from a small section at the ends to a large section near the license plate cut out. The Multi-sections Solid feature will also enable the bumper to wrap around the rear corner of the truck. Only half of this model is created using Multi-sections Solid features. The geometry is then mirrored to create the completed model shown in Figure 4–58.

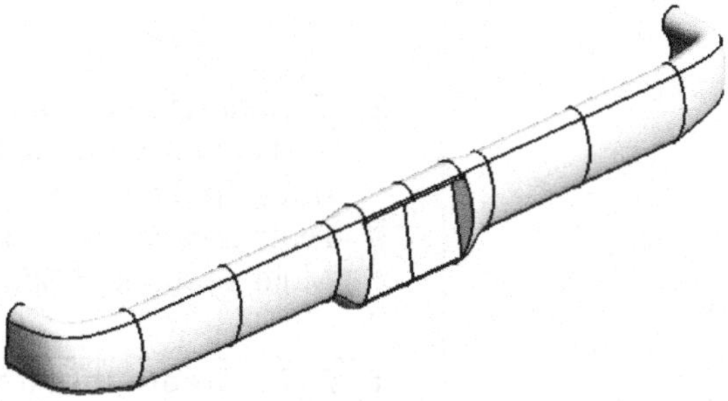

Figure 4–58

You will start with a model that contains the construction geometry required to create the bumper model. The model displays as shown in Figure 4–59.

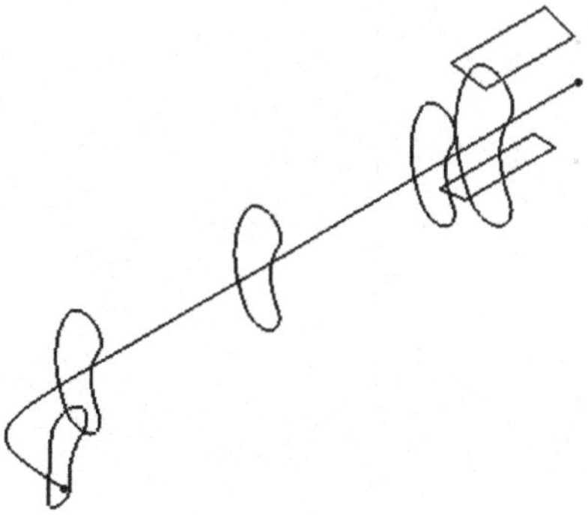

Figure 4–59

Task 1 - Open the part.

1. Import and open **Truck Bumper.3dxml** for editing. When importing, type your initials followed by the dash symbol into the *Duplication string* field (e.g., **IA-**). The model displays as shown in Figure 4–60.

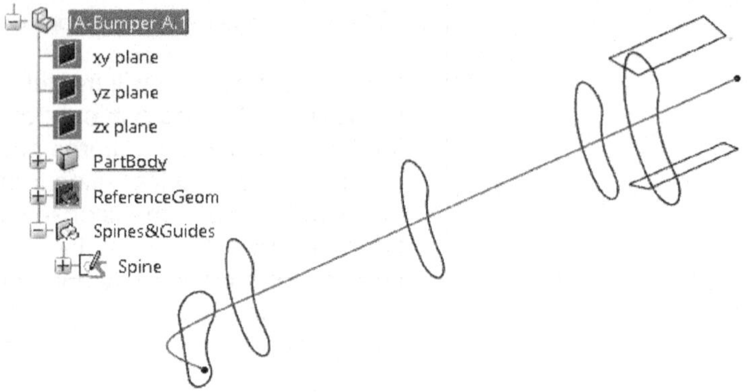

Figure 4–60

2. Expand the specification tree to display the different planes and sketches in the model. Sketches 1 to 5 are used to develop the shape of the bumper. The PlateTop and PlateBottom sketches are used to define a negative Multi-sections Solid, creating a cutout for the license plate.

Task 2 - Create the first Multi-sections Solid.

1. Click  (Multi-sections Solid). The Multi-sections Solid dialog box opens as shown in Figure 4–61.

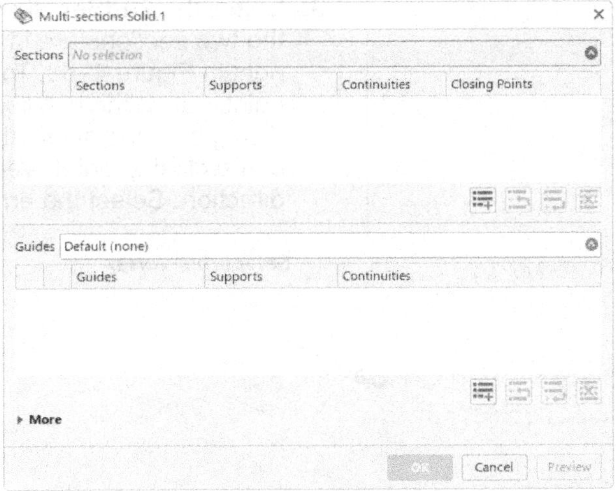

Figure 4–61

2. In the model or specification tree, select the **1stSec** sketch. The section is added to the top field in the Multi-sections Solid dialog box. Note the location of **ClosingPoint1**, as shown in Figure 4–62.

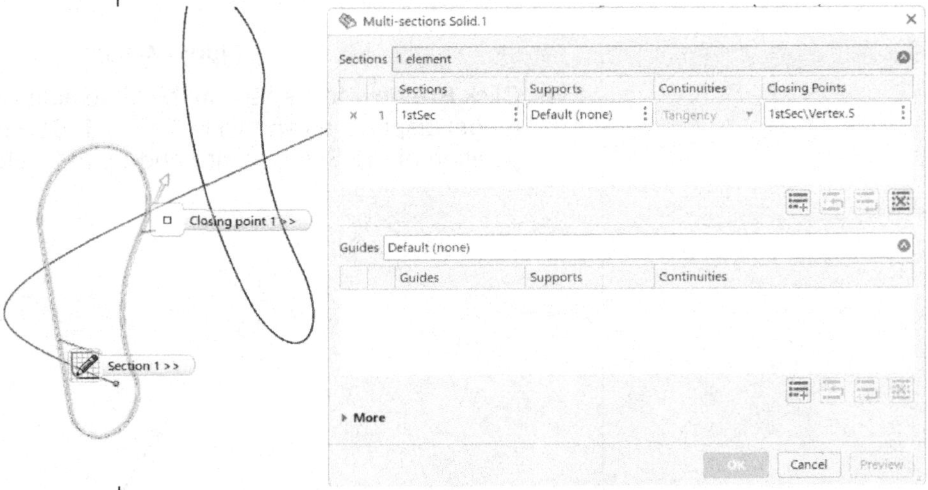

Figure 4–62

3. Select the **2ndSec** sketch. Ensure that the closing points of the two sections are in the same positions, as shown on the right in Figure 4–63. To change the position of the closing point, select the corresponding *Closing Points* field in the dialog box and select the point or vertex for the new location of the closing point. Verify that the arrows point in the same direction. Select the arrow to flip it, if required.

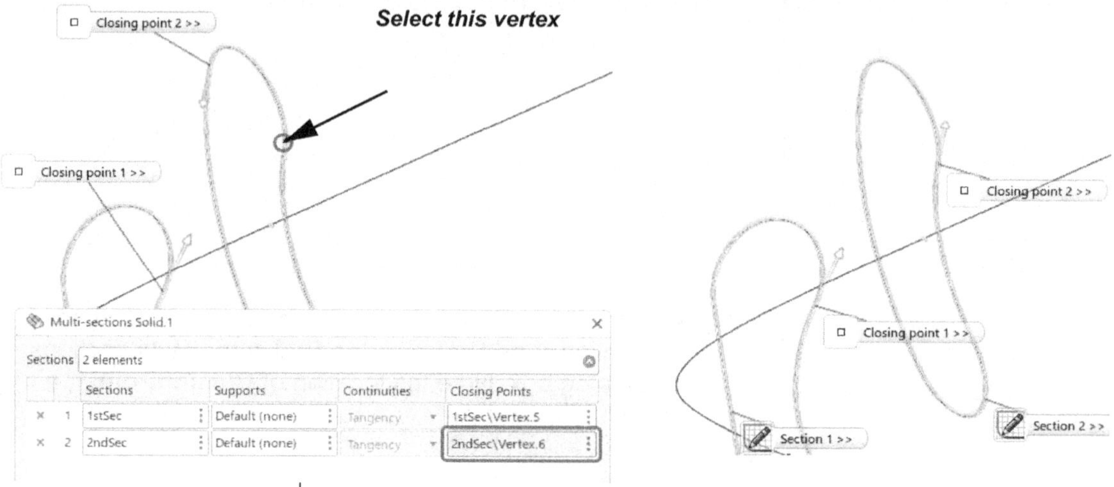

Figure 4–63

4. Click **Preview** to display the Multi-sections Solid feature. The model displays as shown in Figure 4–64. Note the relative position of the Solid feature and Spine sketch feature.

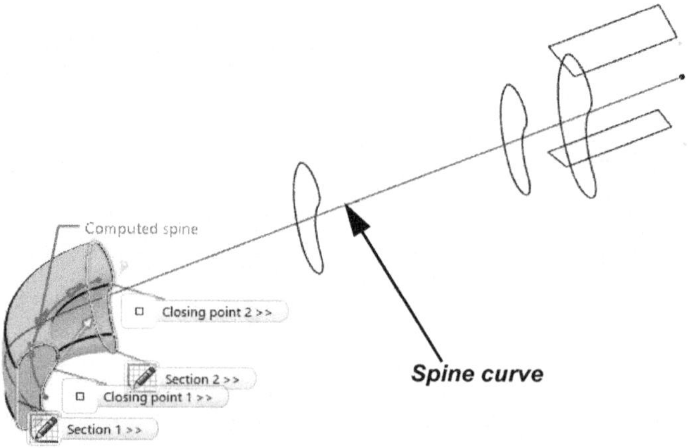

Figure 4–64

The Spine sketch is developed to determine the orientation of the cross-section as the bumper rounds the rear corner of the truck.

5. Click **More** to expand the Multi-sections Solid dialog box and select the *Spine* field. In the **Spines&Guides** geometrical set, select the **Spine** sketch.

6. Click **OK**. The model displays as shown in Figure 4–65. Note that the Spine curve and two sections have been added under the **Multi-sections Solid.1** feature in the specification tree. All of the sketches are hidden automatically to simplify the display of the Solid feature.

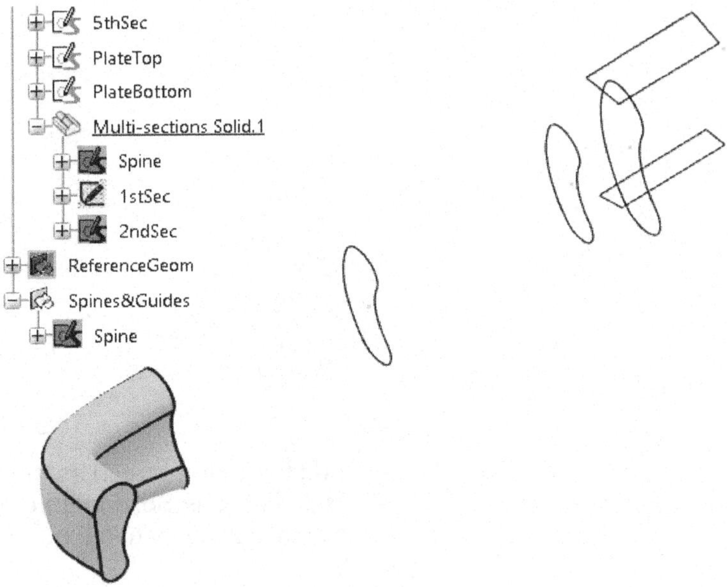

Figure 4–65

7. Show the **2ndSec** and **Spine** sketches. They are used in the next Multi-sections Solid feature.

Task 3 - Create an unrelimited Multi-sections Solid feature.

1. Click (Multi-sections Solid).

2. Select these sections in the following order: **2ndSec**, **3rdSec**, **4thSec**, and **5thSec**.

3. Ensure that the closing points for all of the sections are in the same place and point in the same direction, as shown in Figure 4–66.

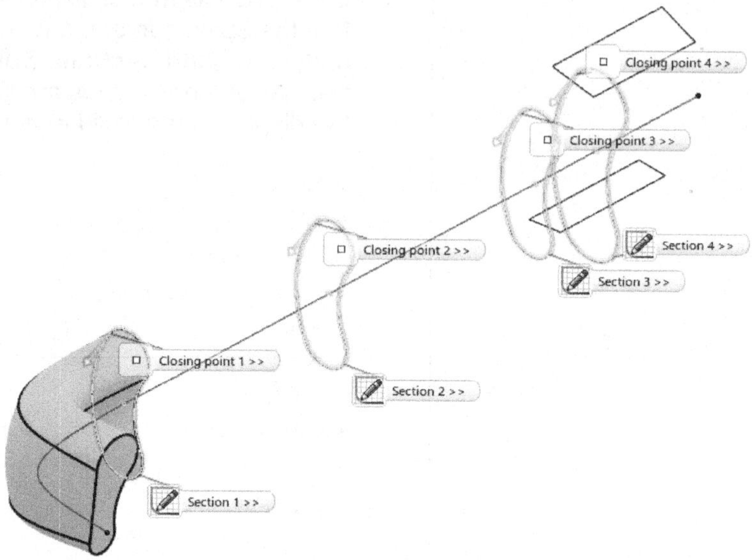

Figure 4–66

4. Add the Spine sketch as the Spine curve for the Multi-sections Solid feature and click **Preview**. The model displays as shown in Figure 4–67.

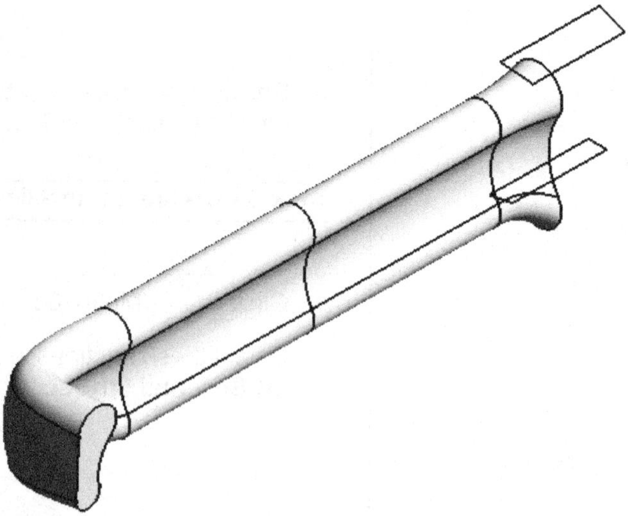

Figure 4–67

5. Clear the **Relimited on end section** option, as shown in Figure 4–68. The Multi-sections Solid turns red, indicating that it needs updating.

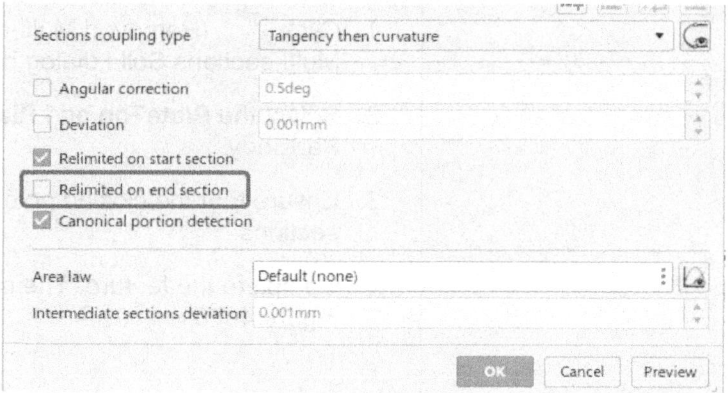

Figure 4–68

6. Click **OK**. The model displays as shown in Figure 4–69. Note that the Multi-sections Solid only extends as far as the longest Spine or Guide curve.

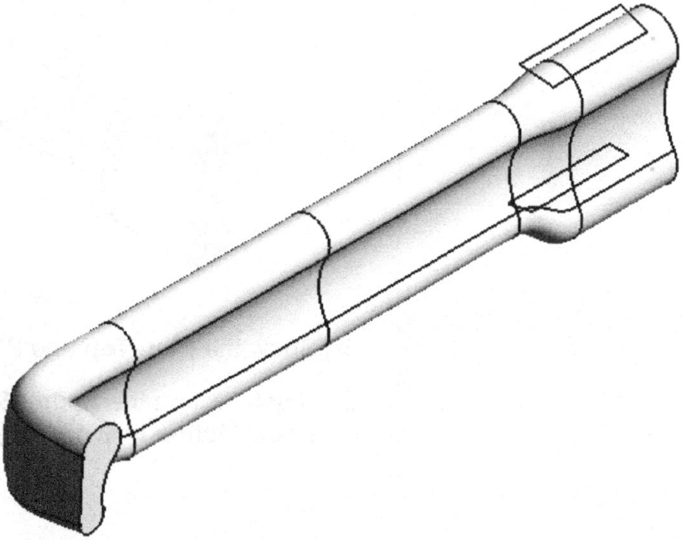

Figure 4–69

7. Save the model.

Task 4 - Create a negative Multi-sections Solid for the license plate space.

1. Click  (Removed Multi-sections Solid). The Multi-sections Solid dialog box opens.
2. Select the **PlateTop** and **PlateBottom** sections from the PartBody.
3. Ensure that the closing points match between the two sections.
4. Complete the feature. The model displays as shown in Figure 4–70.

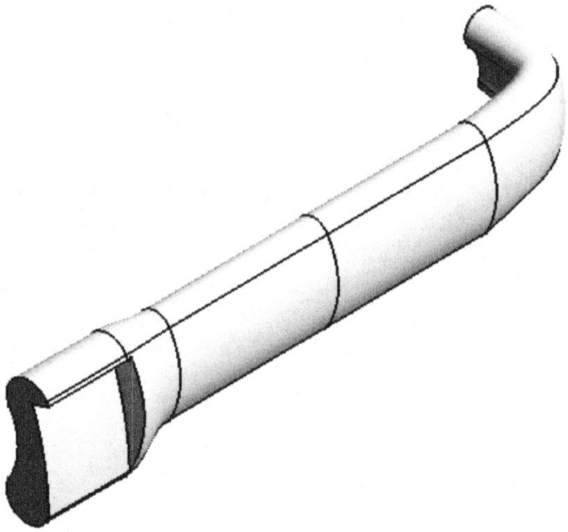

Figure 4–70

5. Show the **PlateTop** and **PlateBottom** sketches.
6. Right-click on the **Spines&Guides** geometrical set and select **Define In Work Object**.

7. Create a line using the Point - Point definition. Select the vertices of the **PlateTop** and **PlateBottom** sketches, as shown in Figure 4–71.

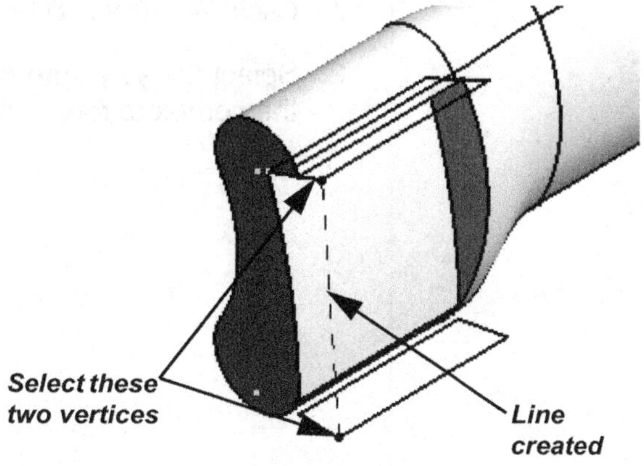

Figure 4–71

8. Rename the line as **PlateGuide**.

9. Edit **Multi-sections Solid.3** and locate the Guides section.

10. Select the *Guides* field. Add **PlateGuide** as a guide curve and complete the feature.

11. Hide all of the sketches and lines used to develop the Multi-sections Solids for this model. The model displays as shown in Figure 4–72.

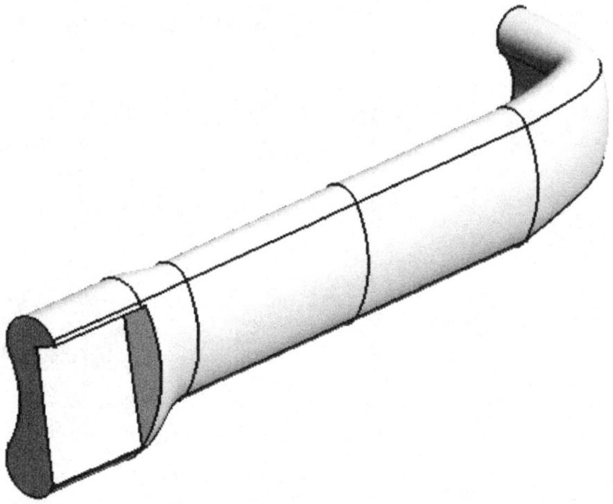

Figure 4–72

12. Right-click on the PartBody and select **Define In Work Object**.

Task 5 - Mirror the bumper.

1. Click  (Mirror) to perform a mirror operation.
2. Select the **yz plane** or an appropriate model surface so that the complete model displays as shown in Figure 4–73.

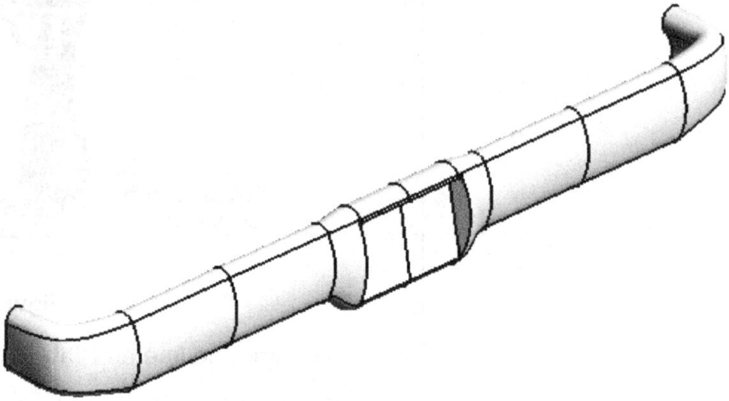

Figure 4–73

3. Save the model.

Task 6 - (Optional) Modify the spine curve.

1. Double-click on the Spine sketch in the **Spines&Guides** geometrical set and zoom in on the spline on the right side of the sketch, as shown in Figure 4–74.

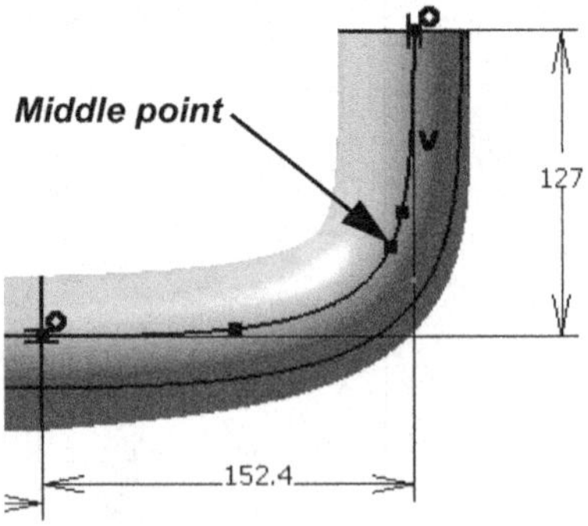

Figure 4–74

The spline has five control points. You will move the middle point to see how it affects the shape of the Multi-sections Solid. Experiment with a variety of locations.

2. Drag the middle control point to a new location and exit the Sketcher. Note how the Multi-sections Solid feature updates. Some examples are shown in Figure 4–75.

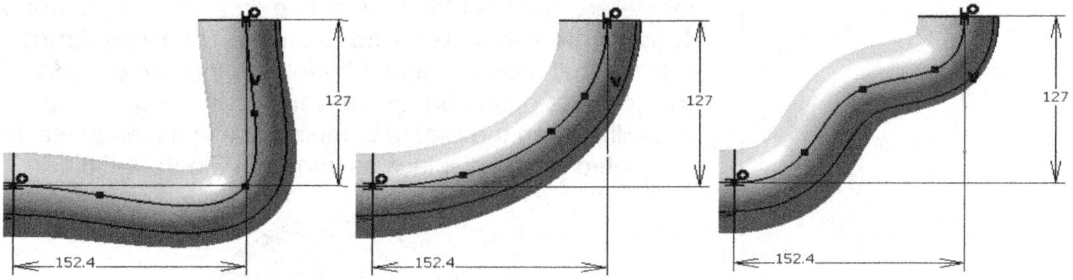

Figure 4–75

3. Close the model without saving.

Practice 4d Speaker Cover

Practice Objective

- Create a Slot feature using the **Keep Angle** option.

In this practice, you will create the vents on a speaker cover for a car stereo. The vent features will be created using a Slot with the **Keep Angle** and **Merge Ends** options. The **Keep Angle** option ensures that the vent geometry follows the center curve. The **Merge Ends** option brings the vents to the edge of the cover. You will pattern the Slot to complete the speaker cover. The completed model displays as shown in Figure 4–76.

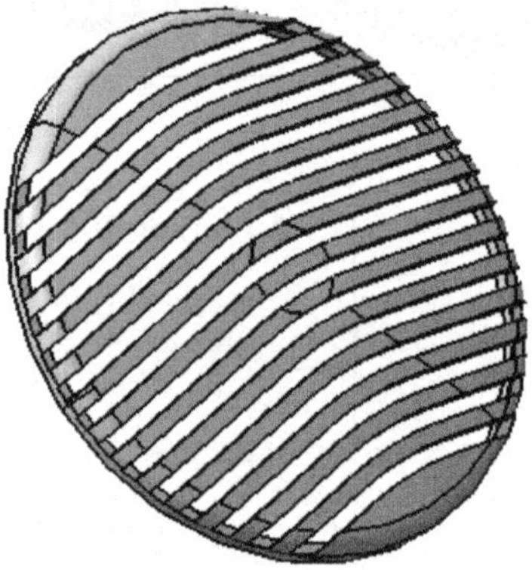

Figure 4–76

Task 1 - Open the part.

1. Import and open for **Speaker.3dxml** for editing. When importing, type your initials followed by the dash symbol into the *Duplication string* field (e.g., **IA-**). The model displays as shown in Figure 4–77.

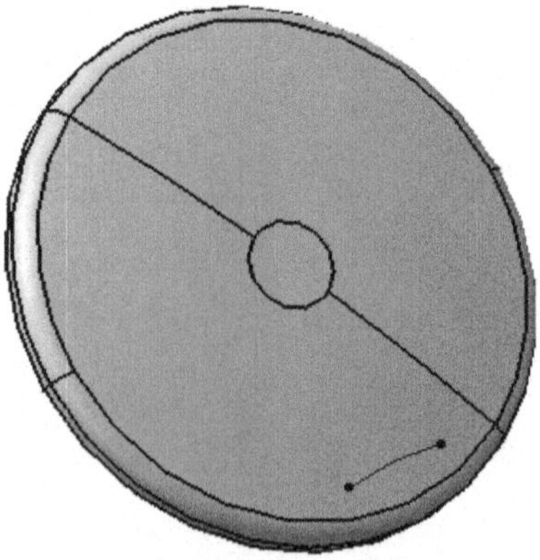

Figure 4–77

Task 2 - Complete reference geometry.

1. Define **ConstrGeom** to be the In Work Object.
2. Create a reference plane for the slot's profile sketch using the following options:
   - *Plane type:* **Normal to curve**
   - *Curve:* **Center Curve**
   - *Point:* **end point of Center Curve**, as shown in Figure 4–78

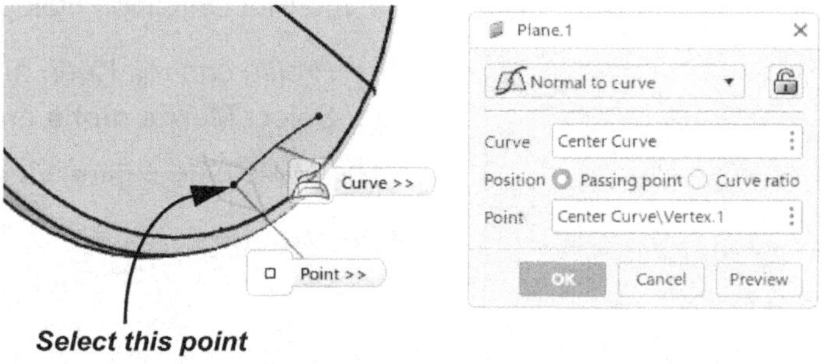

Figure 4–78

3. Rename the plane as **Profile Plane**.
4. Create a sketch on the Profile Plane. Sketch and constrain the section, as shown in Figure 4–79. Note the equidistant constraint between the vertical edges and the end point of the Center Curve.

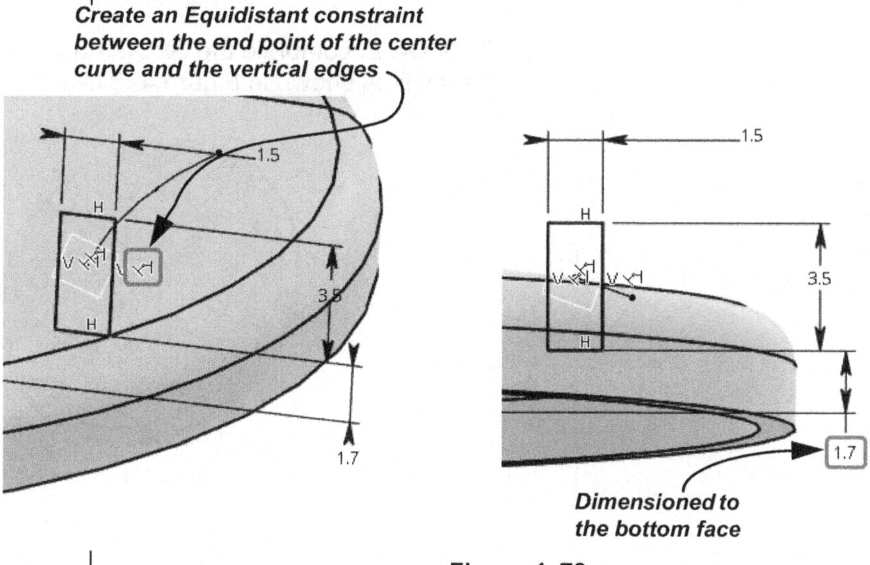

Figure 4–79

5. Exit the Sketcher app.
6. Rename the sketch as **Vent Profile**.

Task 3 - Create the Slot feature.

1. Define the PartBody as in the Work Object.
2. Click  (Slot) to create a Slot. Select the **Vent Profile** feature as the slot profile, and the **Center Curve** feature as the slot center curve, and then make the following selections in the Slot Definition dialog box:
   - *Profile control:* Keep angle
   - Select **Merge slot's ends**.

   The completed settings are shown in Figure 4–80.

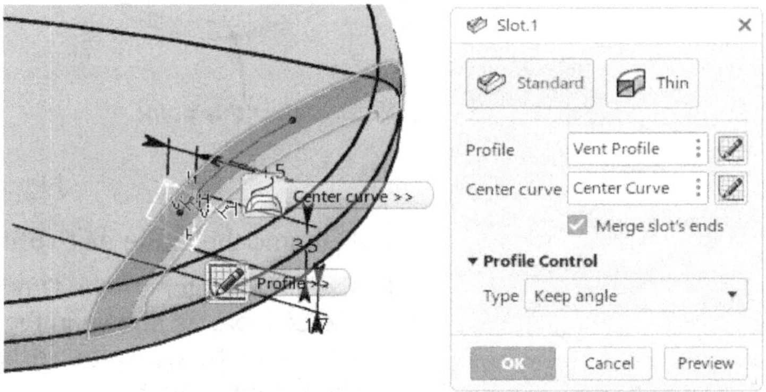

Figure 4–80

3. Click **OK** to complete the Slot feature. The speaker cover displays as shown in Figure 4–81.

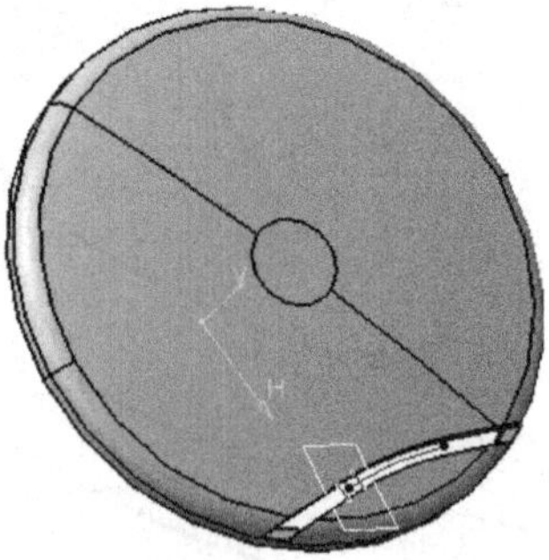

Figure 4–81

Task 4 - Pattern the Slot Rib feature.

1. Preselect the Slot feature and click  (Rectangular Pattern). Make the following selections in the Rectangular Pattern dialog box, as shown in Figure 4–82:

   - *Parameters:* **Instances & Spacing**
   - *Instances:* **14**
   - *Spacing:* **3mm**
   - *Reference element:* **yz plane** (if necessary, reverse the direction of the pattern creation)
   - Select **Keep specifications**.

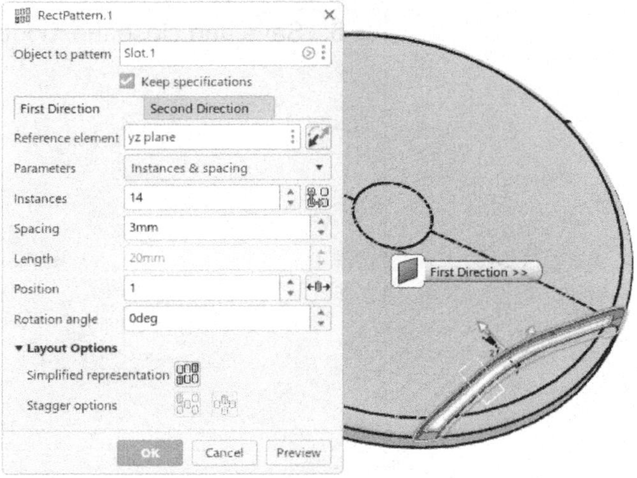

Figure 4–82

2. Click **OK** to complete the Pattern feature.

3. Close the warning dialog box.

4. Hide the Profile Plane. The completed model displays as shown in Figure 4–83.

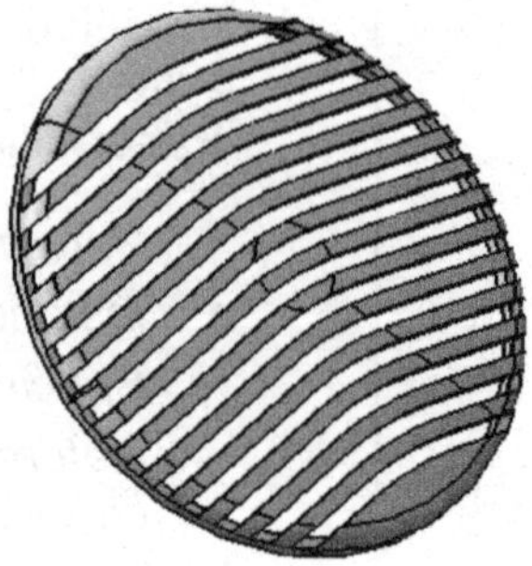

Figure 4–83

5. Save and close the model.

Practice 4e

Turbine Wheel

Practice Objective

- Create a Rib feature using a Reference Surface.

In this practice, you will create a Rib feature using a reference surface. The reference surface is used to achieve the complex airfoil geometry of the turbine compressor blades. You will then pattern the Rib. The completed model display as shown in Figure 4–84.

Figure 4–84

Task 1 - Open the part.

1. Import and open **1stStage.3dxml** in the *Turbine* directory for editing. The model displays as shown in Figure 4–85.

Figure 4–85

2. Note the following features in the specification tree, as shown in Figure 4–86:

   - **Blade Profile** sketch in the PartBody
   - **Lead Edge** spline curve in the Geometrical Set
   - **Trail Edge** spline curve in the Geometrical Set

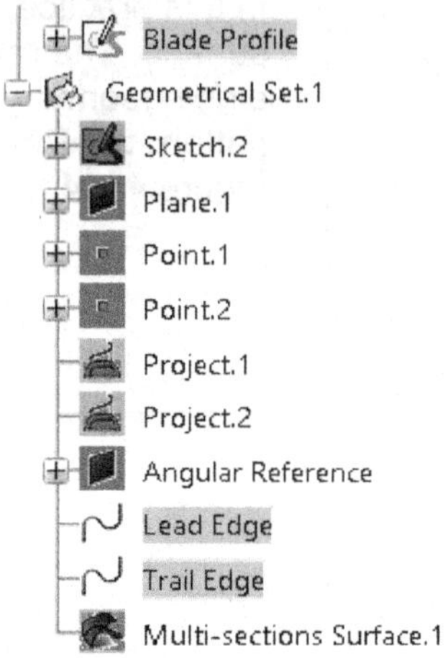

Figure 4–86

Task 2 - Create a Rib feature.

1. Create a Rib by selecting the **Blade Profile** feature as the *Rib Profile* and the **Lead Edge** feature as the *Rib Center curve*, as shown in Figure 4–87.

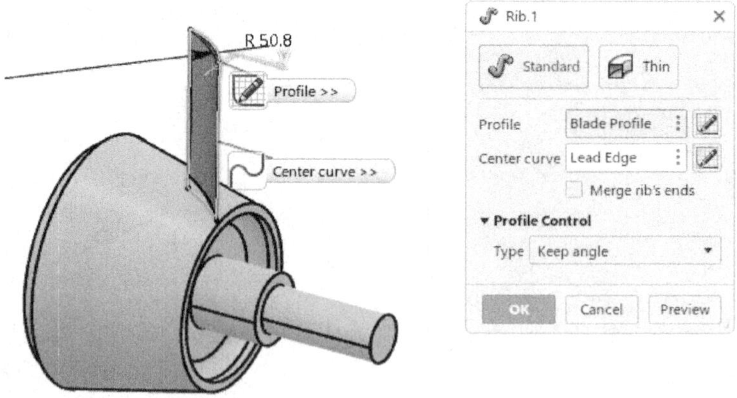

Figure 4–87

2. Keep the default **Keep angle** option selected as the **Profile control** option. This setting will be temporary. You will later modify the Profile control to **Reference Surface** to compare the resultant geometry.

3. Click **OK** to complete the Rib feature.

4. Zoom in on the area shown in Figure 4–88.

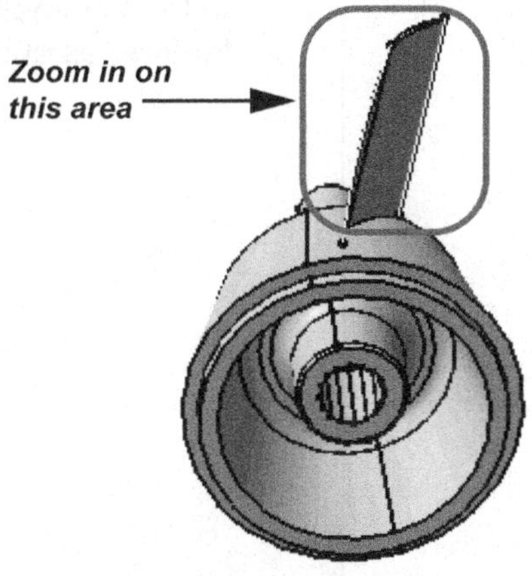

Figure 4–88

5. Show **Multi-sections Surface.1** under Geometrical Set in the specification tree. The Surface feature displays as shown in Figure 4–89.

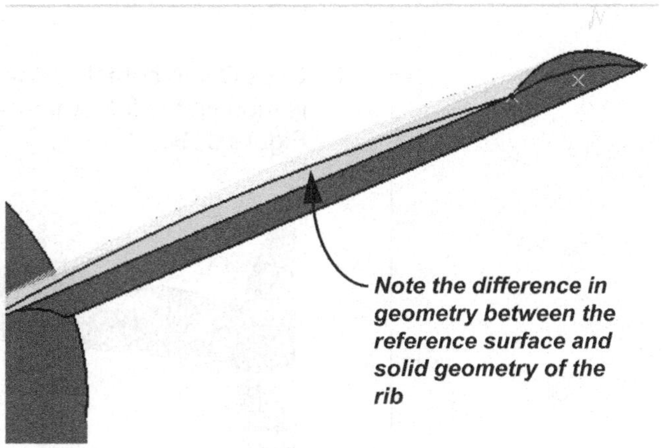

Figure 4–89

Task 3 - Redefine the Rib feature.

1. In the specification tree, double-click on **Rib.1** to redefine the **Profile control** option.

2. In the Profile control drop-down list, select **Reference surface**.

3. In the Geometrical Set, select the **Multi-sections Surface.1** feature, as shown in Figure 4–90.

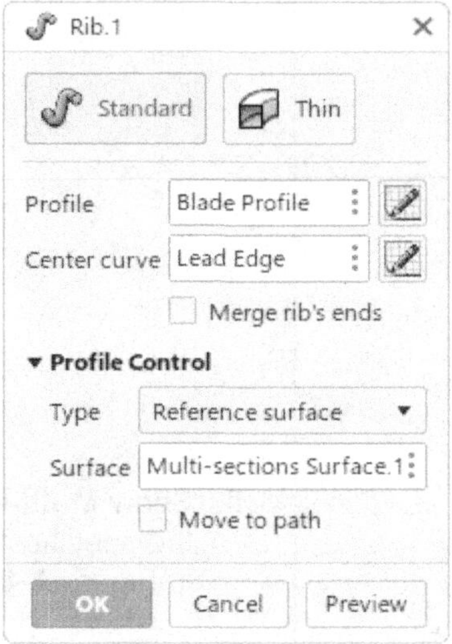

Figure 4–90

4. Click **OK** to complete the Rib feature. The resulting geometry is modified to follow the reference surface shape, as shown in Figure 4–91.

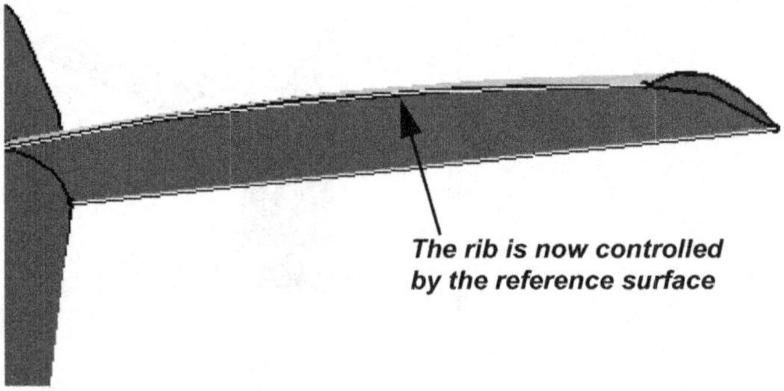

Figure 4–91

Task 4 - Pattern the Rib feature.

1. In the specification tree, select the **Rib.1** feature.

2. Click  (Circular Pattern) to create a circular pattern of the blade.

3. Define the circular pattern as shown in Figure 4–92.

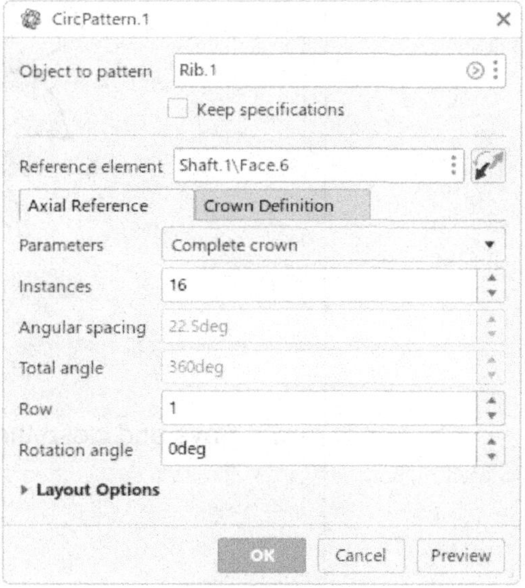

Figure 4–92

4. For the Reference Direction, select the surface shown in Figure 4–93.

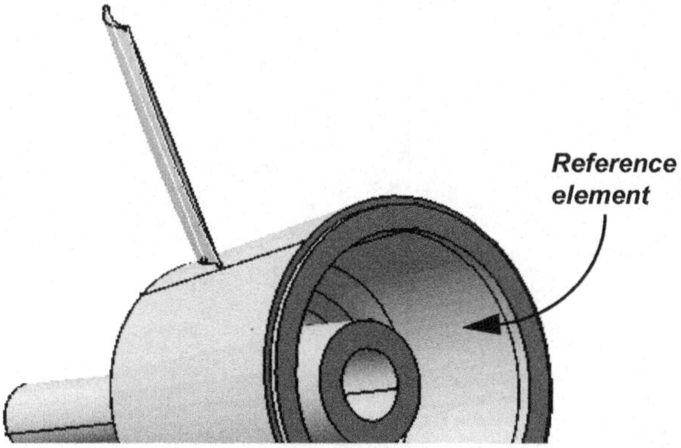

Figure 4–93

5. Click **OK** to complete the Rib feature.

6. Hide the Reference Surface feature (**Multi-sections Surface.1**) in the Geometrical set. The completed model displays as shown Figure 4–94.

Figure 4–94

7. Save and close the model.

Practice 4f

Hammer Head

Practice Objectives

- Create a Multi-sections Solid.
- Create a Rib using pulling direction.

In this practice, you will create the head of a hammer. The Base feature will be a Multi-sections Solid. The claw geometry is created using a Rib with pulling direction profile control and the hammer head geometry is created using a Shaft. The completed model displays as shown in Figure 4–95.

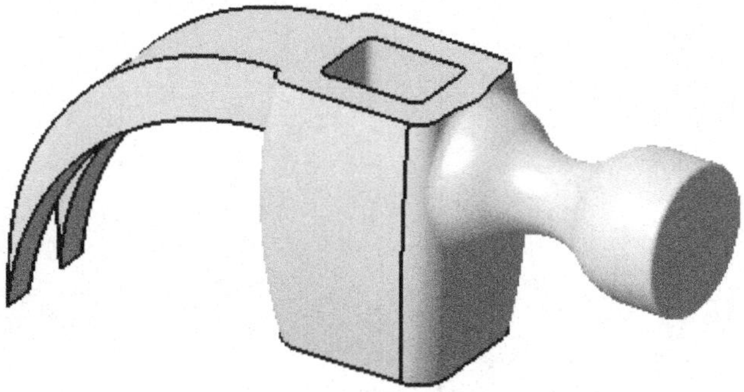

Figure 4–95

Task 1 - Open the part.

1. Import and open **HammerHead.3dxml**, as shown in Figure 4–96. When importing, type your initials followed by the dash symbol into the *Duplication string* field (e.g., **IA-**).

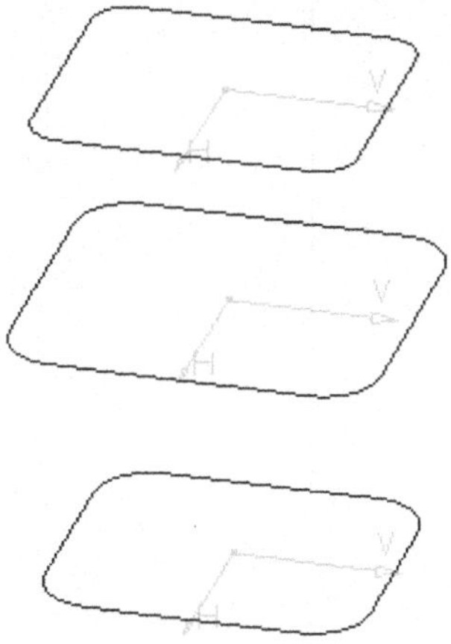

Figure 4–96

2. Click  (Multi-sections Solid). Define the Multi-sections Solid feature by selecting the following sketches, as shown in Figure 4–97:

   - **Sketch.1**
   - **Sketch.2**
   - **Sketch.3**

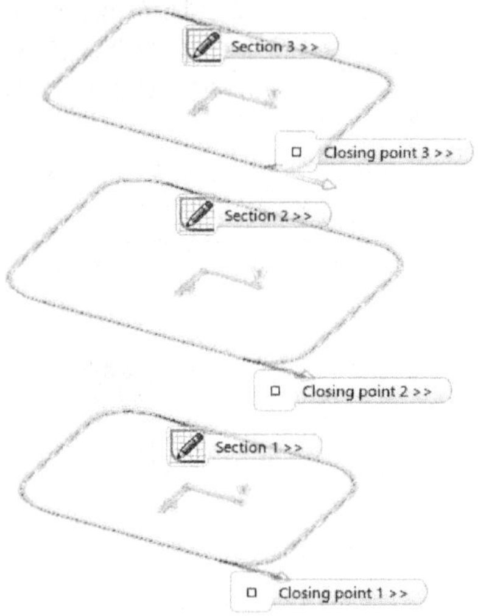

Figure 4–97

The completed Multi-sections Solid displays as shown in Figure 4–98.

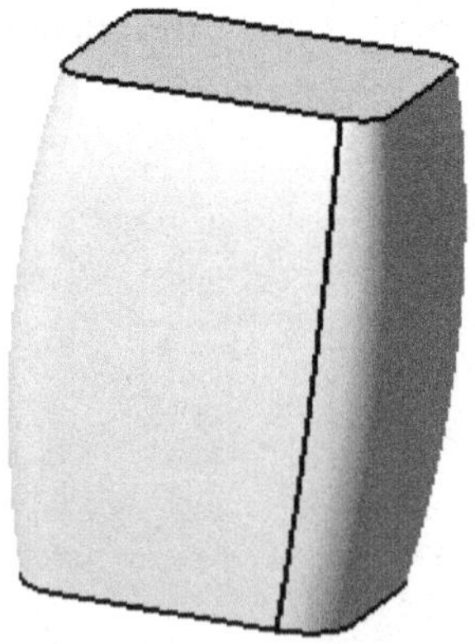

Figure 4–98

Task 2 - Create sketches for a Rib feature.

1. Apply an isometric view, if required.
2. Create a reference plane with the following parameters:
   - *Plane type:* **Through two lines**
   - *Line 1:* (as shown in Figure 4–99)
   - *Line 2:* (as shown in Figure 4–99)

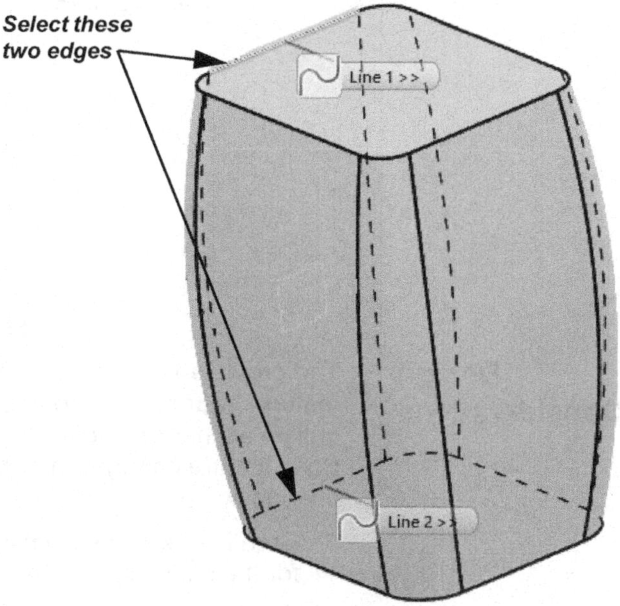

Figure 4–99

3. Select the reference plane that you have just created and activate the Sketcher app.

4. Create the sketch shown in Figure 4–100. Trim the projections with the sketched line.

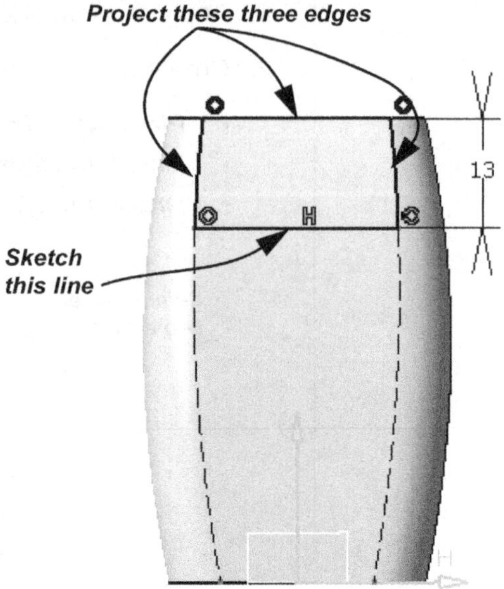

Figure 4–100

Design Considerations

The projected edges help capture the design intent of this feature. Your intent is to ensure that the claw uses the same outline as the Base feature. This also builds in associativity. If the Base feature changes in size, the claw profile will update with the changes.

5. Create a sketch shown in Figure 4–101, using the yz plane for the sketching plane.

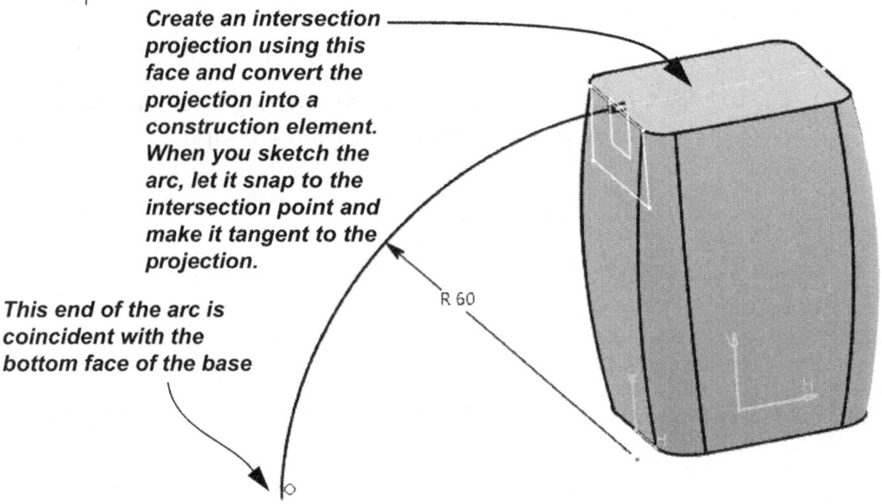

Figure 4–101

Task 3 - Create a Rib feature.

1. Click (Rib). Define the Rib feature by selecting the following sketches:
   - *Profile:* **Sketch.4**
   - *Center curve:* **Sketch.5**
   - *Profile control:* Keep angle

   The completed Rib displays as shown in Figure 4–102.

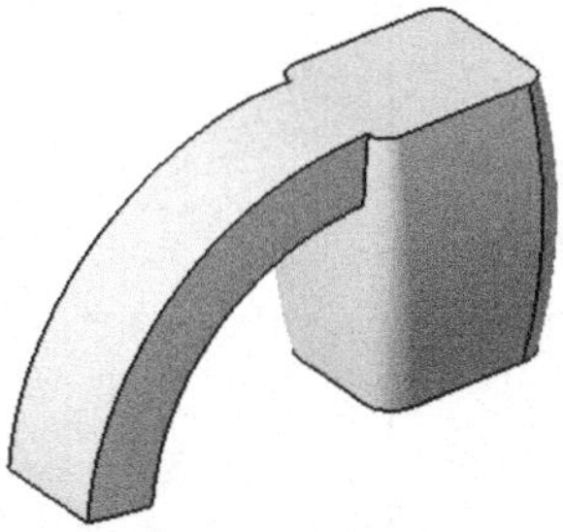

Figure 4–102

2. Edit the Rib feature and make the following change:
   - *Type:* **Pulling direction**
   - *Direction:* Select the surface shown in Figure 4–103.

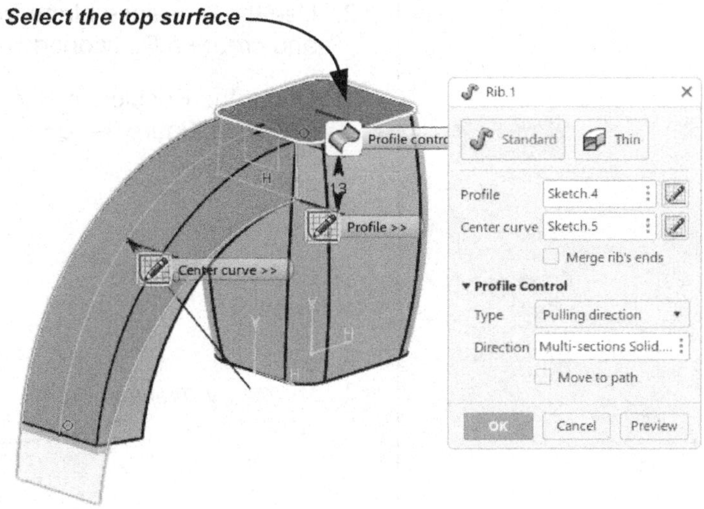

Figure 4–103

3. Complete the Rib feature.

Task 4 - Create a Pocket.

1. Create a reference plane with the following parameters:
   - *Plane type:* Through two lines
   - *Line 1:* (as shown in Figure 4–104)
   - *Line 2:* (as shown in Figure 4–104)

You might need to show ***Geometrical Set.1*** *to display the reference plane.*

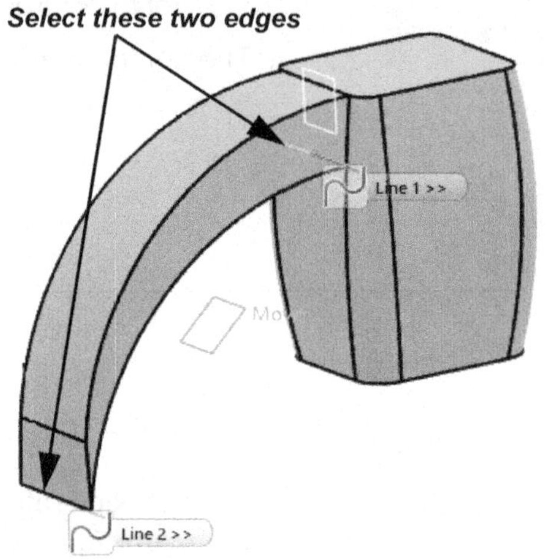

Figure 4–104

2. Use the reference plane from Step 1 as the sketching plane and create a Positioned Sketch.
3. Orient the Positioned Sketch and create the sketch, as shown in Figure 4–105.

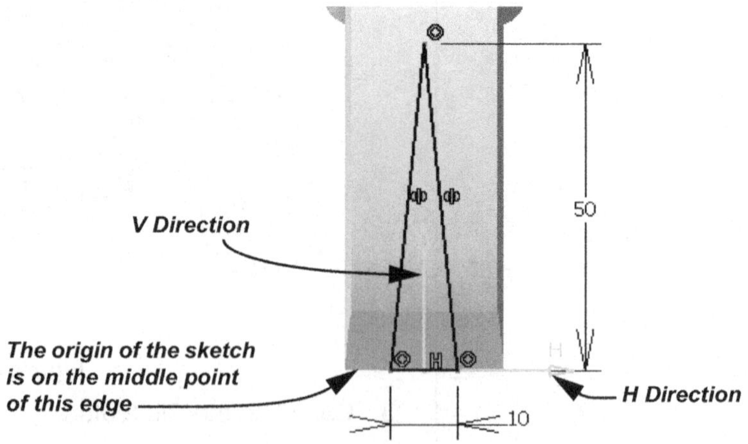

Figure 4–105

4. Create the Pocket shown in Figure 4–106. Select a depth option that best captures your intent.

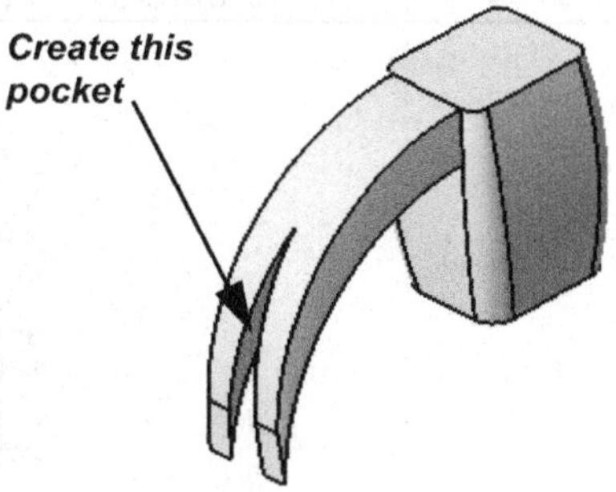

Figure 4–106

Task 5 - Create a Shaft feature.

1. Create the profile shown in Figure 4–107, using a positioned sketch on the yz plane. For the sketch origin, use the **Curve intersection** option and the top edge of the base feature.

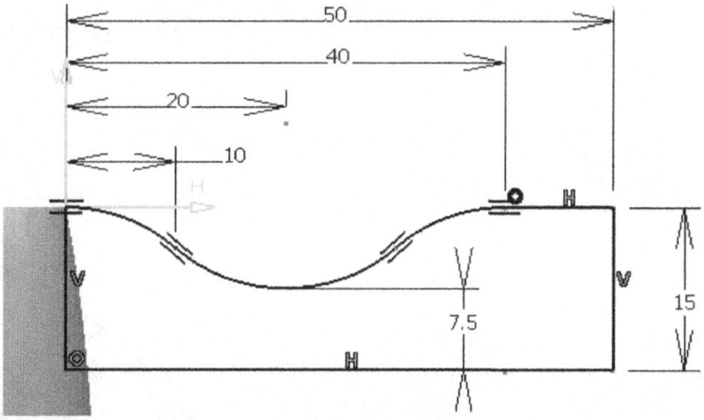

Figure 4–107

2. Create the Shaft shown in Figure 4–108.

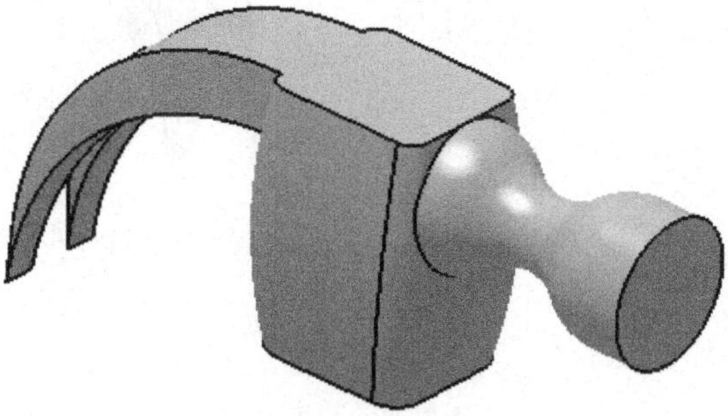

Figure 4–108

Task 6 - Create a Pocket feature.

1. Create the sketch shown in Figure 4–109.

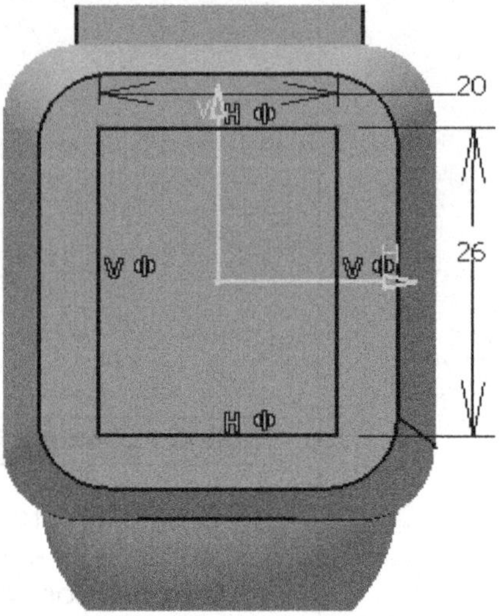

Figure 4–109

2. Create the pocket shown in Figure 4–110.

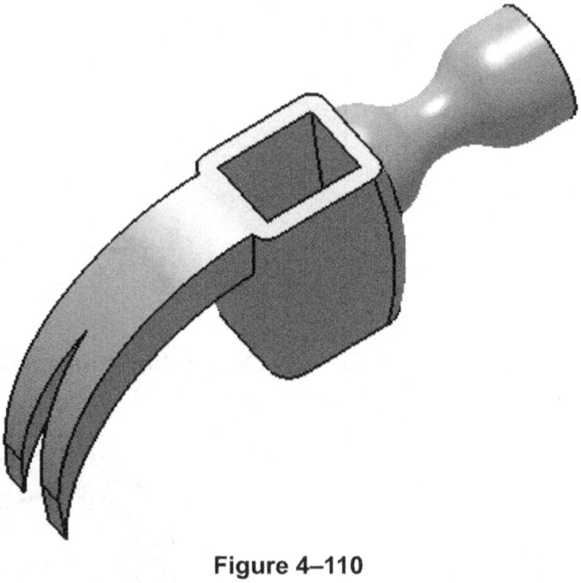

Figure 4–110

Task 7 - Create Dress-Up features.

1. Add draft to the Pocket surfaces.
   - *Angle:* **2**
   - *Face(s) to draft:* (the four surfaces of the Pocket)
   - *Neutral Element:* (surface shown in Figure 4–111)

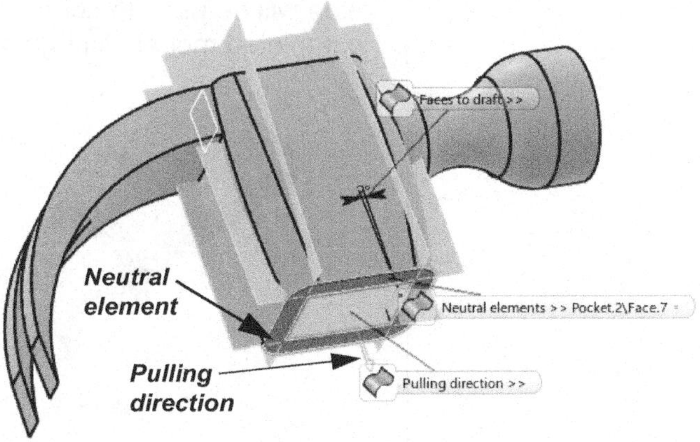

Figure 4–111

2. Create the Fillets shown in Figure 4–112.

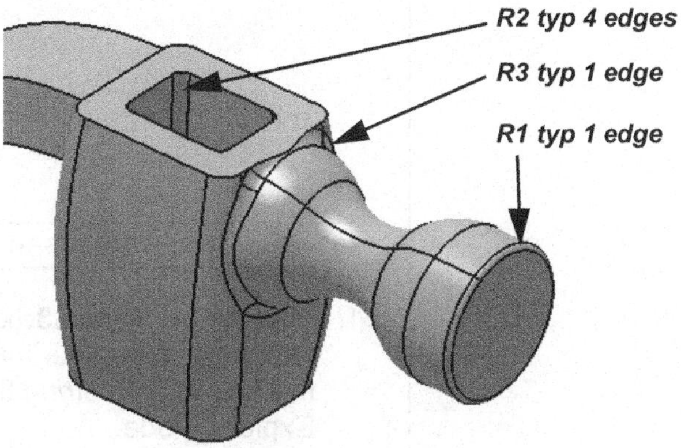

Figure 4–112

3. Save the model and close the window.

Practice 4g Transition Pipe

Practice Objectives

- Create a Multi-sections Solid.
- Creating output elements.

In this practice, you will create a transition pipe. This transition pipe will be used to connect two different types of pipes. The completed model displays as shown in Figure 4–113.

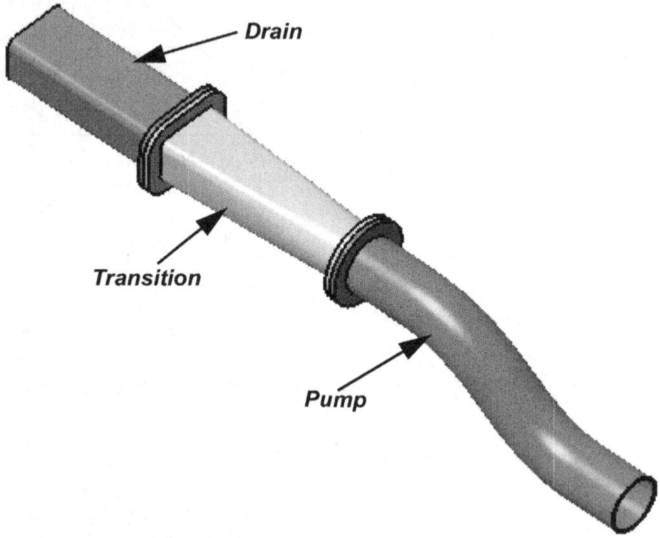

Figure 4–113

Task 1 - Open the assembly and part.

1. Import **The_Pipes.3dxml** from the *Pipe* folder. When importing, type your initials followed by the dash symbol into the *Duplication string* field (e.g., **IA-**). The model opens in Explore mode.

2. Right-click on the root assembly in the specification tree and select **Open**. The assembly opens for editing, as shown in Figure 4–114.

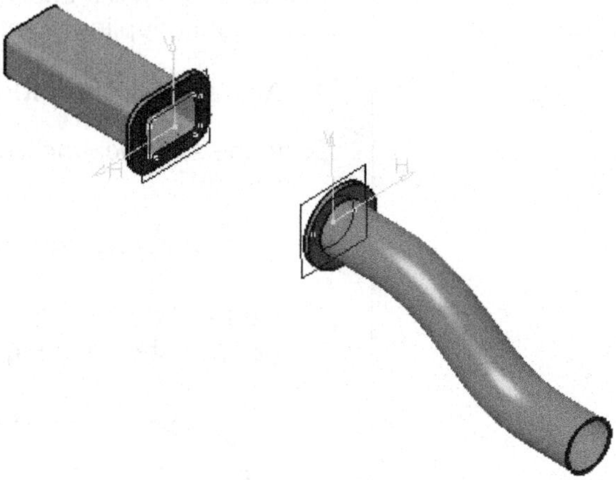

Figure 4–114

3. Switch to the Explore window. Right-click on the **Transition** part in the tree and select **Open With>Open in New App**. The part opens in a separate window, as shown in Figure 4–115. Note that the sections for the connector pipe have already been created.

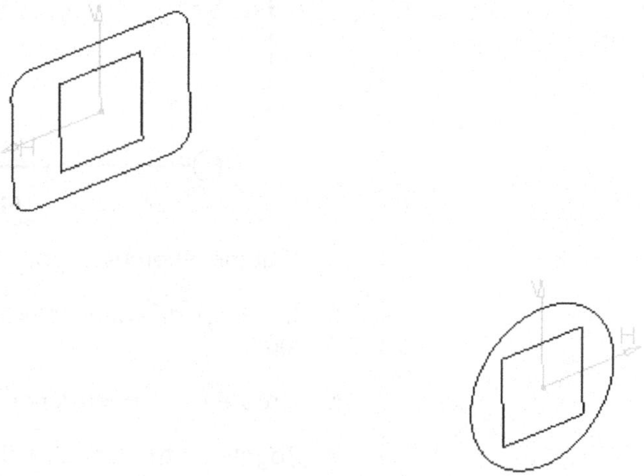

Figure 4–115

Task 2 - Create outputs.

In this task, you will create output points to use as coupling points for the Multi-sections Solid creation. Each section will have eight coupling points.

1. Activate the **Transition** part window.
2. In the specification tree, double-click on **Sketch.1** to enter the sketch.
3. Expand the right end of the Sketch section in the Action Bar.

   Find and double-click on  (Output feature) and select the vertices shown in Figure 4–116.

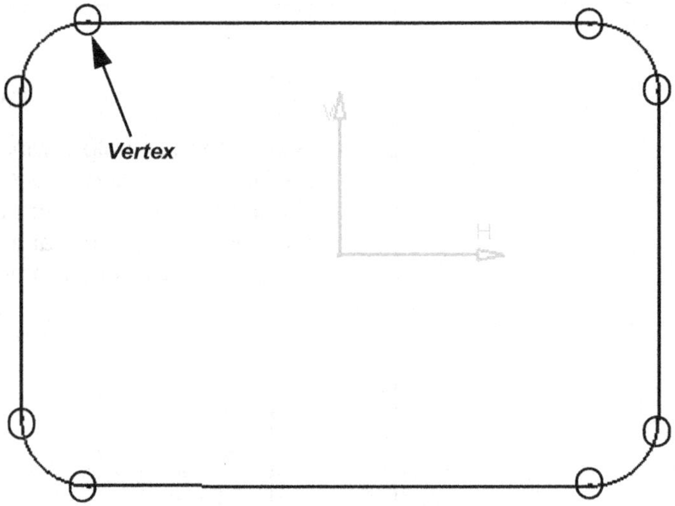

Figure 4–116

4. Exit the Sketcher app.
5. In the specification tree, double-click on **Sketch.2** to enter the sketch.
6. Create four construction lines, as shown in Figure 4–117.
7. Toggle off the Construction mode.

8. Highlight the four construction lines and click

    (Intersection Point), then select the circle to create the points shown in Figure 4–117.

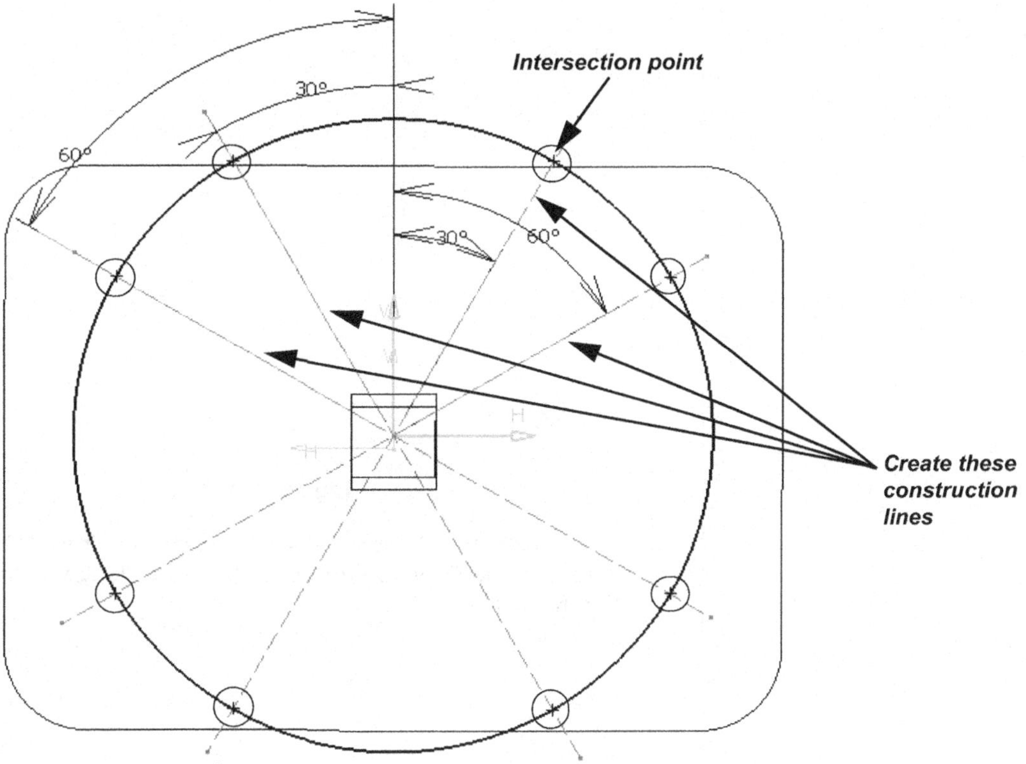

Figure 4–117

9. In the Sketch section of the Action Bar, double-click on

    (Output feature) and select the eight intersection points that you just created.

10. Exit the Sketcher app.

Task 3 - Create a Multi-sections Solid.

In this task, you will create a Multi-sections Solid using coupling curves. The outputs that you created in the previous task will be used as the coupling points to define the transition between the two sections. This enables you to control the shape of the Multi-sections Solid. If you are not satisfied with the results, you can modify the shape of the Multi-sections Solid by editing the position of the output points.

1. Click (Multi-sections Solid). Select the rectangular shaped profile and then select the circular profile from the display. The model displays as shown in Figure 4–118.

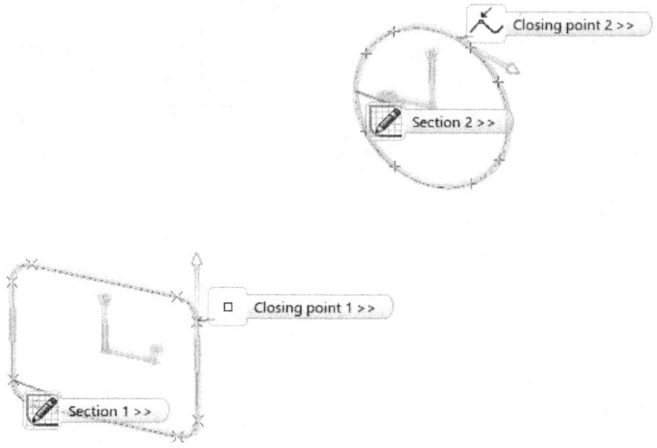

Figure 4–118

2. If required, invert the direction for **Closing Point 2** by selecting the direction arrow. The model displays as shown in Figure 4–119.

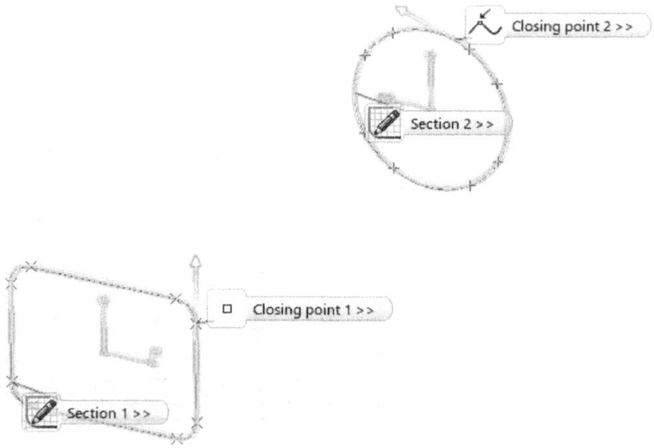

Figure 4–119

3. Click **More** to expand the Multi-sections Solid dialog box.

4. In the Sections coupling drop-down list, select the **Ratio** option.

5. Preview the Multi-sections Solid. The model displays as shown in Figure 4–120. Note that the Multi-sections Solid has a twisted shape. This is not the correct result.

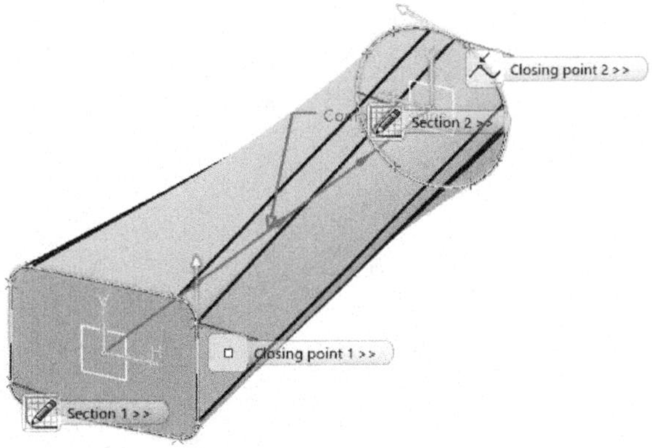

Figure 4–120

6. In the Multi-sections Solid dialog box, click **Cancel**.

7. Click  (Multi-sections Solid). Select the rectangular shaped profile and then select the circular profile.

8. Select the *Closing Points* field for Sketch.2, as shown in Figure 4–121.

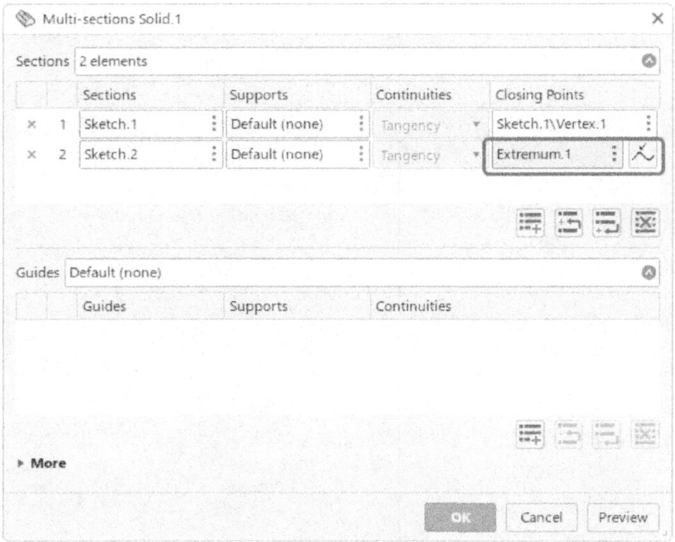

Figure 4–121

9. Select the new coupling point (one of the output points created for Sketch.2 in Task 2) and ensure that the closing point directions are pointing in the same direction. The model displays as shown in Figure 4–122.

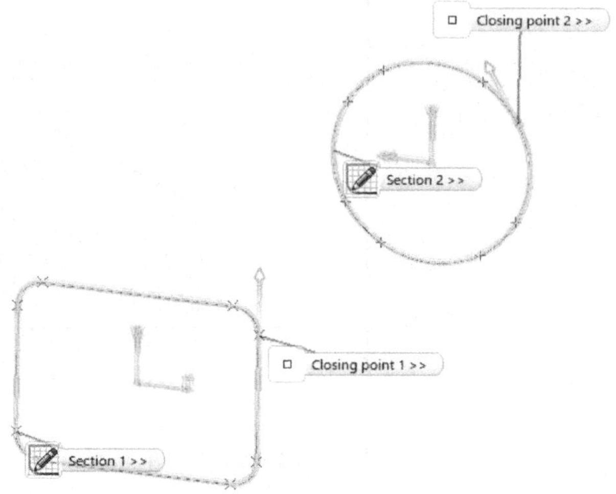

Figure 4–122

10. Click **More** to expand the Multi-sections Solid dialog box and click in the *Couplings* field, as shown in Figure 4–123.

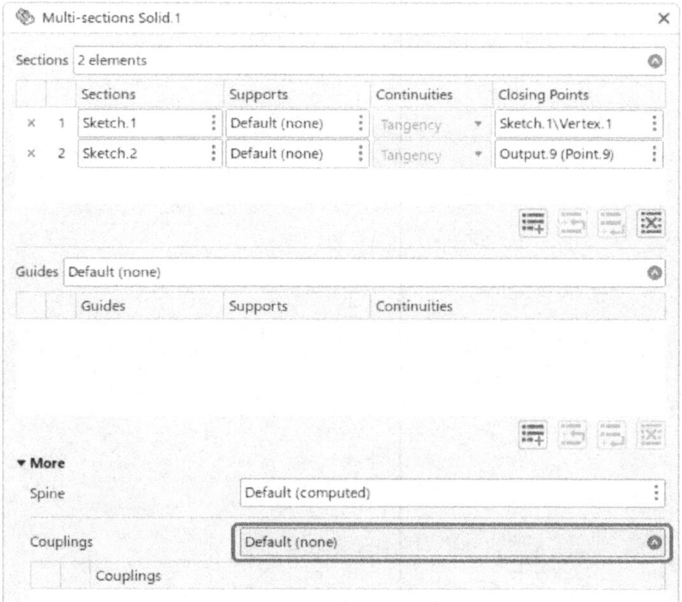

Figure 4–123

11. Select the point shown in Figure 4–124. This is one of the output vertices created for Sketch.1 in Task 2.

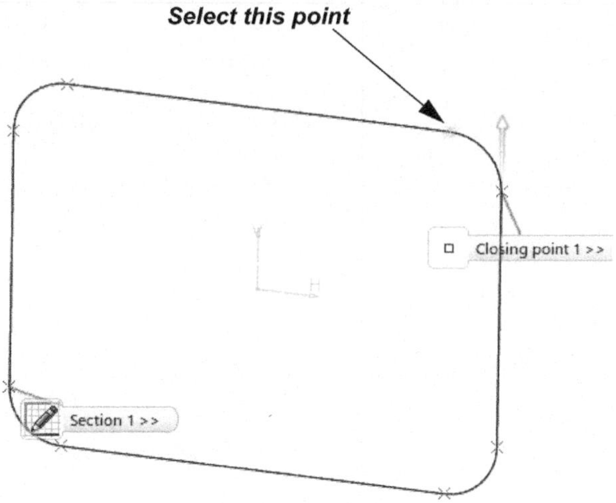

Figure 4–124

12. Select the point shown in Figure 4–125. This is one of the output vertices created for Sketch.2 in Task 2.

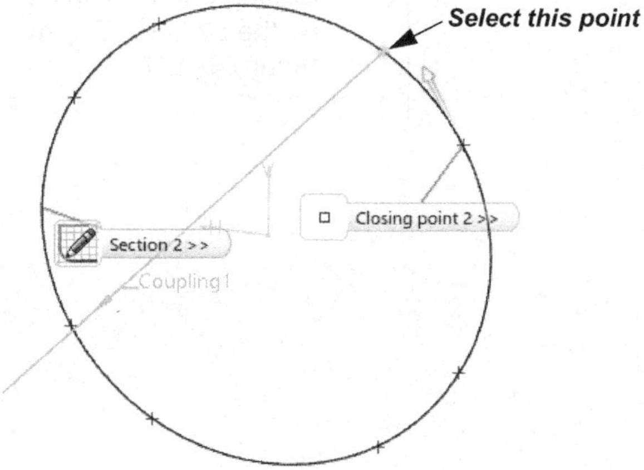

Figure 4–125

The model displays as shown in Figure 4–126.

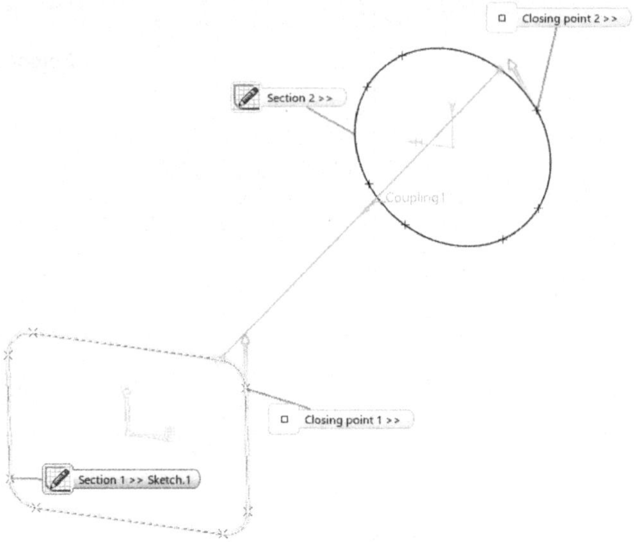

Figure 4–126

13. Create six more coupling curves using the output points. Note that there is no need to create coupling curve for the closing points. The closing points are coupled automatically by the system. The model displays as shown in Figure 4–127.

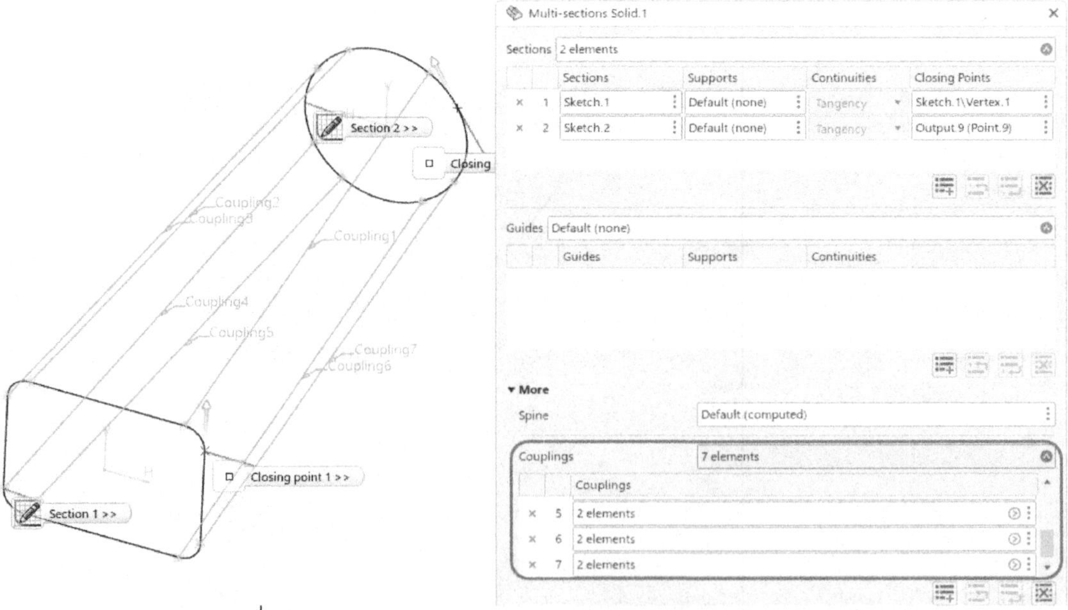

Figure 4–127

14. Click **OK** to complete the feature. The model displays as shown in Figure 4–128.

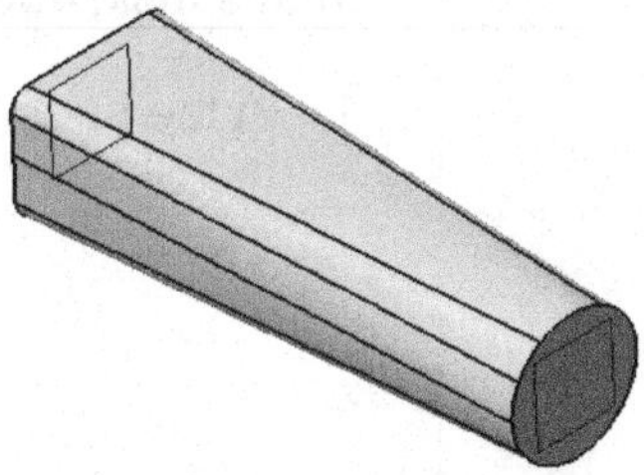

Figure 4–128

15. Hide the eight output points from both **Sketch.1** and **Sketch.2**.

Task 4 - Create a Shell feature.

1. In the Model section of the Action Bar, click  (Shell).
2. Make the selections shown in Figure 4–129.

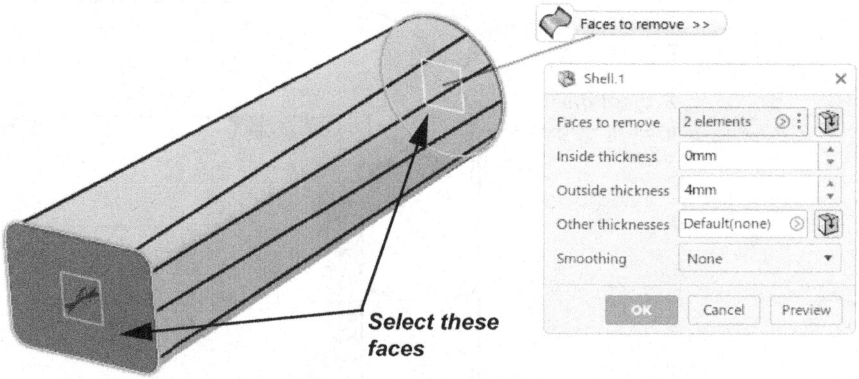

Figure 4–129

3. Click **OK** to complete the feature. The model displays as shown in Figure 4–130.

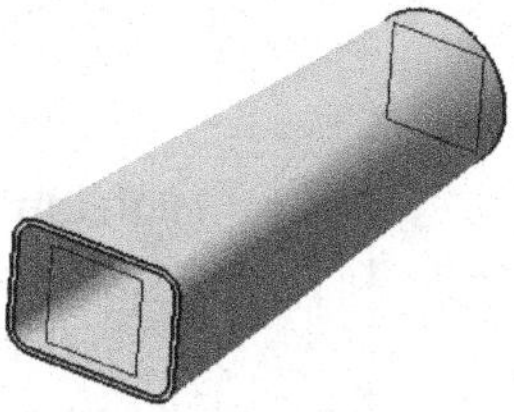

Figure 4–130

Task 5 - Create flange features.

In this task, you will create the flanges to connect the pipes.

1. In the specification tree or model, select **Plane.1** and enter the Sketcher app, as shown in Figure 4–131.

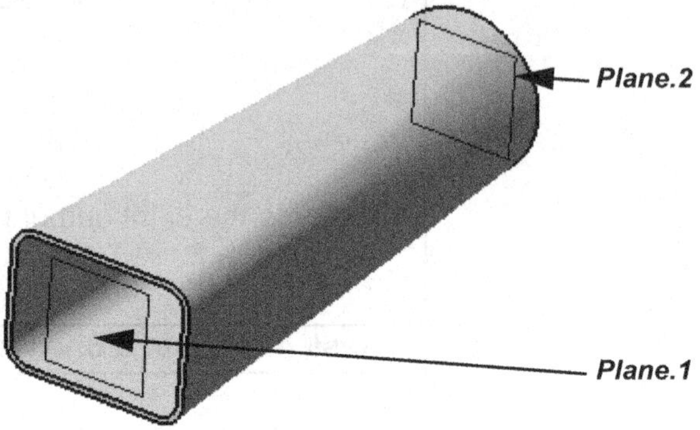

Figure 4–131

2. Sketch the profile shown in Figure 4–132.

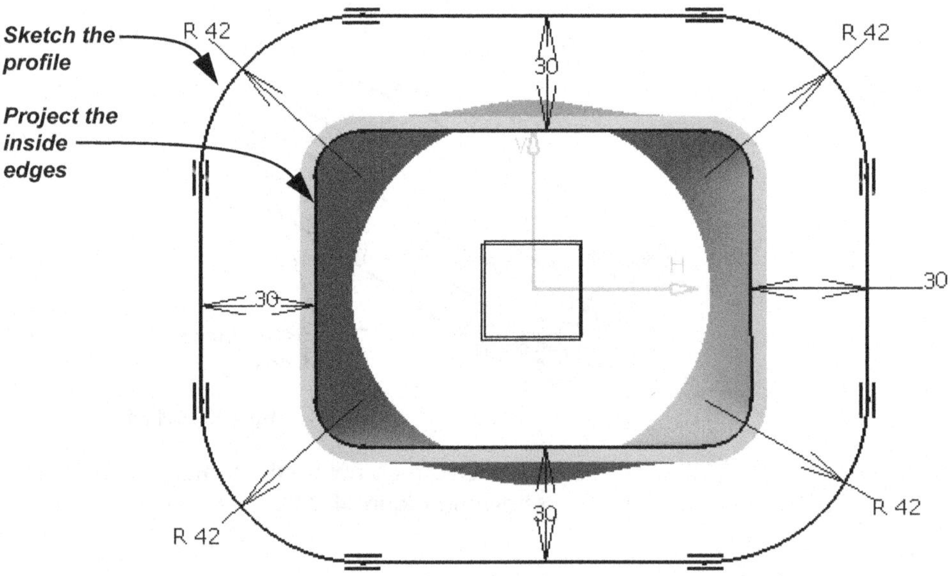

Figure 4–132

3. Highlight the sketch that you just created and click  (Pad).

4. Make the following selections, as shown in Figure 4–133:
   - *Type:* **Dimension**
   - *Length:* **10mm**

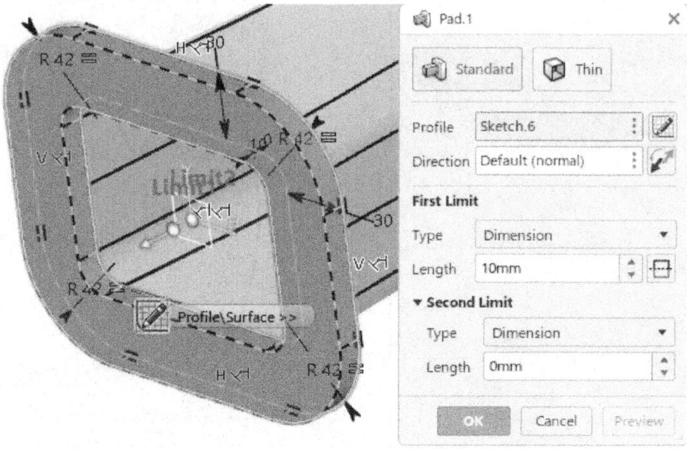

Figure 4–133

5. Click **OK** to complete the feature. The model displays as shown in Figure 4–134.

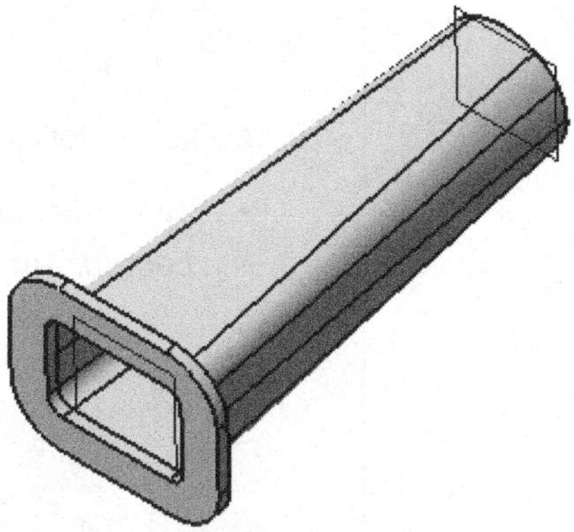

Figure 4–134

6. In the specification tree or model, select **Plane.2** and enter the Sketcher app.

7. Sketch the profile shown in Figure 4–135.

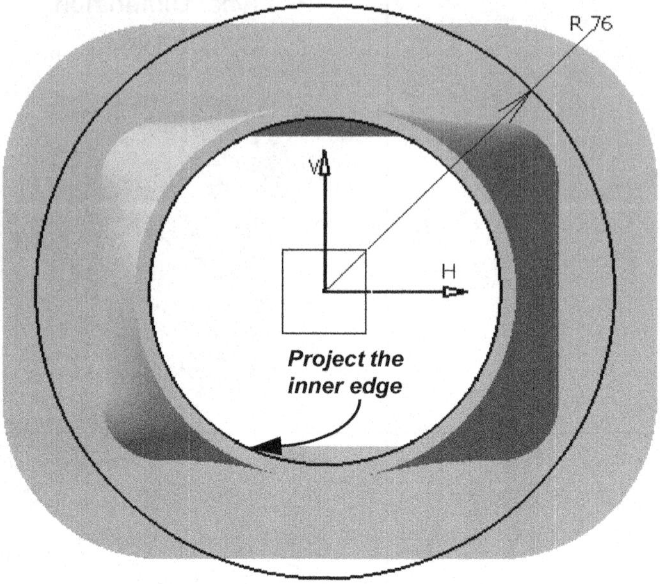

Figure 4–135

8. Highlight the sketch that you just created and click  (Pad).

9. Make the following selections, as shown in Figure 4–136:
   - *Type:* **Dimension**
   - *Length:* **10mm**

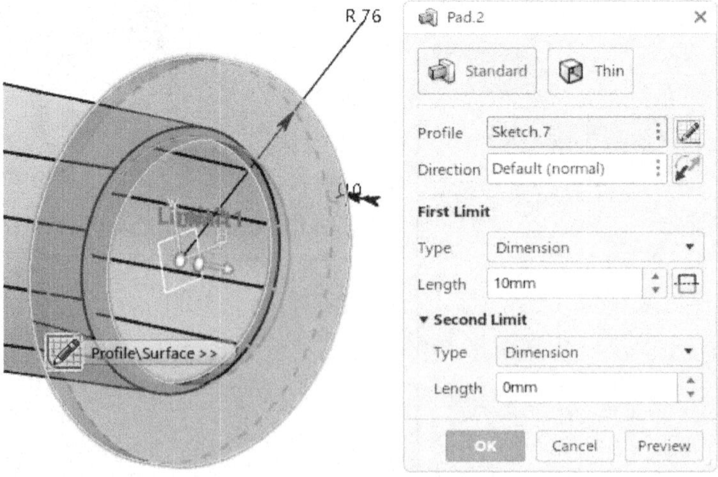

Figure 4–136

10. Click **OK** to complete the feature. The model displays as shown in Figure 4–137.

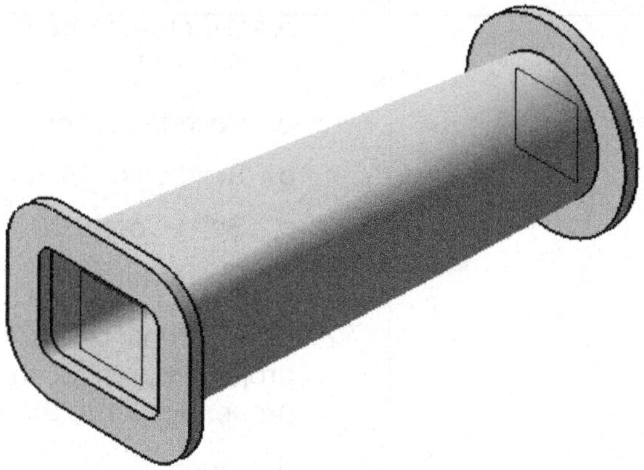

Figure 4–137

11. Activate the **Pipes** assembly window. The model displays as shown in Figure 4–138.

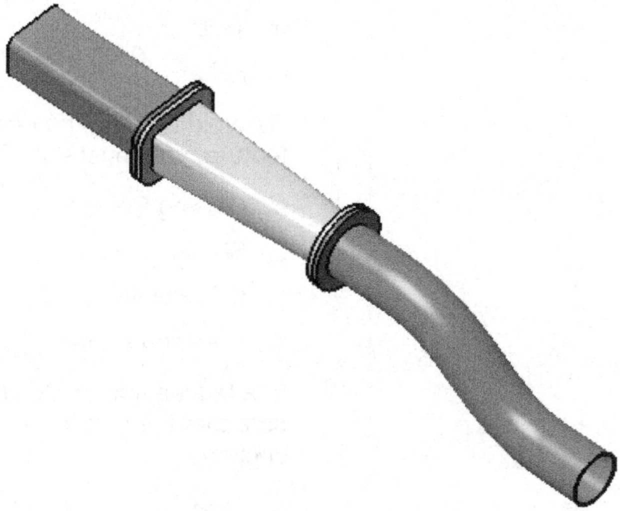

Figure 4–138

12. Save and close the files.

Chapter Review Questions

1. A solid created from the intersection of two projected profiles is referred to as a _______ feature.
   a. Solid Intersect
   b. Solid Join
   c. Solid Combine
   d. Solid Merge
2. When creating a solid feature from the intersection of two projected profiles, the profiles can only be projected perpendicular to the respective profile planes.
   a. True
   b. False
3. A Multi-sections Solid can contain a maximum of two sections.
   a. True
   b. False
4. To avoid twisting the geometry in a Multi-sections Solid feature, you must ensure that the _____ line up.
   a. Closing Points
   b. Starting Points
   c. End Points
   d. Coupling Points
5. In a Multi-sections Solid feature, a Spine curve defines the path that the feature must follow as it transitions between sections.
   a. True
   b. False

6. In a Multi-sections Solid feature, you use _______ to extend the feature beyond the first or last section, up to the shortest guide curve.

   a. Trim
   b. Extend
   c. Relimitation
   d. Crop

7. For Shell features, what does the **Tangency propagation for faces to remove** option do?

   a. Creates the shell by removing all of the selected faces.
   b. Creates the shell by removing only the internal faces.
   c. Creates the shell by removing all of the curved surfaces.
   d. Creates the shell by removing all of the surfaces with edges that are tangent continuous to the selected surface.

Answers: 1c, 2b, 3b, 4a, 5b, 6c, 7d

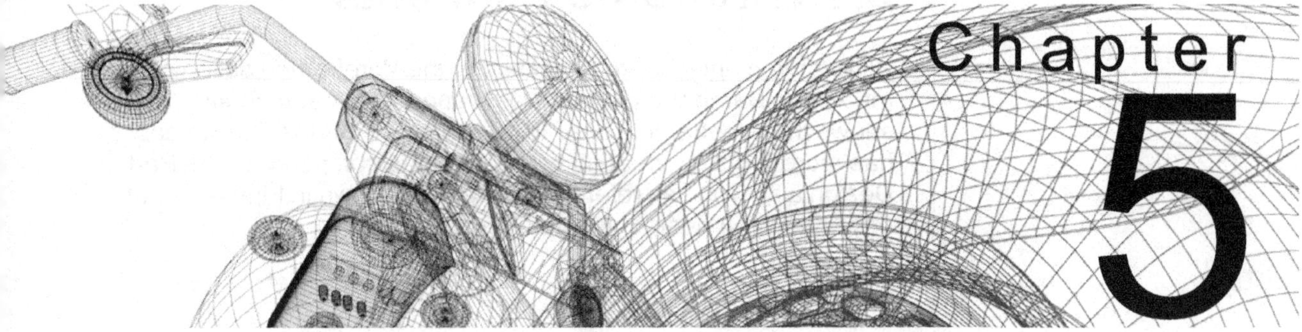

Wireframe Lines and Curves

In this chapter, only wireframe elements that are commonly used during complex, solid-feature creation are discussed.

Learning Objectives in This Chapter

- Understand where to access the Wireframe tools.
- Create points, lines, and planes for Wireframe geometry.
- Create splines for use in creating complex wireframe shapes.
- Learn how a Polyline differs from a Spline.
- Create a Polyline and a Helix Curve.
- Learn how to use a Combine element to create a curve that lies at the intersection of the projection of two curves.
- Understand how to project a curve onto a non-planar support.
- Create a curve at the intersection of two entities.
- Learn how to join two or more curves or surfaces so they can be treated as single entities.
- Extract new surface elements by copying surface or solid faces.
- Learn how to manage situations in which more than one possible solution exists for feature creation.

5.1 Wireframe Elements

Wireframe elements are accessed in the Wireframe section of the Action Bar in the Generative Shape Design app. Figure 5–1 shows the Wireframe icons. The Generative Shape Design app has more tools for creating wireframes, as compared to the Part Design app. You can refer to the example shown in Figure 5–1 at any time if you need to locate a specific tool.

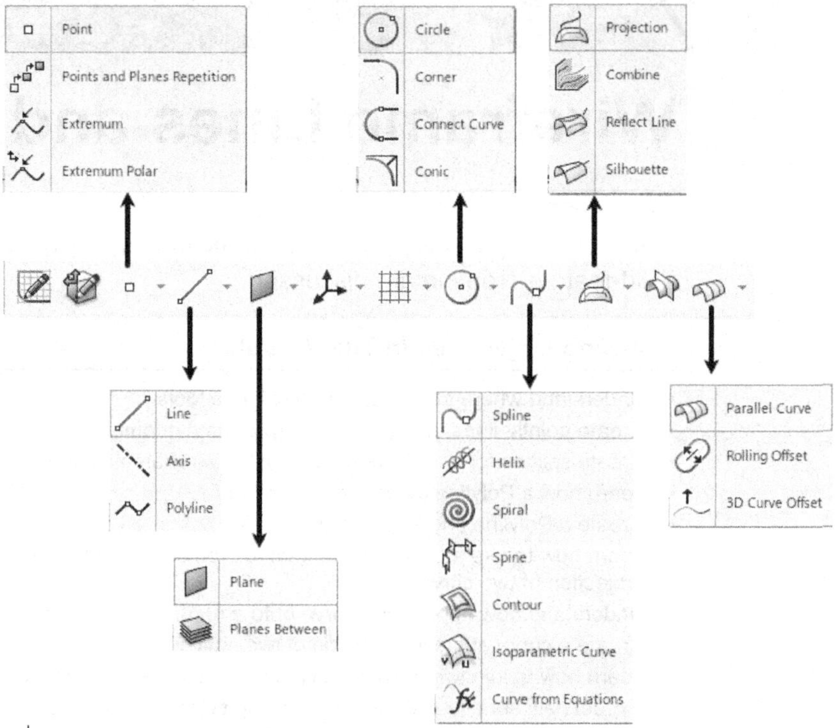

Figure 5–1

5.2 Points, Lines, and Planes

Point, Line, and Plane features are normally used as references that facilitate the creation of other elements.

Points

Points are geometry markers located in 3D space. They can be the building blocks of solid geometry or surface geometry, but are often used to create other wireframe elements.

Click □ (Point) in the Wireframe section of the Action Bar. The Point dialog box opens as shown in Figure 5–2. To create a single Point, select an option in the drop-down list, select required references, enter required parameters, and click **OK**.

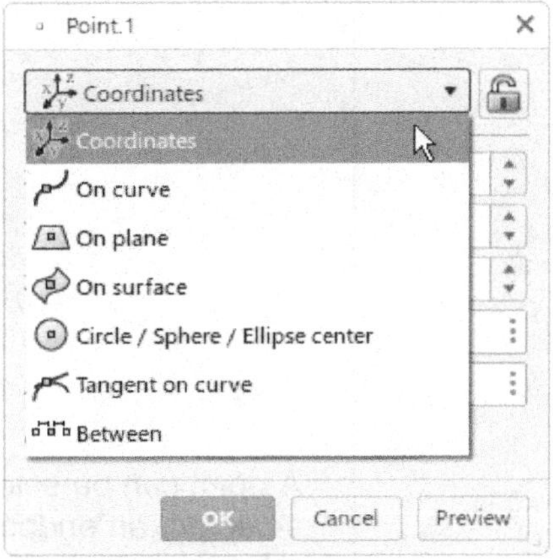

Figure 5–2

To create multiple Points along a Curve, Line, or Edge, click  (Points and Planes Repetition). The Points Repetition dialog box opens as shown in Figure 5–3.

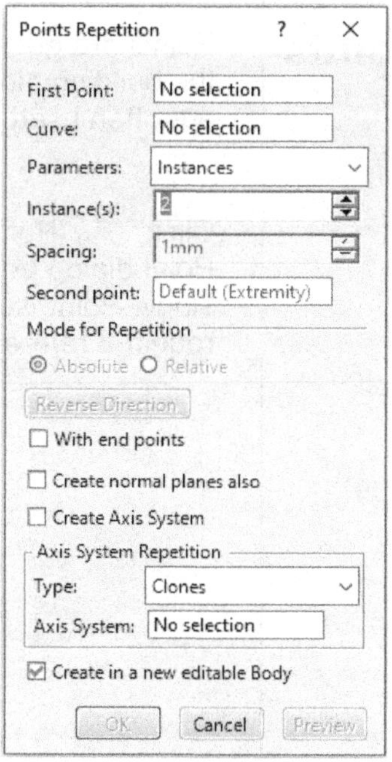

Figure 5–3

A point can be selected for the First Point, but if one is not selected, an endpoint of the Curve is used instead. The reference for the Curve can be an edge, line, or curve.

To obtain evenly-spaced points, select **Instances** in the Parameters drop-down list. Figure 5–4 shows five Points created using the **Instances** option.

Figure 5–4

To obtain Points spaced at a specific distance relative to each other, select **Instances and Spacing** in the Parameters drop-down list. The **Instances and Spacing** option is only available if you have selected a Point to define the start of the repetition. Figure 5–5 shows four Points spaced apart by **0.5 in** using the **Instances and Spacing** option.

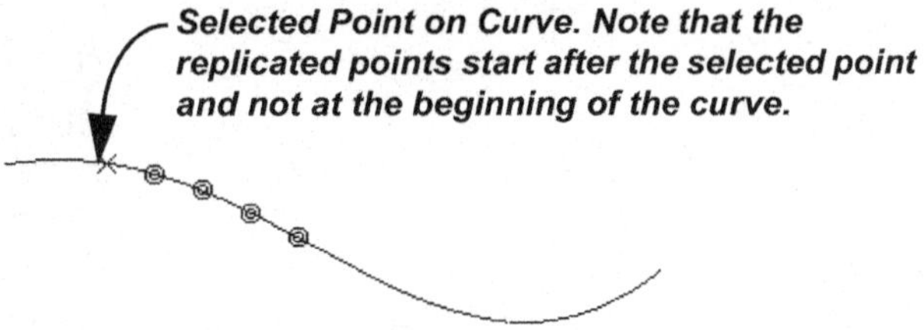

Figure 5–5

Lines

You can use Lines as a reference to align two components in an assembly or as a reference to define a rotational plane in a part model. Click (Line). The Line dialog box opens as shown in Figure 5–6. To create a Line feature, select an option in the Line type drop-down list, select required references, and enter required parameters.

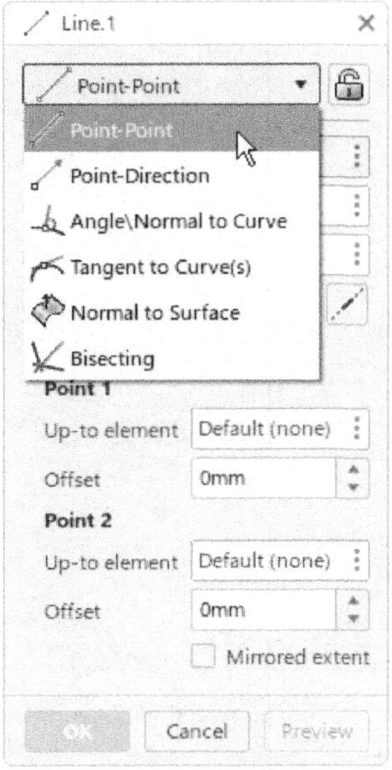

Figure 5–6

Planes

You can use Plane features as a placement and dimensional reference for all types of features. Click  (Plane). The Plane dialog box opens as shown in Figure 5–7. To create a Plane, select an option in the drop-down list.

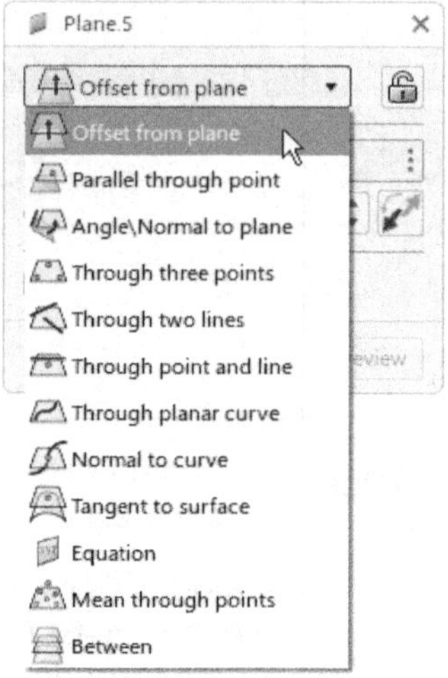

Figure 5–7

5.3 Creating Splines

Splines are curves that pass smoothly through two or more points. The selected points can be point elements or vertices of previous features, including sketched points. These points can be present before you initiate the creation of the Spline, or you can create them on the fly using the shortcut menu. Once the points have been selected, you can insert or replace additional points. You can create a spline as either 2D or 3D. Splines are great tools for creating complex wireframe shapes.

General Steps

Use the following general steps to create a Spline feature:

1. Start the creation of a Spline.
2. Select reference points.
3. Define Spline parameters.
4. Complete the feature.

Step 1 - Start the creation of a Spline.

Click  (Spline). The Spline dialog box opens as shown in Figure 5–8.

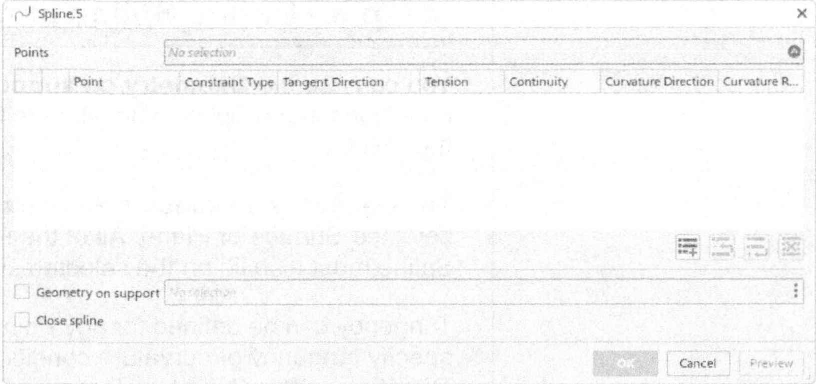

Figure 5–8

Step 2 - Select reference points.

Once you start the creation of the Spline, you can select reference points, end points, and vertices. Add Points to the Spline by selecting them in the specification tree or main window. You can use the options in the Spline dialog box to perform operations on the current, highlighted Point. For example, you can rearrange the order of the Points, close the Spline, or remove a Point.

You can use  to control the position of the next selected Point. You can add Points before or after the current Point. You can also replace the current Point.

The **Close Spline** option automatically selects the last Point of the Spline using the first selected Point to close the Spline.

Figure 5–9 shows a Spline passing through five Points.

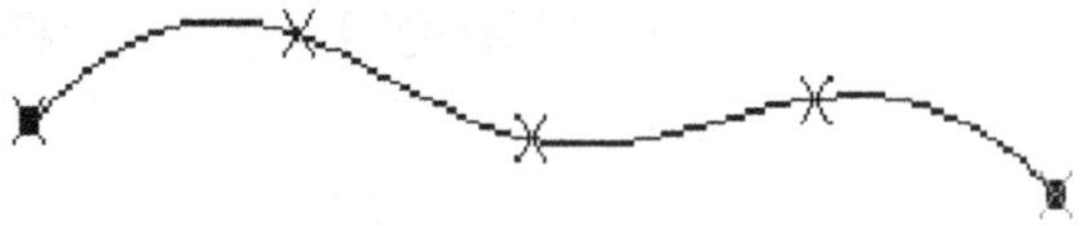

Figure 5–9

Step 3 - Define Spline parameters.

You can use the **Geometry on support** option and tangency conditions in the Spline dialog box to further define the shape of the Spline.

The **Geometry on support** option forces the Spline to lie on the selected Surface or Plane. All of the Points selected for the Spline must also lie on the selected support.

Tangency can be defined for any Point specified in the Spline. To specify tangency or curvature conditions, select *Tangent Direction* and/or *Curvature Direction* field for the Point and then select a Line, Plane, or Curve to which the Spline is going to be tangent at the selected point.

Tangency specification is not limited to end points.

The graphic at the top in Figure 5–10 shows a Spline created between two surfaces with no tangency constraints added. The lower graphic shows a Spline created between the same two surfaces with tangency constraints added at both ends of the Spline. The direction of tangency can be set as required.

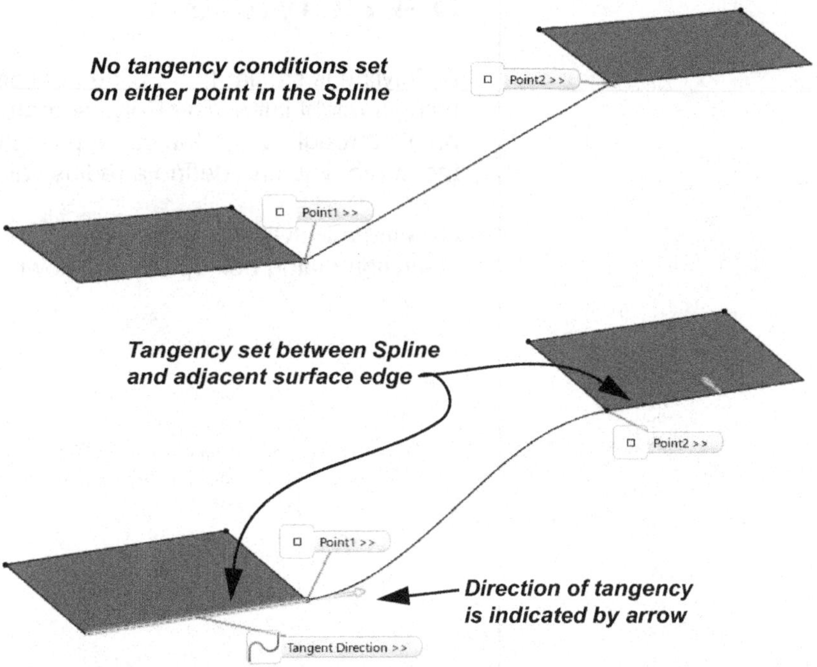

Figure 5–10

Step 4 - Complete the feature.

In the Spline dialog box, click **OK** to complete the feature.

5.4 Polyline

A Polyline is similar to a Spline but connects the selected points using straight lines. The Polyline feature is defined by selecting points through which the curve passes. To control the shape of the curve, you can define a radius value at each point. To start creating a Polyline feature, click 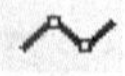 (Polyline). The Polyline Definition dialog box opens as shown in Figure 5–11.

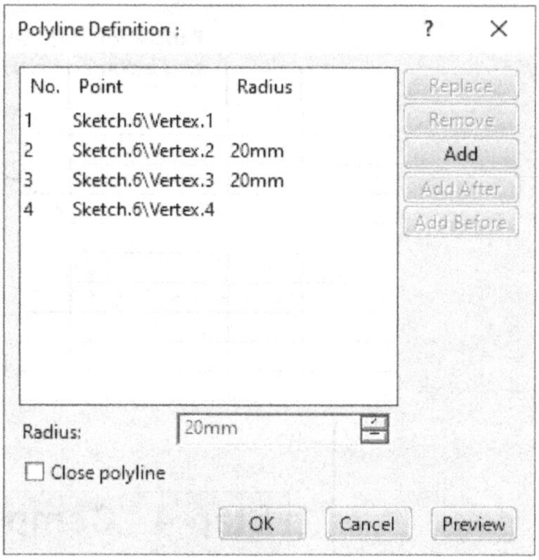

Figure 5–11

The Polyline shown on the left in Figure 5–12 is created using the default straight edges. When a radius is applied at Point 2 and 3 of the Polyline, it displays as shown on the right in Figure 5–12.

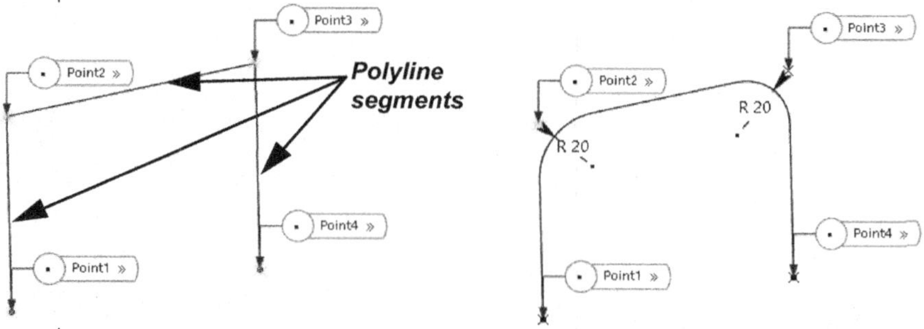

Figure 5–12

5.5 Helix Curve

To start creating a Helix Curve, click  (Helix). The Helix Curve Definition dialog box opens as shown in Figure 5–13.

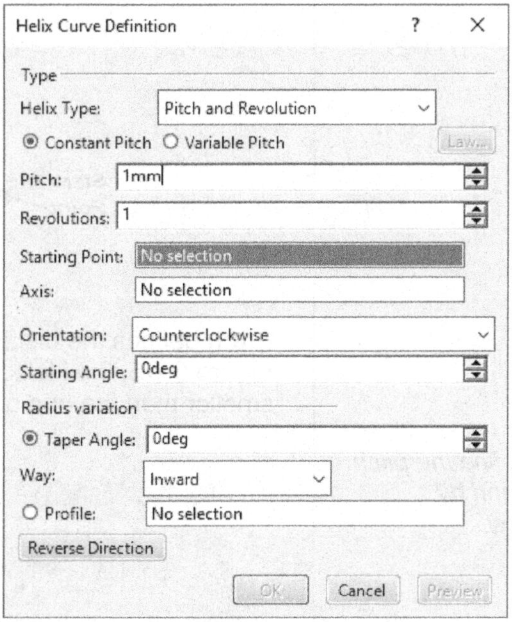

Figure 5–13

A helix is defined by three parameters: **Pitch**, **Revolution** and **Height**. You can create a helix by any two parameters. In the Helix Type drop-down list, select one of the following helix creation methods:

- **Pitch and Revolution**
- **Height and Pitch**
- **Height and Revolution**

Additionally, you must select either **Constant Pitch** or **Variable Pitch**. The **Variable Pitch** option is only available for the **Pitch** and **Revolution** type of helix. When the **Variable Pitch** option is selected, you can define the *Start* pitch value and the *End* pitch value.

A helix can be defined by selecting a starting point and an axis. The starting point defines the radius of the helix and the axis defines the center of the helix, as shown in Figure 5–14. Once specified, you can adjust the remaining parameters to achieve the required results.

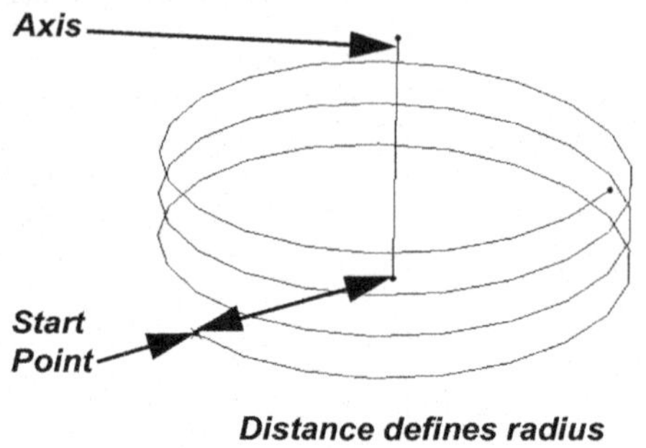

Figure 5–14

Pitch defines the distance between the Helix revolutions. In Figure 5–15, the Helix on the left was created with a pitch smaller than the one on the right.

*You can define the pitch using a graph by clicking **Law**.*

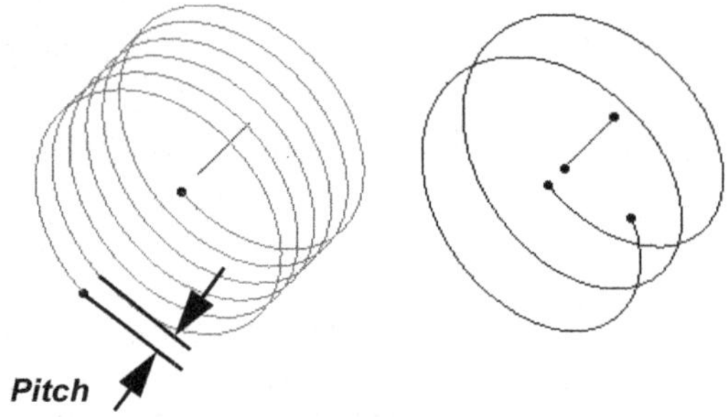

Figure 5–15

Height defines the length of the axis from the start point of the Helix. In Figure 5–16, a smaller height has been defined for the Helix on the right.

Height is not controlled by the selected axis.

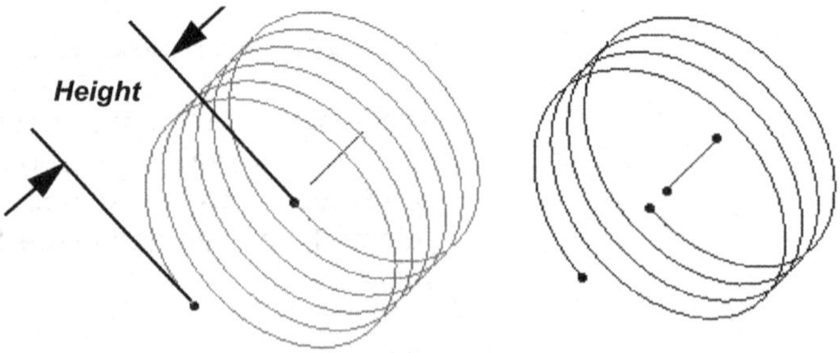

Figure 5–16

Taper Angle defines whether the Helix has a linearly increasing or decreasing diameter. The taper can be defined **Inward** or **Outward** at a specified angle. In Figure 5–17, the Helix on the right tapers inward by 15°.

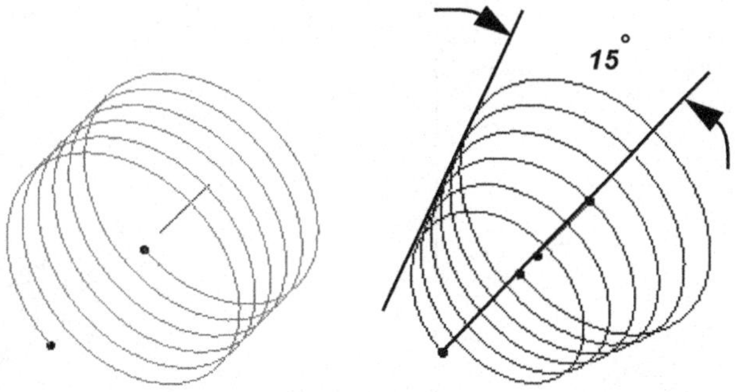

Figure 5–17

Starting Angle starts the Helix offset from the start point, as shown in Figure 5–18.

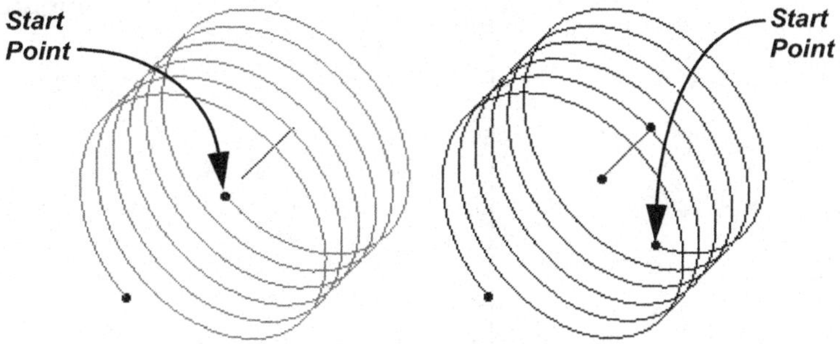

Figure 5–18

In the Helix Curve Definition dialog box, use the options in the *Radius variation* area to further define the Helix Curve. You can use the **Profile** option to define a profile curve that the Helix should follow. An example is shown in Figure 5–19.

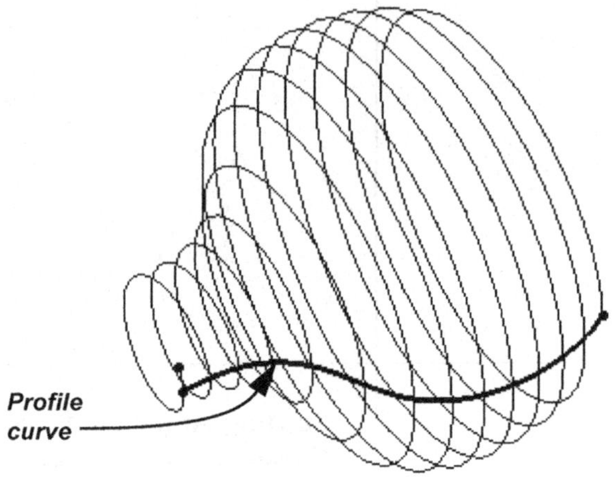

Figure 5–19

5.6 Combine Curve

Combine

A Combine element enables the creation of a curve that lies on the intersection of the projection of two curves or sketches. Each curve or sketch is created independent of the other and can either be projected along the normal or along a specified direction. This method is analogous to creating two extruded surfaces and creating a curve using the intersection element.

A Combine element can be used to define a 3D curve with only 2D information about the curve.

How To: Create a Combine Element

1. Click  (Combine). The Combine dialog box opens as shown in Figure 5–20.

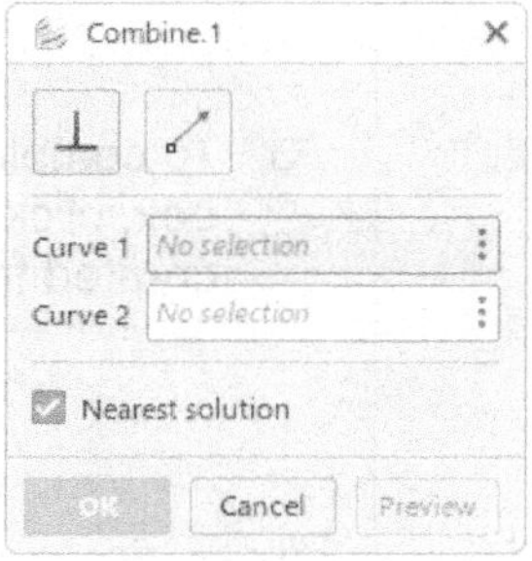

Figure 5–20

2. Specify the Combine type as  (Normal to Curve) or  (Along a direction) and select two curves to define the combine element. Figure 5–21 shows two curves selected to define a Combine element.

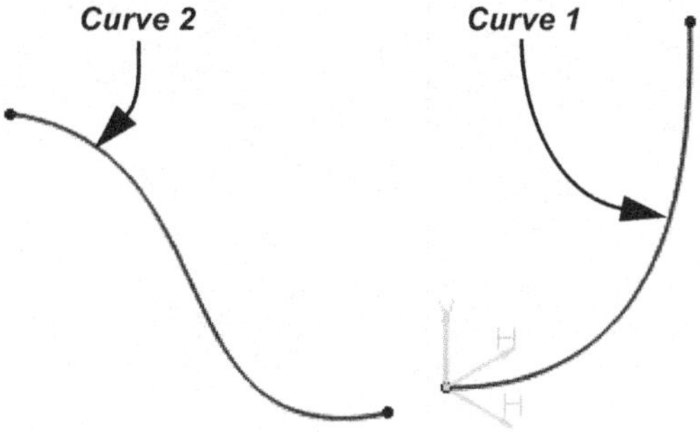

Figure 5–21

Figure 5–22 shows the imaginary extruded surfaces. The resulting intersection defines the location of the combine element.

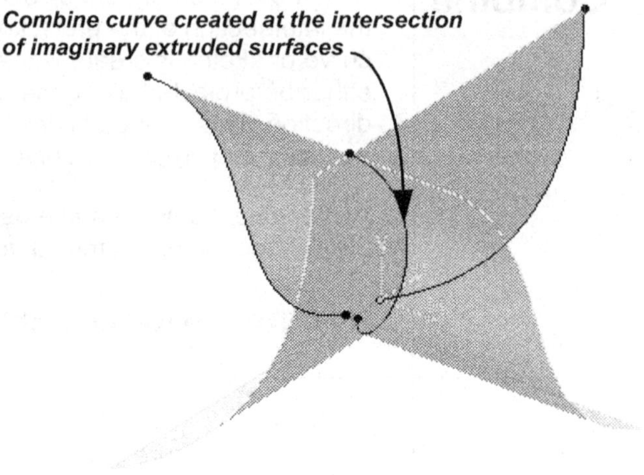

Figure 5–22

3. To complete the Combine element, in the Combine dialog box, click **OK**. Figure 5–23 shows a Combine element created from the two curves shown in Figure 5–23.

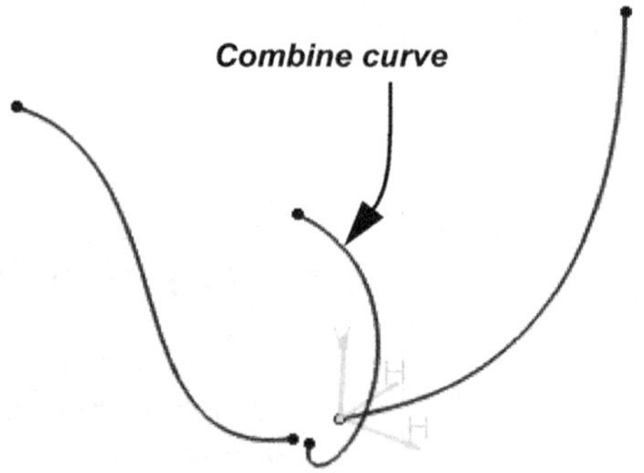

Figure 5–23

If you specify the Combine type as **Along a direction**, you must select direction references for each curve. Planar references denote normal projection, as shown in Figure 5–24.

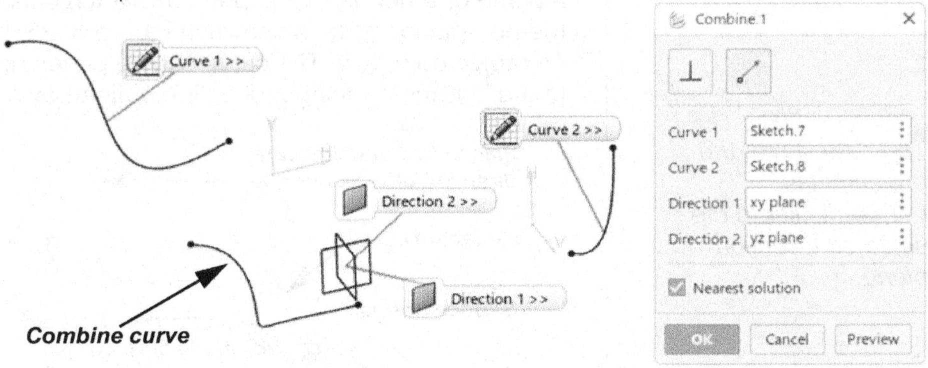

Figure 5–24

5.7 Projection Curve

The Projection feature enables you to project 3D geometry onto a plane or a non-planar support. A sketch cannot be created on the non-planar surface shown in Figure 5–25, but a sketch can be projected onto it. The curve can be projected at points normal to the surface or along a direction defined by a plane or line.

The direction of the projection is perpendicular to the selected Direction plane.

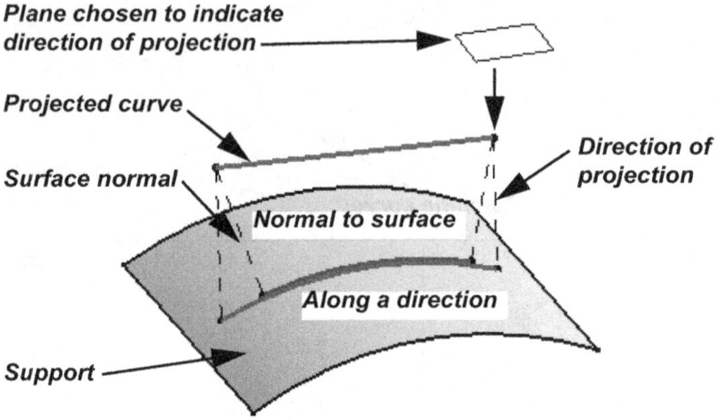

Figure 5–25

To create a projection, click (Projection). The Project dialog box opens. You must specify a curve to be projected and a support on which to project the curve, as shown in Figure 5–26.

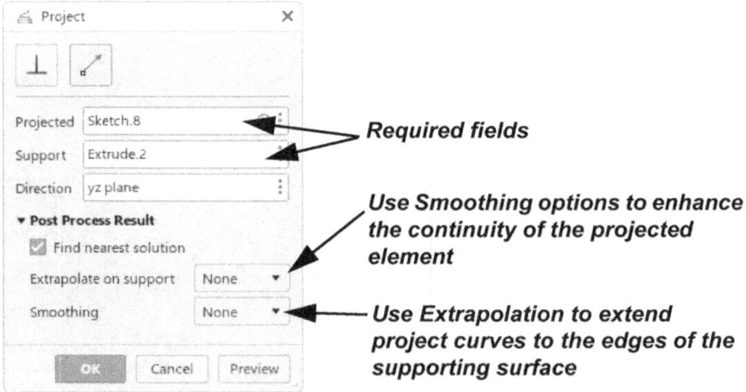

Figure 5–26

Depending on the orientation of the selected curve and support, the resulting feature could be a curve or a point.

5.8 Intersection Curve

The Intersection feature enables you to create geometry at the intersection of two elements. Using this feature, a curve can be created at the intersection of two surface features, as shown in Figure 5–27.

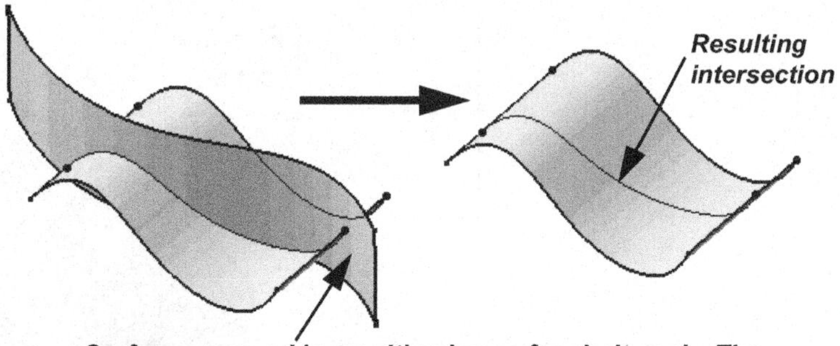

Figure 5–27

How To: Create an Intersection

1. Click (Intersection). The Intersect dialog box opens as shown in Figure 5–28.

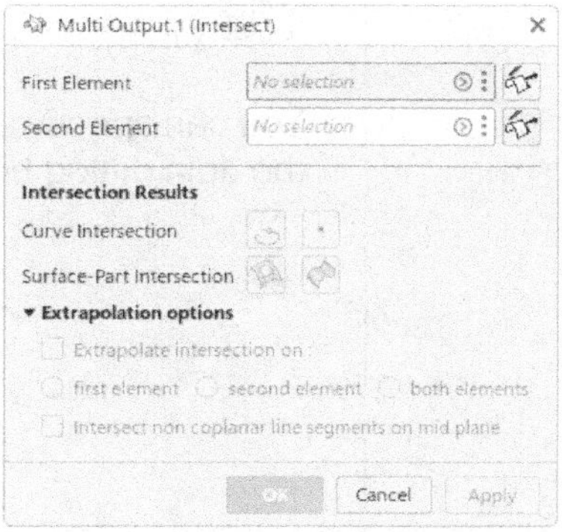

Figure 5–28

2. Select the two elements to intersect. Curves, surfaces, and planes are acceptable elements.
3. Click **OK** to complete the Intersect. The resulting geometry can be curves, points, or a surface area, depending on the options used and the selected geometry.

5.9 Operations

Join

The **Join** operation joins two or more adjacent Curves or Surfaces so that they can be selected as one Curve or Surface. The two Surfaces shown in Figure 5–29 represent two separate features in the specification tree.

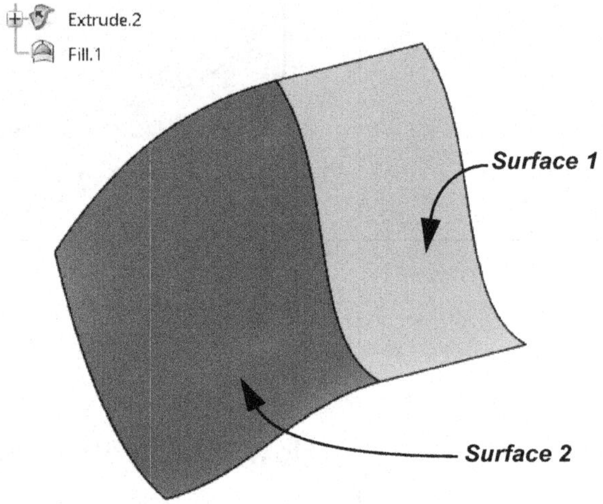

Figure 5–29

To join two surfaces, select both surfaces using <Ctrl> and click

 (Join).

You can specify additional parameters using optional elements in the Join dialog box, as shown in Figure 5–30.

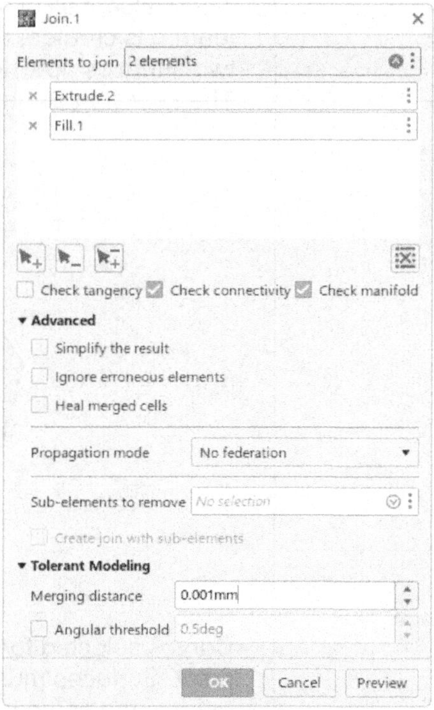

Figure 5–30

Some of the options are described as follows:

Option	Description
Check Connectivity	Checks whether the joined elements are connected, within the Merging distance value.
Simplify the result	Reduces the number of elements in the Join, if possible.
Ignore erroneous elements	Ignores any elements that prevent the creation of the Join feature.
Merging Distance	Determines the maximum separation permitted between elements. The merging distance has a maximum value of 0.1mm.
Propagation mode	Defines groups of elements in the Join. By default, the **No Federation** option is selected. In this situation, each surface in the Join can be selected individually. If the **All** option is selected, all of the elements in the join are selected together.
Sub-Elements to Remove	You can use this tab to exclude sub-elements of elements that have been included in the Join. For example, an individual face of a Surface to be joined can be removed from the Join feature.

If you accept all of the defaults in the Join dialog box, a new Join feature is created, as shown in Figure 5–31. Note that the initial two surfaces now display as grayed out in the specification tree. The new Join Surface represents these two surfaces.

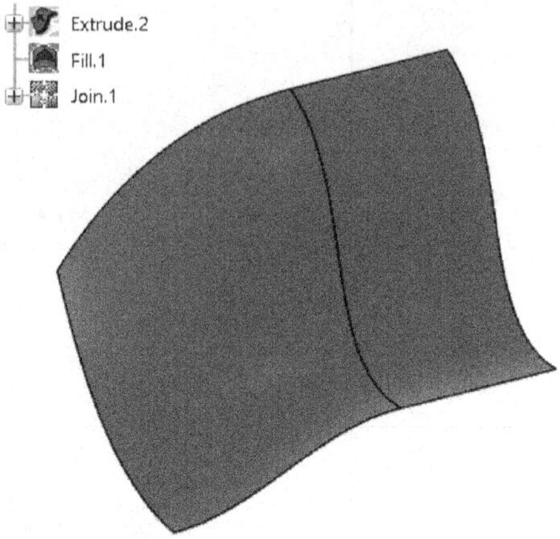

Figure 5–31

Curves selected for a **Join** operation must share a common end point. Surfaces must share an edge, but the edges do not need to have the same length. You can still join features that do not meet these requirements by clearing the **Check connectivity** option.

Extract

The **Extract** operation creates new surface elements by copying surface or solid faces. Curves and edges can also be extracted. The resulting surface is a duplicate of the original element that was selected. An example of the **Extract** tool is shown in Figure 5–32, Figure 5–33, and Figure 5–34.

Figure 5–32 shows the solid model of a bushing.

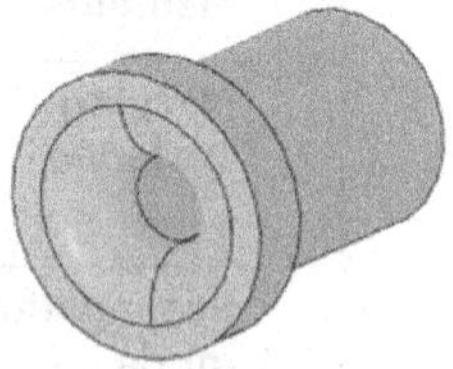

Figure 5–32

Figure 5–33 shows a preview of the surface selected to be extracted.

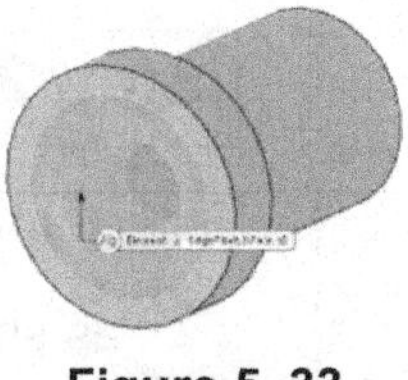

Figure 5–33

Figure 5–34 shows the resulting extracted surface. The solid geometry is hidden.

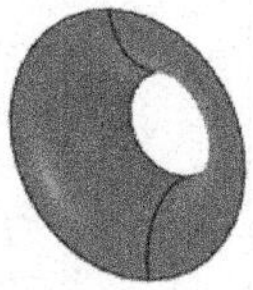

Figure 5–34

General Steps

Use the following general steps to perform an **Extract** operation:

1. Activate the **Extract** tool.
2. Select the entities to extract.
3. Specify the propagation type.
4. (Optional) Define the additional options.

Step 1 - Activate the Extract tool.

Click  (Extract). The Extract Definition dialog box opens as shown in Figure 5–35.

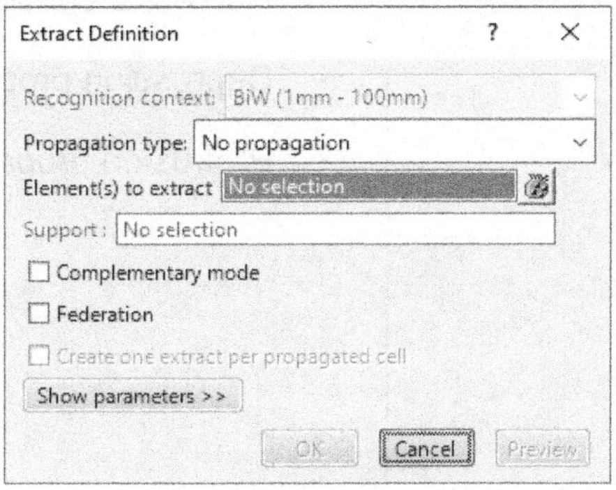

Figure 5–35

Step 2 - Select the entities to extract.

Select a face in the model. You can select multiple faces using , as shown in Figure 5–36. Once the Element(s) to extract dialog box is open, you can select multiple entities.

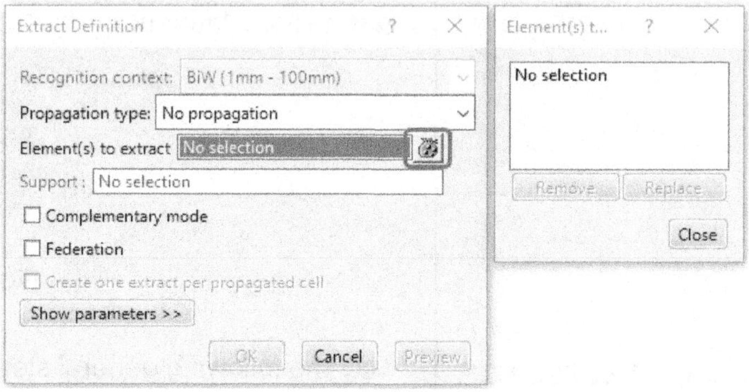

Figure 5–36

Step 3 - Specify the propagation type.

In the Propagation type drop-down list, select one of the following options:

- No propagation
- Point continuity
- Tangent continuity
- Curvature continuity
- Depression propagation
- Protrusion propagation

Figure 5–37 shows some of the different propagation settings used in the **Extract** operation. Only one face was selected in each propagation setting.

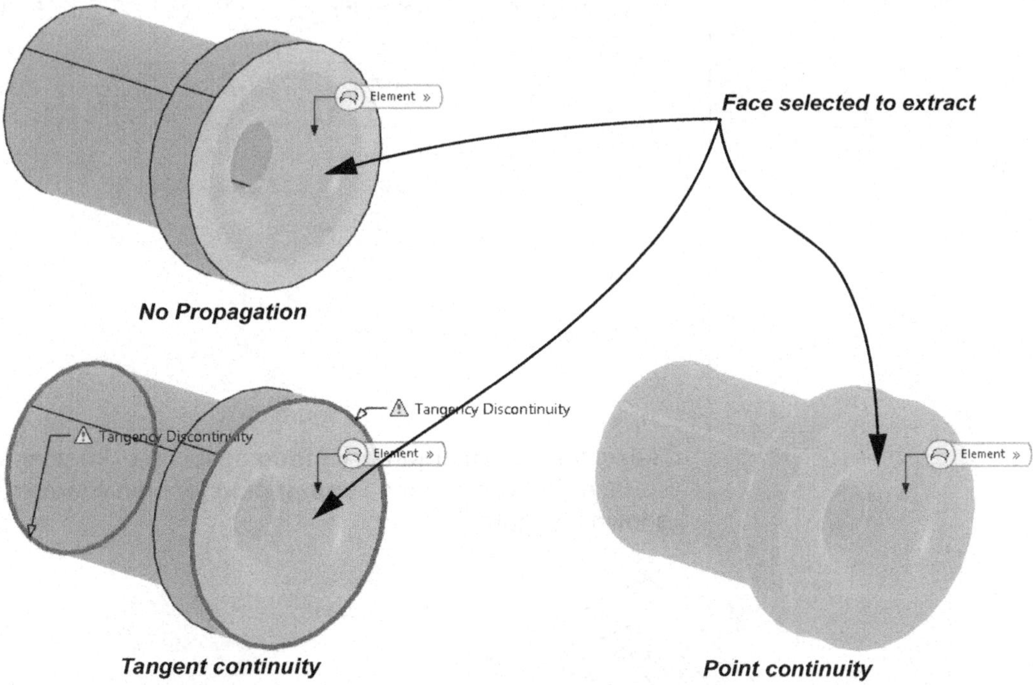

Figure 5–37

Step 4 - (Optional) Define the additional options.

You can apply optional settings, as shown in Figure 5–38.

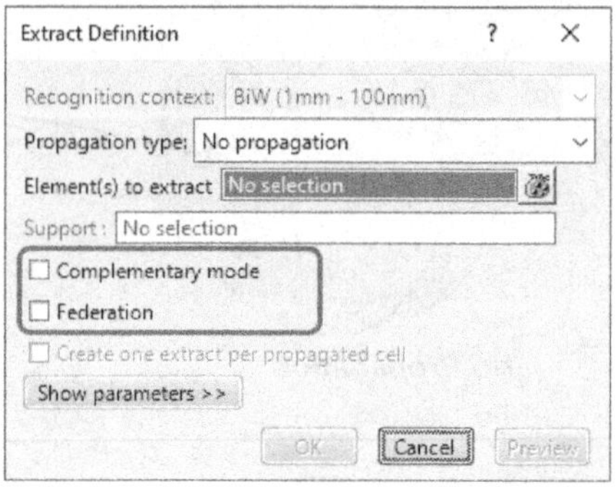

Figure 5–38

Select the **Complementary mode** option to extract the opposite surfaces selected by the **Propagation** tool. An example of this is shown in Figure 5–39.

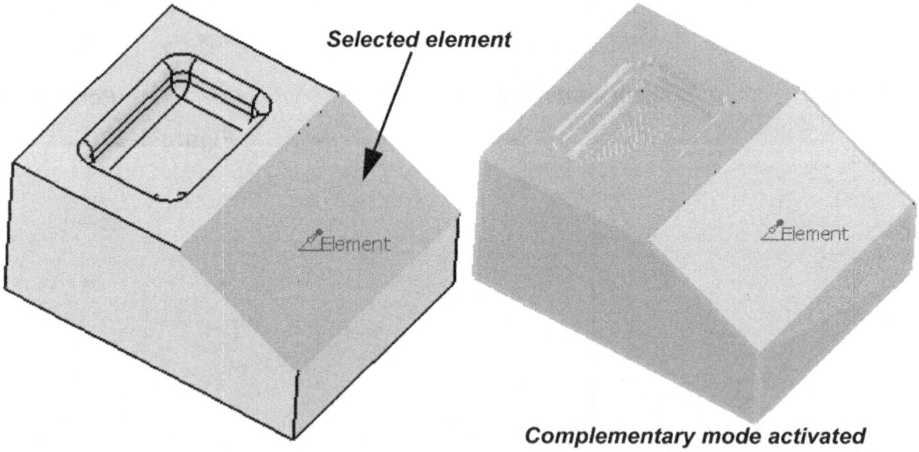

Figure 5–39

Select the **Federation** option if the resultant Surface is considered a representation of all of the Surfaces added to the extract. Do not select the **Federation** option if the resultant Surface is used as a collection of patches representing each individual Surface added to the Extract.

The **Federation** option determines whether the resultant Surface can mathematically represent all of the Surfaces added to the Extract. For example, if a Pad is extruded up to an Extract surface, the **Federation** option should be selected. This enables the stop Surface of the Pad to be calculated at any location on the Extract. If the **Federation** option is not selected and the Pad moves to a new location on the Extract, the Pad feature might fail.

Protrusion/Depression Propagation

Protrusion propagation and **Depression propagation** are available when surfaces are selected to extract. Protrusions and/or depressions of a surface can be selected quickly. When you select a surface, the system will select adjacent convex surfaces for Protrusion propagation, and adjacent concave surfaces for Depression propagation.

When Protrusion or Depression propagation are selected, the **Recognition context** option is available, as shown in Figure 5–40.

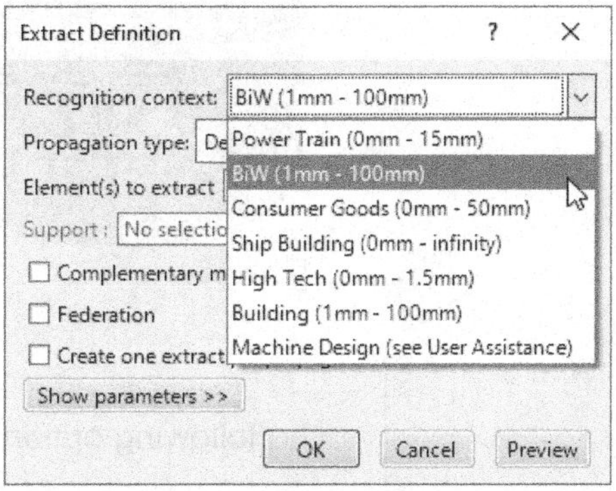

Figure 5–40

The Recognition context options take the industry into consideration by setting the size range of chamfers and fillets that will be recognized.

When the appropriate entities have been selected, click **OK** to complete the Extract.

5.10 Multi-Result Management

Whenever more than one possible solution is available to create a feature, 3DEXPERIENCE prompts you to select the sub-element(s) to keep. The Multi-Result Management dialog box contains new options for selecting which sub-element(s) to keep.

For example, two possible lines can be created when a Plane intersects a cylindrical Surface. Once you have clicked **OK** in the Intersection dialog box, the Multi-Result Management dialog box opens as shown in Figure 5–41.

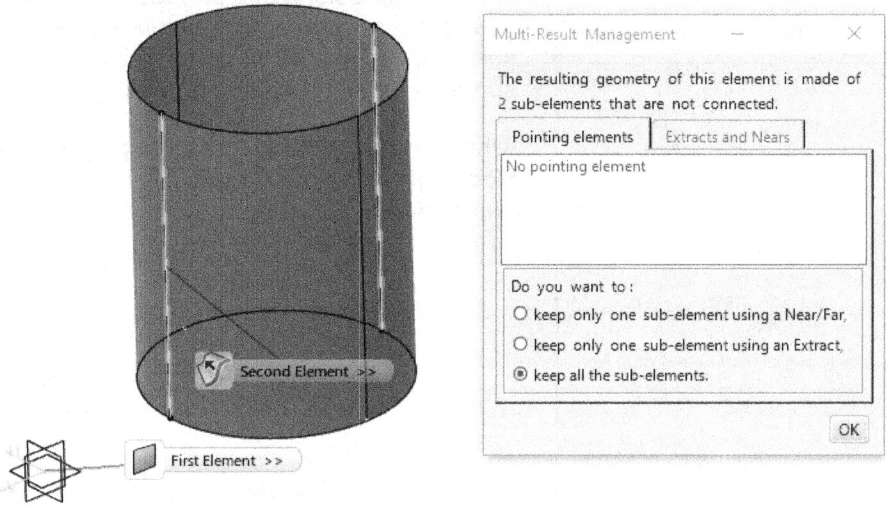

Figure 5–41

The following options are available:

- Keep only one sub-element using a Near/Far
- Keep only one sub-element using an Extract
- Keep all the sub-elements

Keep only one sub-element using a Near/Far

This option opens the Near/Far dialog box in which you select one element that is closest to or farthest from the required output. For example, the xy plane is selected to keep the sub-element shown in Figure 5–42.

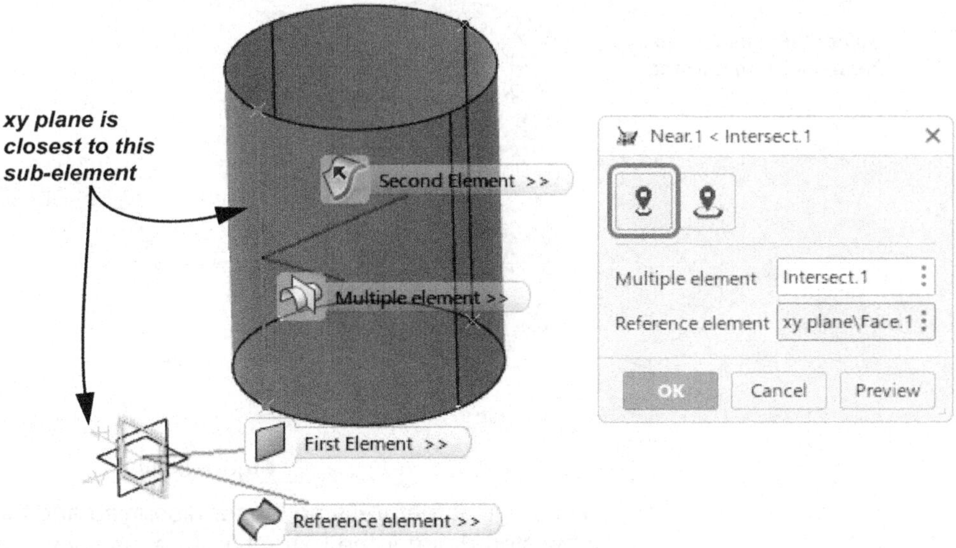

Figure 5–42

The original feature is no longer displayed and the geometry is now stored under the Near feature, as shown in Figure 5–43.

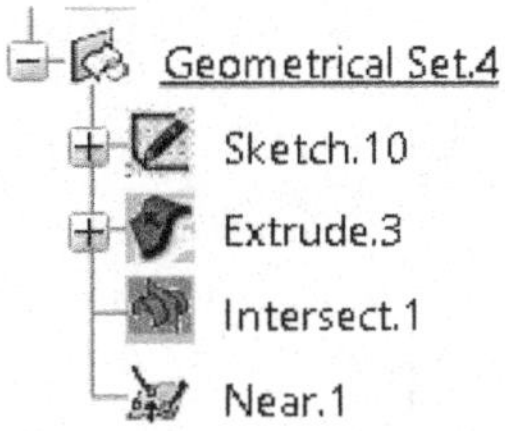

Figure 5–43

Keep only one sub-element using an Extract

You can directly select the element to keep, using an **Extract** operation. This option opens the Extract Definition dialog box, enabling you to select one of multiple results. For example, the opposite line is selected in Figure 5–44.

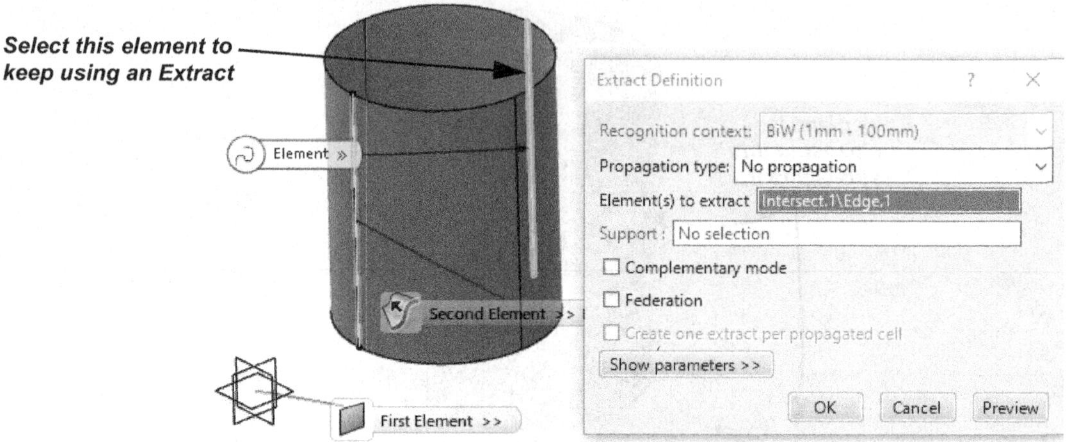

Figure 5–44

The original feature is no longer displayed and the geometry is now stored under the Extract feature, as shown in Figure 5–45.

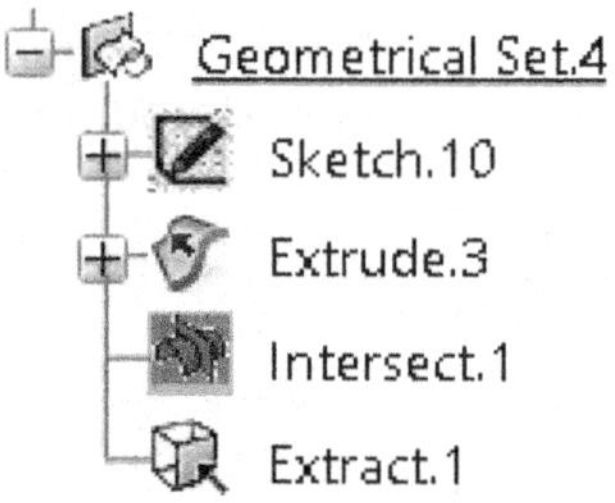

Figure 5–45

Keep all the sub-elements

This option keeps all of the sub-elements. In the case of the intersection of a cylinder and a plane, the Intersection feature consists of two disconnected lines.

Practice 5a

Spline-Polyline

Practice Objective

- Create a Polyline and a Spline.

In this practice, you will create a Polyline and a Spline. You will use these curves to create two Rib features. The completed model displays as shown in Figure 5–46.

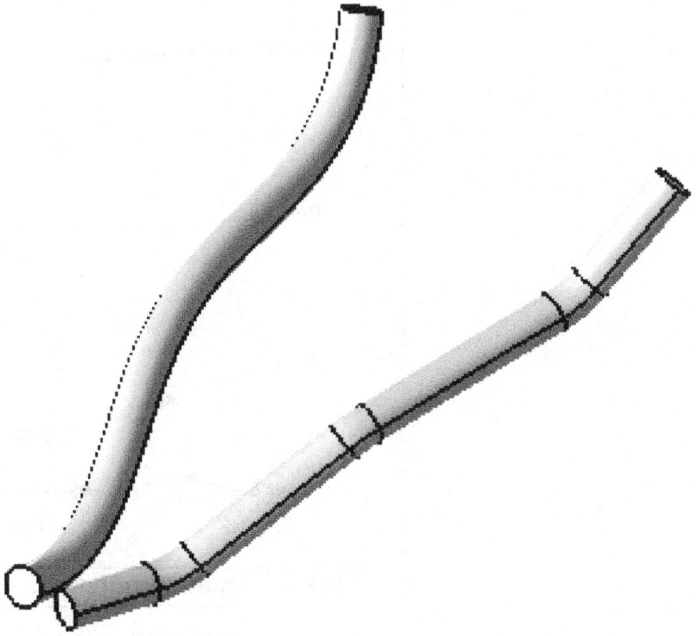

Figure 5–46

Task 1 - Open the part.

1. Import and open **Spline-polyline.3dxml**. When importing, type your initials followed by the dash symbol into the *Duplication string* field (e.g., **IA-**). The points for the formation of the curves have already been created, as shown in Figure 5–47.

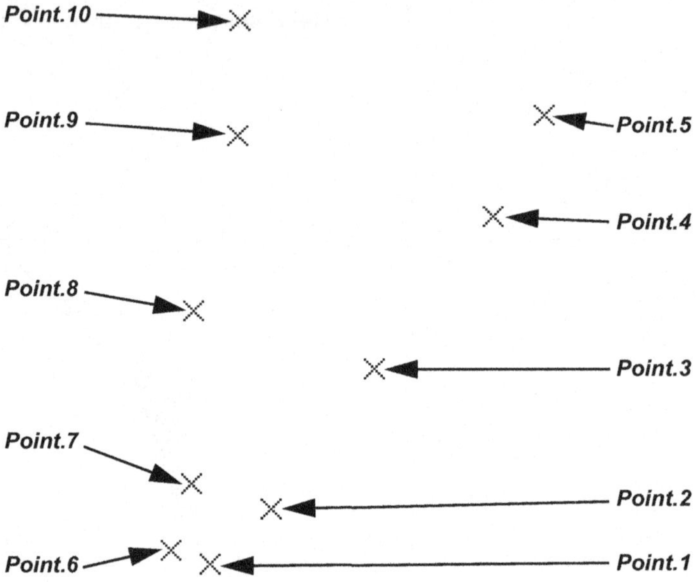

Figure 5–47

Task 2 - Create a polyline.

1. In the 3DEXPERIENCE Compass, select the Outer ring called Roles, Apps, and Solutions Portfolio. Scroll down to My Apps and select the **Generative Shape Design** app. This will display the wireframe and surfacing tools and icons in the Action Bar.

2. In the Wireframe section of the Action Bar, expand the Line flyout and click  (Polyline). The Polyline Definition dialog box opens.

3. Select the following points in the same order:
   - **Point.1**
   - **Point.2**
   - **Point.3**
   - **Point.4**
   - **Point.5**

4. In the Polyline Definition dialog box, select **Point.2**. In the *Radius* field, enter **300** as shown in Figure 5–48.

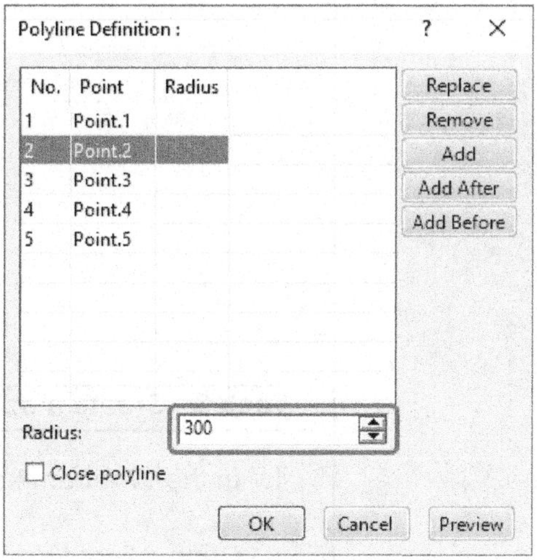

Figure 5–48

5. Select **Point.3** and **Point.4**. In the *Radius* field, enter **300**.

6. Click **Preview**. The model and Polyline Definition dialog box open as shown in Figure 5–49.

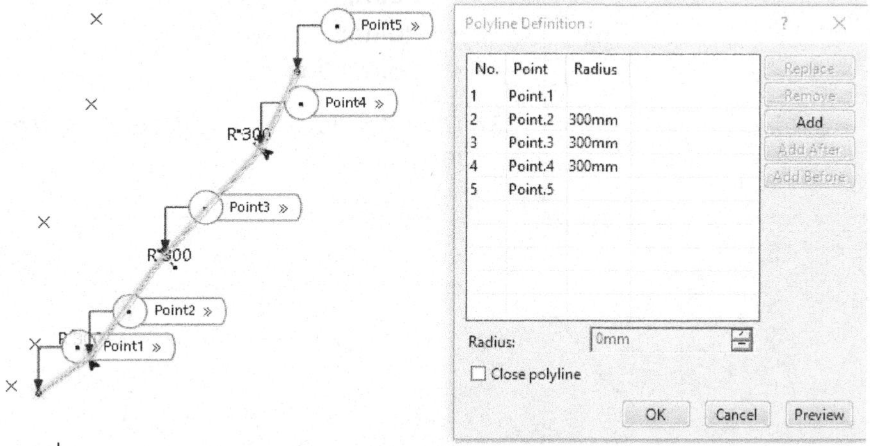

Figure 5–49

7. Click **OK** to complete the feature, which displays as shown in Figure 5–50.

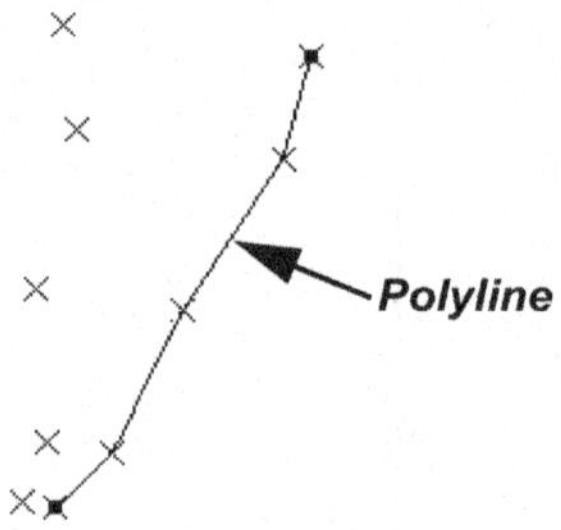

Figure 5–50

Task 3 - Create a spline.

1. In the Wireframe section of the Action Bar, expand the Curves flyout and click  (Spline). The Spline dialog box opens.

2. Select the following points in the same order:

   - **Point.6**
   - **Point.7**
   - **Point.8**
   - **Point.9**
   - **Point.10**

3. Click **Preview**. The model and the dialog box open as shown in Figure 5–51.

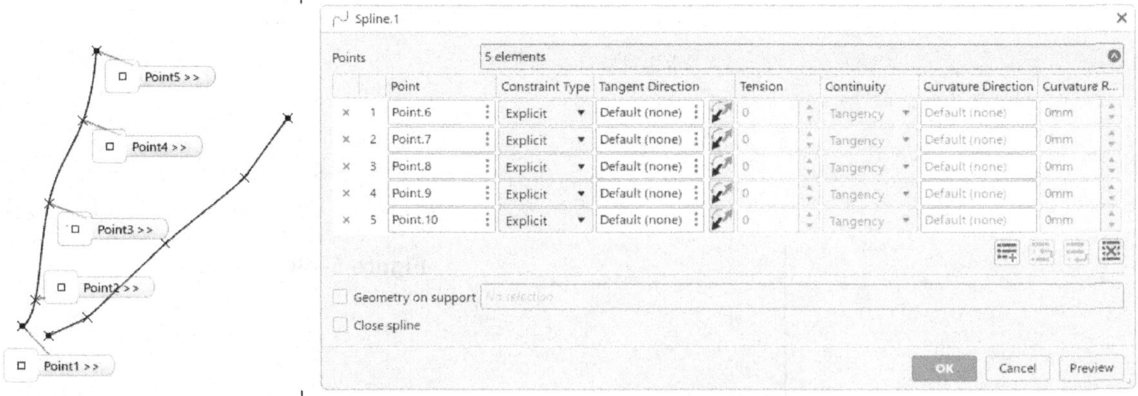

Figure 5–51

4. Click **OK** to complete the feature, which displays as shown in Figure 5–52.

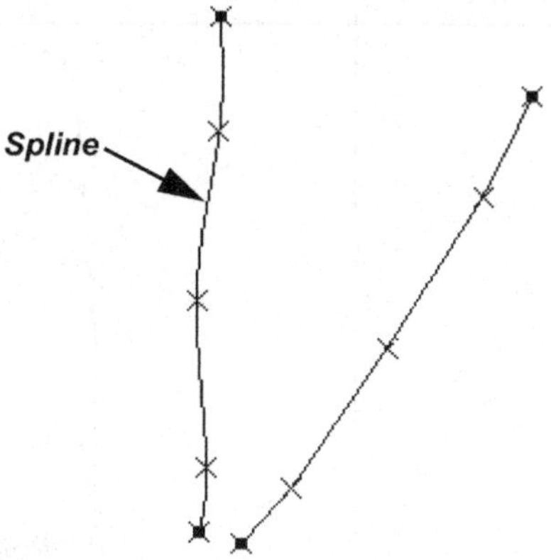

Figure 5–52

Task 4 - Create two Rib features.

In this task, you will create two Rib features with the Polyline and Spline that you created in the previous tasks.

1. Create a Plane using the plane type **Normal to curve**. Use the options shown in Figure 5–53 to define the Plane.

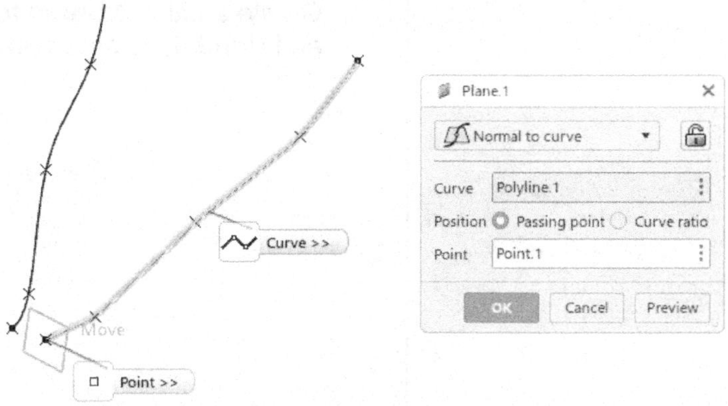

Figure 5–53

2. Create a circle profile, as shown in Figure 5–54 using a positioned sketch. Ensure that the origin of the sketch is positioned at **Point.1**.

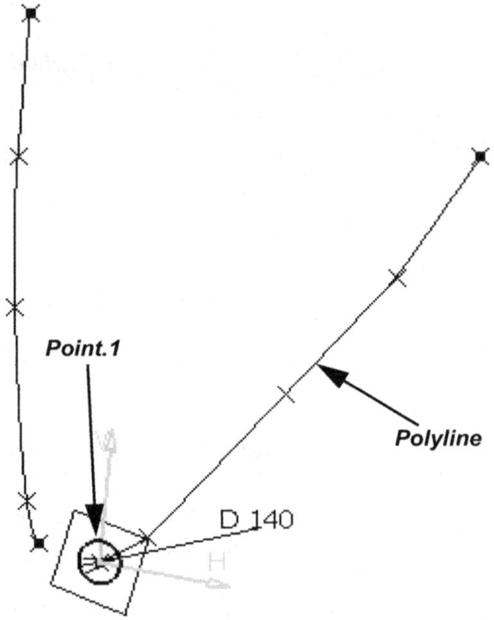

Figure 5–54

3. Create another **Normal to curve** type plane using the Spline and **Point.6**, as shown in Figure 5–55.

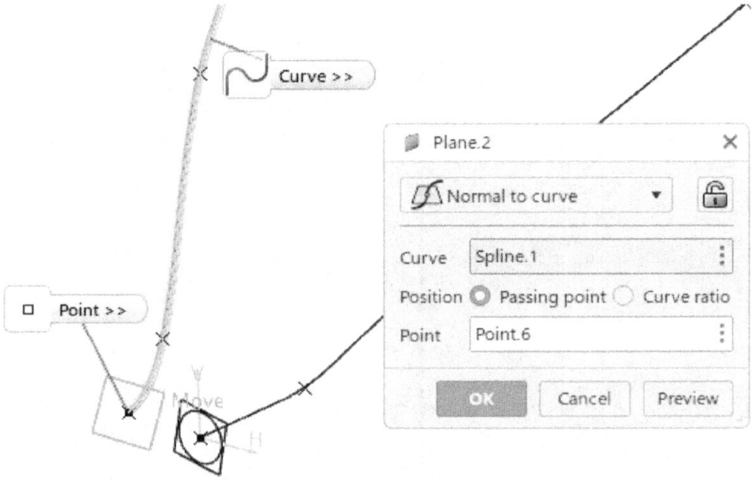

Figure 5–55

4. Using the newly created Plane, create a positioned sketch. Use **Point.6** as the origin of the sketch.

5. Sketch a circular profile as shown in Figure 5–56.

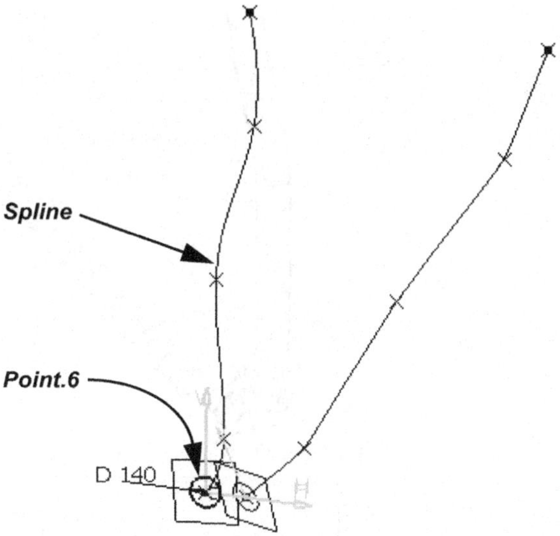

Figure 5–56

6. Switch to the Part Design app.

7. Define the PartBody to be the work object.

8. Create a Rib feature, as shown in Figure 5–57.

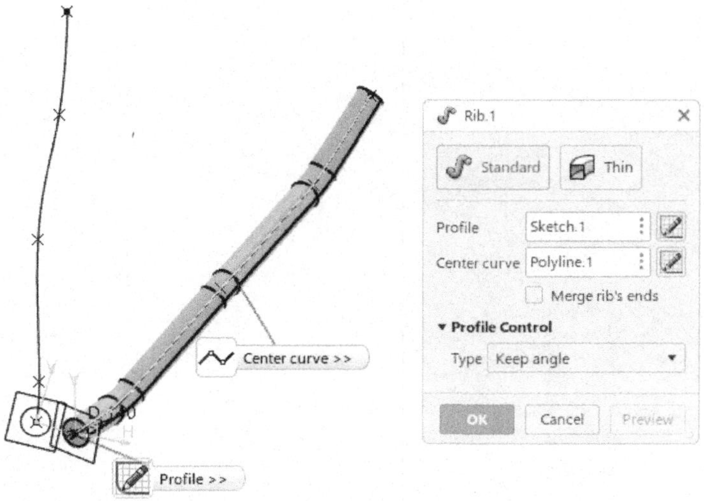

Figure 5–57

9. Create a Rib feature, as shown in Figure 5–58.

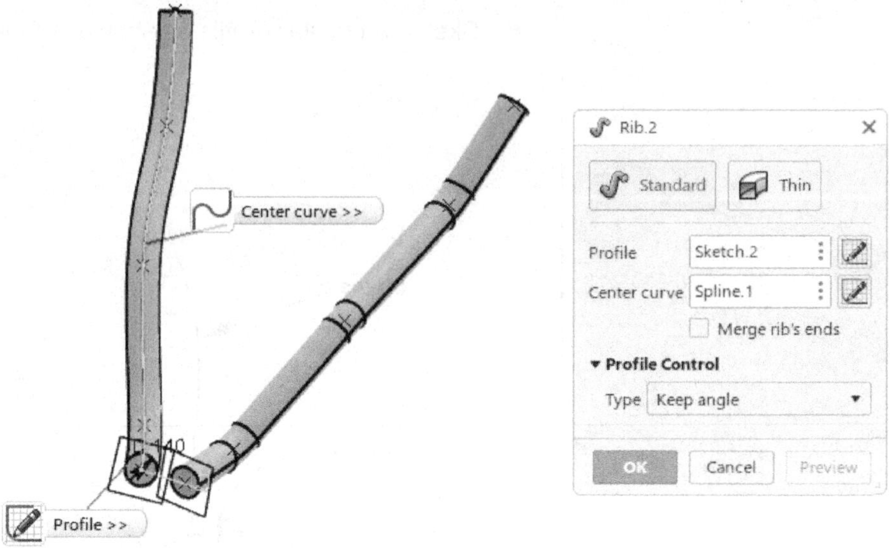

Figure 5–58

10. Hide **Geometrical Set.1**.

11. Save and close the model.

Practice 5b Projection Curve

Practice Objectives

- Create a Projection curve.
- Create a Join Surface.

In this practice, you will create a wavy washer using isolated surfaces. The center curve for the Rib feature is created by projecting the profile onto the surface. The completed model displays as shown in Figure 5–59.

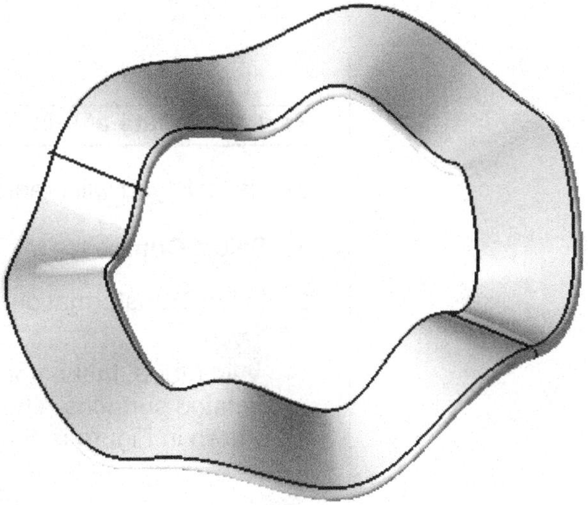

Figure 5–59

Task 1 - Open the part.

1. In the Top Bar, click (Add)>**Import**.
2. In the Format drop-down list, select **IGES3D (*.igs)**.
3. Click on the **Open** icon in the *Filename* field.
4. Browse and select **Wavy_washer.igs**.

5. Click **OK** to import the model.The model displays as shown in Figure 5–60.

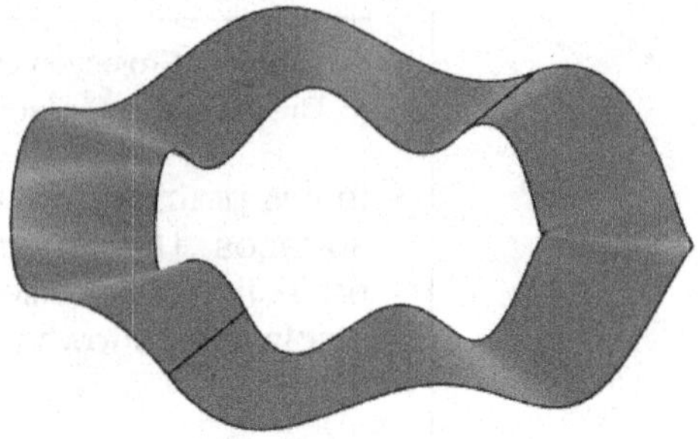

Figure 5–60

Task 2 - Create a Join.

In this task, you will create a Join with the isolated surfaces.

1. Select **Compass>My Apps>Generative Shape Design**.
2. In the Transformation section of the Action Bar, click  (Join). In the specification tree or model, select the two isolated surfaces. The Join Definition dialog box displays as shown in Figure 5–61.

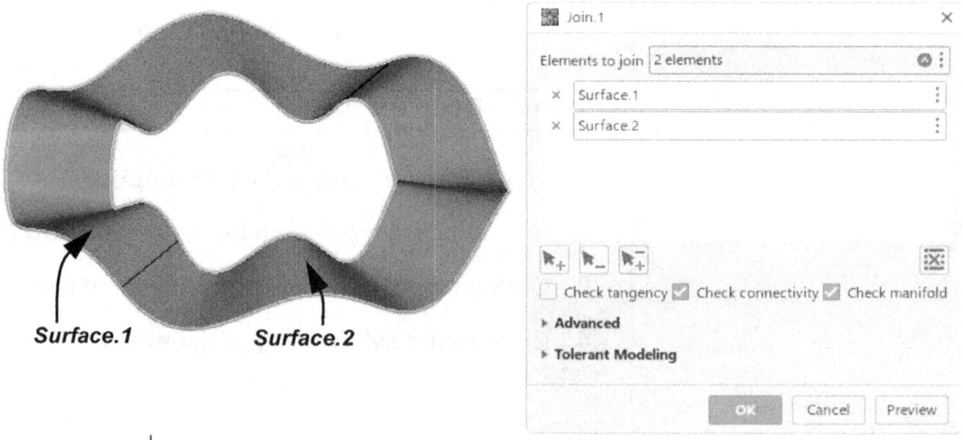

Figure 5–61

3. Click **OK** to complete the feature, which displays in the specification tree as shown in Figure 5–62.

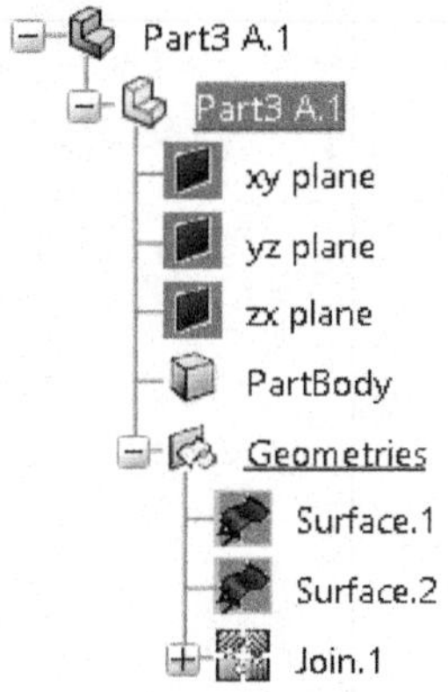

Figure 5–62

Task 3 - Create a Profile.

In this task, you will create a profile that will be projected onto the surface.

1. Create an offset Plane as shown in Figure 5–63.

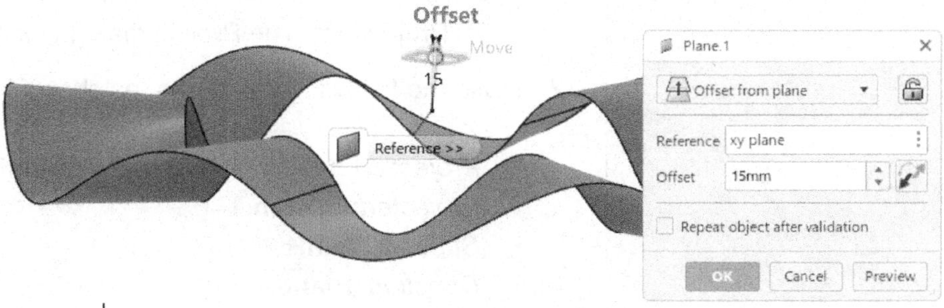

Figure 5–63

2. Sketch a circular profile on the newly created Plane, as shown in Figure 5–64.

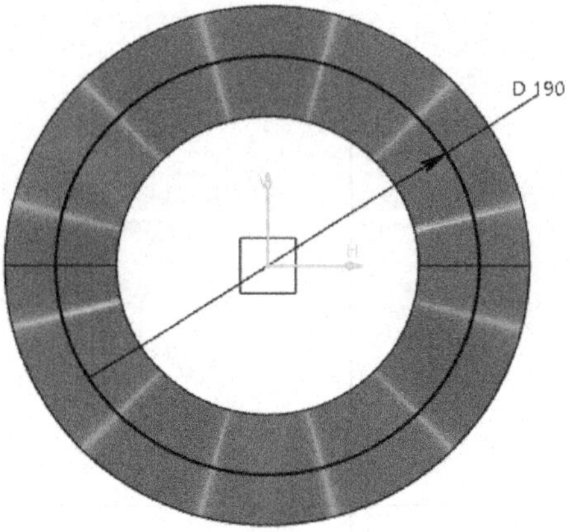

Figure 5–64

Task 4 - Create a Projection curve.

In this task, you will create a projection curve with the profile that you just created.

1. In the Wireframe section of the Action Bar, click  (Projection). The Project dialog box opens.
2. Make the following selections, as shown in Figure 5–65:
   - *Projection type:*  **(Along a direction)**
   - *Projected:* **Sketch.1**
   - *Support:* **Join.1**
   - *Direction:* **Plane.1**

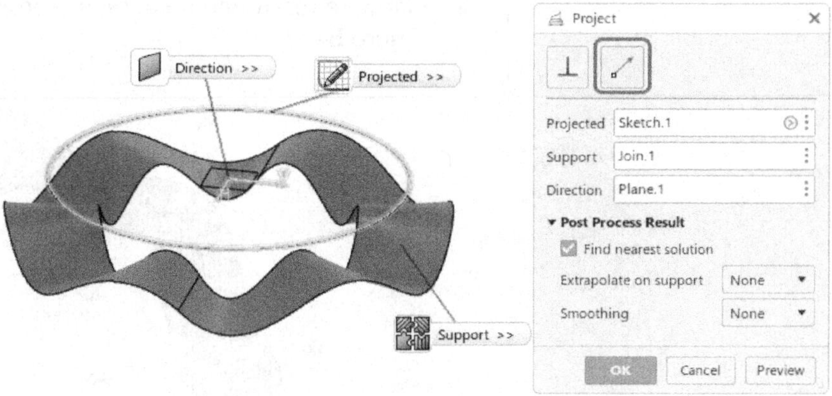

Figure 5–65

3. Click **OK** to complete the feature, which displays as shown in Figure 5–66.

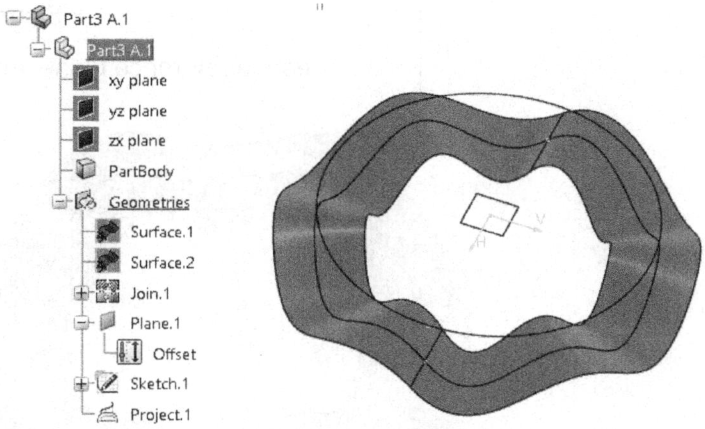

Figure 5–66

Task 5 - Create a Rib feature.

In this task, you will create a profile for Rib creation.

1. Hide **Sketch.1**.

2. Create a reference point on the projection curve, as shown in Figure 5–67.

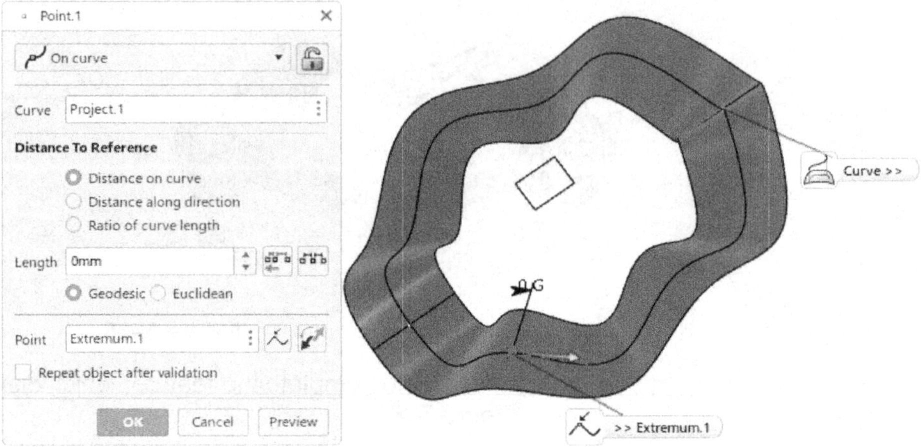

Figure 5–67

3. Create a reference plane, as shown in Figure 5–68.

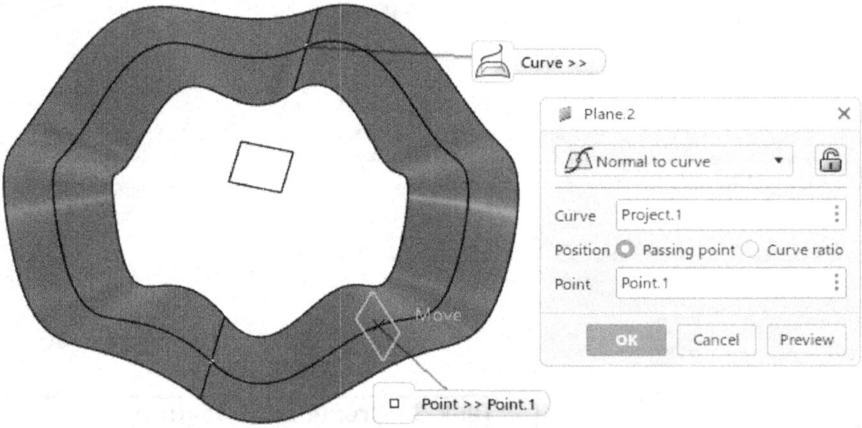

Figure 5–68

4. Create a positioned sketch on the plane that you just created. Ensure that the origin of the sketch is located at **Point.1**, as shown in Figure 5–69.

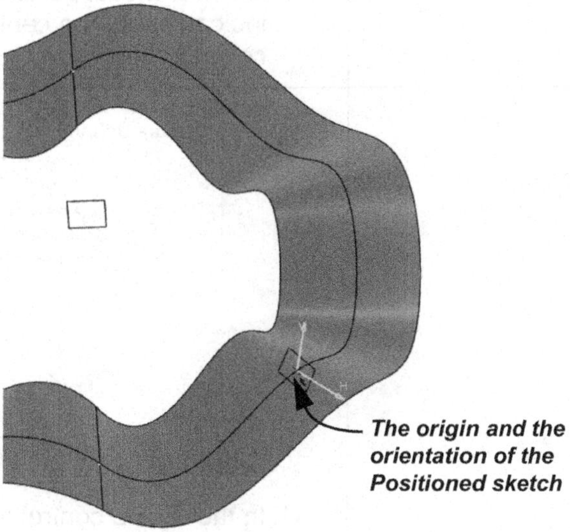

Figure 5–69

5. Create the profile, as shown in Figure 5–70.

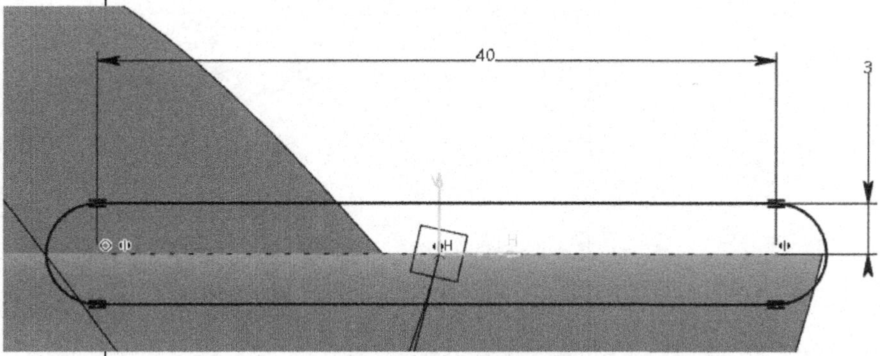

Figure 5–70

6. Switch to the Part Design app.
7. Define the **PartBody** to be the In Work Object.
8. Create a Rib feature using the following specifications:
   - *Profile:* **Sketch.2**
   - *Center curve:* **Project.1**

9. An error message opens as shown in Figure 5–71. It indicates that the center curve curvature leads to a twist configuration.

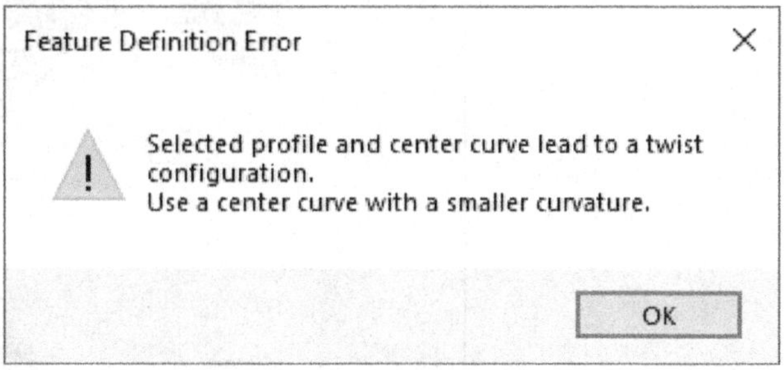

Figure 5–71

10. Close the Feature Definition Error dialog box.

11. In the Profile control drop-down list, select the **Pulling direction** option. In the specification tree or model, select **Plane.1**. The Rib dialog box opens as shown in Figure 5–72.

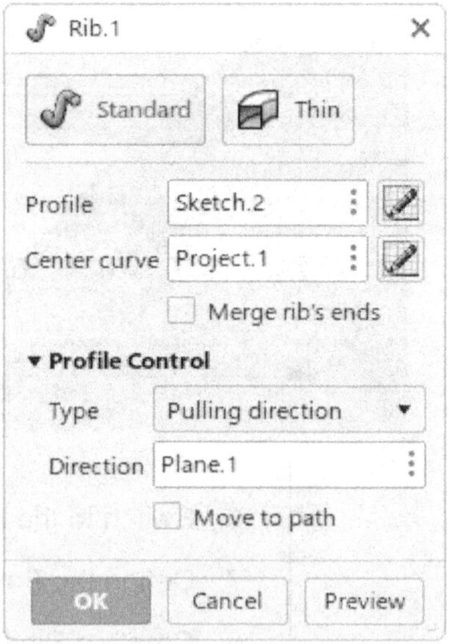

Figure 5–72

12. Click **OK** to complete the feature.

13. Click **Close** in the Warnings dialog box.

14. Hide the **Geometries** geometrical set.

15. Save and close the model.

Practice 5c Handle

Practice Objectives

- Create intersection elements.
- Create a Near.
- Create a Join curve.
- Create a Spline curve.
- Create a Combine curve.
- Create a Helix.

In this practice, you will create a handle for a barbeque. First you will create the required 3D profile to create the Rib, and then the profiles to create the threads. The completed model displays as shown in Figure 5–73.

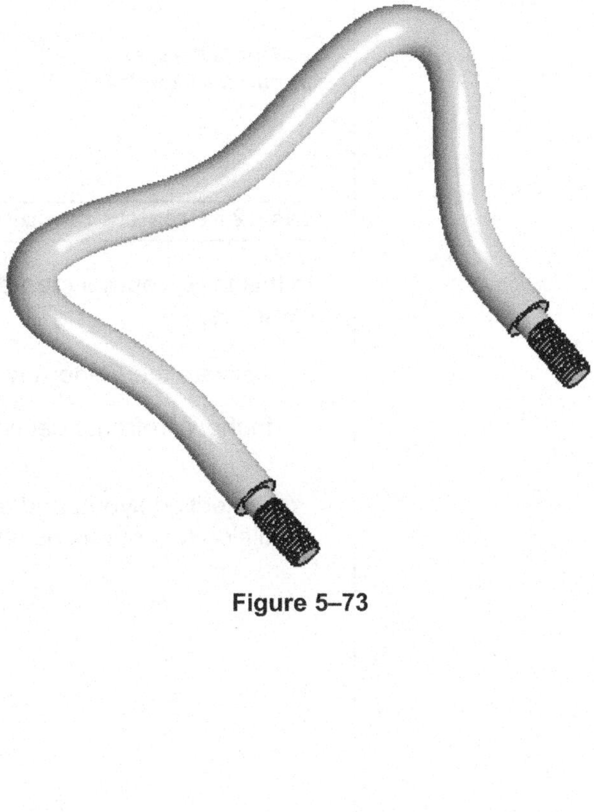

Figure 5–73

Task 1 - Open the part.

1. Import and open **Handle.3dxml**. When importing, type your initials followed by the dash symbol into the *Duplication string* field (e.g., **IA-**). There are two sketches in the model that you will use to create a Combine feature. The model displays as shown in Figure 5–74.

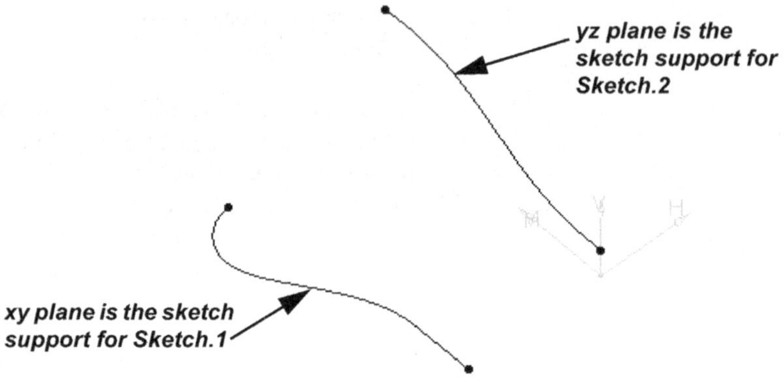

Figure 5–74

Task 2 - Create a combine curve.

In this task, you will create a combine curve with the provided sketches.

1. Activate the Generative Shape Design app.
2. In the Wireframe section of the Action Bar, expand the Projection flyout, and click  (Combine). The Combine dialog box opens as shown in Figure 5–75.

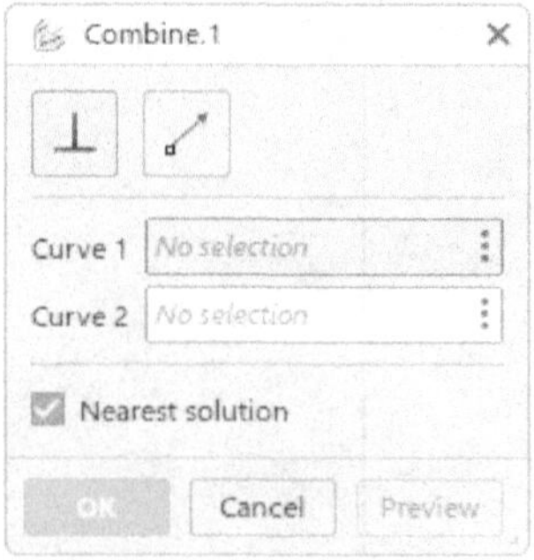

Figure 5–75

3. In the specification tree or model, for *Curve1*, select **Sketch.1** and for *Curve2*, select **Sketch.2**, as shown in Figure 5–76.

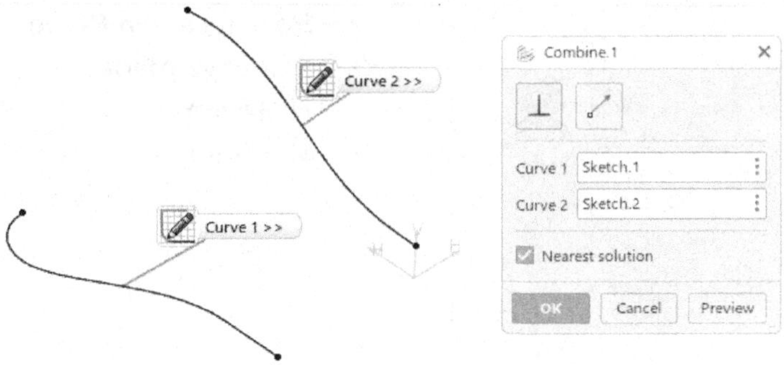

Figure 5–76

4. Click **OK** to complete the feature. The combine curve displays as shown in Figure 5–77.

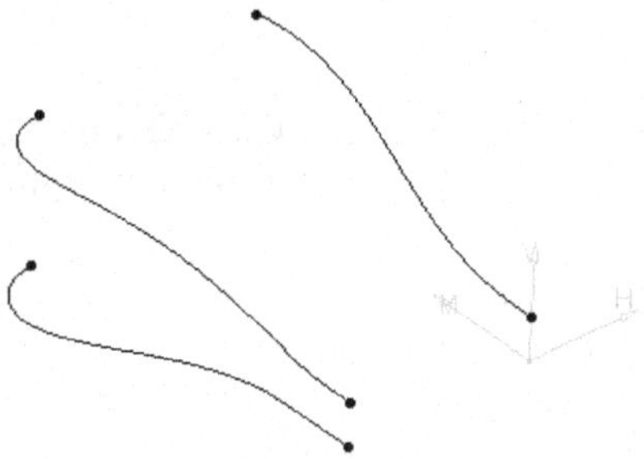

Figure 5–77

Task 3 - Create a spline curve.

In this task, you will create two Points that will be used to create a Spline.

1. Click (Point) and make the following selections, as shown in Figure 5–78:
   - *Point type:* **On Plane**
   - *Plane:* **yz plane**
   - *H:* **34mm**
   - *V:* **13mm**

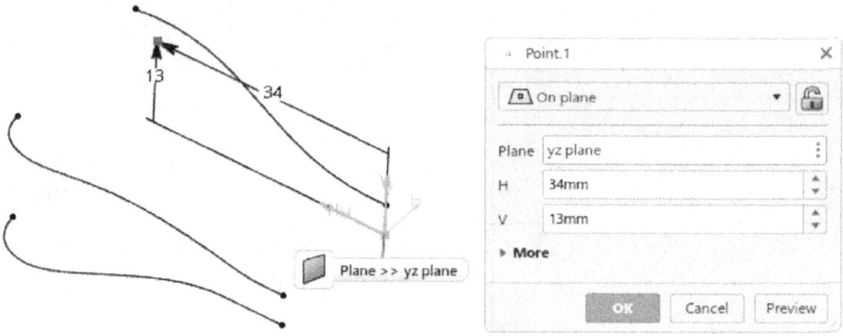

Figure 5–78

2. Click **OK** to complete the feature. The point displays as shown in Figure 5–79.

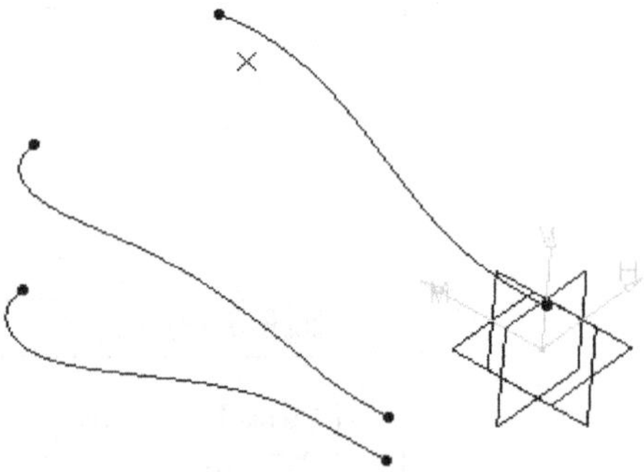

Figure 5–79

3. Create a Point, as specified in Figure 5–80.

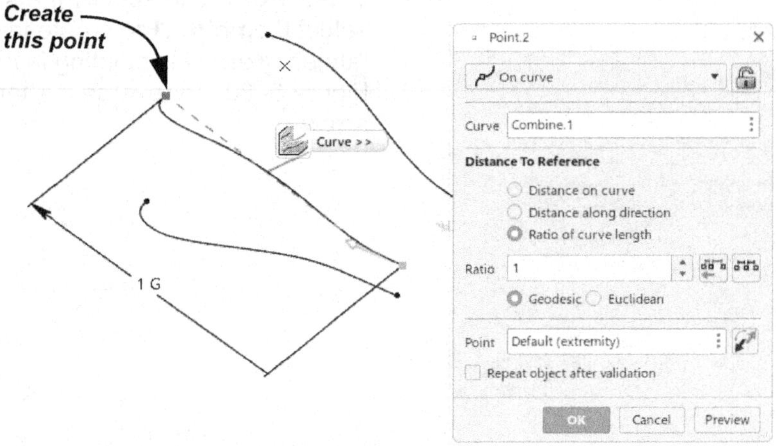

Figure 5–80

4. Create another Point, as specified in Figure 5–81.

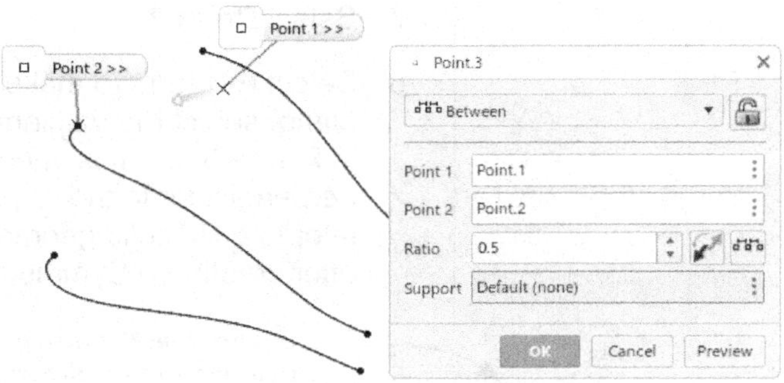

Figure 5–81

The result displays as shown in Figure 5–82.

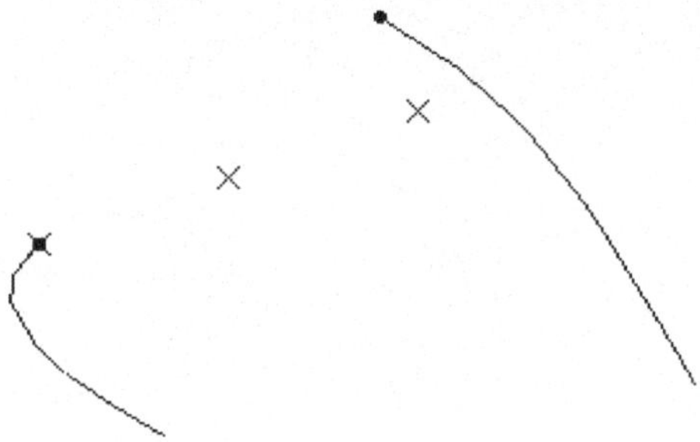

Figure 5–82

5. In the Wireframe section of the Action Bar, expand the Curves flyout, and click (Spline). The Spline Definition dialog box opens.

6. Select **Point.2** to specify the start point of the Spline, then select **Combine.1** to create tangency. Ensure that the tangency arrow is pointing in the same direction, as shown in Figure 5–83. To reverse the tangency direction, select the arrow.

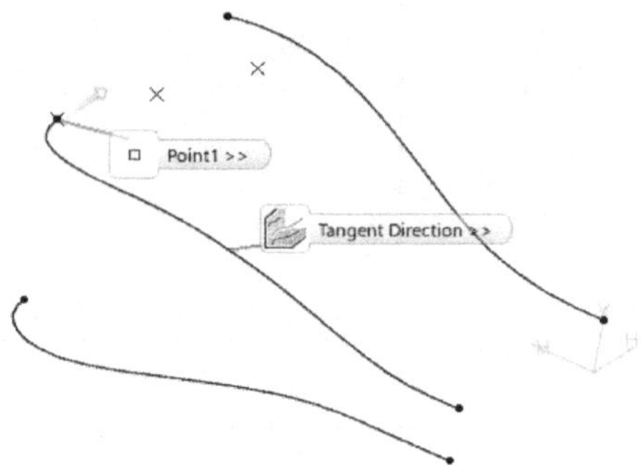

Figure 5–83

7. Select **Point.3**.

8. Select **Point.1**. To make the spline perpendicular to the yz plane, select the yz plane in the specification tree, as shown in Figure 5–84. It is important to have the spline perpendicular to the yz plane, because the spline will be used later to build solid geometry. This is to ensure a smooth result after creating a Symmetry feature.

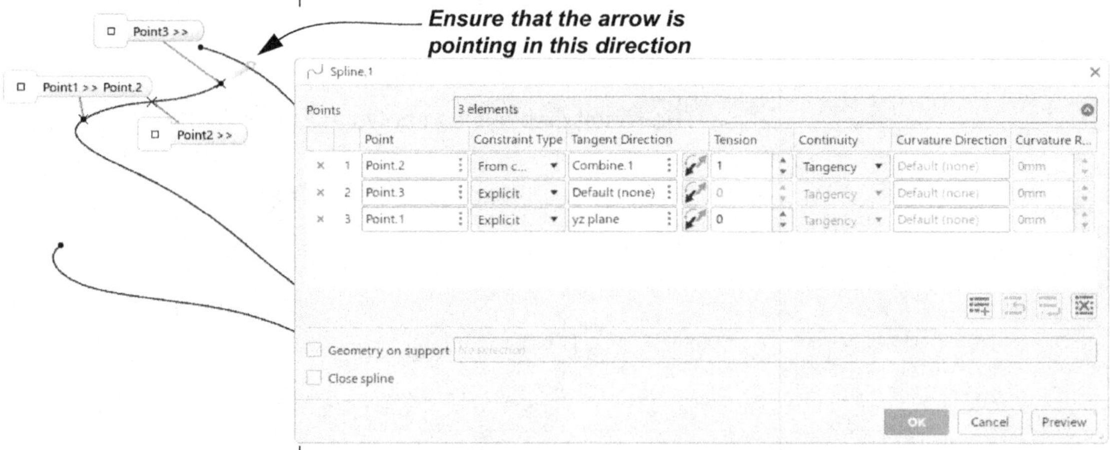

Figure 5–84

9. Click **OK** to complete the feature. The Spline displays as shown in Figure 5–85.

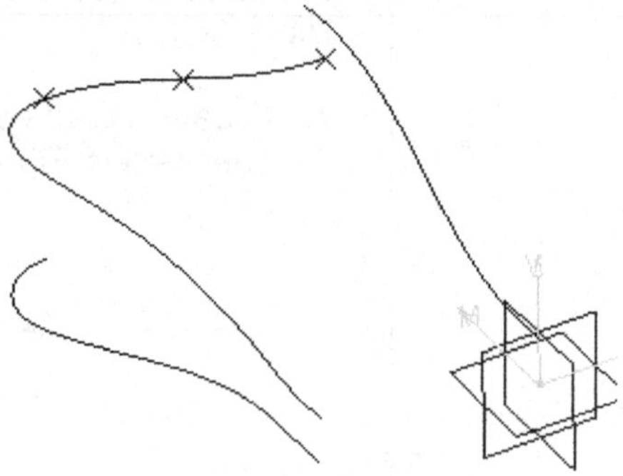

Figure 5–85

Task 4 - Create a Joined curve.

In this task, you will join the Combine curve with the Spline curve. You will use this Joined curve as the center curve during the Rib creation.

1. Hide the sketches.
2. In the Essentials section of the Action Bar, click (Join).
3. In the specification tree or model, select the **Combine.1** and the **Spline.1** curves. The Join Definition dialog box opens as shown in Figure 5–86.

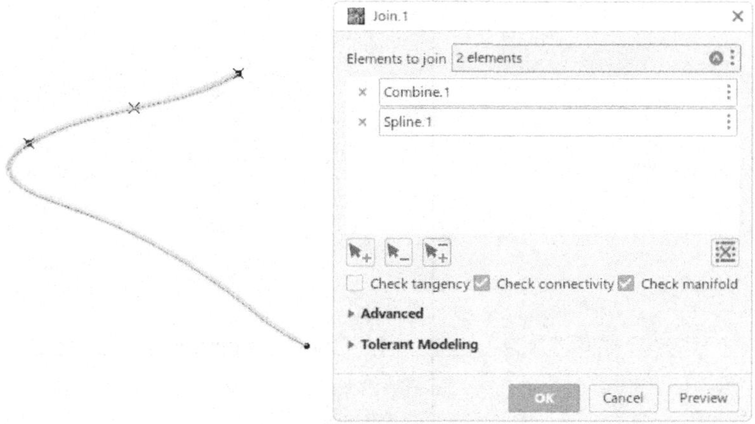

Figure 5–86

4. Click **OK** to complete the feature. The Join feature displays in the specification tree. Note that the Combine curve and the Spline curve are hidden automatically.

Task 5 - Create a Rib feature.

In this task, you will first create the Rib profile and then create a Rib feature.

1. Create a plane using the **Parallel through point** type as specified in Figure 5–87.

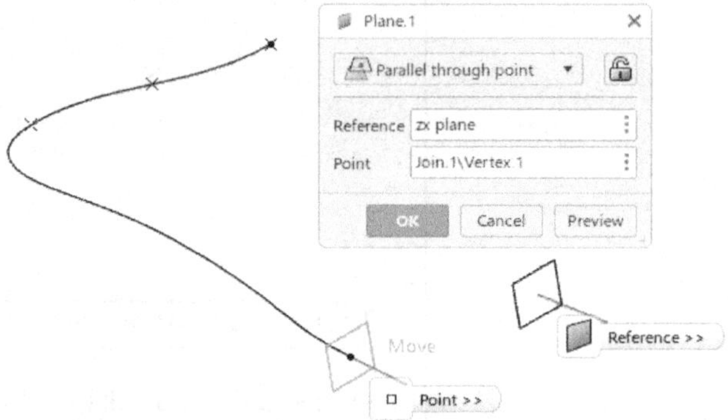

Figure 5–87

2. Rename the reference plane as **Refplane1**.

3. Create a positioned sketch on **Refplane1** as shown in Figure 5–88.

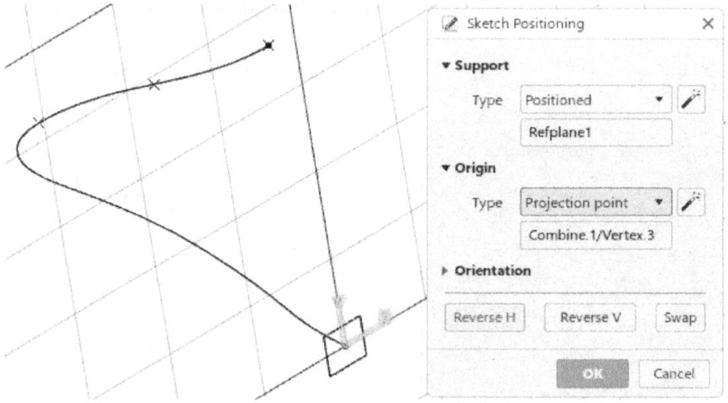

Figure 5–88

4. Create a circle profile, as shown in Figure 5–89.

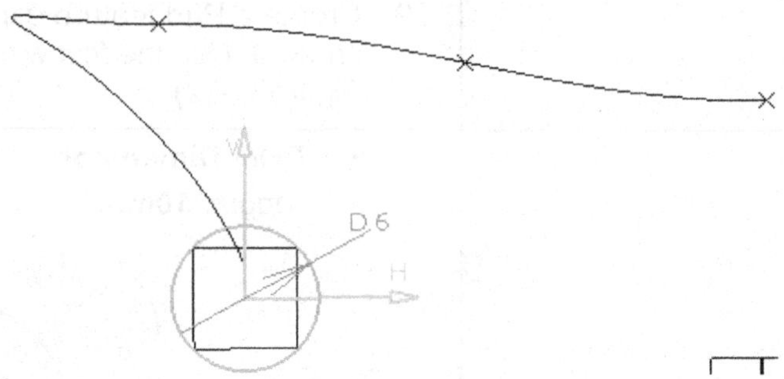

Figure 5–89

5. Switch from Generative Shape Design app to the Part Design app. Define the **PartBody** to be the In Work Object.

6. Create a Rib using the circle profile and joined curve, as shown in Figure 5–90.

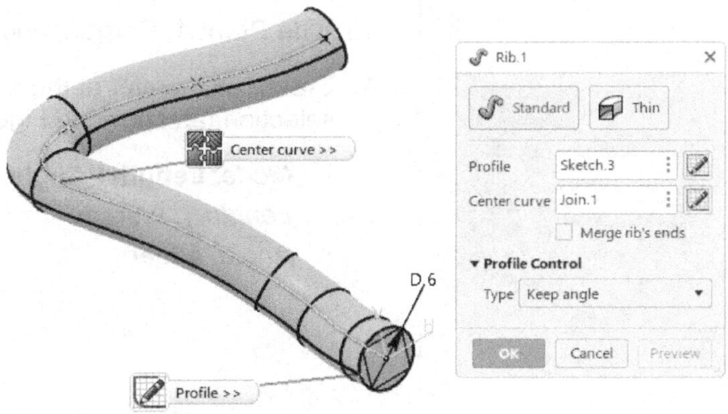

Figure 5–90

7. Complete the Rib feature.

8. Create a positioned sketch on **Refplane1** and then sketch a circular profile, as shown in Figure 5–91. Use the **Projection point** option and the end point of the **Combine.1** curve for the *Origin* of the sketch.

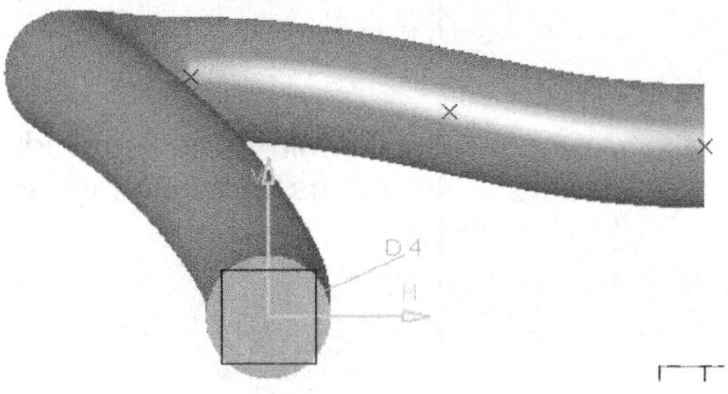

Figure 5–91

9. Create a Pad feature using the profile that you have just created. Use the following specifications (as shown in Figure 5–92).

   - *Type:* **Dimension**
   - *Length:* **10mm**

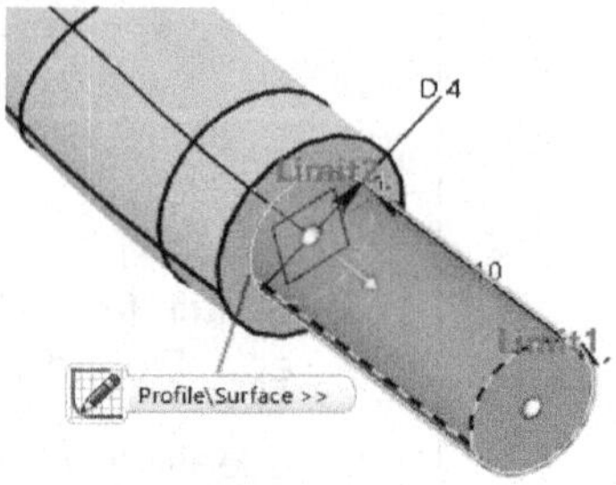

Figure 5–92

10. Hide **Point.1**, **Point.2**, and **Point.3**.

11. Create a Chamfer at the edge of the Pad with following selection (as shown in Figure 5–93).

   - *Mode:* **Length1/Angle**
   - *Length 1:* **0.3mm**
   - *Angle:* **45deg**

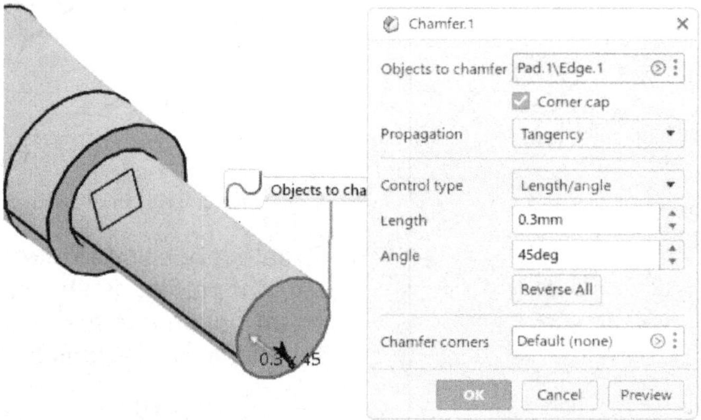

Figure 5–93

12. Mirror the PartBody about the yz plane. The model displays as shown in Figure 5–94.

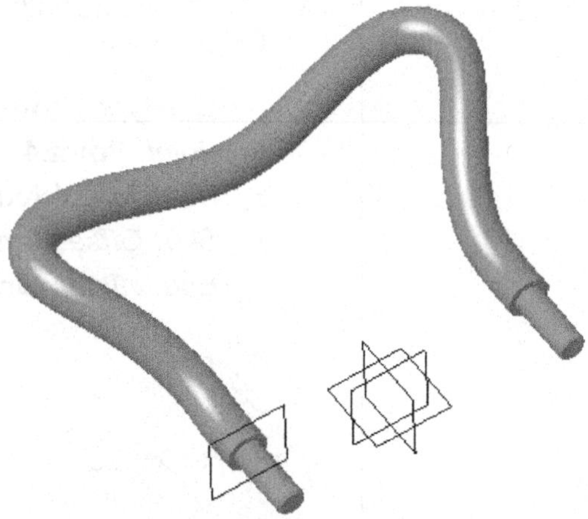

Figure 5–94

Task 6 - Create Wireframe features.

In this task, you will create a Line that will be used as the Helix axis, an intersection point that will be used as the starting point of the Helix, and a profile that defines the shape of the Helix.

1. Activate the Generative Shape Design app.
2. Show the Join feature.
3. Create an **On curve** type point, as shown in Figure 5–95.

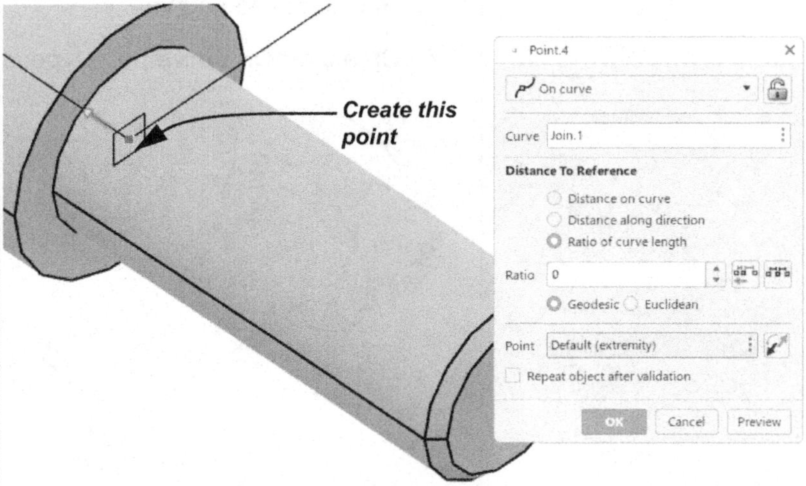

Figure 5–95

4. Create a Line with the following selections, as shown in Figure 5–96:

   - *Line type:* **Point-Direction**
   - *Point:* **Point.4**
   - *Direction:* **Y Axis** (in the shortcut menu)
   - *Start Offset:* **0mm**
   - *End Offset:* **10mm**

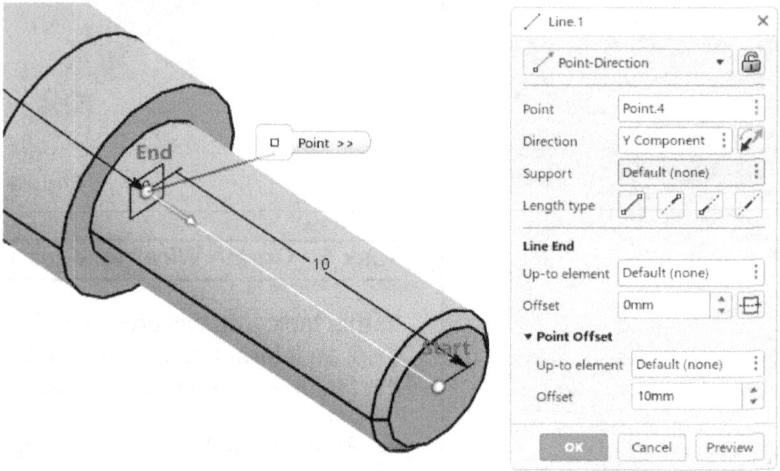

Figure 5–96

5. Rename the line as **Axis**.

6. Hide the joined curve.

7. Create an **On curve** point type, as shown in Figure 5–97.

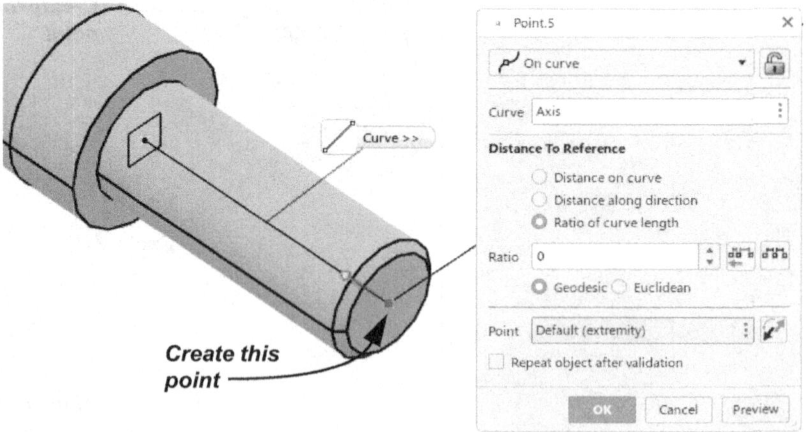

Figure 5–97

8. Create a **Parallel through point** plane type as specified in Figure 5–98.

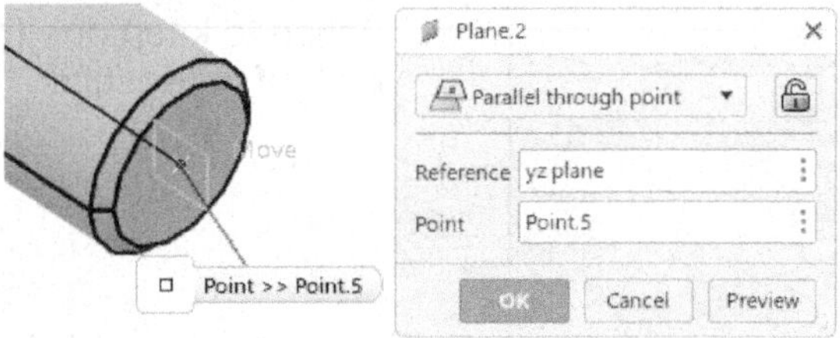

Figure 5–98

9. Rename the reference plane as **Refplane2**.

Task 7 - Create an Intersection feature.

1. In the Wireframe section of the Action Bar, click

    (Intersection).

2. Select the edge of the chamfer as the first element and the reference plane that you just created as the second element, as shown in Figure 5–99.

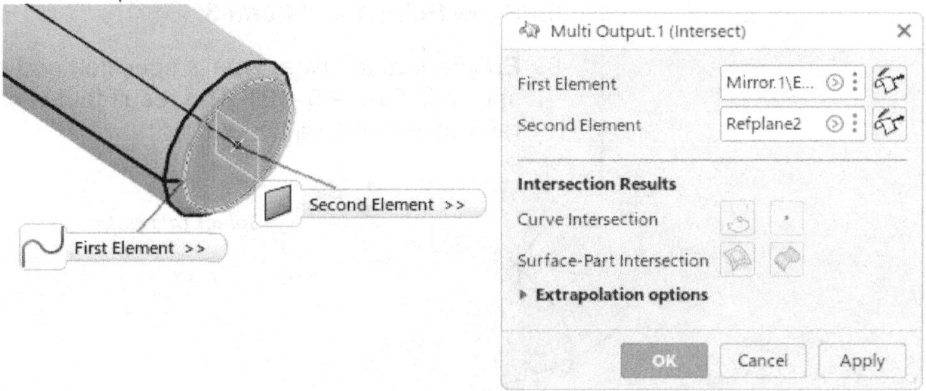

Figure 5–99

3. Click **OK** to continue. Because there are two results for this action, the Multi-Result Management dialog box opens as shown in Figure 5–100. In this dialog box, you can select an option to keep one (by specifying a reference element) or both of the results.

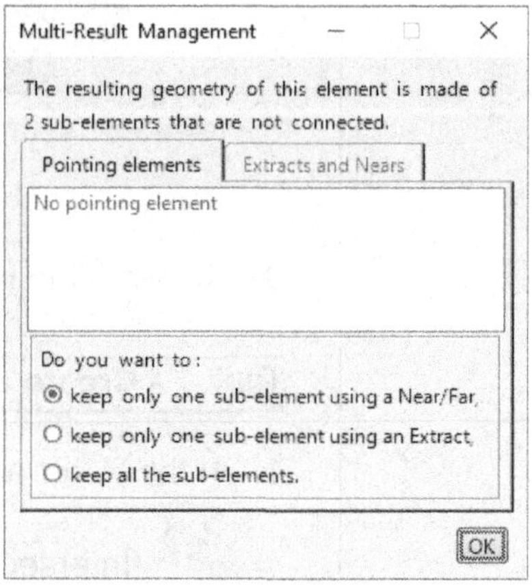

Figure 5–100

4. Ensure that the **keep only one sub-element using a Near/Far** option is selected, and click **OK**.

5. Show **Point.1** and **Point.3**.

6. Ensure that the *Near* type is specified and select the point shown in Figure 5–101. The result that is closest to this reference point will be kept.

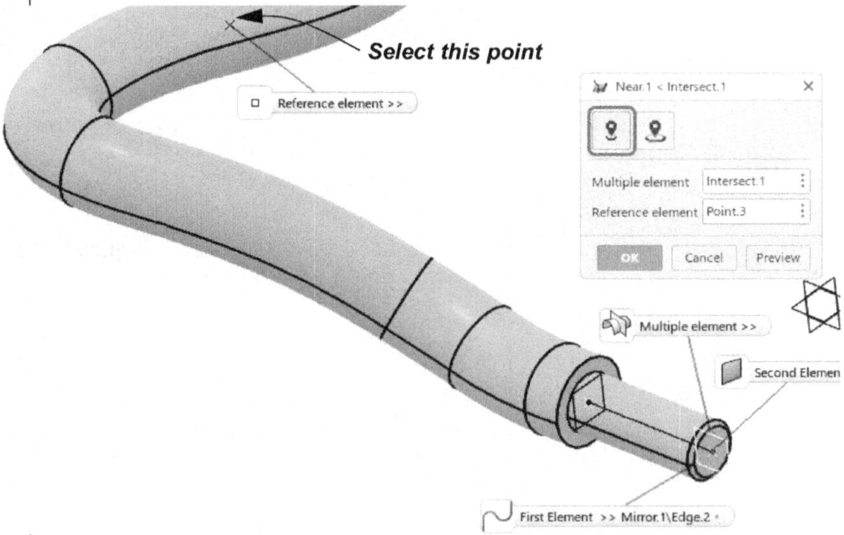

Figure 5–101

7. Click **OK** to complete the feature. The point displays as shown in Figure 5–102.

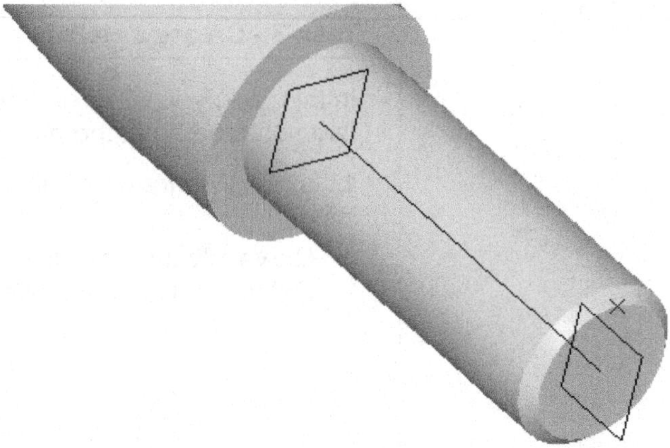

Figure 5–102

Note that the Intersection feature and Near feature display in the specification tree.

8. Rename the Near feature as **Startpoint**.

9. Select **Refplane2** and enter the Sketcher app.

10. Sketch the profile on **RefPlane2**, as shown in Figure 5–103.

Dimension point is created by intersecting the horizontal line with the angled line.

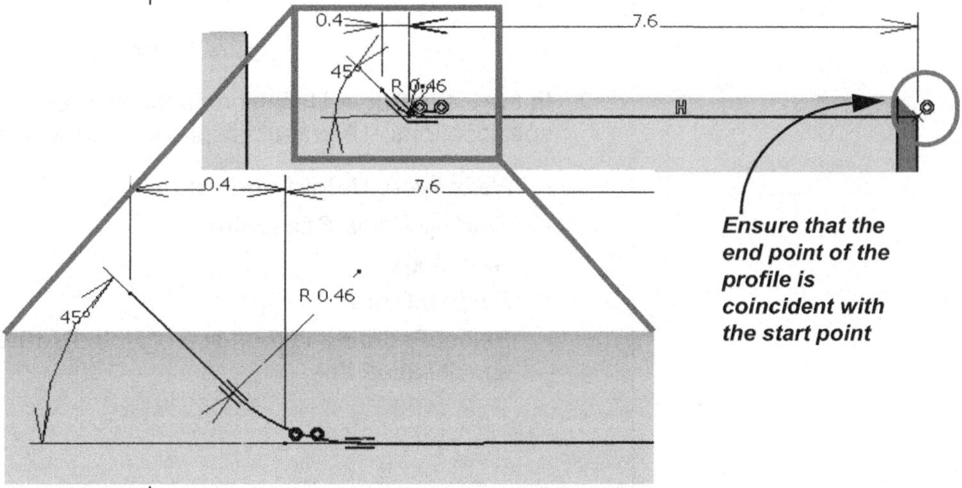

Figure 5–103

11. Complete the sketch.
12. Rename the sketch as **HelixProfile**.

Task 8 - Create a Helix.

In this task, you will create a Helix using the wireframe elements that you created in the previous tasks.

1. In the Wireframe section of the Action Bar, expand the Curves flyout, and click  (Helix). The Helix Curve Definition dialog box opens as shown in Figure 5–104.

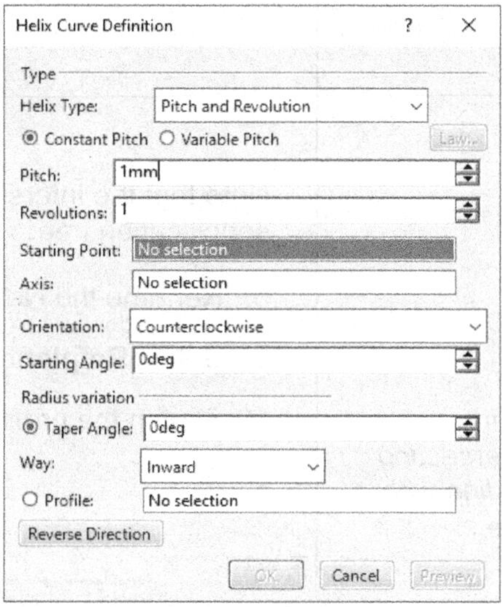

Figure 5–104

2. In the Helix Curve Definition dialog box, enter the following specifications. The result displays as shown in Figure 5–105:
   - *Helix Type:* **Height and Pitch**
   - *Starting Point:* **Startpoint**
   - *Axis:* **Axis**
   - *Pitch:* **0.6mm**
   - Select **Profile** and then select **HelixProfile** in the specification tree.

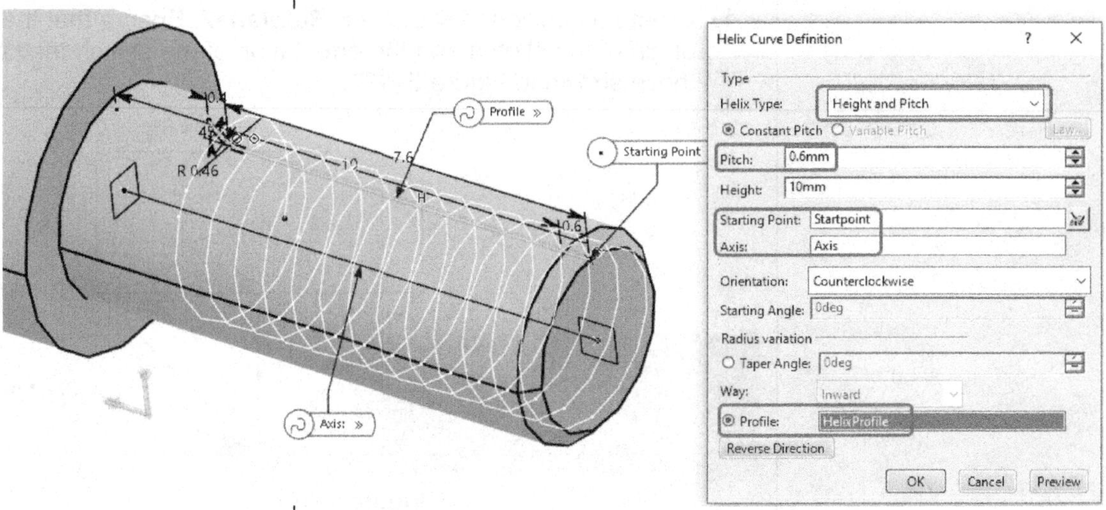

Figure 5–105

3. Click **OK** to complete the feature. The Helix displays as shown in Figure 5–106.

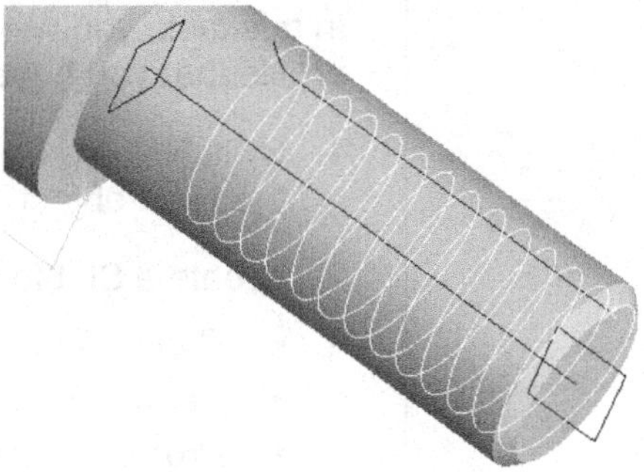

Figure 5–106

Task 9 - Create a Profile.

In this task, you will create a Profile that defines the shape of the thread.

1. Create a positioned sketch on **Refplane2**. Ensure that the origin of the sketch and the orientation of the sketch match those shown in Figure 5–107.

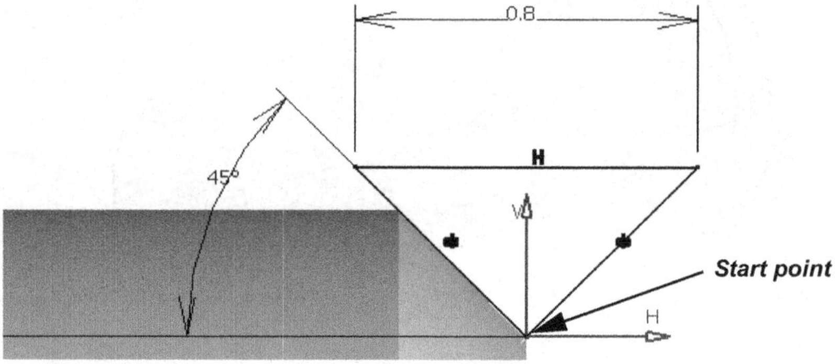

Figure 5–107

2. Rename the sketch as **ThreadProfile**.

Task 10 - Create the thread.

In this task, you will create the thread using the Helix and the profile that you have created in the previous tasks.

1. Switch to the Part Design app and define the **PartBody** as the work object.

2. Create a Slot feature with the following selections:
   - *Profile:* **ThreadProfile**
   - *Center curve:* **Helix.1**
   - *Profile control:* **Pulling direction**
   - *Selection:* **Refplane1**

   The model displays as shown in Figure 5–108.

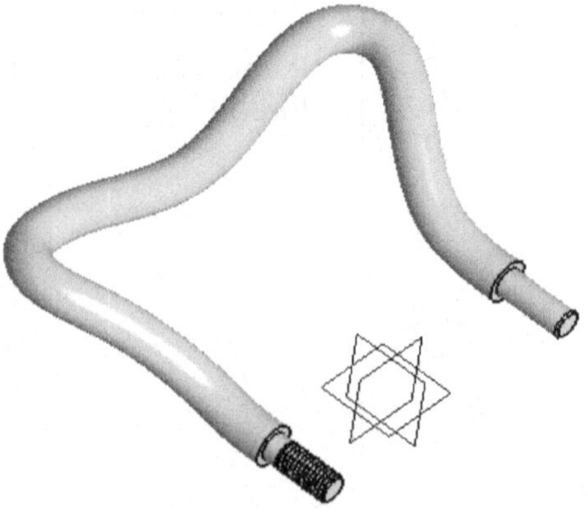

Figure 5–108

3. Save the file.

Task 11 - (Optional) Create another thread.

In this task, you will create another thread for the mirrored side of the model. Note that you cannot just mirror the thread created on the first end of the handle. That would create a left-handed thread on the other end.

1. Create the required wireframe elements.
2. Create the Helix.
3. Create the thread profile.
4. Create the thread.
5. Save and close the model.

   The completed model displays as shown in Figure 5–109.

Figure 5–109

Practice 5d Sailboat Keel

Practice Objectives

- Create intersection elements.
- Extract elements.
- Create splines.
- Create a Multi-sections Solid feature using a Spline.

In this practice, you will create the keel of a racing sailboat. The keel consists of a hydrodynamic foil and a bulb that holds ballast. You will model the foil using a Multi-sections Solid feature. You will then construct the required wireframe elements to create the bulb, using a Multi-sections Solid feature. The completed model displays as shown in Figure 5–110.

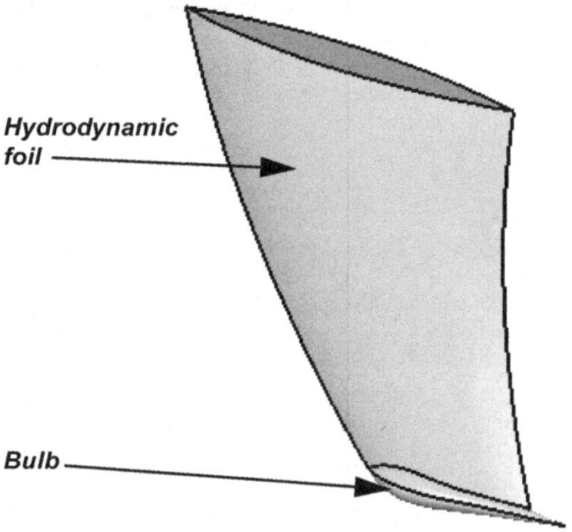

Figure 5–110

Task 1 - Open the part.

1. Import and open **SailboatKeel.3dxml**. When importing, type your initials followed by the dash symbol into the *Duplication string* field (e.g., **IA-**). The foil sections have already been created, as shown in Figure 5–111.

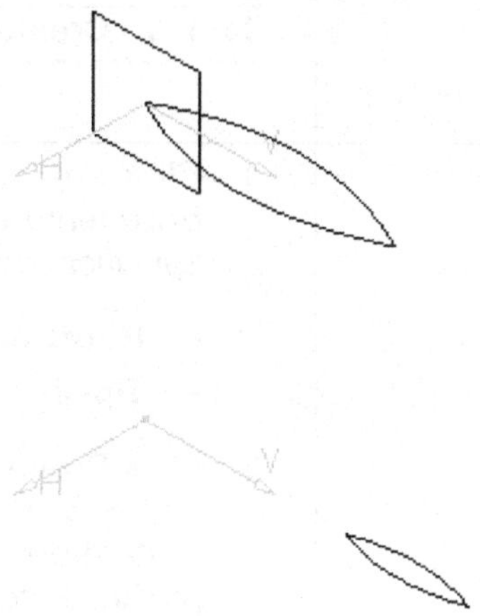

Figure 5–111

Task 2 - Create a profile.

In this task, you will create a profile that will be used to create the Multi-sections Solid.

1. Sketch an arc on the yz plane, similar to the one shown in Figure 5–112.

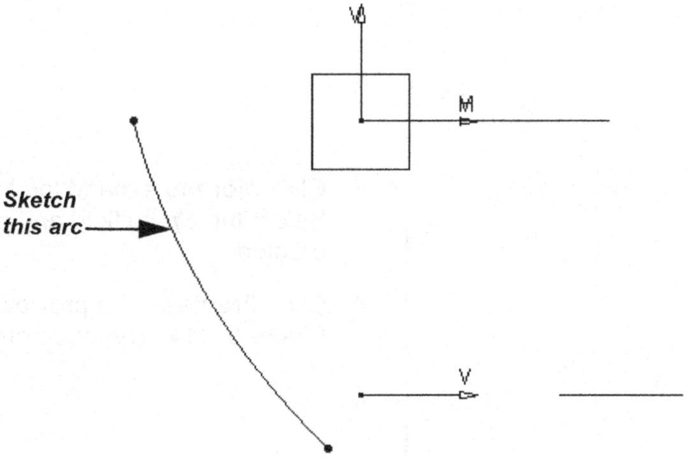

Figure 5–112

Task 3 - Create a Multi-sections Solid.

1. Click  (Multi-sections Solid). Define the Multi-sections Solid feature by selecting the following sketches in the specification tree or model:
   - **RootChord**
   - **TipChord**
2. Click **Preview**. The preview displays as shown in Figure 5–113. The transition between sections is system-defined. Note how different it is compared to the profile sketch in Task 2.

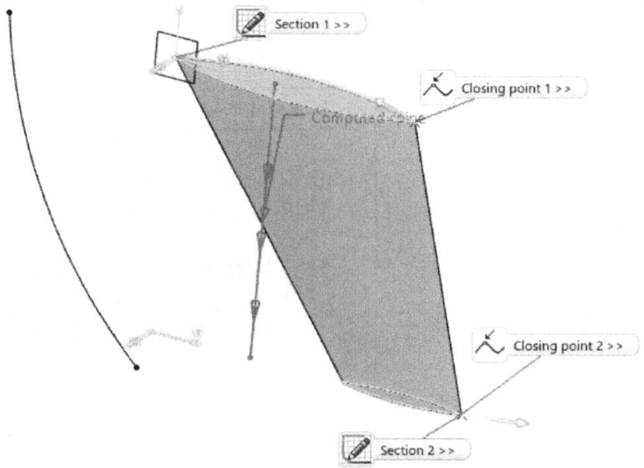

Figure 5–113

3. Click **More** to expand the Multi-sections Solid dialog box. Select the *Spine* field and select the profile that you just created.
4. Click **Preview**. The preview displays as shown in Figure 5–114. The geometry is forced to follow the Spine.

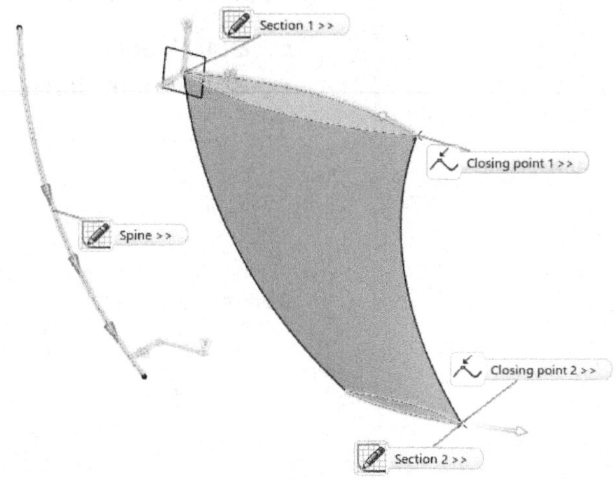

Figure 5–114

5. Complete the feature and hide the yz plane. The Multi-sections Solid feature displays as shown in Figure 5–115.

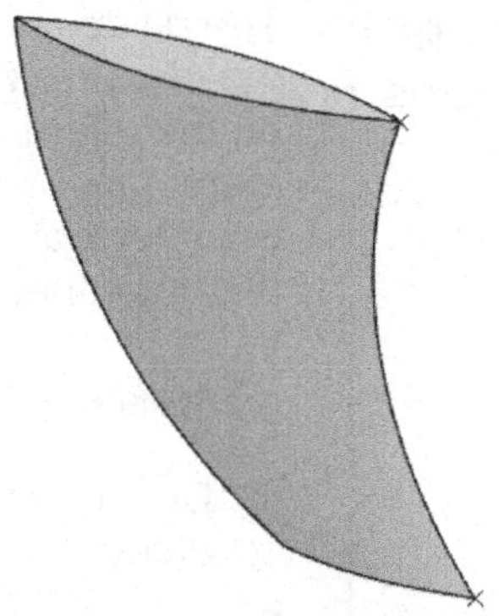

Figure 5–115

6. Save the model.

Task 4 - Create reference elements for the bulb.

In this task, you will create reference points. You will use these points to create guide curves and as closing points for the Multi-sections Solid creation.

1. Hide the **PartBody** and **KeelProfiles** geometrical set.

2. Show the following geometrical sets:

    - **BulbProfiles**
    - **BulbPointsPlanes**

    The model displays as shown in Figure 5–116.

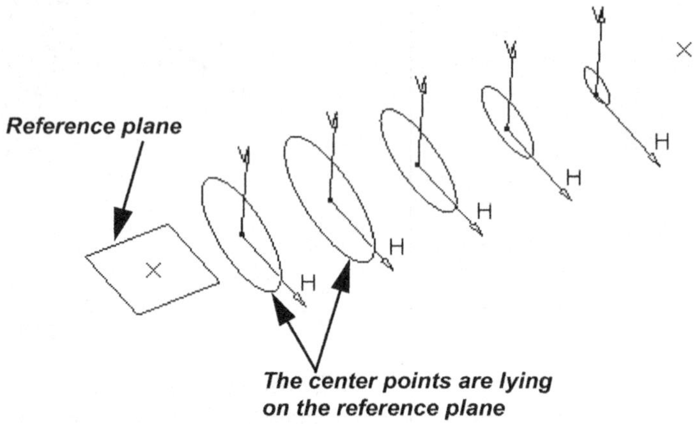

Figure 5–116

Design Considerations

The guide curves will be created using the extremum points of the ellipses. The center points for the first two ellipses are lying on the reference plane. You can make the creation of the extremum points for these two ellipses easier and faster using the Intersection and Extract features. The extremum points of the other three ellipses will be created using the Point feature.

3. Switch to the **Generative Shape Design** app.
4. Define the **BulbGuideCurves** geometrical set to be the work object.
5. In the Essentials section of the Action Bar, click  (Intersection).
6. In the *First Element* field, click ⊙ to open the selection collector box, and select the first two profiles as the First Element. Select the reference plane as the Second Element to create the intersection points, as shown in Figure 5–117.

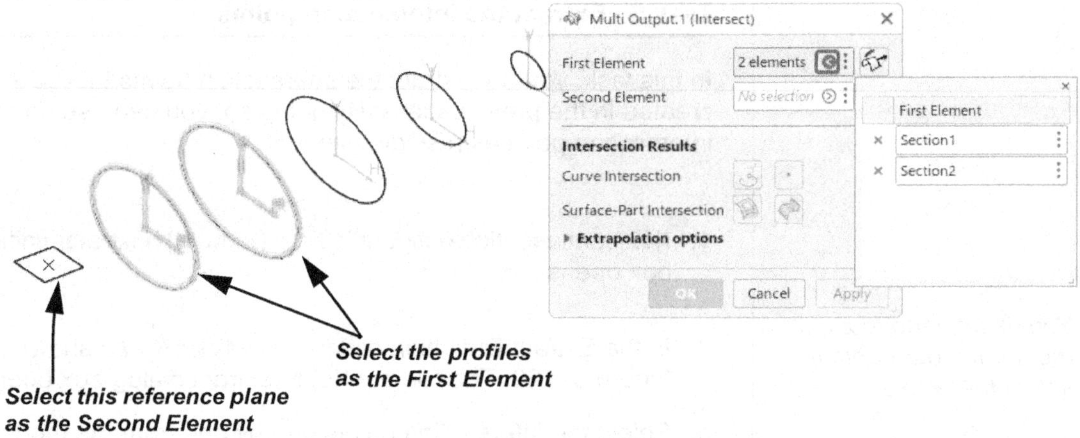

Figure 5–117

7. Click **OK**. The Multi Result Management dialog box opens as shown in Figure 5–118. Click **No**.

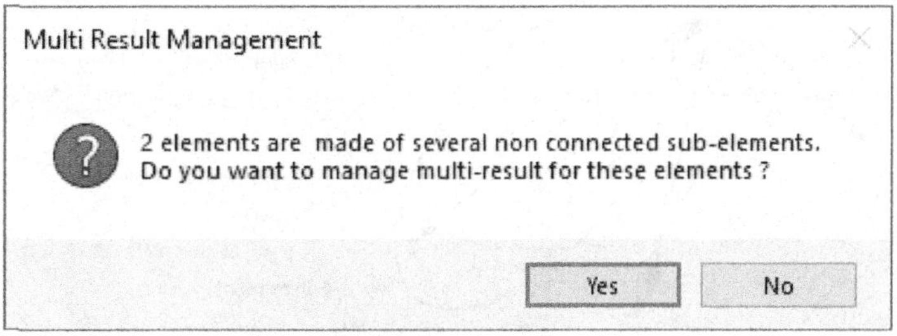

Figure 5–118

The model displays as shown in Figure 5–119.

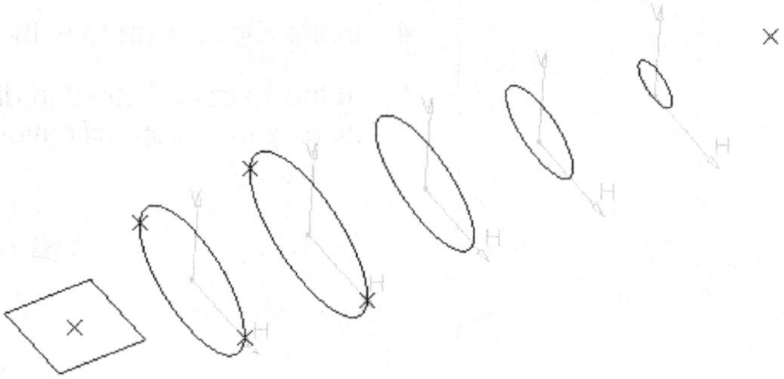

Figure 5–119

Task 5 - Extract the intersection points.

In this task, you will extract the intersection points that you created in the previous task. By doing so, you can use each intersection point as a single element.

1. In the Essentials section of the Action Bar, click (Extract). The Extract Definition dialog box opens.

You might need to zoom the model to be able to select the points.

2. In the Extract Definition dialog box, click , as shown in Figure 5–120. The Element(s) to extract dialog box opens.
3. Select the intersection points one by one from the model. Four elements display in the Element(s) to extract dialog box, as shown in Figure 5–120.

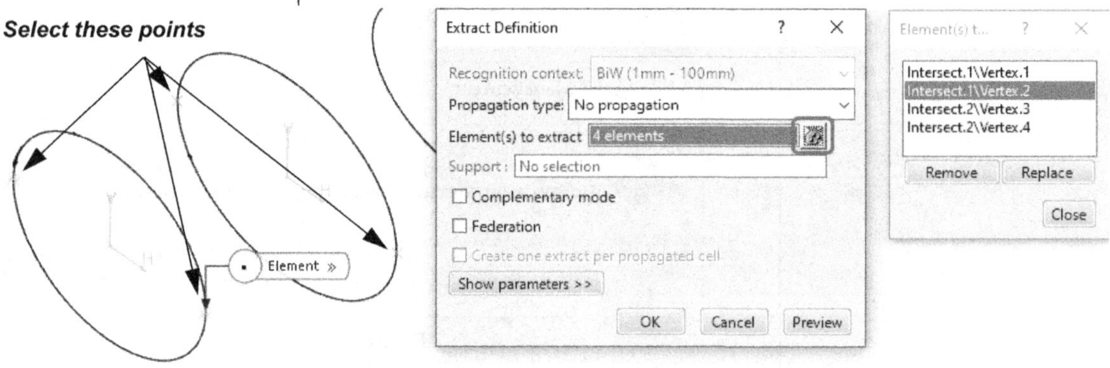

Figure 5–120

4. In the Element(s) to extract dialog box, click **Close**.
5. In the Extract Definition dialog box, click **OK**. The points display in the specification tree, as shown in Figure 5–121.

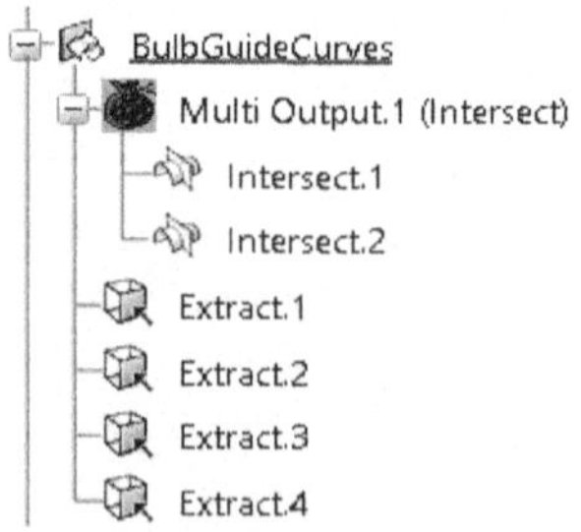

Figure 5–121

6. In the specification tree, hide the **Intersect.1** and **Intersect.2** intersection points.

Task 6 - Create the extremum points.

1. Click (Point). Make the following selections in the Point dialog box (as shown in Figure 5–122).
   - *Point type:* **On curve**
   - *Curve:* **Section3**
   - *Distance To Reference:* **Ratio of curve length**
   - *Ratio:* **0.25**
   - *Reference Point:* **Point.1**

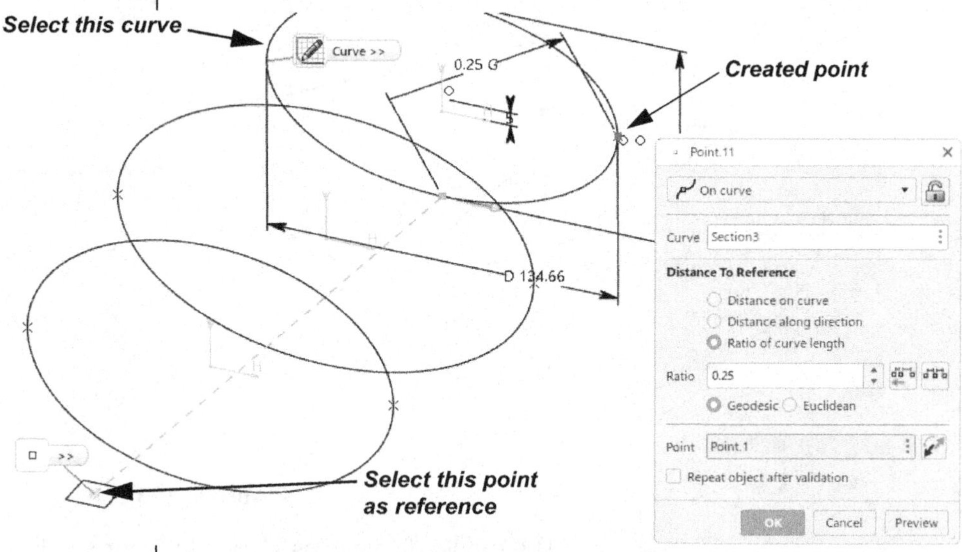

Figure 5–122

2. Click ▫ (Point). Make the following selections in the Point dialog box, as shown in Figure 5–123:

   - *Point type:* **On curve**
   - *Curve:* **Section3**
   - *Distance To Reference:* **Ratio of curve length**
   - *Ratio:* **0.5**
   - *Reference Point:* **Point.11**

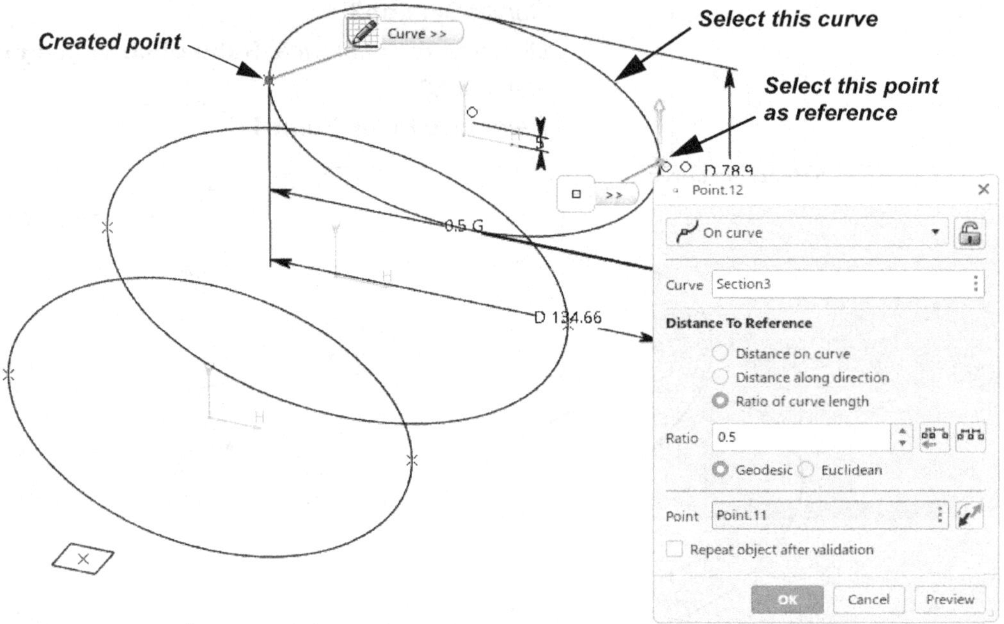

Figure 5–123

The model displays as shown in Figure 5–124.

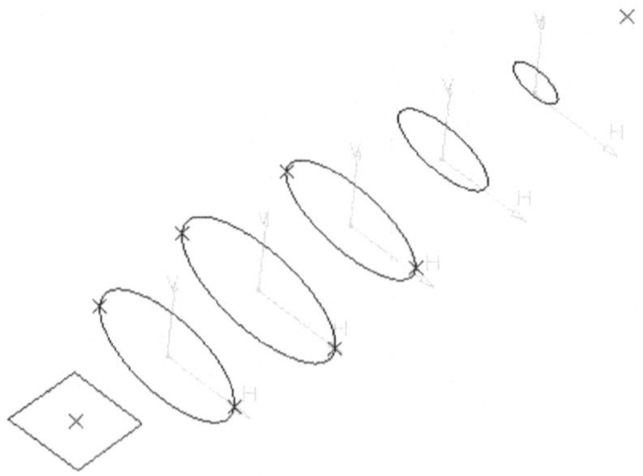

Figure 5–124

3. Using Steps 1 and 2 as the guideline, create four more points on the **Section4** and **Section5** curves, as shown in Figure 5–125.

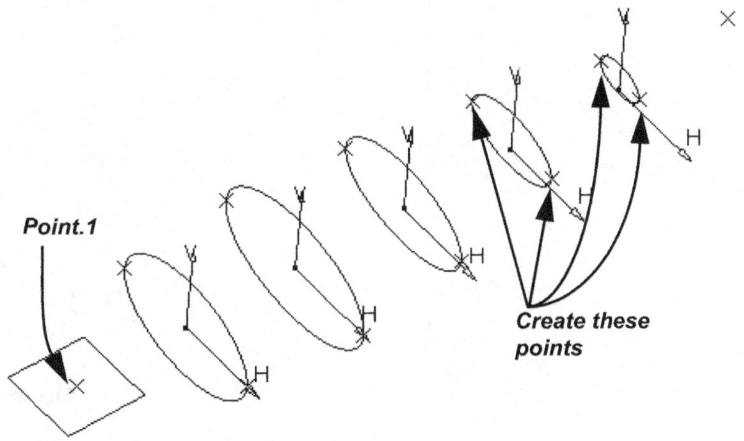

Figure 5–125

Task 7 - Create the guide lines.

In this task, you will create the guide lines. You will use these lines in the next task, during the Multi-sections Solid creation.

1. Click  (Spline).
2. In the specification tree or display, select the points as shown in Figure 5–126.

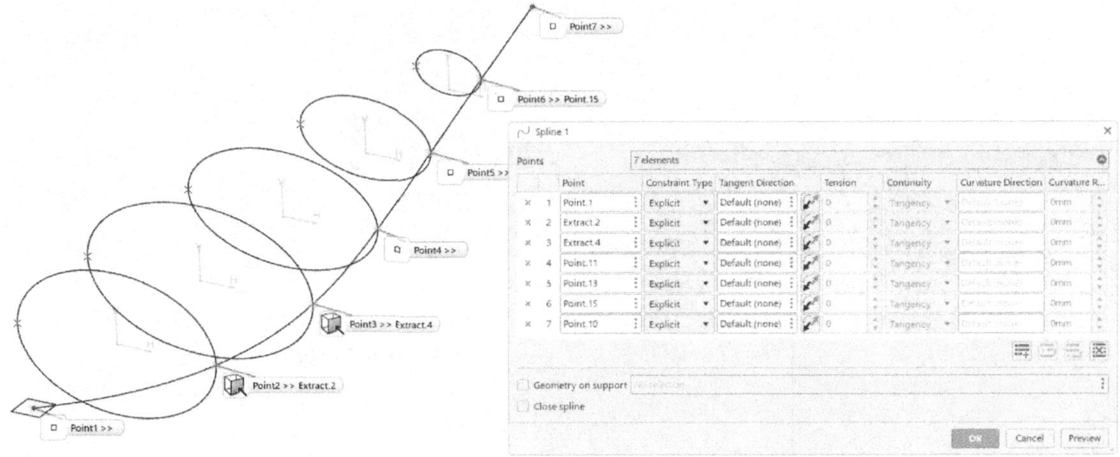

Figure 5–126

3. Click **OK** to complete the feature. The curve displays as shown in Figure 5–127.

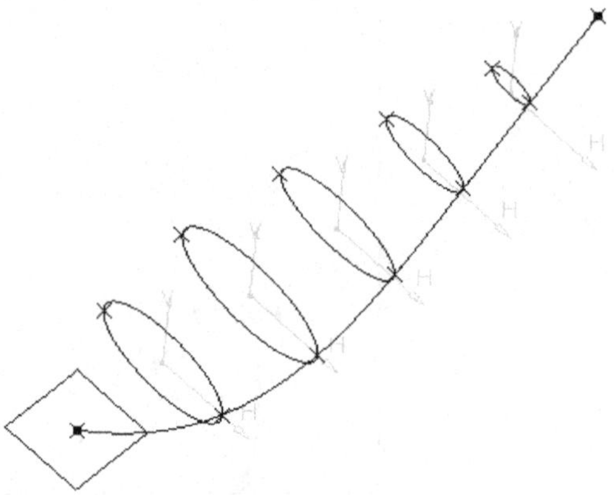

Figure 5–127

4. Rename the spline as **guide1**.

5. Create another Spline as shown in Figure 5–128. Rename the Spline as **guide2**.

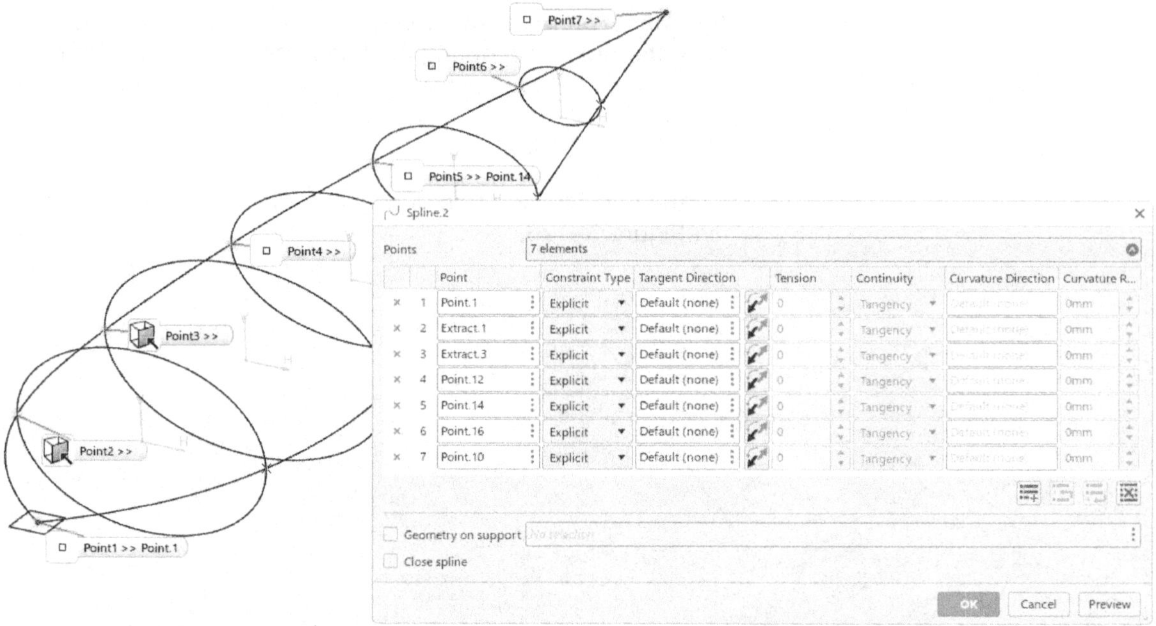

Figure 5–128

Task 8 - Create a Multi-sections Solid.

In this task, you will create a Multi-sections Solid using the profiles, guide curves, and extremum points.

1. Define the **PartBody** to be the work object.
2. Switch to the **Part Design** app.
3. Click  (Multi-sections Solid). The Multi-Sections Solid Definition dialog box opens. In the specification tree or model, select the following sketches:
   - **Section1**
   - **Section2**
   - **Section3**
   - **Section4**
   - **Section5**
4. Select the *Guides* field. Select the following splines as the guide curves, as shown in Figure 5–129:
   - **guide1**
   - **guide2**

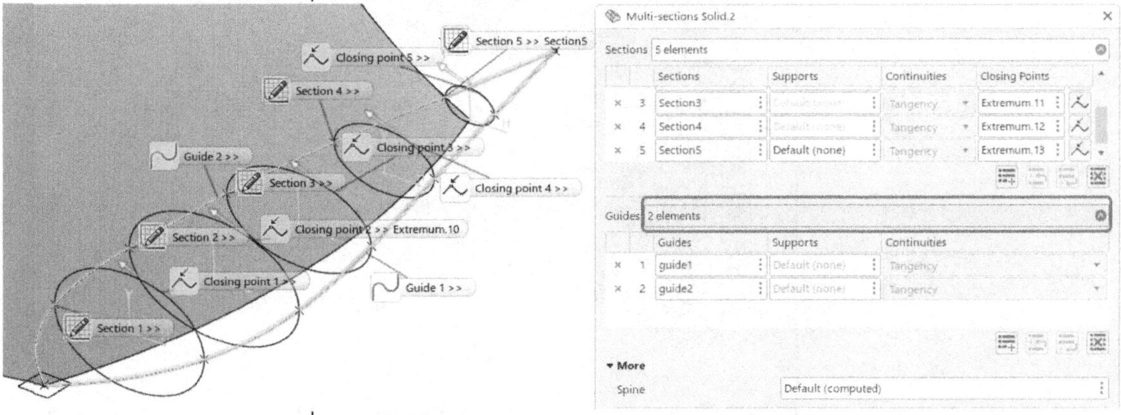

Figure 5–129

5. Click in the *Closing Points* field for **Section5**.

6. Select the extremum point. The closing point is now located at the extremum point, as shown in Figure 5–130.

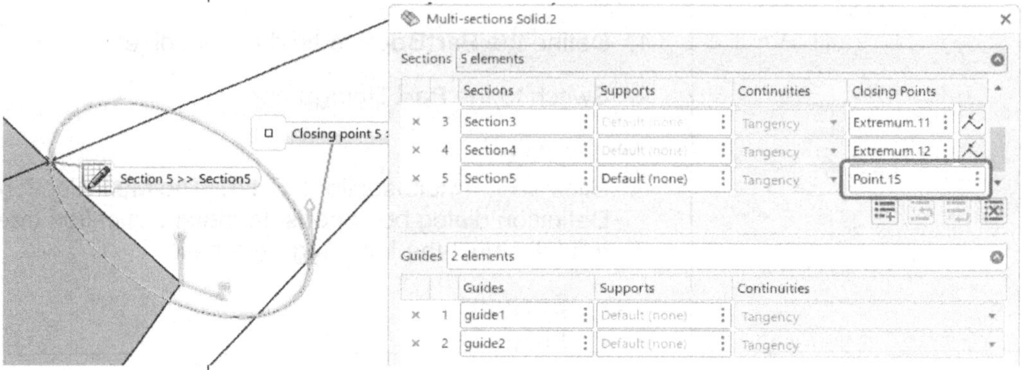

Figure 5–130

7. Replace the rest of the closing points and ensure that they are all pointing in the same direction, as shown in Figure 5–131.

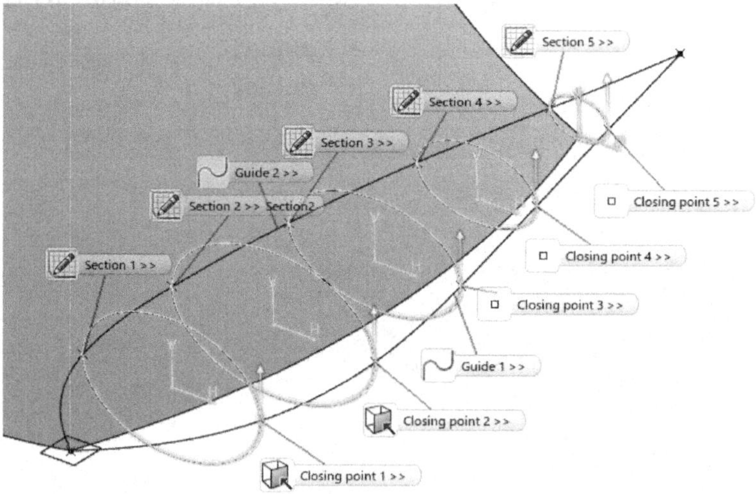

Figure 5–131

8. In the Multi-sections Solid dialog box, click **Preview**. The preview displays, as shown in Figure 5–132.

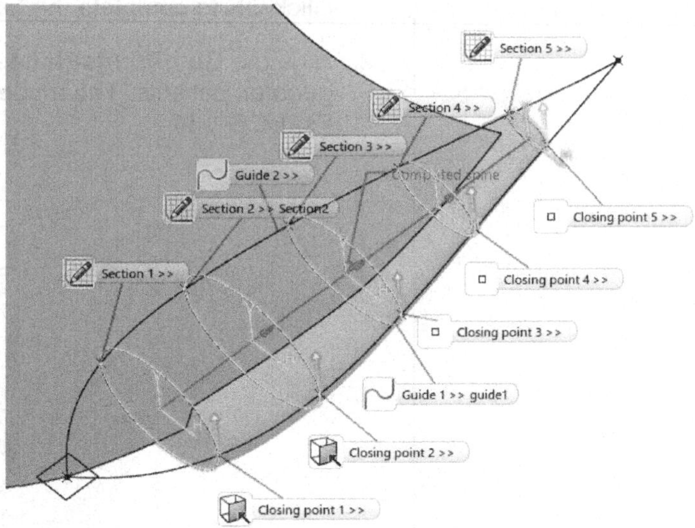

Figure 5–132

9. The solid is only created between the sections. To create the whole bulb, click **More** to expand the Multi-sections Solid dialog box and clear the following options, as shown in Figure 5–133:

   * **Relimited on start section**
   * **Relimited on end section**

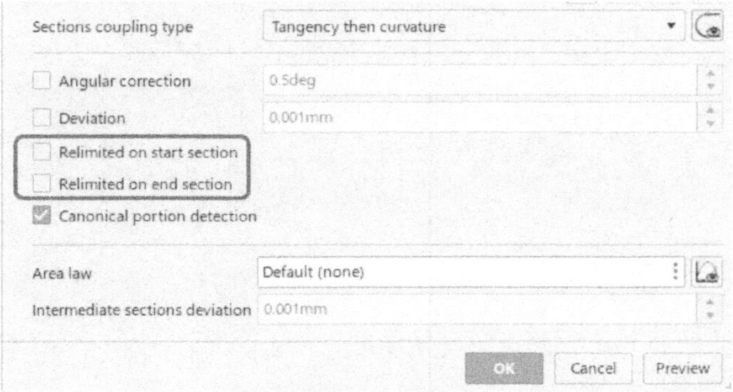

Figure 5–133

Task 9 - Complete the feature.

1. Click **OK** to complete the feature.
2. Hide the **BulbPointsPlanes** and **BulbGuideCurves** geometrical sets. The model displays as shown in Figure 5–134.

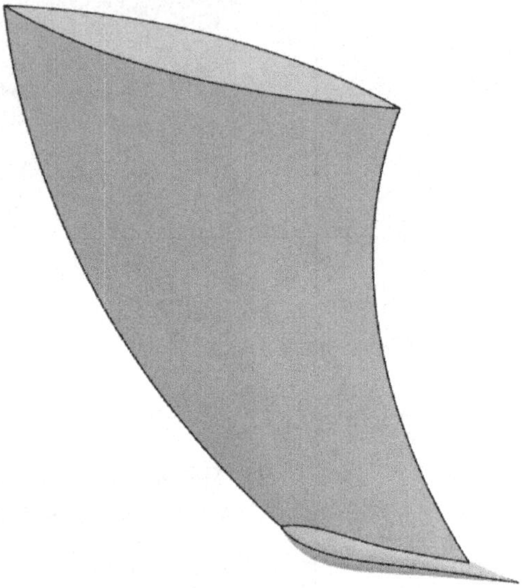

Figure 5–134

3. Save the model and close the window.

Chapter Review Questions

1. To create multiple points along a curve, line, or edge, click
    a. 
    b. 
    c. 
    d. None of the above.
2. Which of the following options is valid when creating a line?
    a. Point-Point
    b. Point-Direction
    c. Tangent to curve
    d. All of the above.
3. A spline requires a minimum of three points.
    a. True
    b. False
4. Which of the following options is valid for use as points in a spline?
    a. Reference points
    b. End points
    c. Vertices
    d. All of the above.

5. What can be inferred about the spline curve shown in Figure 5–135?

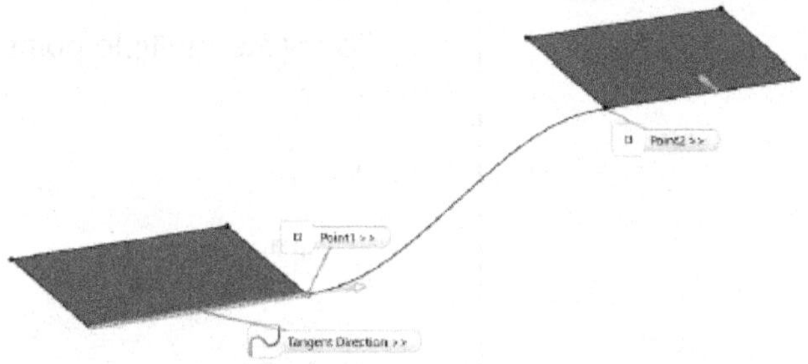

Figure 5–135

   a. There is tangency set between the spline and the adjacent surface edges, at Point1 and Point2.
   b. The arrow indicates the direction of tangency between the spline and the edge of the surface on the left.
   c. Both a and b.
   d. None of the above.

6. The main difference between a Spline and a Polyline, is that a Polyline connects the points with straight lines rather than curves, but can also have a radius defined at each point to control the shape.
   a. True
   b. False

7. The axis of a Helix can be straight or curved.
   a. True
   b. False

8. Once the Axis and Start Point of a Helix have been defined, you can then define _____.
   a. The Pitch
   b. The Height
   c. The Taper
   d. The Starting Angle
   e. All of the above.

9. The curves used to create a Combine are always projected perpendicular to each other.

    a. True

    b. False

Answers: 1b, 2d, 3b, 4d, 5c, 6a, 7b, 8e, 9b,

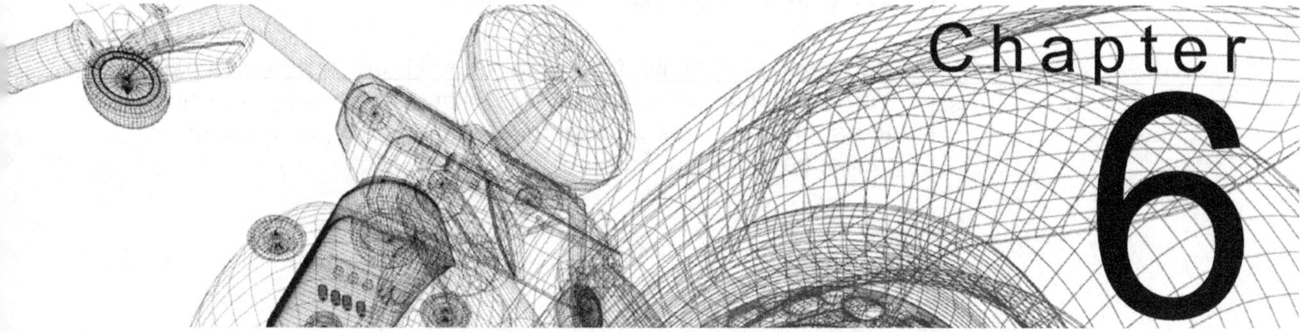

Advanced Fillets and Drafts

Dress-up features do not require the creation of a sketch to determine their shape. By default, the underlying geometry of the dress-up feature determines the shape of the resulting geometry. Advanced options for the Fillet and Draft features provide additional control over their shape and propagation. These options also enable you to create the features over more complex geometry.

Learning Objectives in This Chapter

- Understand the advance fillet options for controlling the shape of a fillet.
- Learn about additional types of fillets, including Variable Radius, Chordal, and Face-Face.
- Understand the reflect line draft.
- Learn how advanced draft can provide additional capabilities over regular draft.
- Understand how to manage any failures that occur when creating or editing draft and fillets.

6.1 Advanced Fillets

You can use the Fillet feature to round sharp corners of a part. You can define fillets in the Edge Fillet dialog box by selecting the appropriate reference geometry and specifying a radius value, as shown in Figure 6–1.

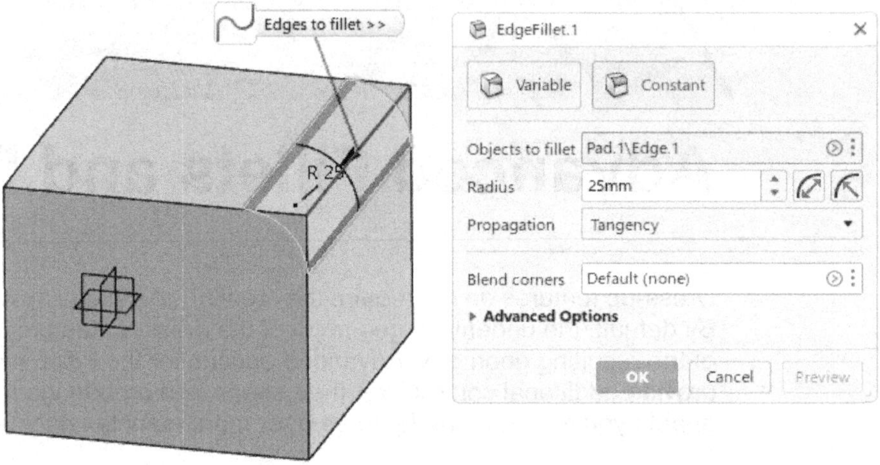

Figure 6–1

You can create fillets using the icons in the Refine section of the Action Bar shown in Figure 6–2.

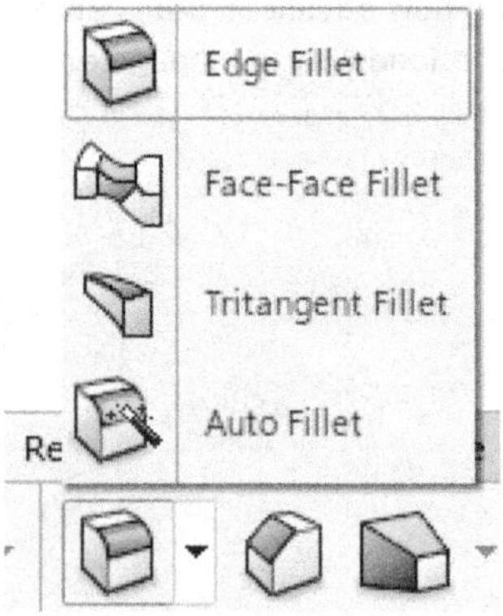

Figure 6–2

In the Edge Fillet dialog box, click **Advanced Options** to display the advanced Fillet options. You can use the advanced options to further define the shape and propagation of the Fillet feature. The options vary for each type of Fillet feature:

- Edge Fillet
- Face to Face Fillet
- Tritangent Fillet

Edge Fillet

Note that next time you create an edge fillet, the system will remember whether the dialog box was expanded or not.

The expanded Edge Fillet dialog box is shown in Figure 6–3.

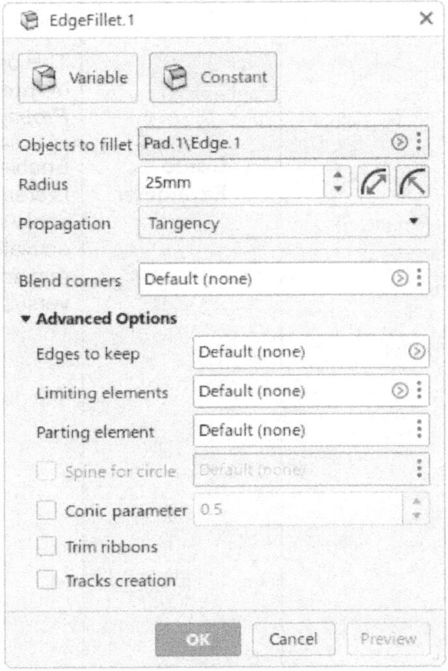

Figure 6–3

The options in the expanded Edge Fillet dialog box are as follows.

Option	Description
Trim Ribbons	Trims overlapping fillets at their intersections. 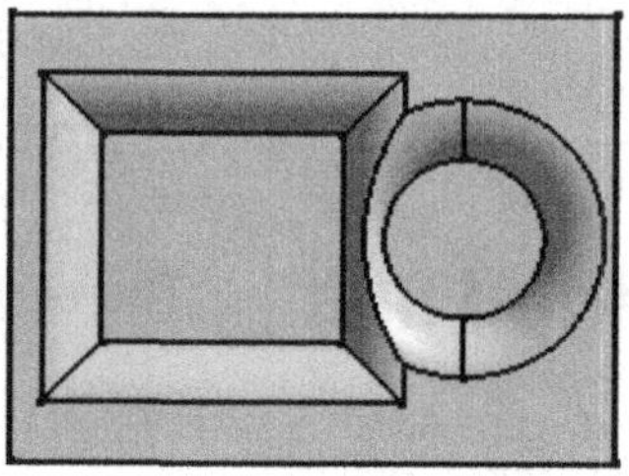 This option is only available when you use either **Tangency** or **Intersection with selected features** option in the *Propagation* field.
Conic Parameter	Enables you to create conic shaped fillets. By default, a fillet is created with a radial cross-section. To create conic-shaped fillets, the **Conic parameter** option must be activated. The examples show fillet geometry and their respective cross-sections to demonstrate a radial fillet versus a conic fillet. 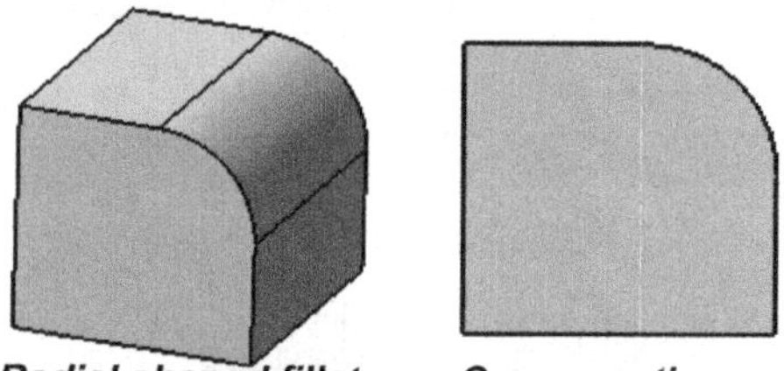 ***Radial shaped fillet*** ***Cross-section*** 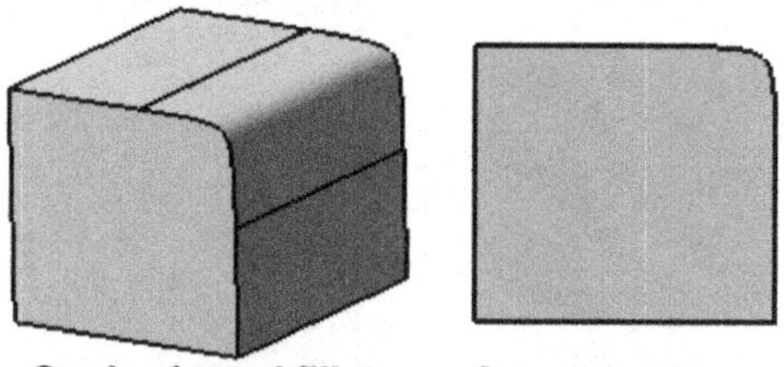 ***Conic shaped fillet*** ***Cross-section***
Edge(s) to Keep	Stops the fillet at the selected part edge. You can add more than one reference. This option is useful when the fillet extends past the boundary of the part geometry.

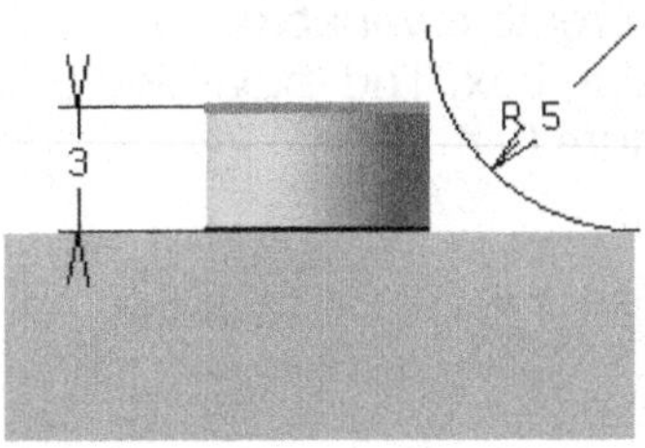

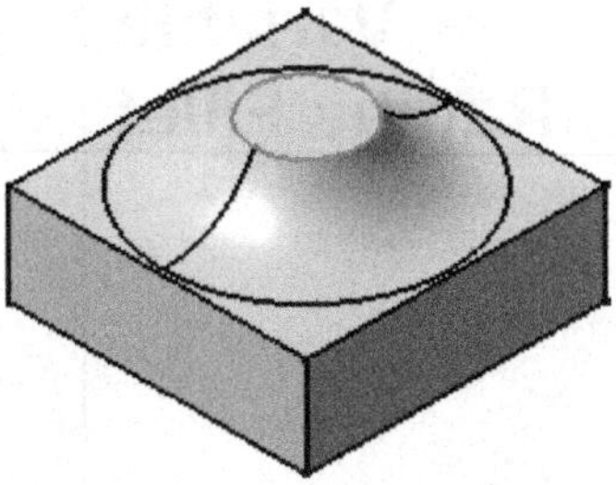

Limiting Elements

Stops the propagation of the fillet at the selected geometry. This geometry can be a reference plane or model surface. The direction of material to be kept is indicated by an arrow.

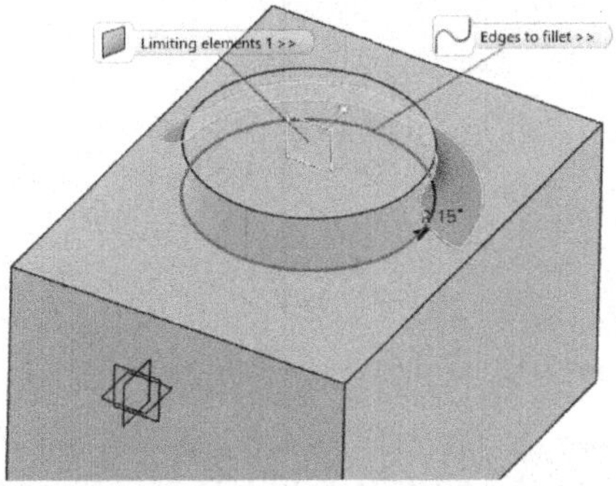

Blend Corners

When more than two edges transition into a corner of a Fillet feature, the **Blend Corner** option is available. It reshapes the way the fillet edges transition together.

How To: Use Blend Corner

1. Select the *Blend corners* area and select a vertex.
2. Enter a value for the setback distance. The setback distance defines where the fillet shape begins blending into the other fillet shapes.

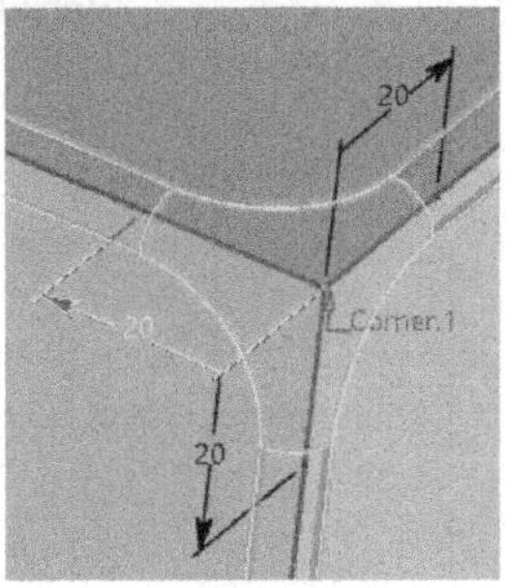

Variable Radius Fillet

To create a variable radius fillet, click 

in the Edge Fillet dialog box. The expanded Edge Fillet dialog box is shown in Figure 6–4.

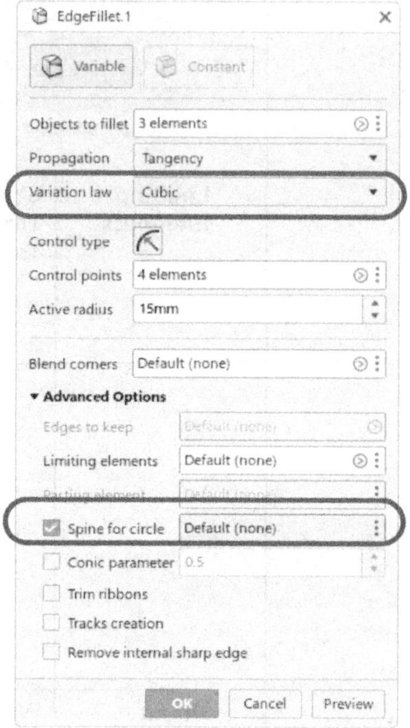

Figure 6–4

The Edge Fillet dialog box updates to enable some additional parameters that were grayed out when the 

option was selected.

Option	Description
Variation Law	Determines the shape of the fillet as it blends between two different radii. 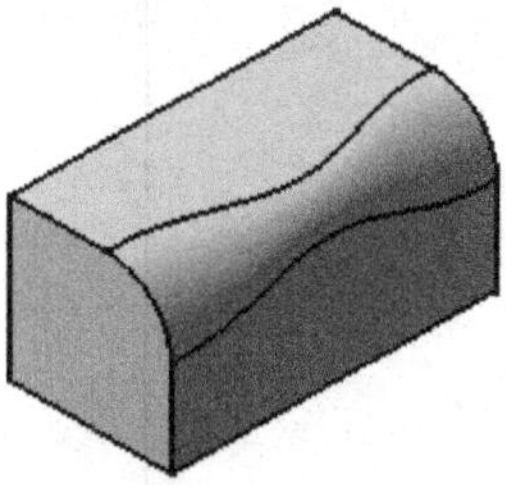 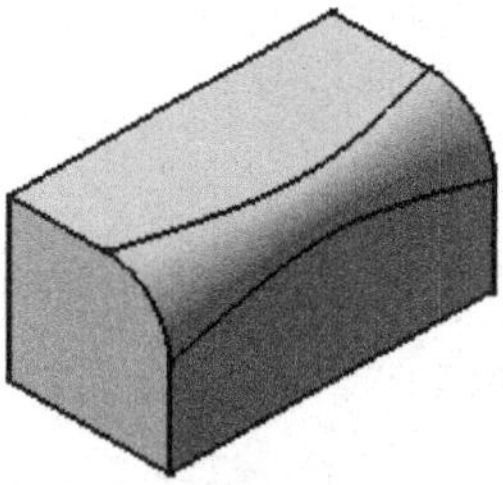 ***Cubic*** ***Linear*** You can select from the following two options:

	Cubic	A third order polynomial curve is fitted between the two radii.
	Linear	A first order polynomial curve is fitted between the two radii.
Spine for circle		Provides control over the shape of a Variable Radius Fillet. The radius of the fillet is always perpendicular to the spine. 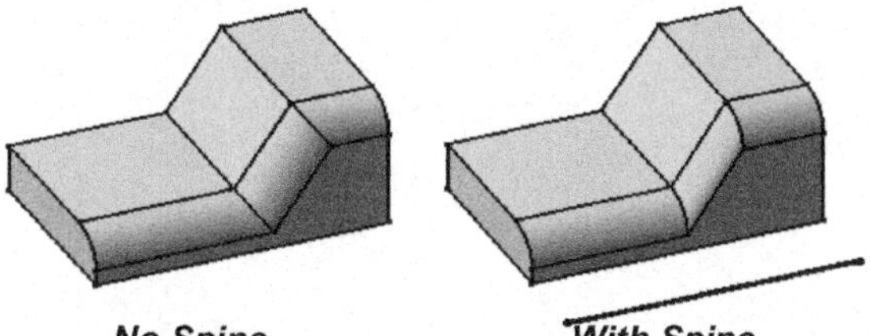 ***No Spine*** ***With Spine*** The selection of the spine is disabled by default. To enable selection of a spine, you must first select the **Spine for circle** checkbox.

The variable radius fillet can have unique radii at each point or vertex along the edges being filleted. You can select the radius dimension in the model and enter the new value in the *Active radius* field, as shown in Figure 6–5.

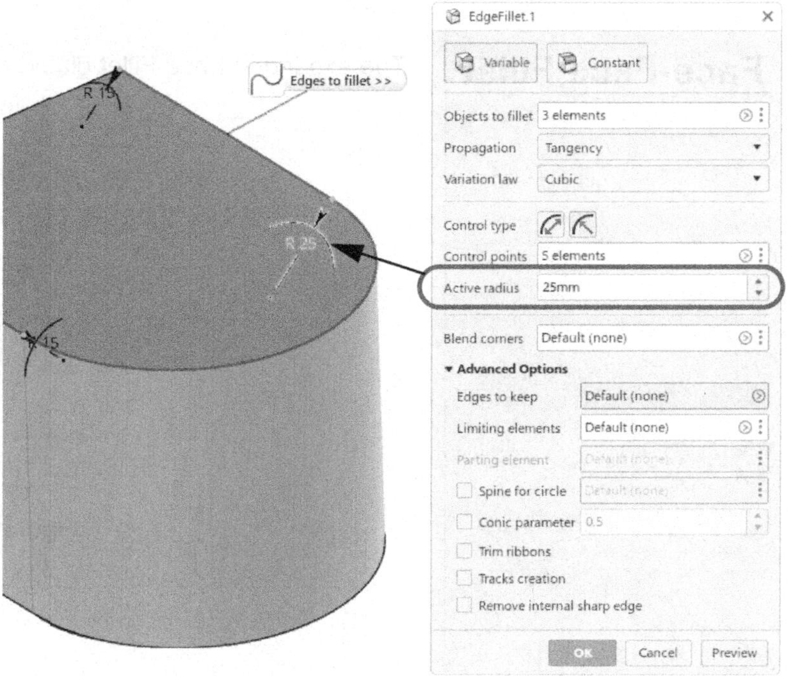

Figure 6–5

Chordal Fillet

To create a chordal fillet, click (Edge Fillet) to open the Edge Fillet dialog box, then click (Chordal). The expanded Edge Fillet dialog box is shown in Figure 6–6.

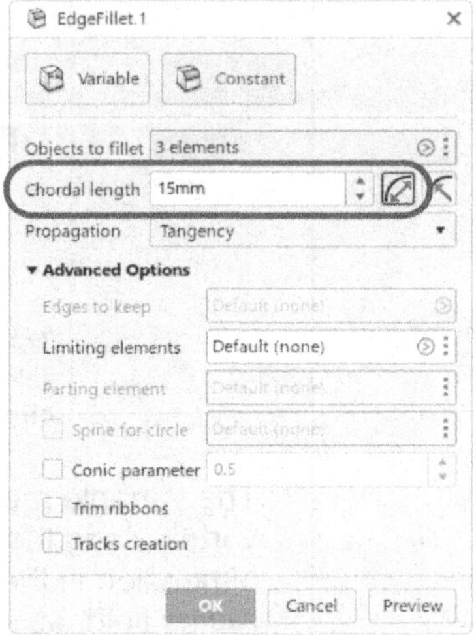

Figure 6–6

Face-Face Fillet

The expanded Face Fillet dialog box is shown in Figure 6–7.

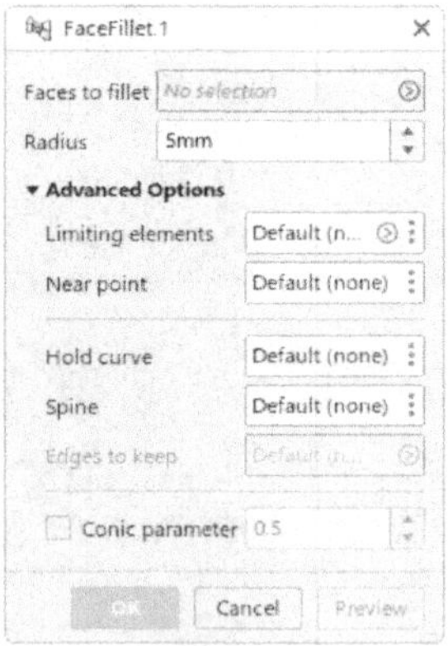

Figure 6–7

In addition to the **Limiting elements** option, the Face Fillet dialog box enables you to specify a Hold Curve and Spine. You can use the **Hold Curve** option to specify the radius of the fillet by selecting a sketch or curve created in the Wireframe and Surface app. To define the hold curve, you must select a spine. An example is shown in Figure 6–8.

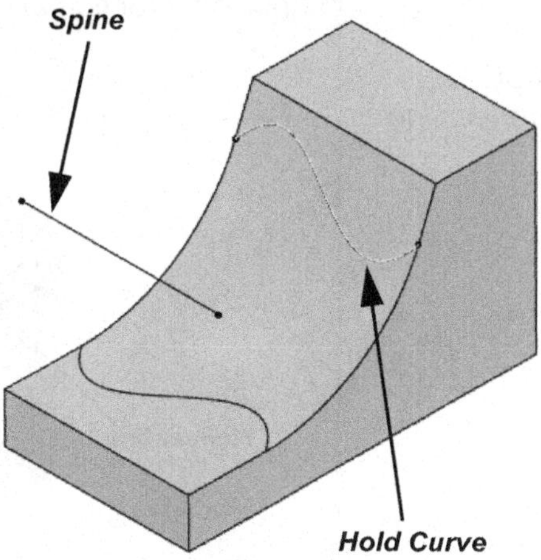

Figure 6–8

6.2 Creating Reflect Line Draft

A reflect line is the external edge of a non-planar face when viewed from a specific direction. Reflect Line Draft uses the reflect lines as neutral lines when drafting the selected faces. The system determines the reflect lines based on the specified pulling direction and Draft angle, as shown in Figure 6–9.

3DEXPERIENCE highlights the reflect line in magenta.

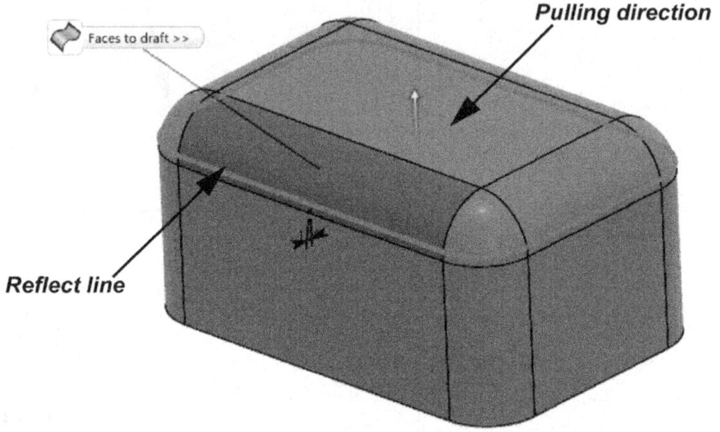

Figure 6–9

Reflect Line Draft is useful when drafting complex models, because their geometry is typically non-planar. This type of Draft enables you to place draft on faces that are already filleted.

General Steps

Use the following general steps to create a Reflect Line Draft:

1. Start Draft creation.
2. Specify Reflect Line Draft elements.

Step 1 - Start Draft creation.

To create a Reflect Line Draft feature, click (Draft Reflect Line) in the Refine section of the Action Bar. The expanded Draft dialog box opens as shown in Figure 6–10.

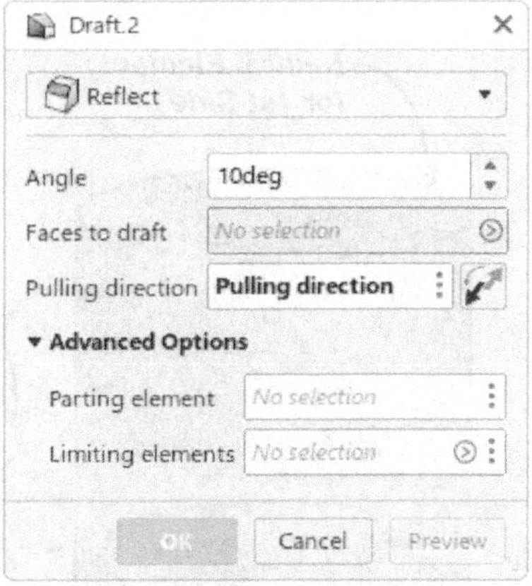

Figure 6–10

Step 2 - Specify Reflect Line Draft elements.

The Draft requires you to enter the following information:

- Draft angle
- Faces to draft
- Pulling direction
- Parting element, if applicable.
- Limiting element(s), if applicable.

Click **OK** to complete the feature.

6.3 Creating Advanced Draft

The Advanced Draft feature provides additional control and functionality over the Constant Draft feature. Advanced Draft incorporates all of the functionality of the constant and variable Drafts. Additionally, different Draft angles can be specified for either side of the parting element, as shown in Figure 6–11.

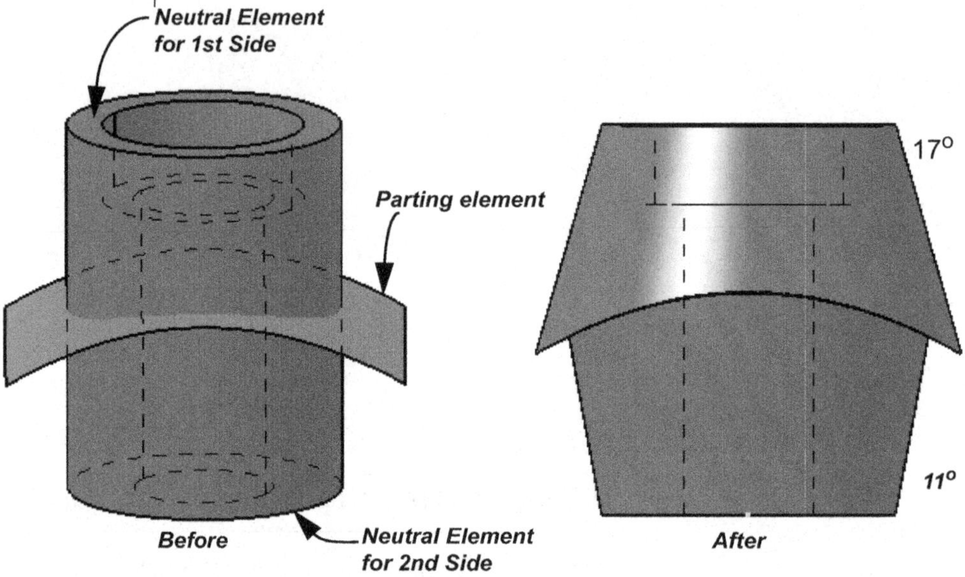

Figure 6–11

General Steps

Use the following general steps to create an Advanced Reflect Line Draft:

1. Start the creation of an Advanced Draft feature.
2. Define the Draft angle conditions.
3. Select the faces to draft.
4. Select a neutral element in the first direction.
5. Select a pulling direction.
6. Select a parting element.
7. Select a neutral element in the second direction.

Step 1 - Start the creation of an Advanced Draft feature.

Click  (Advanced Draft) in the Refine section of the Action Bar. The Draft Definition (Advanced) dialog box opens as shown in Figure 6–12.

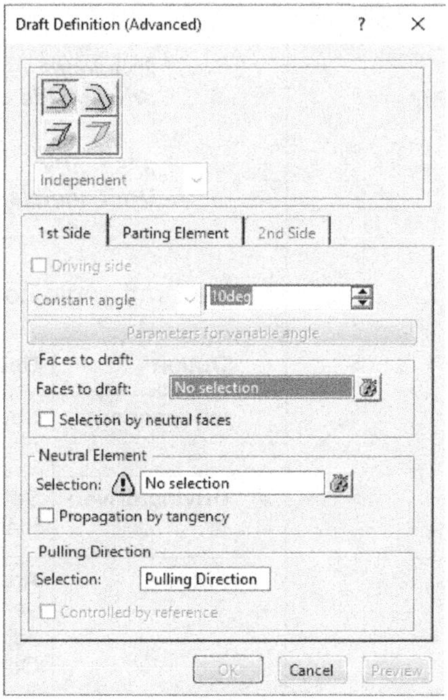

Figure 6–12

Click the required icons in the top of the dialog box. The icons are described as follows:

Icon	Description
	Create a one-sided Draft feature.
	Create a two-sided Draft feature.
	Create a one-sided Draft Reflect Line feature.
	Create a two-sided Draft Reflect Line feature.

Step 2 - Define the Draft angle conditions.

For the two-sided Draft Reflect line, define the Draft angle conditions, as shown in Figure 6–13.

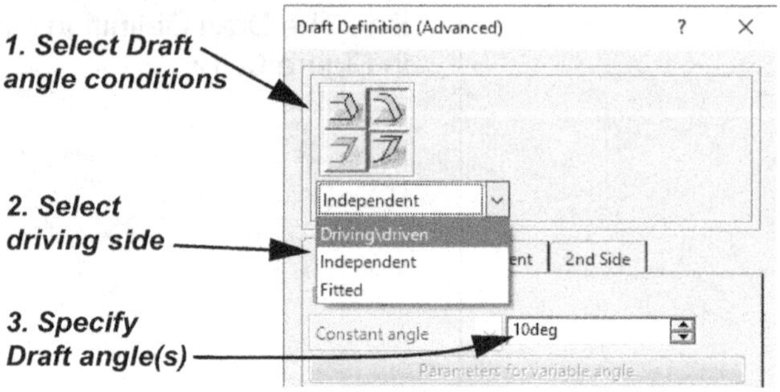

Figure 6–13

The Draft angle conditions can be specified, as follows:

Option	Description
Independent	Specifies the Draft angle independently for each direction.
Driving/driven	Selects a direction as the driving side. The Draft angle that you specify controls draft in both directions.
Fitted	Applies draft symmetrically on two opposite sides of the parting line. Using this option, you can apply a parting line adjustment. This option requires a Cast & Forged Part Optimizer license.

Step 3 - Select the faces to draft.

Select the *Faces to draft* field and select the faces on the model.

Step 4 - Select a neutral element in the first direction.

Select the *Neutral Element* field and select the neutral element in the model. If you activate the **Propagation by tangency** option, tangent surfaces to the selected neutral element are automatically included in the selection.

Step 5 - Select a pulling direction.

Select a pulling direction. This option determines the direction in which the mold is pulled away from the part. You can select a reference plane, planar face, or surface. An arrow displays, indicating the pulling direction. You can flip the direction using the arrow.

Step 6 - Select a parting element.

Select the *Parting Element* tab in the Draft Definition (Advanced) dialog box. The parting element determines the surface at which the top and bottom of the mold meet. You can select a reference plane or model face. A parting element is required for a Draft in two directions.

Step 7 - Select a neutral element in the second direction.

Select the *2nd Side* tab in the Draft Definition (Advanced) dialog box. In the *Neutral Element* field, select in the model the neutral element for the second side.

6.4 Draft and Fillet Failure Resolution

Fillet Failure Resolution

When a fillet fails, you can use a variety of methods to investigate and resolve the failure. Check the error message reported by the system to determine the cause of the problem. Based on the error message, try one of the following techniques to resolve the error:

- Ensure that the model is of good quality by inspecting it for short edges and very small surfaces that might cause unnecessary complications.
- Reduce the radius of the fillet feature. A large radius often causes the fillet to intersect itself or other complex geometry, which causes it to fail. Create the fillet with a smaller radius and then visualize what the fillet would look like with a larger radius.
- Carefully check your references. When creating large and complex fillets, an incorrect reference is often selected or an important reference is missing. Try breaking a complex fillet into smaller features that are easier to manage.
- Select edges to fillet iteratively by selecting one or two edges and clicking **Preview**, and then selecting more edges as required.
- Fillet the part in a different order. For example, if you have a vertical and horizontal edge that meet, and the vertical edge was filleted first, try filleting the horizontal edge first.
- Try using one of the other types of fillets.
- Extract surface features of a failed fillet and use surface features and surface operations to create the geometry (use this method as a last resort).

Common Filleting Errors and Possible Fixes:

- **Twisted Fillet Error:** Indicates that the radius of the fillet you are attempting is too large for the radius of curvature of the edge you are trying to fillet. A possible solution is to reduce the fillet radius.
- **More than (3) Edges on a Vertex Error:** Indicates that the fillet cannot be re-limited to the point at which the edges come to a point. The solution is to move one of the fillets further up in the specification tree.

- **Interrupted Fillet Error:** Think of the filleting process as a marble rolling between two surfaces. An interrupted fillet is a fillet where the marble cannot stay in contact with the two surfaces through the entire length of the edge. The solution here is to try a smaller radius fillet or a different style of fillet.
- **Coupling:** Indicates that the underlying surfaces and faces cannot be trimmed to complete a closure of the volume. A situation where a fillet is not limited is shown in Figure 6–14.

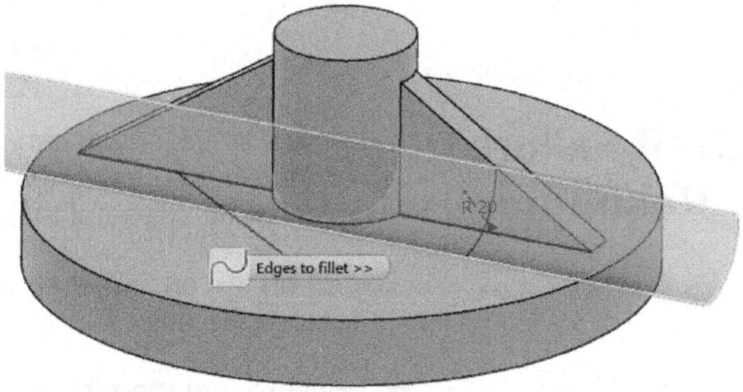

Figure 6–14

The Update Error dialog box opens as shown in Figure 6–15.

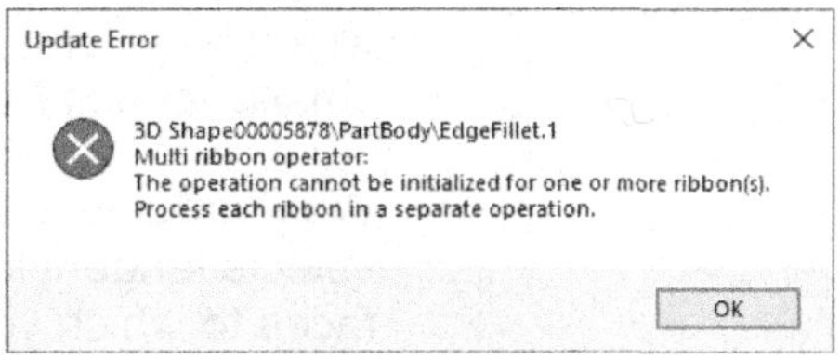

Figure 6–15

Possible solutions:

- Fillet the part in a different order as shown in Figure 6–16.

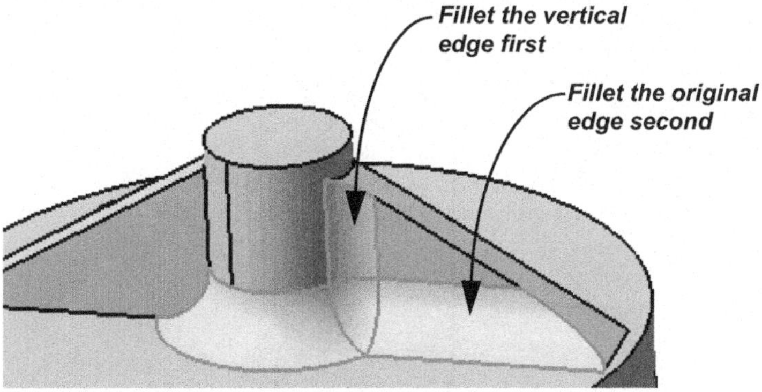

Figure 6–16

- Reduce the fillet radius as shown in Figure 6–17.

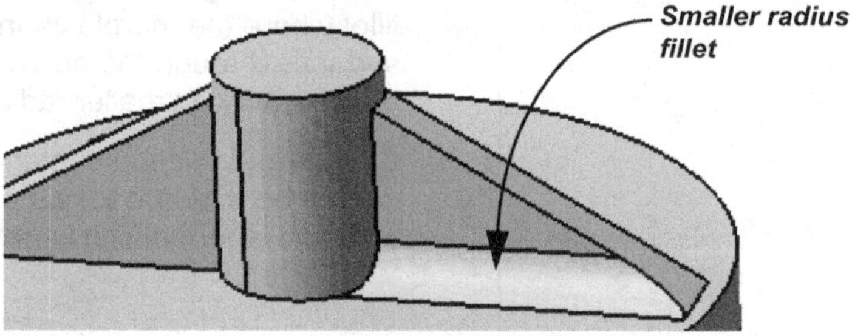

Figure 6–17

Draft Failure Resolution

When a draft fails, you can use a variety of available methods to investigate and resolve the failure. Check the error message to determine the cause of the problem.

Based on the error message, try one of the following techniques to resolve the error:

- Ensure that the model is of good quality by inspecting it for short edges and very small surfaces that might cause unnecessary complications.
- Reduce the angle of the Draft feature. If the Draft feature fails with a large angular value, try to create the draft with a smaller angular value.
- When adding a draft to a model, the system automatically selects tangent faces. Ensure that you have only selected the faces to which you want to add a draft.
- Extract Surface features of a failed draft and use Surface features and Surface operations to create the geometry (use this method as a last resort).

Practice 6a Advanced Fillet Creation

Practice Objectives

- Use Limiting Elements.
- Use Circle Fillet with Spine.
- Specify the edge(s) to keep.

In this practice, you will create a series of fillets on an existing part. Throughout this practice, be aware of the order in which the fillets are created, and also the type of fillet and fillet options that are used. The completed model displays as shown in Figure 6–18.

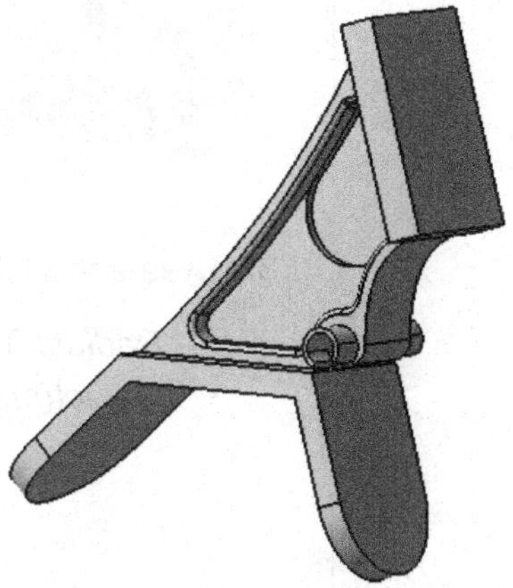

Figure 6–18

Task 1 - Open the part.

1. Import and open **Support.3dxml**. When importing, type your initials followed by the dash symbol into the *Duplication string* field (e.g., **IA-**). The model displays as shown in Figure 6–19.

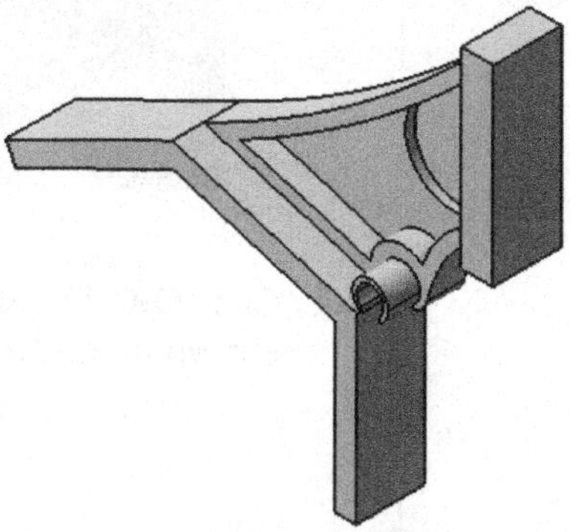

Figure 6–19

2. Create the following Edge Fillet:
   - *Radius:* **3**
   - *Object(s) to fillet:* **5 Edges** (as shown in Figure 6–20)

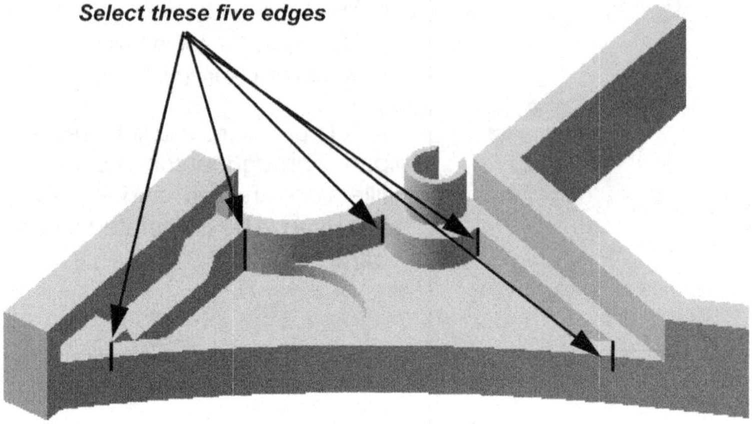

Figure 6–20

3. Create the following Edge Fillet:
   - *Radius:* 3
   - *Object(s) to fillet:* **1 Edge** (as shown in Figure 6–21)

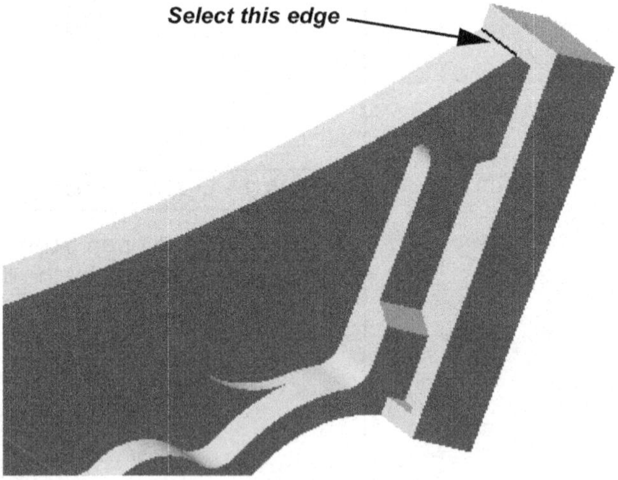

Figure 6–21

4. Click **OK**. The fillet fails due to **Impossible relimitation** as shown in the Update Error dialog box in Figure 6–22.

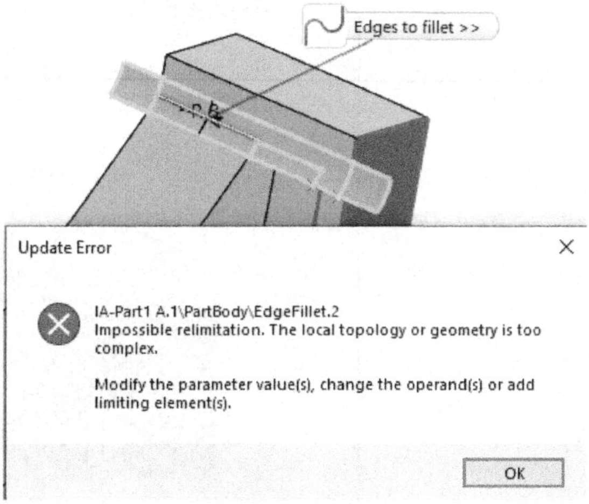

Figure 6–22

5. Click **OK**.

6. In the Edge Fillet dialog box, click **Options**, if required, to expand it, and make the following change:

   - *Limiting elements:* Select the planar face shown in Figure 6–23.

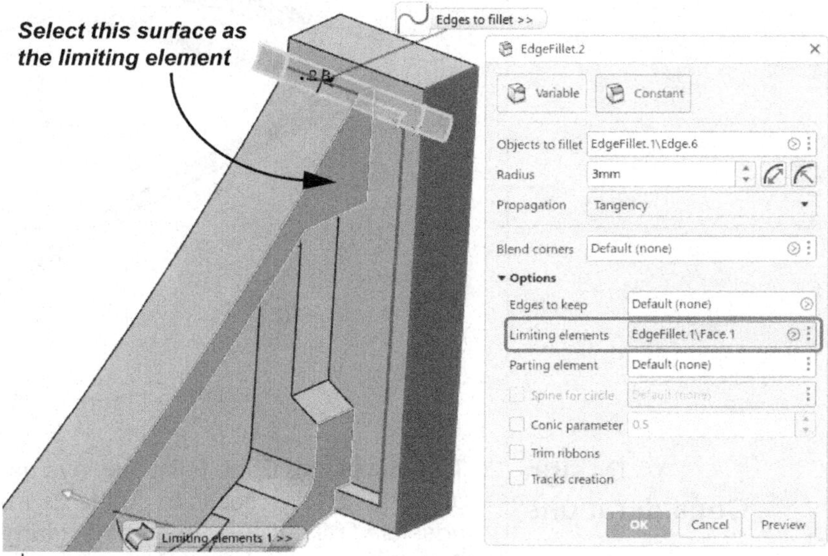

Figure 6–23

7. Click **OK**. The limited Edge Fillet displays as shown in Figure 6–24.

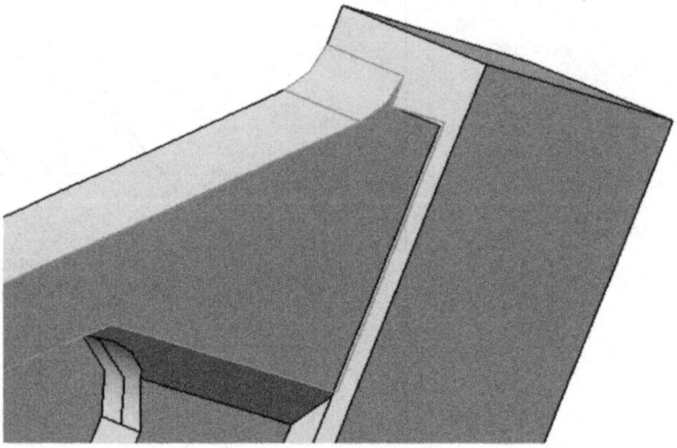

Figure 6–24

8. Create the following Edge Fillet:
   - *Radius:* **1**
   - *Object(s) to fillet:* **7 Edges** (as shown in Figure 6–25)

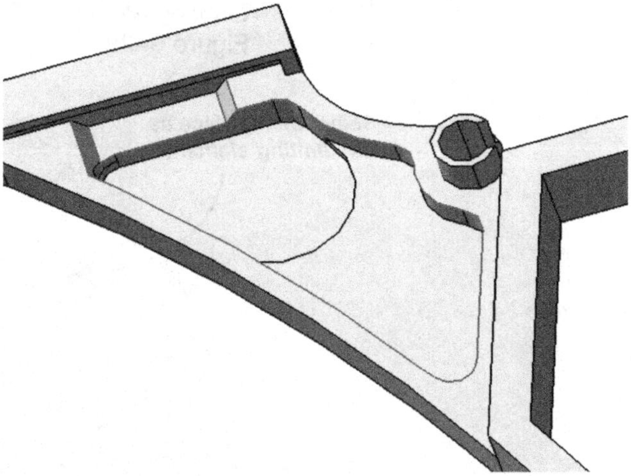

Figure 6–25

Design Considerations

The completed Edge Fillet displays as shown in Figure 6–26. A good design practice is to create as many large radius fillets as possible first, followed by the next largest, etc. If you select the **Tangency** option in the *Propagation* field, the system permits efficient edge selection.

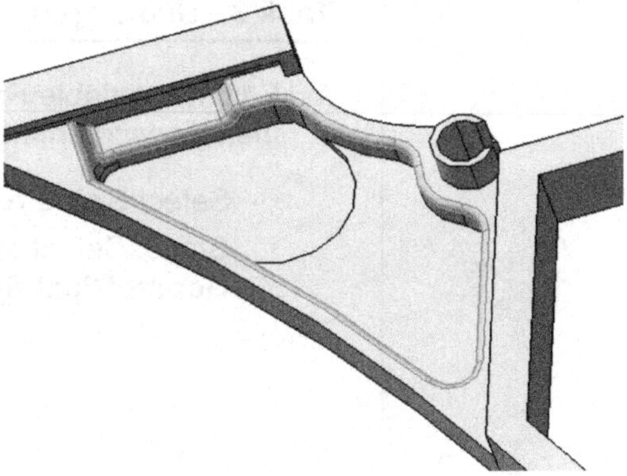

Figure 6–26

Task 2 - Create a Variable Radius Edge Fillet.

1. Click  (Edge Fillet) and click 

. In the Edge Fillet dialog box, apply the following parameters:

   - *Radius:* **1**
   - *Object(s) to fillet:* **1 Edge** (as shown in Figure 6–27)

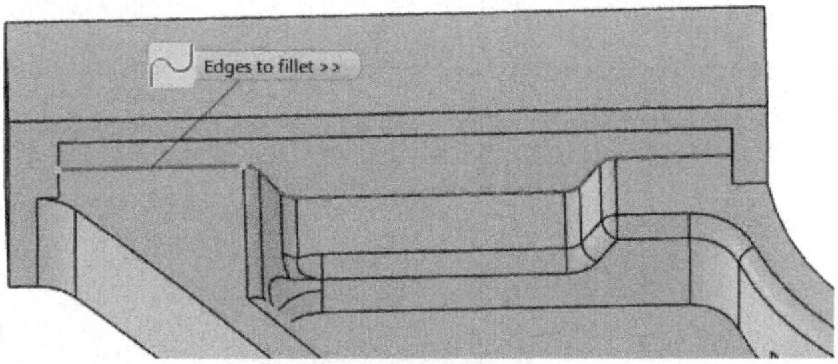

Figure 6–27

The completed Variable Radius Fillet displays as shown in Figure 6–28.

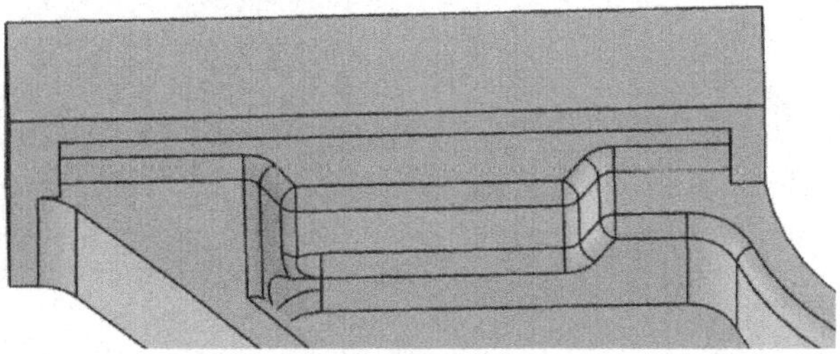

Figure 6–28

Task 3 - Use a spine to control an Edge Fillet.

1. Edit the Variable Radius Fillet that you just created and make the following changes, as shown in Figure 6–29:

    - Select **Spine for circle** option.
    - *Spine:* Select the Line feature named **Spine** under **Geometrical Set.1**

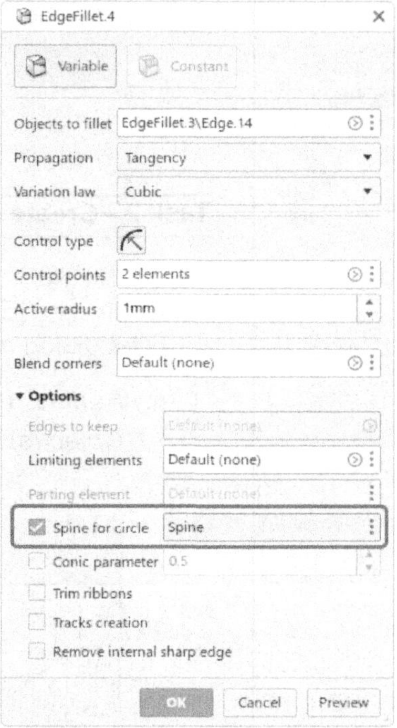

Figure 6–29

The completed fillet displays as shown in Figure 6–30.

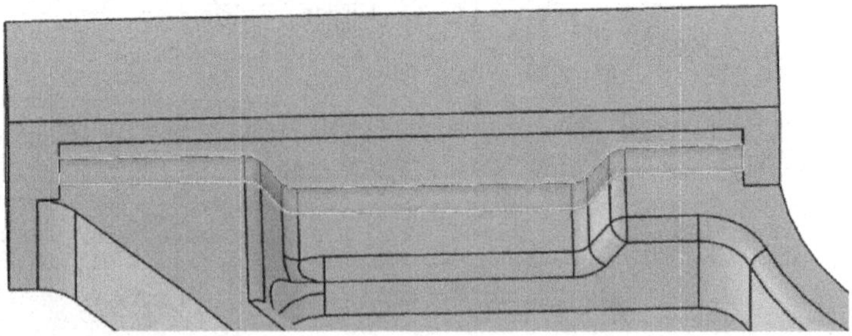

Figure 6–30

2. Show the Spine feature.

Design Considerations

When you use a spine to control the fillet, the fillet remains normal to the selected spine, as shown in Figure 6–31. You cannot use a spine to control a Constant Radius Fillet feature. Note that this fillet was created as a Variable Radius Fillet.

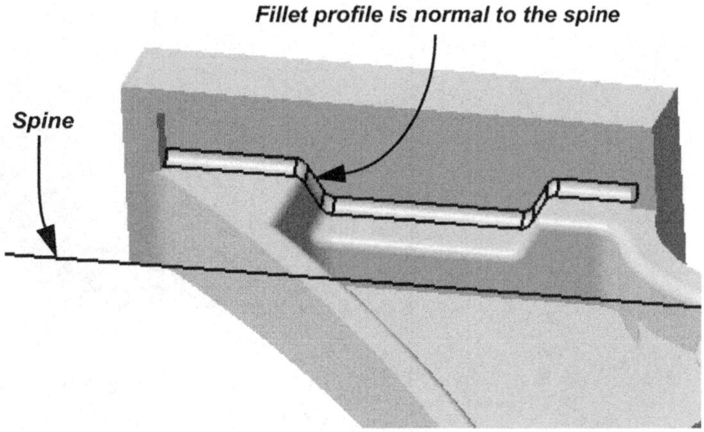

Figure 6–31

3. Hide the Spine.

Task 4 - Use the edge(s) to keep option.

1. Zoom in to the area shown in Figure 6–32.

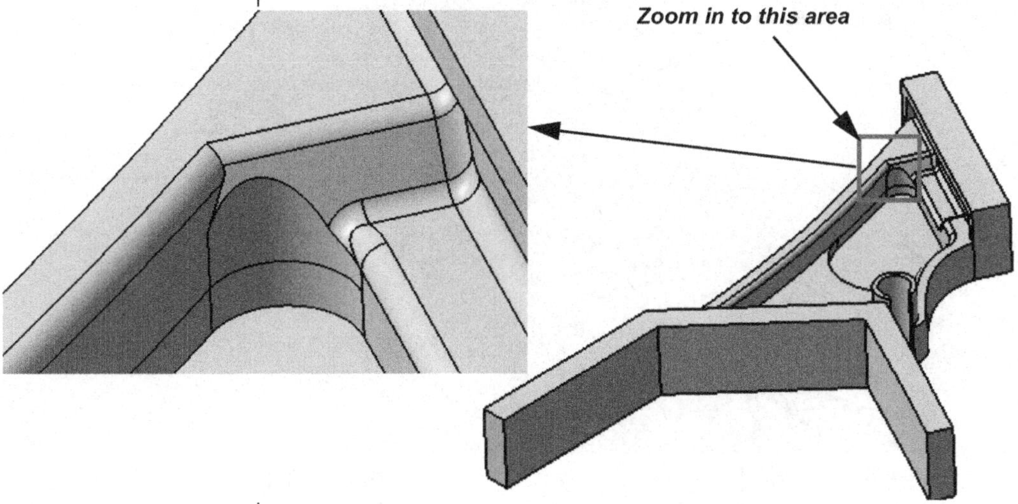

Figure 6–32

2. Edit the fillet shown in Figure 6–33.

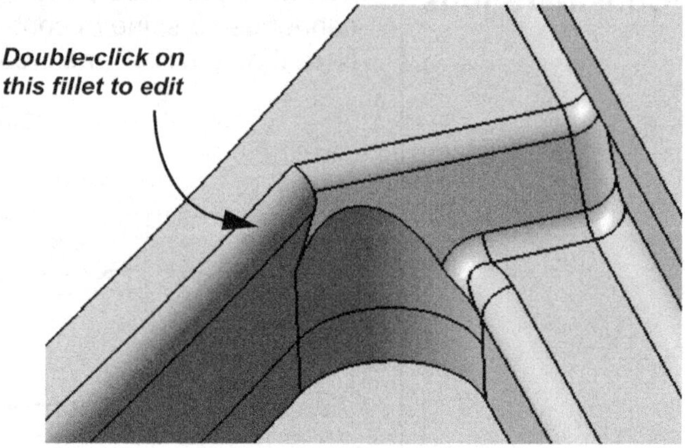

Figure 6–33

3. In the Edge Fillet dialog box, click **Options** if required, to expand it. Click in the *Edges to keep* field, then select the edge shown in Figure 6–34.

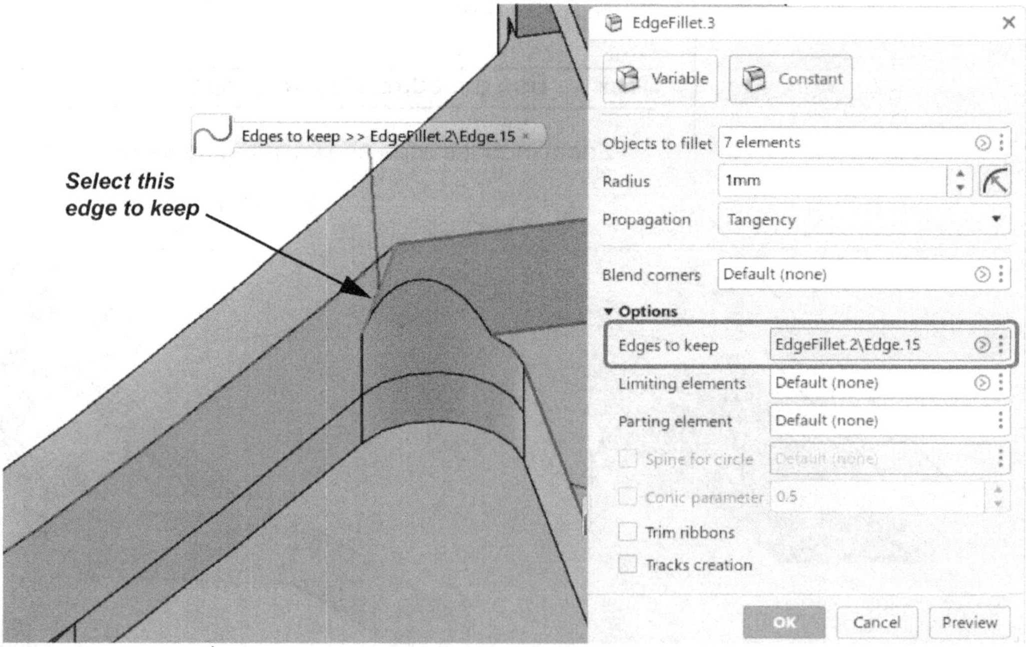

Figure 6–34

4. Click **OK**. Note the difference in the fillet transition, as shown in Figure 6–35.

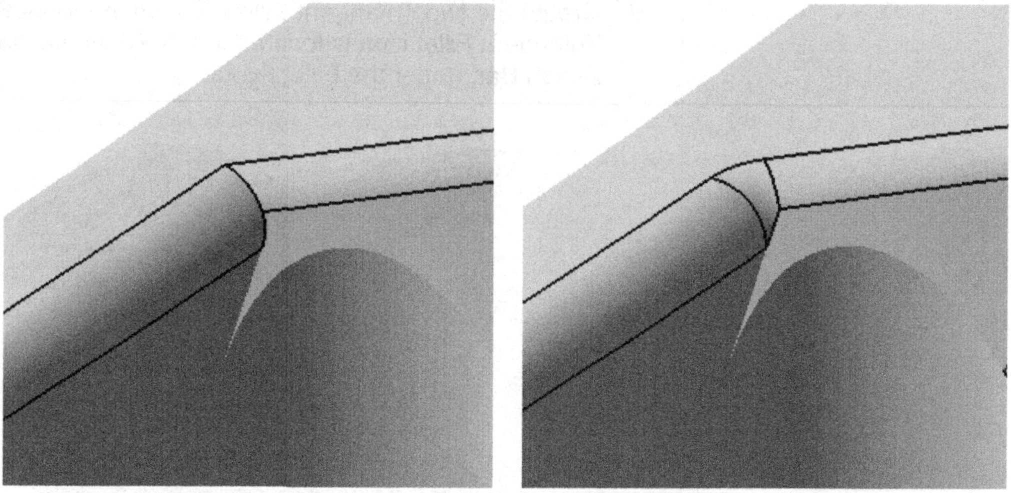

Before Edges to keep selection ***After Edges to keep selection***

Figure 6–35

Task 5 - Mirror the geometry.

1. Click  (Mirror) to mirror the part geometry about the yz plane. The model displays as shown in Figure 6–36.

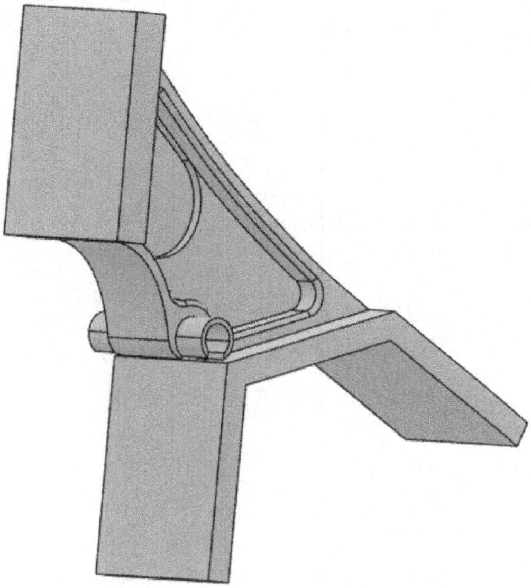

Figure 6–36

2. Create the two Tritangent Fillets shown in Figure 6–37. The Tritangent Fillet icon is located in the Refine section of the Action Bar, under the Fillet flyout.

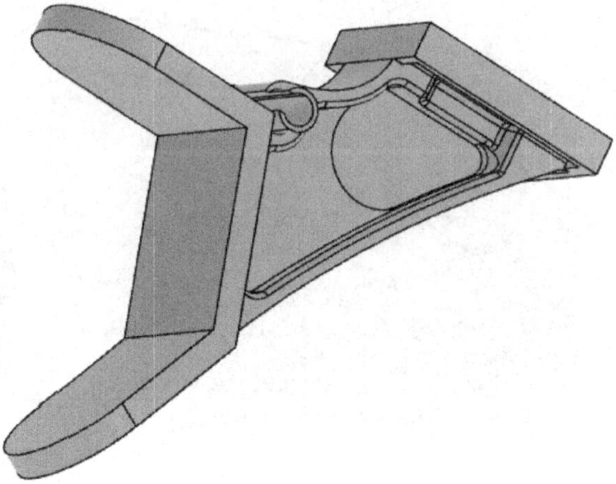

Figure 6–37

3. Save the model and close the window.

Practice 6b Blended Fillets

Practice Objectives

- Use Blend Corner.
- Use Setback distance.
- Trim Ribbons.

In this practice, you will practice creating blended corners. The completed model displays as shown in Figure 6–38.

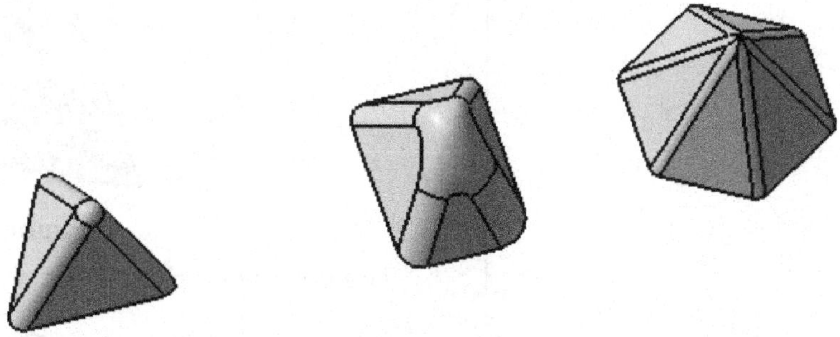

Figure 6–38

Task 1 - Open the part.

1. Import and open **BlendedCorner.3dxml**. When importing, type your initials followed by the dash symbol into the *Duplication string* field (e.g., **IA-**). The model displays as shown in Figure 6–39.

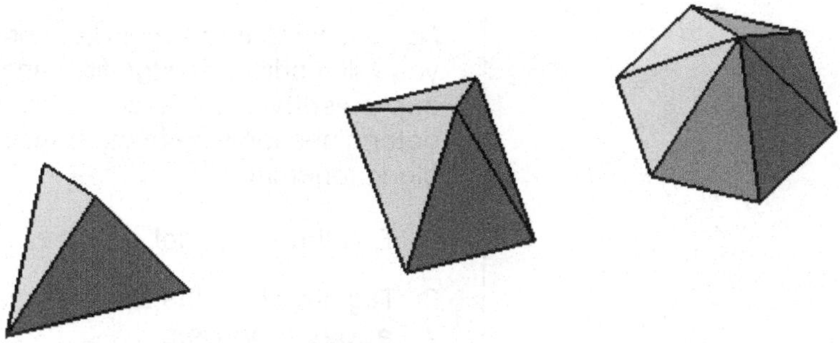

Figure 6–39

Task 2 - Create an Edge Fillet.

1. Click  (Edge Fillet) to open the Edge Fillet dialog box, then click . Create a **2mm** edge fillet along the three edges shown in Figure 6–40.

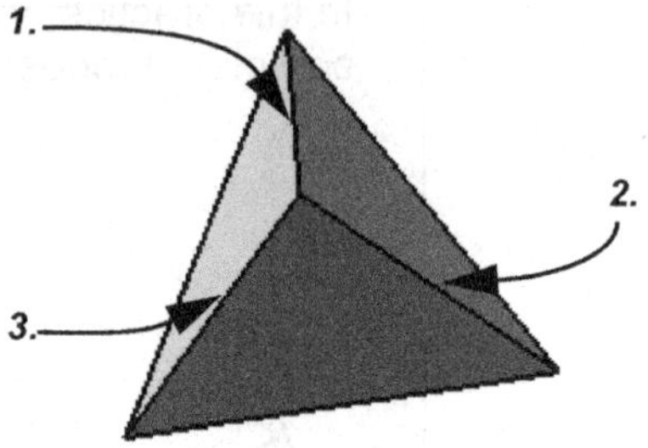

Figure 6–40

The completed Edge Fillet displays as shown in Figure 6–41.

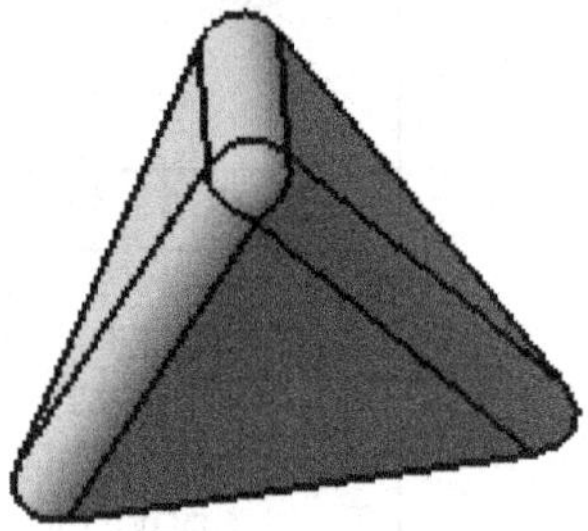

Figure 6–41

Note how the three fillets converge at the top. In the next steps you will modify the edge fillet and use the **Blend Corners** tool to apply a setback distance. A setback distance is a dimension that determines the size of the transition zone where the fillet edges blend together.

2. Edit the edge fillet.
3. Right-click on the *Blend corner(s)* field and select **Create by edges or vertex**.
4. Click **Preview**.

The setback distance defines where the fillet shape begins blending into the other fillet shapes.

5. Note the shape of the fillet with a setback distance of **10mm**.

6. Modify the Setback distance to **6mm** and click **OK**. The model displays as shown in Figure 6–42.

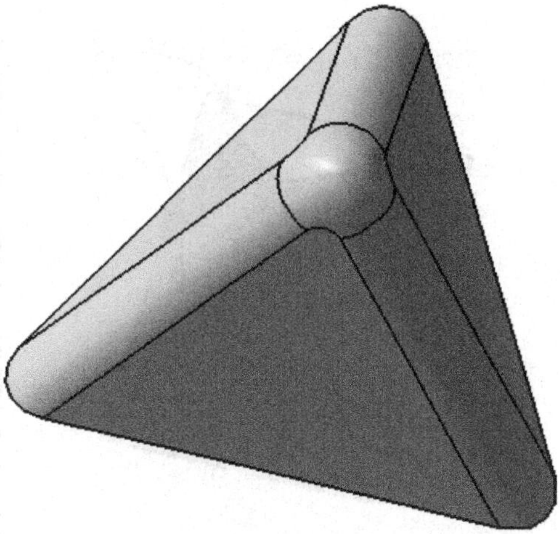

Figure 6–42

Task 3 - Create a Variable Radius Edge Fillet.

1. Click  (Edge Fillet) to open the Edge Fillet Definition dialog box, then click 

.

2. Select the edge labeled **1** in Figure 6–43. In the Edge Fillet dialog box, enter an *Active Radius* of **2mm** and press <Tab> to update the radius values of both vertices for the first edge segment.

3. Select the edge labeled **2** in Figure 6–43. In the Edge Fillet dialog box, enter a *Radius* of **3mm** and press <Tab> to update the radius values of both vertices for the second edge segment.

4. Select the edge labeled **3** in Figure 6–43. In the Variable Radius Fillet Definition dialog box, enter an *Active Radius* of **3.5mm** and press <Tab> to update the radius values of both vertices for the third edge segment.

5. Select the edge labeled 4 in Figure 6–43. In the Edge Fillet dialog box, enter a radius of **5.5mm** and press <Tab> to update the radius values of both vertices for the fourth edge segment.

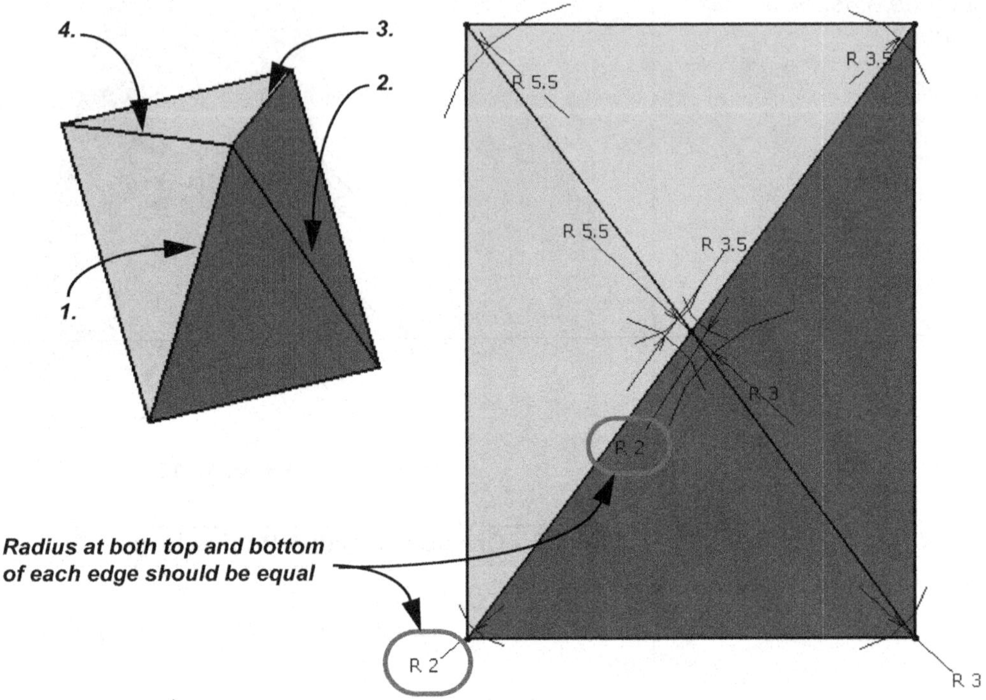

Figure 6–43

6. Click **OK**. The model displays as shown in Figure 6–44.

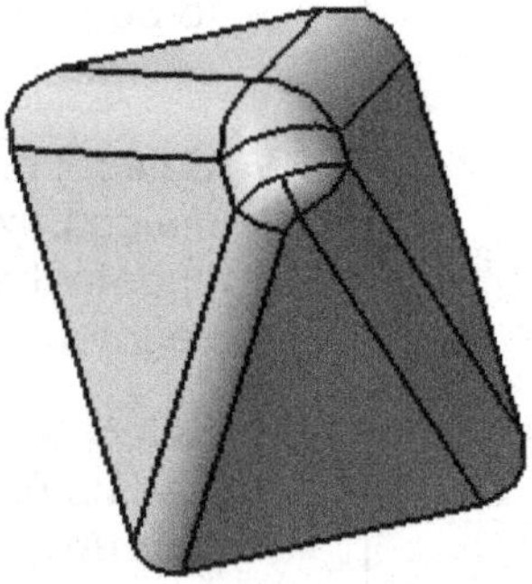

Figure 6–44

7. Edit the Variable Radius Fillet.

8. Right-click on the *Blend corner(s)* field and select **Create by edges or vertex**. In the *Active Setback* field, enter **10**.

9. Click **OK**. The model displays as shown in Figure 6–45.

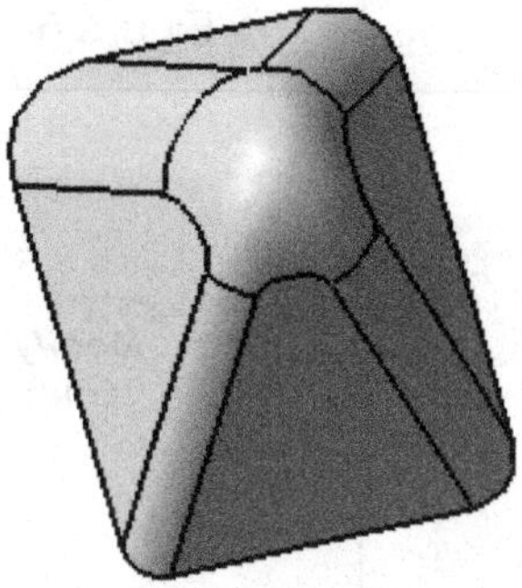

Figure 6–45

10. Rotate the model as shown in Figure 6–46. Note the way the fillets blend into each other at the back of the model. This is not correct and in the next task you will change the setback distance to fix this.

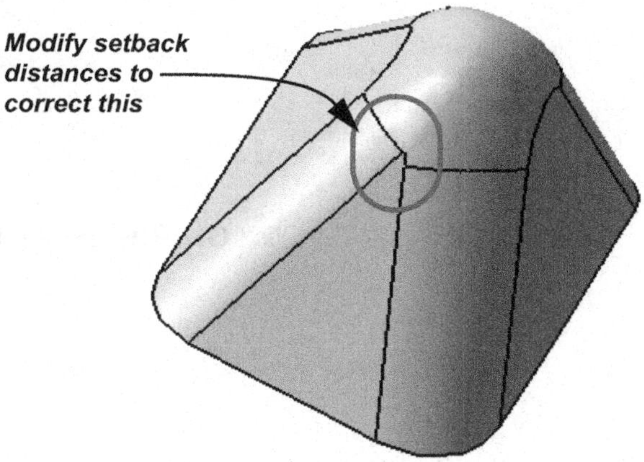

Figure 6–46

Task 4 - Modify the Setback distance.

1. Edit the Variable Radius Fillet.

2. Double-click on the setback distance for the two values surrounding the area that needs to be corrected, as shown in Figure 6–47, and change both values to **14**.

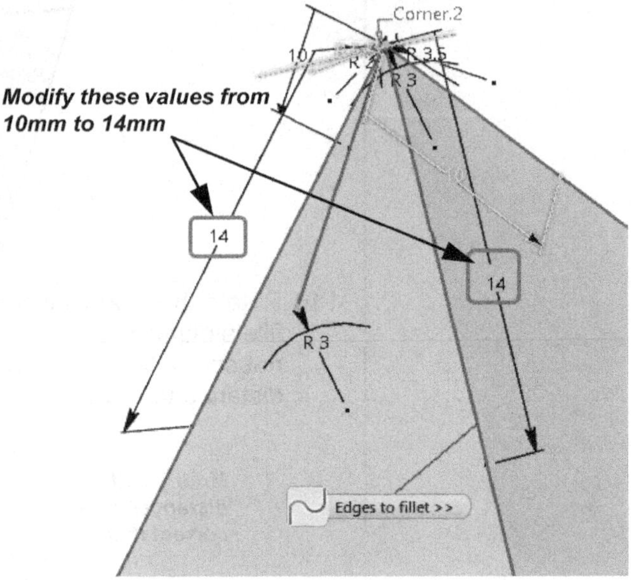

Figure 6–47

3. Click **OK**. The model displays as shown in Figure 6–48.

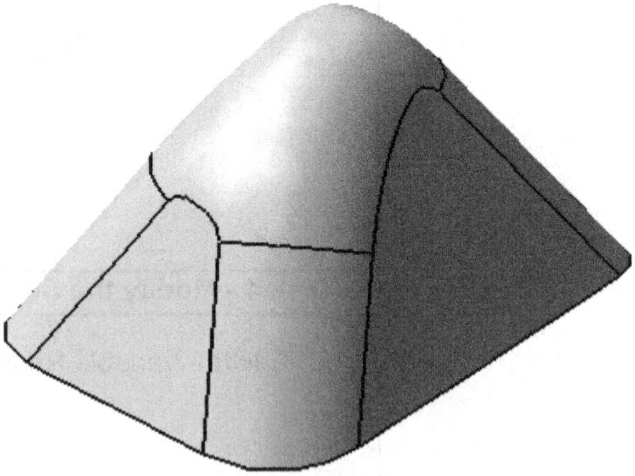

Figure 6–48

Task 5 - Create an Edge Fillet.

1. Click  (Edge Fillet). Create a **2mm** fillet on all 6 edges as shown in Figure 6–49.

2. Click **OK**. The model displays as shown in Figure 6–49.

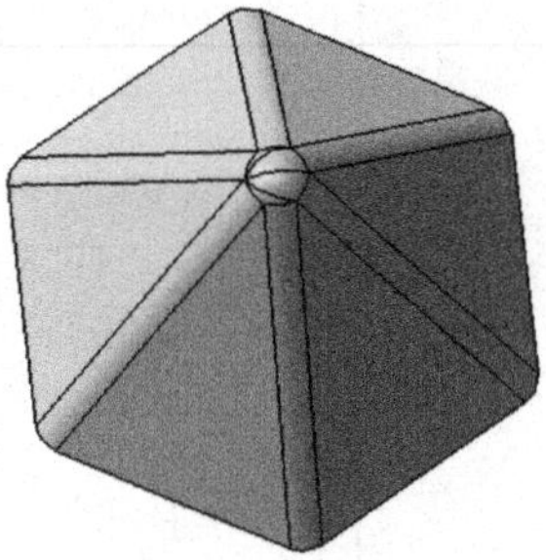

Figure 6–49

Task 6 - Apply the Trim Ribbons option.

In this task, you will modify the fillet created in the last task and apply the **Trim ribbons** option to demonstrate how it will affect the fillet. The **Trim ribbons** option trims overlapping fillets at their intersections.

1. Edit the Edge Fillet created in the last task.

2. If necessary, click **Options** to expand the Edge Fillet dialog box. Select the **Trim ribbons** option as shown in Figure 6–50.

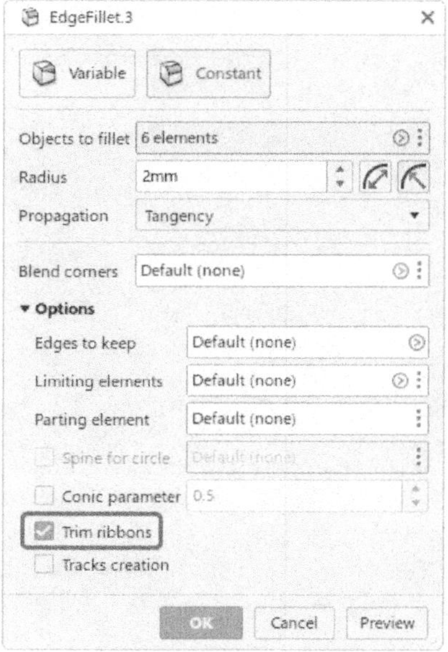

Figure 6–50

3. Click **OK**. The model displays as shown in Figure 6–51.

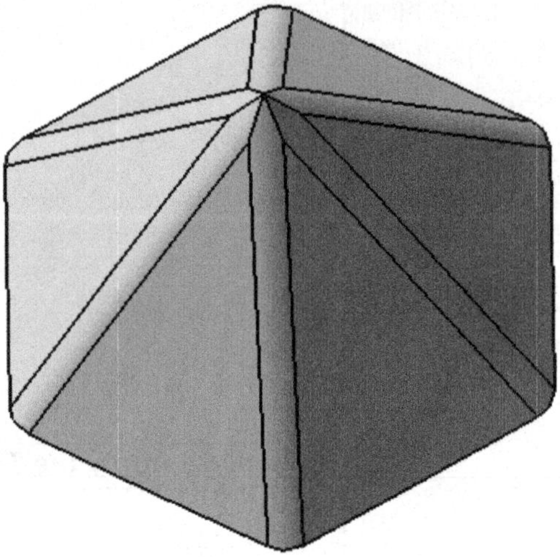

Figure 6–51

4. Save and close the model.

Practice 6c

Advanced Fillet and Draft

Practice Objectives

- Create a Fillet with a hold curve and spine.
- Create a Reflect Line Draft with a parting element.

In this practice, you will add Draft and Fillet to the plastic injection molded front cover for a small speaker. You will use advanced Fillet and Draft options to create the final geometry of the part, as shown in Figure 6–52.

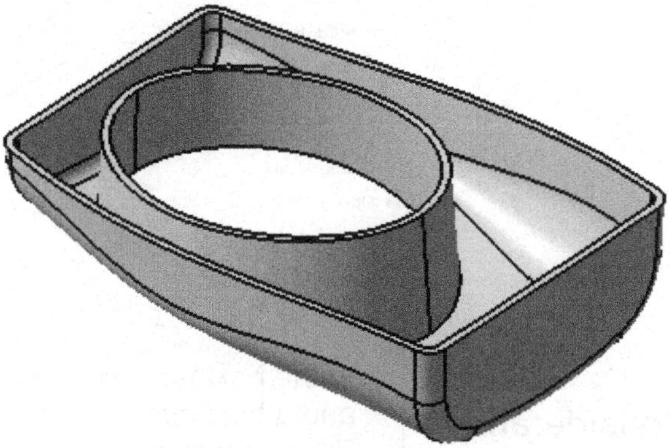

Figure 6–52

Task 1 - Open the part.

1. Import and open **SpeakerCover.3dxml**. When importing, type your initials followed by the dash symbol into the *Duplication string* field (e.g., **IA-**). The model displays as shown in Figure 6–53.

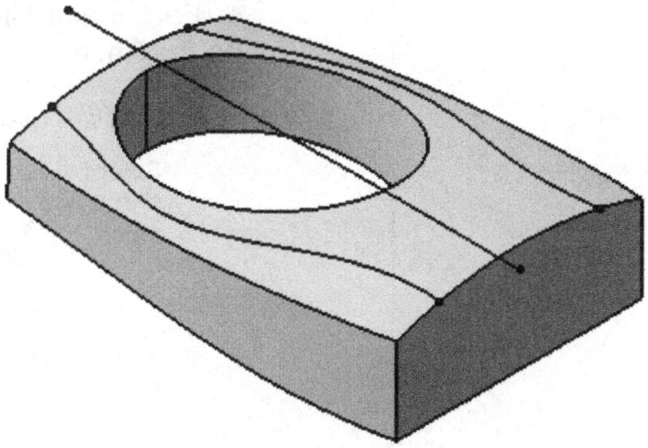

Figure 6–53

Task 2 - Investigate the fillet control curves.

1. In the specification tree, locate the **FilletControlCurves** geometrical set.
2. Hover the cursor over **Line.1**, **HoldCurve1**, and **HoldCurve2** to highlight them on the model, as shown in Figure 6–54.

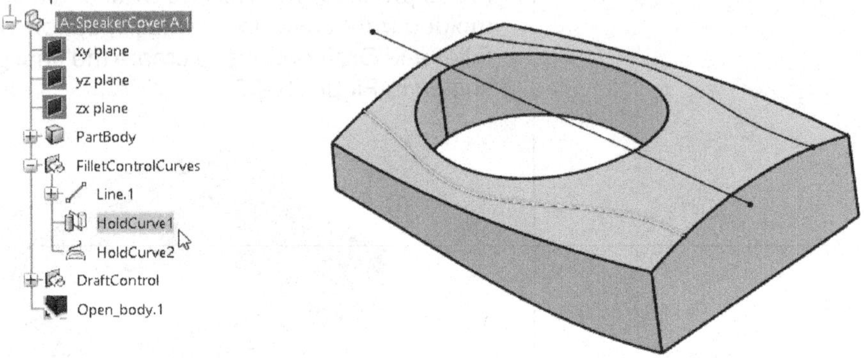

Figure 6–54

Design Considerations

In the next task, you will create a Face-Face Fillet using a spine and a hold curve. A hold curve controls the tangent line of the Fillet. In this case, the hold curve is created to control the formation of the Fillet around the Pocket. The Line will be used as a spine for the Fillet. Note that the profile of the Fillet will stay normal to the spine.

Task 3 - Create a fillet with spine and hold curve.

1. In the Refine section of the Action Bar, Fillet flyout, click  (Face-Face Fillet). In the Face-Face Fillet dialog box, define the Face-Face Fillet as follows:
   - *Faces to fillet:* Select the two faces shown in Figure 6–55

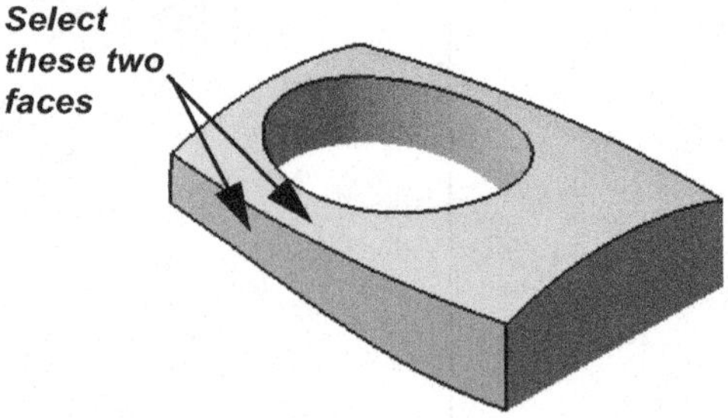

Figure 6–55

2. Click **Options** and define the following (as shown in Figure 6–56).
   - *Hold curve:* **HoldCurve1**
   - *Spine:* **Line.1**

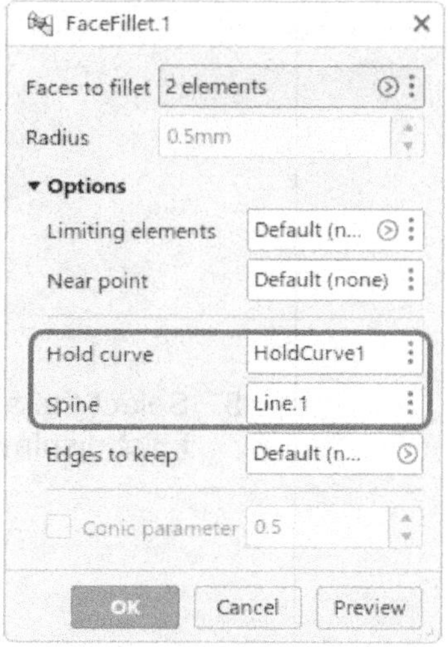

Figure 6–56

3. Click **OK**. The Face-Face Fillet using hold curve and spine displays as shown in Figure 6–57.

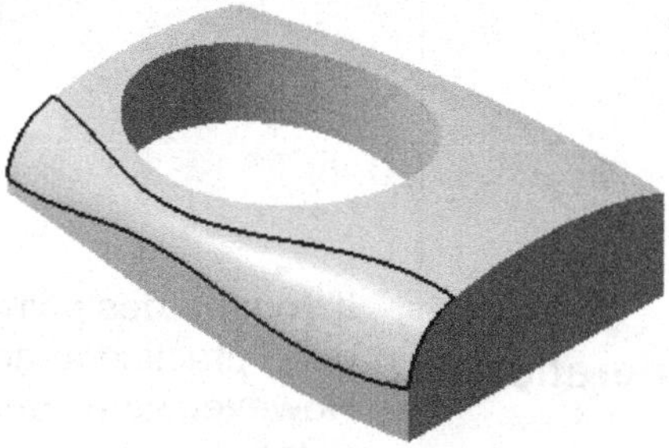

Figure 6–57

4. Create a second Face-Face Fillet by selecting the two faces shown in Figure 6–58.

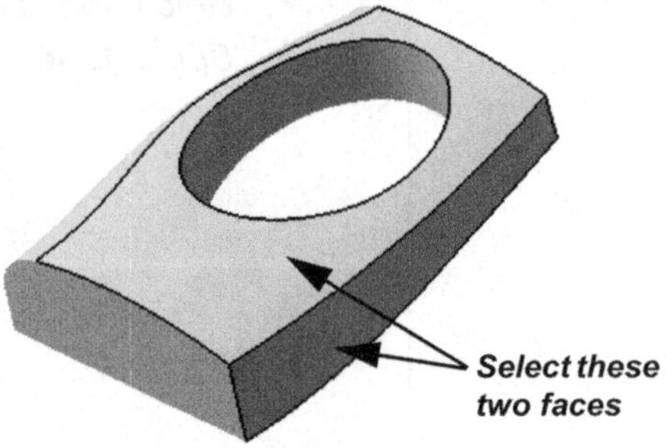

Figure 6–58

5. Select the appropriate hold curve and spine. The completed Fillet displays as shown in Figure 6–59.

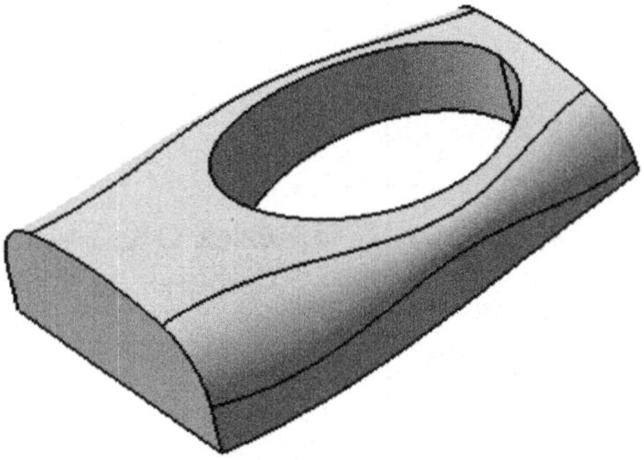

Figure 6–59

Design Considerations

If you are designing a part that requires draft, it is considered good practice to add draft to the model before creating fillets. However, some design scenarios (such as working with imported data) require you to add draft to a model in which some fillet geometry exists. The **Reflect Line Draft** option can be used in this case.

Task 4 - Create reflect line draft.

1. In the Refine section of the Action Bar, Draft flyout, click  (Advanced Draft). In the Draft Definition (Advanced) dialog box, click  (Draft Reflect Line (1st Side)), as shown in Figure 6–60.

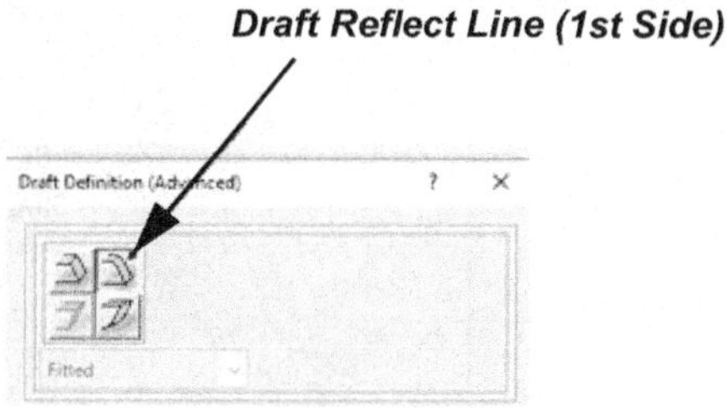

Figure 6–60

2. Make the following selections:
   - *Angle:* **3deg**
   - *Neutral Element Selection:* Select the Face-Face Fillets shown in Figure 6–61

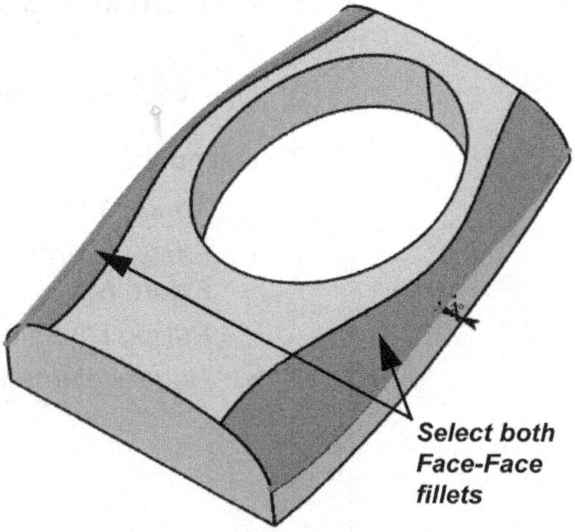

Figure 6–61

3. Click **Preview**. The Reflect Line Draft preview displays as shown in Figure 6–62.

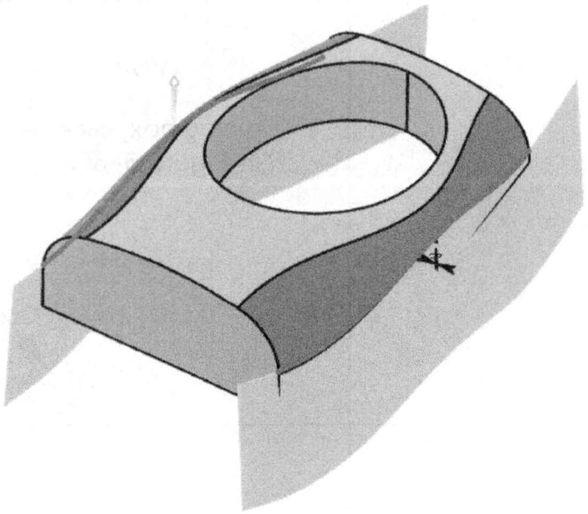

Figure 6–62

4. Click **OK** to complete the feature.

Task 5 - Create Draft that uses a parting element.

1. In the **DraftControl** geometrical set, show **PartingElement**.
2. Use  (Draft Angle) to create a standard Draft.
3. Define the Draft with the following parameters:
   - *Angle:* **3deg**
   - *Faces to draft:* Select the three faces shown in Figure 6–63
   - *Pulling Direction:* **xy plane**
   - *Neutral elements selection:* **PartingElement**

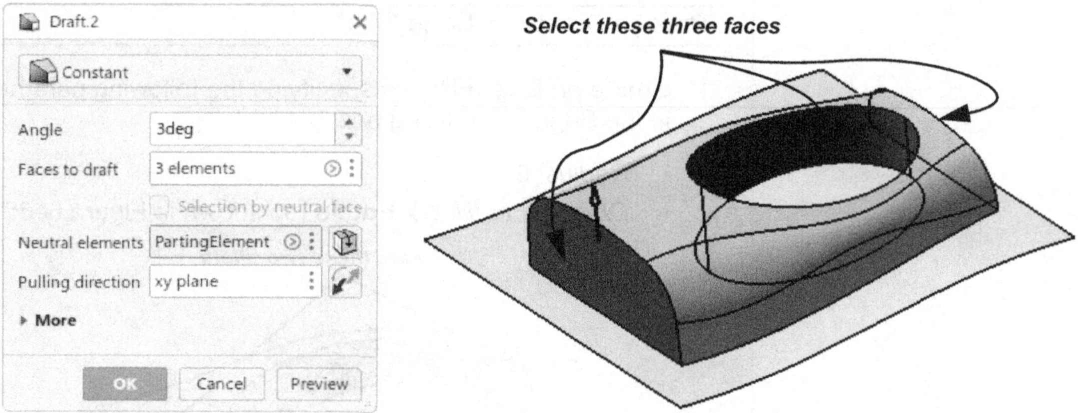

Figure 6–63

4. Click **OK**.
5. In the specification tree, hide the **PartingElement**.
6. Display the model and note the effect of adding draft to the geometry, as shown in Figure 6–64.

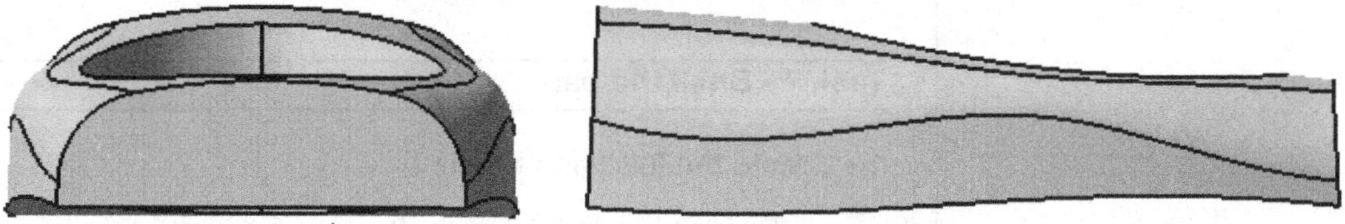

Figure 6–64

Task 6 - Create an Edge Fillet.

1. Create an Edge Fillet by specifying the following parameters in the Edge Fillet dialog box:

   - *Radius:* **5**
   - *Object(s) to fillet:* **2 Edges** (as shown in Figure 6–65)

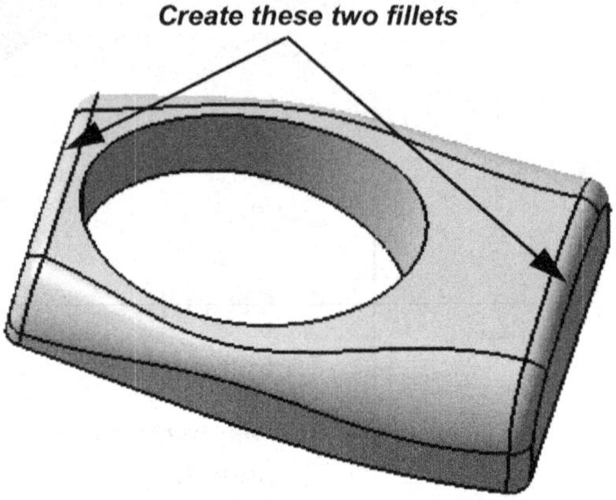

Figure 6–65

Task 7 - Shell the part.

1. Create the following Shell:

   - *Default inside thickness:* **2**
   - *Faces to remove:* **1 Face** (select the face shown in Figure 6–66)

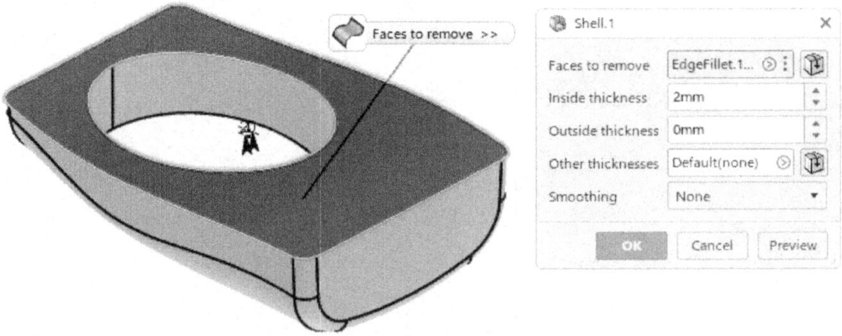

Figure 6–66

The shelled part displays as shown in Figure 6–67.

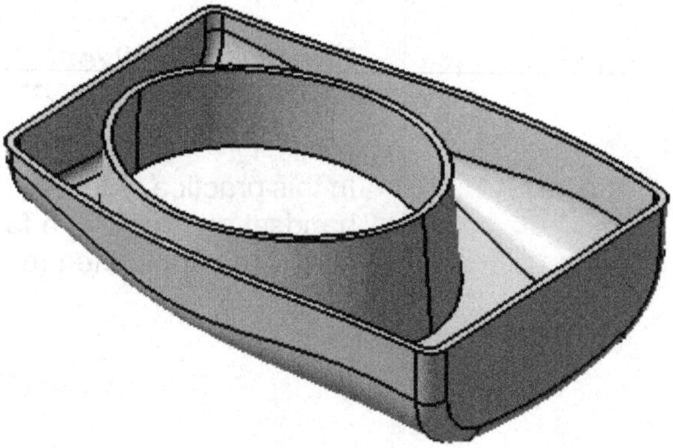

Figure 6–67

Design Considerations

Use **Reflect Line Draft** when the Fillet geometry is created first. Otherwise, you should add draft to the model as required and create Fillets as late in the design cycle as possible, beginning with the largest radius Fillets first. Typically, a model is shelled after Fillet creation.

2. Hide the **FilletControlCurves** geometrical set.
3. Click  (Isometric View) to return to the isometric view, as shown in Figure 6–68.

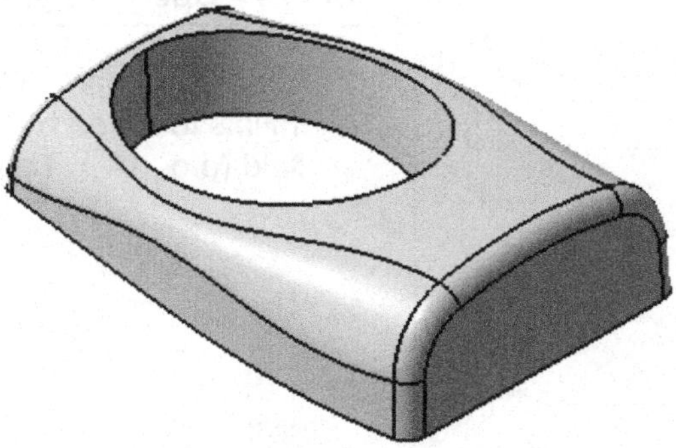

Figure 6–68

4. Save the model and close the file.

Practice 6d Advanced Draft Creation

Practice Objective

- Use the Standard Draft 1st and 2nd side options.

In this practice, you will create an advanced Draft on a telephone handset and resolve a failure during the creation of another Draft. The completed model displays as shown in Figure 6–69.

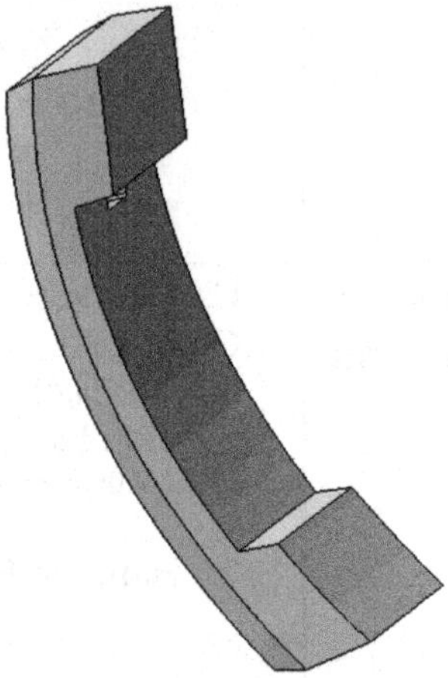

Figure 6–69

Task 1 - Open the part.

1. Import and open **Phone.3dxml**. When importing, type your initials followed by the dash symbol into the *Duplication string* field (e.g., **IA-**). The model displays as shown in Figure 6–70.

Figure 6–70

Task 2 - Create a Standard Draft on both sides.

1. In the Refine section of the Action Bar, in the Drafts flyout, click  (Advanced Draft). The Draft Definition (Advanced) dialog box opens as shown in Figure 6–71.

Figure 6–71

2. Create a two-sided Draft feature by clicking  (Standard Draft (1st Side)) and  (Standard Draft (2nd Side)).
3. Enter a *Draft angle* of **5**.

4. Select the *Face(s) to draft* field and select the four surfaces shown in Figure 6–72 (including the hidden one).

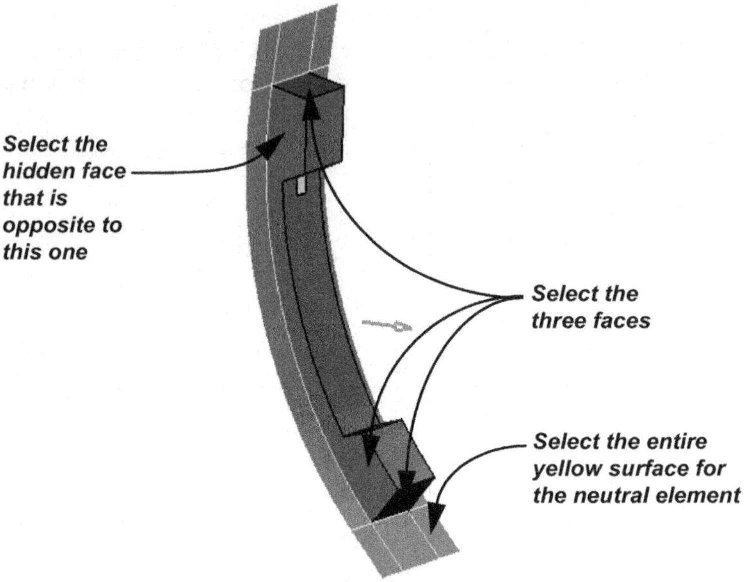

Figure 6–72

5. Select the *Neutral Element Selection* field and select **Join.5** in **Geometrical Set.1**, which is the entire yellow surface for the neutral element.
6. Click on the *Pulling Direction Selection* field and select **xy plane**.
7. Select the *Parting Element* tab and select the *Selection* field.
8. Select the **Join.5** surface that was used for the neutral element.
9. Select the *2nd Side* tab.
10. For the *draft angle*, enter **10**.
11. Select the *Neutral Element Selection* field and select **Join.5** for the neutral element.

12. Click **OK** to complete the feature. The part displays as shown in Figure 6–73.

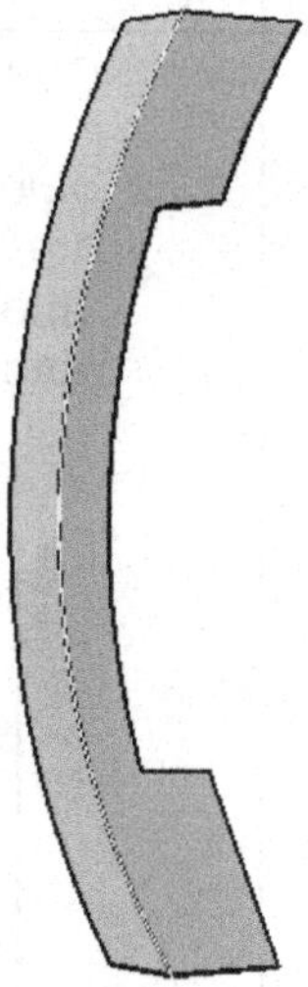

Figure 6–73

13. Hide the yellow surface used as the neutral plane in draft.

Task 3 - Add fillets.

1. Click  (Edge Fillet). The Edge Fillet dialog box opens.
2. Select the four edges shown in Figure 6–74.

Figure 6–74

3. Enter a *Radius* of **1mm**.
4. Complete the feature.

Task 4 - Draft additional surfaces and resolve the Draft failure.

1. Click  (Draft). The Draft dialog box opens.
2. Select one of the inside faces of the Pocket as the *Faces to draft*. Because the vertical surfaces are tangent to each other, all of the inside vertical surfaces of the Pocket are automatically selected, as shown in Figure 6–75.

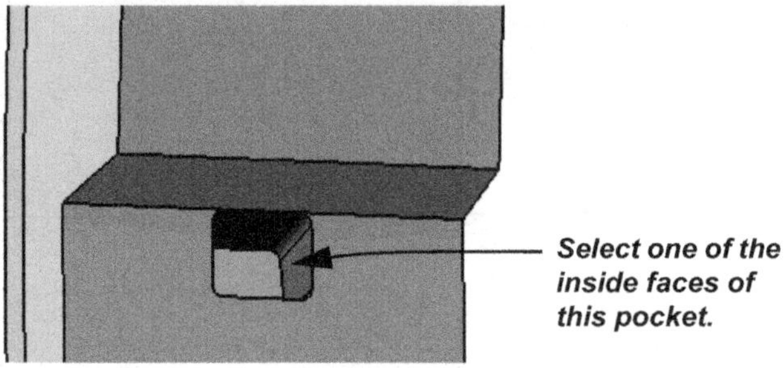

Figure 6–75

3. For the *Draft angle*, enter **7**.
4. For the *Neutral Element*, select **Plane.5**.
5. Ensure that the pulling direction displays as shown in Figure 6–76. If not, click the pulling direction arrow to reverse the direction.

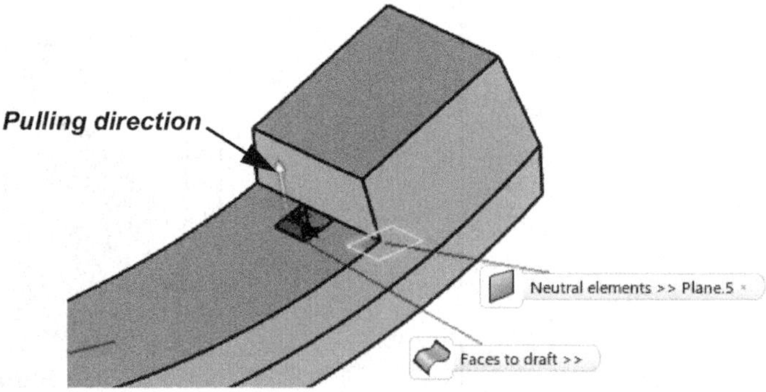

Figure 6–76

6. Preview the Draft feature. The model displays as shown in Figure 6–77. Note that the Draft edges overlap.

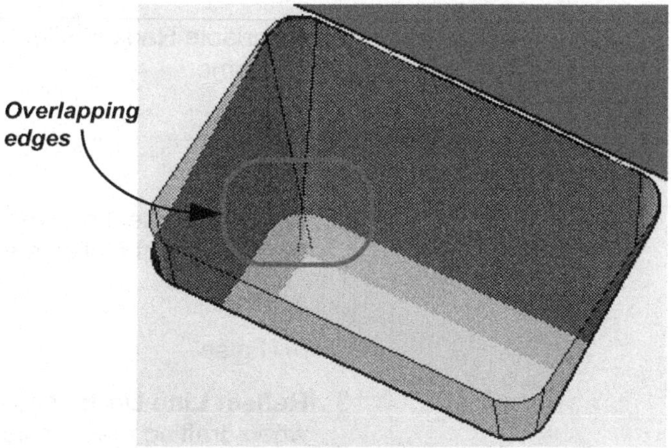

Figure 6–77

7. Click **OK**. An Update Error message opens, indicating that there are twisted faces during the feature creation.
8. Close the Update Error dialog box. The Feature Definition Error dialog box opens, prompting you to deactivate the Draft and extract the geometry, as shown in Figure 6–78.

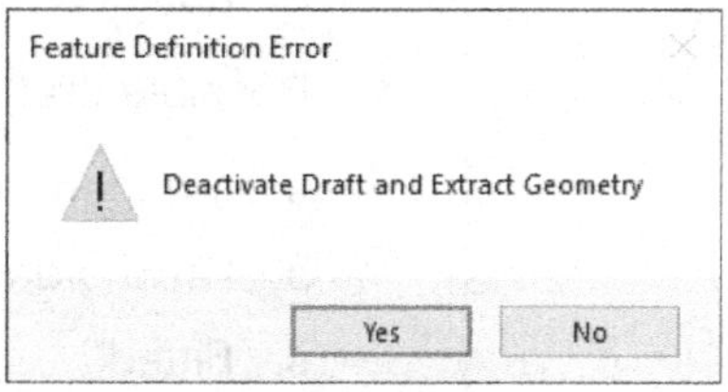

Figure 6–78

9. Click **No**.
10. Modify the *Draft angle* to **5** and complete the feature.
11. Save the model and close the window.

Chapter Review Questions

1. A Variable Radius Fillet requires the start and end radii to be the same.

    a. True

    b. False

2. When you select a Spine curve with a Variable Radius Fillet, the radius of the fillet is always perpendicular to the spine.

    a. True

    b. False

3. **Reflect Line Draft** uses the reflect lines as neutral lines when drafting the selected faces.

    a. True

    b. False

4. **Advanced Draft** allows for different draft angles on either side of the parting line.

    a. True

    b. False

5. Possible draft angle conditions are:

    a. Independent

    b. Driving/driven

    c. Fitted

    d. All of the above.

Answers: 1b, 2a, 3a, 4a, 5d

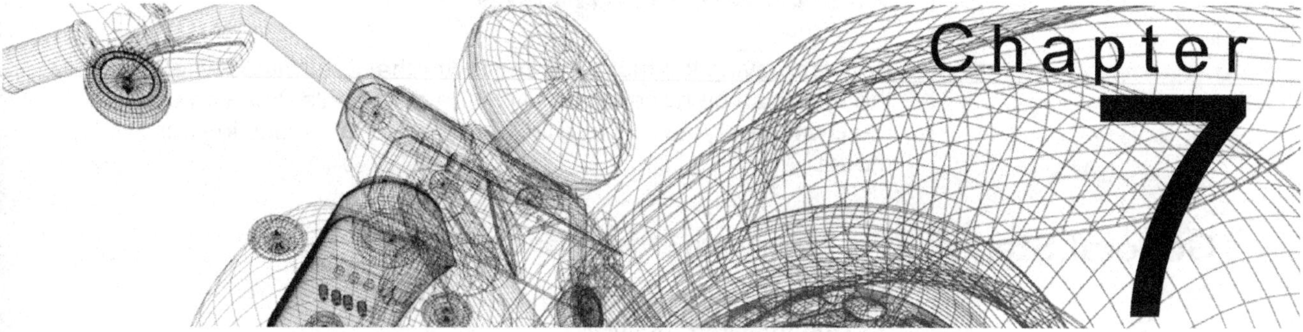

Chapter 7

Analysis Tools

After you complete the modeling, you can run the Analysis tools on the model to verify that the intended design has been achieved.

Learning Objectives in This Chapter

- Learn to use Draft Analysis to check draft angles.
- Create Thread and Tap features.
- Learn to use Thread/Tap Analysis to review threads and taps in your model.
- Understand how to filter the model using the Parameterization Analysis tool.

7.1 Draft Analysis

While removing the mold, the key factor that determines whether the mold can be removed easily is the draft angle. You can use the **Draft Analysis** tool to check all of the draft angles in your model.

General Steps

Use the following general steps to run a Draft analysis:

1. Change the display settings and View mode.
2. Run the Draft Analysis.
3. Specify the mode.
4. Specify the display settings.
5. Specify the direction.
6. Complete the analysis.

Step 1 - Change the display settings and View mode.

The analysis is only displayed in the Shading with Material View mode. To change the View mode to **Shading with Materials**, click (View Modes) and select (Shading with Materials).

Step 2 - Run the Draft Analysis.

Click (Draft Analysis) in the Review section of the Action Bar and select a face on the model.

The color of the model changes to display the analysis results, and the Draft Analysis and Draft Analysis.* dialog boxes open, as shown in Figure 7–1.

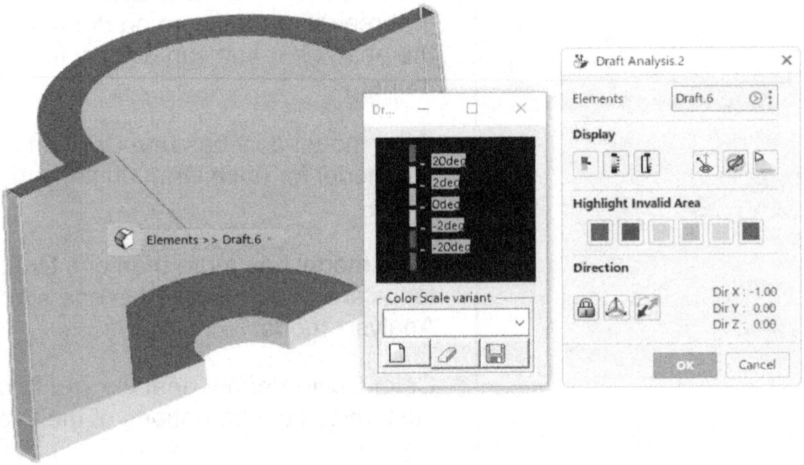

Figure 7–1

Step 3 - Specify the mode.

There are two different types of analysis modes: Quick Analysis mode (indicated by ) and Full Analysis mode (indicated by ), as shown in Figure 7–2.

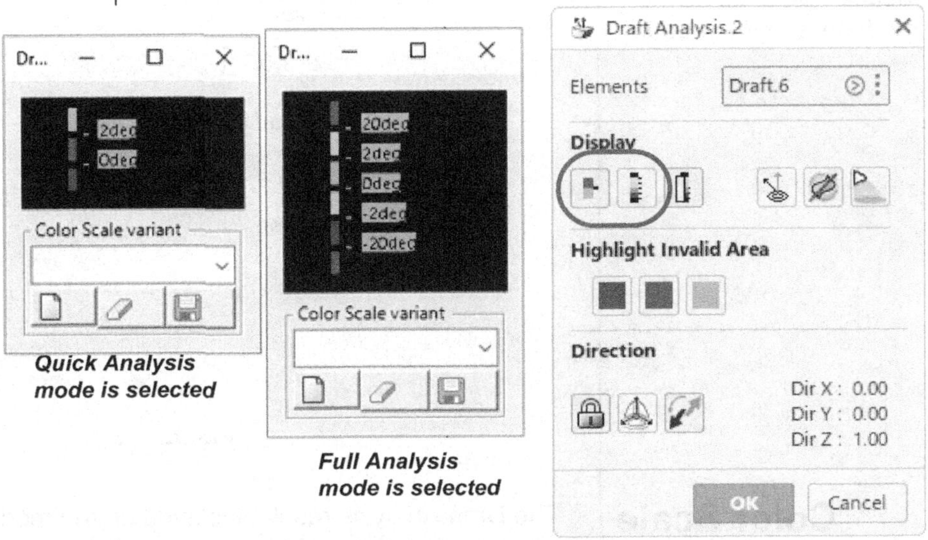

Figure 7–2

In the Quick Analysis mode, the analysis result can display in up to three different colors on the model. In the Full Analysis mode, the analysis result can display in up to six different colors on the model.

If the model only has one Draft angle, or if you want to analyze the model for each Draft angle, you can use the Quick Analysis mode.

If the model has more than one Draft angle, and all of the drafted faces are to be analyzed in one step, you can use the Full Analysis mode.

Color Scale Variant enables you to create, delete, and save customized configurations of the Draft Analysis display.

Step 4 - Specify the display settings.

Use the tools in the display section in the Draft Analysis dialog box to better understand and clarify your results, as shown in Figure 7–3.

 highlights representations on the model.  controls the brightness of the model.

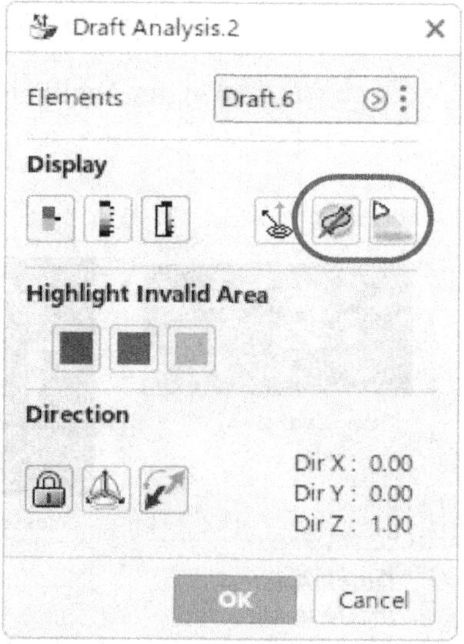

Figure 7–3

Color Scale

The Draft Analysis result displayed on the model depends on which scale values and colors are used in the Draft Analysis.* dialog box.

In the Draft Analysis dialog box, click  to open the Draft Analysis.* dialog box. The color can be changed by double-clicking on it and selecting a different color in the Color dialog box, as shown in Figure 7–4.

Figure 7–4

The default scale values increase linearly. However, it is possible to modify the scale value by double-clicking on it and entering the required value in the Edit dialog box, as shown in Figure 7–5. When the scale value is modified, a green frame displays on the scale value. To use a linear value, right-click on the value and select **Unfreeze**.

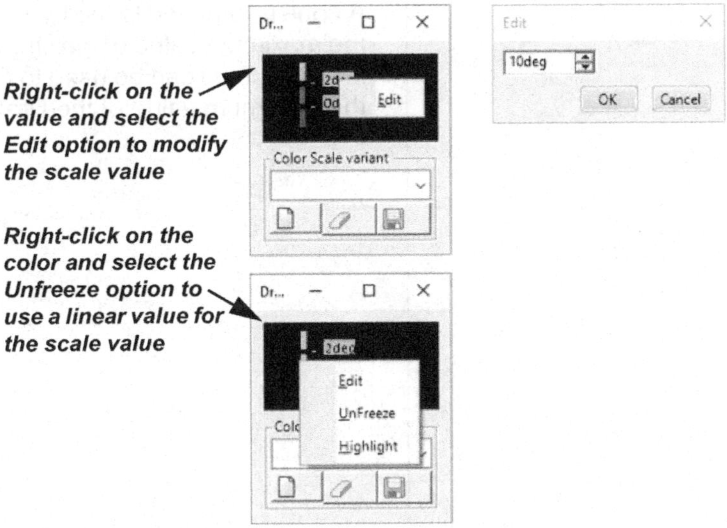

Figure 7–5

On The Fly

If you click  in the Draft Analysis dialog box, the analysis result displays for any location in the model. Three arrows display on the model, as shown in Figure 7–6.

Figure 7–6

The arrows are described as follows:

Type	Description
Red Arrow	Draft direction.
Blue Arrow	Tangent direction.
Green Arrow	Normal direction.

A cone is attached to the Draft direction arrow, which depends on the maximum value of the Draft analysis scale. This cone (shown in Figure 7–7) can be used to compare different Draft angles with the maximum value of the Draft analysis scale.

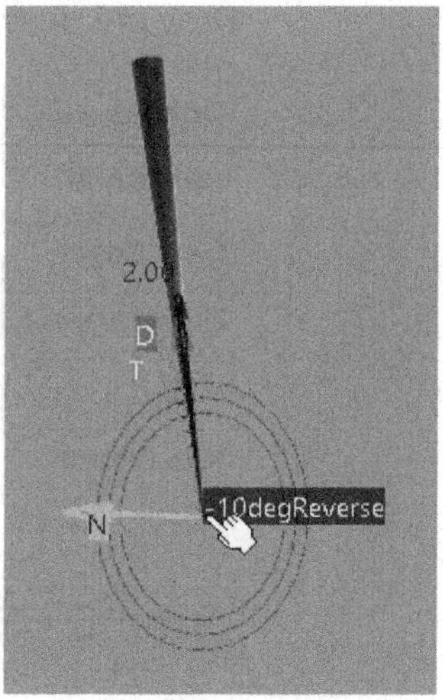

Figure 7–7

If you right-click on the draft direction arrow, the options shown in Figure 7–8 display.

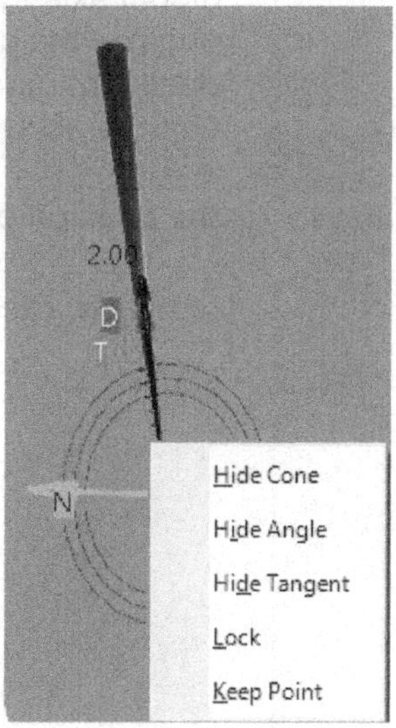

Figure 7–8

They are described as follows:

Options	Description
Hide Cone	Hides the cone.
Hide Angle	Hides the angle.
Hide Tangent	Hides the circles that show the tangent plane.
Lock	Locks the position.
Keep Point	Creates a point for the selected location.

Step 5 - Specify the direction.

In the Draft Analysis dialog box, in the *Direction* area, there are three options that control the reference Draft direction. The Draft analysis results are generated according to the Z-direction of the global axis system. When you click , the robot snaps to the origin of the global axis system. To use a different reference Draft direction, manipulate the robot. The results of the analysis change according to the position of the robot. You can also lock the position of the robot by clicking . To change the draft direction, click , as shown in Figure 7–9.

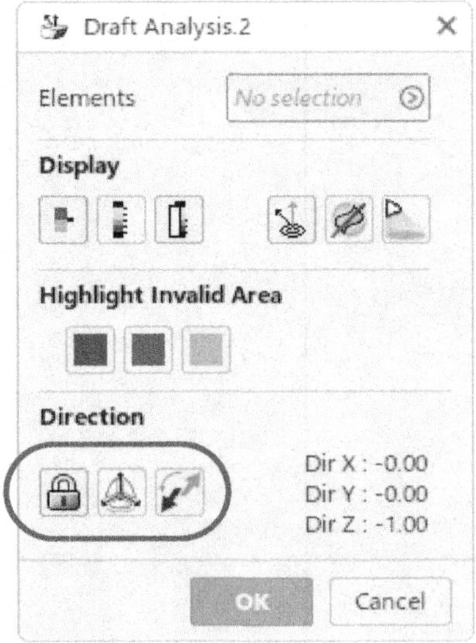

Figure 7–9

Step 6 - Complete the analysis.

To complete the analysis, click **OK**. The analysis result is saved in the specification tree, as shown in Figure 7–10.

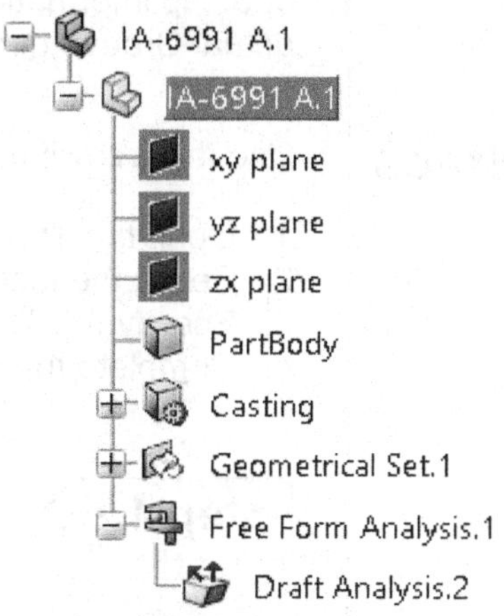

Figure 7–10

Having a smaller 3D accuracy setting enables you to have better visualization while zooming into the model, but it affects the performance of your system. There are two different options: **Proportional** and **Fixed**. Select the **Proportional** option if you are working on an area that is not smaller than the overall model. Select the **Fixed** option if the working surface area is too small when compared to the overall size of the model.

To change the 3D accuracy settings, select **Me>Preferences> Common Preferences>2D 3D View Display>Performance**, as shown in Figure 7–11.

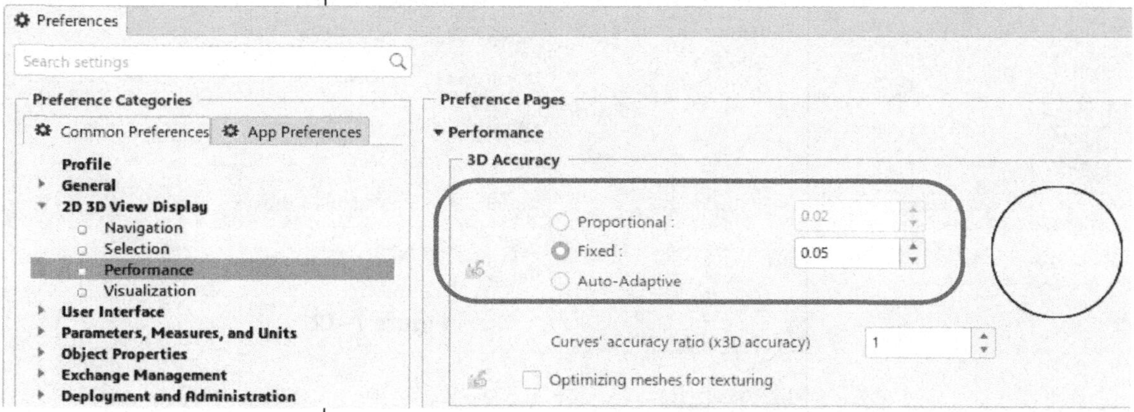

Figure 7–11

7.2 Threads and Taps

You can create Thread and Tap features on cylindrical surfaces. These features are only used to simulate a Helical Groove. They are non-solid features and their purpose is to store the Thread and Tap information, which is then shown on a drawing. The actual Groove geometry is not created.

General Steps

Use the following general steps to create a Thread feature:

1. Open the Thread dialog box.
2. Select the face(s) to be threaded or tapped.
3. Specify the Thread type and depth.
4. Complete the feature.

Step 1 - Open the Thread dialog box.

Click  (Thread/Tap). The Thread dialog box opens as shown in Figure 7–12.

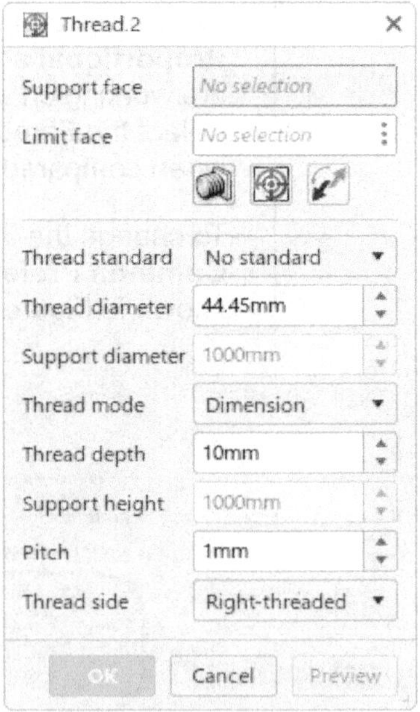

Figure 7–12

Step 2 - Select the face(s) to be threaded or tapped.

Select a support face (cylindrical surface) to place the Threads, and a limit face to define the start of the Threads.

Step 3 - Specify the Thread type and depth.

You can apply any of the standard Threads loaded into 3DEXPERIENCE. Alternatively, you can create a special, non-standard Thread. The depth of the Thread is calculated from the limit face to the specified Thread depth.

Step 4 - Complete the feature.

Click **OK** to complete the feature. The Thread displays in the specification tree. When you select the Thread feature in the specification tree, it is also highlighted on the model, as shown in Figure 7–13.

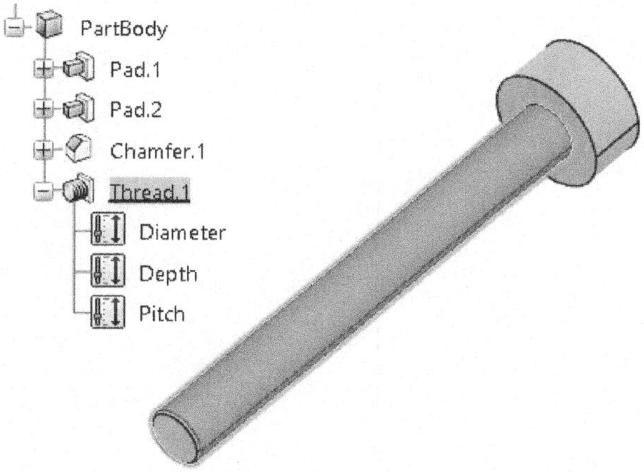

Figure 7–13

7.3 Thread/Tap Analysis

Since Threads and Taps are not displayed as solid geometry, it can sometimes be difficult to keep track of them. You can use the Thread/Tap Analysis to explore the Threads/Taps in your model.

General Steps

Use the following general steps to run a Thread/Tap Analysis:

1. Open the Thread/Tap Analysis dialog box.
2. Run the Thread/Tap Analysis.

Step 1 - Open the Thread/Tap Analysis dialog box.

Click  (Thread/Tap Analysis) in the Review section of the Action Bar. The Thread/Tap Analysis dialog box opens as shown in Figure 7–14. The area at the top of the box reports the number of Thread and Tap features that are present in the model. Any Hole features that have Thread parameters defined are included in the reported Taps.

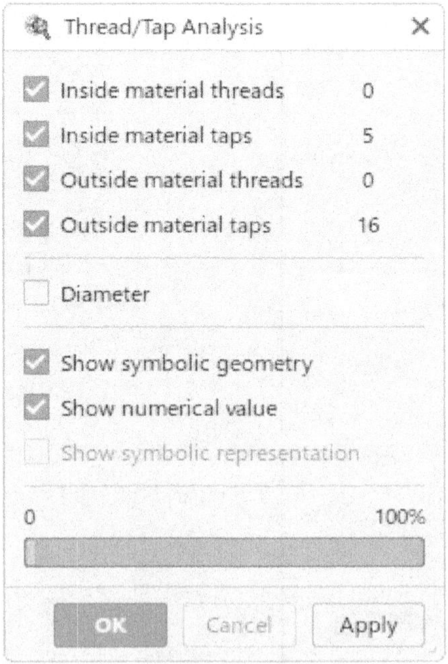

Figure 7–14

Step 2 - Run the Thread/Tap Analysis.

To run the analysis, click **Apply**. By default, the system displays a symbolic surface and parameter information for each Thread or Tap on the model, as shown in Figure 7–15.

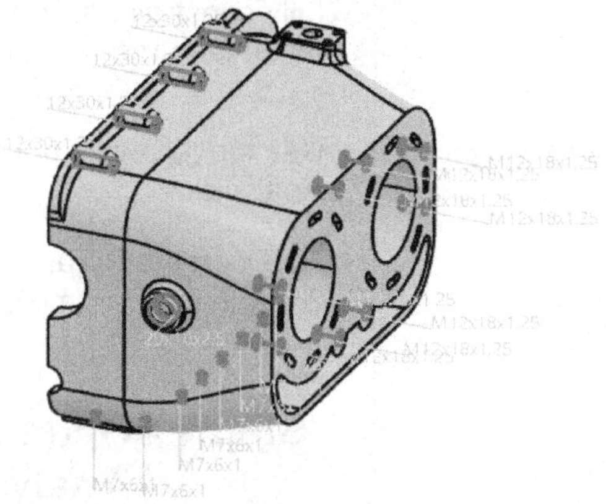

Figure 7–15

The bottom of the Thread/Tap Analysis dialog box contains the **Show symbolic geometry** and **Show numerical value** options. These options enable you to control the display of the symbolic surface and parameter information, respectively.

The middle of the dialog box contains the **Diameter** option. This can be used as a filter to only display the Thread/Taps with a diameter that you specify. For example, if you enter **20** in the *Diameter* field, as shown in Figure 7–16, only the Thread features of 20 display.

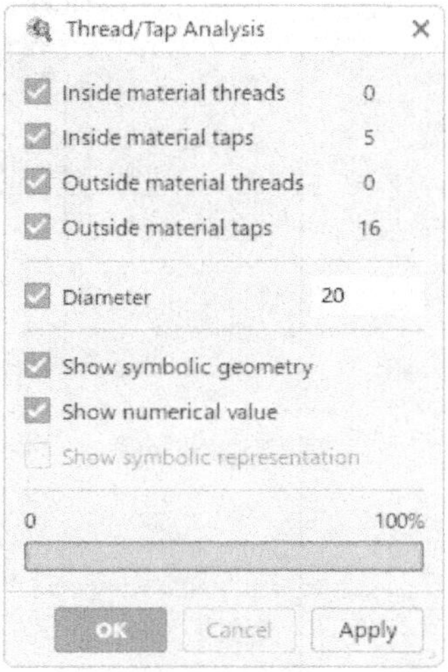

Figure 7–16

7.4 Parameterization Analysis

In a complex model with several features, it can become difficult to manage and investigate the specification tree. The **Parameterization Analysis** tool can filter the model and locate specific features in the tree. For example, you can search for fully constrained sketches, under-constrained sketches, and failed features in a model.

General Steps

Use the following general steps to run a Parameterization Analysis:

1. Open the Parameterization Analysis dialog box.
2. Run the Parameterization Analysis.

Step 1 - Open the Parameterization Analysis dialog box.

Select  (Parameterization Analysis) in the Review section of the Action Bar.

The Parameterization Analysis dialog box opens as shown in Figure 7–17.

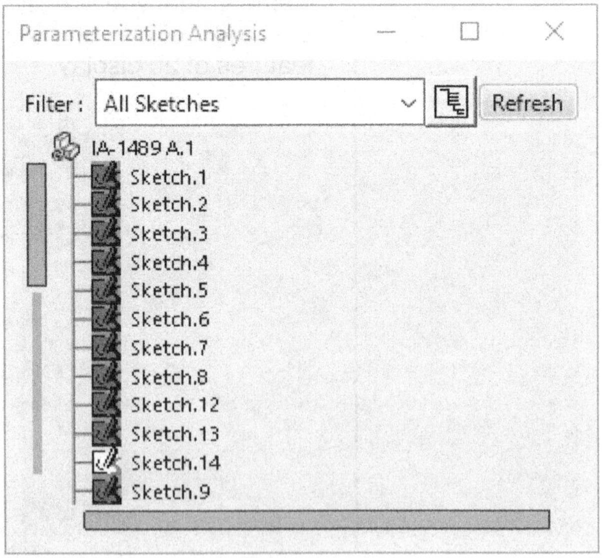

Figure 7–17

Step 2 - Run the Parameterization Analysis.

In the Parameterization Analysis dialog box, select a filter type in the Filter drop-down list, as shown in Figure 7–18.

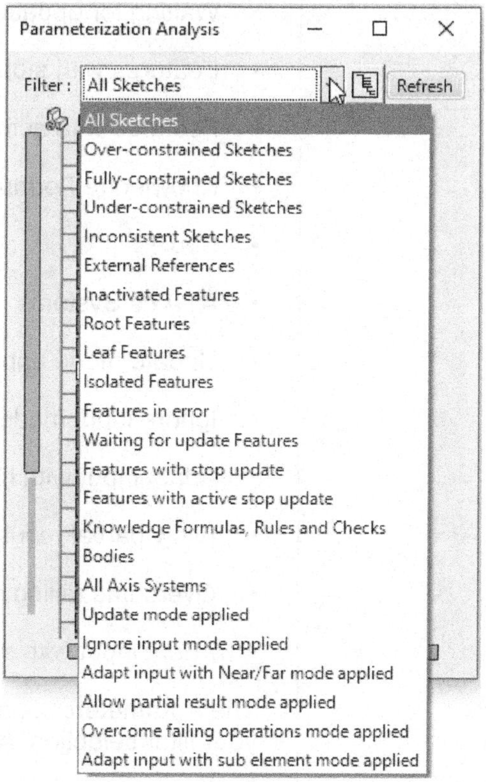

Figure 7–18

The following options are available in the Filter drop-down list.

- All Sketches
- Over-constrained Sketches
- Fully-constrained Sketches
- Under-constrained Sketches
- Inconsistent Sketches
- External References
- Inactivated Features
- Root Features

- Leaf Features
- Isolated Features
- Features in error
- Waiting for update Features
- Features with stop update
- Features with active stop update
- Knowledge Formulas, Rules and Checks
- Bodies
- All Axis Systems
- Update mode applied
- Ignore input mode applied
- Adapt input with Near/Far mode applied
- Allow partial result mode applied
- Overcome failing operations mode applied
- Adapt input with sub element mode applied

The Parameterization Analysis dialog box updates according to your filter selection. An example is shown in Figure 7–19.

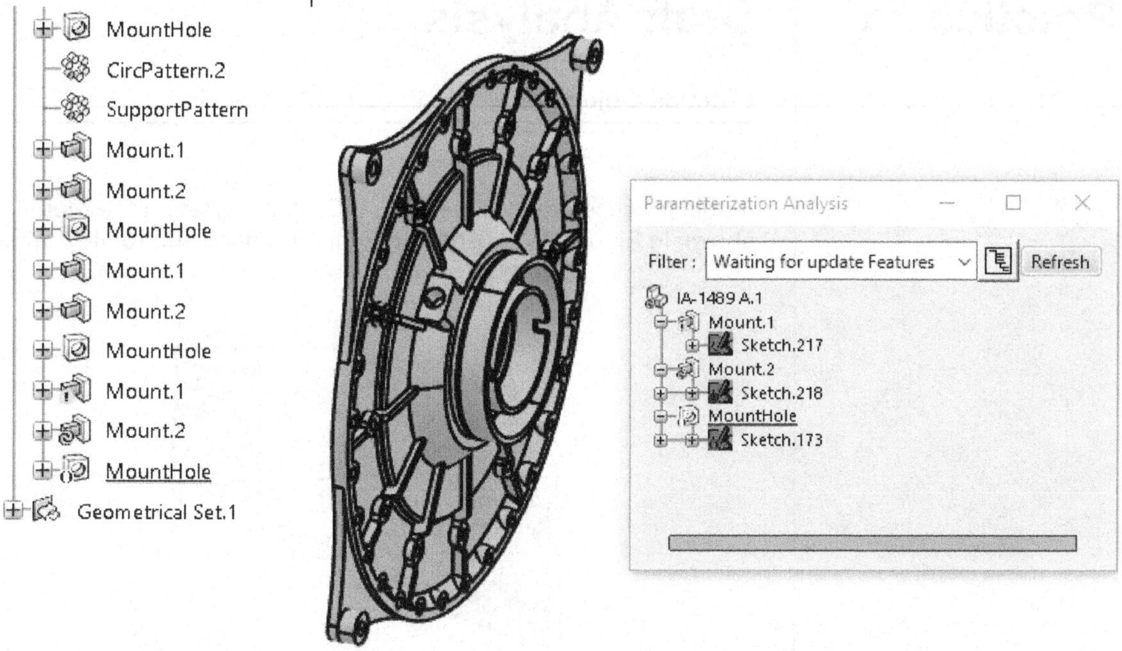

Figure 7–19

To display the body structure in the same order as in the specification tree, click (Displays body structure), as shown in Figure 7–20.

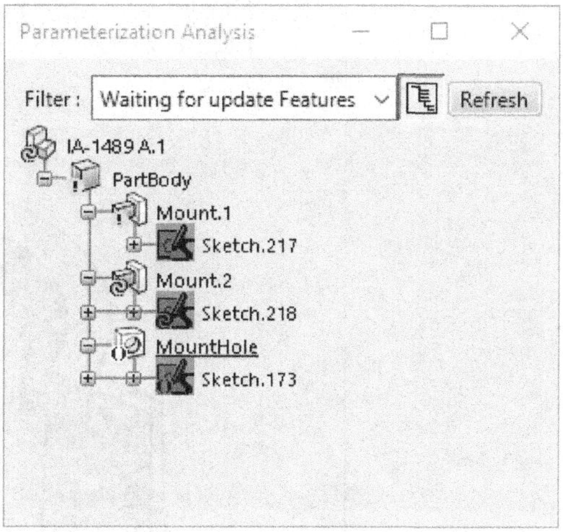

Figure 7–20

Practice 7a

Draft Analysis

Practice Objective

- Perform a Draft Analysis.

In this practice, you will perform a Draft analysis on the model shown in Figure 7–21, and verify that the part is correctly drafted.

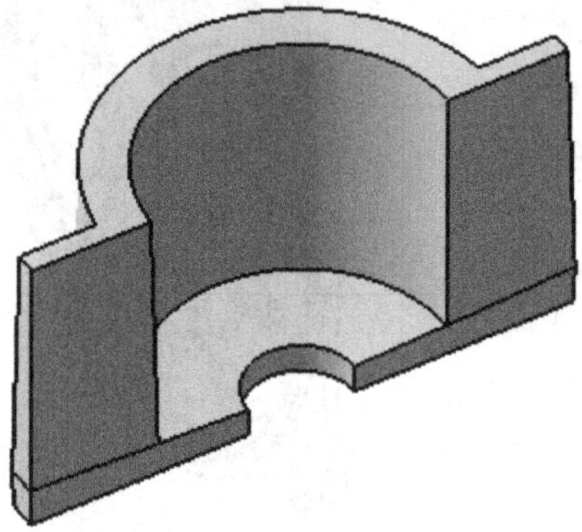

Figure 7–21

Task 1 - Open the part.

1. Import and open **Draft_Analysis.3dxml**. When importing, type your initials followed by the dash symbol into the *Duplication string* field.The model displays as shown in Figure 7–22.

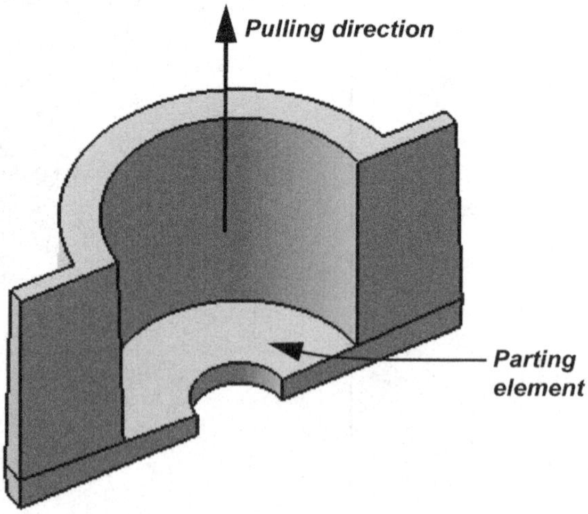

Figure 7–22

Task 2 - Change the View mode.

In the View section of the Action Bar, click  (View Modes) and then select  (Shading with Materials).

Task 3 - Perform a Draft analysis.

1. In the Review section of the Action Bar, click  (Draft Analysis) and select one of the faces of the model. The analysis result displays on the model, as shown in Figure 7–23.

The inside surface should be green. If it is blue, click  ***in the Draft Analysis dialog box to invert the draft direction.***

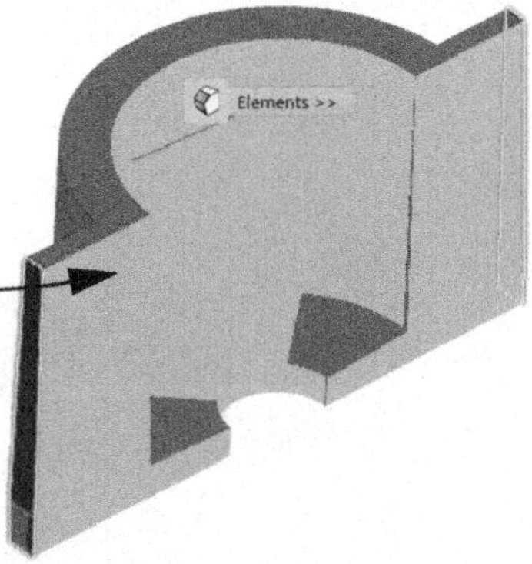

Figure 7–23

2. If necessary, in the Draft Analysis dialog box, click  to toggle off the light effect.

3. In the Draft Analysis dialog box, ensure that  (Quick Analysis mode) is selected. The Draft Analysis and Draft Analysis.1 dialog boxes open as shown in Figure 7–24.

If you do not see the Draft Analysis.1 dialog box (i.e., the color scale), click .

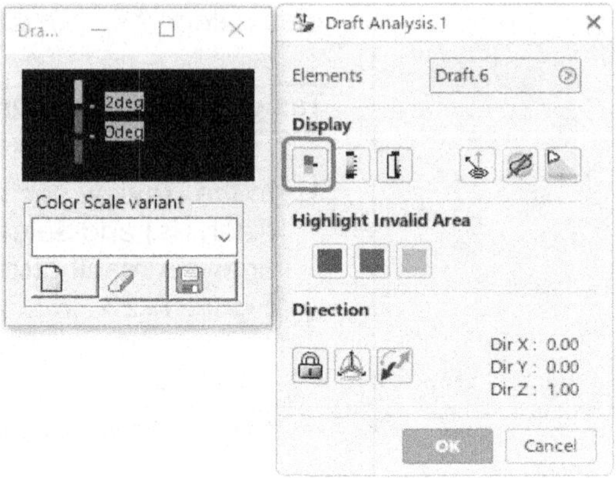

Figure 7–24

4. In the *Display* area, click , and drag the cursor over the model. In Figure 7–25, note that the draft direction is not pointing to the right. If your results are the inverse of those shown in Figure 7–25, click  in the Draft Analysis dialog box to invert the draft direction.

Note that your images will vary slightly from those in this section, depending on your model's orientation and where you select.

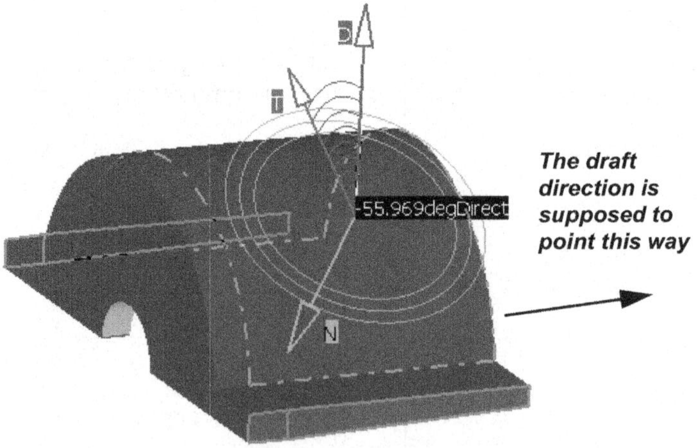

Figure 7–25

5. In the Draft Analysis dialog box, click . The robot will snap to the origin of the global axis system.

6. Locate the robot, as shown in Figure 7–26.

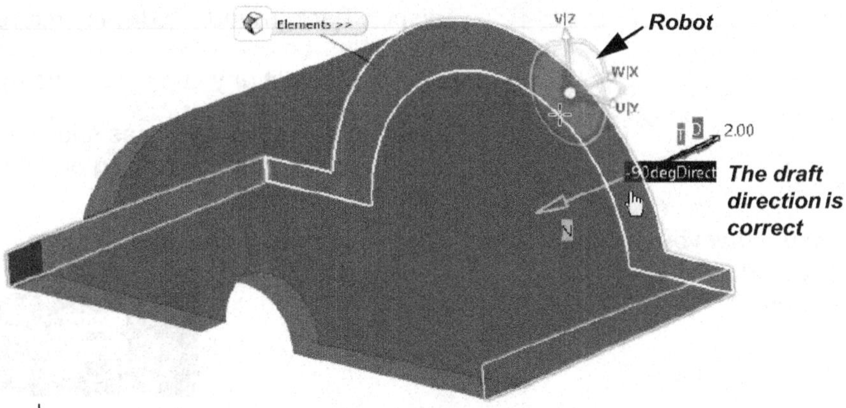

Figure 7–26

7. In the Draft Analysis dialog box, click [lock icon] to lock the position of the robot.

Design Considerations

Both sides of the part (above and below the parting element shown in Figure 7–22) are drafted using **1deg** draft angle. To display the drafted faces with **1deg**, the scale values need to be modified.

8. Double-click on **0deg**. The Edit dialog box opens as shown in Figure 7–27. In the Edit dialog box, enter **0.25**. The colors of the model update automatically.

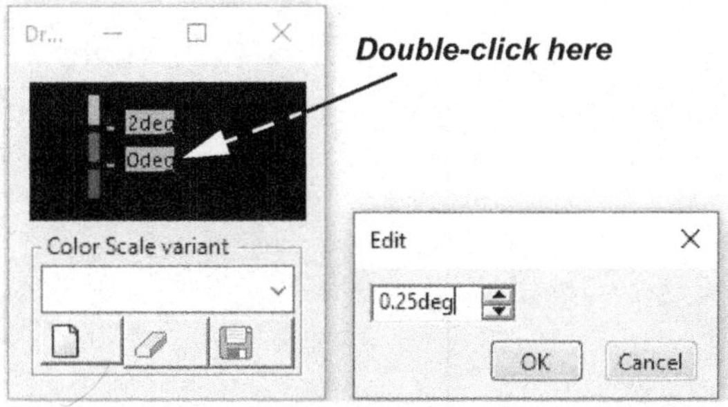

Figure 7–27

9. All of the red faces displayed on the model have a draft angle between 0.25deg and 2deg. This means that all of the red faces are drafted with a 1deg angle value.

10. Explore the model to note the faces that display in red.

    The colors on the model might disappear if you select in the display background. To display the results again, clear  and select any surface on the model.

11. Change the scale values as shown in Figure 7–28. Change the *0.25deg* value to **-1.5deg** and then change the *2deg* value to **-0.25deg**.

Ensure that you edit the values in the order listed in Step 11.

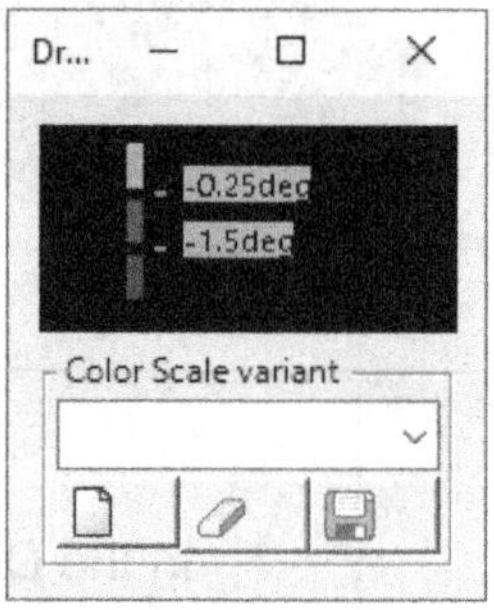

Figure 7–28

12. All of the red faces displayed on the model have a draft angle between -1.5deg and -0.25deg. This means all of the red faces are drafted with a -1deg angle value.

13. In the Draft Analysis dialog box, click  (Full Analysis mode). The Draft Analysis.1 dialog box displays as shown in Figure 7–29.

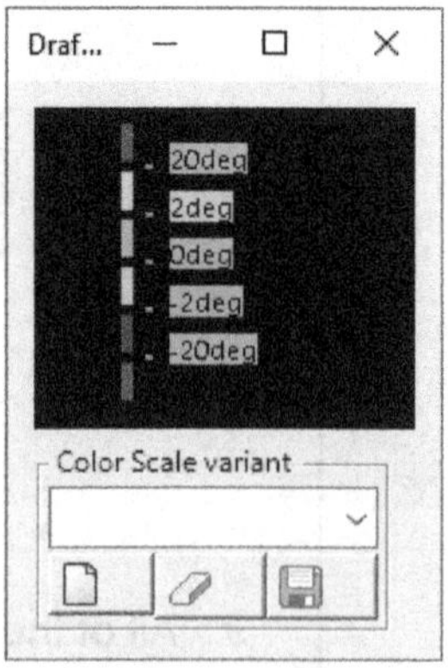

Figure 7–29

14. Edit the values as follows:

- *0deg:* **0.25**
- *2deg:* **0.75**
- *20 deg:* **1.25**
- *-2deg:* **-0.5**
- *-20deg:* **-1.25**

15. The Draft Analysis dialog box displays as shown in Figure 7–30.

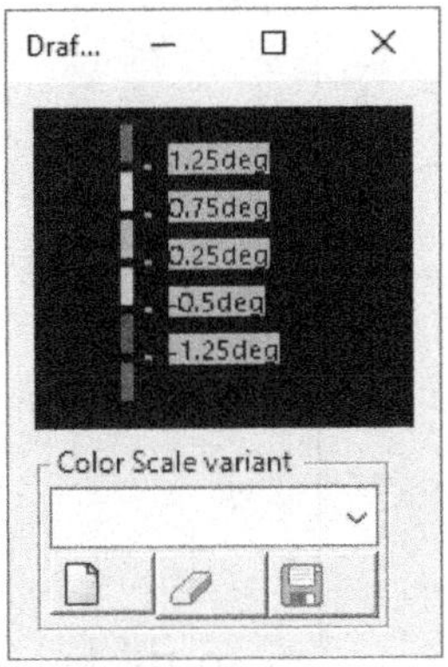

Figure 7–30

16. Double-click on the red color, which is the last color on the scale. The Color dialog box opens as shown in Figure 7–31.

17. Change the color to pink.

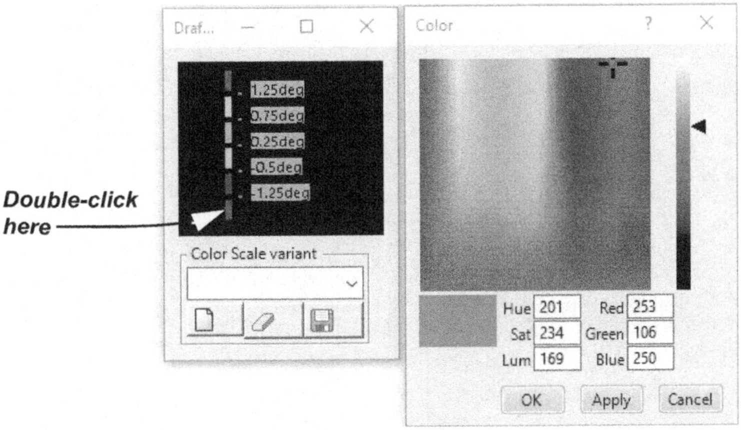

Figure 7–31

18. Click **OK**. The model displays as shown in Figure 7–32.

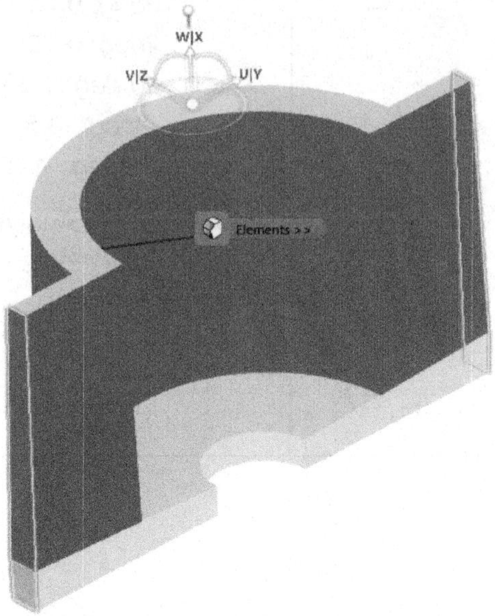

Figure 7–32

19. Explore all of the faces and the colors of the model. The part is supposed to be drafted with 1deg draft angle. Verify that the part has been drafted correctly. If not, try to determine which faces need to be drafted.

20. Save and close the model.

Practice 7b

Creating Threads and Taps

Practice Objectives

- Create a Thread.
- Create a Tap.
- Modify a Hole to include a Tap.

In this practice, you will use the **Thread/Tap** tool to add Threads and Taps to the model shown in Figure 7–33.

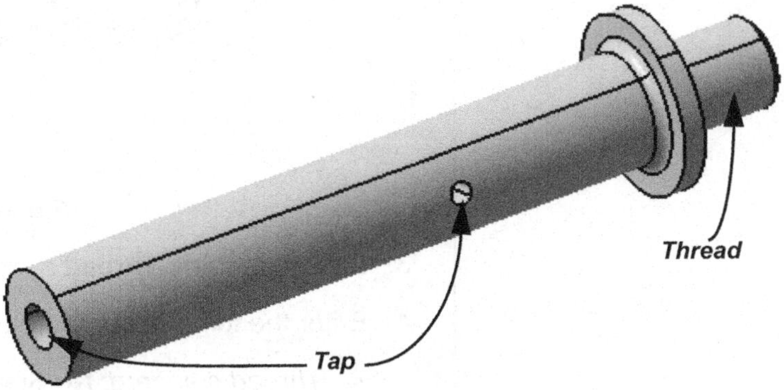

Figure 7–33

Task 1 - Open the part.

1. Import and open **ThreadTap.3dxml**. When importing, type your initials followed by the dash symbol into the *Duplication string* field.

Task 2 - Create a thread.

 *can be found in the Model section of the Action Bar.*

1. Click  (Thread/Tap) to open the Thread dialog box.

2. Select geometry for the Support face and Limit face as shown in Figure 7–34.

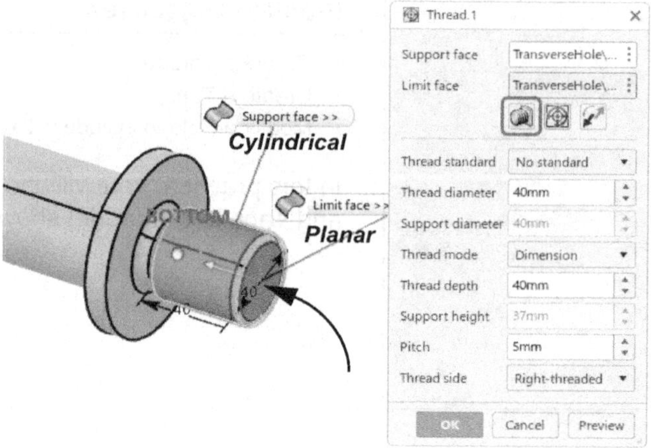

Figure 7–34

3. Ensure that the **Thread** option is selected.

4. Enter the following parameter values:

   - *Thread standard:* **No Standard**
   - *Thread diameter:* **40mm**
   - *Thread depth:* **40mm**
   - *Pitch:* **5mm**
   - Thread side: **Right-threaded**

5. Click **OK** to complete the Thread feature. Note that there is no visual representation for the Thread, but the information is stored in the specification tree, as shown in Figure 7–35.

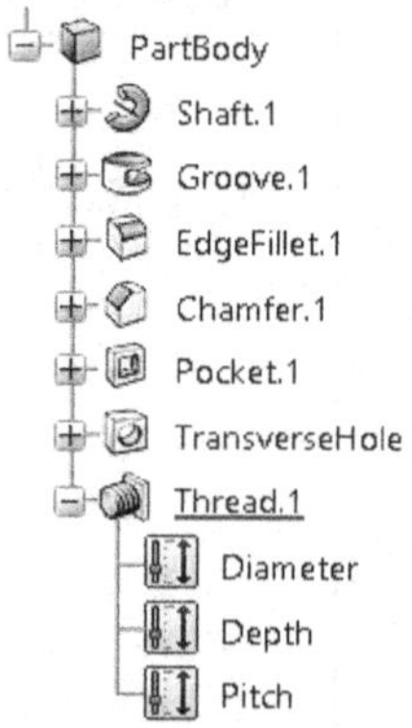

Figure 7–35

6. Rename the *Thread.1* feature as **ShaftThread**.

Task 3 - Create a tap.

1. Click  (Thread/Tap).
2. Ensure that the **Tap** option is selected.
3. Select geometry for the support face and limit face, as shown in Figure 7–36.

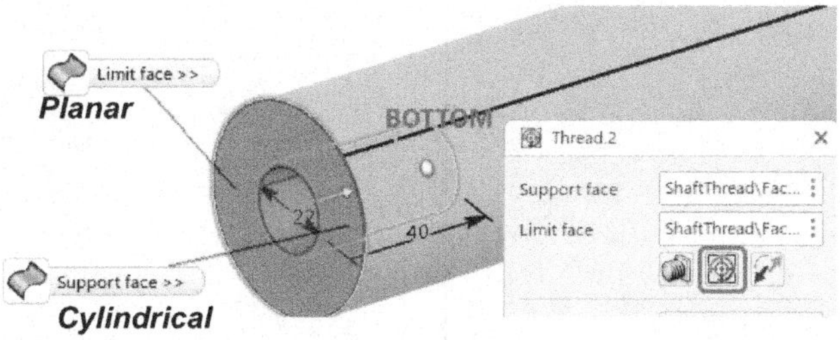

Figure 7–36

4. In the Thread standard drop-down list, select **Metric Thick Pitch**. The Feature Definition Error dialog box opens when this selection is made, as shown in Figure 7–37.

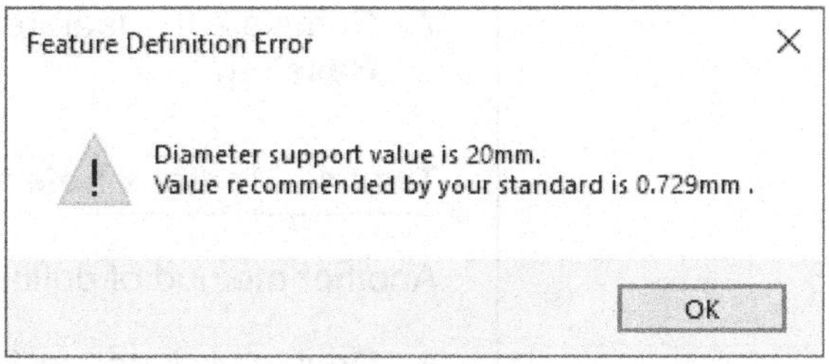

Figure 7–37

Design Considerations

The Feature Definition Error dialog box provides an automatic reference to ISO standards. The recommended value of 0.729mm is the ISO standard for the minor diameter of the M1 thread/tap. Because the diameter of the Pocket feature is 20mm, the M22 Thread Description is best suited for this application.

5. Click **OK** to close the dialog box. The system automatically selects the **M1** standard for the Thread Description. Change the Thread Description to **M22.**

6. Make the following selections:

    - *Thread depth:* **40mm**
    - *Thread side*: **Right-threaded**

    The Thread dialog box displays, as shown in Figure 7–38.

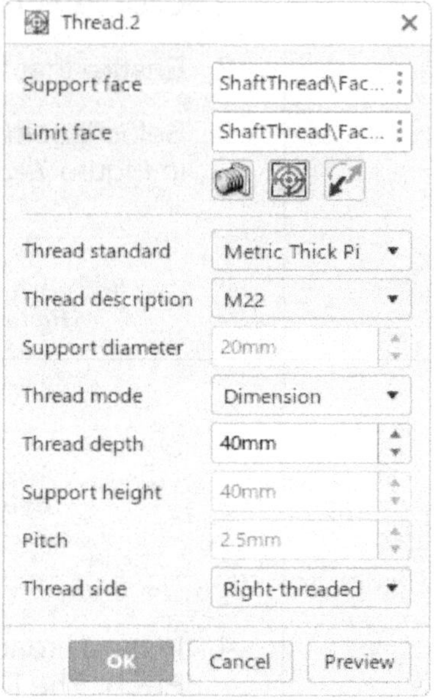

Figure 7–38

7. Complete the feature and rename the Thread.2 feature as **BaseTap**.

Task 4 - Modify a hole to include a tap.

Another method of defining a Tap is through the Hole dialog box.

1. Double-click on the Transverse Hole feature to open the Hole dialog box.
2. Select the  **Threaded** option.
3. Enter the following parameter values:

    - *Thread standard:* **Metric Thick Pitch**
    - *Thread description:* **M12**
    - *Thread side:* **Left-threaded**

4. To define the thread depth, right-click on the *Thread Depth* field and select **Edit Formula**.

5. With the Formula Editor dialog box open, double-click the **45mm** dimension shown in Figure 7–39. This will set the thread depth equal to the hole depth.

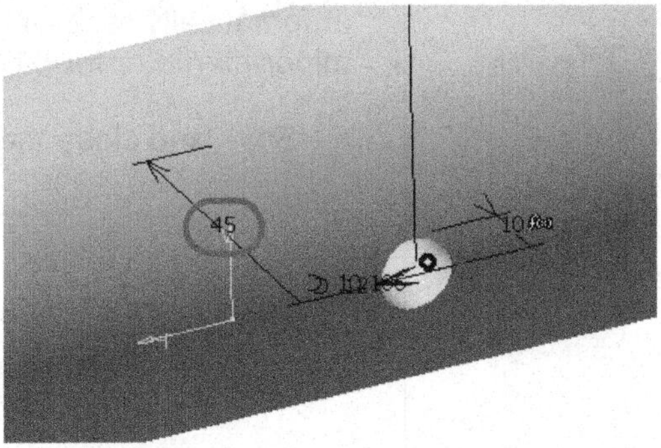

Figure 7–39

6. In the Formula Editor dialog box, click **OK** to complete the formula. The Hole dialog box opens as shown in Figure 7–40.

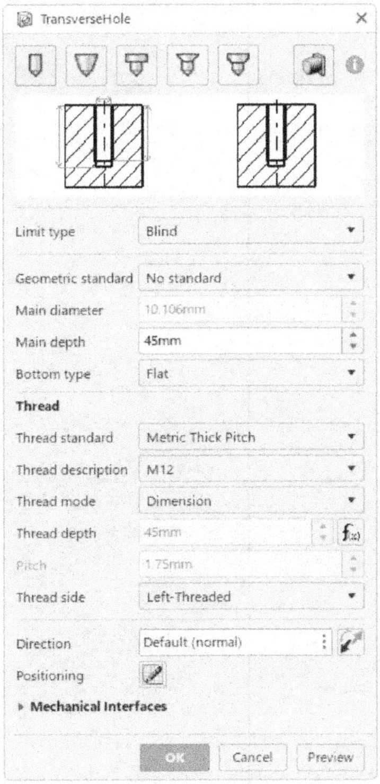

Figure 7–40

7. Click **OK** to complete the Tap feature.

Design Consideration

Rather than creating a Pocket and applying a Tap, you can create a threaded hole using the Hole Definition dialog box. This reduces the model feature count. Additionally, the **Thread Description** option in the Hole Definition dialog box automatically resizes the Hole diameter to the ISO standard minor-diameter for the selected Thread Description.

8. Save and close the model.

Practice 7c Thread/Tap Analysis

Practice Objective

- Analyze the Taps and Threads that are in a model.

In this practice, you will use the **Thread/Tap Analysis** tool to review the Taps that have been applied to the part shown in Figure 7–41.

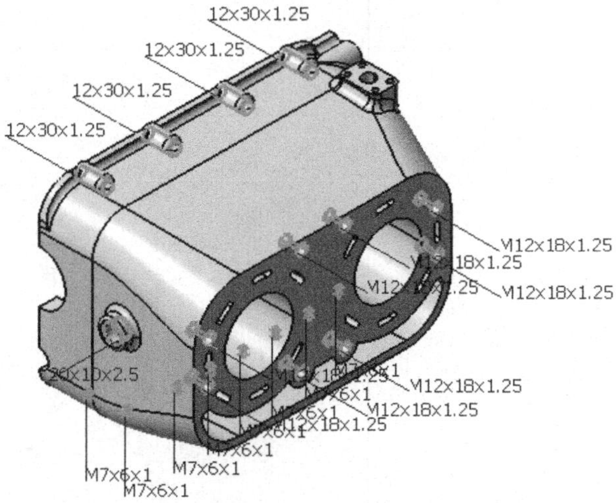

Figure 7–41

Task 1 - Open the part.

1. Import and open **ThreadAnalysis.3dxml**. When importing, type your initials followed by the dash symbol into the *Duplication string* field. The model displays as shown in Figure 7–42.

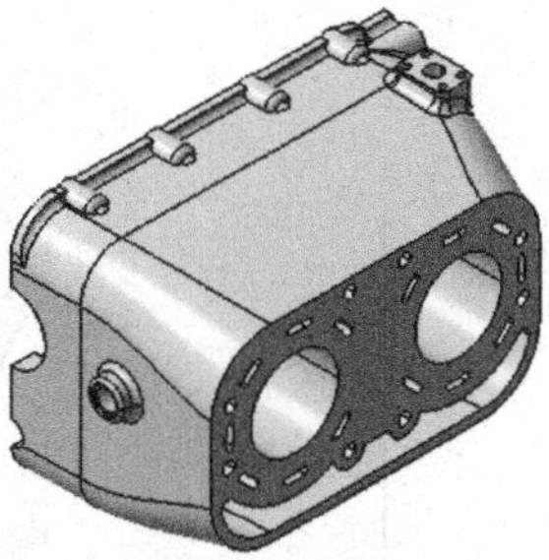

Figure 7–42

Although Tap features are present in the model, there is no visual indication that they are present when reviewing the geometry.

Task 2 - Perform a Thread/Tap Analysis.

1. In the Review section of the Action Bar, Analysis flyout, click  (Tap-Thread Analysis).

2. The Thread/Tap Analysis dialog box opens as shown in Figure 7–43. The number of Threads and Taps display in the dialog box. By default, the **Show symbolic geometry** and **Show numerical value** options are selected.

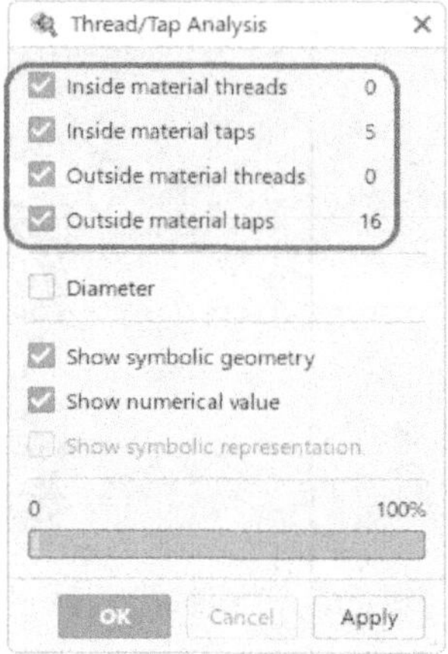

Figure 7–43

3. Click **Apply**. The Tap and Thread information displays on the model. Since the **Thread/Tap Analysis** options were set to display both geometry and values, each Tap is highlighted and the Tap information displays, as shown in Figure 7–44.

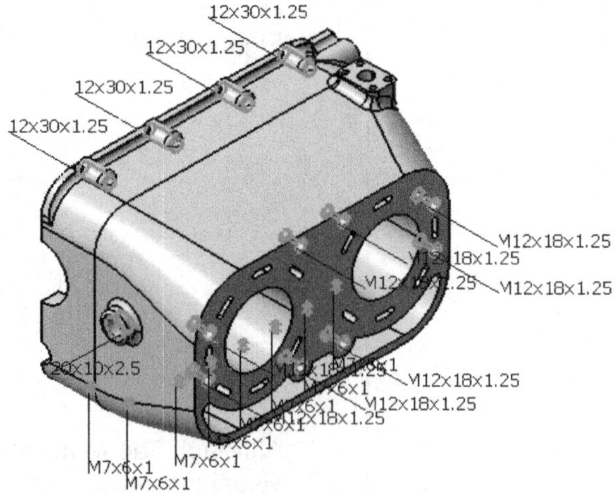

Figure 7–44

Task 3 - Modify the tap analysis parameters.

In this task, you will modify the parameters in the Thread/Tap Analysis dialog box to locate specific taps on the model.

1. Select **Diameter**. This option enables you to specify the diameter of the Tap or Thread to report.
2. In the *Value* field, enter **7** and click **Apply**. The model displays as shown in Figure 7–45.

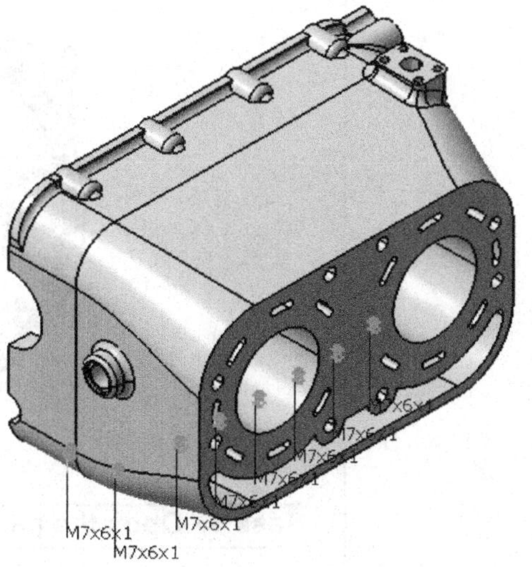

Figure 7–45

3. Close the Thread/Tap Analysis dialog box.
4. Close the model. Since no modifications were made, the model does not need to be saved.

Practice 7d Parameterization Analysis

Practice Objective

- Perform a Parameterization Analysis.

In this practice, you will perform a parameterization analysis on the model shown in Figure 7–46.

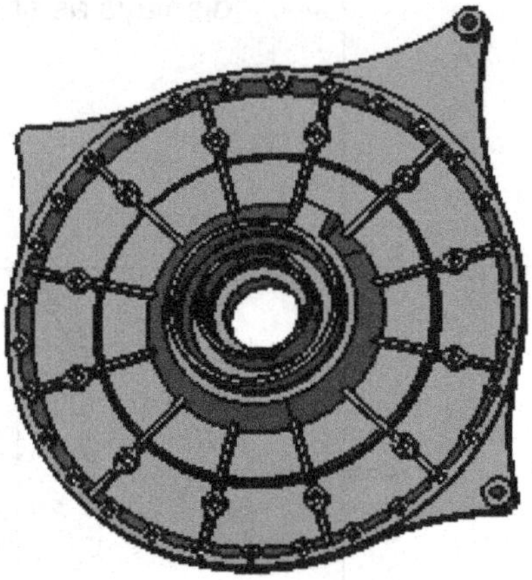

Figure 7–46

Task 1 - Open the part.

1. Import and open **Aft_Cover.3dxml**. When importing, type your initials followed by the dash symbol into the *Duplication string* field.The model displays as shown in Figure 7–47.

Figure 7–47

Task 2 - Perform a Parameterization Analysis.

1. In the Review section of the Action Bar, click  (Parameterization Analysis). The Parameterization Analysis dialog box opens. The **All Sketches** option is the default filter. This option displays all of the sketches that currently exist in the model.
2. In the Filter drop-down list, select the **Fully-constrained Sketches** option to display the fully constrained sketches, as shown in Figure 7–48. The Parameterization Analysis dialog box only lists the sketches that are fully constrained.

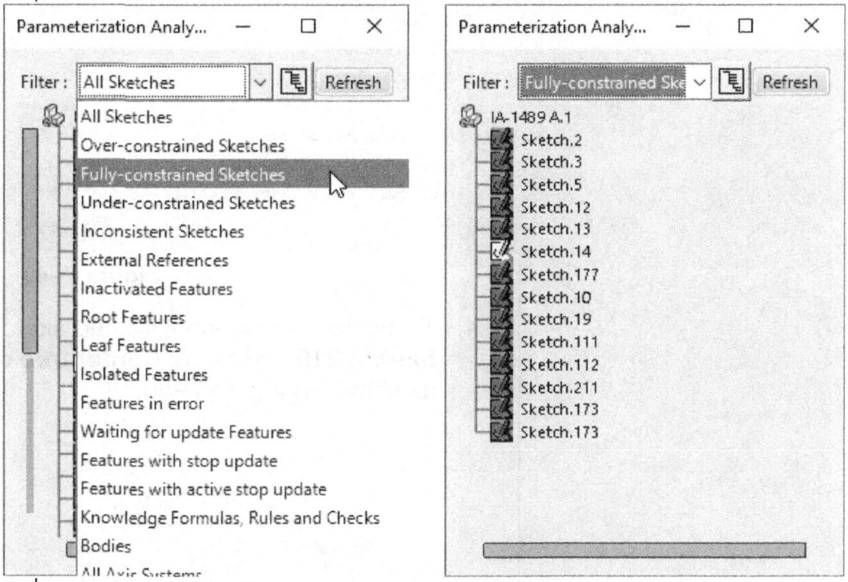

Figure 7–48

3. In the Filter drop-down list, select the **Over-constrained Sketches** option to display the over-constrained sketches, as shown in Figure 7–49.

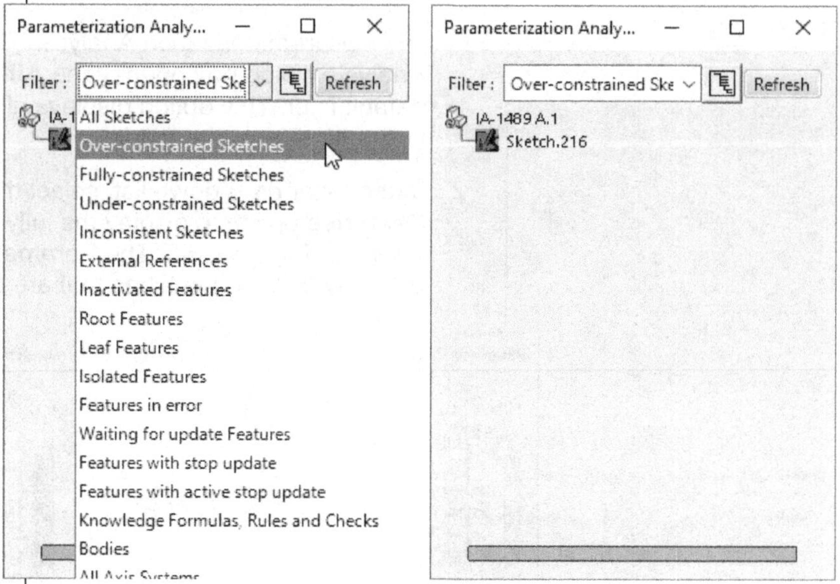

Figure 7–49

4. To locate the over-constrained sketch, right-click on **Sketch.216** and select **Center tree on Preselected Objects**, as shown in Figure 7–50.

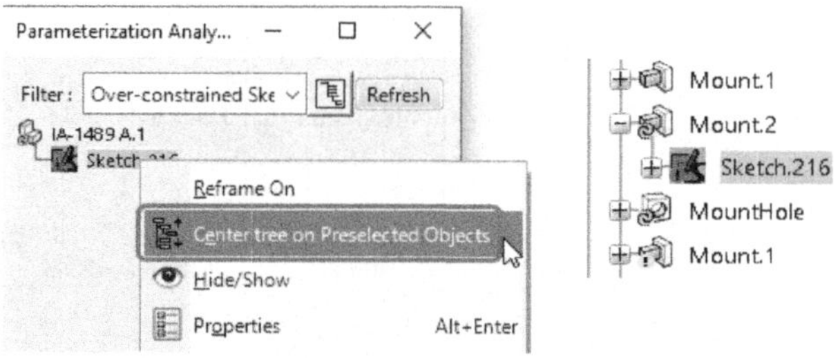

Figure 7–50

5. Double-click on **Sketch.216** to enter the Sketcher app.

6. Delete the dimension shown in Figure 7–51, and exit the Sketcher.

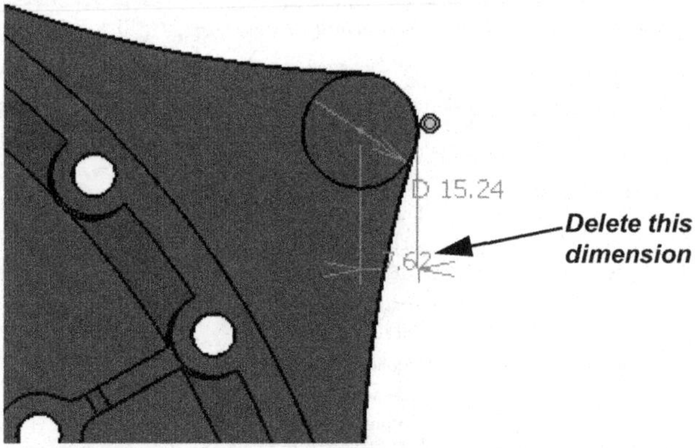

Figure 7–51

7. The Update Diagnosis: Sketch.216 dialog box opens, indicating that the profile used for Mount.1 is not a closed profile.

Design Considerations

The focus of this practice is to show you how to use the **Parameterization Analysis** tool. The problems in the model will not be fixed.

8. Click **Close**.

9. Run the Parameterization Analysis to display the over-constrained sketches. There are no over-constrained sketches in the specification tree, as shown in Figure 7–52.

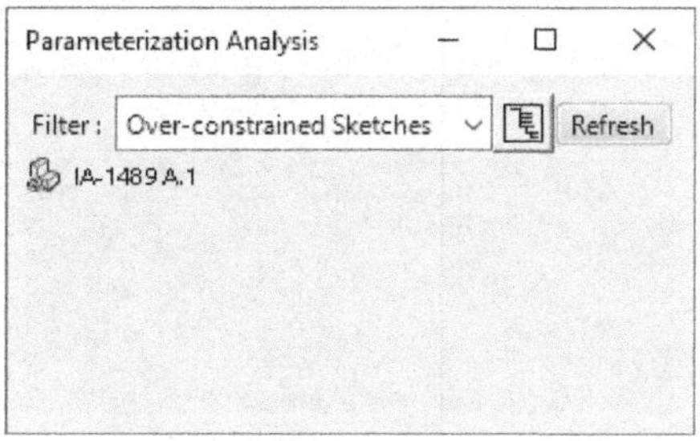

Figure 7–52

10. In the Filter drop-down list, select **Waiting for update Features**, as shown in Figure 7–53.

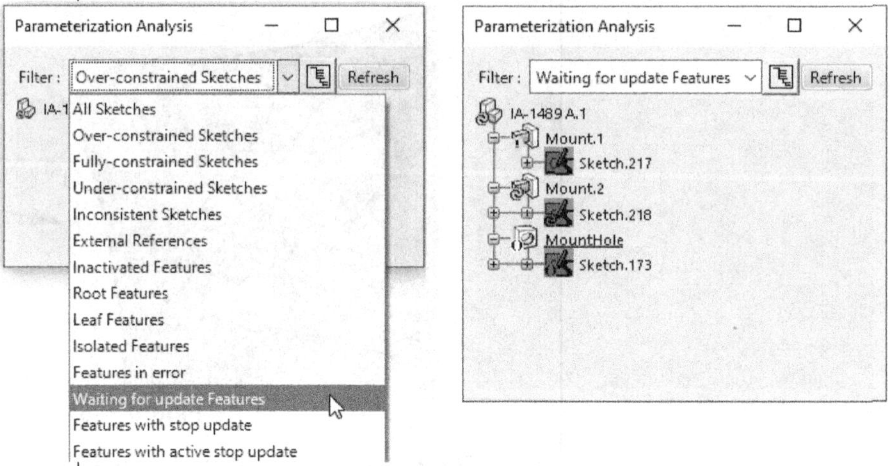

Figure 7–53

11. To display the body structure in the same order as in the specification tree, click  (Display body structure). In the Parameterization Analysis dialog box, the body structure display changes as shown in Figure 7–54.

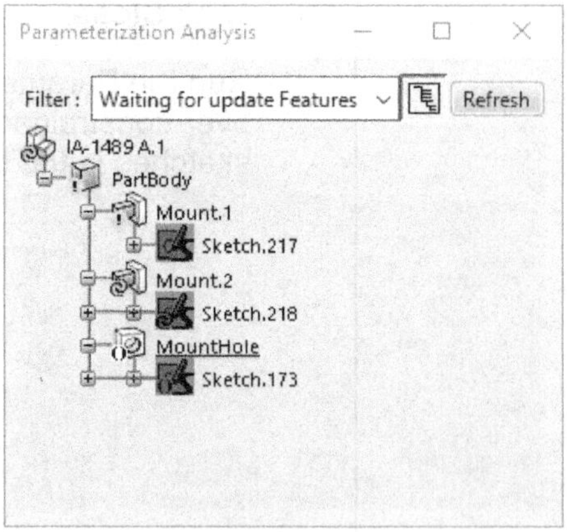

Figure 7–54

12. Save and close the model.

Chapter Review Questions

1. The **Draft Analysis** tool checks all of the draft angles in your model.
   a. True
   b. False
2. To display draft analysis results, the display mode has to be set to_____.
   a. Shading
   b. Shading with Edges
   c. Shading with Material
   d. Shading with Edges and Hidden Edges
3. Thread and Tap features create solid geometry to represent threaded cylinders or tapped holes.
   a. True
   b. False
4. What does the limit face do when defining a thread?
   a. Defines the start of the thread.
   b. Defines the end of the thread.
   c. Defines the pitch of the thread.
   d. None of the above.
5. You can use Thread/Tap Analysis to investigate the Thread and Tap features in the model.
   a. True
   b. False
6. The **Parameterization Analysis** tool can be used to filter the specification tree to locate specific features. You can filter for:
   a. Fully-constrained Sketches
   b. Isolated Features
   c. External References
   d. All of the above.

Answers: 1a, 2c, 3b, 4b, 5a, 6d

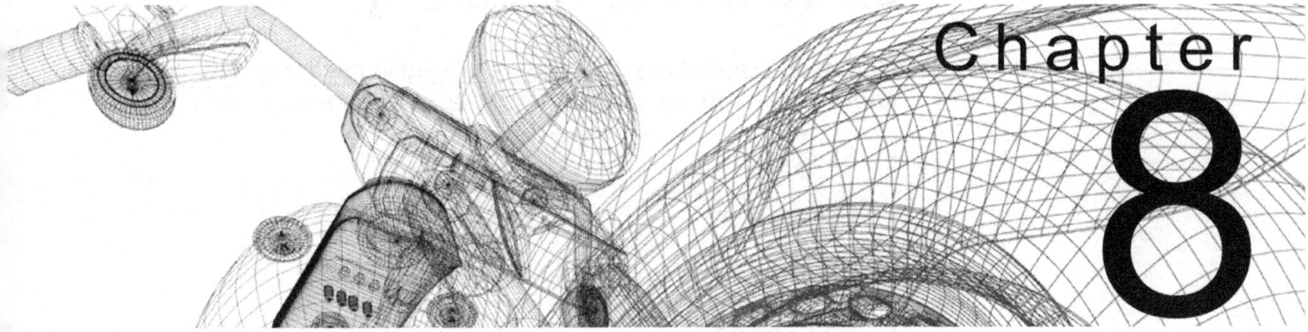

Multi-Model Links

You can reuse an existing design by copying and pasting a part body from one part to another part. If a geometry link is required between the part bodies, you can use special Paste options. The geometry link can be valuable when changes to the source part are expected.

Learning Objectives in This Chapter

- Understand the difference between Paste and Paste Special.
- Learn about the various Paste Special options.
- Use links to create references to other documents.
- Use Publications to identify and select externally linked elements.
- Review the best practices for managing links.

8.1 Reuse of Geometry

Geometry created in a part can be reused in the same part file or another file. You can copy many types of elements, including:

- Sketches
- Solid features
- Wireframe and Surface features
- Part Bodies
- Geometrical Sets
- Ordered Geometrical Sets

You can copy these features into the same or another part. When you use the standard **Paste** command, the copy includes all of the parameters and information, without a link to the original geometry. When you use the **Paste Special** command, you can create the copy with or without a link to the original element, and with or without all of the specifications.

Advantages

- Copying and pasting geometry reduces re-work time, because you can use preexisting data to create similar parts.
- By preserving links between the original geometry and the copy, you can update multiple parts by only modifying one part.
- By severing links, you can create variations of a part while preserving the original features and dimensions.

Disadvantages

- If you create a copy without a link to the original, you cannot update the copy to reflect changes to the original.
- If you create a copy that is linked to the original and someone else changes the original without investigating the links, more parts end up changed than were intended.

8.2 Copy and Paste Special

Regular **Copy** and **Paste** options work well if you require a non-associative copy of a part body from another part. If you want to have a geometrical link between the source part body and the target part, you can use the **Paste Special** option.

General Steps

Use the following general steps to copy a body from one model and paste it into a second model with an external link.

1. Copy a body from the first model.
2. Paste the body into the second model using the **Paste Special** option.

Step 1 - Copy a body from the first model.

To copy a body from one model to another, select the body to be copied and select  (Copy) from the Standard section of the Action Bar, as shown in Figure 8–1.

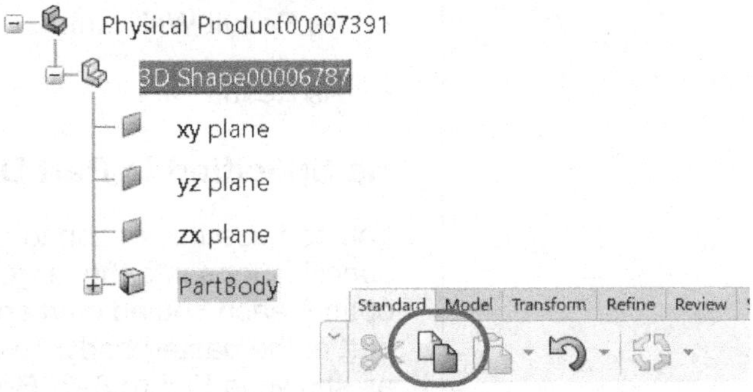

Figure 8–1

Step 2 - Paste the body into the second model using the Paste Special option.

Activate the model in which you want to paste the body and select  (Paste Special). The Paste Special dialog box opens as shown in Figure 8–2.

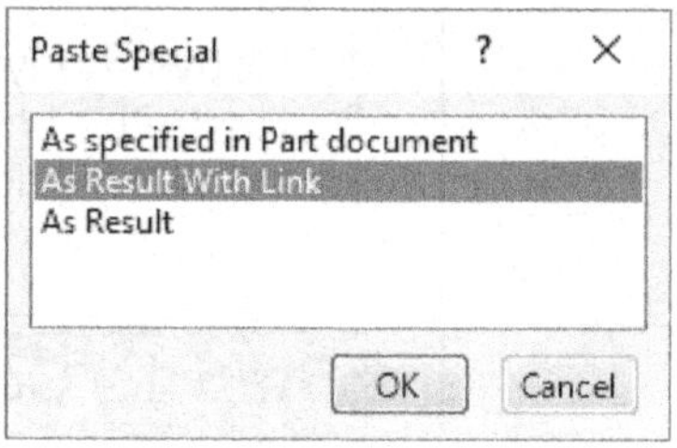

Figure 8–2

You can paste the body into the new document using one of the following options:

- As specified in Part document
- As Result With Link
- As Result

As Specified in Part Document

You can use this option to paste the body with its design specifications into the target document. When you use this option, each copied element displays in the specification tree as part of the pasted body. Two bodies are copied into a document, as shown in Figure 8–3. **Body.2** is pasted using **As Result**, and Body.3 is pasted using **As specified in Part document**.

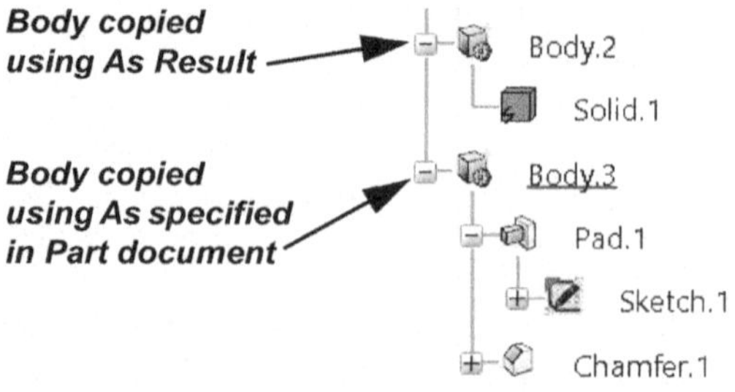

Figure 8–3

As Result With Link

You can use this option to paste the body without its design specifications and to maintain a link between the original and the copy. This means that if the original is modified, the copy can be updated to reflect the changes.

The body in Figure 8–4 is copied from another document and displays as Solid.1 in the specification tree.

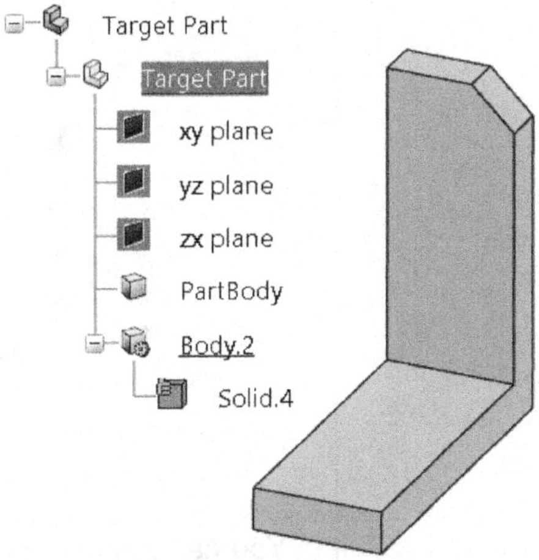

Figure 8–4

If the original body is modified, a red thumbs down symbol displays in the specification tree to the left of the copied body (Solid.4), as shown in Figure 8–5. This red thumbs down symbol indicates that changes have been made to the original body and that the copied element must be updated to display these changes.

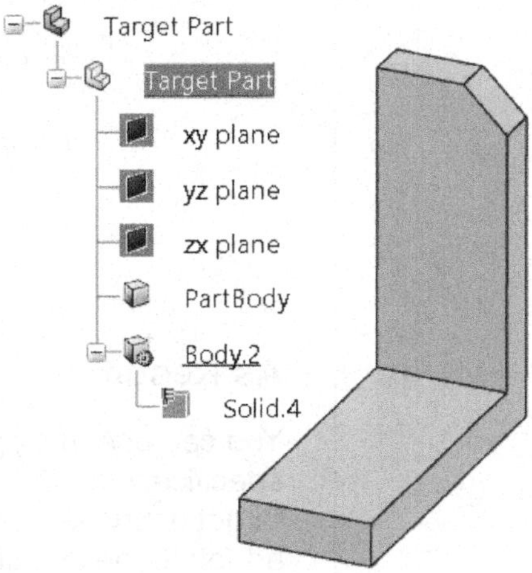

Figure 8–5

To update the model, activate the Physical Product level of the specification tree by double-clicking on it, then click  (Update) or press <Ctrl>+<U>. Figure 8–6 shows the copied document after updating. The symbol to the left of Solid.4 in the specification tree has returned to its original form.

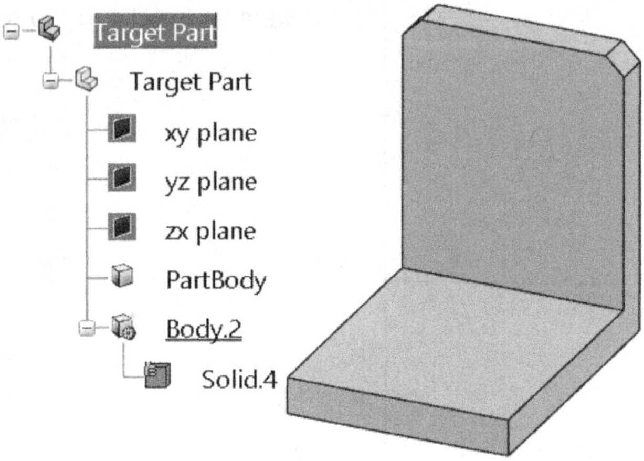

Figure 8–6

You can restrict the ability of elements to be linked between models. Select **Me>Preferences>Common Preferences>Object Properties>3D Shape>Infrastructure>General**. In the *External References* area, select the **Restrict external selection with link to published elements** option. By doing so, you enable only published elements to be pasted with a link between models. If you select this option and then attempt a paste using the **As Result With Link** option, the error message shown in Figure 8–7 opens.

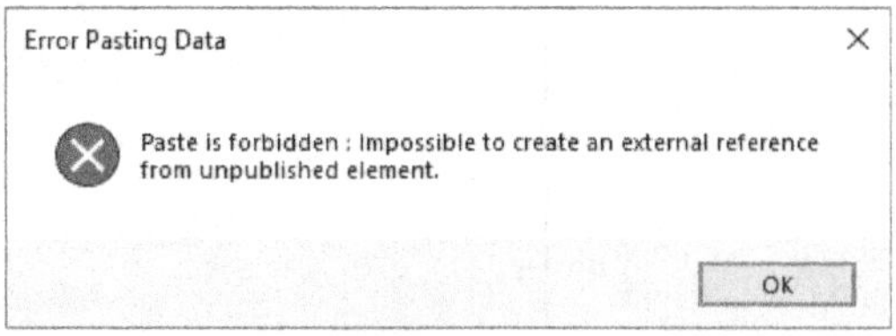

Figure 8–7

As Result

You can use this option to paste the body without its design specifications and without making a link between the source and target documents. When you use this option, one element is added to the specification tree of the target document, regardless of the number of elements copied.

This option is useful if you do not plan to make changes to the element, and it simplifies the display of the specification tree. The copied items display in the specification tree as solid.***x*** (where ***x*** indicates the number of that particular element inserted into the model), as shown in Figure 8–8.

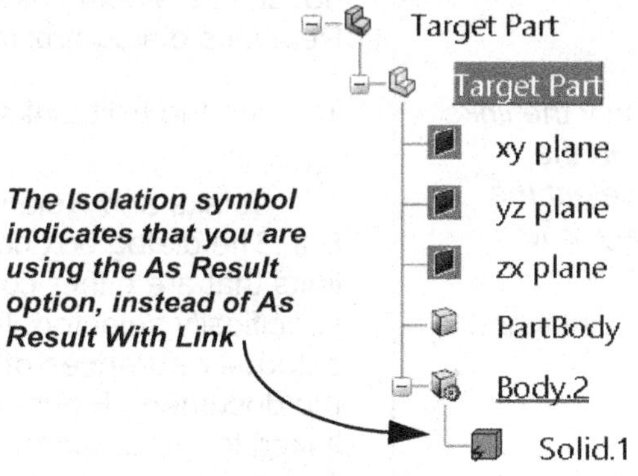

Figure 8–8

Referenced Geometry Symbols

The referenced geometry link status symbols are described as follows:

Link Status Symbol	Description
	Copied geometry is synchronized and open in session.
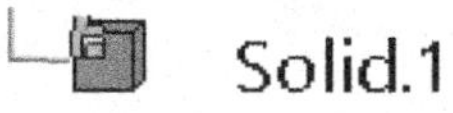	Pointed document is synchronized but not open in session.
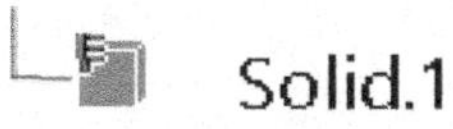	Source geometry has been modified but is open in session. Target body is not synchronized.
	Source geometry has been modified and is not open in session. Target body is not synchronized.
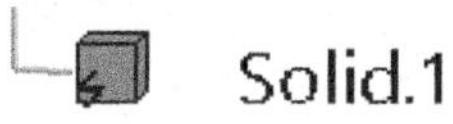	External link has been isolated.

8.3 External Links

You can create references to other documents to ensure that designs are consistent. As the number of documents increases, it becomes difficult to remember where information in a document is being read from. You can use the Edit Links and Relations dialog box to manage external links in documents.

To display only the links of one body in the document, select the required body, and select  (Links and Relations)

To open the Edit Links and Relations dialog box, select

 (Links and Relations) from the Tools section of the Action Bar. The dialog box contains a list of components, relations, or links that are either contained in the model or that have been specifically selected. In the dialog box, you can review the external references of an entire document or of just one body in the document. Figure 8–9 shows that the selected Target Part is linked to the Original 3D Shape because of the Solid.1 PartBody. The red arrow pointing to Target Part indicates that the pointed object impacts the pointing component, meaning that changes to the Original 3D Shape will affect the Target Part. This information can be found by expanding the + icons to the left of the line items.

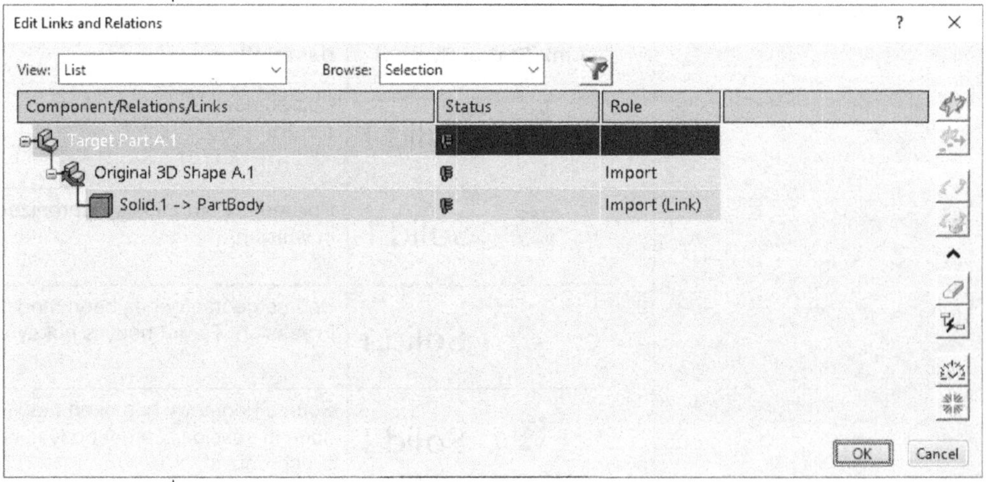

Figure 8–9

If the document you are reviewing has a number of external references, try using (Filter) to find the required reference. You can filter the information to include or exclude based on *Role* or *Status* values.

To manage links, use the following icons on the right side of the window.

(Automatic Reconnection)	Reconnects links automatically.
(Switch to minor in session)	Replaces the pointed component in a relation with another minor version in session of this component.
(Manual Reconnection)	Reconnects links manually.
(Change Version)	Replaces the pointed component in a relation with another major version of the same component.
(Delete Pointed element)	Deletes the pointing component in the link.
(Isolate Links)	Removes the link between the referenced document and the current document. Once a link is isolated, it no longer displays in the dialog box and cannot be re-linked. To recreate a link, you must copy the referenced element again and delete the element that was isolated.
(Synchronize links)	Displays if changes are made to the reference document while the link was deactivated.
(Disable/Enable Synchronization)	Disables or enables a link. Disabling a link temporarily breaks the association between the copied element and its reference. This prevents the element from synchronizing with the reference document while the body is being updated. To enable a link, click the button again.

If a folder is displayed in the *Status* column, that means that the original reference model of the link is not open in session. By right-clicking on the item in the Edit Links and Relations window, you can select **Open**. This will open the original pointed reference without having to search the database for it.

Figure 8–10 shows that the Original 3D Shape part is not synchronized and the reference body is not in session.

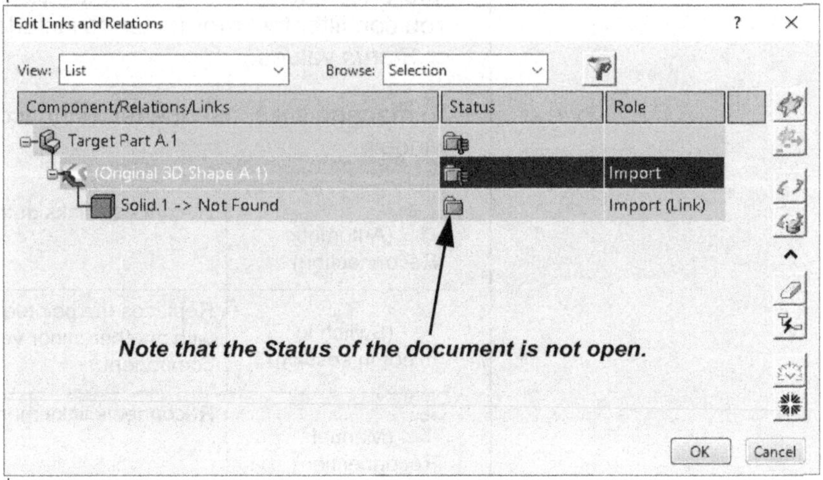

Figure 8–10

Figure 8–11 shows that an open option becomes available by right-clicking on a reference object in the Edit Links and Relations window. This way, changes to the original can be viewed or made as needed.

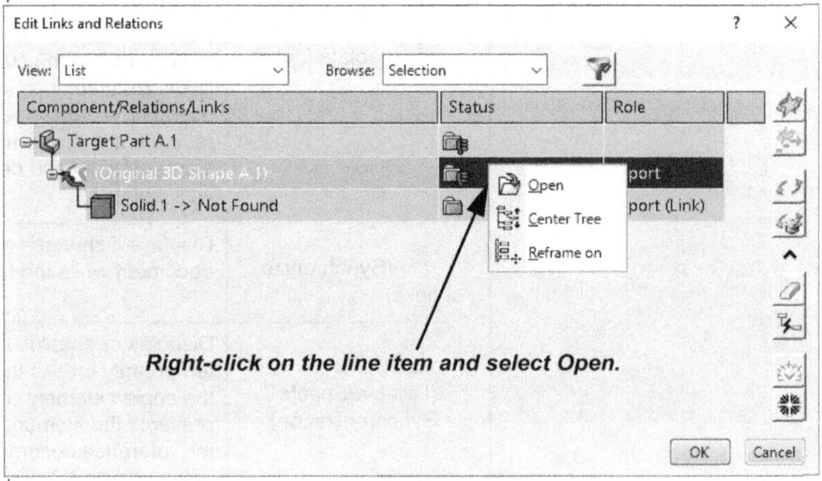

Figure 8–11

A link is also synchronized when the body is updated, as long as the linked documents are open in session and the link is active.

You can click (Synchronize link) to update a link. If you make a change in the linked element, the copied element in the current document must be synchronized to the referencing document so that the changes are reflected. **Synchronize link** is only available if the highlighted link needs to be updated. If a link requires synchronization, its *Status* is (Not synchronized), as shown in Figure 8–12. Once a link has been synchronized, its Status changes to (Synchronized).

Note the Status indicates Not synchronized

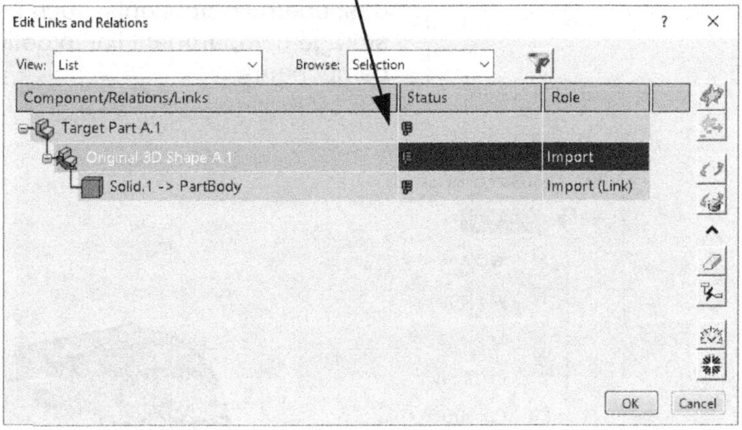

Figure 8–12

8.4 Publications

A publication is an organizational and reference management tool that you can use to identify and select elements that are externally referenced. When an element is published, it is added to a new Publications branch in the specification tree. You can then rename it, so that it can be easily identified and selected by other designers.

For example, the dashboard surface for an automobile has been published in the DashSkel component shown in Figure 8–13. This publication can then be referenced externally by any of the dashboard components, such as the HVAC vent bezel or the storage compartment lid, to define the shape of these components.

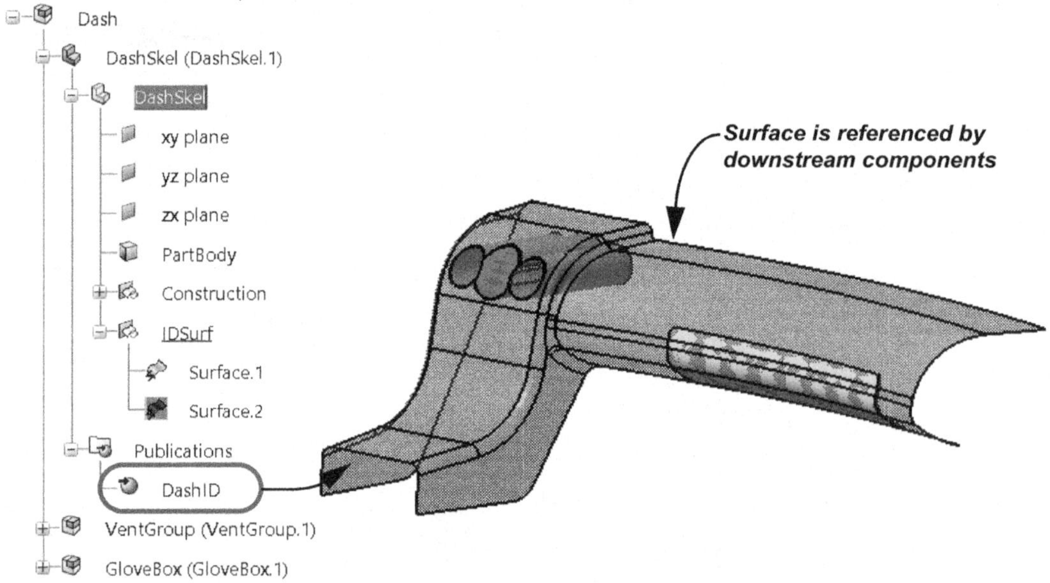

Figure 8–13

Creating this contextual link between elements helps to ensure that the shape of the dashboard components always matches the design intent defined by the styling department that created the published surface. The use of publications in performing this operation is similar to a controlling mechanism that defines which geometry can be externally referenced, and facilitates its selection by placing it in a separate branch in the tree.

Another benefit of publishing data is seen during integration with the 3DEXPERIENCE. The use of publications places the geometry at a higher level of importance within the modeling process. Therefore, the publication is viewed with the same weight as an actual part file. This facilitates the management of links through the use of publications.

You can publish the following types of elements:

- Reference elements, such as Points, Planes, Lines, and Splines
- Features
- Sketches
- Bodies
- Surfaces
- Parameters
- Sub-elements, such as faces, edges, and axes

Many companies enforce a design standard that requires the publication of any element that is going to be externally referenced. This is to ensure that no undesired parent-child relationships are developed.

There are two ways in which reference selections can be made:

- External References
- Constraint Creation

External References

The options that control the use of publications for external references are highlighted in Figure 8–14 and Figure 8–15. To locate the options in Figure 8–14, select **Me>Preferences>Common Preferences>Object Properties> 3D Shape>Infrastructure>General** and go to the *External References* area.

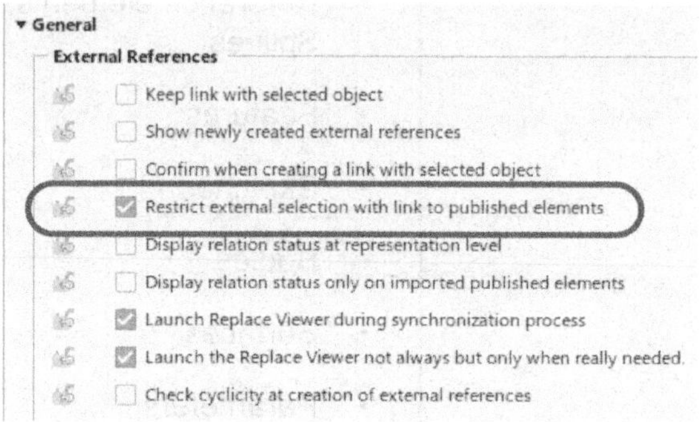

Figure 8–14

To locate the options for Figure 8–15, go to **Me>Preferences> App Preferences>3D Modeling>Systems Architecture>Publication** and go to the *Selection* area.

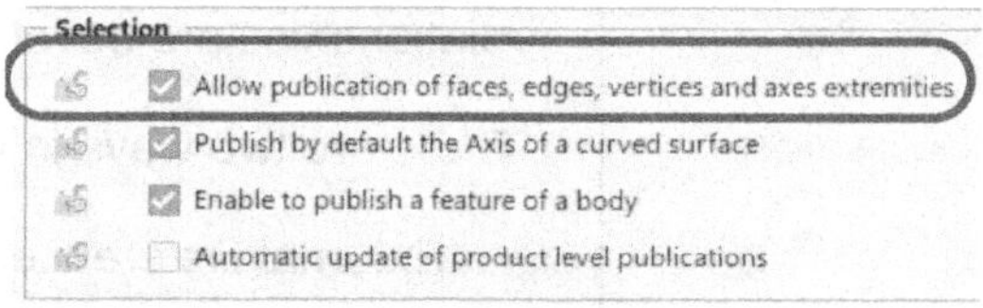

Figure 8–15

The highlighted options are as follows:

Option	Description
Restrict external selection with link to published elements	When this option is selected, external references can only be developed by selecting a published element.
Allow publication of faces, edges, vertices, and axes extremities	You must select this option to publish individual sub-elements of features, such as the face, edge, or vertex of a Pad. When this option is disabled, sub-elements cannot be published, thus restricting users from making boundary representation selections.

8.5 Best Practices

Link Management

You must create references to other documents to ensure that designs are consistent. As the number of documents increases, it is difficult to remember where information in a document is being read from. Avoid creating any unnecessary external references.

You can use the Edit Links and Relations dialog box to manage external links in documents. The use of publications to create external references inhibits the creation of unnecessary links, and only required links are created between parts.

Breaking Links

After the model is finalized, you must isolate all of the external references that were created during modeling of the part. Doing so ensures that if one of the referencing models is used and modified in a different assembly, the final model is not impacted by the changes.

3DEXPERIENCE Considerations

Because 3DEXPERIENCE automatically handles links between components, some might think that Publications are not as useful as they once were. However, by using publications on specific important objects in a model, they can help keep a project organized. Allowing external links to just any feature can quickly become get out of hand when a team of users are working on the same project. Publications also allow for a permission structure to be created within a project so that only certain users are allowed to create and reference them, while others are restricted from being able to create external links completely.

Practice 8a Paste Special Options

Practice Objective

- Understand the differences between the Paste Special options.

In this practice, you will use the three Paste Special options to copy part bodies from one 3DPart to another. You will see the different results produced by the three Paste Special options:

- **As specified in Part document**
- **As Result With Link**
- **As Result**

The completed model displays as shown in Figure 8–16.

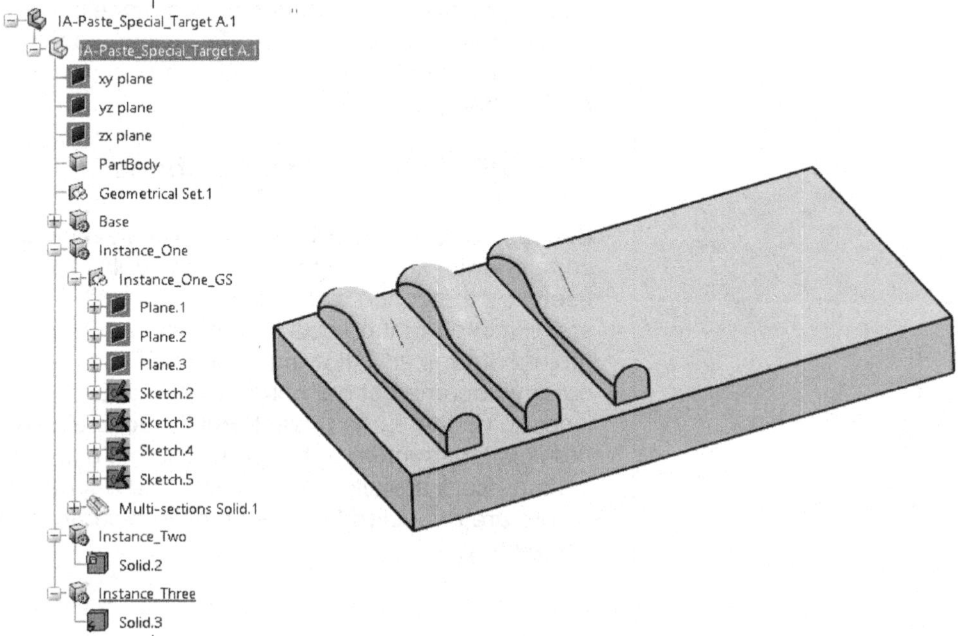

Figure 8–16

Task 1 - Open the part from which to copy the part bodies.

1. Import and open **Paste_Special_Original.3dxml**. The model contains a PartBody as well as three copies of a Multi-sections Solid feature, as shown in Figure 8–17.

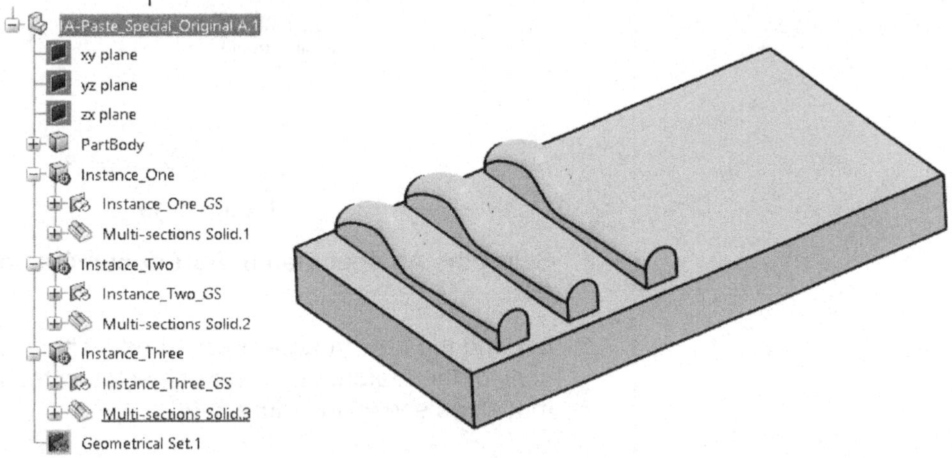

Figure 8–17

Task 2 - Paste using the As specified in Part document option.

1. Select the **Instance_One** body, then right-click and select **Copy**.
2. While keeping the **Paste_Special_Original** window open, import and open **Paste_Special_Target.3dxml**. The model contains a base part body, as shown in Figure 8–18.

Figure 8–18

3. Select the **Paste_Special_Target** part in the tree (the item one level down from the root object), right-click, and select **Paste Special**. The Paste Special dialog box opens as shown in Figure 8–19.

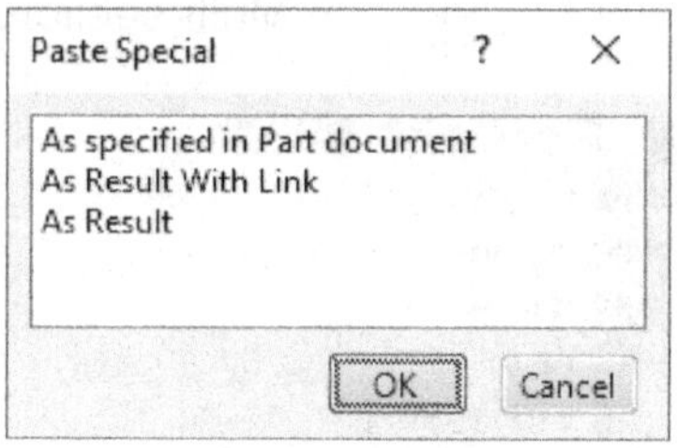

Figure 8–19

4. Select the **As specified in Part document** option and click **OK**.

5. Expand the new **Instance_One** body. The body contains a copy of the features that were selected in the referenced model, as shown in Figure 8–20.

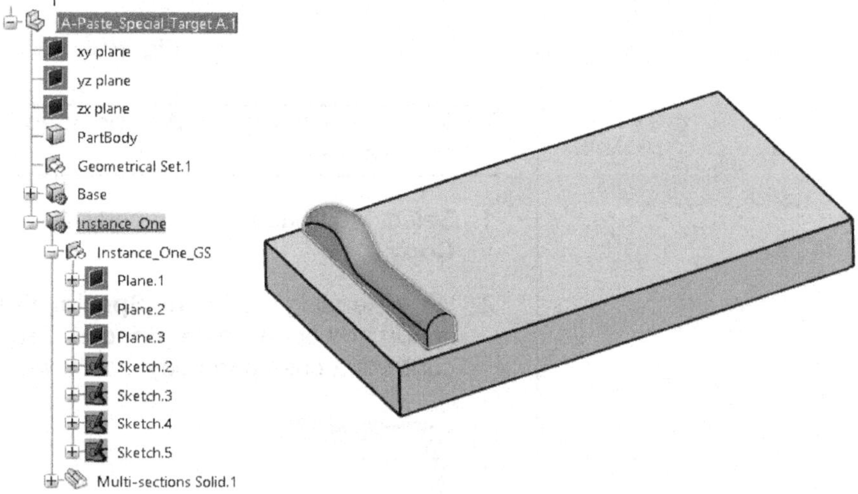

Figure 8–20

Task 3 - Paste using the As Result With Link option.

1. Activate the **Paste_Special_Original** window.

2. Copy the **Instance_Two** body.

3. Activate the **Paste_Special_Target** window, select the **Paste_Special_Target** part in the tree, right-click, and select **Paste Special**.

4. In the Paste Special dialog box, select **As Result With Link**.
5. Click **OK**. The new body is added, as shown in Figure 8–21. The **As Result With Link** option places a linked solid feature into the new body.

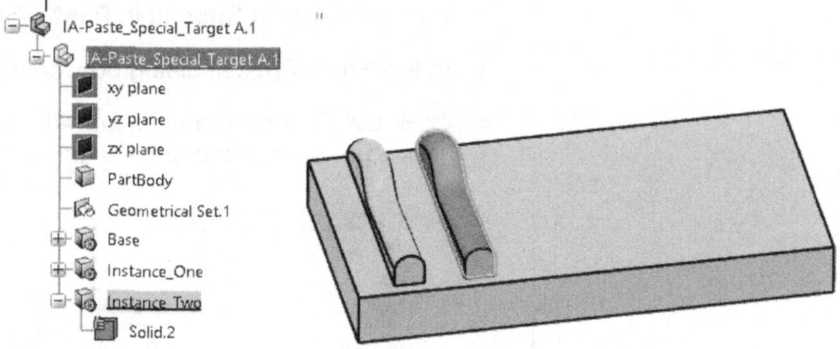

Figure 8–21

Task 4 - Investigate the links.

1. In the Tools section of the Action Bar, select . The Edit Links and Relations dialog box opens as shown in Figure 8–22. Expand the tree in the box as shown in Figure 8–22.

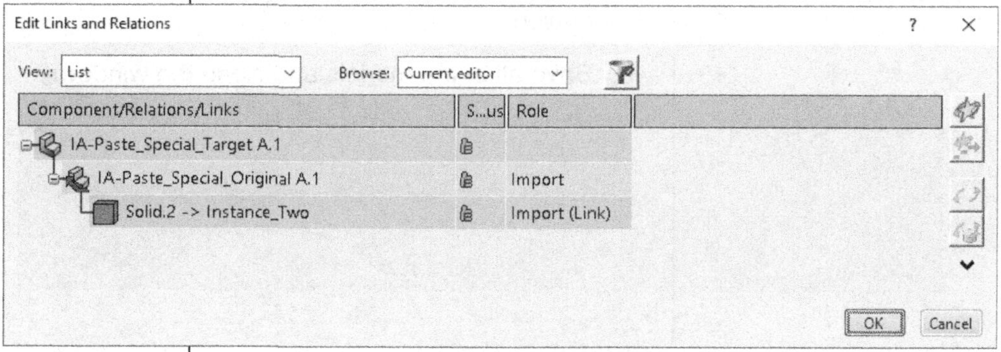

Figure 8–22

Design Considerations

This dialog box indicates any links that exist in the model. The system shows that the **Solid.2** element is linked to the **Instance_Two** element in the **Paste_Special_Original** model. The dialog box also indicates that this link has a *Status* of **OK** ( ).

2. Close the Links and Relations dialog box.

Task 5 - Paste using the As Result option.

1. Activate **Paste_Special_Original** and copy the **Instance_Three** body.
2. Perform a **Paste Special** in **Paste_Special_Target**.
3. In the Paste Special dialog box, select the **As Result** option.
4. Click **OK**. The new body is added, as shown in Figure 8–23. This time, an isolated solid is added to the body.

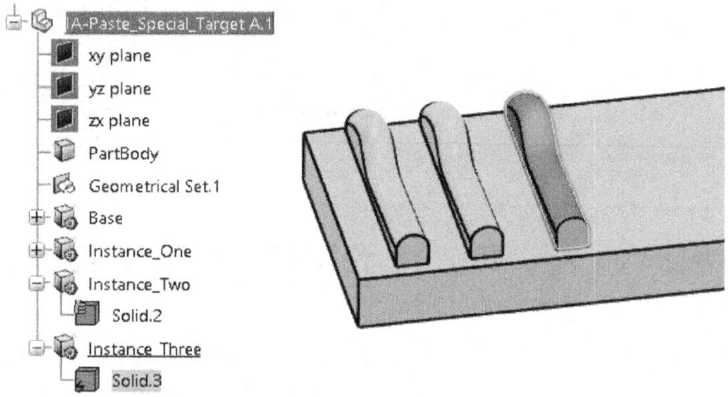

Figure 8–23

5. Compare the results among the three instances that were copied.
6. Save all of the models and close the windows.

Practice 8b Multi-Model Links

Practice Objective

- Copy geometry between part models while keeping the link.

In this practice, you will create a link between a cover and a bushing using the **As Result With Link** option. You will also synchronize the parts shown in Figure 8–24. You will see how the linked components interact when dimensions are changed.

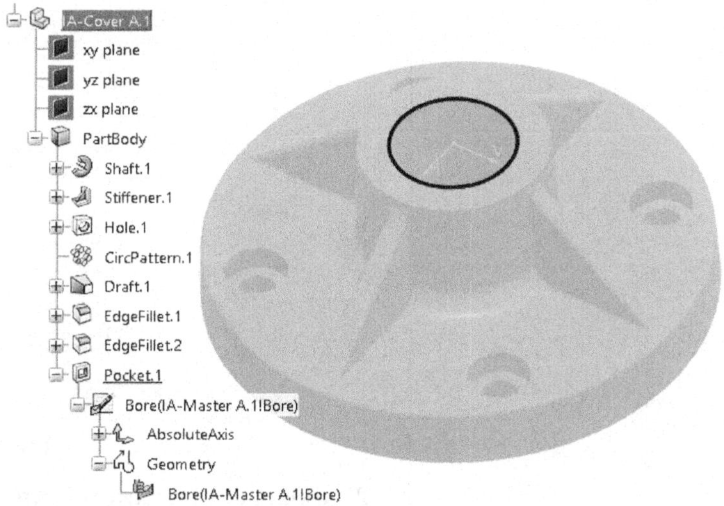

Figure 8–24

Task 1 - Set the required options.

1. Open the Preferences dialog box and select **Common Preferences>Object Properties>3D Shape> Infrastructure**. In the *General* area, select **Keep link with selected object** and **Restrict external selection with link to published elements.** In the *Update* area, select **Synchronize all external references when updating the 3D shape**, as shown in Figure 8–25.

Design Considerations

- The **Keep link with selected object** option enables creation of external links between the models.
- The **Restrict external selection with link to published elements** option disables creation of links between non-published elements.

- The **Synchronize all external references when updating the 3D shape** option enables automatic synchronization of external links between the pointing (i.e., the "child") and the pointed (i.e., the "parent") parts upon an update of the child part geometry. Otherwise, the external links would need to be manually synchronized whenever the parent part is modified.

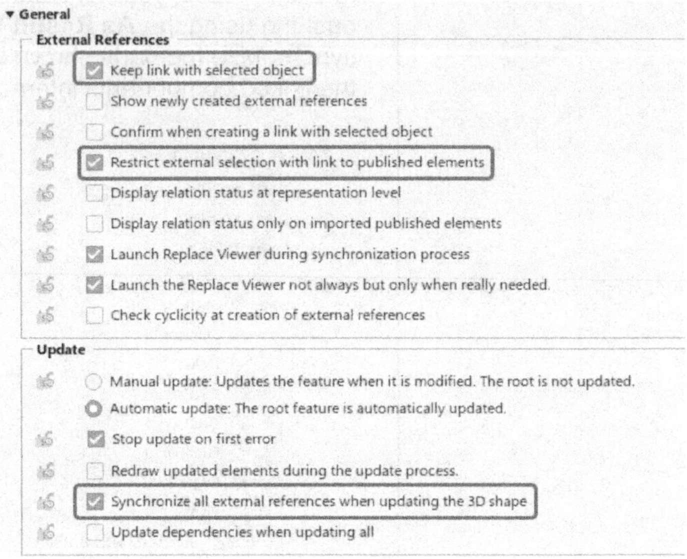

Figure 8–25

2. Select the **Common Preferences>Object Properties>3D Shape>Infrastructure>Display** section.

3. Select **Parameters** and **Relations**, as shown in Figure 8–26.

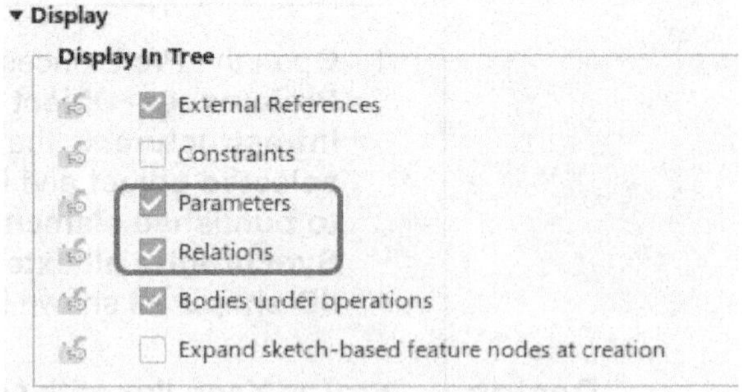

Figure 8–26

Design Considerations

These options make parameters and formulas visible in the part specification tree.

4. Select **App Preferences>3D Modeling>Systems Architecture** section.
5. In the *Publication* area, select **Automatic update of product level publications**, as shown in Figure 8–27.

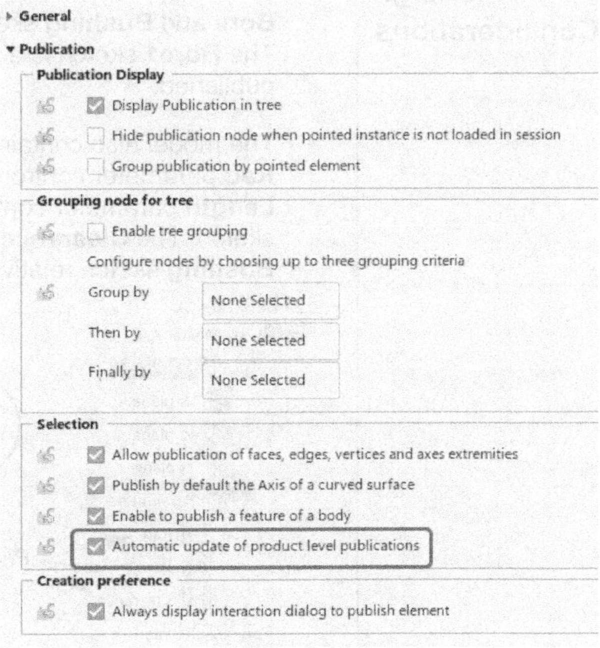

Figure 8–27

6. Click **OK** to close the Preferences dialog box.

Task 2 - Open a part file.

1. Import and open **Master.3dxml** from the *MultiModelLinks* folder. When importing, type your initials followed by the dash symbol into the *Duplication string* field. The model displays as shown in Figure 8–28.

Design Considerations

- The model contains three sketches and two publications. The **Bore** and **Bushing** sketches are the published geometries. The **Bore1** sketch is a copy of the **Bore** sketch, but it is not published.
- The model also contains three user-defined parameters. The **Rad** parameter controls the radius of the **Bore** sketch. The **Length** parameter controls the vertical size of the **Bushing** sketch. The **Clearance** parameter controls the position of the **Bushing** sketch relatively to the **Bore** sketch.

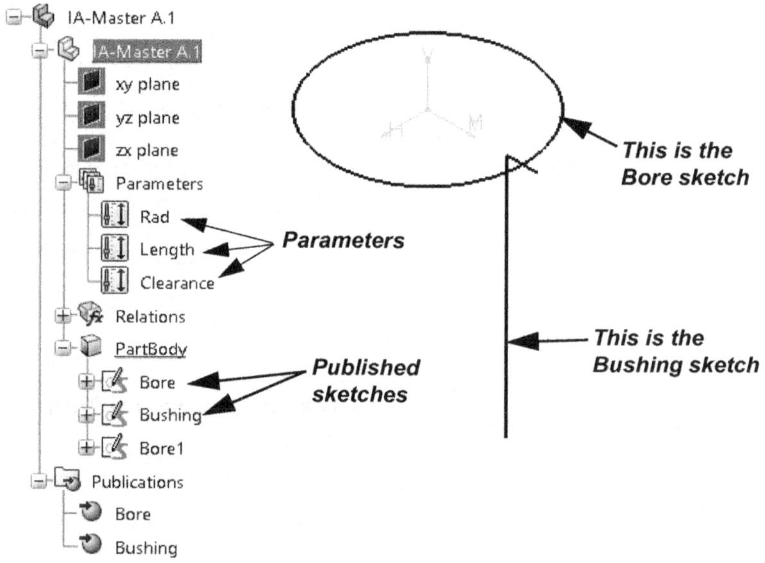

Figure 8–28

2. Double-click on the **Clearance** parameter. The Edit Parameter dialog box opens.

3. Change the parameter value to **20mm**, as shown in Figure 8–29.

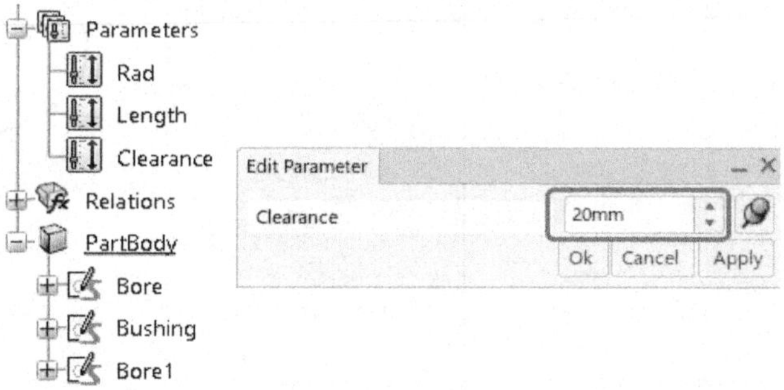

Figure 8–29

The Bushing sketch updates, as shown in Figure 8–30.

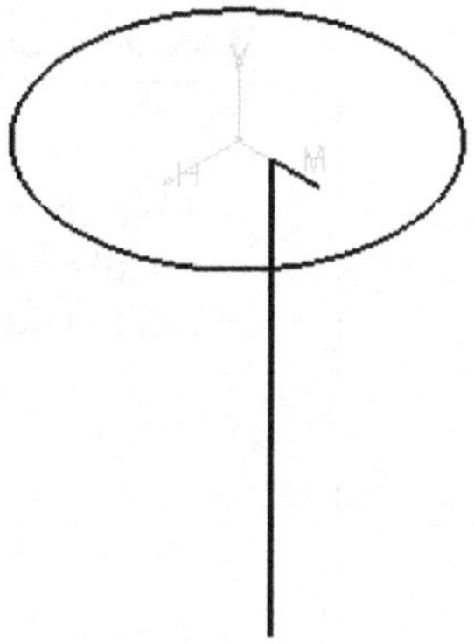

Figure 8–30

4. Change the **Clearance** parameter value to **4mm**, as shown in Figure 8–31.

Figure 8–31

The Bushing sketch updates, as shown in Figure 8–32.

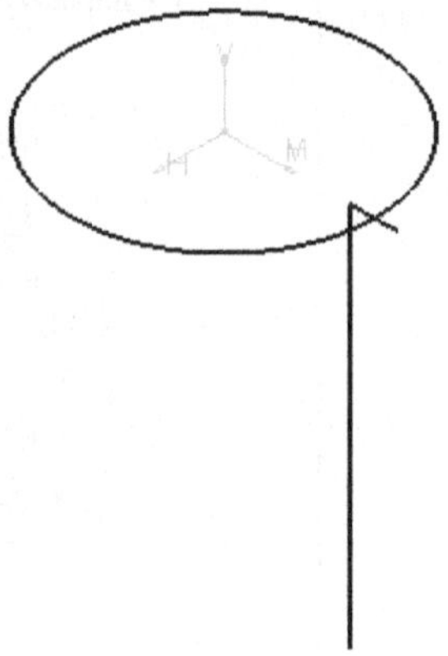

Figure 8–32

Task 3 - Open a part file.

1. Keep the Master part open. Import and open **Cover.3dxml** from the *MultiModelLinks* folder. When importing, type your initials followed by the dash symbol into the *Duplication string* field. The model displays as shown in Figure 8–33.

Figure 8–33

2. In the Tools section of the Action Bar, select  to verify whether the part has any external links. The Edit Links and Relations dialog box opens indicating that the part does not have external links, as shown in Figure 8–34.

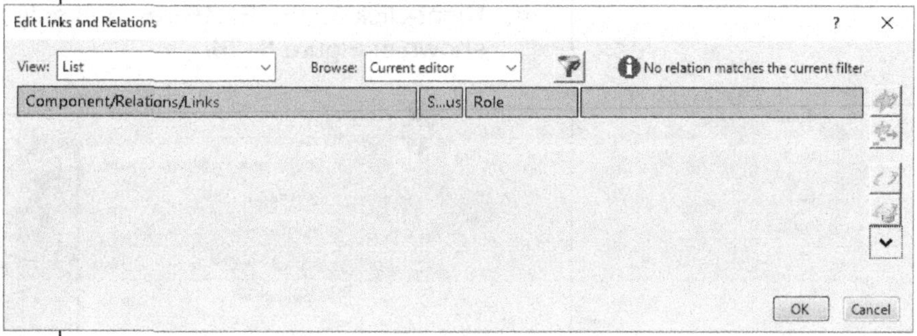

Figure 8–34

Task 4 - Copy and paste a sketch between parts.

1. Activate the **Master** part window.
2. In the specification tree, right-click on the **Bore1** sketch and select **Copy**, as shown in Figure 8–35.

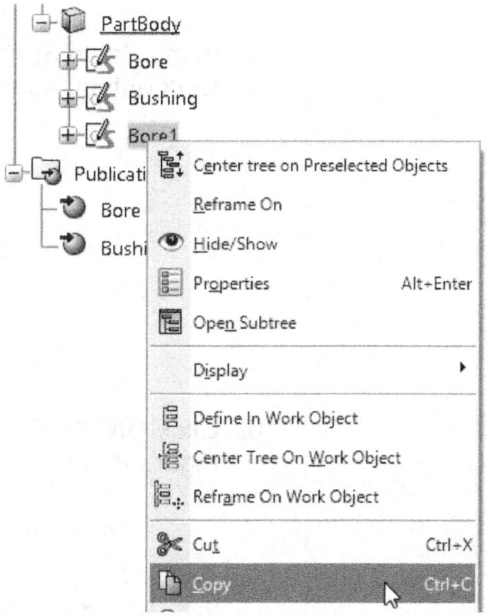

Figure 8–35

3. Activate the **Cover** part window.

4. Right-click on the **PartBody** and select **Paste Special**, as shown in Figure 8–36.

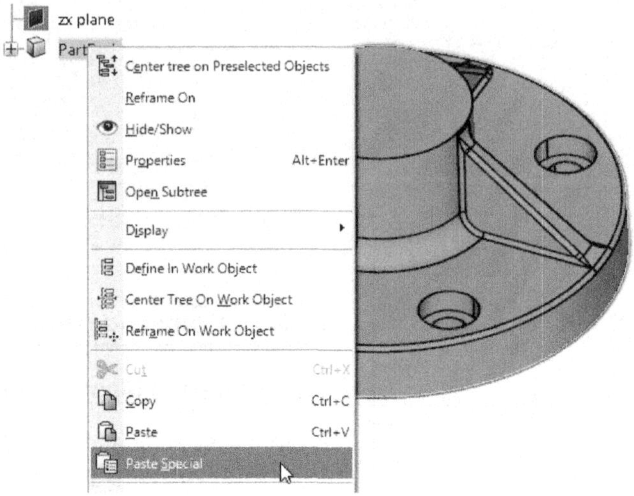

Figure 8–36

5. In the Paste Special dialog box, select the **As Result With Link** option, as shown in Figure 8–37.

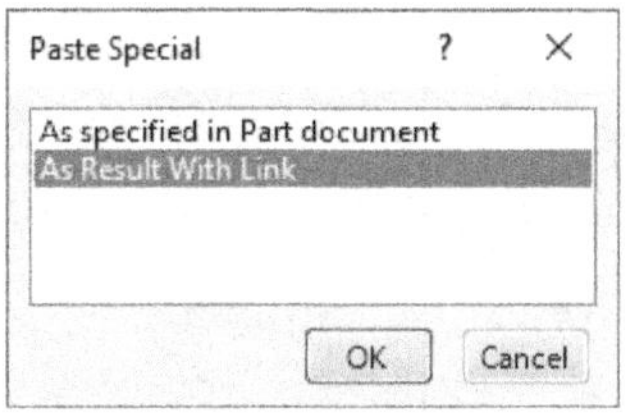

Figure 8–37

6. Click **OK**. An Error dialog box opens as shown in Figure 8–38.

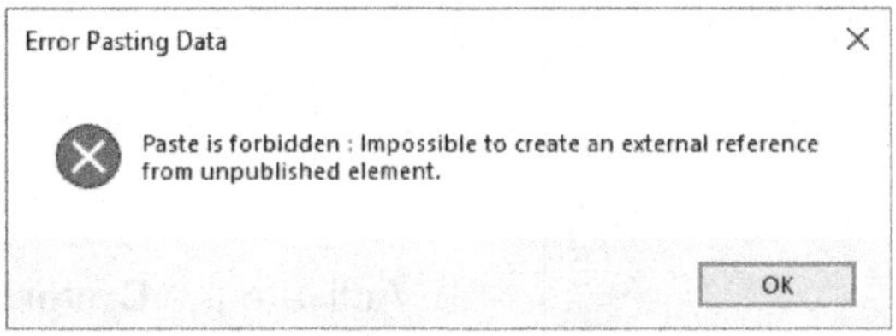

Figure 8–38

Design Considerations

Use of published elements restricts external reference creation. The Bore1 sketch is not published. That is why the Copy/Paste has failed.

7. Close the Error dialog box.
8. Activate the **Master** part window.
9. Copy the Bore published geometry, as shown in Figure 8–39. Note that when the Bore published element is selected, the Bore sketch is highlighted as well.

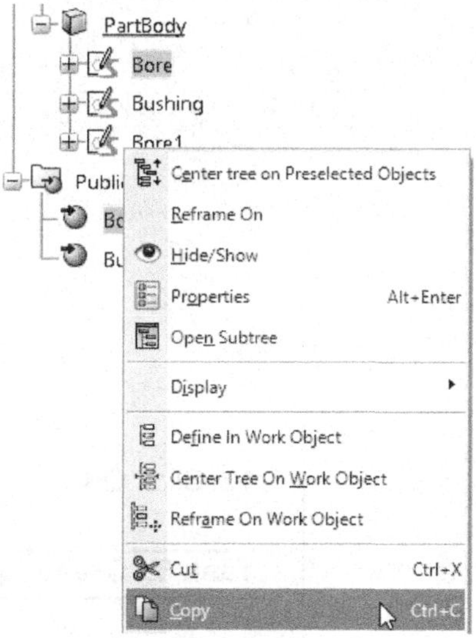

Figure 8–39

10. Activate the **Cover** part window.
11. Paste the Bore sketch into the PartBody using the **As Result With Link** option.

Design Considerations

The pasted sketch displays as a result in the specification tree. The green symbol shown in Figure 8–40 indicates that this sketch maintains a link with the original sketch.

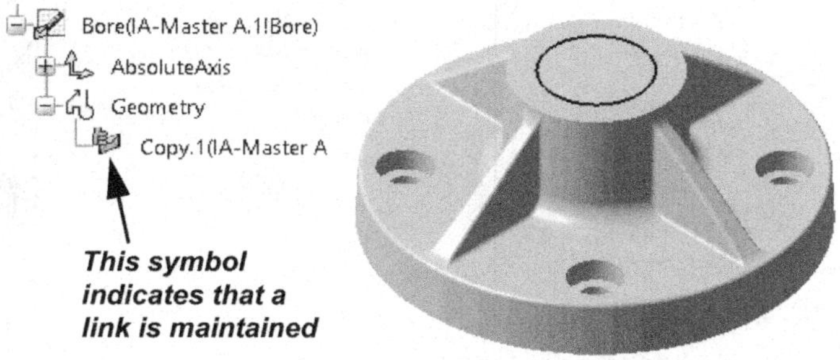

Figure 8–40

12. Investigate the resulting links by selecting . The Edit Links and Relations dialog box shown in Figure 8–41 indicates that this part has a link to the published element in the Master part that has been copied and pasted using one of the **Paste Special** options.

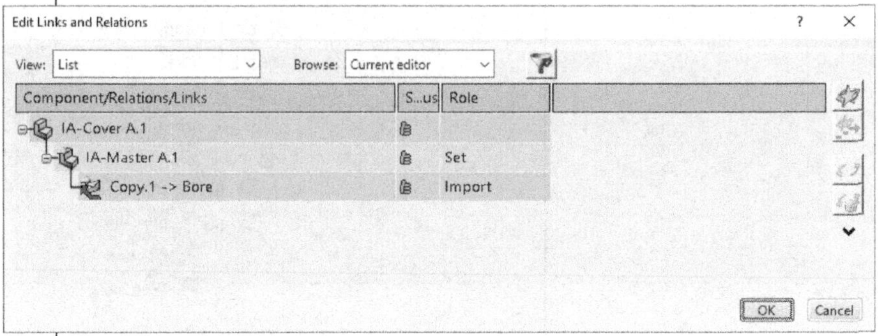

Figure 8–41

13. Click **OK**.

Task 5 - Create geometry from a pasted sketch.

1. Select the pasted sketch and create the Pocket feature shown in Figure 8–42.

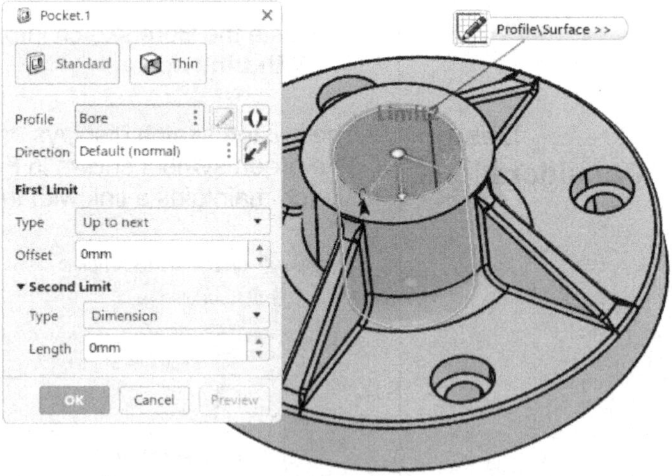

Figure 8–42

The Cover part model is now linked to the Master part.

2. Use the **Save All** option to save **Cover** and then close the window. Leave the Master part file open.

Task 6 - Open a part file.

1. Import and open **Bushing.3dxml**. When importing, type your initials followed by the dash symbol into the *Duplication string* field. The model does not contain any geometry. It displays as shown in Figure 8–43.

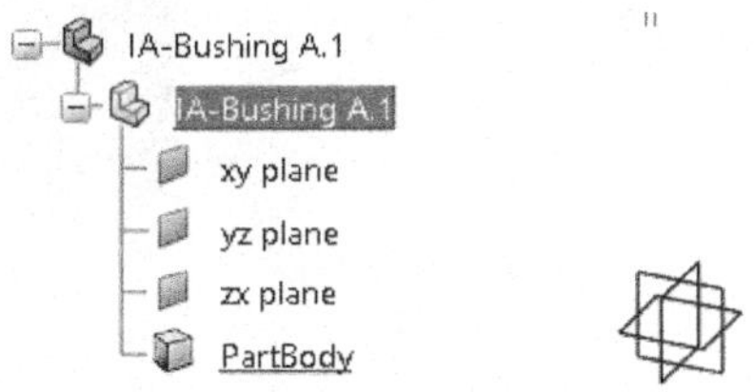

Figure 8–43

2. Copy and paste the Bushing published geometry into the Bushing part file using the **As Result With Link** option. The resulting geometry displays as shown in Figure 8–44.

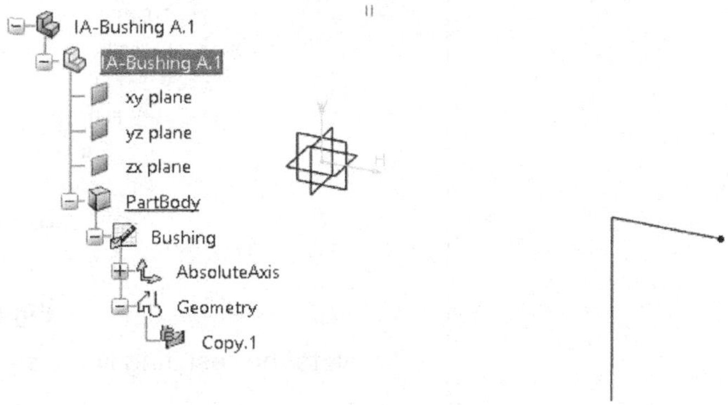

Figure 8–44

3. Create a thin Shaft feature from the pasted sketch with the parameters shown in Figure 8–45.

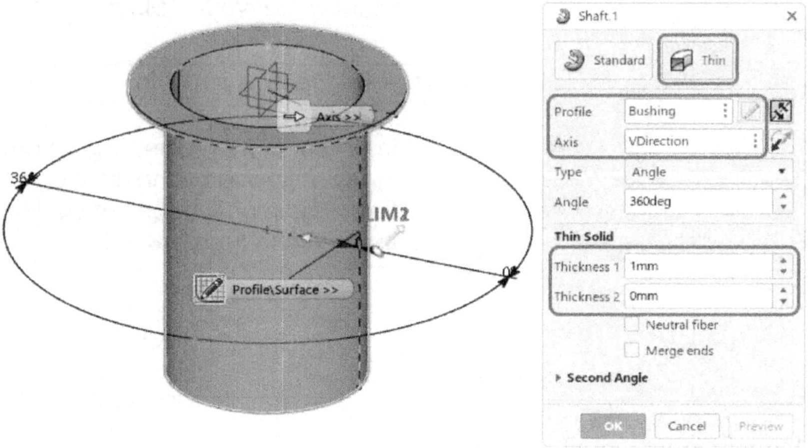

Figure 8–45

The completed bushing part displays as shown in Figure 8–46.

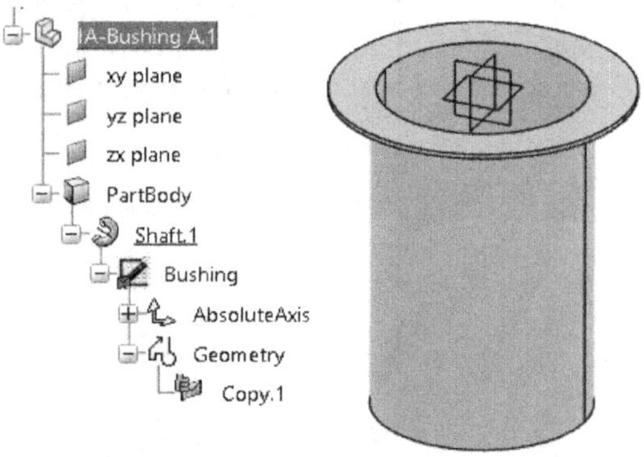

Figure 8–46

4. Note the resulting links, as shown in Figure 8–47.

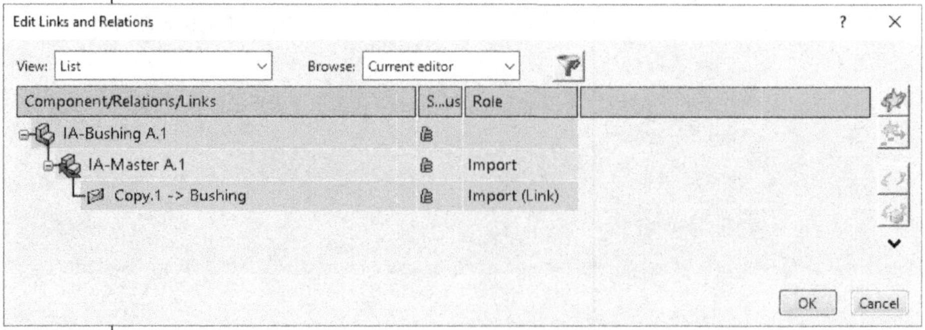

Figure 8–47

5. Save the Bushing part.

Task 7 - Modify the Master part and update the Cover.

1. Close all of the models except for the Master part, as shown in Figure 8–48.

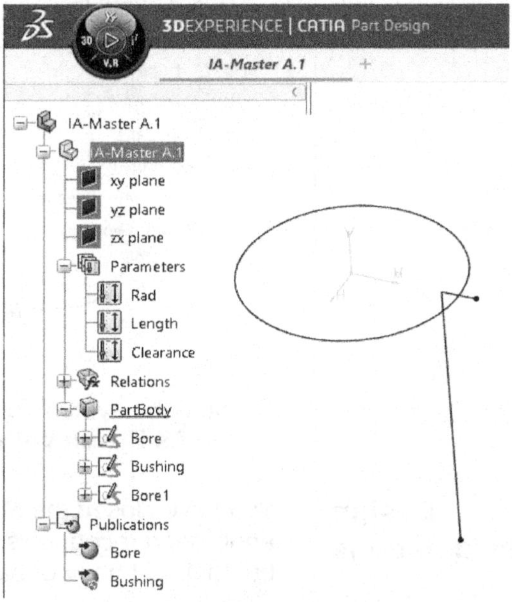

Figure 8–48

2. Change the radius of the Bore sketch by changing the value of the **Rad** parameter to **30mm**, as shown in Figure 8–49.

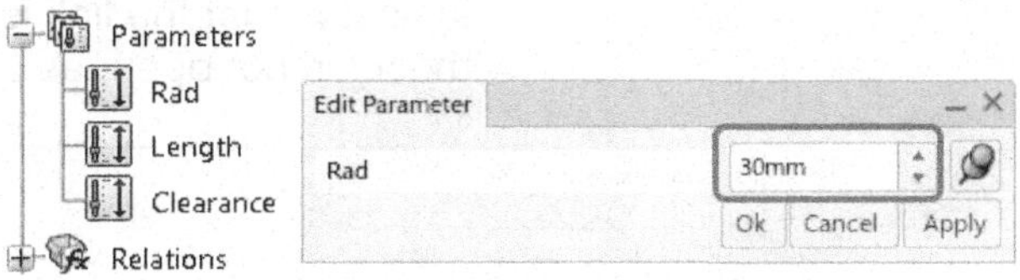

Figure 8–49

3. Save and close the Master part.

4. Using the 3DEXPERIENCE search tool, search for and open **<*YourInitials*>-Cover**. Show the **Bore** sketch under the Pocket.1 feature. The model displays as shown in Figure 8–50.

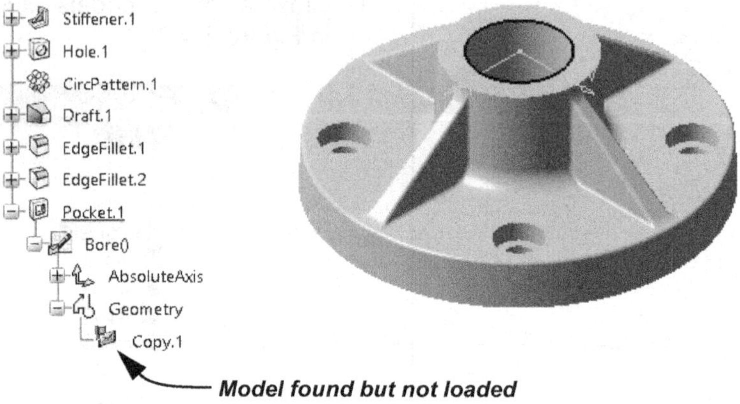

Figure 8–50

5. Note the symbol for the sketch that has been pasted using the **As Result With Link** option.

Design Considerations

You have closed the **Master** part and opened **Cover**. The application recognizes that a link to another part (Master) exists, but that part has not been loaded. Therefore, the link has not been synchronized. This status is indicated by .

6. Investigate the links by selecting . The *Status* column indicates that the link is unsynchronized since the parent model is not open, as shown in Figure 8–51.

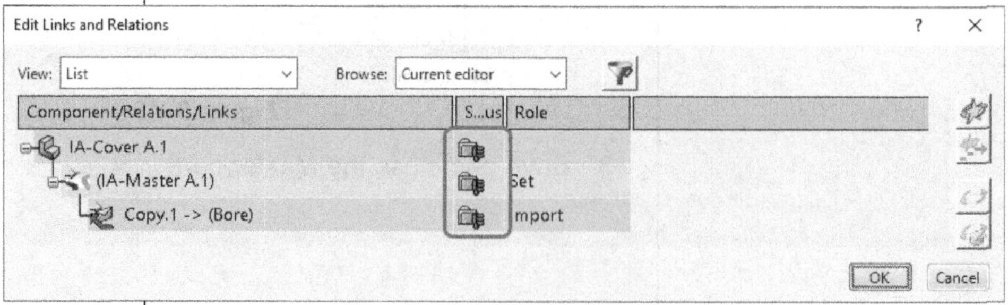

Figure 8–51

7. Right-click on the link and select **Open** to open the pointed document. The Open Advanced dialog box opens. Click **OK** to proceed. The Master part opens in a separate window.

8. Switch to the **Cover** window and display the Edit Links and Relations dialog box. Note that the *Status* column still shows **Unsynchronized**, as shown in Figure 8–52. Click  (Synchronize link).

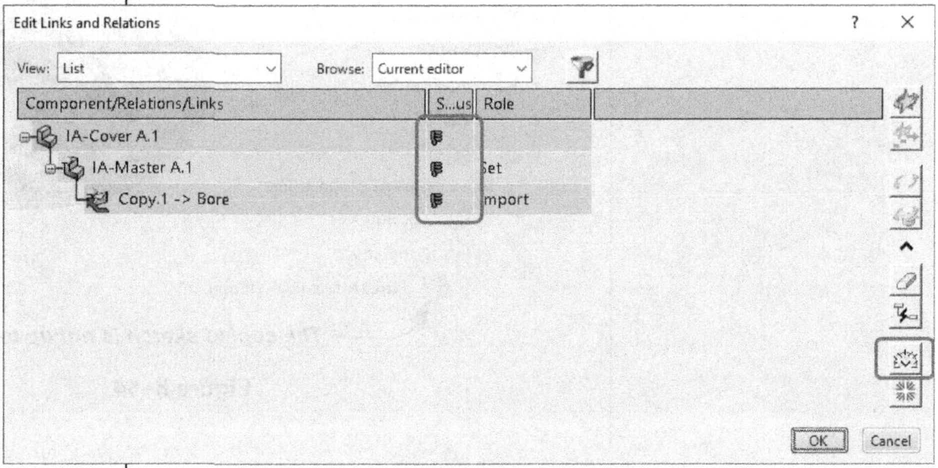

Figure 8–52

9. The status of the link changes to **Synchronized**, as shown in Figure 8–53.

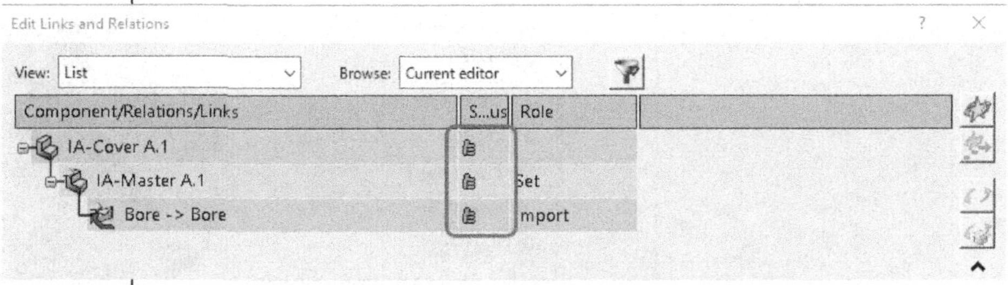

Figure 8–53

10. Click **OK** to close the Edit Links and Relations dialog box.

Design Considerations

Now that you have loaded the information from the pointed document, the application recognizes that changes have been made (you changed the **Rad** parameter of **Master** to **30mm**) and that the result of the **Paste Special** element is not up to date. The **Cover** part displays in red, indicating that an update is required, as shown in Figure 8–54.

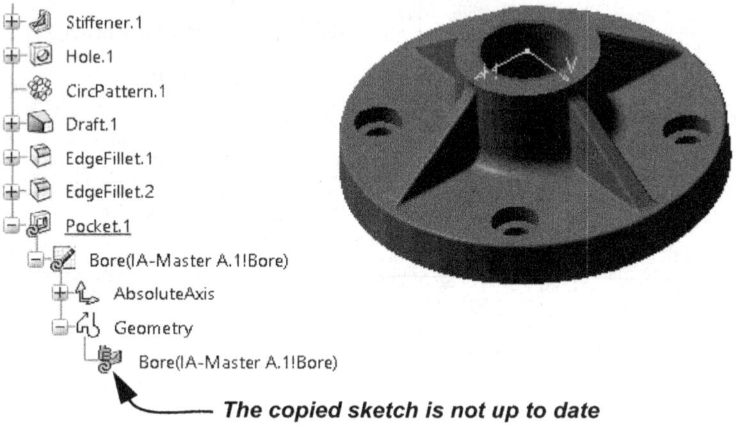

Figure 8–54

11. Click  to update the model. The model updates with the changes made to the pointed document and the symbol indicates that the result is up to date, as shown in Figure 8–55.

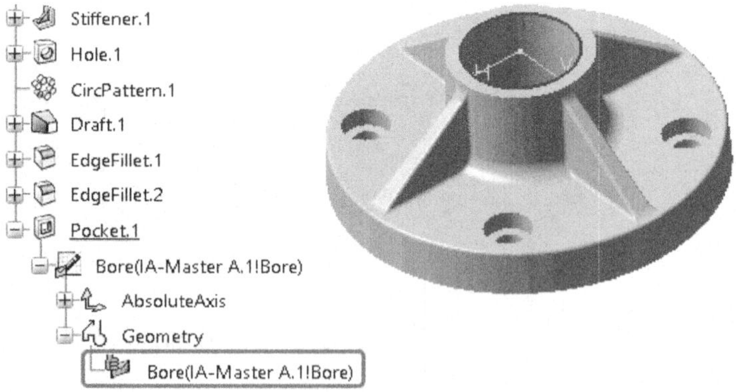

Figure 8–55

Task 8 - Update the Bushing part.

In this task, you will open the Bushing part for updating. Since the pointed document will already be in session, all that is required is an update of the target document.

1. Search for and open <***YourInitials***>**-Bushing**. The part displays as shown in Figure 8–56.

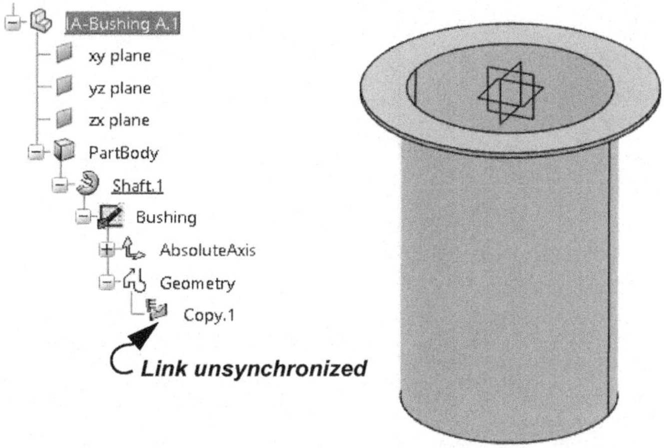

Figure 8–56

2. Click . The model updates to reflect the changes made to the pointed document. The model displays as shown in Figure 8–57.

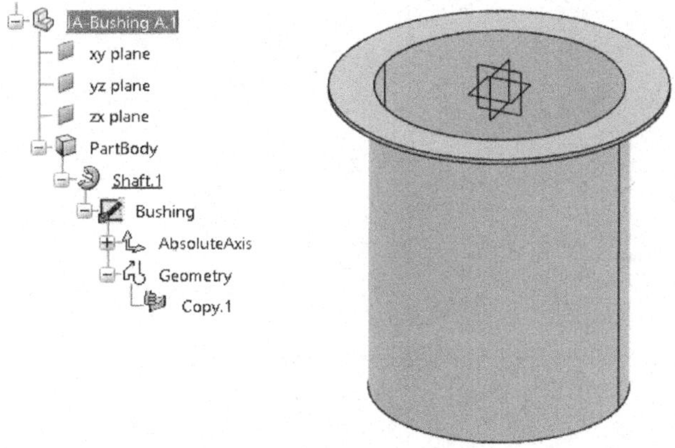

Figure 8–57

This practice shows you that design intent can be captured in a single part model, and that information can be used to drive the geometry of any number of parts using the **Paste Special** and **As Result With Link** options.

3. Save all models.

4. If time permits, leave the models open and continue with the next practice, otherwise, close all models.

Practice 8c Managing Multi-Model Links

Practice Objective

- Manage multi-document link.

In this practice, you will use the bushing shown in Figure 8–58 to explore and manage multi-model linking by editing linked parts in an assembly and using the **Isolate** command.

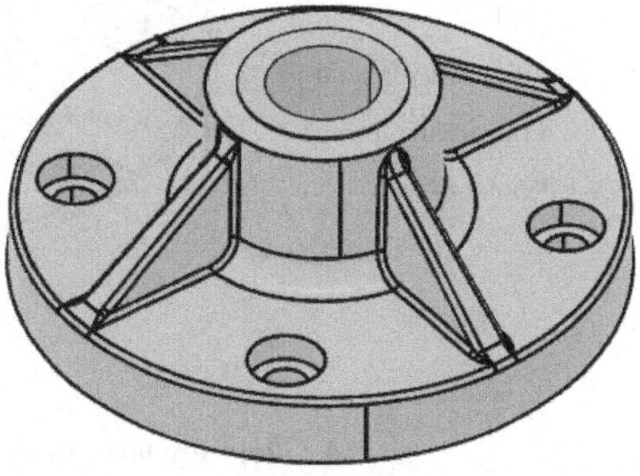

Figure 8–58

Task 1 - Open the assembly.

1. Open a new Physical Product, named <***YourInitials>_ FrontCover***.

2. Assemble the **Cover** part (that you have had open in your session since Practice 8b) using the Fix constraint. The assembly displays as shown in Figure 8–59.

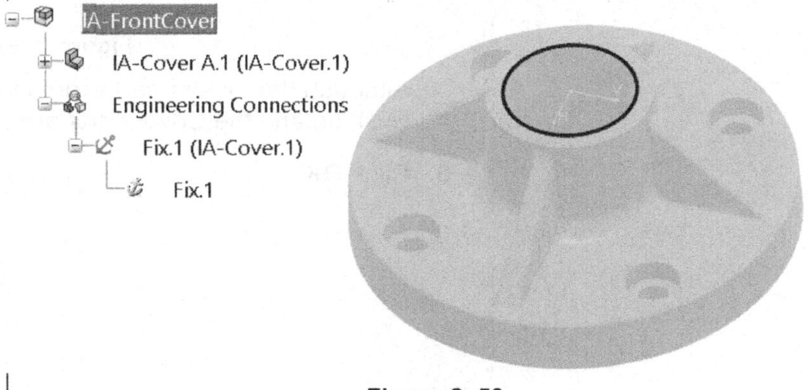

Figure 8–59

3. Assemble **Bushing** using a coincidence and contact constraint, as shown in Figure 8–60.

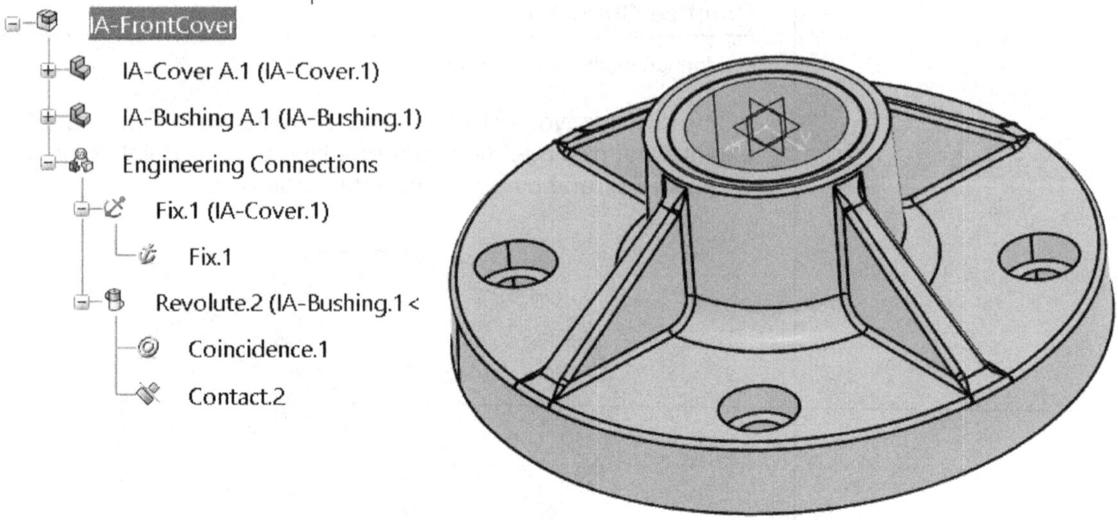

Figure 8–60

4. Note the links to the Master part, as shown in Figure 8–61.

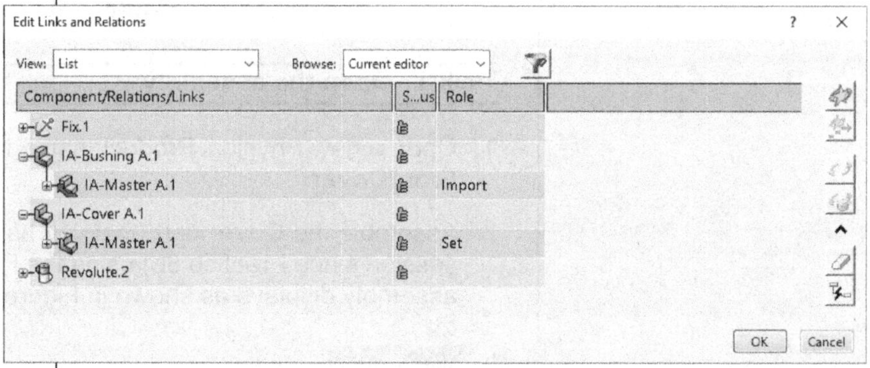

Figure 8–61

Although the Master part is not included in the assembly, the Bushing and the Cover parts are still linked to it.

5. Click **OK**.

Task 2 - Modify the pointed document.

1. Switch to the **Master** part window.
2. Modify the **Rad** parameter to **20mm**, as shown in Figure 8–62.

*If the Warnings dialog box opens, click **Close**.*

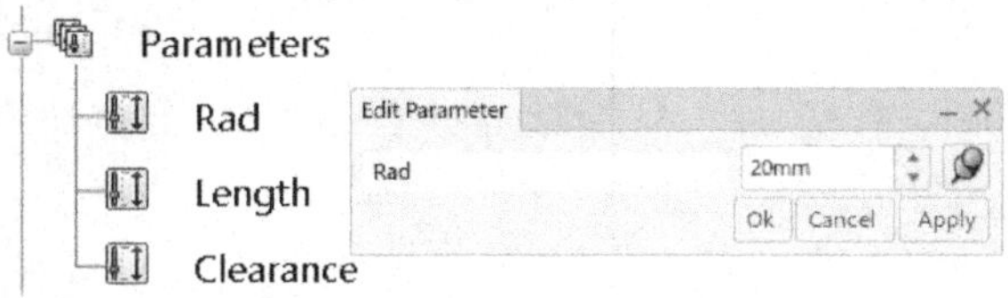

Figure 8–62

3. Save the Master part.
4. Activate the **FrontCover** product window and update the assembly, as shown in Figure 8–63.

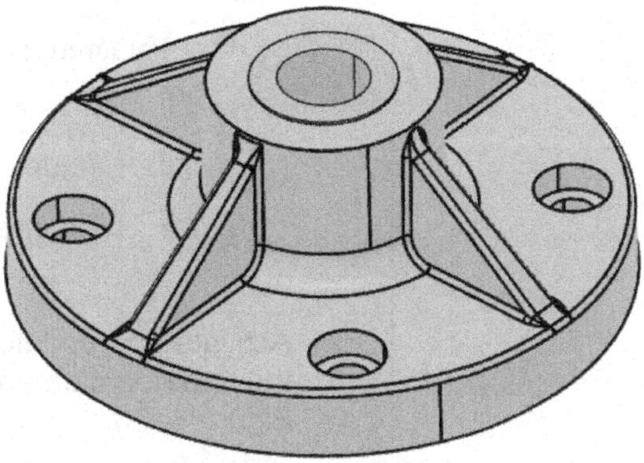

Figure 8–63

Design Considerations

The product does not directly point to the Master part. However, the Master part controls the individual parts through the part-to-part links established in the previous practice. Using the **Paste Special** and **As Result With Link** options is a great method for sharing information between parts, and for capturing assembly design intent. In the following steps, you will see how the clearance between two parts can be controlled using this technique.

5. Rotate the product so that you can see the clearance between the two parts, as shown in Figure 8–64.

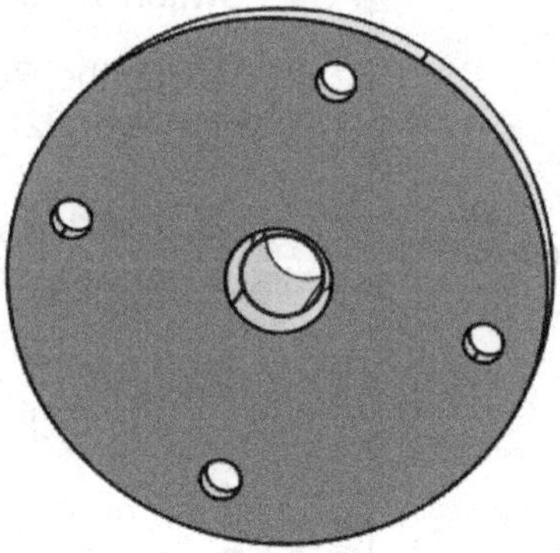

Figure 8–64

6. Activate the **Master** part window and modify the **Clearance** parameter to **0.5mm**, as shown in Figure 8–65.

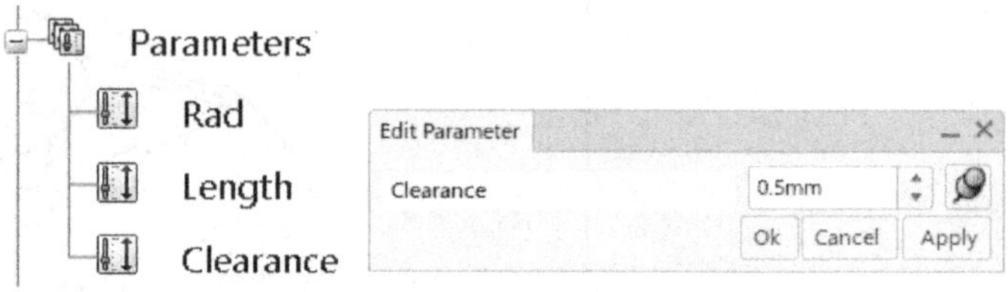

Figure 8–65

7. Activate and update the **FrontCover** product window. Note the updated clearance between the parts, as shown in Figure 8–66.

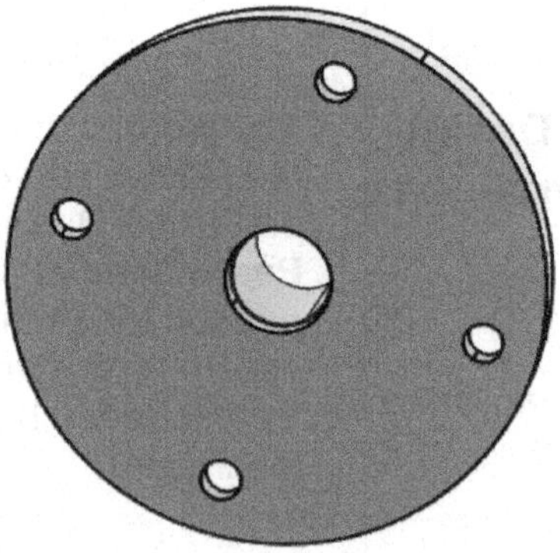

Figure 8–66

Task 3 - Manage links.

Design Considerations

Using the **As Result With Link** option can be a valuable technique in the early stages of a design, as changes made to the Master part will be reflected in the parts that point to it. However, as the design matures and the final component configuration has been achieved, links to the pointed document can be isolated as required. Keep in mind that once a link has been isolated, it cannot be re-established.

1. Switch to the **Bushing** window.
2. Open the Edit Links and Relations dialog box. It will display as shown in Figure 8–67.

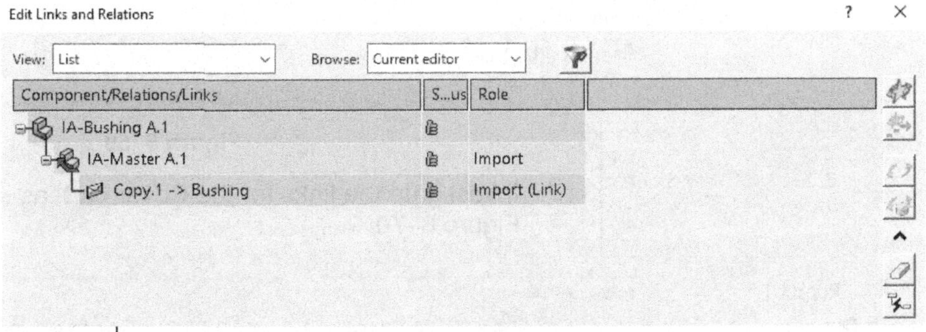

Figure 8–67

3. Isolate the link by selecting the last line and clicking  (Isolate). The link is removed from the list and the sketch geometry icon shows that it is now an isolated copy, as shown in Figure 8–68.

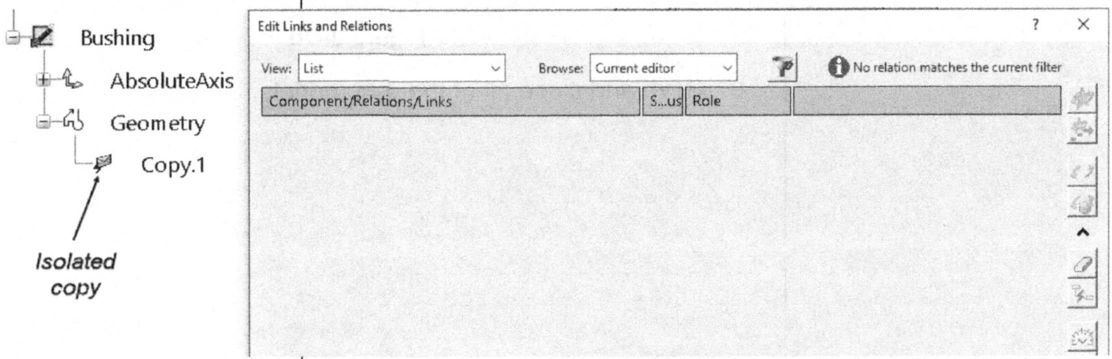

Figure 8–68

4. Click **OK**.

5. Switch to the **Cover** window.

6. Right-click on the **Bore** sketch and isolate it, as shown in Figure 8–69.

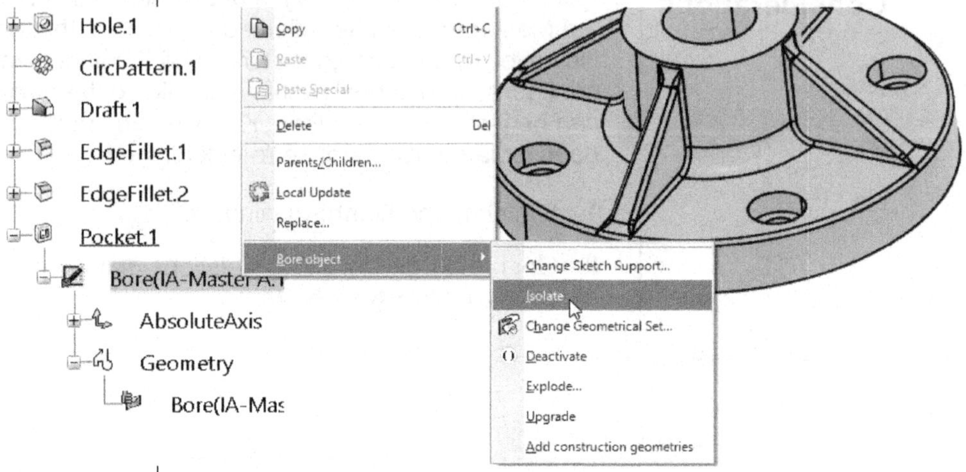

Figure 8–69

7. Investigate the links for the Cover part, as shown in Figure 8–70.

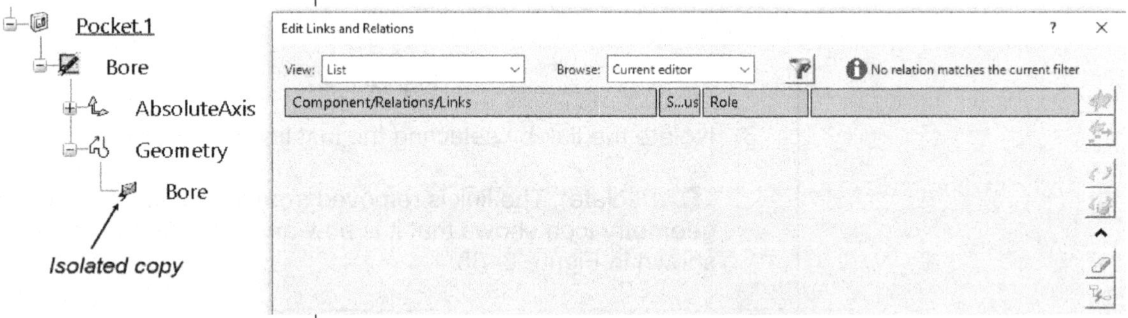

Figure 8–70

8. Save and close all of the part models.

Design Considerations

Use of multi-model links is an effective method of communicating design intent between parts. Once the design is finalized and the links between parts are isolated, models can act as independent parts. You can reuse these parts in other designs without being concerned about maintaining the multi-model links. At this stage in the design, the Master part is no longer required and can be deleted. The result is shown in Figure 8–71.

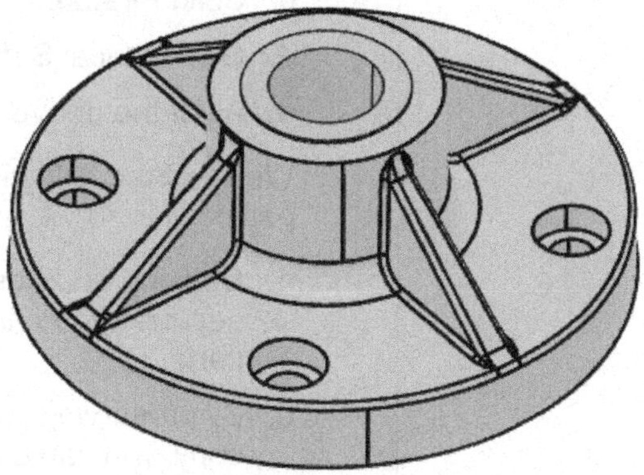

Figure 8–71

9. Save the assembly and close the window.

Chapter Review Questions

1. Which of the following can be copied in a part?
    a. Sketches
    b. Part Bodies
    c. Solid Features
    d. Geometrical Sets
    e. All of the above
2. Which of the following are advantages of copying and pasting?
    a. Copying and pasting geometry reduces re-work time because you can use pre-existing data to create similar parts.
    b. By preserving links between the original geometry and the copy, you can update multiple parts by only modifying one part.
    c. By severing links, you can create variations of a part while preserving the original features and dimensions.
    d. All of the above.
3. When using **Paste Special**, what does the **As Result** option do?
    a. Pastes the body with its design specifications into the target document.
    b. Pastes the body without its design specifications and maintains a link between the original and the copy.
    c. Pastes the body without its design specifications and without making a link between the source and target documents
    d. None of the above.
4. The Edit Links and Relations dialog box lists the external references of an entire document or only one body in the document.
    a. True
    b. False

5. One method for reusing a group of elements that are externally referenced is to create a _____?
    a. Document
    b. Guide
    c. Publication
    d. None of the above.

Answers: 1e, 2d, 3c, 4a, 7c

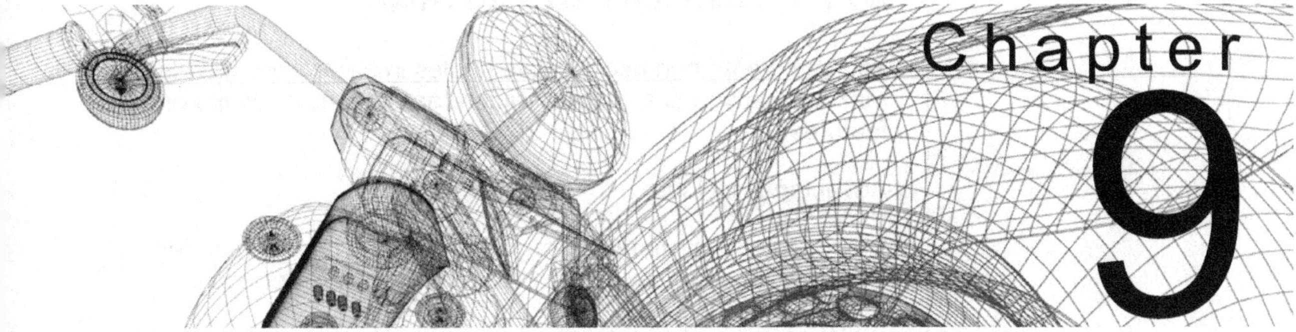

Boolean Operations

Boolean operations in CATIA are powerful design tools. The ability to combine feature-based modeling with boolean operations enables the creation of robust geometry. You can work with various bodies in a single part file. This provides flexibility in design scenarios, promotes concurrent engineering, and enables viewing and manipulation of multiple model states.

Learning Objectives in This Chapter

- Learn how to create and use multiple bodies in a part.
- Understand how multiple bodies can be used to both organize your model geometry and to facilitate boolean operations.
- Understand boolean operations.
- Understand 3D constraints.

9.1 Creation of Bodies

You can create and use multiple bodies in a Part model. This makes it easy to create the structure and organize groups of features.

Advantages include:

- You can improve model organization by grouping features in separate bodies with respect to their function or position.
- You can create each body in a separate part model and then paste it into the finished model. Using this feature, a number of designers working concurrently can build a model.
- A single part model can contain and display a variety of model states (i.e., cast and machined state).

General Steps

Use the following general steps when working with part bodies:

1. Insert the bodies.
2. Rename the bodies.
3. Create the features.

Step 1 - Insert the bodies.

Select  (Body) from the Structure section of the Action Bar. Inserted bodies display as shown in Figure 9–1.

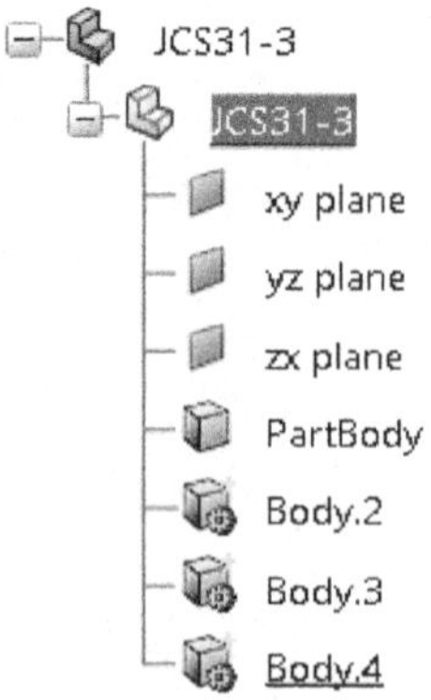

Figure 9–1

To add an existing feature to a part body, select the feature, right-click, and select ***object>Insert in New...**, as shown in Figure 9–2.

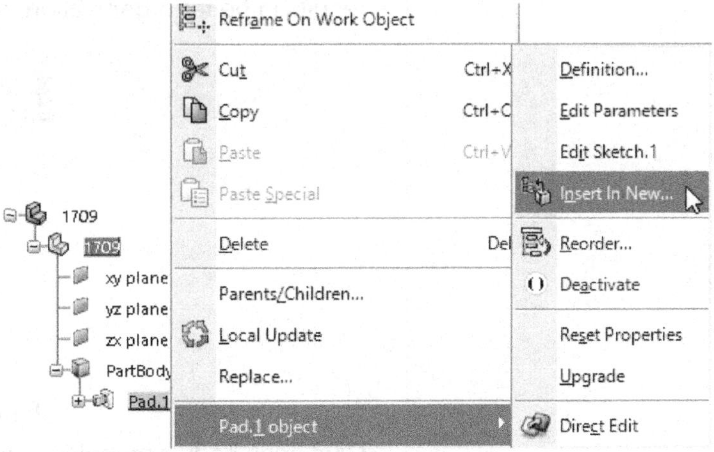

Figure 9–2

The feature is added to a new body and automatically assembled to the PartBody using the **Assemble Boolean** operation, as shown in Figure 9–3.

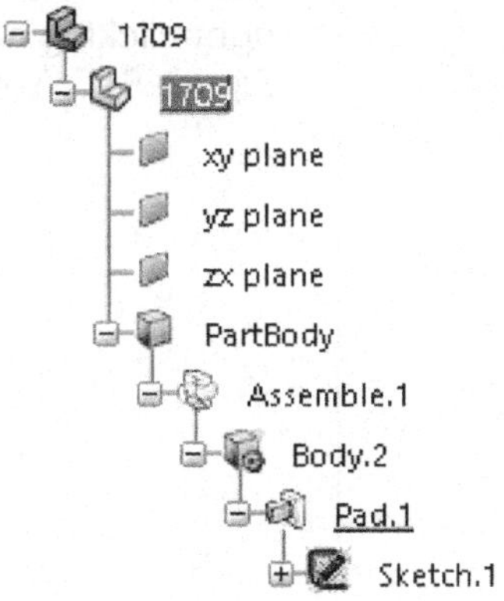

Figure 9–3

Alternatively, select  (Insert in New) from the Structure section of the Action Bar.

Step 2 - Rename the bodies.

It is considered good practice to rename new bodies. Doing so results in better organization, as shown in Figure 9–4.

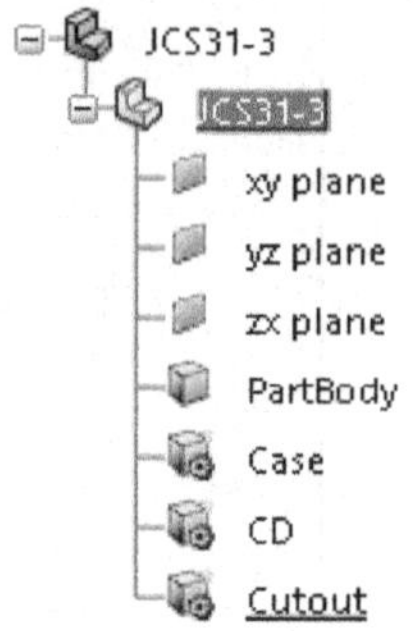

Figure 9–4

Give each body a meaningful name that is easily recognizable by other users.

Step 3 - Create the features.

Activate the appropriate body by selecting the body, and then right-clicking and selecting **Define In Work Object**, as shown in Figure 9–5. You can now create features in the body.

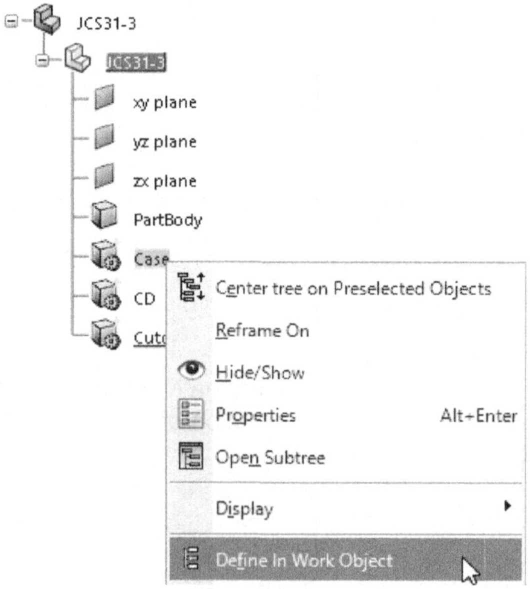

Figure 9–5

Alternatively, when a body that is not active is selected, a context menu is displayed. From this menu, you can select  (Define in work Object), as shown in Figure 9–6.

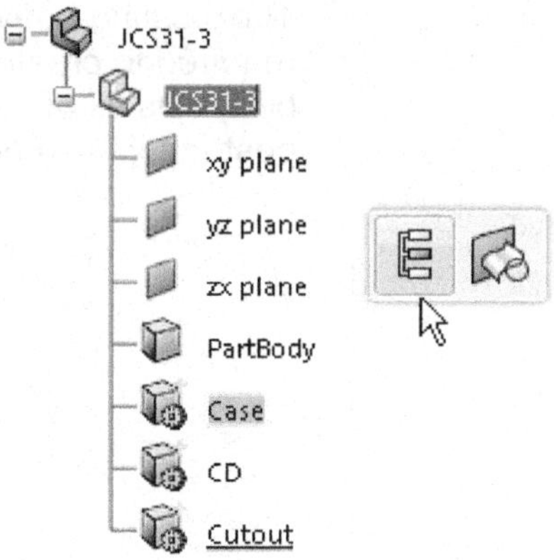

Figure 9–6

9.2 Feature Organization

Using various bodies not only facilitates boolean operations, but helps keep the part geometry organized. Consider the example shown in Figure 9–7. The specification tree depicts a cast part. The Casting body contains all of the bodies and features required to create the cast geometry. The MachiningOperations body lists all of the bodies and features required to achieve post-machining geometry.

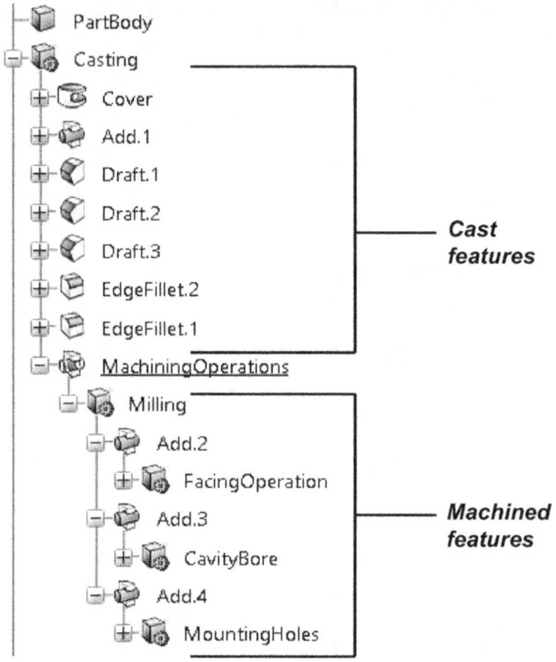

Figure 9–7

PartBody

A PartBody can only be used as the operand, not the operator.

Geometrical Set

It is suggested that you insert a geometrical set for each body. This helps in better organization of the features of the model. All of the sketches and wireframe elements can be stored under the geometrical set(s).

As the part becomes more complex, it is more difficult to keep track of the features. If there are several designers working on the same model, all of the designers can use the geometrical set(s) to understand how the model is built. Use of geometrical sets also makes it easier to find the required sketches and wireframe elements to make the required modifications.

Axis System

You must create an axis system for each body. All of the elements and features for a body should be referenced by its axis system. If you need to move a body, you can do so easily by changing the position of its axis system.

Design Considerations

While designing the bodies, you must ensure that the features do not reference the other bodies before the boolean operations, unless it is required. If the reference body is deleted, moved, or modified, the children of the reference body are most likely to cause an update failure. Therefore, you must ensure that non-required external links to the other bodies are isolated.

Activate and Deactivate

You can deactivate individual part bodies to reduce update time, and to display a model in various states. The models in Figure 9–8 are shown in a cast pre-machined state (MachiningOperations deactivated) and in a post-machined state.

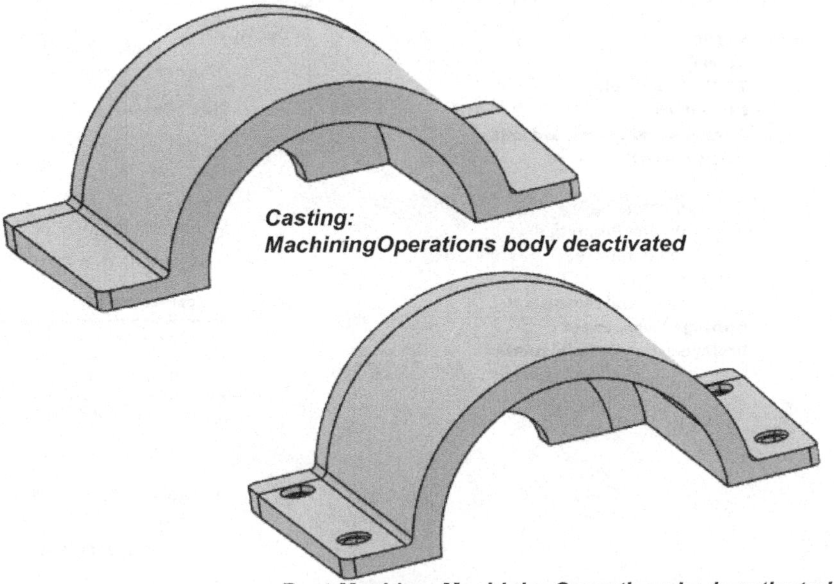

Figure 9–8

Hide and Show

Hiding bodies might be a convenient method of simplifying the display of a complex model. You can only hide bodies independently if they have not been used in a boolean operation.

Color

To differentiate between bodies, it is suggested that you apply different colors for each body. You can do this by adjusting the graphic properties for each body.

Geometry Display Options

You can control the display of the model based on the activated body or geometrical set by using the settings in the Preferences dialog box. To open the Preferences dialog box, select **Me>Preferences>Common Preferences**. Expand **Object Properties<3D Shape>Display**. The **Only the current operated solid** and **Only current body** options are shown in Figure 9–9. These options enable the designer to focus on the geometry of the active body or geometrical set, and are useful for organizing the display of a complex, multi-body part.

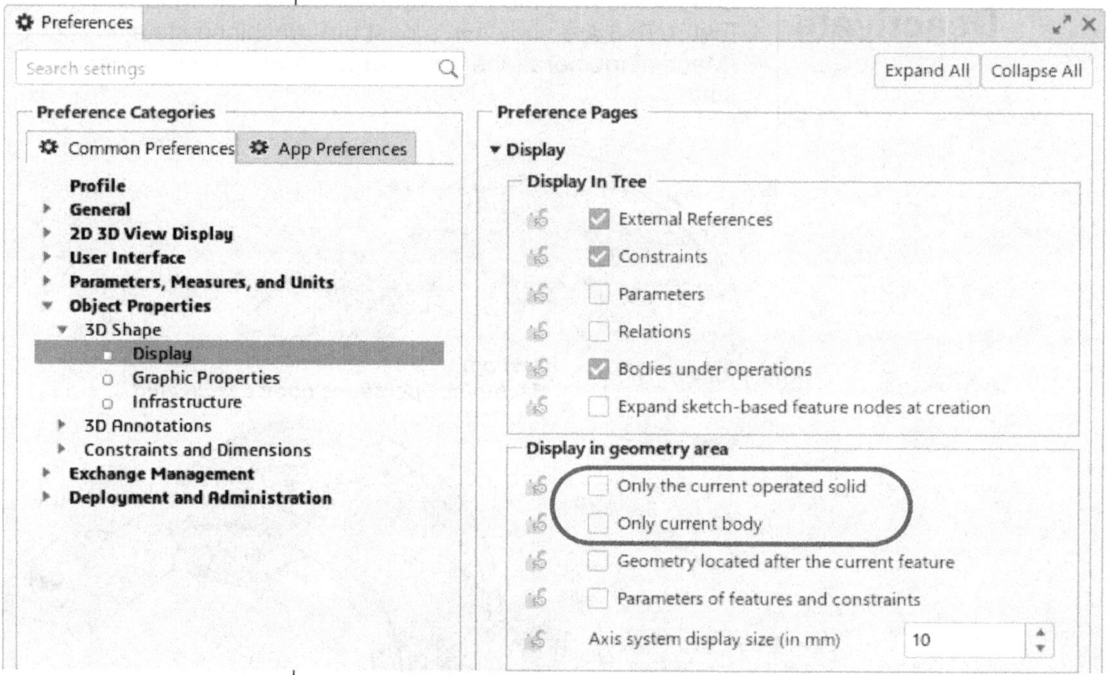

Figure 9–9

The options are also located in the App Options window, as shown in Figure 9–10.  (App Options) can be found in the Tools section of the Action Bar.

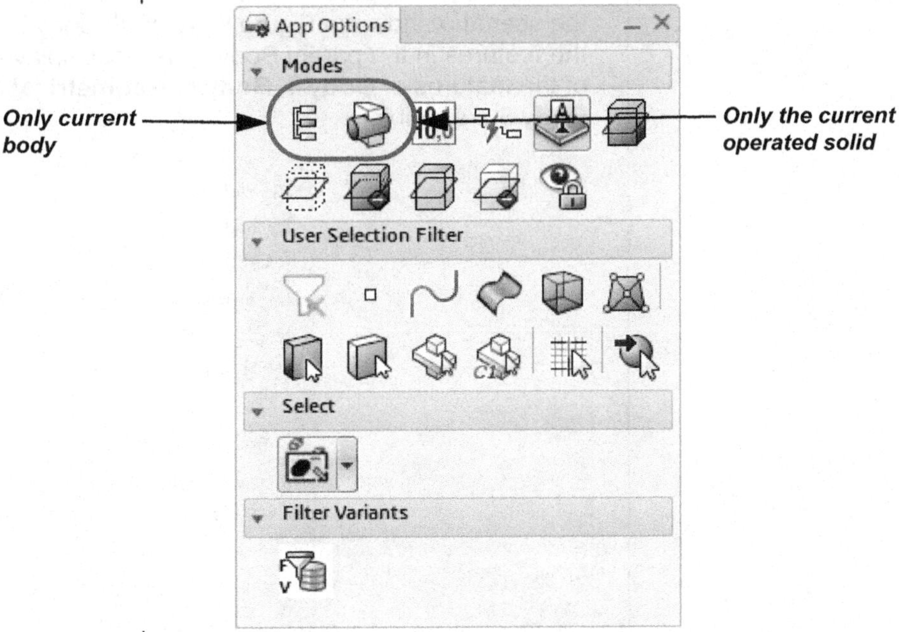

Figure 9–10

Only the Current Operated Solid

When you select this option, all of the bodies and geometrical sets display, except for any parent bodies. For example, consider the scenario shown in Figure 9–11. With Body.3 activated, all of the features in the parent Body.2 are not displayed. However, all of the features of **Body.3**, **Body.4**, **Geometrical Set.1**, and **Body.5** are visible.

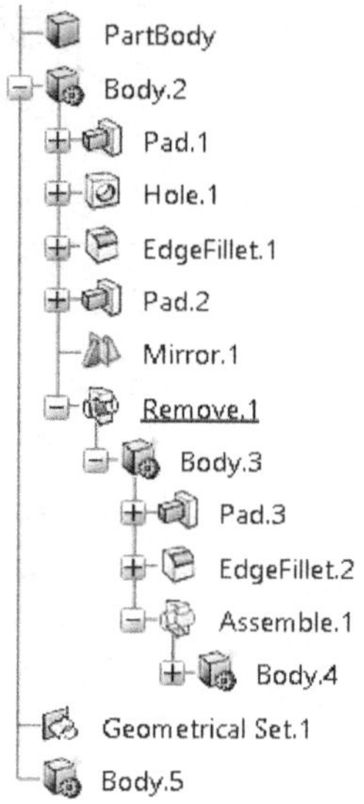

Figure 9–11

Only Current Body

When you select this option, only the geometry of the active geometrical set or solid body displays. Any bodies that are located beneath the active body (through a **Boolean** operation) are also displayed. If you consider the same scenario shown in Figure 9–11, if the **Only current body** option is selected, only the geometry of **Body.3** and **Body.4** would be visible. Since **Geometrical Set.1** and **Body.5** do not belong to **Body.3**, they would be hidden.

9.3 Boolean Operations

The Boolean Operations can be found in the Structure section of the Action Bar. All of the boolean operation icons are shown in Figure 9–12.

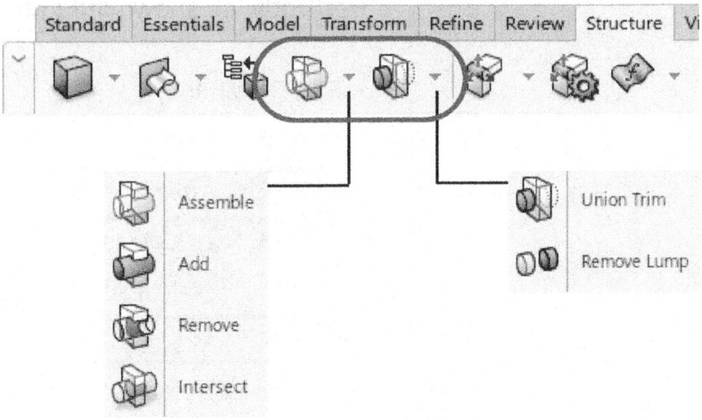

Figure 9–12

The following types of boolean operations are discussed, using the example model shown in Figure 9–13:

- Assemble
- Add
- Remove
- Intersect
- Union Trim
- Remove Lump

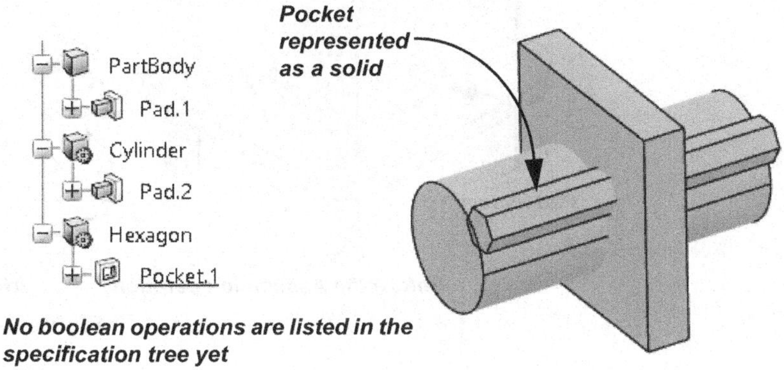

Figure 9–13

Assemble

 (Assemble) assembles the selected body into another body. Because the features are assembled, they are not altered in any way. For example, **Pad.2** of the Cylinder body results in the addition of geometry to the PartBody, and **Pocket.1** of the Hexagon body results in the removal of geometry from the PartBody, as shown in Figure 9–14 and Figure 9–15.

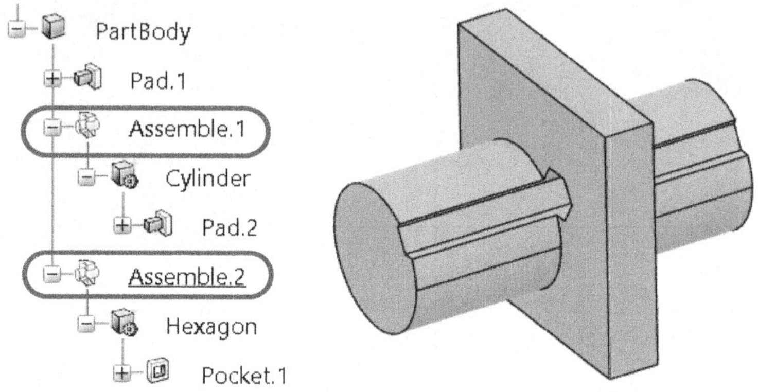

Figure 9–14

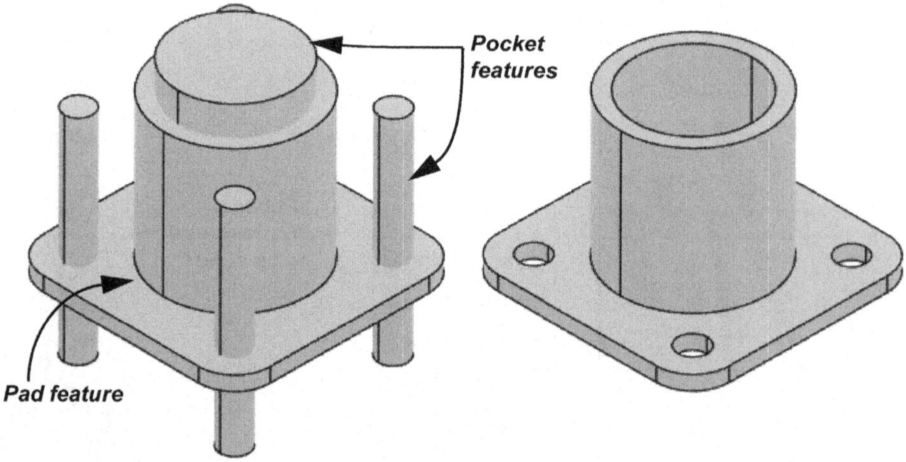

Before the Assemble operation ***After the Assemble operation***

Figure 9–15

Add

 (Add) considers all of the features of a body to be additive. Therefore, both the Pad and Pocket features from the original bodies add material to the PartBody, as shown in Figure 9–16.

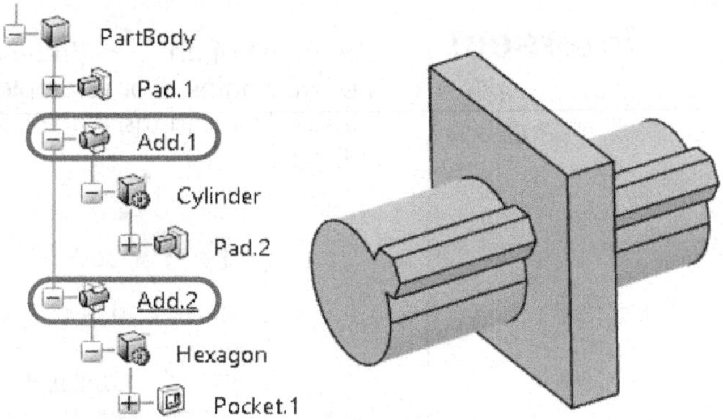

Figure 9–16

Remove

 (Remove) considers all of the features of a body to be subtractive. Therefore, both the Pad and Pocket features from the original bodies remove material from the PartBody, as shown in Figure 9–17 and Figure 9–18.

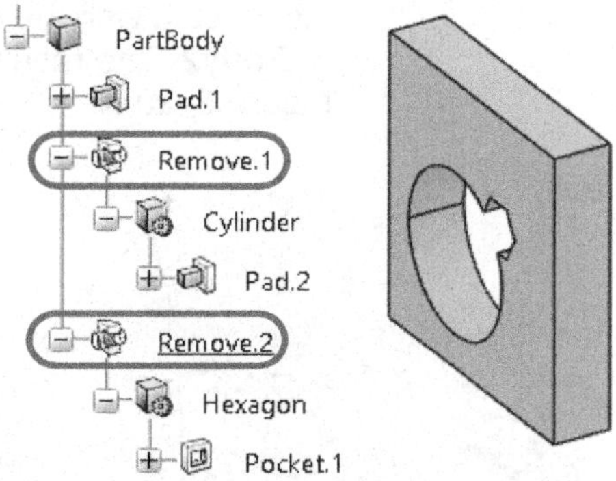

Figure 9–17

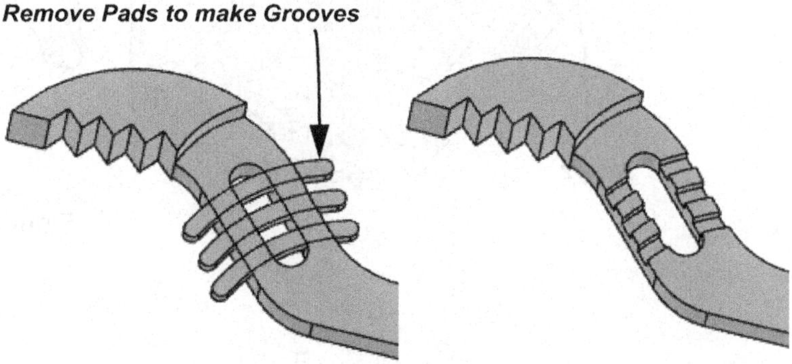

Figure 9–18

Intersect

The result of an  (Intersect) is the shared volume between the two bodies. For example, if the Cylinder body were intersected with the PartBody, the result would display as shown in Figure 9–19.

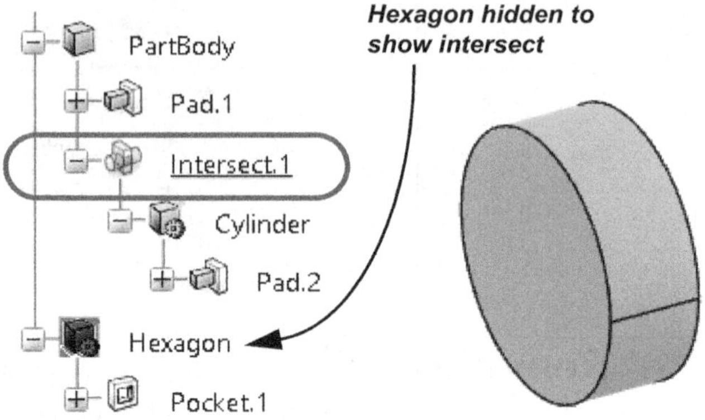

Figure 9–19

In another example, an engine block model located in **Body1** is intersected with the geometry of a transmission interface located in **Body2**. The resulting intersection displays as shown in Figure 9–20.

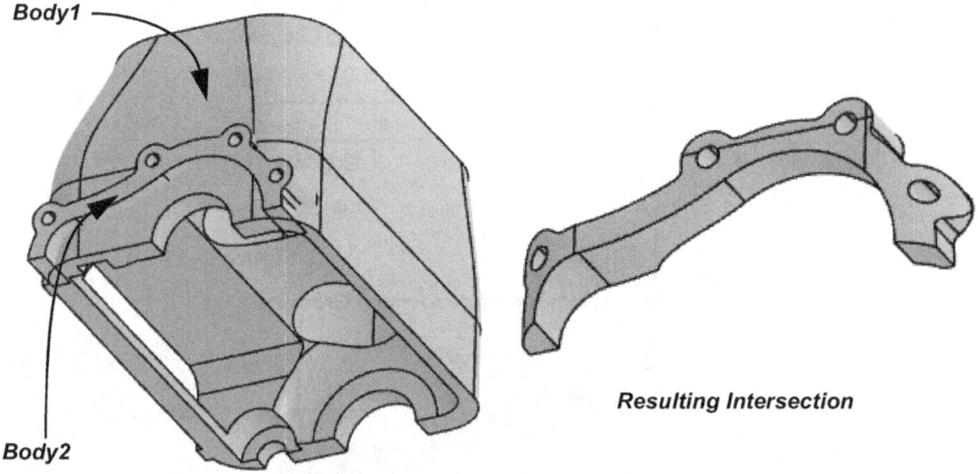

Figure 9–20

Union Trim

 (Union Trim) is similar to an **Add** operation, with the ability to remove or keep selected faces on the two bodies. For example, if you select to remove the faces from the frame and circle geometry, the resulting geometry displays as shown in Figure 9–21.

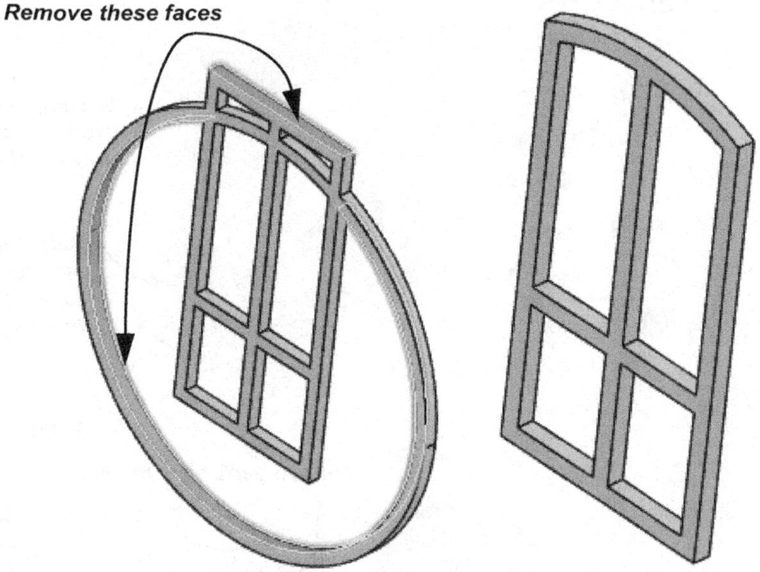

Figure 9–21

Remove Lump

(Remove Lump) removes growths and gaps and reshapes the body by selecting faces that you can remove and keep. The example models demonstrate the **Remove Lump** operation, as shown in Figure 9–22 and Figure 9–23.

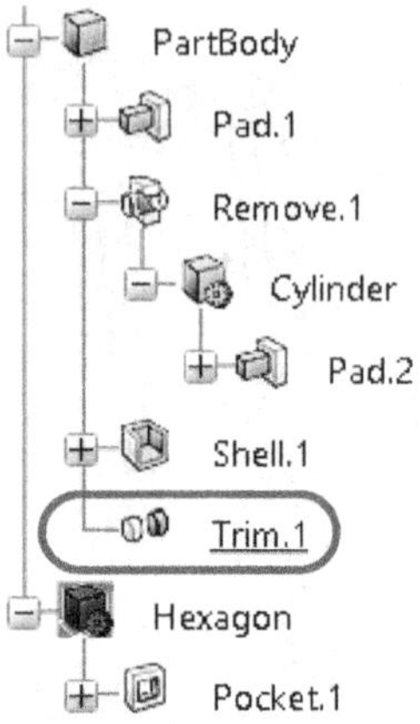

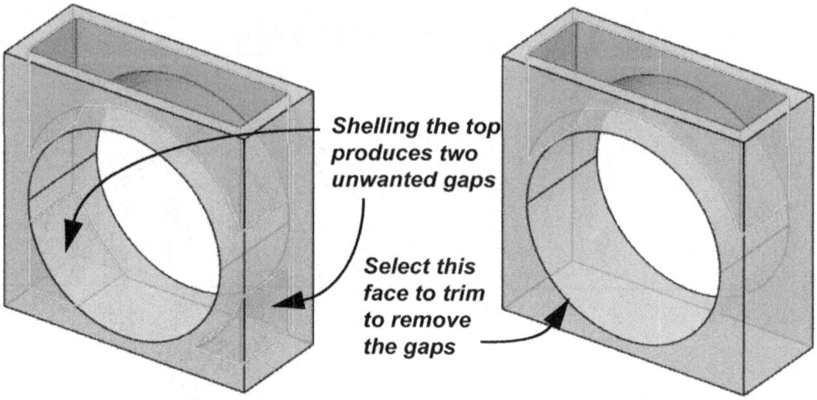

Figure 9–22

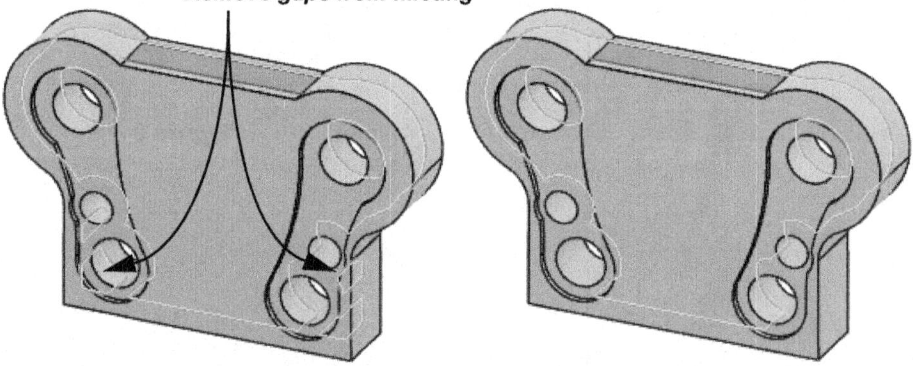

Figure 9–23

Boolean Operation Summary

The different types of Boolean operations and their results are described as follows:

Operation	Result
(Assemble)	Pocket = Pocket Pad = Pad
(Add)	Pocket = Pad Pad = Pad
(Remove)	Pocket = Pocket Pad = Pocket
(Intersect)	Shared volume.
(Union Trim)	Select faces to keep and/or remove (adds part of selected body).
(Remove Lump)	Reshape a body by selecting faces to remove and/or keep.

Naming Conventions

When you perform a Boolean operation, the original body is represented by the Boolean feature in the top level in the specification tree. For example, when **CutOut** is added to the PartBody using an **Assemble** operation, **Assemble.1** displays in the specification tree, as shown in Figure 9–24.

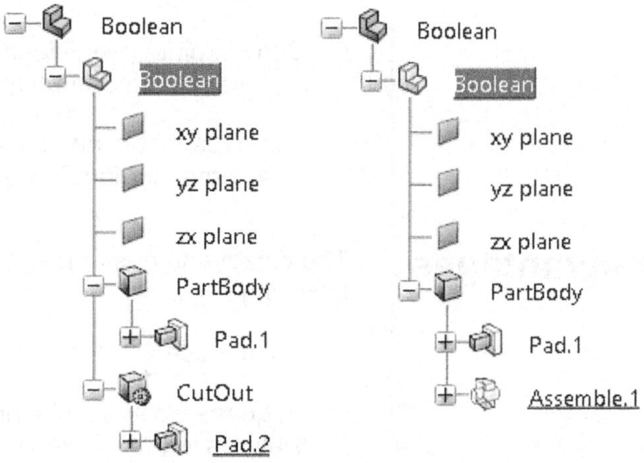

Figure 9–24

To simplify the location of bodies in the tree and make the model easier to understand for other designers, you must rename the Boolean feature after the body that was operated on. For example, the Boolean feature from the previous example could be renamed as **CutOut (Assemble)**, as shown in Figure 9–25.

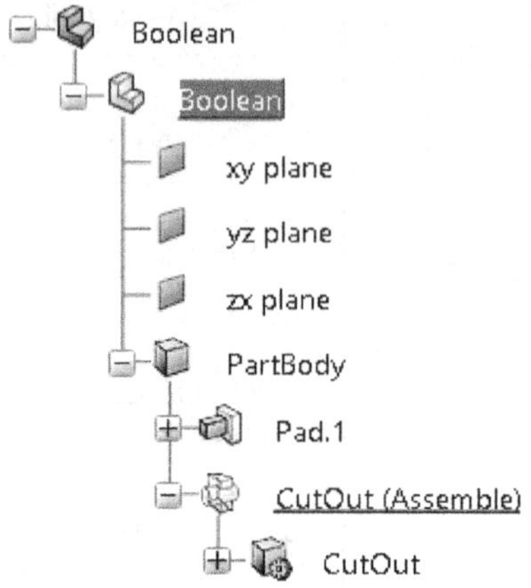

Figure 9–25

Advantages

The advantages of using Boolean operations include the following:

- Increases flexibility in the combination of part bodies and their geometry.
- Provides an extension of parametric, feature-based modeling practices.
- Can simulate core injection molding, cavity injection molding, and machining operations.
- Improves modeling and system performance when working with complex models that have a large number of features.

Disadvantages

The disadvantages of using Boolean operations include the following:

- Cannot use PartBody as an operator.
- Requires strategic planning on the position and structure of features in the model.
- Using bodies with features that are tangent to each other can result in geometric instabilities.

9.4 3D Constraints

Copied features can be positioned relative to other geometry using 3D constraints. This is useful if geometry is reused in a different location or orientation than the original.

3D constraints can only be applied to copies that do not have stored history. Therefore, features created with the **As Result** and **As Result with Link** options can be positioned in space in this manner. 3D constraints have the same appearance as sketch constraints, as shown in Figure 9–26.

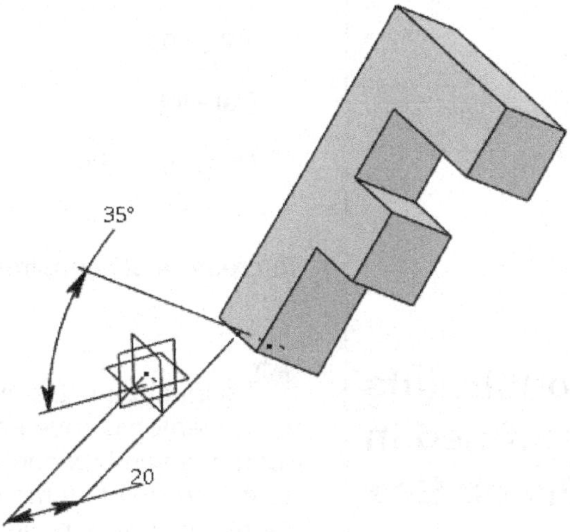

Figure 9–26

If a constraint is created on or between features with design history, the constraint becomes a reference that reflects the dimension without letting the dimension be changed. References are denoted by parentheses around the value, as shown in Figure 9–27.

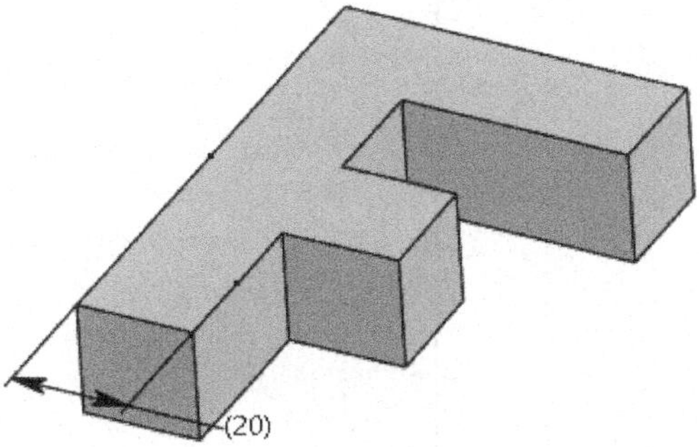

Figure 9–27

Eight 3D constraint types can be created. These constraints are similar to Sketcher constraints, but they are used to constrain 3D geometry rather than sketched elements.

- Fix
- Length
- Distance
- Angle
- Coincidence
- Tangency
- Parallel
- Perpendicular

To create a 3D constraint, use  or .

Constraints Defined in Dialog Box

 (Constraints Defined in Dialog Box) is available after one or more elements have been selected. You can click this icon to open a dialog box containing the types of constraints available for the group of elements that were selected. The dialog box opens as shown in Figure 9–28.

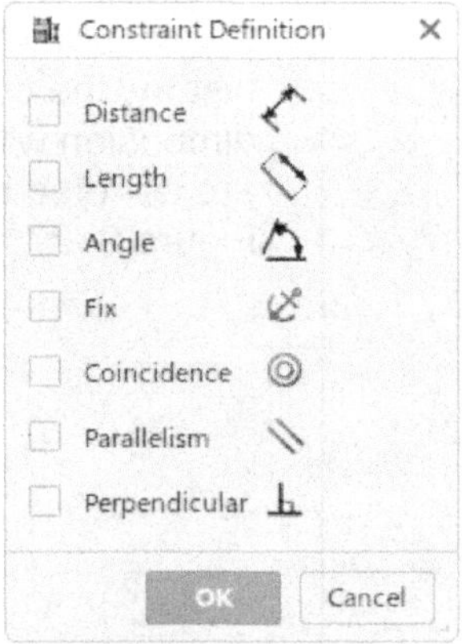

Figure 9–28

Constraint

 (Constraint) automatically determines a default constraint type based on the types of elements selected. Select the constraint to accept the default constraint type. To change the constraint type, right-click on the constraint and select the constraint type, as shown in Figure 9–29.

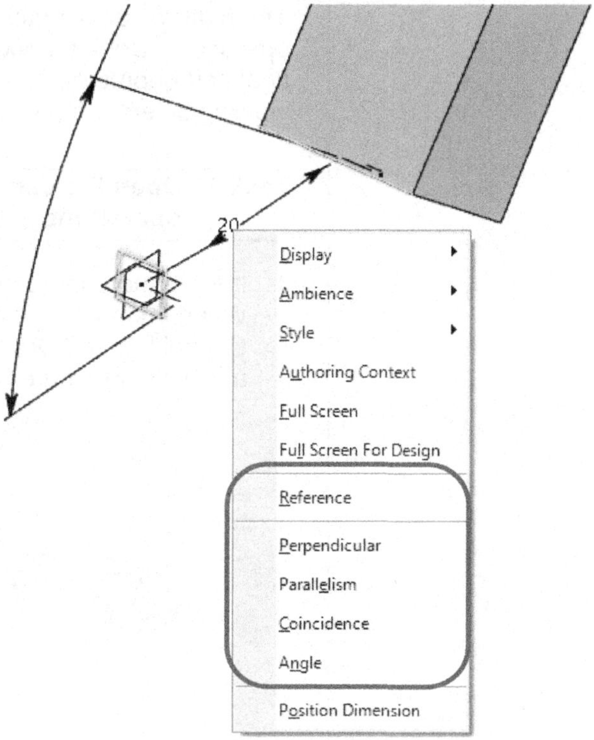

Figure 9–29

Practice 9a Boolean Operations Overview

Practice Objective

- Review the Boolean operations of a model.

In this practice, you will open a part file of a cast/machined part. The features are organized by using casting and machining operations. Boolean operations have been used to achieve the final part geometry, and inherently provide flexibility in terms of viewing different states of the model.

Task 1 - Open the part and investigate the boolean operations.

1. Import and open **Cover.3dxml** from the *Boolean* directory. When importing, type your initials followed by the dash symbol into the *Duplication string* field. The model displays as shown in Figure 9–30.

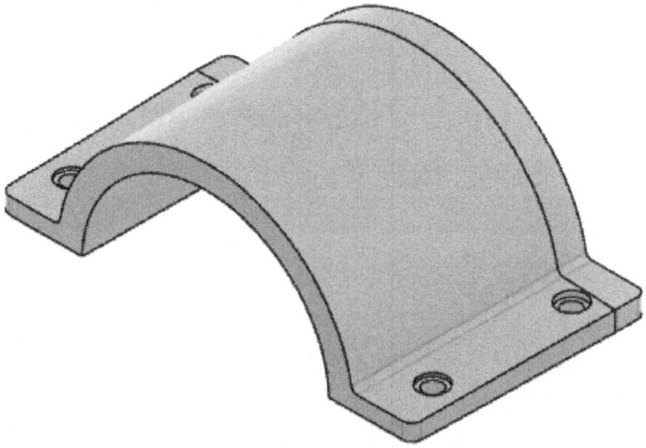

Figure 9–30

2. In the specification tree, note that no geometry has been created in the PartBody. When using **Boolean** operations, you must ensure that no geometry is created in the PartBody. This provides more flexibility in that the PartBody can only be used as the operand, and not the operator (i.e., a PartBody cannot be removed from an inserted body).

3. Expand the specification tree and note the features listed under the **Casting** body, as shown in Figure 9–31.

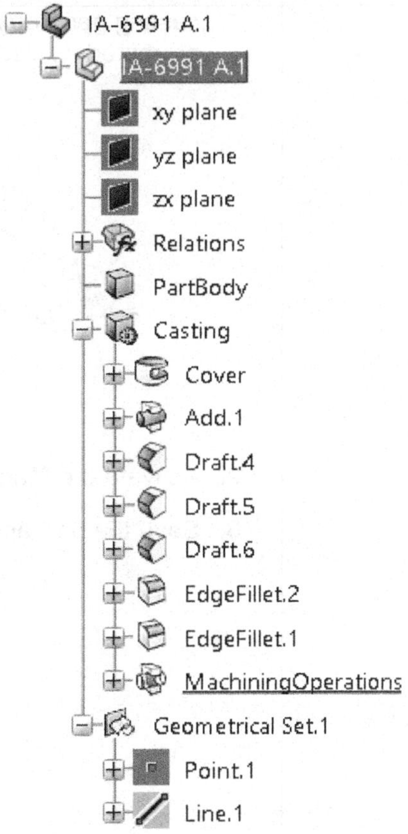

Figure 9–31

4. Expand the **MachiningOperations** feature and note the bodies and features listed.

Task 2 - Deactivate a body.

1. Deactivate the **MachiningOperations** feature and note the casting geometry, as shown in Figure 9–32. Click **OK**, if prompted, to deactivate aggregated elements.

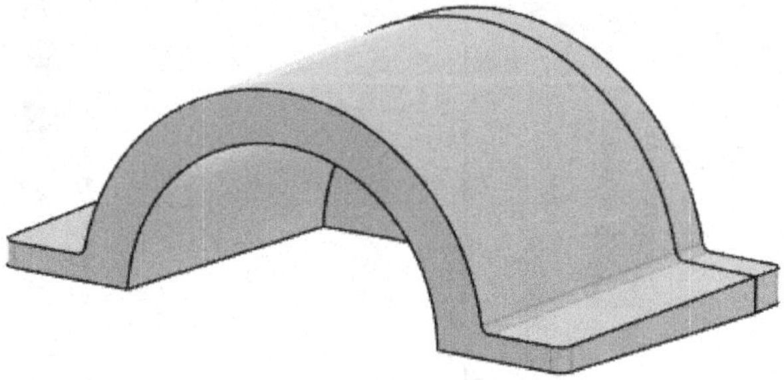

Figure 9–32

2. Activate the **MachiningOperations** feature.
3. Save the part and close the window.

Practice 9b Boolean Operations

Practice Objective

- Model using Boolean operations.

In this practice, you will create a part file and structure the part by creating the required bodies. Geometry is created in the appropriate bodies, and **Boolean** operations are used to achieve the final configuration.

Task 1 - Create a new part.

1. Create a new 3D Part called **###-JCS31-3** where ### represents your initials. Ensure that the **Enable hybrid design** option in the *Characteristics* tab is cleared.

Task 2 - Insert bodies.

1. In the Essentials section of the Action Bar, select  (Body) to insert a body. Repeat the operation two more times.
2. Rename the three new bodies as **Case**, **CD**, and **Cutout**, as shown in Figure 9–33.

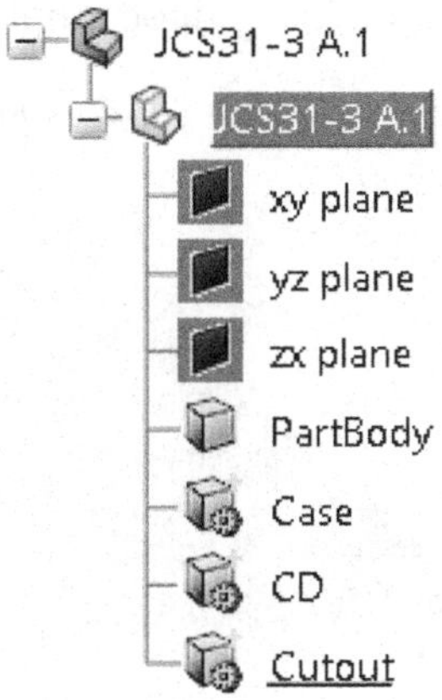

Figure 9–33

3. Ensure that the units are set to **Millimeter** (mm).
4. Define the **Case** body as the In Work Object.

Task 3 - Create a Pad feature.

1. Select the **xy plane** as the sketch support and activate the Sketcher app.
2. Sketch a rectangle. Define the symmetry with the vertical and horizontal axes and create two dimensions with the values, as shown in Figure 9–34.

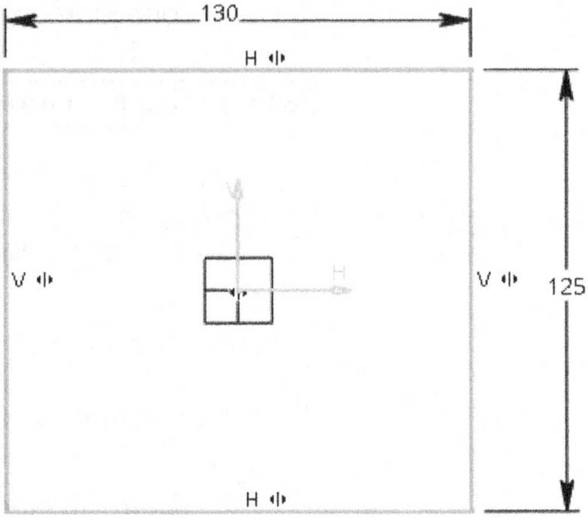

Figure 9–34

3. Exit Sketcher.
4. Create a Pad. In the *Length* field, enter **4**. Ensure that the directional arrow points up, as shown in Figure 9–35.

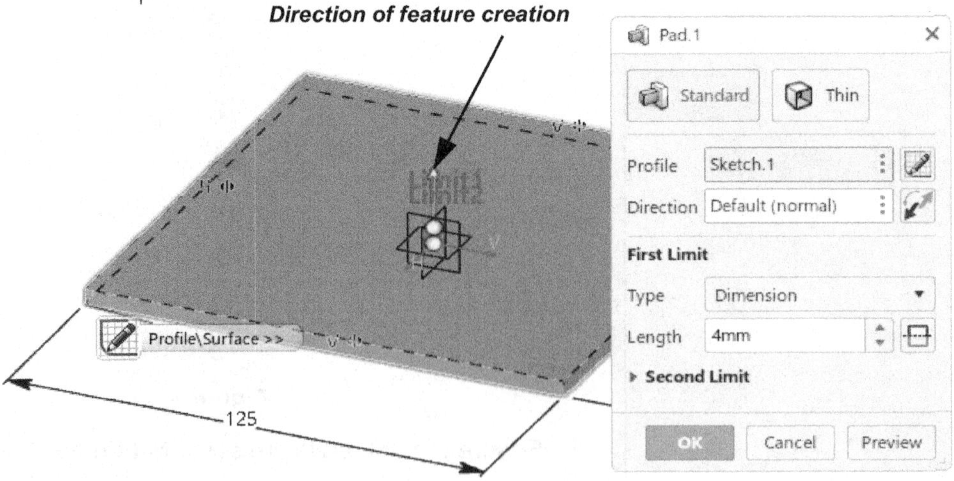

Figure 9–35

Task 4 - Create a reference plane.

1. Create a reference plane offset from the xy plane by **2.5**. Ensure that the directional arrow points up, as shown in Figure 9–36.

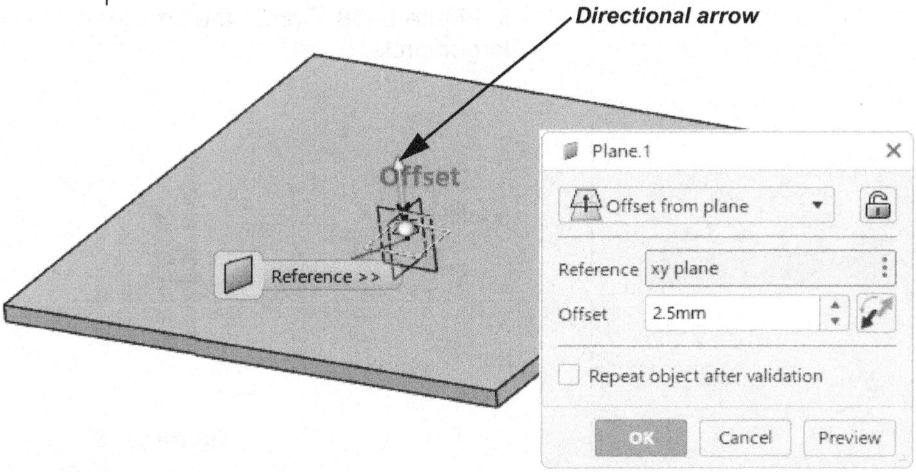

Figure 9–36

2. Rename the plane as **CDPlane**.

3. Define the **CD** body as the Work Object. The specification tree displays as shown in Figure 9–37.

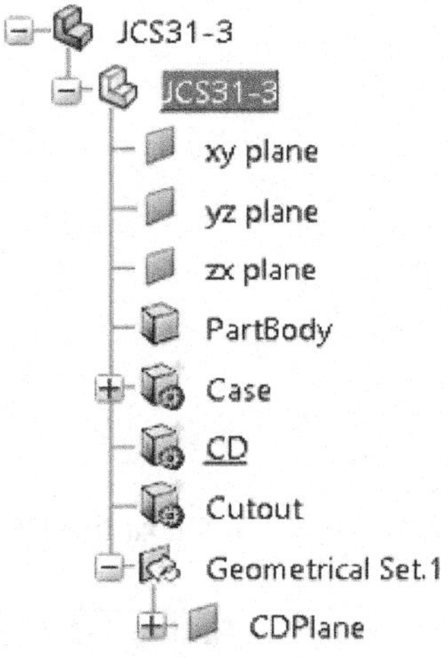

Figure 9–37

4. Hide the **Case** body.

Task 5 - Create a sketch.

1. Select **CDPlane** and activate the Sketcher app.
2. Create two circles. Ensure that the centers of the circles are located at the origin of the sketch and dimensioned as shown in Figure 9–38. Create the smaller circle first and then the larger circle.

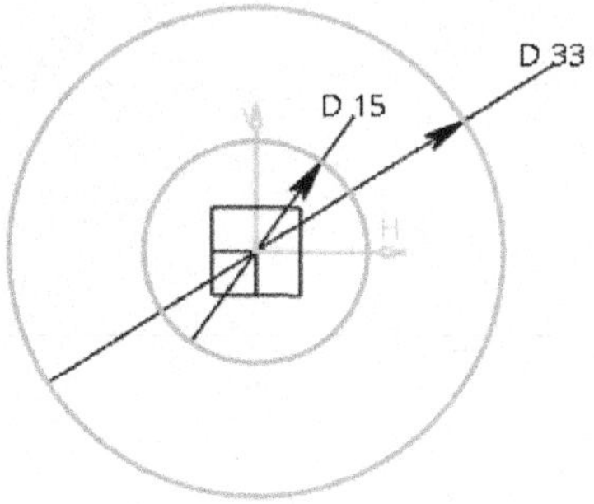

Figure 9–38

3. Sketch a third circle and dimension it as **120**, as shown in Figure 9–39.

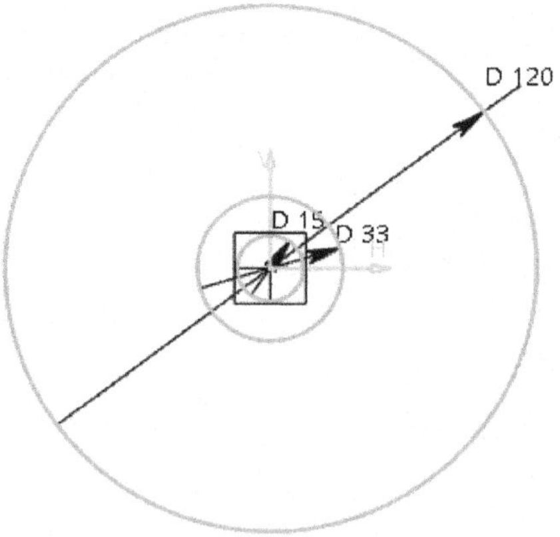

Figure 9–39

4. Exit the Sketcher app.

Task 6 - Create a Multi-pad.

1. In the Model section of the Action Bar, click  (Multi-Pad) to create a Multi-pad.

2. For *Domain 1 and Domain 2*, set the following, as shown in Figure 9–40:

   Domain 1:

   - In the *Limit 1* field, enter **1.5mm**.
   - In the *Limit 2* field, enter **4mm**.

   Domain 2:

   - In the *Limit 1* field, enter **1mm**.
   - In the *Limit 2* field, enter **4mm**.

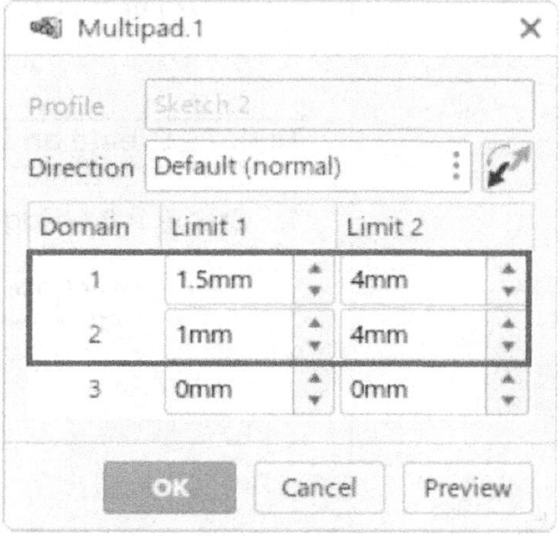

Figure 9–40

3. Ensure that the direction of feature creation points down, as shown in Figure 9–41.

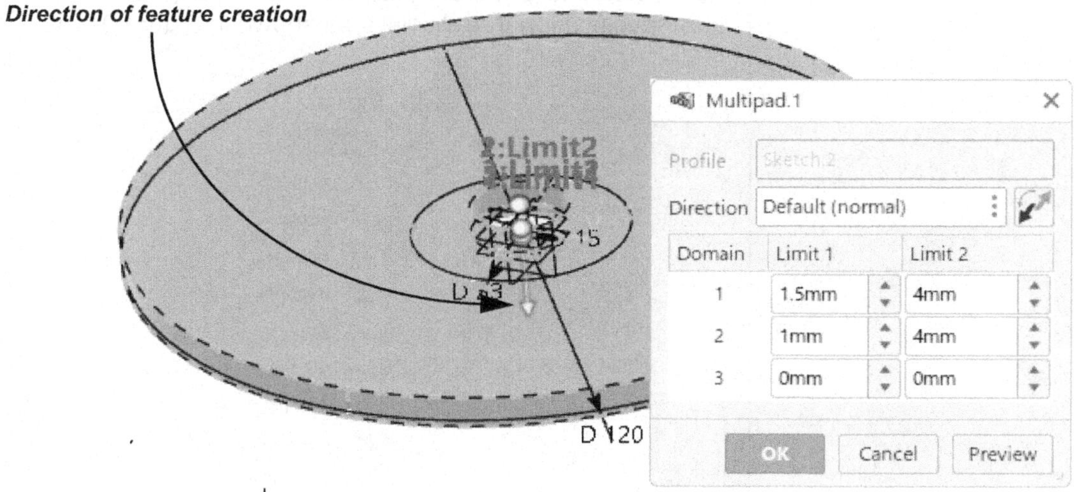

Figure 9–41

4. Click **OK**. The Multi-pad feature displays as shown in Figure 9–42.

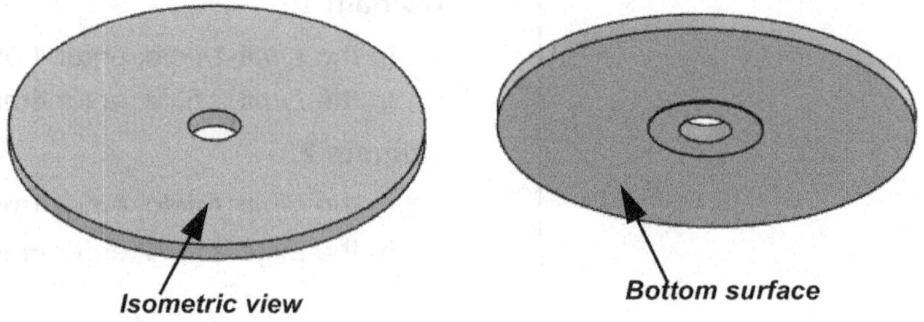

Figure 9–42

Task 7 - Create an Edge Fillet.

1. Create a **0.5** Edge Fillet on the edge shown in Figure 9–43.

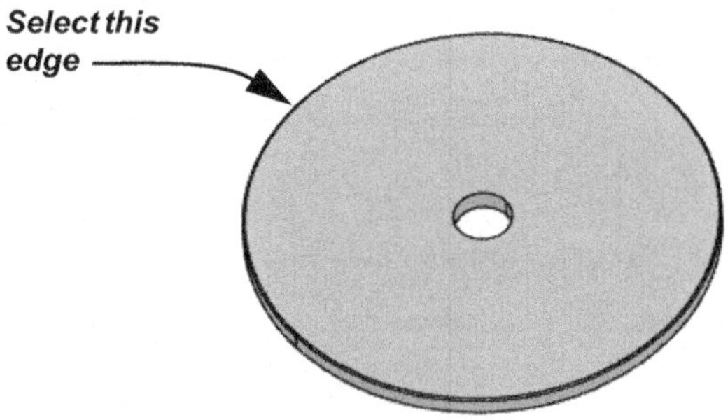

Figure 9–43

2. Define the **Case** body to be the Work Object. The specification tree displays as shown in Figure 9–44.

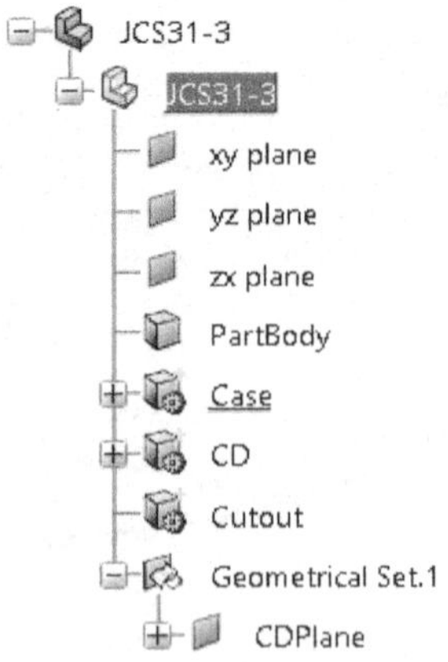

Figure 9–44

Task 8 - Perform a Boolean operation.

1. Select the background of the display to make sure nothing is pre-selected.
2. In the Essentials section of the Action Bar, click  (Remove).
3. Select the **CD** body. The Remove dialog box opens as shown in Figure 9–45.

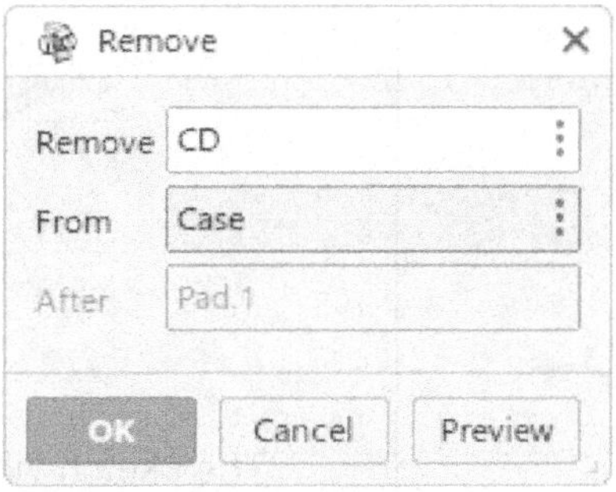

Figure 9–45

4. Click **OK** to complete the operation.
5. The model displays in Isometric view as shown in Figure 9–46.

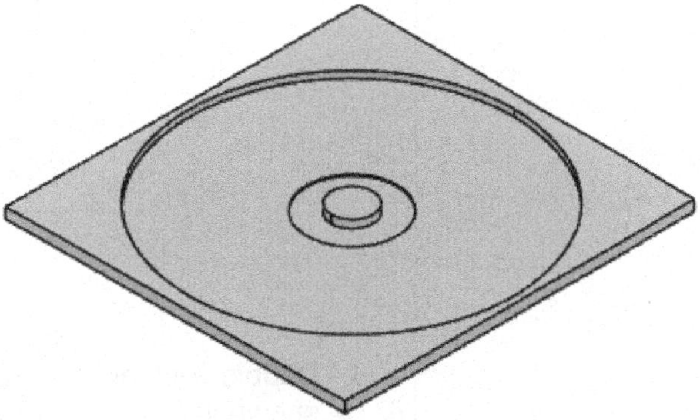

Figure 9–46

Task 9 - Create cutout geometry.

1. Define the **Cutout** body as the Work Object.
2. Select the top surface as shown in Figure 9–47, and enter the Sketcher app.

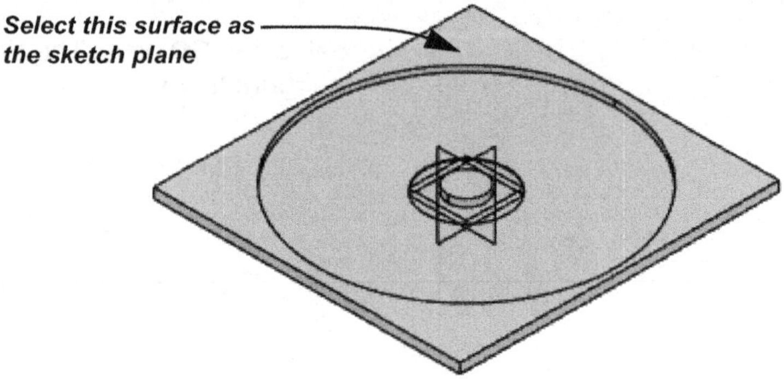

Figure 9–47

The sketch view displays as shown in Figure 9–48.

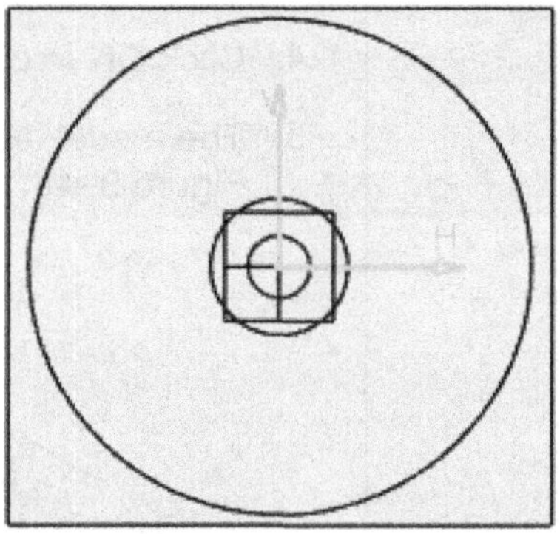

Figure 9–48

3. Double-click on  (Offset) and offset the three edges shown in Figure 9–49 by **1** to the inside of the geometry.

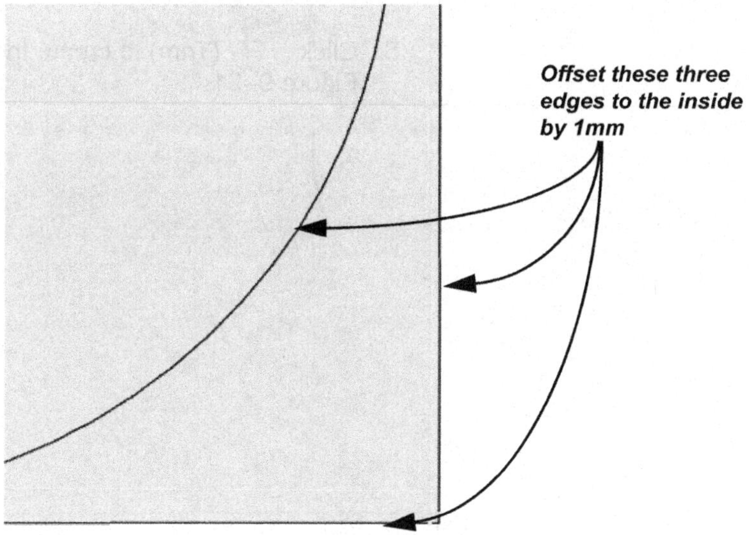

Figure 9–49

4. Sketch a horizontal and a vertical line. Dimension the horizontal line by **55** and the vertical line by **45**, as shown in Figure 9–50.

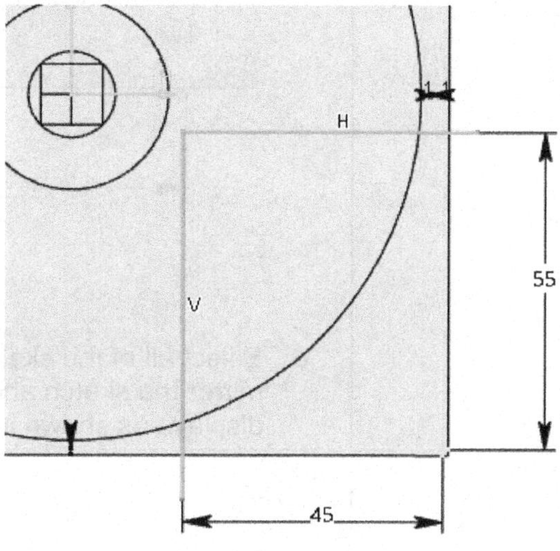

Figure 9–50

5. Click (Trim) to create the sketch geometry shown in Figure 9–51.

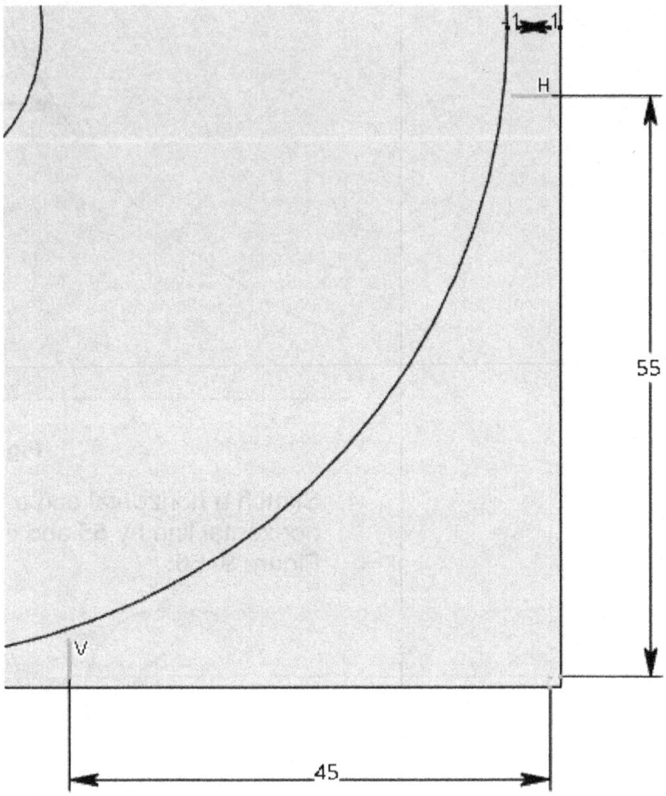

Figure 9–51

6. Select all of the sketch geometry and use (Mirror) to mirror the sketch about the horizontal axis. The sketch displays as shown in Figure 9–52.

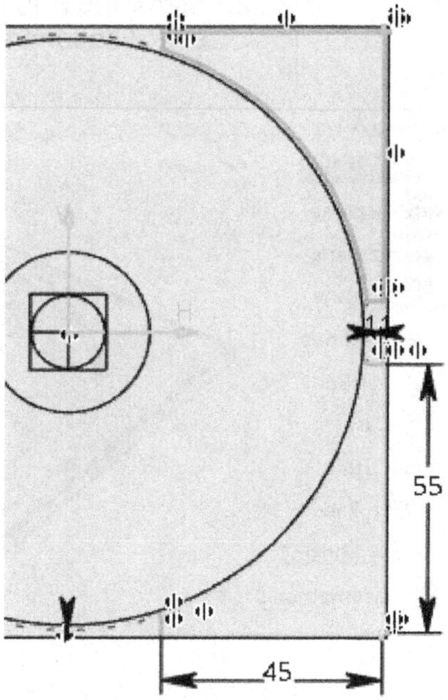

Figure 9–52

7. Exit the Sketcher app.

Task 10 - Create solid geometry.

1. Create a Pad **2mm** in length in the direction shown in Figure 9–53.

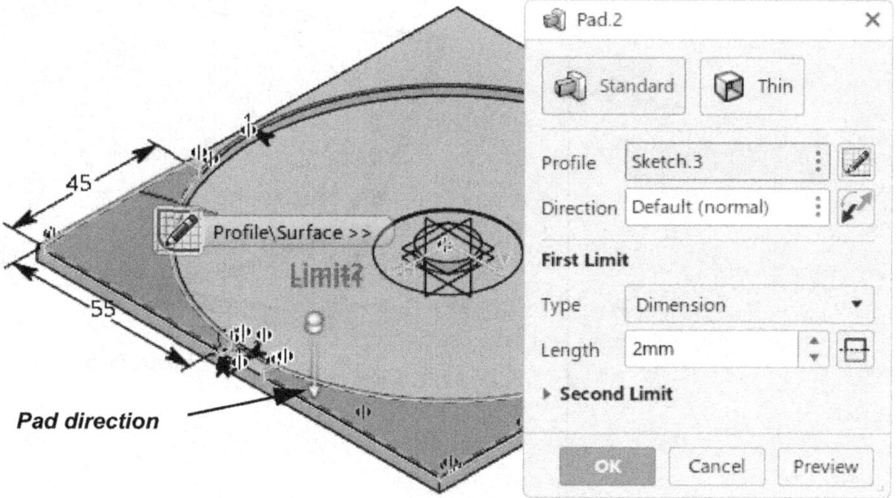

Figure 9–53

2. Mirror the Pad feature about the yz plane. The model and the specification tree display as shown in Figure 9–54.

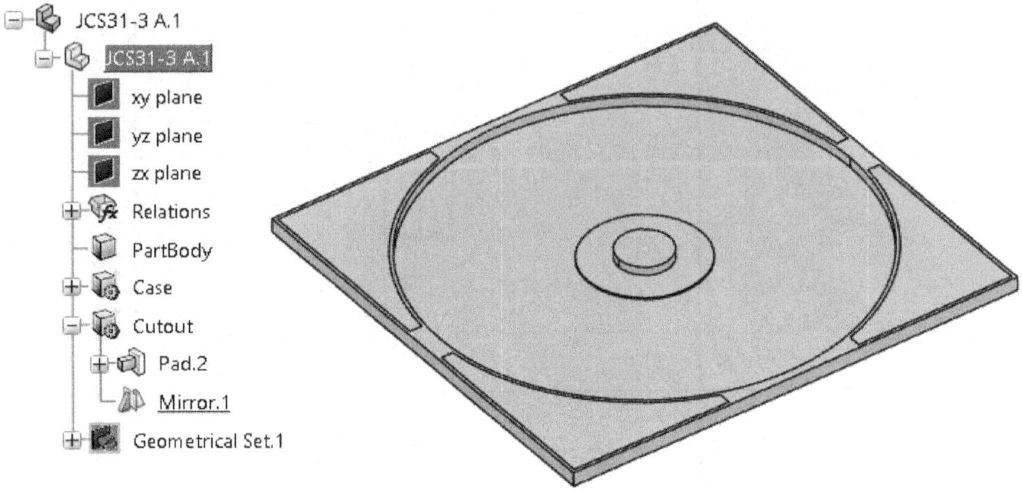

Figure 9–54

3. Define the **Case** body as the Work Object, and clear the **Case** body by selecting the background of the display.

4. Click  (Remove) to remove the **Cutout** body from the **Case** body. The model displays as shown in Figure 9–55.

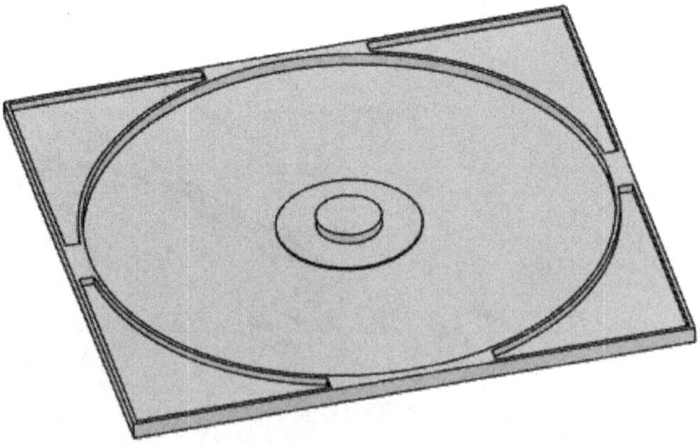

Figure 9–55

Task 11 - Create a sketch.

1. Select the planar surface shown in Figure 9–56 and activate the Sketcher app.

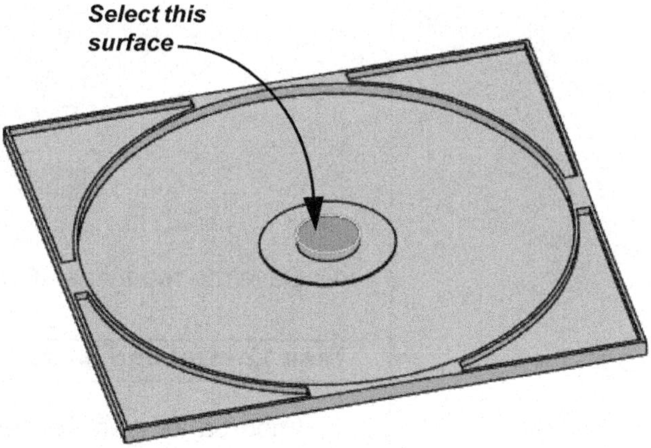

Figure 9–56

2. Use  (Offset) to offset the circular edge to the inside by **1**, as shown in Figure 9–57.

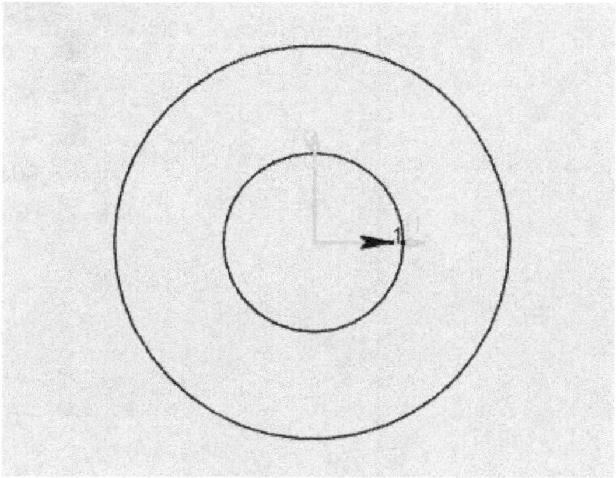

Figure 9–57

3. Create a Pocket feature **2.5** deep using the sketch you just created. The Pocket feature displays as shown in Figure 9–58.

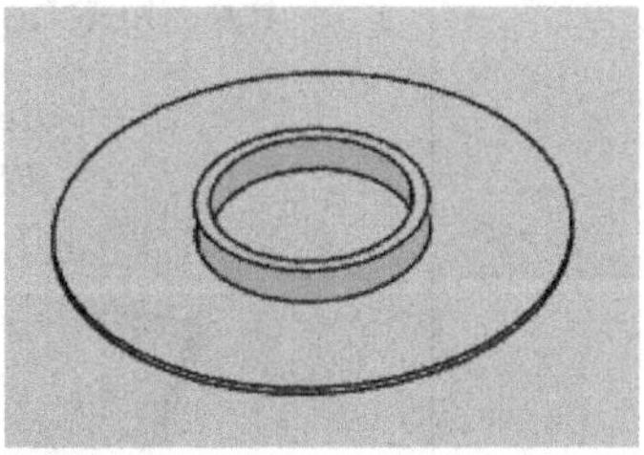

Figure 9–58

4. Save the model as **JCS31-3**, but do not close the window.

Task 12 - Cut and paste a body.

1. Import and open **CenterCutOut.3dxml** from the *Boolean* directory. When importing, type your initials followed by the dash symbol into the *Duplication string* field.

2. Copy the **CenterCutOut** body as shown in Figure 9–59.

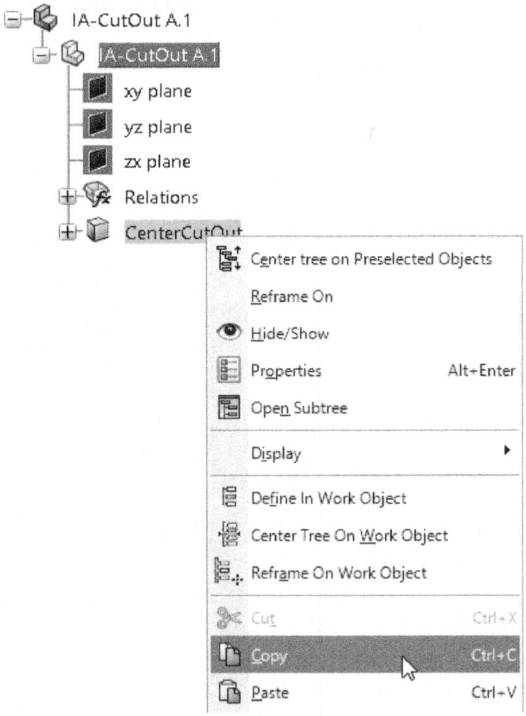

Figure 9–59

3. Activate the **JCS31-3** window.

4. Paste **CenterCutOut** body into the 3D Shape level of the specification tree, as shown in Figure 9–60.

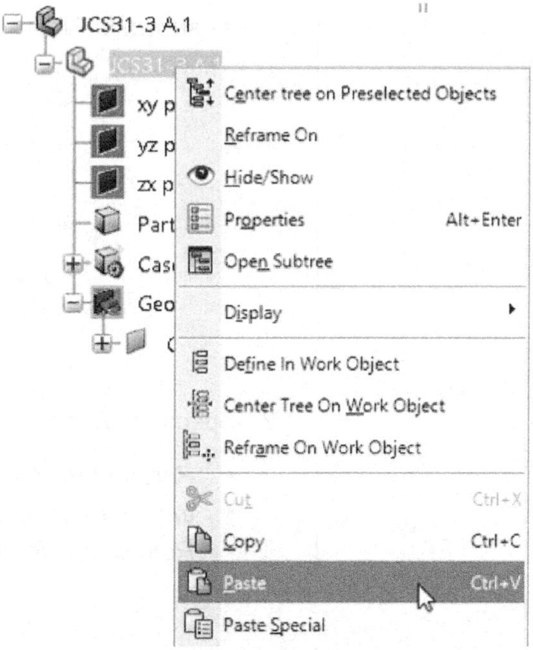

Figure 9–60

The body displays at the bottom of the specification tree.

5. Zoom in and note the pasted geometry, as shown in Figure 9–61.

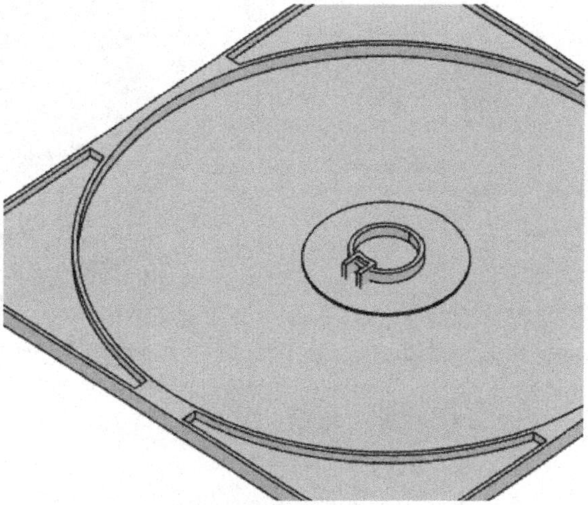

Figure 9–61

Task 13 - Create a pattern.

1. Select the Pad feature under the pasted **CenterCutOut** body, as shown in Figure 9–62, and click  (Circular Pattern).

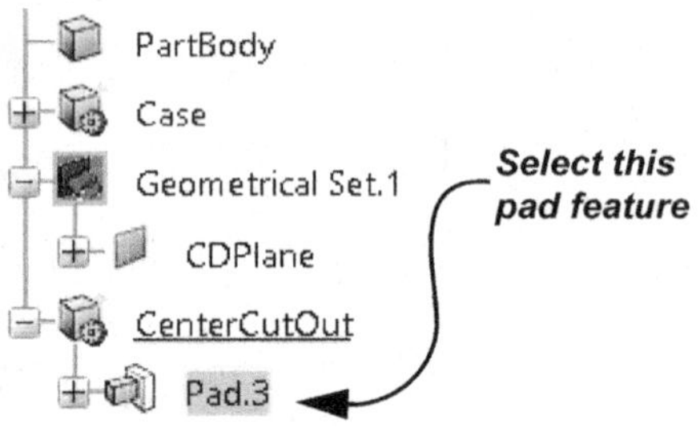

Figure 9–62

2. Specify the pattern using the following values:

   - *Parameters:* **Complete crown**
   - *Instances:* **3**
   - *Reference element:* as shown in Figure 9–63

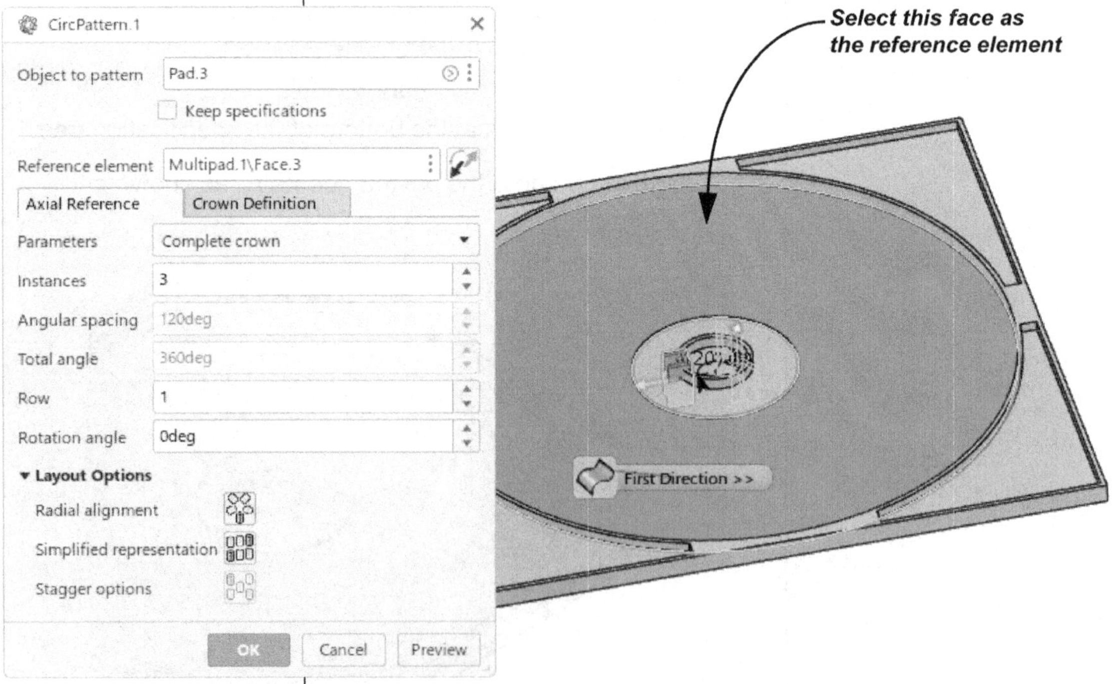

Figure 9–63

3. Click **OK**. The pattern displays as shown in Figure 9–64.

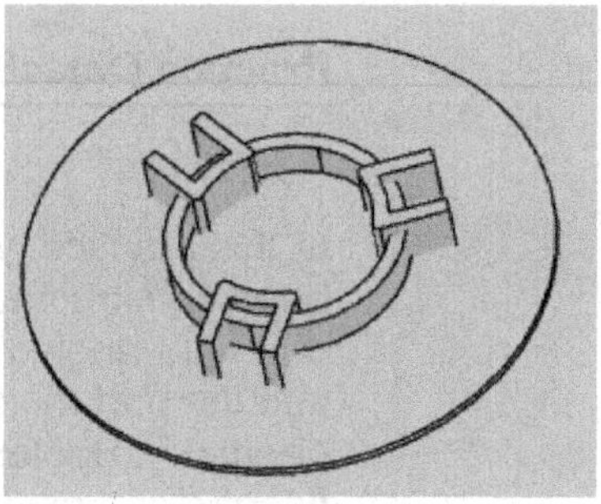

Figure 9–64

4. Remove the **CenterCutOut** body from the **Case** body. The model and the specification tree display, as shown in Figure 9–65.

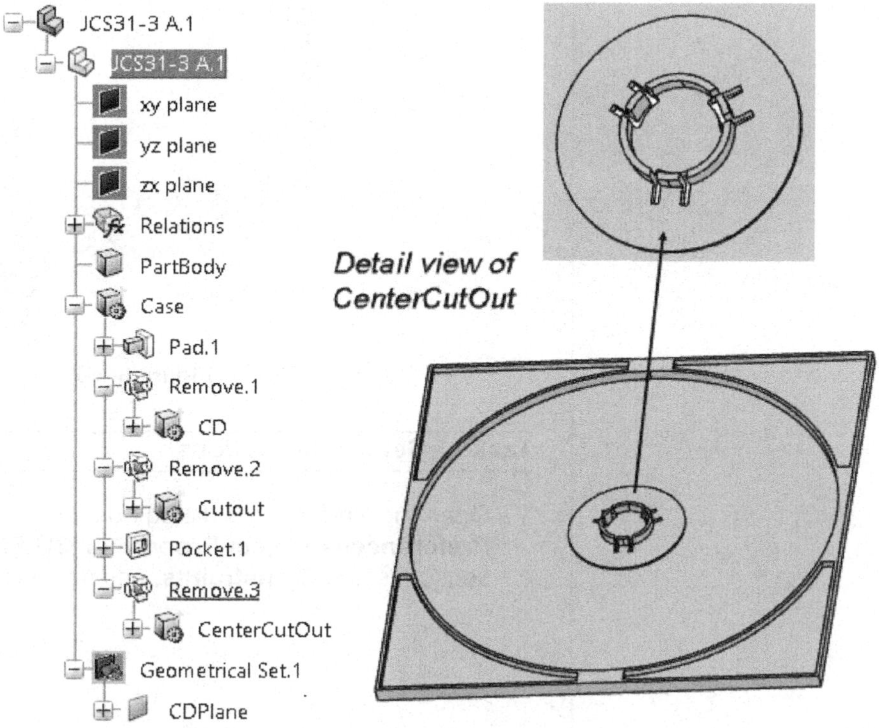

Figure 9–65

5. Save and close the model.

Practice 9c 3D Constraints

Practice Objective

- Use 3D constraints to position the copied geometry.

In this practice, you will use the geometry of a flange that has been constructed in a separate part model to develop the ends of a right-angled pipe. You will copy and paste the flange twice into the part model, and use constraints to position the new geometry. Boolean operations will be used to assemble the flanges and pipe. The final result is shown in Figure 9–66.

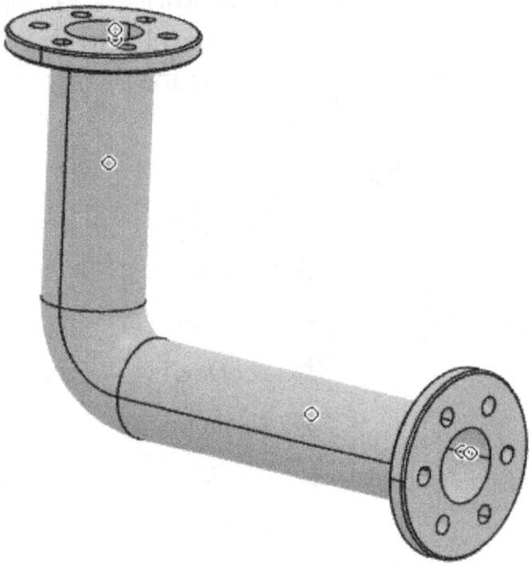

Figure 9–66

Task 1 - Set display options.

1. Open the Preferences dialog box, and select **Common Preferences> Object Properties>3D Shape**. In the *Display* section, select **Constraints**, as shown in Figure 9–67.

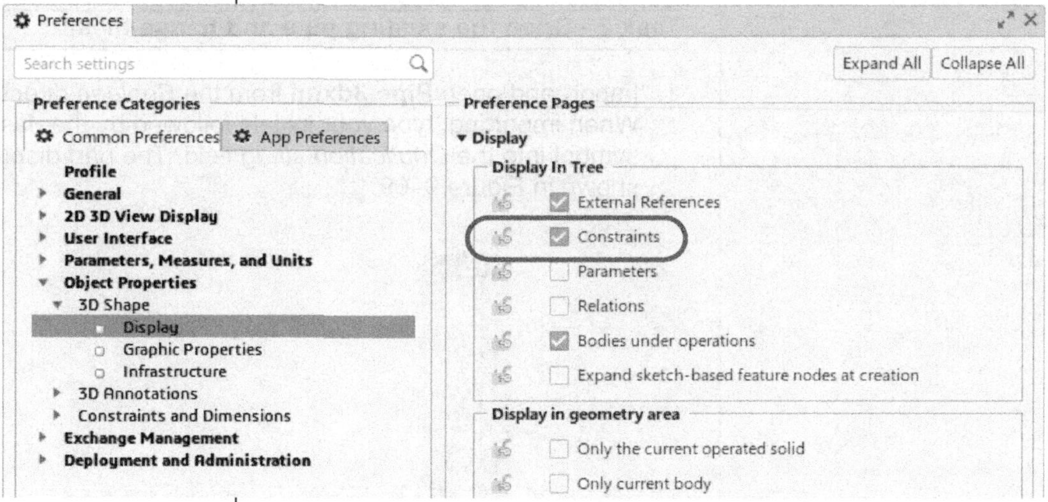

Figure 9–67

2. In the *Infrastructure* section, clear the **Restrict external selection with link to published elements** option, as shown in Figure 9–68.

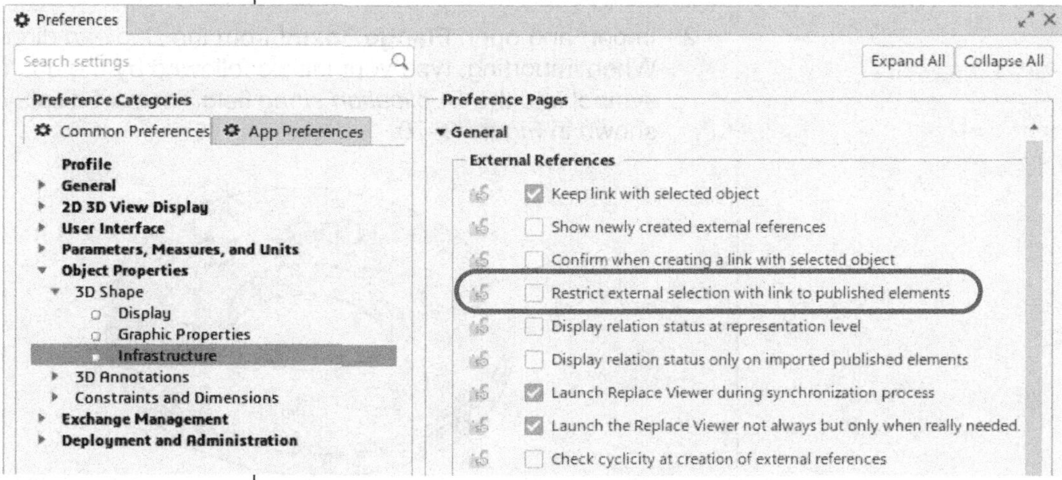

Figure 9–68

3. Click **OK**.

Task 2 - Open the existing pipe and flange files.

1. Import and open **Pipe.3dxml** from the *Boolean* directory. When importing, type your initials followed by the dash symbol into the *Duplication string* field. The part displays as shown in Figure 9–69.

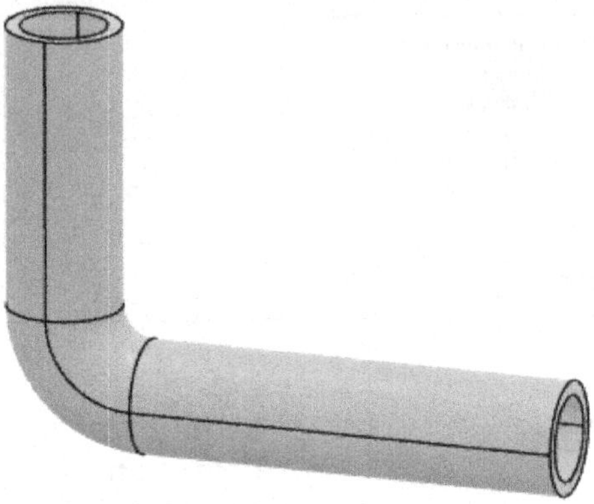

Figure 9–69

2. Import and open **Flange.3dxml** from the *Boolean* directory. When importing, type your initials followed by the dash symbol into the *Duplication string* field.The part displays as shown in Figure 9–70.

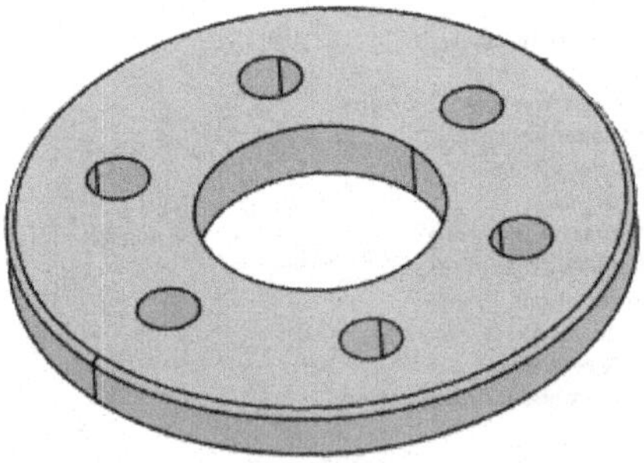

Figure 9–70

Task 3 - Copy the flange into the pipe file.

1. In the Flange part window, right-click on the **PartBody**, and select **Copy**.

2. Activate the **Pipe** part window. Select the 3D Shape object in the tree, then right-click and select **Paste Special**.

3. Select **As Result with Link**.

4. Click **OK**. The part displays as shown in Figure 9–71.

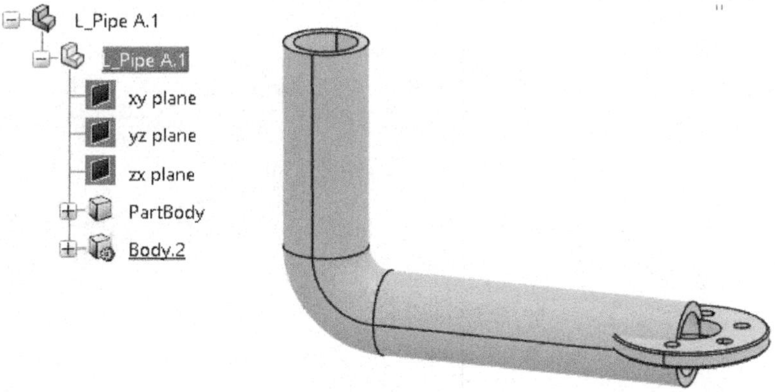

Figure 9–71

Task 4 - Position the flange on the end of the pipe with 3D constraints.

1. Press and hold <Ctrl> and select the top of the flange and the end of the pipe, as shown in Figure 9–72.

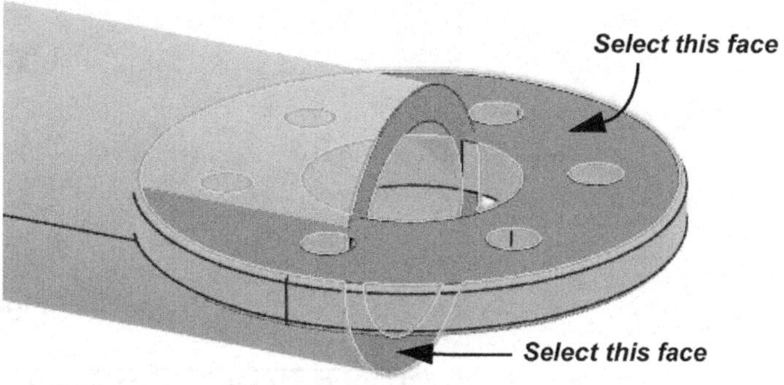

Figure 9–72

2. In the Transform section of the Action Bar, click  (Constraint Defined in a Dialog Box) to create a constraint.

3. Select **Coincidence** in the list. The flange moves, as shown in Figure 9–73.

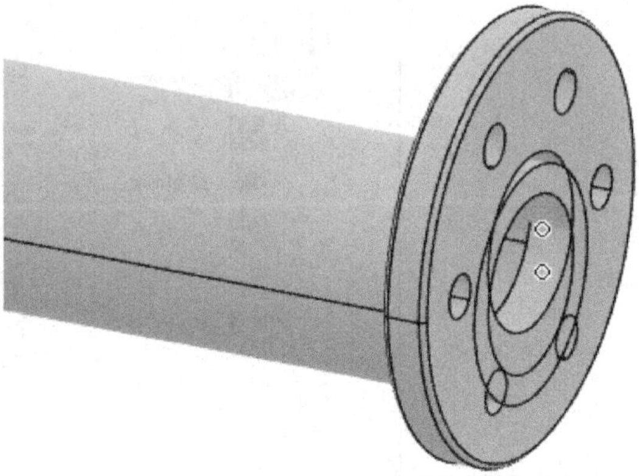

Figure 9–73

4. In the specification tree, expand the **Constraints** branch to display the Coincidence constraint, as shown in Figure 9–74.

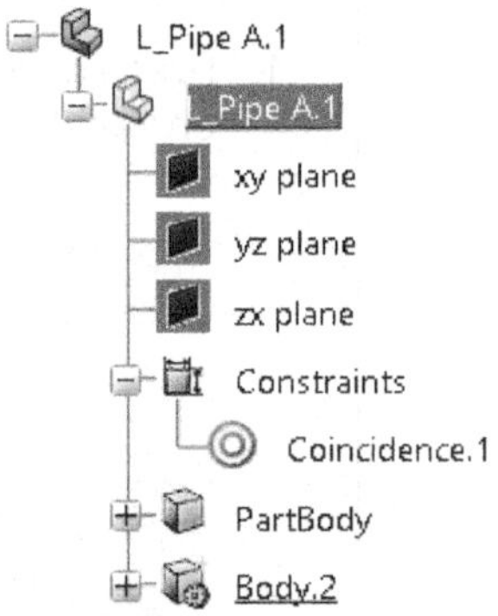

Figure 9–74

Task 5 - Modify a 3D constraint.

By default, the Coincidence constraint will set a normal vector for both faces to point in the same direction. To have the flange mate with the end of the pipe, you must modify the Coincidence constraint and set the normal directions to be opposite.

1. Double-click on the **Coincidence** constraint.

2. In the **Orientation** menu, select **Opposite**.

3. Click **OK**. The part updates, as shown in Figure 9–75.

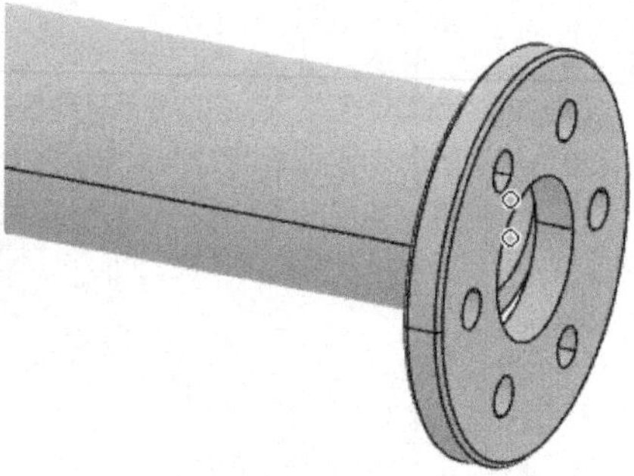

Figure 9–75

Task 6 - Align the axis of the flange with the axis of the pipe.

1. In the Transformation section of the Action Bar, click  (Constraint) to create a new constraint.
2. Click the inner cylindrical surface of the flange. Note that the central axis of the flange is selected.
3. Click the inner cylindrical surface of the pipe to select the central axis.
4. CATIA automatically selects a Distance constraint. To change this to a Coincidence, right-click on the constraint and select **Coincidence**, as shown in Figure 9–76.

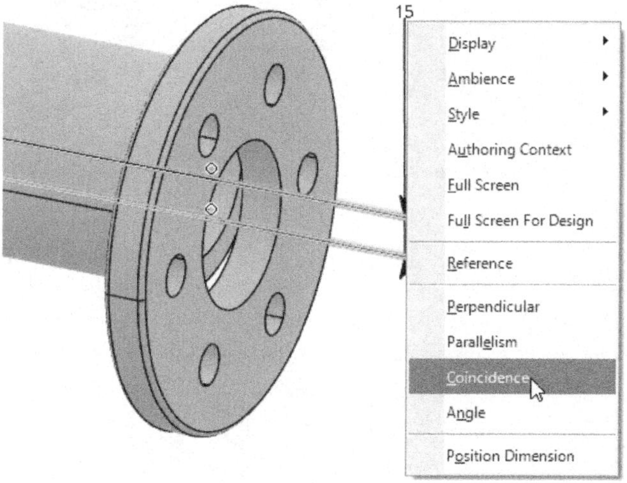

Figure 9–76

The flange moves to a coaxial position with the pipe, as shown in Figure 9–77.

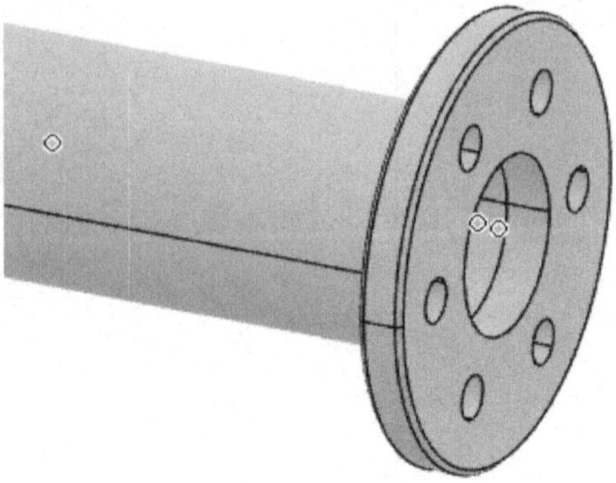

Figure 9–77

Task 7 - Paste and position another flange into the pipe file.

1. Repeat Tasks 2 to 6 to place another flange on the other end of the pipe. The required result is shown in Figure 9–78.

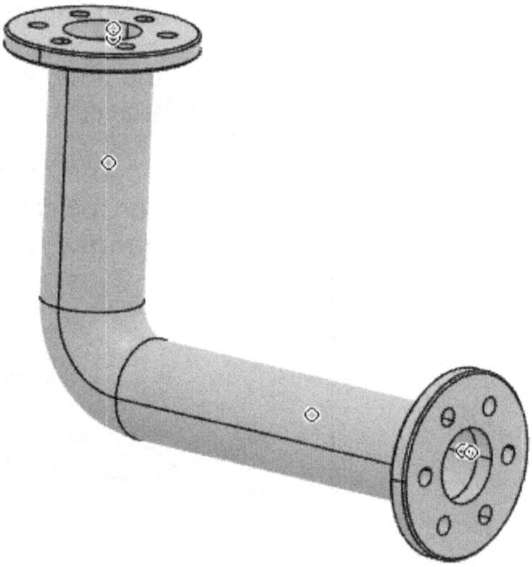

Figure 9–78

Task 8 - Assemble the flanges to the pipe.

1. In the Essentials section of the Action Bar, click  (Assemble).
2. Select **Body.2** and select the **PartBody**.
3. Click **OK**. The flange will be assembled into the pipe.
4. Repeat the **Assemble** operation to assemble **Body.3** into the **PartBody**. The part displays as shown in Figure 9–79.

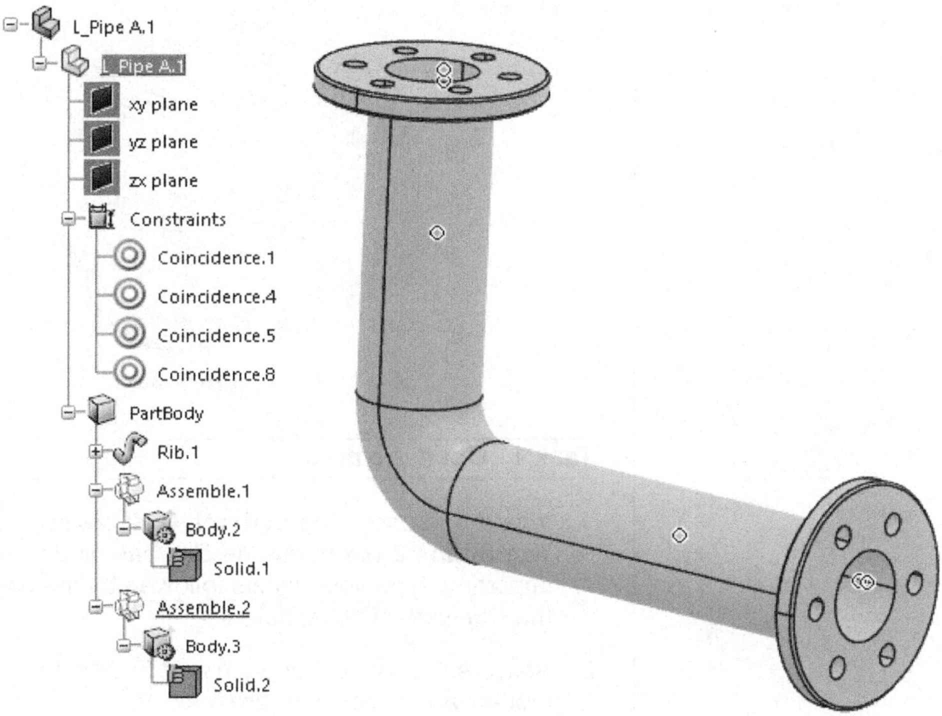

Figure 9–79

5. Save both models and close all of the windows.

Practice 9d (Optional) Importing Bodies

Practice Objective

- Work with multiple bodies.

In this practice, you will use the geometry of existing parts to design an air vent for the passenger side dash of an automobile. The known geometry includes the curved surface of the dash, the general shape of the vent, and the size and configuration of the air flow slots, as shown in Figure 9–80.

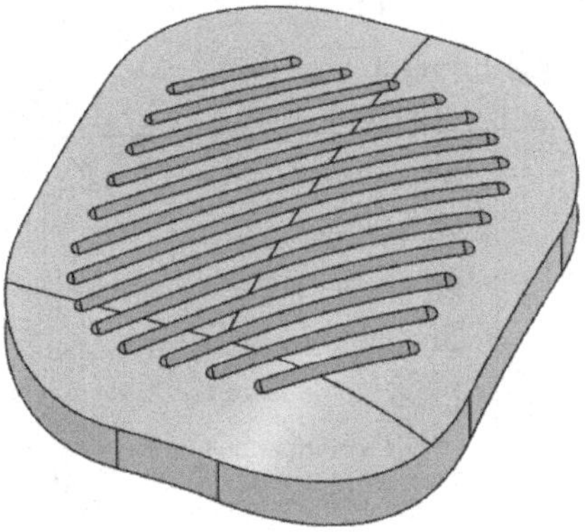

Figure 9–80

Task 1 - Open the part.

1. Import and open **Dash.3dxml**, **Grill.3dxml** and **VentShape.3dxml** from the *Boolean* directory. When importing, type your initials followed by the dash symbol into the *Duplication string* field.

2. Activate the window of each part to display the three part models as shown in Figure 9–81.

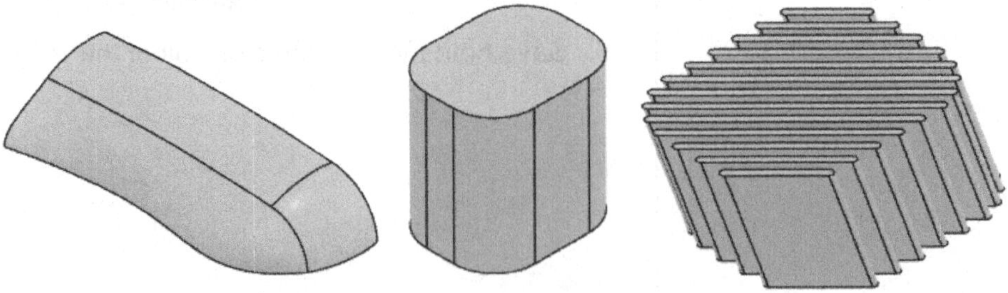

Figure 9–81

Task 2 - Create a new part file.

1. Activate the **Dash** window.

2. In the *Essentials* section, click  (Axis System). The Axis System Definition dialog box opens as shown in Figure 9–82.

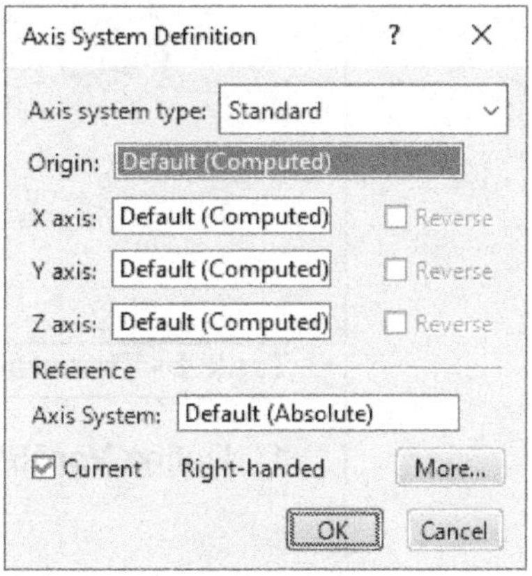

Figure 9–82

3. Click **OK** to accept the default axis definition settings.

Task 3 - Copy a body.

1. Activate the **VentShape** window.

2. Copy the **VentShape** body shown in Figure 9–83.

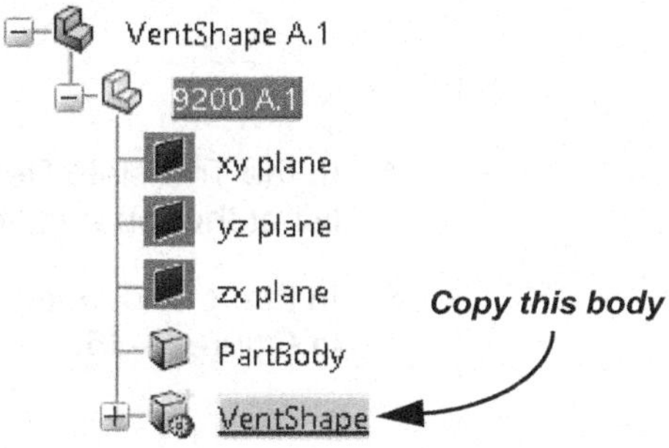

Figure 9–83

3. Activate the **Dash** window and paste the **VentShape** body into the top-most level. The model displays as shown in Figure 9–84.

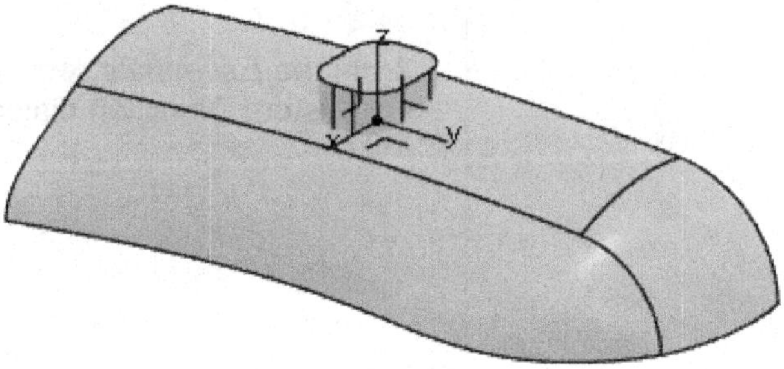

Figure 9–84

Task 4 - Translate a body.

1. Define **VentShape** body as the Work Object.

2. In the *Transform* section, click  (Translation).

3. In the Question window, click **Yes**, as shown in Figure 9–85.

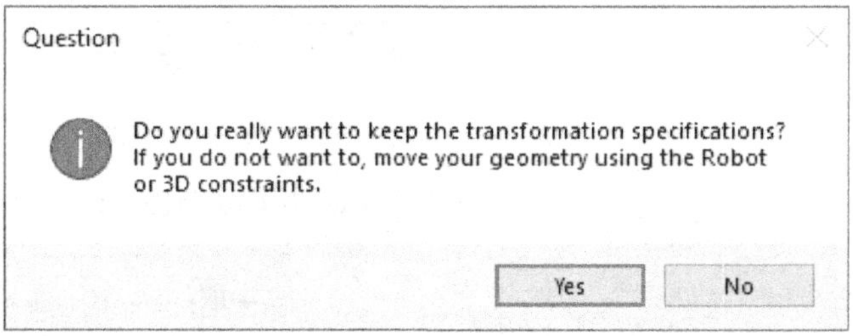

Figure 9–85

4. In the Translate Definition dialog box, expand the drop-down list at the top and select **Coordinates**.

5. In the *X* field, enter **40** and in the *Y* field, enter **260**, as shown in Figure 9–86.

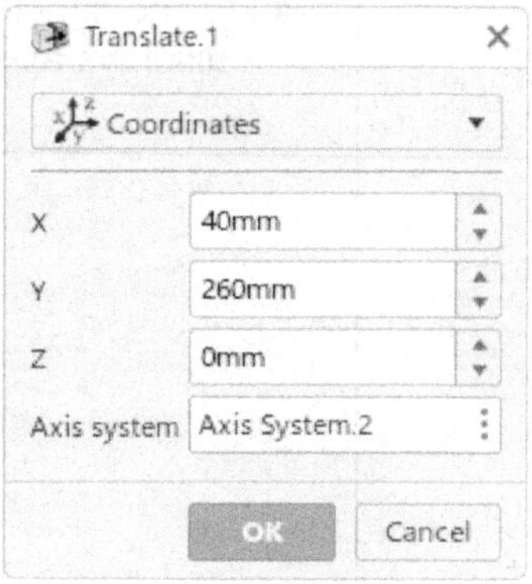

Figure 9–86

6. Click **OK**. The model displays as shown in Figure 9–87.

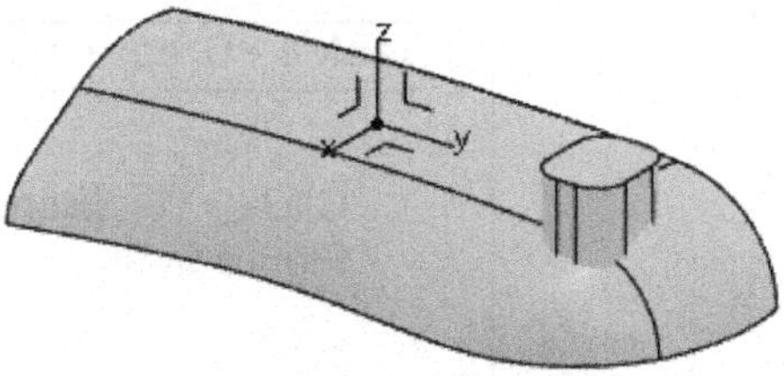

Figure 9–87

Task 5 - Manipulate geometry with another body.

1. In the Essentials section of the Action Bar, click  (Intersect). The Intersect dialog box opens.

2. In the *Intersect* field, select the **Dash** body. In the *With* field, **VentShape** should be selected automatically, and in the After field, **Translate.1** should be selected automatically as shown in Figure 9–88.

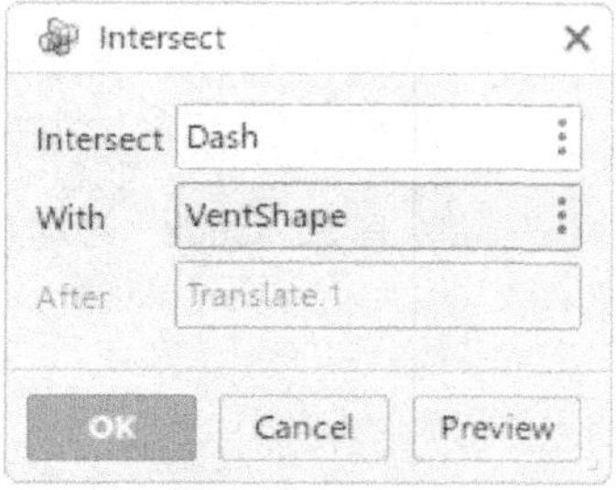

Figure 9–88

3. To complete the operation, click **OK**.

4. In the specification tree, hide **Group-DashGeom**. The model displays as shown in Figure 9–89.

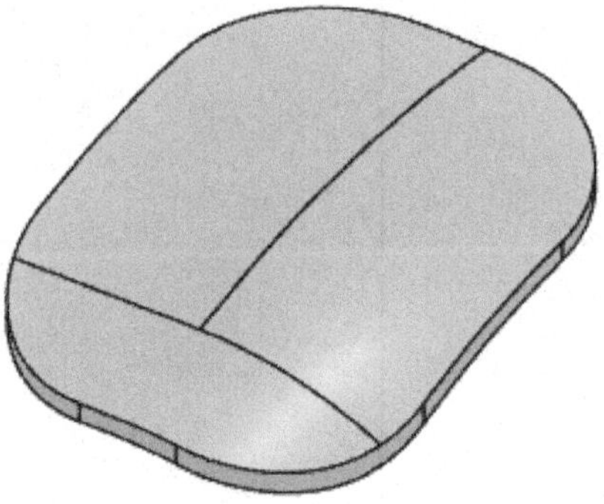

Figure 9–89

Task 6 - Create a Shell feature.

1. Click  (Bottom View). The model displays as shown in Figure 9–90.

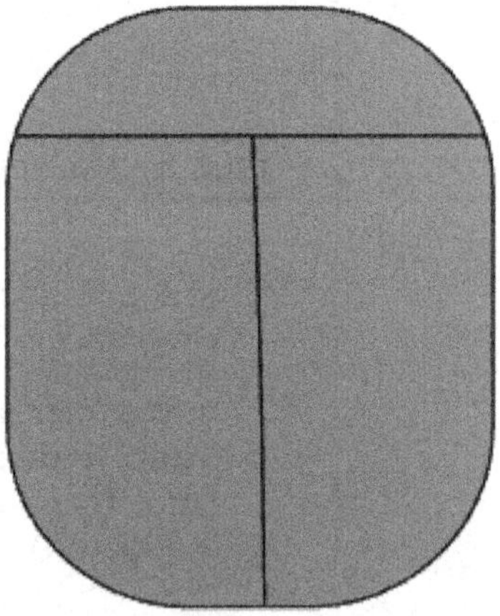

Figure 9–90

2. Click  (Shell). The Shell Definition dialog box opens.

3. Select the face as shown in Figure 9–91. All of the tangent faces will be selected automatically.

4. In the Shell Definition dialog box, in the *Default Outside thickness* field, enter **4**.

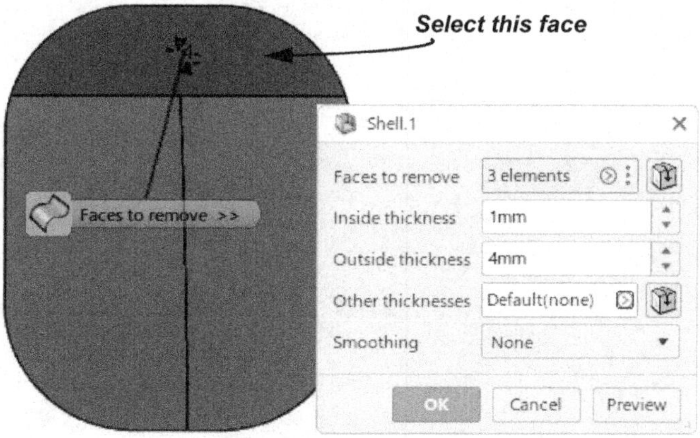

Figure 9–91

5. Click **OK**. The model displays as shown in Figure 9–92.

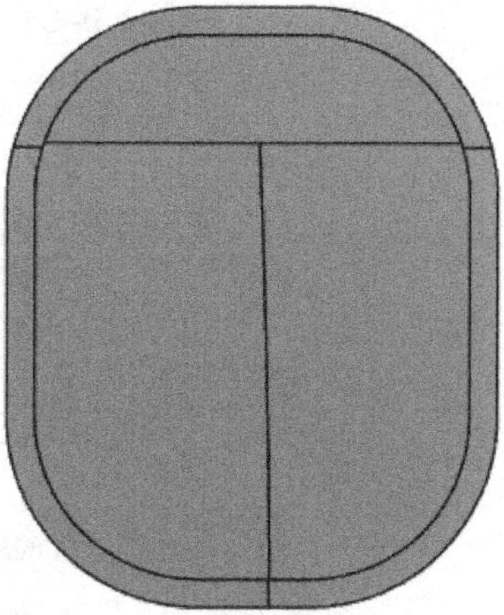

Figure 9–92

6. Click  (iso) to display the model in isometric view.

Task 7 - Import a body with link.

1. Activate the **Grill** window and copy the **GrillSlots** Publication shown in Figure 9–93.

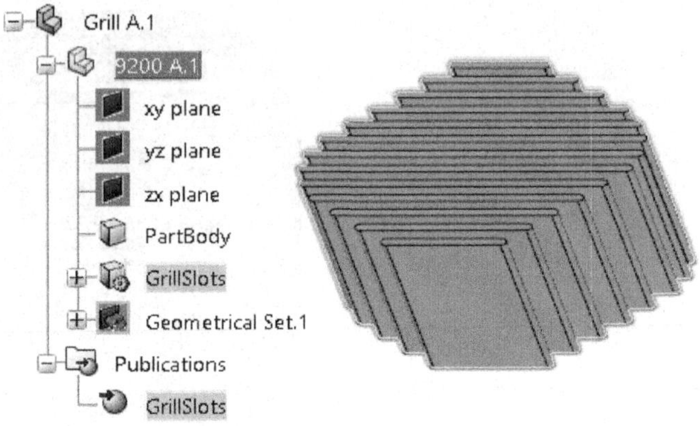

Figure 9–93

2. Activate the **Dash** window.

3. Insert the **GrillSlots** body using **Paste Special**, as shown in Figure 9–94.

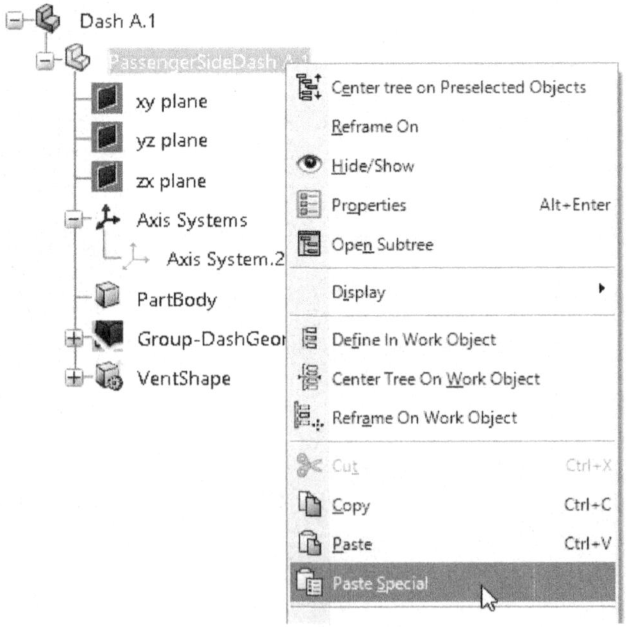

Figure 9–94

4. In the Paste Special dialog box, select **As Result With Link**, as shown in Figure 9–95, and click **OK**.

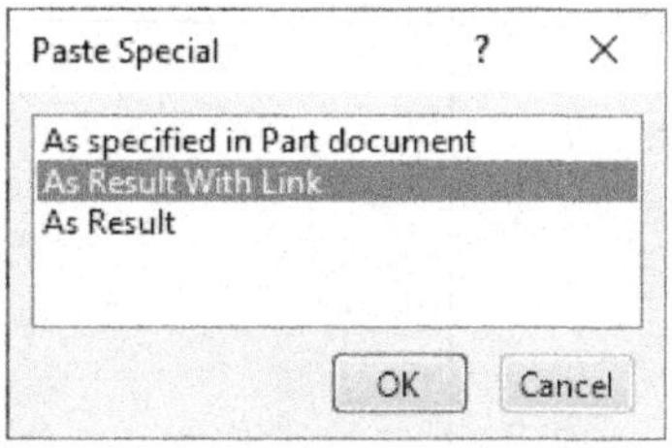

Figure 9–95

5. Translate the **GrillSlots** body by **40** in the *X* direction and **260** in the *Y* direction, as shown in Figure 9–96.

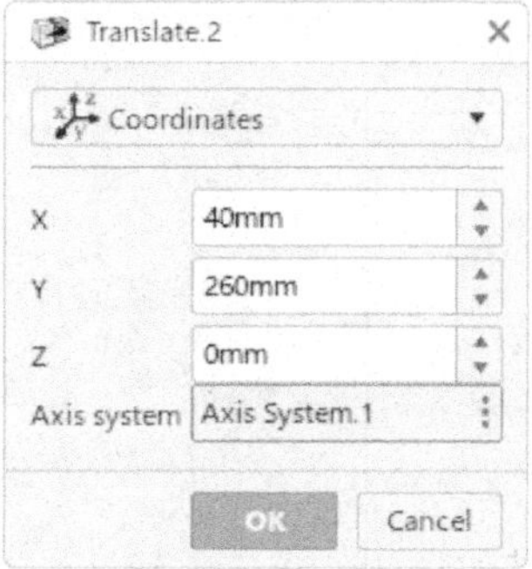

Figure 9–96

6. Click **OK**. The model displays as shown in Figure 9–97.

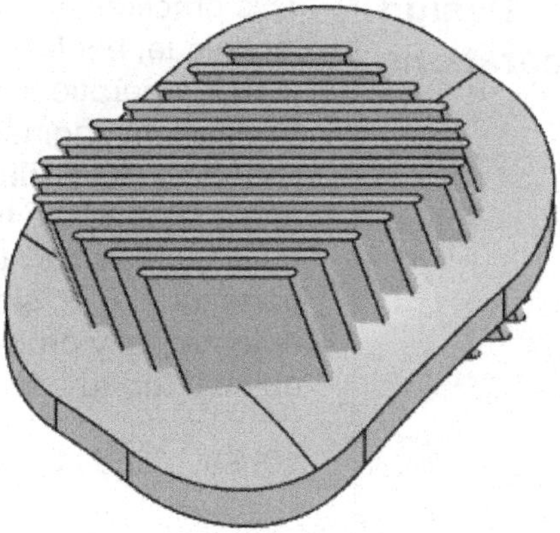

Figure 9–97

7. Define **VentShape** to be the Work Object.

8. Use the Boolean **Remove** operation to remove the **GrillSlots** body, as shown in Figure 9–98.

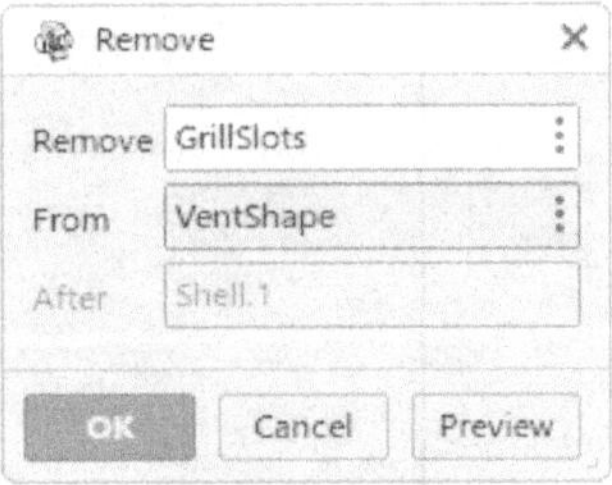

Figure 9–98

9. Click **OK**. The model displays as shown in Figure 9–99.

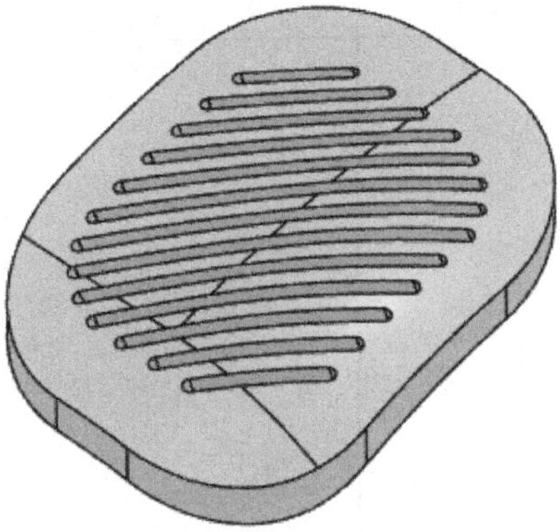

Figure 9–99

Design Considerations

This practice shows you the power of combining multi-body technique, boolean (**Intersect** and **Remove**), and feature-based (**Shell**) operations to achieve the required part geometry. Concurrent engineering is promoted using **Paste Special** when importing the **GrillSlots** body. An engineer might still need to make changes to the **GrillSlots** due to the results of some maximum air flow calculations. If changes are made to the **Grill** part model (i.e., slots become wider), then those changes are automatically propagated to the **Dash** part. This results in a fully defined, up-to-date part.

10. Save and close all models.

Chapter Review Questions

1. What are the advantages of using multiple bodies in a model?
   a. You can improve model organization by grouping features in separate bodies with respect to their function or position.
   b. You can create each body in a separate part file and then paste it into the finished model.
   c. A single part file can contain and display a variety of model states.
   d. All of the above.
2. You must always create an axis system for a body so that If you need to move a body, you can do so easily by changing the position of the axis system.
   a. True
   b. False
3. You can deactivate individual part bodies to reduce update time and display a model in various states.
   a. True.
   b. False
4. Which of the following is NOT a Boolean Operation?
   a. Assemble
   b. Intersect
   c. Divide
   d. Remove
5. When using the **Add** boolean operator, the software combines the bodies. Therefore, any pad features add material and any pocket features remove material.
   a. True
   b. False

6. Which of the following are advantages of using Boolean operations?
    a. Increases flexibility in the combination of part bodies and their geometry.
    b. Provides an extension of parametric, feature-based modeling practices.
    c. Requires strategic planning on the position and structure of features in the model.
    d. Improves modeling and system performance when working with complex models that have a large number of features.
    e. All of the above.

Answers: 1d, 2a, 3a, 4c, 5b, 6e

Feature Failure Resolution

Feature failures can be caused by incorrect selections or settings. Failures can also occur when a part is changed and updated. For update failures, the problem might not be with the feature itself, but with another feature that it relies on. By becoming familiar with the software, you can efficiently resolve these failures.

Learning Objectives in This Chapter

- Learn how features fail during creation.
- Understand the methods used to resolve failures.
- Learn how models can fail on update.
- Understand the methods used to resolve the failures.

10.1 Failures During Feature Creation

Features can fail during creation because the incorrect options have been set or inappropriate elements have been selected. In such cases, you might have to modify the geometry of the feature. You must resolve the failure before you continue with the feature creation.

General Steps

Use the following general steps to resolve failures:

1. Read the failure messages.
2. Investigate the failure.
3. Modify the geometry.

Step 1 - Read the failure messages.

During feature creation, if the selected geometry is not suitable for the feature, a Feature Definition Error dialog box opens as shown in Figure 10–1.

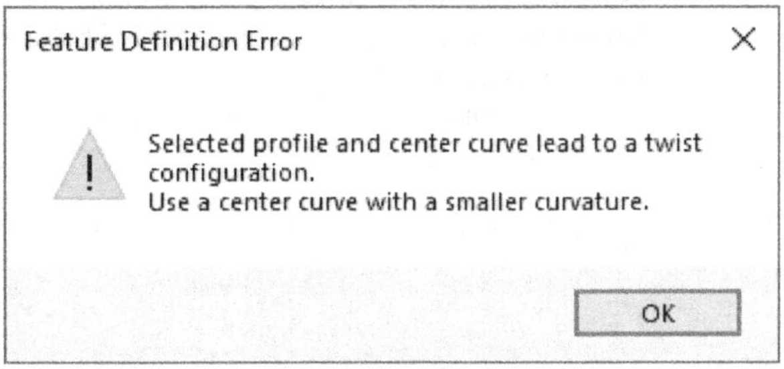

Figure 10–1

Step 2 - Investigate the failure.

When features fail, you can modify and correct them instead of deleting and reconstructing them. An example is shown in Figure 10–2. A Rib feature creation has failed because its profile overlaps during the solid creation. A message box opens describing the error.

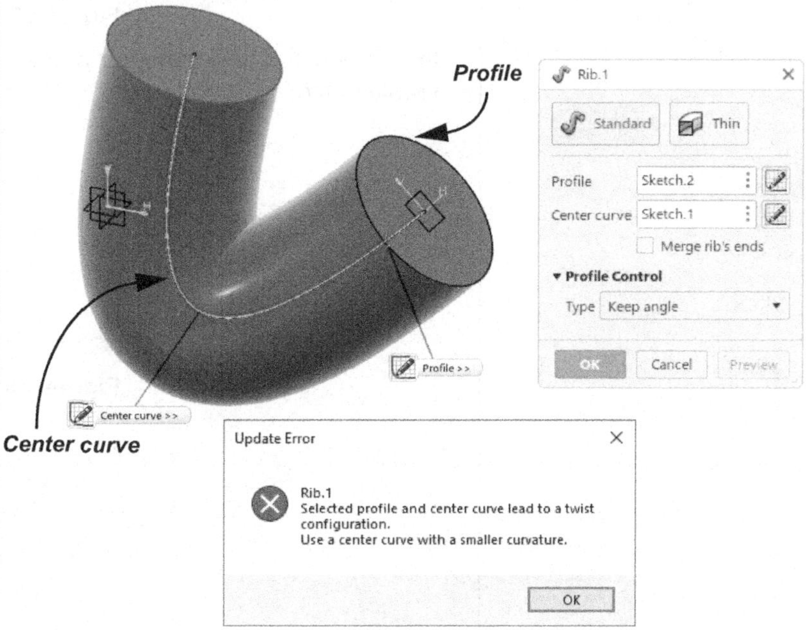

Figure 10–2

Step 3 - Modify the geometry.

Based on the error message, perform the required modifications to resolve the failure. This might require changes to the immediate feature or changes to the supporting geometry used to build the feature. If a sketch is the cause of the problem, use the **Sketch Analysis** tool to verify that any problems with the sketch have been resolved.

In Figure 10–2, the failure could be resolved by reducing the curvature of the center curve, or by reducing the diameter of the profile.

Figure 10-3 shows the center curve with a lower curvature.

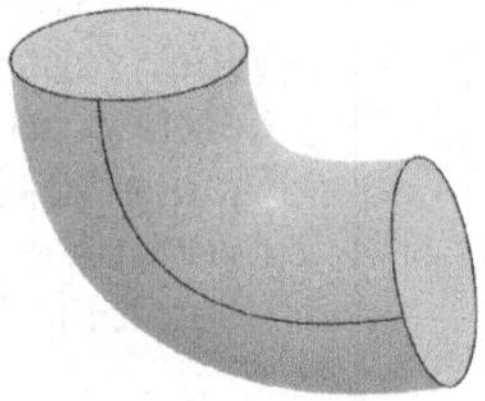

Figure 10–3

In Figure 10–4, the diameter of the profile is changed to a smaller size.

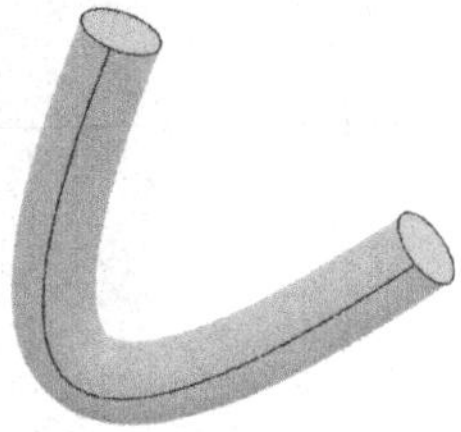

Figure 10–4

10.2 Resolution of Update Failures

When you update a model, failures can occur for a variety of reasons (i.e., geometry cannot be created due to invalid or missing references, dimensional changes result in geometry that cannot be calculated, etc.). The failed feature displays in the specification tree with a yellow warning sign. Until it is fixed, the children of the feature display with an update sign, as shown in Figure 10–5. When a failure occurs, you must resolve the failure before continuing.

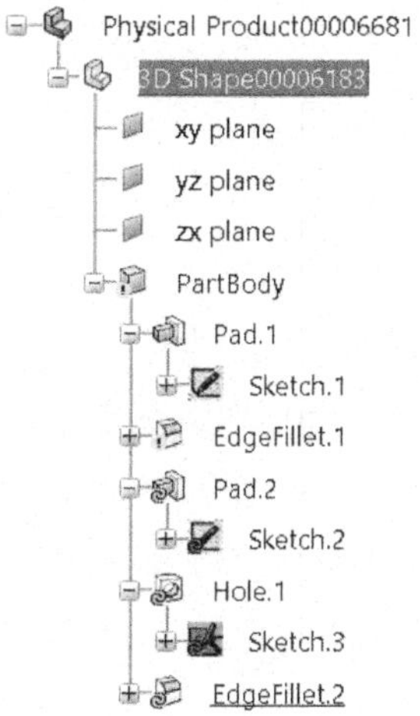

Figure 10–5

General Steps

Use the following general steps to resolve failures:

1. Investigate the failure.
2. (Optional) Undo the changes.
3. Resolve the failure.

Step 1 - Investigate the failure.

Investigate the geometry and try to understand what might have caused the failure. There are several reasons that might cause the Update failure, such as:

- Update Cycle
- Links
- Boundary Representations

Update Cycle

The creation order of the features can cause the feature failures. The features should reference each other in one direction. An example is shown in Figure 10–6. **Pad.1** is the base feature of the model and is created using the **Dimension** option. **Point.1** is created using the **On plane** option. This point is referenced by the top face of the **Pad.1** feature. **Point.2** and **Point.3** are created using **Point.1** as the reference point. **Spline** is created using these three reference points and **Plane.1** is created with the **Normal to curve** option. The Parents and Children relation for **Plane.1** is shown in Figure 10–7.

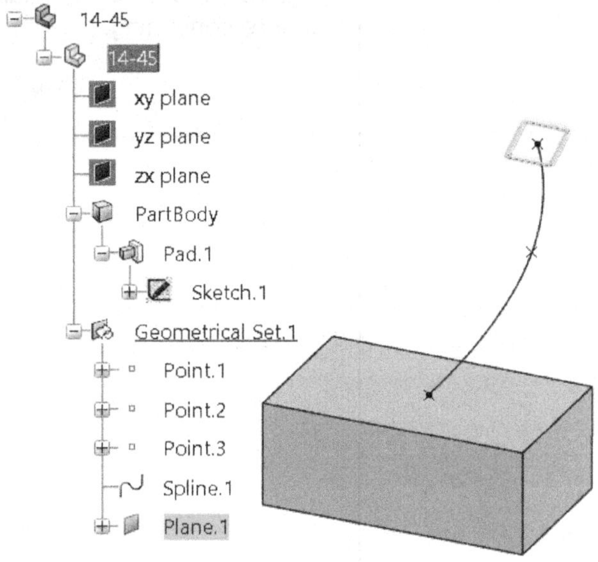

Figure 10–6

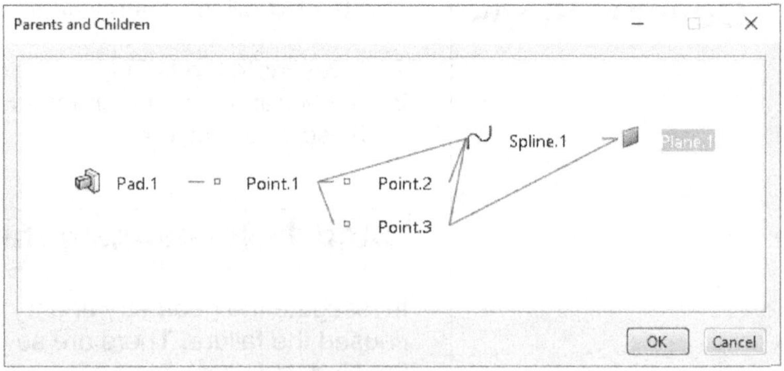

Figure 10–7

If you change the limit type of **Pad.1** from *Dimension* to **Up to surface**, as shown in Figure 10–8, using **Plane.1** as the limiting element, an Update cycle error occurs. This is because **Plane.1** is created using **Point.1**, and **Point.1** is created using the face of the Pad feature. This means that the two features are referencing each other in an endless cycle.

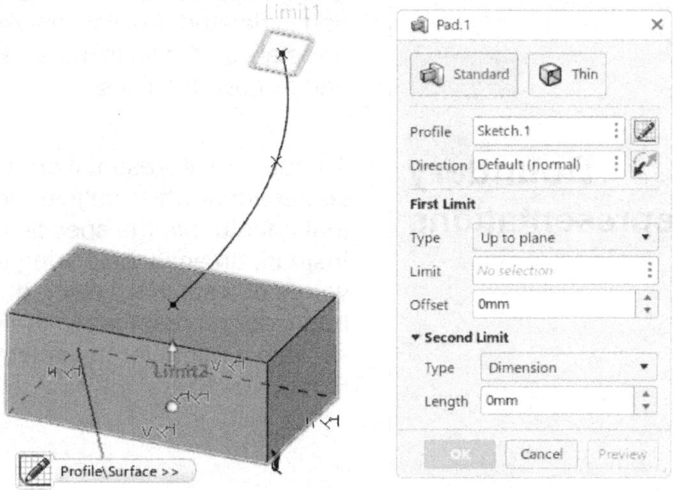

Figure 10–8

The Update cycle error is shown in Figure 10–9.

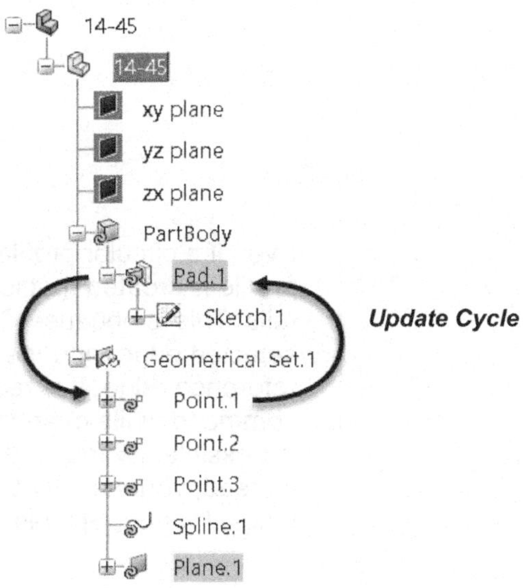

Figure 10–9

To resolve this error, check the Parent-Child relationship of the features. When you find the feature(s) causing the problem, you can modify or isolate them.

Links

Links are commonly established between parts. You can create links in the Assembly app using contextual design or in the Part Design app using the **Paste Special** option. If the referencing part is deleted, the link breaks and the feature fails. You can re-establish the links if they are required. If not, you can isolate and remove the links.

Boundary Representations

A boundary representation refers to the selection of any sub-element when defining references for a feature. This means that a feature in the specification tree is not directly referenced. Instead, an entity belonging to the feature, such as the edge or vertex of a solid, is selected. The EdgeFillet feature uses the boundary representation (selecting an edge of a solid). CATIA assigns a name for the selected sub-elements, as shown in Figure 10–10.

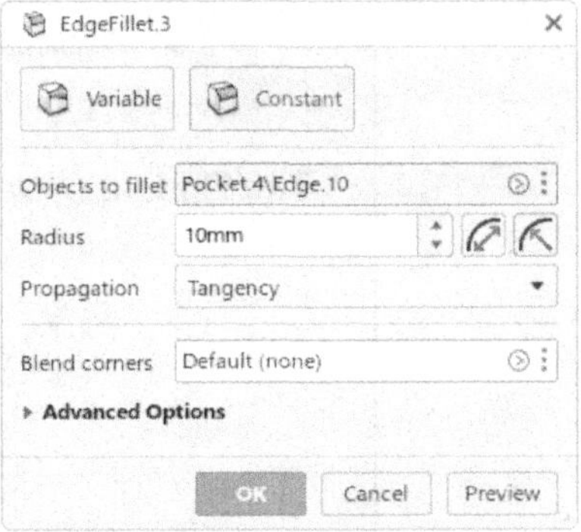

Figure 10–10

Even if a circular profile of a Pad feature is deleted and a new profile is created that is identical to the previous one, the feature fails. This is because CATIA generates a new name for the selected edge, and the EdgeFillet feature fails in finding the reference edge. It is recommended that you use the **Replace** command while changing the existing profile with a new one. If it is possible, try to avoid using the boundary representations. Instead, you must try to create the reference elements (Points, Lines, Planes, Splines, Extracts, etc.).

The Update Diagnosis dialog box provides information on why a feature has failed. Therefore, the content in the Update Diagnosis dialog box is dependent on the error that caused the problem. The items listed under the feature provide you with notes to help determine why the feature could not be created. Select one item at a time to review the information in the lower frame of the window. Items with yellow warning signs indicate errors. In general, warnings provide solutions, while errors explain why the current combination of references and values failed.

In Figure 10–11, the model was created using a Pad and an EdgeFillet feature. The profile for the Pad feature is circular. The edge of the Pad feature is used to create the EdgeFillet feature.

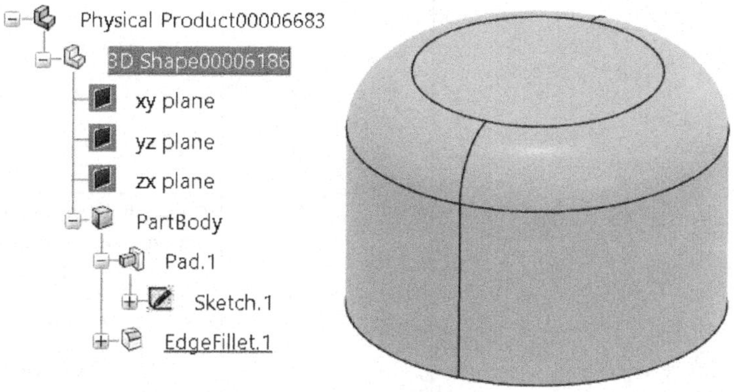

Figure 10–11

If the profile of the Pad feature is changed to a rectangular profile, the EdgeFillet feature fails, because it cannot find the referencing edge, as shown in Figure 10–12.

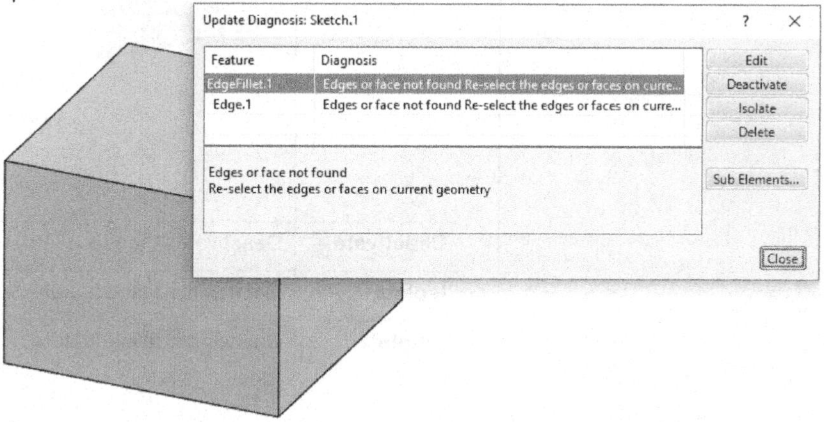

Figure 10–12

The options in the Update Diagnosis dialog box are described as follows:

Option	Description
Edit	When you click **Edit**, a Feature Definition Error message opens, as shown below. It displays a message that describes the reason for the failure. 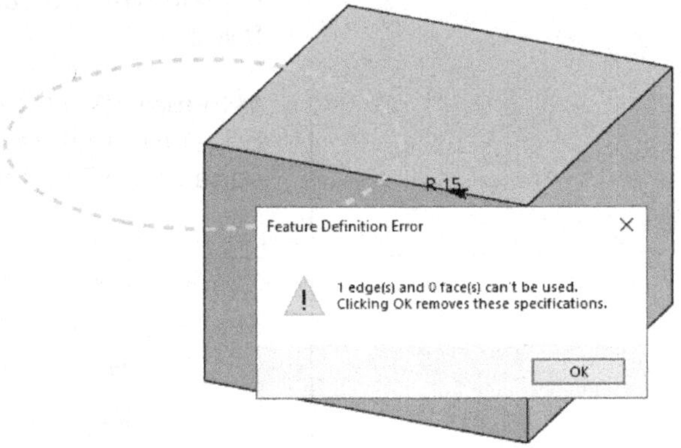
	Click **OK** to close the message box. The Feature Definition dialog box of the failed feature opens as shown below. 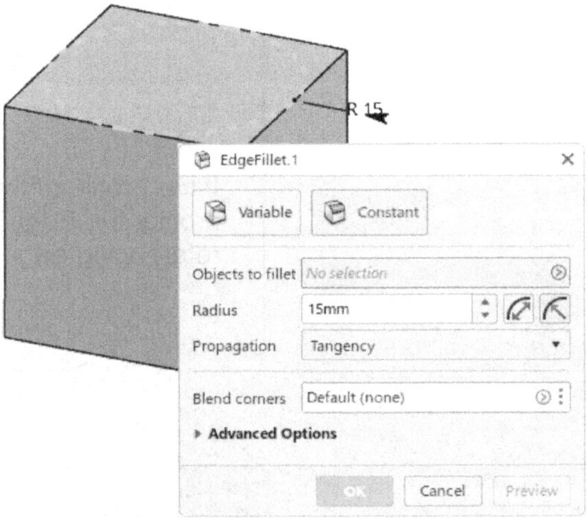
Deactivate	Deactivates the failed feature.
Isolate	Isolates the failed feature.
Delete	Deletes the failed feature.

Step 2 - (Optional) Undo the changes.

You can undo the changes that you have made to the model. The model then automatically updates and returns to its pre-failure state.

Step 3 - Resolve the failure.

Once you have investigated the reason for the failure, the next step is to resolve it. After investigation, perform the required modifications to resolve the failure. This might require making changes to the immediate feature, re-establishing links, isolating links, re-ordering the features, replacing the profiles, etc.

Practice 10a Update Cycle

Practice Objective

- Resolve Update Cycle failures.

In this practice, you will make the modifications to the model shown in Figure 10–13. The feature you are modifying will cause Update cycle failure that must be resolved using a different approach.

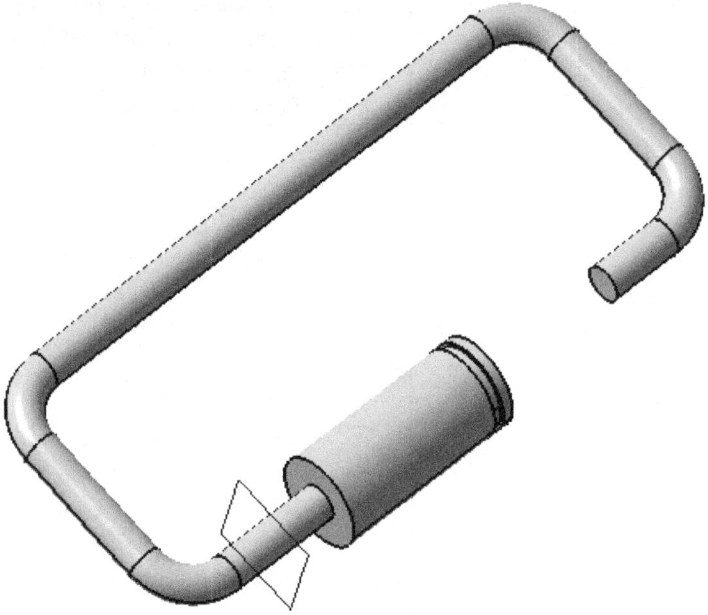

Figure 10–13

Task 1 - Open the part.

1. Import and open **SP-hook.3dxml**. When importing, type your initials followed by the dash symbol into the *Duplication string* field.
2. Investigate the model features.

Task 2 - Modify the Pad.1 feature.

1. Double-click on **Pad.1**.

2. In the Pad dialog box that opens, expand the Type drop-down list and select **Up to surface**. The dialog box and model display as shown in Figure 10–14.

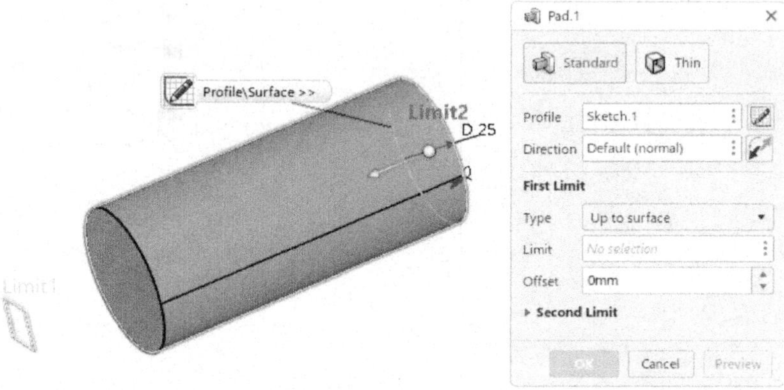

Figure 10–14

3. For the *Limit*, select Plane.1. The Feature Definition Error dialog box opens as shown in Figure 10–15.

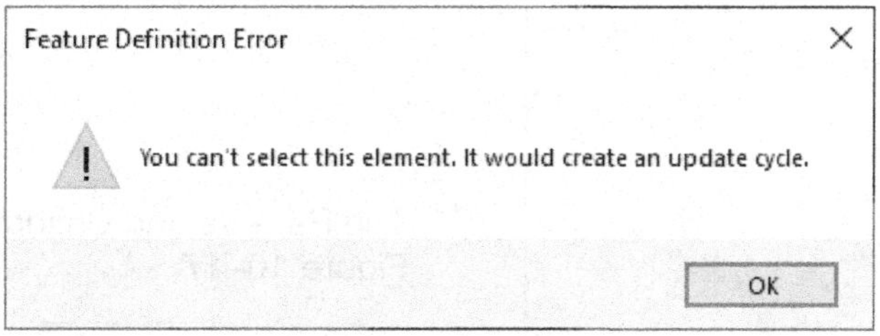

Figure 10–15

The error message indicates that there is an update cycle problem. There are two features that need to be investigated: **Pad.1** and **Plane.1**.

Task 3 - Investigate the error.

In this task, you will investigate the Parent-Child relation of **Plane.1**. This will help you to see what is causing the problem.

1. Click **OK** in the Feature Definition Error dialog box.

2. Click **Cancel** in the Pad dialog box.

3. Right-click on **Plane.1** and select **Parents/Children...**, as shown in Figure 10–16.

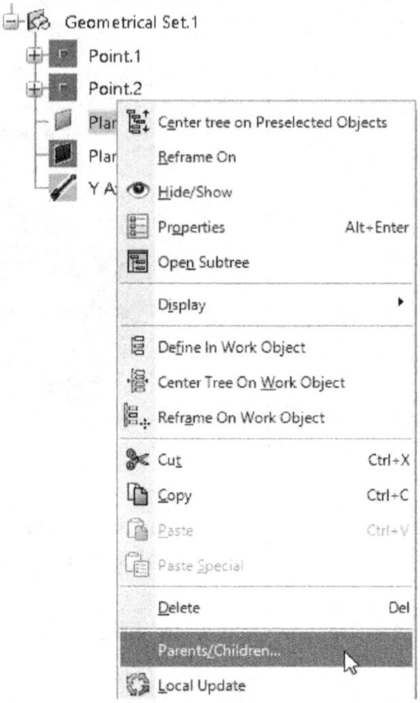

Figure 10–16

The Parents and Children dialog box opens as shown in Figure 10–17.

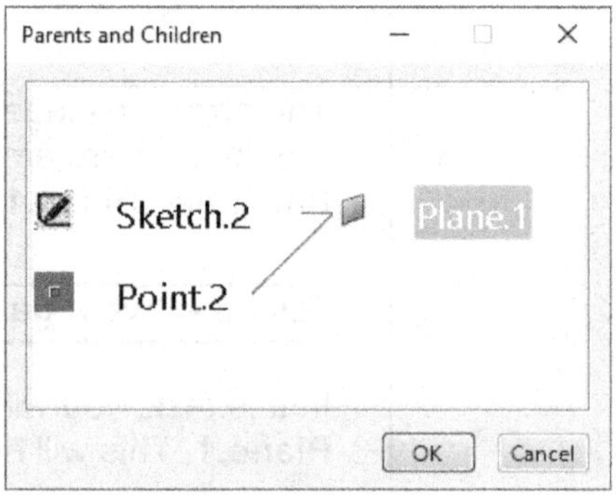

Figure 10–17

4. In the Parents and Children dialog box, double-click on **Sketch.2**, as shown in Figure 10–18.

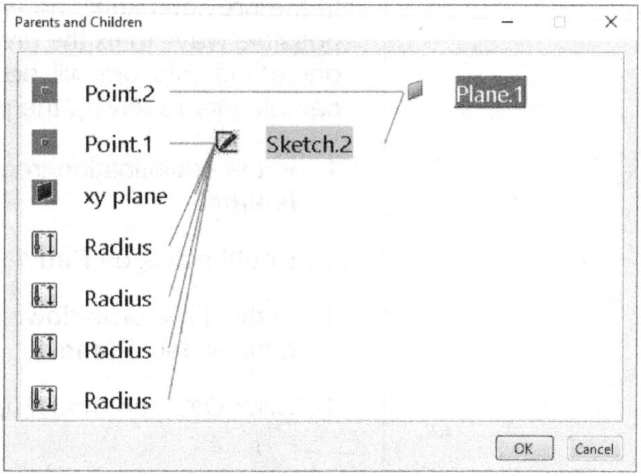

Figure 10–18

5. In the Parents and Children dialog box, double-click on **Point.1**, as shown in Figure 10–19.

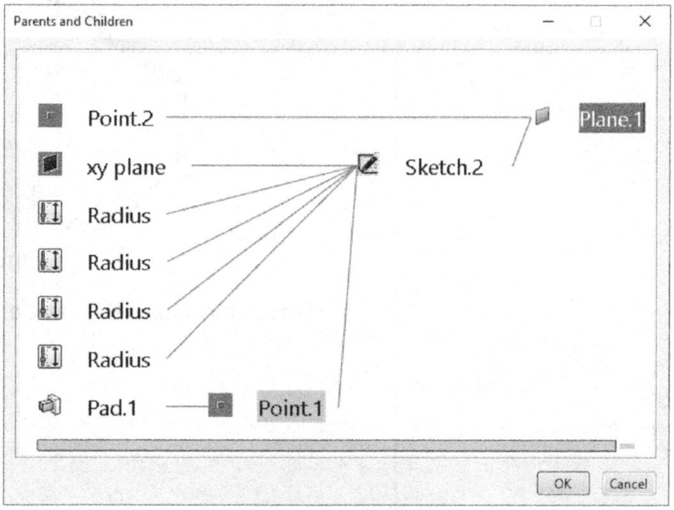

Figure 10–19

As you can see, **Pad.1** is one of the parents of **Plane.1**. The two features are referencing each other in an endless cycle. To resolve this issue, there are three options: extending the Pad by using a bigger dimension, creating a new reference plane which is not related to **Pad.1**, or isolating **Plane.1**.

6. Close the Parent and Children dialog box.

Task 4 - Resolve the update cycle.

In the previous task, the error was investigated and three possible ways to fix the problem were indicated. In this task, only one of the solutions will be applied. However, if time permits, you can also try resolving the problem using the other solutions.

1. In the specification tree, right-click on **Plane.1** and select **Isolate**.
2. Double-click on **Pad.1**.
3. In the Type drop-down list, select **Up to Surface**. For the *Limit*, select **Plane.1**.
4. Click **OK**. The model updates as shown in Figure 10–20.

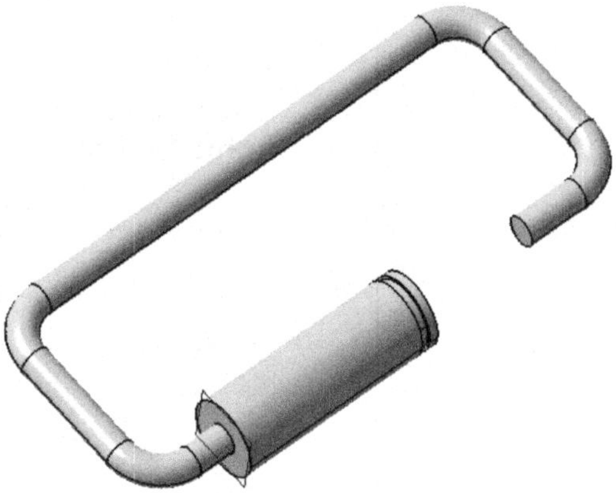

Figure 10–20

5. Save and close the model.

Chapter Review Questions

1. In general to resolve a failure, you:
   a. Read the failure message.
   b. Investigate the failure.
   c. Modify the geometry.
   d. All of the above.
2. If a sketch causes a failure, you can use the ________ to verify that any problems have been resolved.
   a. Sketch Diagnosis tool.
   b. Sketch Resolve tool.
   c. Sketch Analysis tool.
   d. None of the above.
3. Models can fail during creation or after modifications have been made.
   a. True
   b. False
4. The feature creation order is not relevant to feature failures.
   a. True
   b. False

5. What does the yellow icon next to the EdgeFillet.1 (shown in Figure 10–21) indicate?

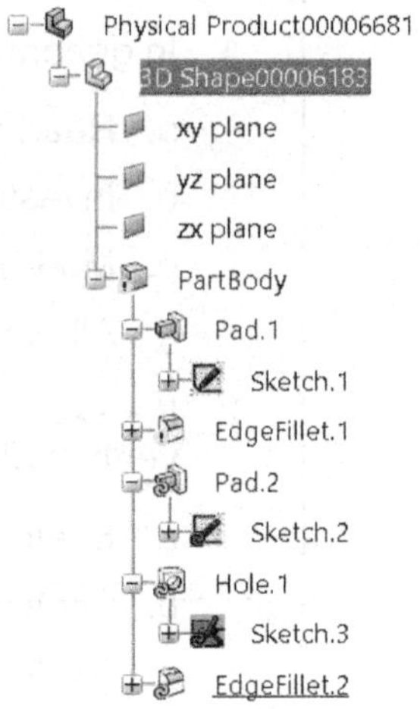

Figure 10–21

a. The feature needs to be updated.
b. The feature has failed.
c. The feature has a failed child.
d. None of the above.

Answers: 1d, 2c, 3a, 4b, 5b

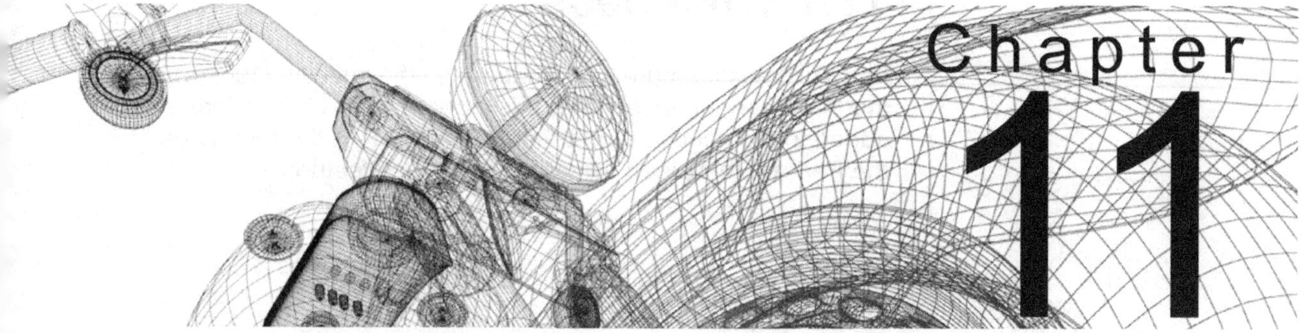

Additional Features

When you import files from a different CAD system using neutral file formats (STP or IGES), feature history is not available for the model. The features introduced in this chapter can be used to modify models that do not have history.

Learning Objectives in This Chapter

- Learn how to use the Thickness feature to add material to the faces of a model.
- Remove faces from Parts or imported data.
- Replace a model face with another face or surface.

11.1 Thickness

The Thickness feature adds material to the specified face(s) of a model. When the face(s) are thickened, the Thickness feature is added to the specification tree. In Figure 11–1, the four faces of the Pad are thickened using the Thickness feature.

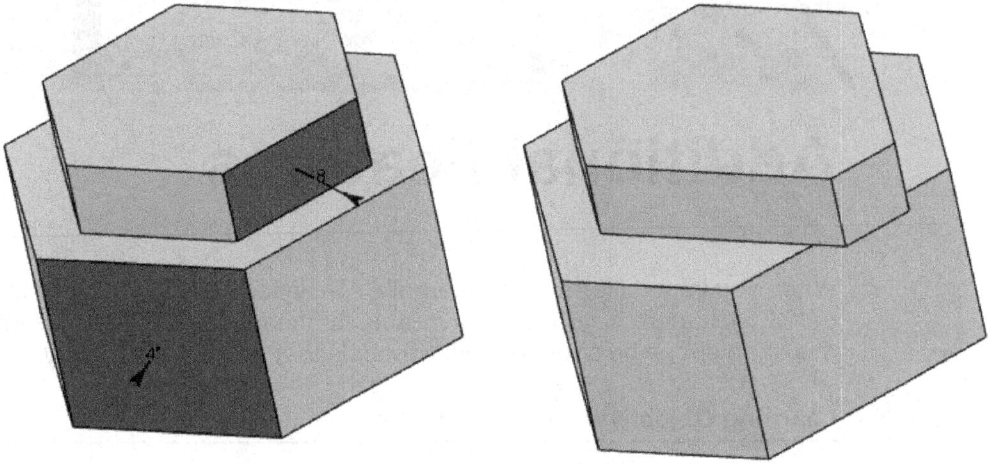

Before ***After: Material added to the four faces of the model***

Figure 11–1

General Steps

Use the following general steps to add material on the face(s):

1. Open the Thickness Definition dialog box.
2. Select the face(s) to which to add material.
3. Complete the feature.

Step 1 - Open the Thickness Definition dialog box.

Click (Thickness). The Thickness Definition dialog box opens as shown in Figure 11–2.

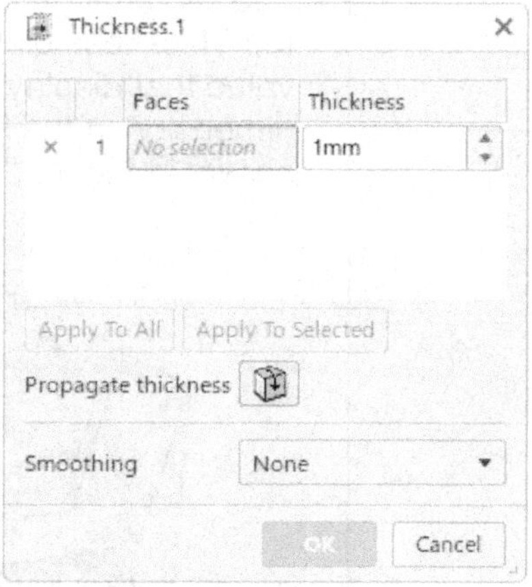

Figure 11–2

Step 2 - Select the face(s) to which to add material.

When you select a face, the faces that are tangent to the selected face are also selected automatically. The values for each selected face display on the model, as shown in Figure 11–3.

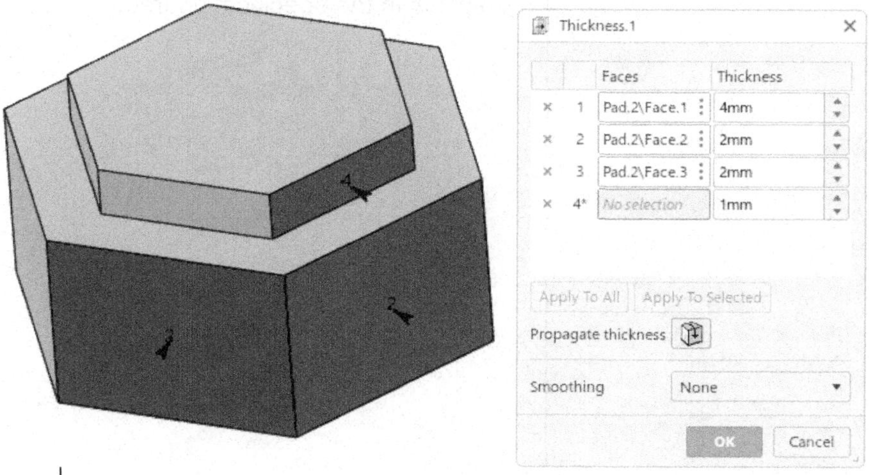

Figure 11–3

You can change the thicknesses either by entering new values in the Thickness dialog box or by double-clicking on the thickness value that displays on the model and entering the required dimension in the Parameter Definition dialog box that opens, as shown in Figure 11–4.

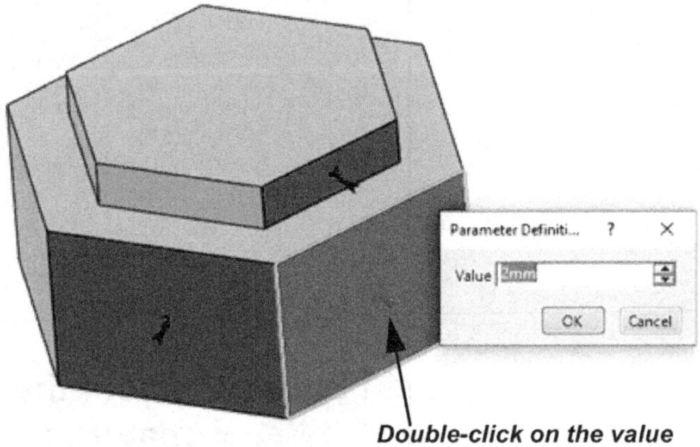

Figure 11–4

Step 3 - Complete the feature.

Click **OK** to complete the feature. The Thickness feature displays in the specification tree.

11.2 Face Removal

This feature removes the selected faces of a model, whether it is a Part or imported data. In Figure 11–5, the interior face of the model is removed using the Remove Face feature.

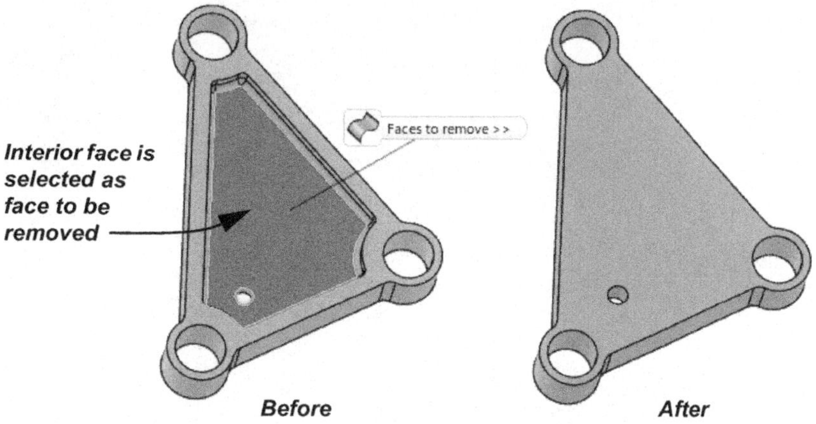

Figure 11–5

General Steps

Use the following general steps to remove face(s):

1. Open the Remove Face dialog box.
2. Select the face(s) to remove.
3. Complete the feature.

Step 1 - Open the Remove Face dialog box.

Click (Remove Face). The Remove Face dialog box opens as shown in Figure 11–6.

Figure 11–6

Step 2 - Select the face(s) to remove.

Select the face(s) to remove and/or keep on the model. To enable the selection to be cleared, you can right-click in the *Faces to remove* field and select **Clear selection**, as shown in Figure 11–7. To auto-select all of the faces that are tangent to the selection, select **Tangency Propagation**. To preview the selection, in the Remove Face dialog box, select (Show all faces to remove).

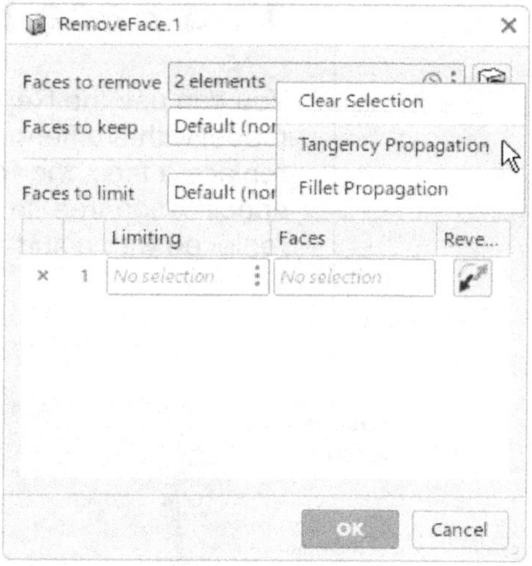

Figure 11–7

When you have selected more than one face, the *Faces to Remove* field changes to list the number of faces selected, rather than listing the individual faces.

To display a list of the individual elements that have been selected, select the arrow icon in the *Faces to remove* field, which opens the dialog box shown in Figure 11–8. You can also use this dialog box to remove or replace any of the selected elements.

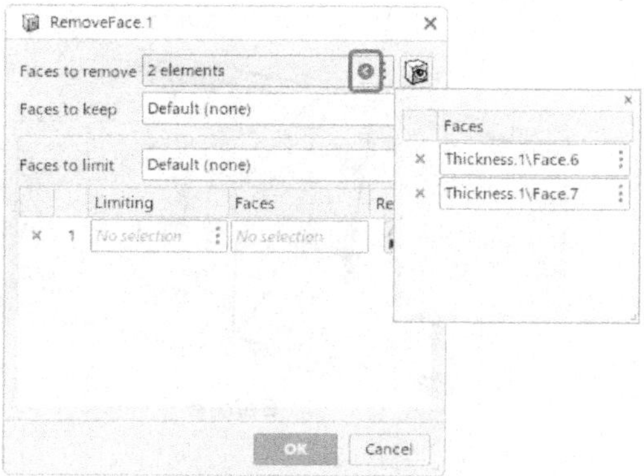

Figure 11–8

Step 3 - Complete the feature.

Click **OK** to complete the feature. The Remove Face feature displays in the specification tree.

11.3 Face Replacement

You can use the Replace Face feature to replace a face of the model with a different surface or face of the model. When you replace a face, the Replace Face feature is added to the specification tree. In Figure 11–9, the face of the model is replaced with a surface.

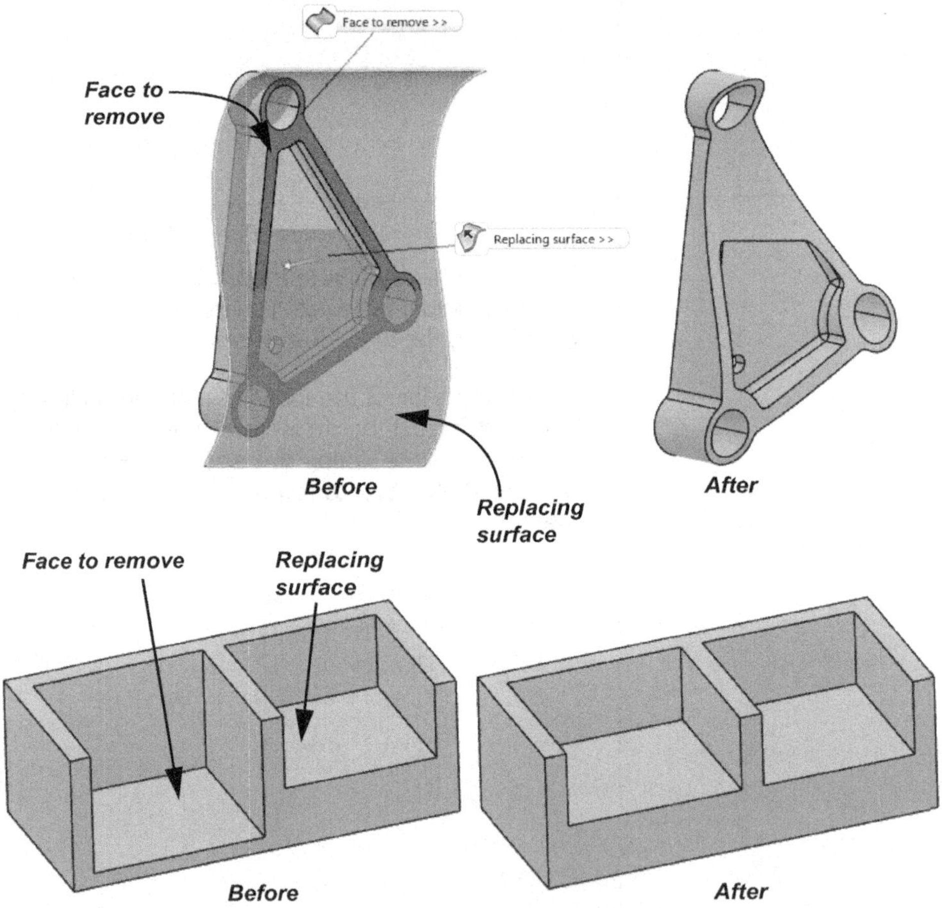

Figure 11–9

General Steps

Use the following general steps to replace the face(s):

1. Open the Replace Face dialog box.
2. Select a replacing surface and a face to remove.
3. Complete the feature.

Step 1 - Open the Replace Face dialog box.

Click (Replace Face). The Replace Face dialog box opens as shown in Figure 11–10.

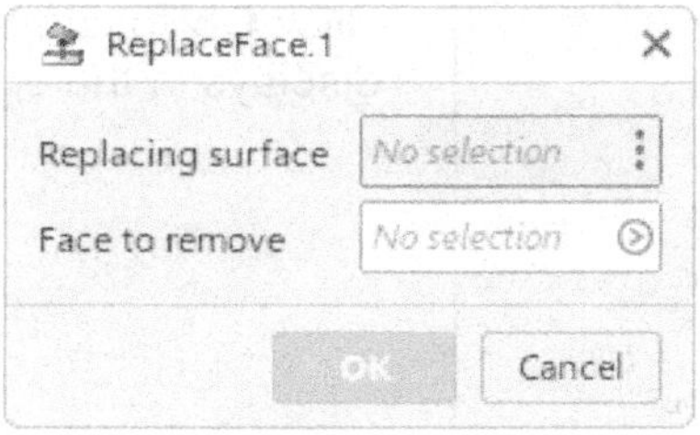

Figure 11–10

Step 2 - Select a replacing surface and a face to remove.

Select a replacing surface and a face to remove. Verify that the material direction is toward the model, as shown in Figure 11–11.

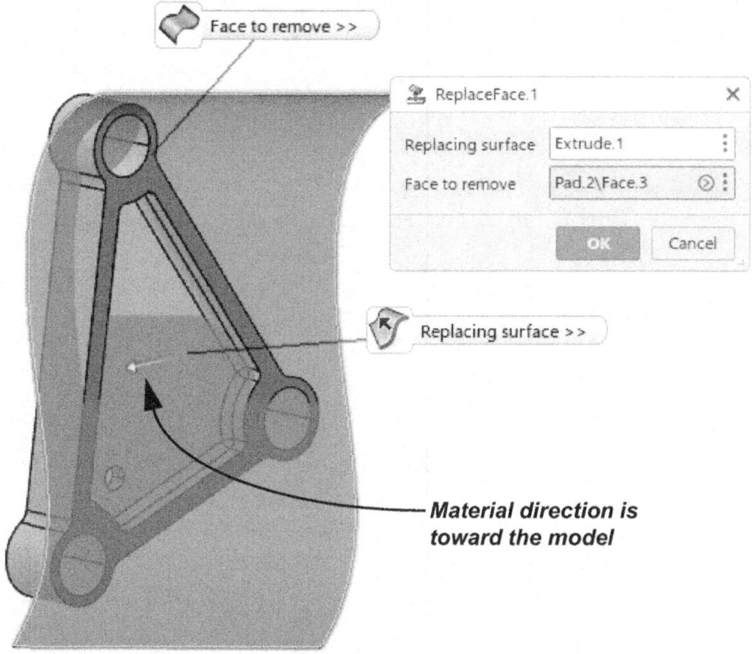

Figure 11–11

Only a planar face of the model can be used as the Replacing surface.

Step 3 - Complete the feature.

Click **OK** to complete the feature. The Replace Face feature displays in the specification tree.

Practice 11a Thickness

Practice Objective

- Use the Thickness feature.

In this practice, you will create a molded model for a finished part. You will add material to the faces of the model using the Thickness feature. The completed model displays as shown in Figure 11–12.

Figure 11–12

Task 1 - Open the part.

1. Import and open **Link10205.3dxml**. When importing, type your initials followed by the dash symbol into the *Duplication string* field. The model displays as shown in Figure 11–13.

Figure 11–13

Task 2 - Copy and paste the body.

In this task, you will copy the **Completed Model** body and paste it under a body using the **Paste Special** option. This way, it is possible to create a link between the original and the molded part. For example, if the completed model is modified, the molded part will be updated automatically according to the changes.

1. Copy the **Completed Model** body.
2. In the specification tree, right-click on the **Link_10205** 3DShape and select **Paste Special**.
3. Select the **As Result With Link** option.
4. Click **OK**.
5. Rename the copied body as **Completed Model**, as shown in Figure 11–14.

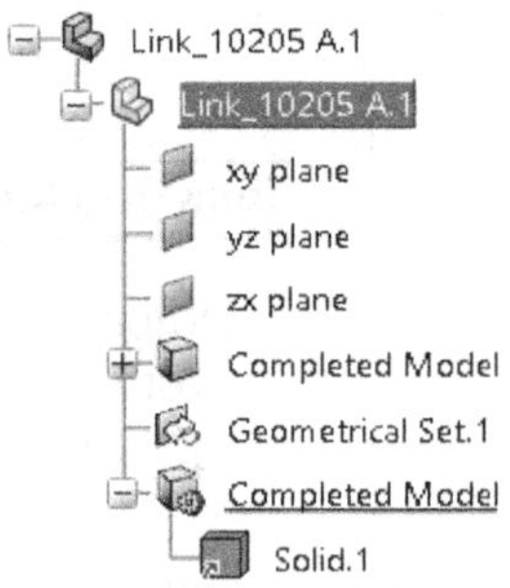

Figure 11–14

6. Hide the **Completed Model** body.

Task 3 - Create Thickness.

In this task, you will add additional material on the faces that will be machined.

1. In the Refine section of the Action Bar, click  (Thickness). The Thickness Definition dialog box opens as shown in Figure 11–15.

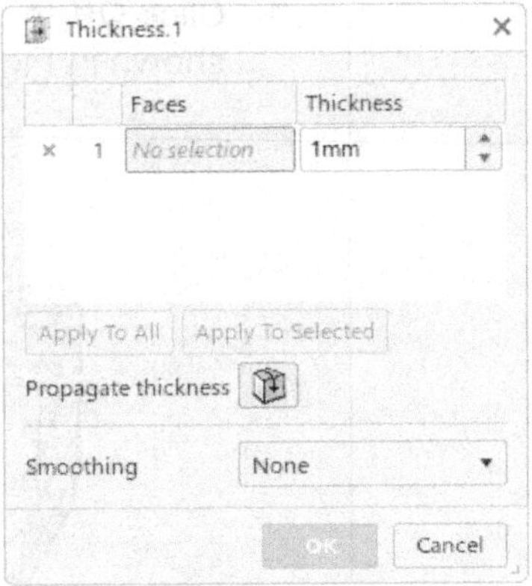

Figure 11–15

2. Select the top and bottom faces of the model to add **2mm** of material, as shown in Figure 11–16.

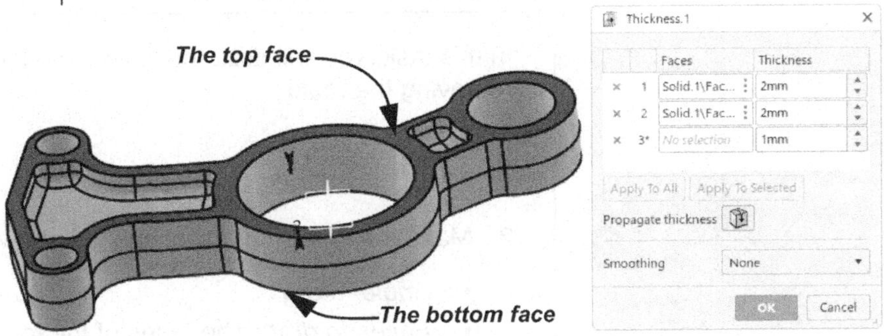

Figure 11–16

3. Select the holes and add **3mm** of material, as shown in Figure 11–17.

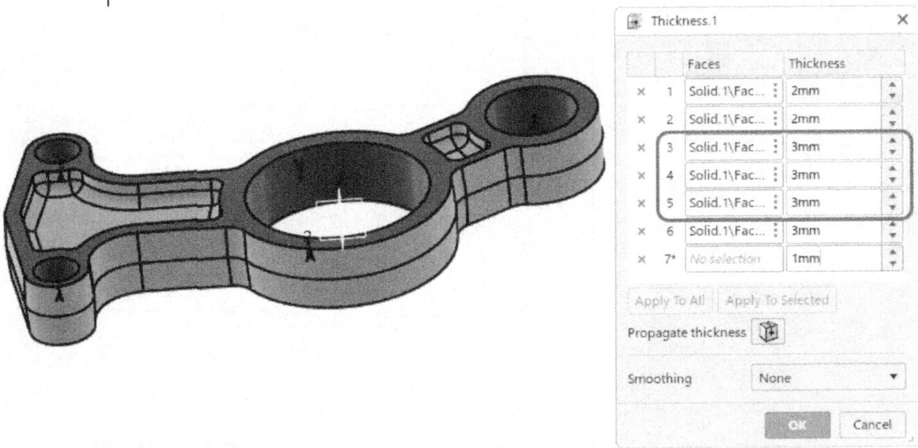

Figure 11–17

4. Click **OK** to complete the feature. The model displays as shown in Figure 11–18.

Figure 11–18

Task 4 - Create Draft.

In this task, you will draft the Holes to ease the process of removing the mold.

1. Click  (Draft) and then click **More**.
2. Make the following selections, as shown in Figure 11–19:
   - *Angle:* **3deg**
   - *Faces to draft:* The faces of the four holes
   - *Neutral Element:* **yz plane**
   - *Parting options:* **Draft both sides**

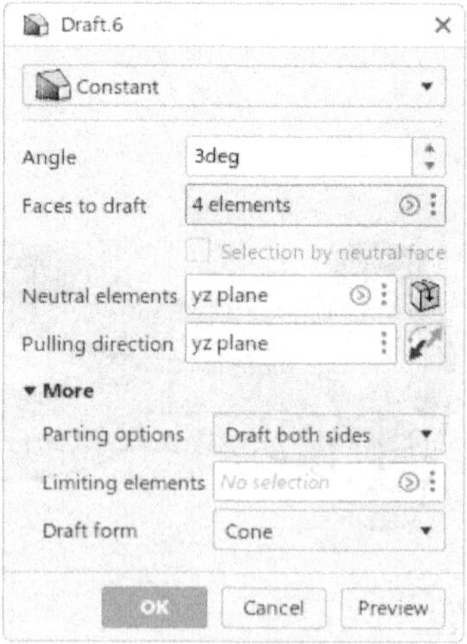

Figure 11–19

3. Click **OK** to complete the feature. The model displays as shown in Figure 11–20.

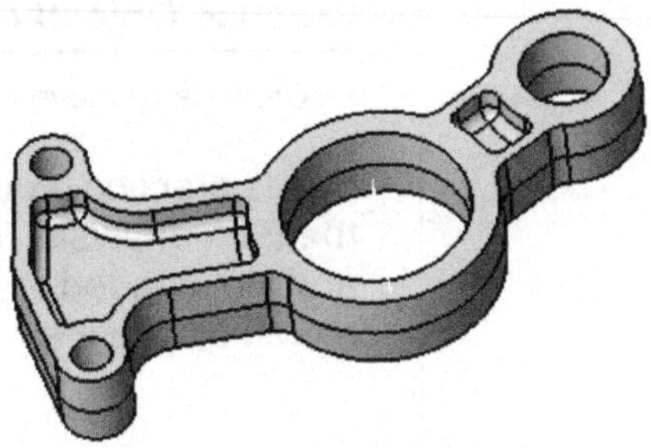

Figure 11–20

4. Right-click on **Molded Model** and select **Properties**. The Properties dialog box opens.

5. In the Properties dialog box, select the *Graphic* tab, and set the *Transparency* value to **150**, as shown in Figure 11–21.

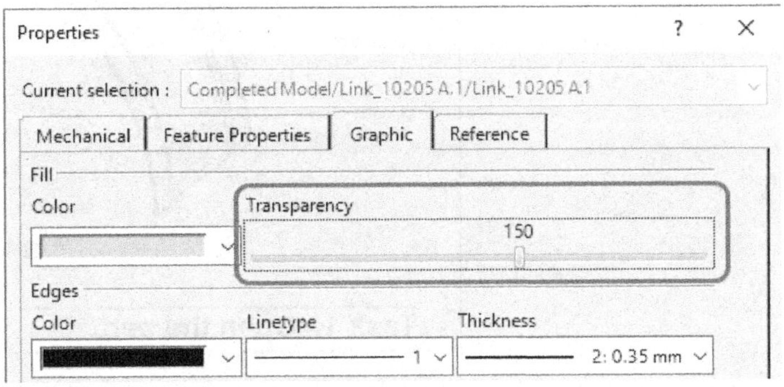

Figure 11–21

6. Show the **Completed Model** body. The model displays as shown in Figure 11–22.

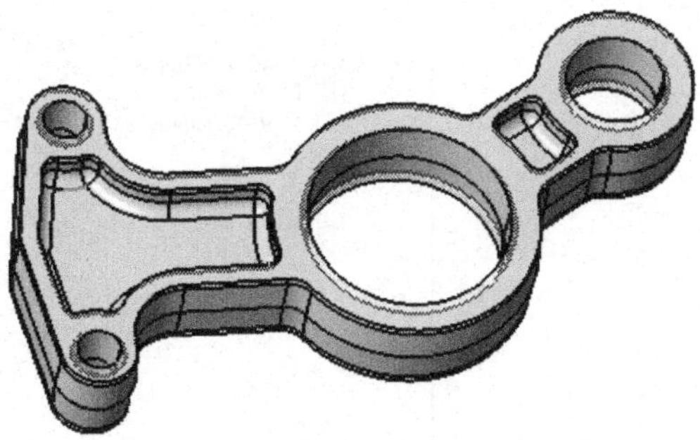

Figure 11–22

7. Save and close the model.

Practice 11b Remove Face

Practice Objective

- Create a Remove Face feature.

In this practice, you will modify an imported part to prepare for the FEA analysis. To mesh the part homogeneously, the Fillets and Holes need to be removed from the model. The completed model displays as shown in Figure 11–23.

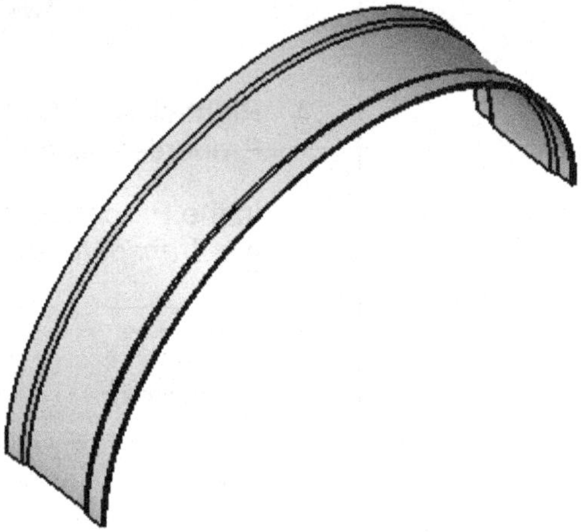

Figure 11–23

Task 1 - Open the part.

1. Import **Stator_Band.stp**. The Stator_Band.stp message box opens as shown in Figure 11–24 indicating that the part has been opened successfully.

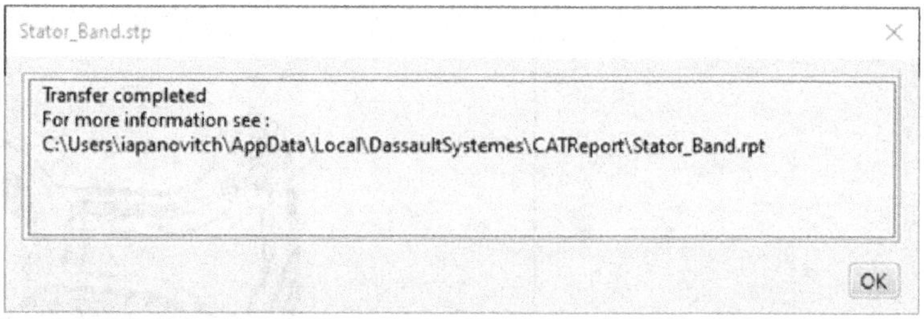

Figure 11–24

2. Click **OK**. The model displays as shown in Figure 11–25.

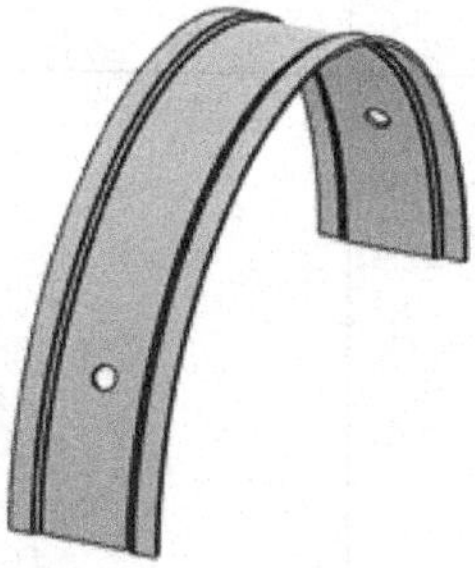

Figure 11–25

Task 2 - Create a Remove Face Feature.

In this task, you will remove the Fillets and the Holes.

1. In the Refine section of the Action Bar, click  (Remove Face). The Remove Face dialog box opens as shown in Figure 11–26.

Figure 11–26

2. Select all of the faces of the Fillets and Holes. There should be 20 selected faces, as shown in Figure 11–27.

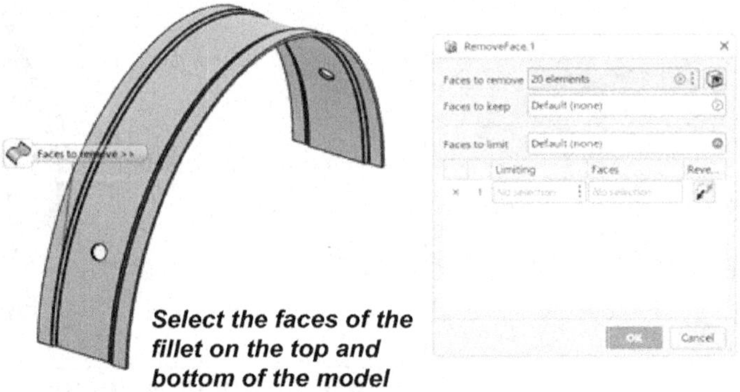

Figure 11–27

3. Click **OK** to complete the feature. The model displays as shown in Figure 11–28.

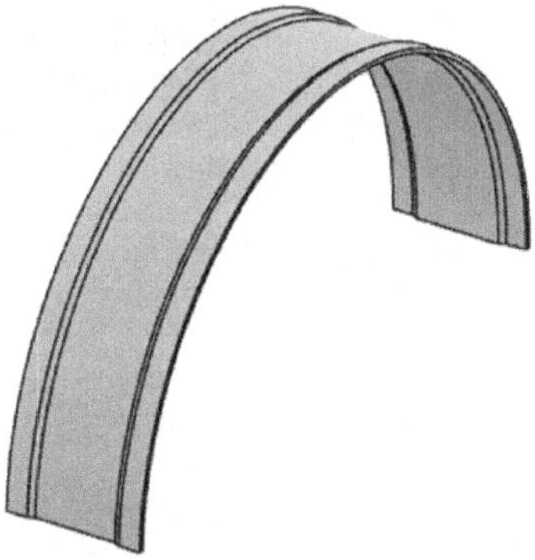

Figure 11–28

4. Save and close the model.

Practice 11c Replace Face

Practice Objectives

- Create a Replace Face feature.
- Create a Remove Face feature.

In this practice, you will modify an imported part using the Replace Face and Remove Face features. The completed model displays as shown in Figure 11–29.

Figure 11–29

Task 1 - Open the part.

1. Import **Replace_face.stp**. The Replace_face.stp message box opens as shown in Figure 11–30 indicating that the part has been opened successfully.

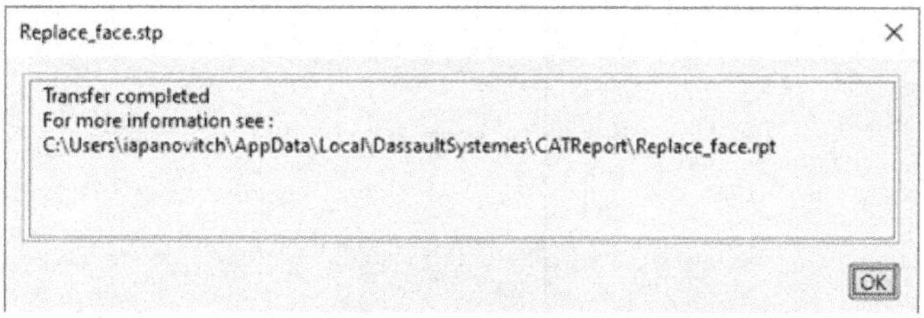

Figure 11–30

2. Click **OK**. The model displays as shown in Figure 11–31.

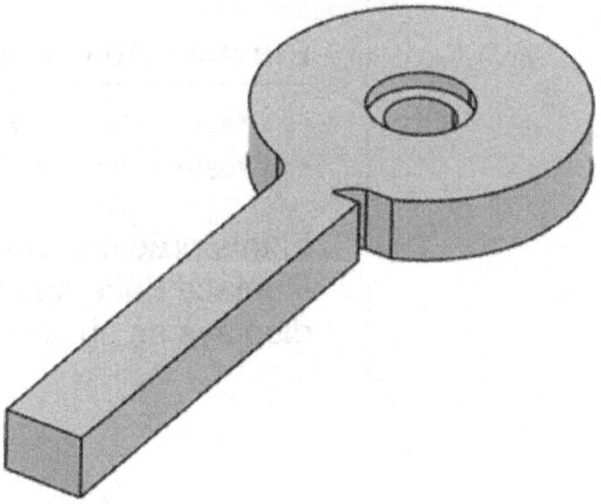

Figure 11–31

Task 2 - Create a Replace Face Feature.

1. In the Refine section of the Action Bar, click  (Replace Face). The Replace Face dialog box opens as shown in Figure 11–32.

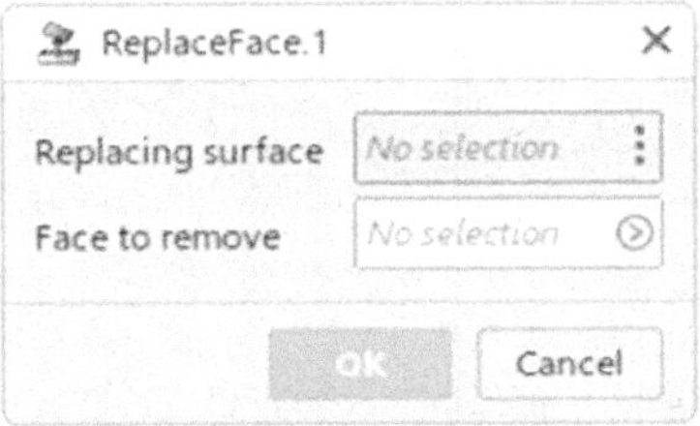

Figure 11–32

2. Select the face that defines the Replacing surface and the Face to remove, as shown in Figure 11–33.

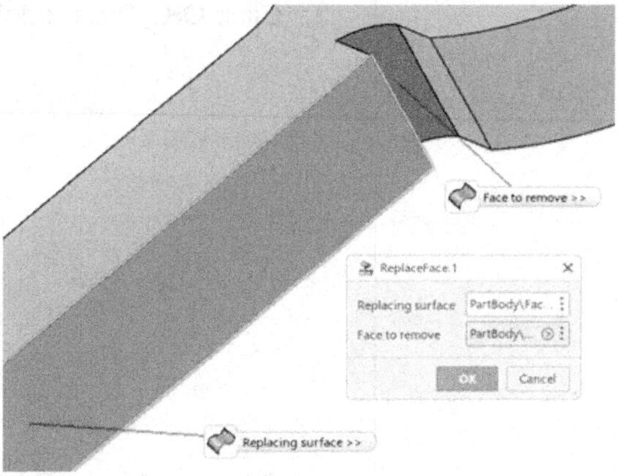

Figure 11–33

3. Click **OK** to complete the feature. The model displays as shown in Figure 11–34.

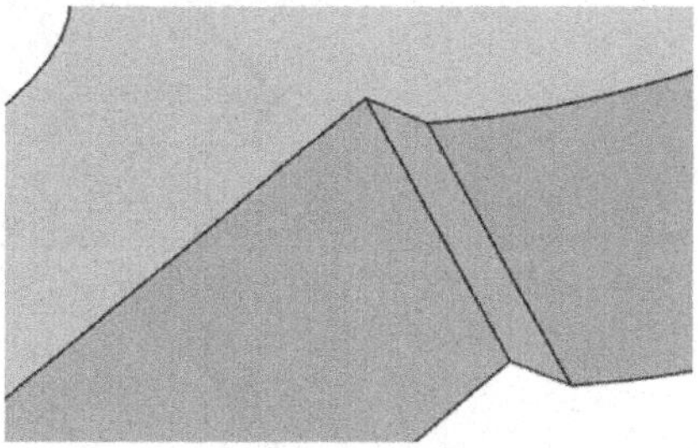

Figure 11–34

Task 3 - Create a Remove Face Feature.

1. In the Refine section of the Action Bar, click  (Remove Face).

2. Select the face of the model, as shown in Figure 11–35.

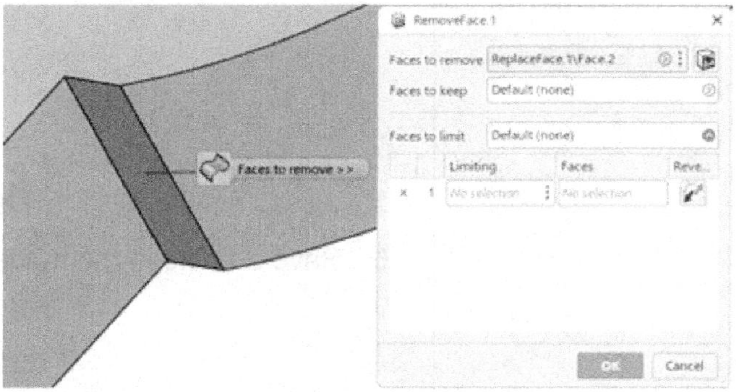

Figure 11–35

3. Click **OK**. The model displays as shown in Figure 11–36.

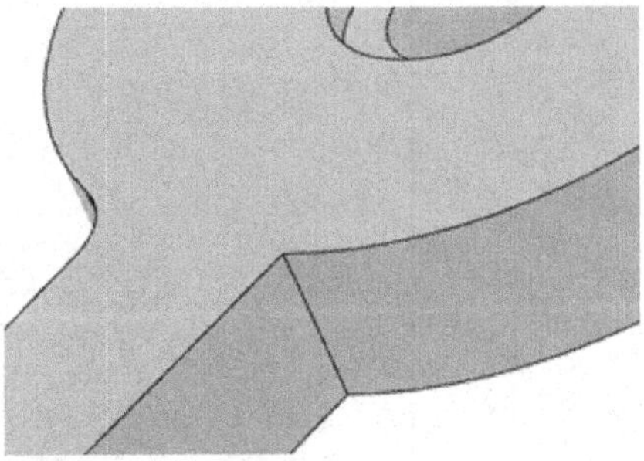

Figure 11–36

4. Create a **10mm** Edge Fillet, as shown in Figure 11–37.

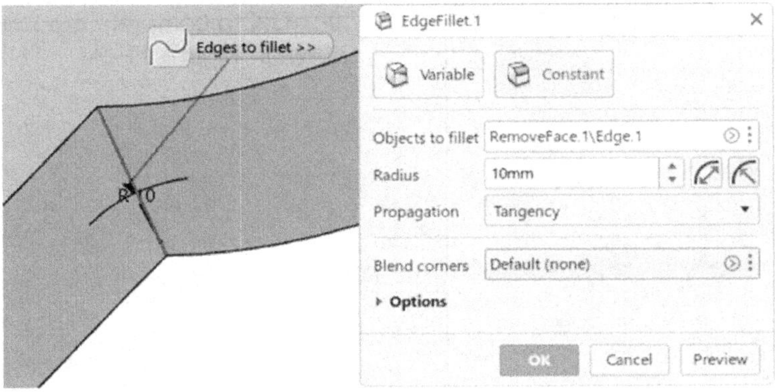

Figure 11–37

5. Click **OK**. The model displays as shown in Figure 11–38.

Figure 11–38

6. Save and close the model.

Chapter Review Questions

1. You can add material to specified faces of a model using the Thickness feature.
   a. True
   b. False
2. Thickness features add the same thickness to all of the selected faces.
   a. True
   b. False
3. **Remove Face** is used to remove pocket features from the model.
   a. True
   b. False
4. You substitute one surface for another using _____.
   a. Remove Face
   b. Switch Face
   c. Swap Face
   d. Replace Face
5. When replacing a surface, it is important that _____.
   a. The replacing surface is planar.
   b. The material direction is toward the model.
   c. The replacing surface falls within the boundary of the face to be removed.
   d. All of the above.

Answers: 1a, 2a, 3b, 4d, 5b

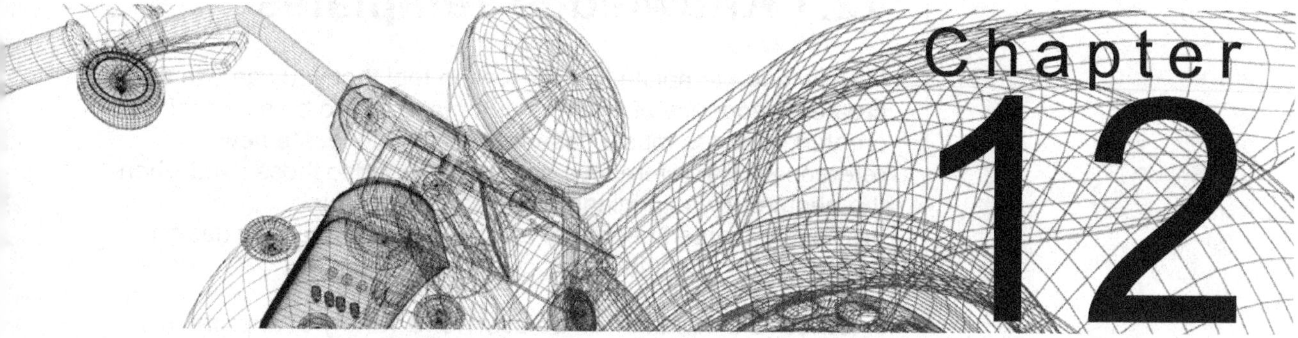

Knowledge Templates

Reuse of existing information saves time and ensures consistency. This chapter introduces two types of knowledge templates: Power Copy and User Feature. The Power Copy template enables you to use features in other documents, and provides more control over the placement of data than simply copying and pasting. User Feature templates are similar in function. However, use of the User Feature template results in a single representative feature, whereas the Power Copy template can result in a group of features.

Learning Objectives in This Chapter

- Understand knowledge templates.
- Create a Power Copy.
- Learn how to use a Power Copy and a User Feature in other models.
- Create a User Feature.

12.1 Knowledge Templates

A knowledge template is a replication tool that you can use to create a sequence of features automatically. To be successfully created, features must possess the ability to locate new references. The references must correspond to those used when the geometry was originally created. In this way, previously-created geometry can be adapted to a new design that is similar in context.

Knowledge templates can be used for a variety of applications, including:

- Adding frequently created features to a part. These features can be modified to apply to the design intent and context of the new part.
- Adding a complete and validated sequence of features to a part. Once positioned in the new part, these features are ready to use and do not require modification.
- Creating a series of customized features for a specific field of activity.

This chapter introduces the two types of knowledge templates in CATIA 3DEXPERIENCE. These templates are as follows:

Knowledge Template	Description	Result	Applications
Power Copy	Copies a selection of features and parameters from the source model into a template that can be applied to target part models.	Copies the entire list of features into the target model. Features have an identical behavior to the original features, and can be modified.	Redundant creation of features that require modification in the target model.
User Feature	Copies a selection of features and parameters from the source model into a template that can be applied to target part models.	Places a single feature into the target model that contains the geometry of all of the selected features. Only published parameters can be modified.	Redundant creation of features that do not require modification in the target model.

12.2 Creation of a Power Copy

Power Copies can be very useful when a feature or group of features is required in several models. Rather than recreate the same features in each model, you can create them once and then use Power Copy to copy the original feature(s) into another model. Unlike the **Paste** option, you can also control the referencing features and dimensions while placing the feature(s).

Carefully consider which references to select when you create features for a Power Copy. Consider the following tips:

- When creating sketches, try to constrain the sketch to edges and faces rather than to reference planes. This technique makes it easier to place the Power Copy, because some reference planes might no longer exist.
- Avoid constraining features that you plan to use in a Power Copy with respect to the Horizontal-Vertical (H-V) absolute axis. This is because the origin and orientation of the absolute axis cannot be controlled. Therefore, the results of placing the Power Copy are unreliable.
- Avoid using projections and intersections in a sketch that you plan to use in a Power Copy.
- Ensure that your sketch is ISO-constrained, (i.e., the sketched entities are green) so that the results of the Power Copy are as expected.

General Steps

Use the following general steps to create a Power Copy:

1. Start the creation of the Power Copy.
2. Add features to the Power Copy.
3. Rename the features.
4. Set the variable parameters, if required.
5. Set an icon or preview for the Power Copy.
6. Complete the Power Copy.

Step 1 - Start the creation of the Power Copy.

Once all of the features for the Power Copy have been created, ensure that the model has been saved.

To open the Power Copy Definition dialog box, select **Tools>**  (Power Copy), as shown in Figure 12–1.

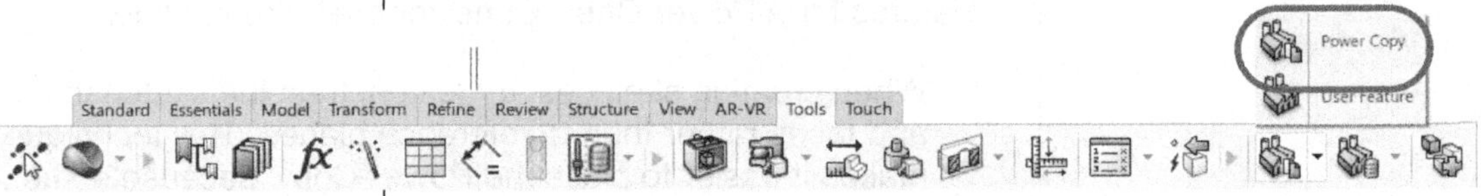

Figure 12–1

The Power Copy Definition dialog box opens as shown in Figure 12–2.

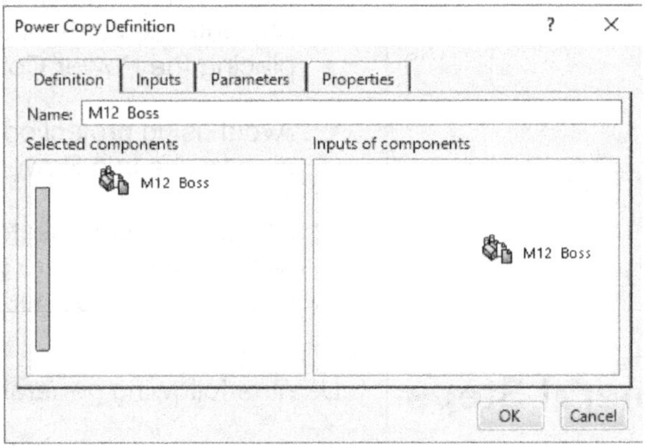

Figure 12–2

In the *Name* field, enter a descriptive name for the Power Copy and press <Enter>.

Step 2 - Add features to the Power Copy.

To begin adding features to the Power Copy, select the *Definition* tab in the Power Copy Definition dialog box.

If you accidentally select a feature you do not want to include in the Power Copy, select the feature again in the specification tree to remove it.

A Power Copy can contain a variety of features, such as geometric features, formulas, and constraints. To add a feature to a Power Copy, select it in the specification tree. Once selected, the feature displays in the *Components* area in the Power Copy Definition dialog box. Any references used when the feature was created are listed in the *Inputs of components* area, as shown in Figure 12–3.

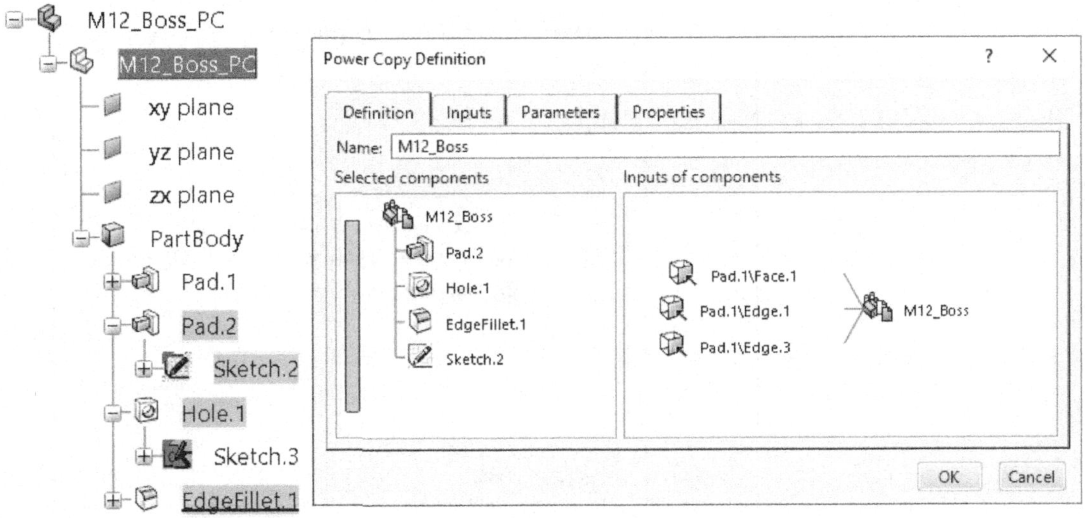

Figure 12–3

These references are used as inputs when the Power Copy is placed in another model.

Try not to add a large number of features to the Power Copy. This avoids complications in the Power Copy and problems that could occur when placing the Power Copy later.

Step 3 - Rename the features.

Once you finish adding the features to the Power Copy, it is a good idea to enter descriptive names for the features. This makes it easier to place the Power Copy later.

To rename an input, select the *Input* tab. Select the feature in the Inputs window and enter a new name in the *Name* field at the bottom of the dialog box. The original name of the feature remains in brackets in the Inputs window, as shown in Figure 12–4.

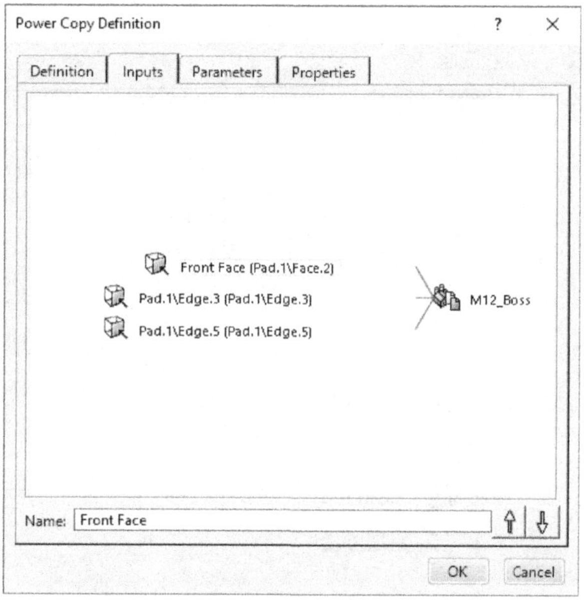

Figure 12–4

Step 4 - Set the variable parameters, if required.

Select the *Parameters* tab to define which parameter values you want to be variable when you are placing the Power Copy feature. You can change the value of a variable parameter to suit the model in which it is placed.

To create a modifiable parameter, select the parameter and select the **Published** option. The *Name* field displays. Enter a descriptive name for the feature. This name can be used when the Power Copy is placed in the new model.

The remaining values associated with the Power Copy are not published. Therefore, their values are not modifiable during placement.

For example, the parameter selected in Figure 12–5 is published. This parameter is now variable.

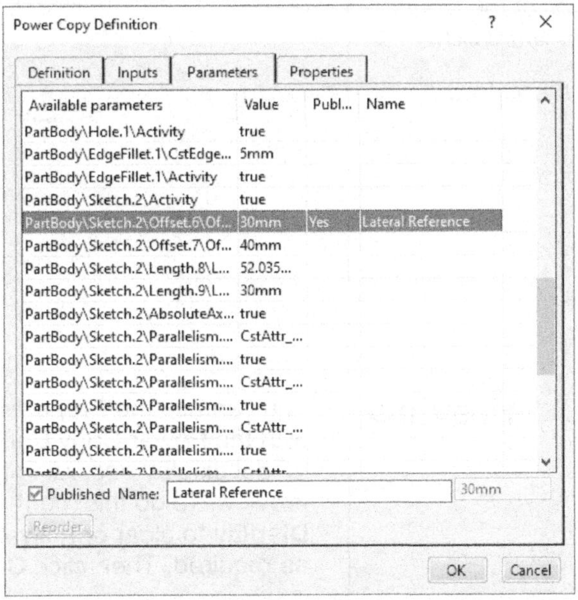

Figure 12–5

Step 5 - Set an icon or preview for the Power Copy.

Select the *Properties* tab and select an icon by which you can identify the Power Copy in the specification tree. Click  to expand the flyout of commonly selected icons, as shown in Figure 12–6.

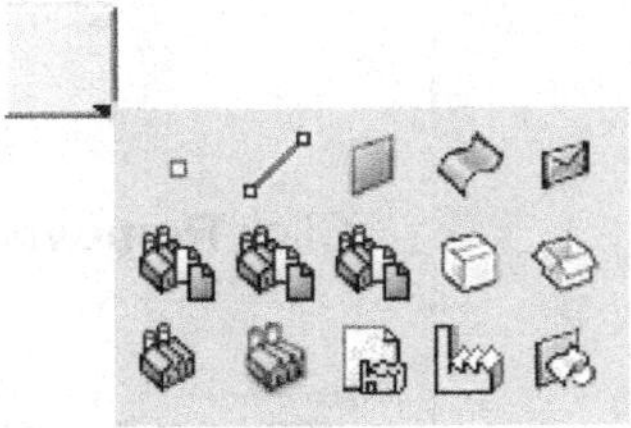

Figure 12–6

You can also browse through all of the icons loaded in your CATIA session by clicking ... .

The selected icon is shown in Figure 12–7.

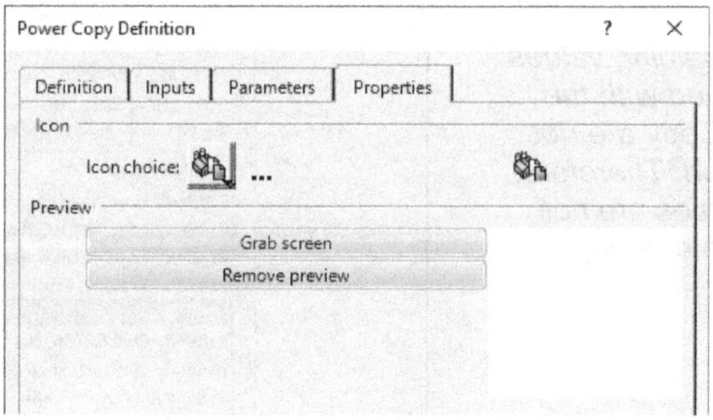

Figure 12–7

Preview

You can use the *Properties* tab to create a preview that is stored with the Power Copy Definition. To create a preview, set up the model display according to how you want it to display in the preview. To do this, right-click on **Display** and select **Tree Display** to clear or activate the display of the specification tree, as required. Then click **Grab screen** to take a screen shot.

This screen shot is used as the preview, as shown in Figure 12–8.

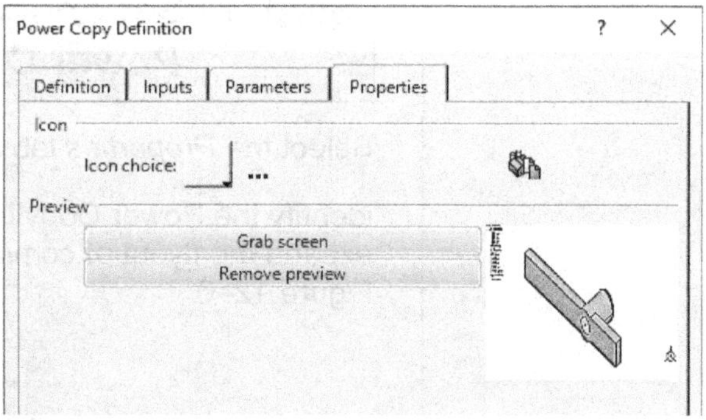

Figure 12–8

Click **Remove preview** to remove the preview.

Step 6 - Complete the Power Copy.

Once you have completed the Power Copy Definition, click **OK** to close the dialog box.

12.3 Instantiation of a Power Copy

Once a Power Copy has been created, you can use it in other models. You can modify any variable parameters to suit the new model.

General Steps

Use the following steps to instantiate the Power Copy.

1. Select the Power Copy to be instantiated.
2. Place the Power Copy.
3. Change the parameters and complete the instantiation.

Step 1 - Select the Power Copy to be instantiated.

In the target model (where you are placing the Power Copy),

select **Tools>**  (Instantiation From Representation), as shown in Figure 12–9.

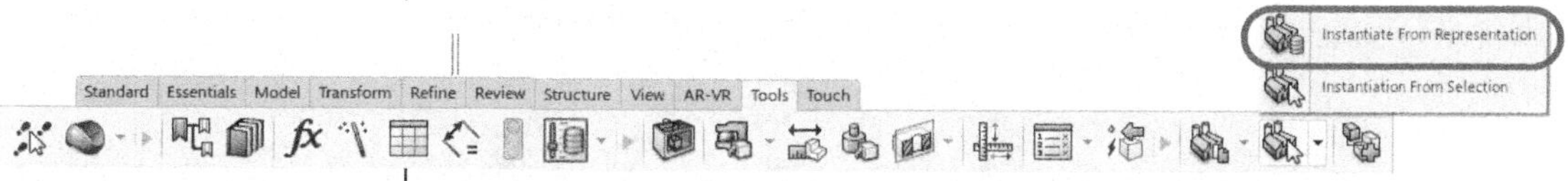

Figure 12–9

The Select or search an object window will appear as shown in Figure 12–10. The part that contains the Power Copy can either be search and selected from within the search field, or if it is already open in a different tab, the top of the parts tree can be directly selected from that tab.

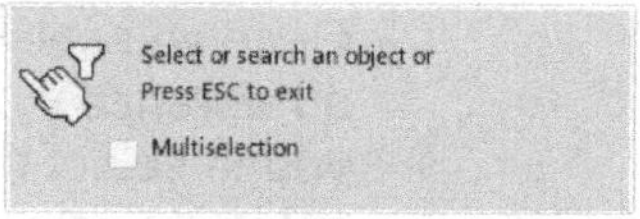

Figure 12–10

Step 2 - Place the Power Copy.

When you select the part, the Insert Object dialog box opens as shown in Figure 12–11. In the Reference drop-down list, select the correct Power Copy (if more than one exists in the source document).

You can also specify the destination of the geometry by selecting **Inside** or **After** in the Destination drop-down list. In the *Reference* field, you can define the geometrical set or PartBody in which the features can be located.

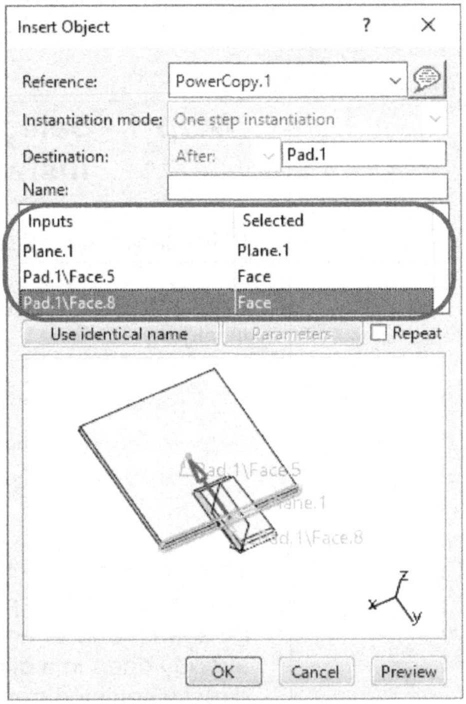

Figure 12–11

Once you select the Power Copy to reference, CATIA highlights a reference in the *Inputs* column in the dialog box and waits for you to select the corresponding feature in the new model. This selection process is repeated until all of the references have been selected and the Power Copy is successfully positioned.

At this point, you can display the Power Copy with the model by clicking **Preview**.

A slide cover and clip being inserted onto the end of the bed are shown in Figure 12–12. The references indicated on the model are selected to correspond to the references listed as inputs in the dialog box.

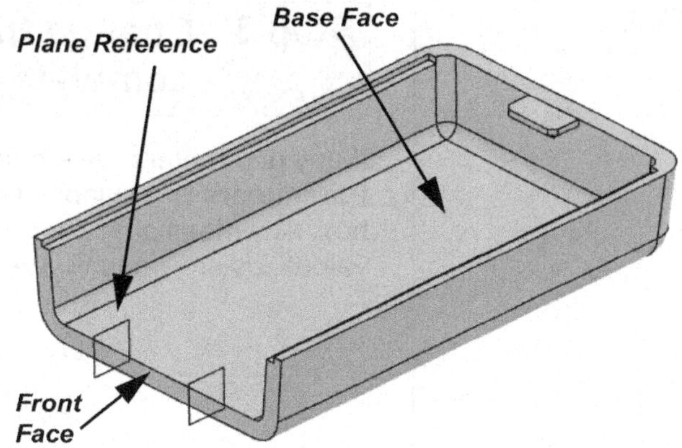

Figure 12–12

If the name of the reference in the target model is the same as in the source model, you can also place references by clicking **Use identical name**. CATIA automatically places the reference by matching the reference name in the Power Copy to the reference name in the new model. For example, the **Plane.1** listed in the dialog box uses the **Plane.1** in the model as a reference for placement, as shown in Figure 12–13.

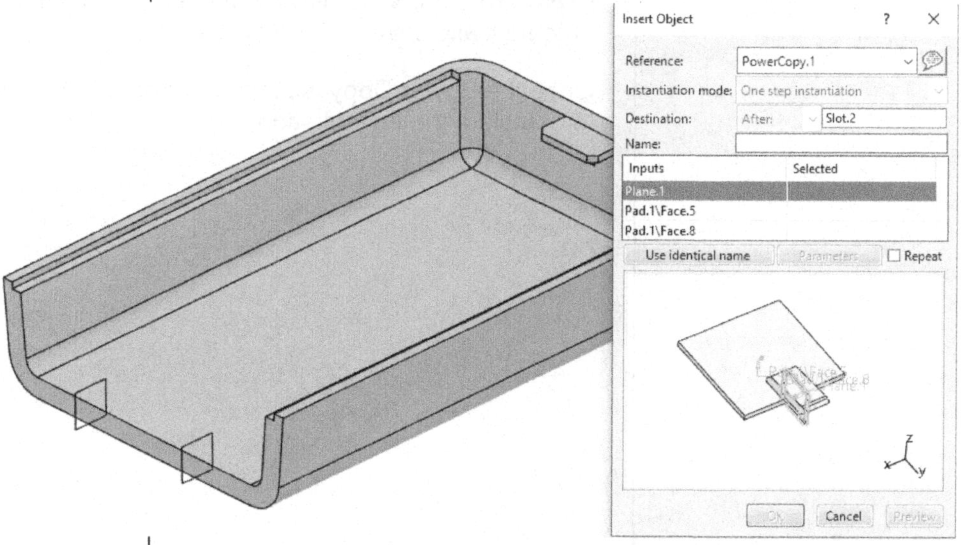

Figure 12–13

Once instantiated, each feature of a Power Copy becomes a separate feature and is no longer linked to the original Power Copy.

If you place more than one of the same object, you can select the **Repeat** option to save time. Once you complete placing the Power Copy, the dialog box remains open to place another one.

Step 3 - Change the parameters and complete the instantiation.

If any parameters have been published with the Power Copy, **Parameters** is available. Click it to open the Parameters dialog box. Any modifiable parameters are listed with the default values, as shown in Figure 12–14.

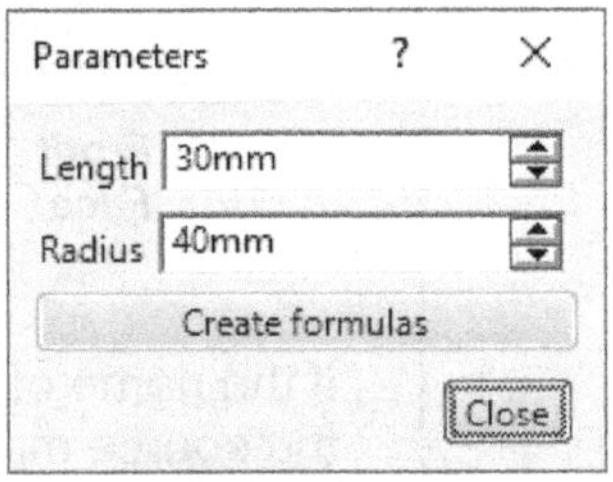

Figure 12–14

Click **Create formulas** to automatically create a formula for any parameter in the model with the same name as a parameter in the Power Copy. When the Power Copy is instantiated in a model with the parameter of the same name and you click **Create formulas**, the length of the rectangular box is automatically driven by the new value.

Once the Power Copy is placed correctly in the model, click **OK** to complete the instantiation.

12.4 Creation of User Features

The process of creation and instantiation of a User Feature is similar to that of a Power Copy. The difference between the two Knowledge Templates is in the result. While a Power Copy adds all of the copied features to the target model, the User Feature only adds geometry as a single feature in the specification tree. This feature cannot be modified. Only parameters that have been published during feature creation can be changed.

Creating a User Feature

To create a User Feature, select **Tools>** (User Feature). The User Feature Definition dialog box opens as shown in Figure 12–15.

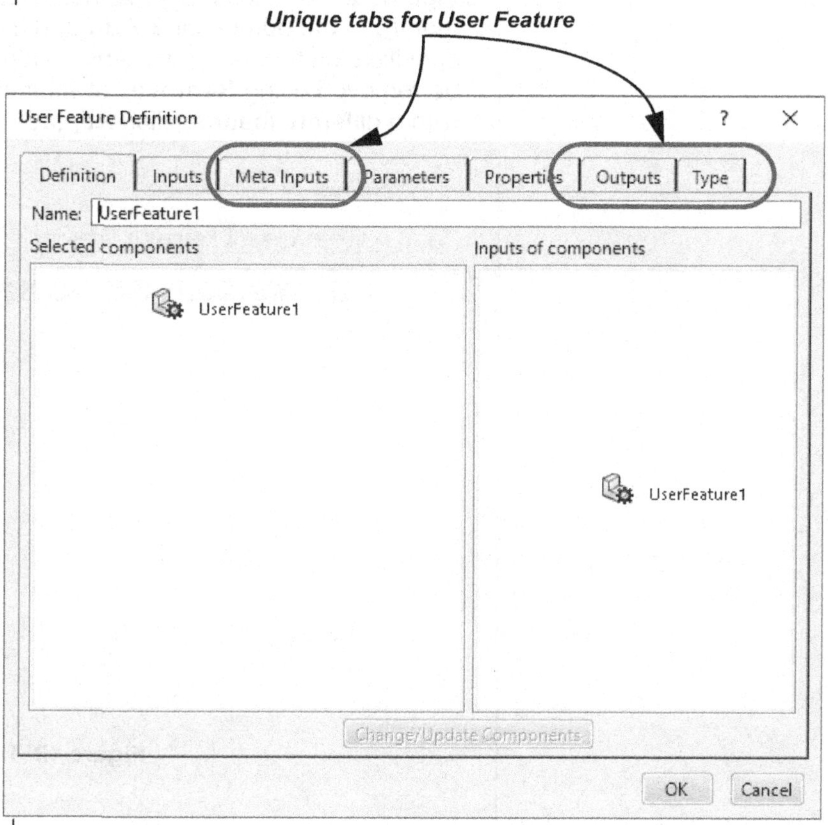

Figure 12–15

You can create a User Feature using the methods described for a Power Copy. The User Feature Definition dialog box is identical to the Power Copy Definition dialog box, except for three additional tabs: *Meta Inputs*, *Outputs*, and *Type*.

Meta Inputs Tab

You can use meta inputs to instantiate entire parts or part bodies efficiently. Using meta inputs, CATIA automatically assigns all of the inputs when instantiating.

Outputs Tab

You can use the *Outputs* tab to define features that are carried forward when the User Feature is instantiated in another model. For example, you could use the *Outputs* tab if you added a Pad feature, but only wanted the sketch used by the Pad to be brought into the new model.

Select the *Outputs* tab to specify an output, as shown in Figure 12–16, and select the Main Result in the list. To add a feature to the output, click **Add** and then select a feature in the specification tree or model. Any feature that has been added can be removed using **Remove**. To replace the default Main Result with a different feature, click **Replace**.

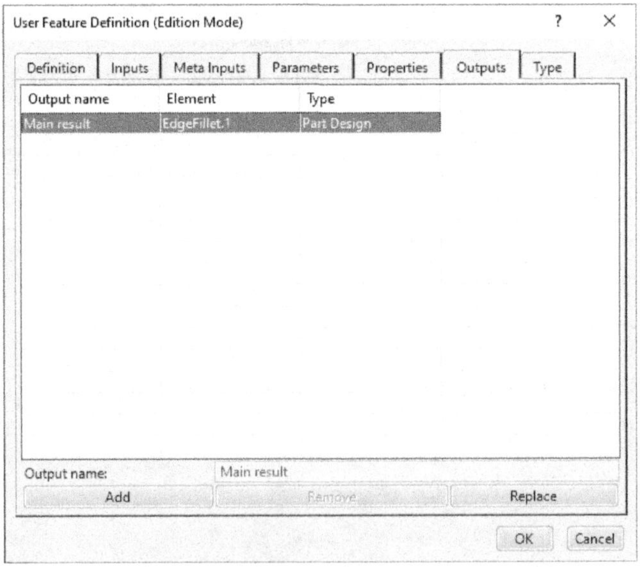

Figure 12–16

Type Tab

When a User Feature is instantiated in a new model, it displays as a single entry in the specification tree, although it might contain a variety of features. The *Type* tab enables you to define a type that you can associate with the User Feature so that it can be located when performing a search. For example, you could associate the type Pad with the User Feature so that it can be located when searching for Pads. The *Type* tab displays as shown in Figure 12–17.

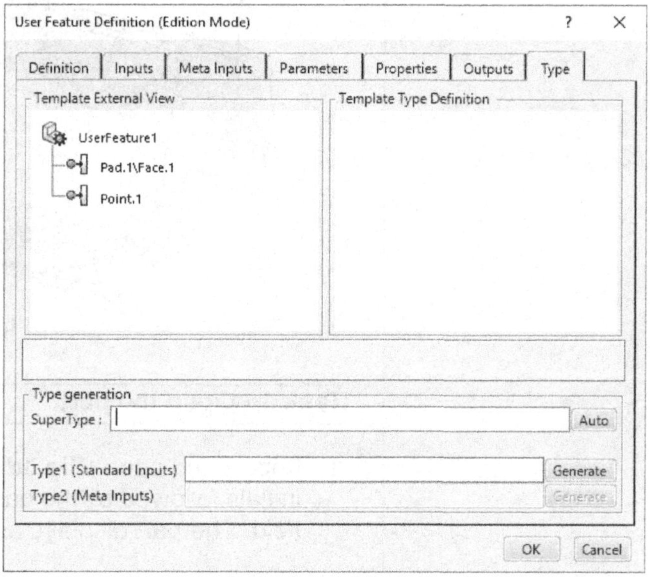

Figure 12–17

Instantiating a User Feature

You can instantiate User Features in another model using the same method as for a Power Copy.

The result of a User Feature instantiation displays as a single feature in the specification tree, as shown in Figure 12–18. The only parts of a User Feature that can be modified are the parameters that have been published.

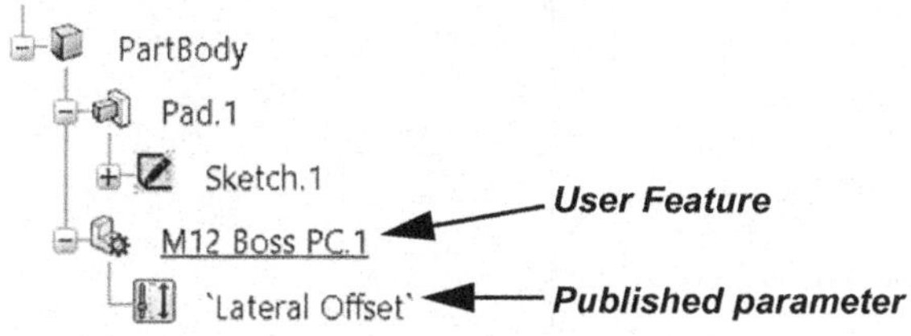

Figure 12–18

Practice 12a Power Copy Creation

Practice Objective

- Instantiate a Power Copy.

In this practice, you will instantiate a Power Copy twice, as shown in Figure 12–19.

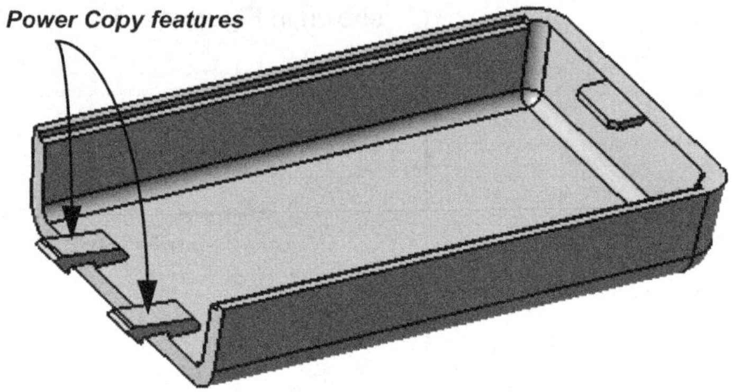

Figure 12–19

Task 1 - Open the part.

1. Import and open **Clip.3dxml**. When importing, type your initials followed by the dash symbol into the *Duplication string* field. The part displays as shown in Figure 12–20.

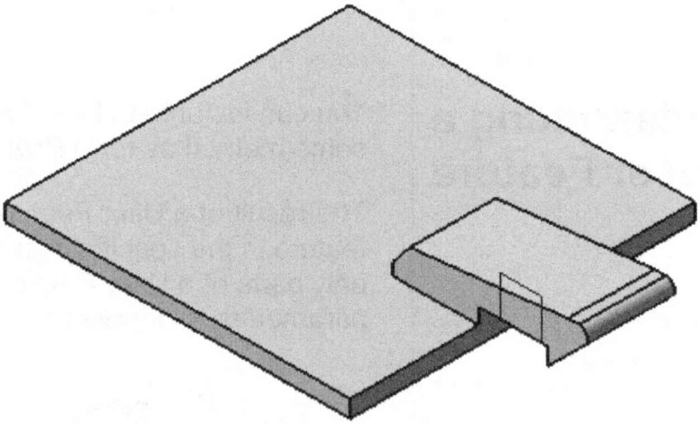

Figure 12–20

Task 2 - Explain the geometry of the Power Copy.

Design Considerations

This model was created as a source model of the Power Copy so that you can insert the geometry of the clip into other models using similar references. The Power Copy Geometry and Support Geometry are shown in Figure 12–21.

Support Geometry

The support geometry consists of the following:

- **Pad.1:** Pad.1 was created so that you can select appropriate sketcher references when creating **Sketch.2**.
- **Plane.1:** Plane.1 was used as a sketching plane for **Sketch.2**.

Each time this Power Copy is placed, a plane or a planar surface must be selected as the new sketch plane for **Sketch.2**.

Power Copy Geometry

The Power Copy consists of the following three features:

- **Pad.2** (and **Sketch.2**)
- **Chamfer.1**
- **EdgeFillet.1**

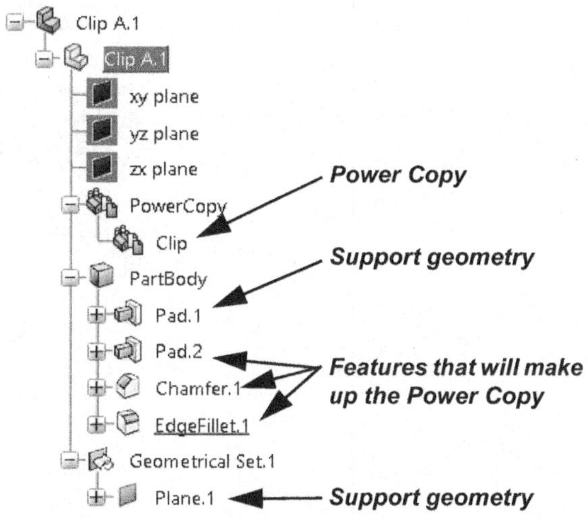

Figure 12–21

2. Keep the model open.

Task 3 - Instantiate a Power Copy.

1. Import and open **SlideCover.3dxml**. When importing, type your initials followed by the dash symbol into the *Duplication string* field. The model displays as shown in Figure 12–22.

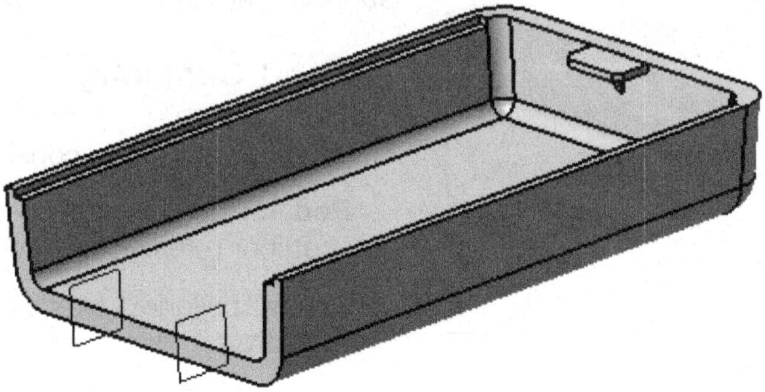

Figure 12–22

2. In the Tools section of the Action Bar, select  (Instantiate From Selection).

3. Activate the **Clip** window and select the **Clip Power Copy** in the tree. The **SlideCover** model window is automatically activated, and the Insert Object dialog box opens as shown in Figure 12–23.

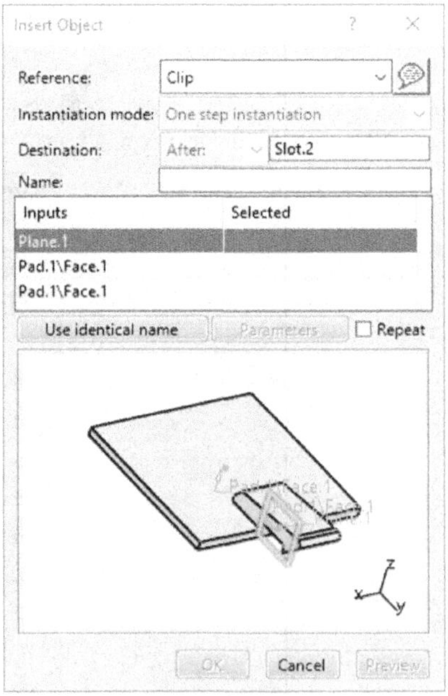

Figure 12–23

Design Considerations

The *Inputs* area in the dialog box lists the references required to place the Power Copy. The **Plane.1** input is highlighted. You must select a reference that corresponds to **Plane.1**.

4. Select **Plane.1** for the plane placement reference, as shown in Figure 12–24.

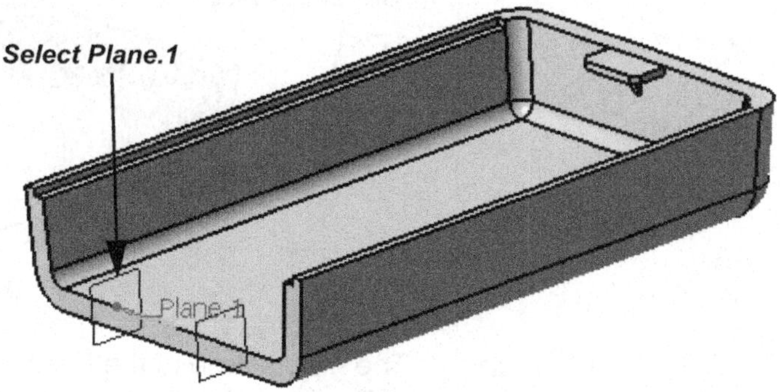

Figure 12–24

5. You must select a planar surface as the next placement reference. Select the top surface of the model, as shown in Figure 12–25.

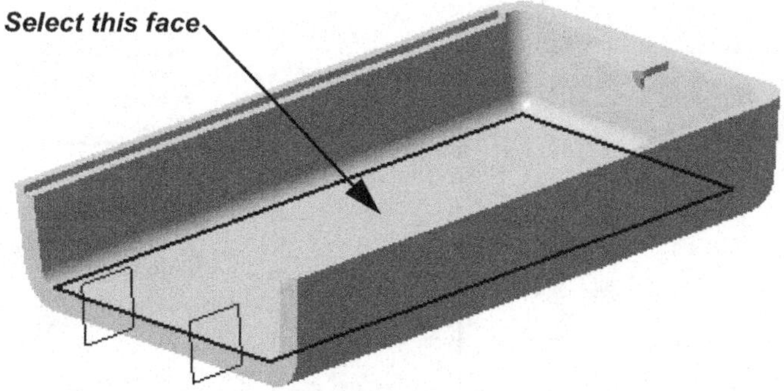

Figure 12–25

6. Select a planar surface as the third and final required placement reference. Select the end surface of the model, as shown in Figure 12–26.

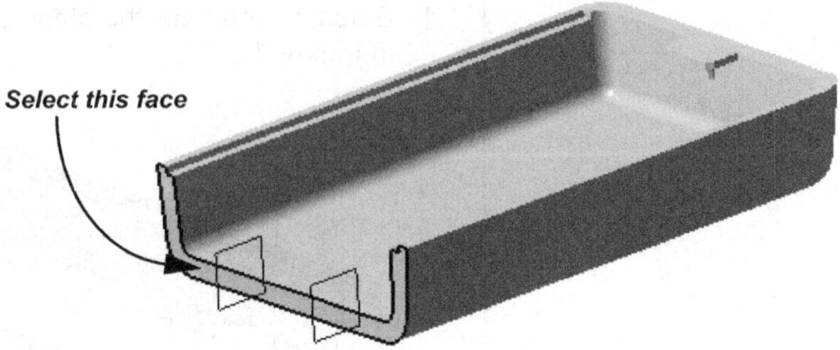

Figure 12–26

Design Considerations

The *Inputs* area in the Insert Object dialog box indicates that all of the inputs have a corresponding reference selected, as shown in Figure 12–27. The Power Copy can now be placed successfully.

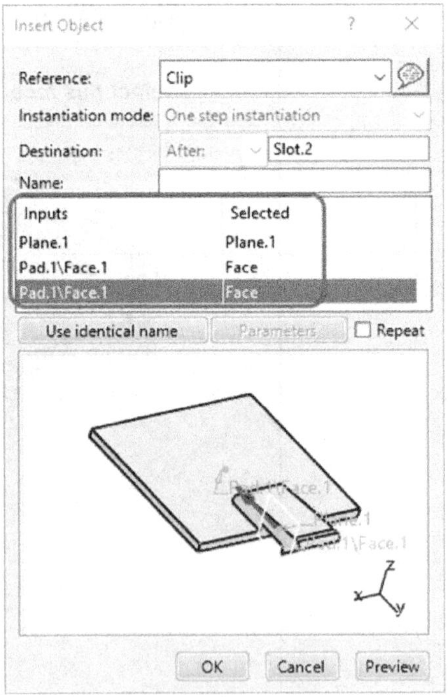

Figure 12–27

7. Click **OK** to complete the instantiation of the Clip Power Copy. The model displays as shown in Figure 12–28.

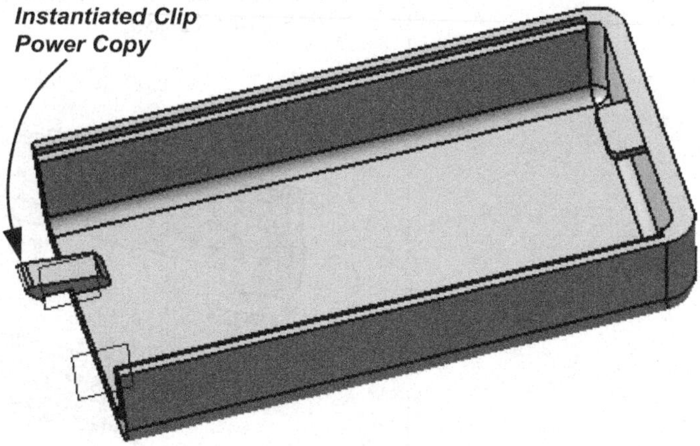

Figure 12–28

Task 4 - Instantiate another instance of the Clip Power Copy.

1. Repeat Steps 2 to 4 in Task 3 to instantiate another instance of the Clip Power Copy.

2. Select **Plane.2** as the corresponding plane reference, as shown in Figure 12–29.

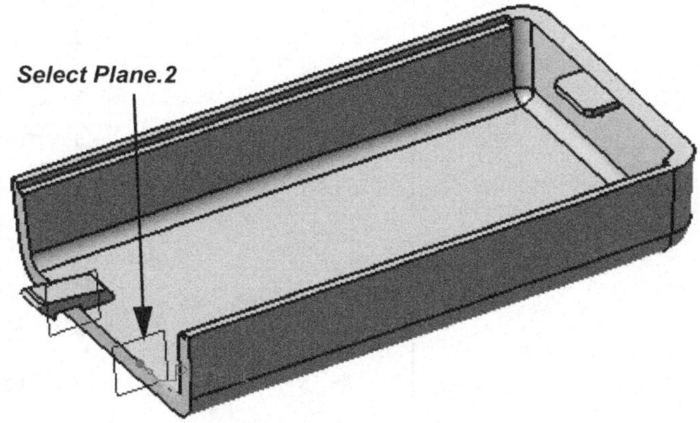

Figure 12–29

3. Select the appropriate placement references to instantiate another instance of the Clip Power Copy. (Hint: The same surfaces as before.) The completed model displays as shown in Figure 12–30.

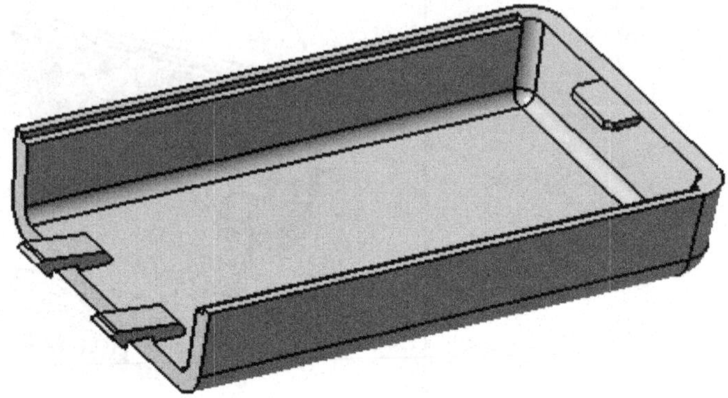

Figure 12–30

Design Considerations

Expand the specification tree to displays the feature list. In Figure 12–31, note that the features that make up the Clip Power Copy are listed as separate, modifiable features.

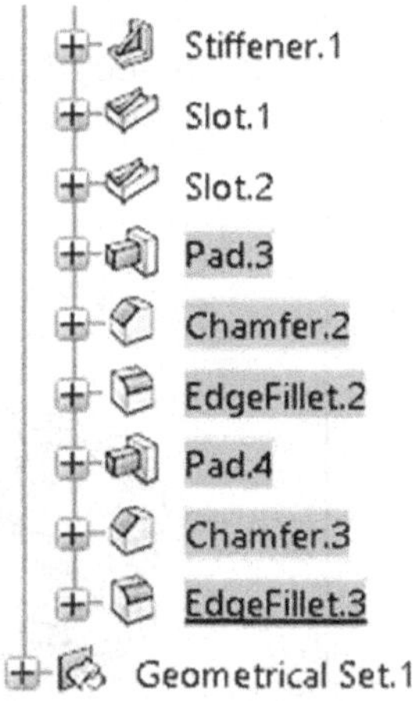

Figure 12–31

4. Save and close both models.

Practice 12b Working with Power Copies

Practice Objectives

- Create features for a Power Copy.
- Instantiate a Power Copy from a document.

In this practice, you will create features for a Power Copy, create the Power Copy, and then instantiate it four times from a document. An example of Power Copy features is shown in Figure 12–32.

Figure 12–32

Task 1 - Open the part.

1. Import and open **Lid.3dxml**. When importing, type your initials followed by the dash symbol into the *Duplication string* field. The model displays as shown in Figure 12–33.

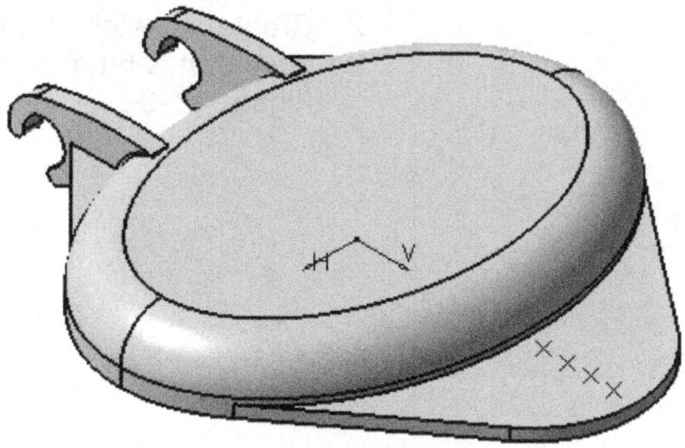

Figure 12–33

Design Considerations

The **Lid** part has a sketch called **GripLocation**, which consists of four sketch points. These points provide a location reference for the Power Copy that you will create. The Power Copy will consist of a Pad and a Tritangent Fillet, which represent the thumb grip texture on the pull-tab of the **Lid Pad**. One instance of the **Grip** Power Copy is shown in Figure 12–34. The location of the grip is defined by one of four sketch points. In this practice, four grip Power Copies are instantiated (one per sketch point).

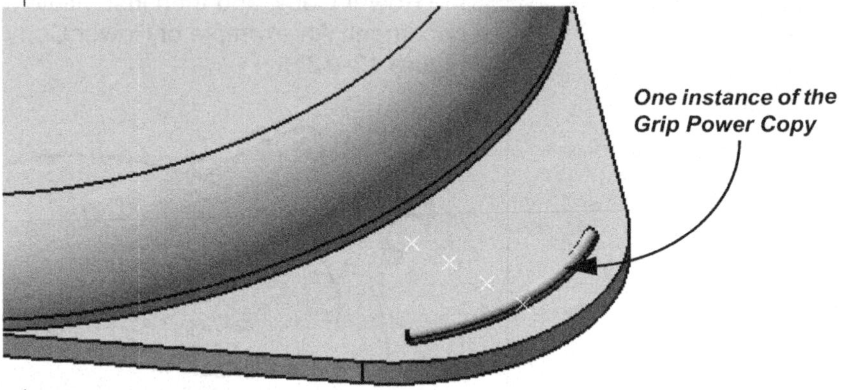

Figure 12–34

2. Leave the **Lid** model open.

Task 2 - Create a part.

In this task, you will create a new part and create the features for the **Grip** Power Copy.

1. Create a new 3D Part and save it with the name **<*YourInitials*>-LidGrip**.
2. Create a sketch on the xy plane and sketch a single sketch point that is 5mm away from the sketch origin, as shown in Figure 12–35.

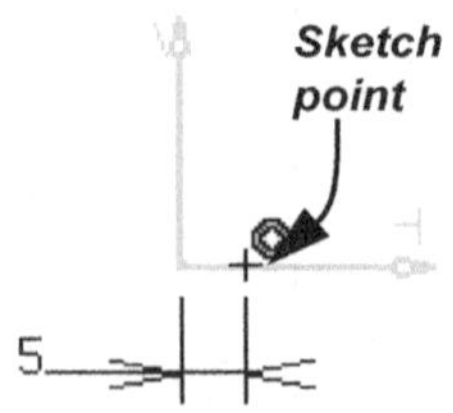

Figure 12–35

3. Exit the Sketcher app.

4. Hide the xy, yz, and zx planes, as shown in Figure 12–36.

Figure 12–36

5. Create another sketch on the xy plane (select the xy plane in the specification tree).

Design Considerations

The reference planes are hidden so that you cannot select them for dimensional references. For this Power Copy creation, all dimensional references and constraints should be to the sketch point of **Sketch.1**.

6. Create a horizontal axis, 20mm long and equidistant with respect to the sketch point, as shown in Figure 12–37.

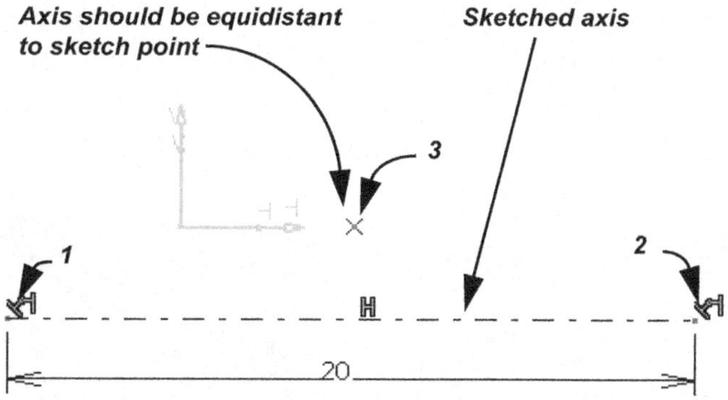

To create the equidistant constraint, hold <Ctrl> and select points 1, 2 and 3. Select the Constraints Defined in Dialog Box option.

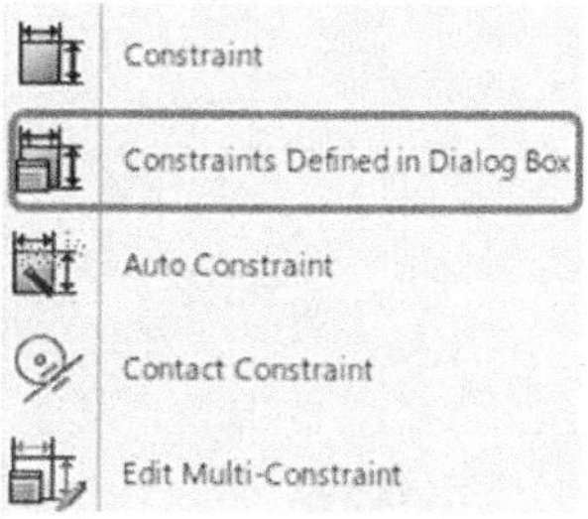

Figure 12–37

7. Sketch an R20 arc, passing through the sketch point (**Sketch.1**), with the end points at each end of the axis, as shown in Figure 12–38.

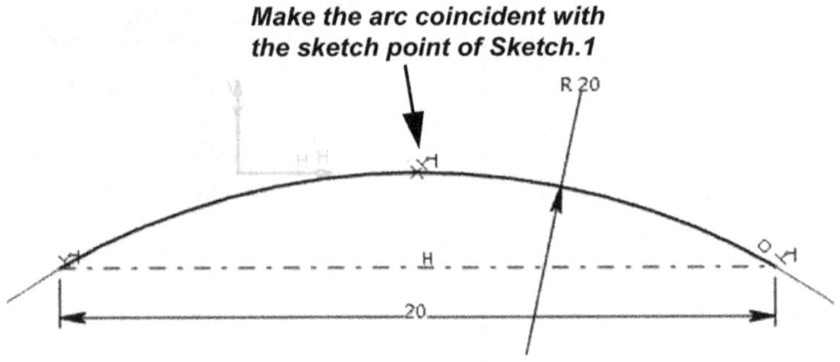

Figure 12–38

8. Create a Thin Pad with the parameters shown in Figure 12–39.

- *Length:* **1mm**
- Select **Thin**.
- *Thickness 1:* **1mm**
- Select **Neutral fiber**.

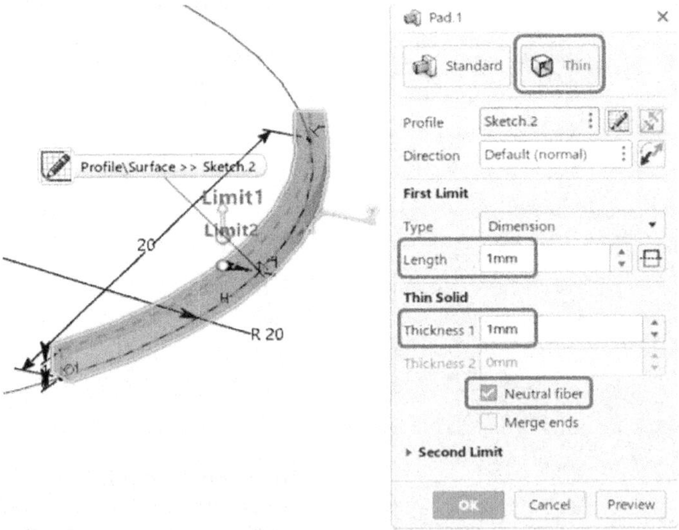

Figure 12–39

Task 3 - Create a Tritangent Fillet.

1. Create the Tritangent Fillet shown in Figure 12–40.

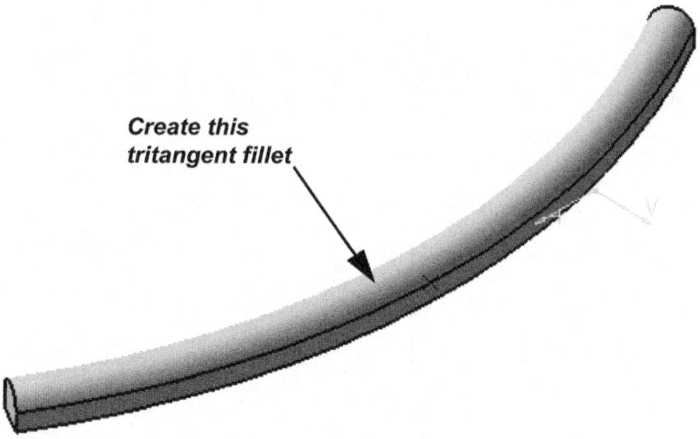

Figure 12–40

Design Considerations

Consider the references that you selected to create the Pad:

- The xy plane was selected as a sketching plane.
- All dimensional references and constraints for the Pad have been created to the sketched point of **Sketch.1**.

The Pad only references two elements: the xy plane and the sketched point. Therefore, only two references are required to place a Power Copy of the Pad. The Tritangent Fillet only references the Pad.

Task 4 - Create a Power Copy.

1. In the Tools section of the Action Bar, select  (Power Copy).
2. Define the Power Copy with the following parameters:
   - *Name:* **Grip**
   - *Selected components:* **Pad.1**, **Sketch.2**, and **TritangentFillet.1**

3. Select the *Inputs* tab and rename the following inputs, as shown in Figure 12–41:
   - *xy plane:* **PlacementPlane**
   - *Sketch.1:* **LocationPoint**

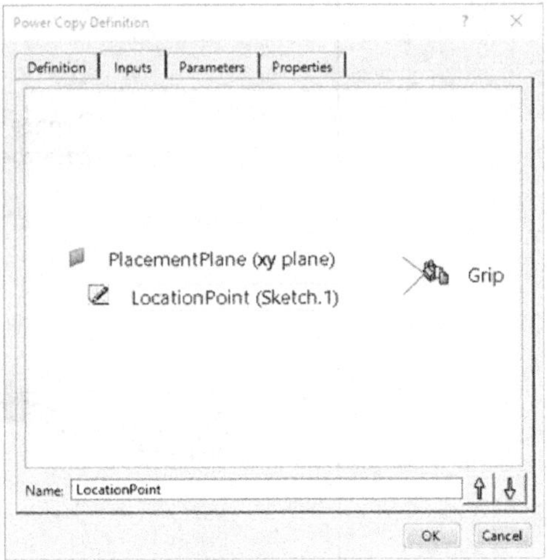

Figure 12–41

4. Select the *Parameters* tab. Publish and rename the following parameters, as shown in Figure 12–42:
   - *PartBody\Sketch.2\ ... \Length\20mm:* **Length**
   - Select **Published Name**.
   - *PartBody\ Sketch.2\ ... \Radius\20mm:* **Radius**
   - Select **Published Name**.

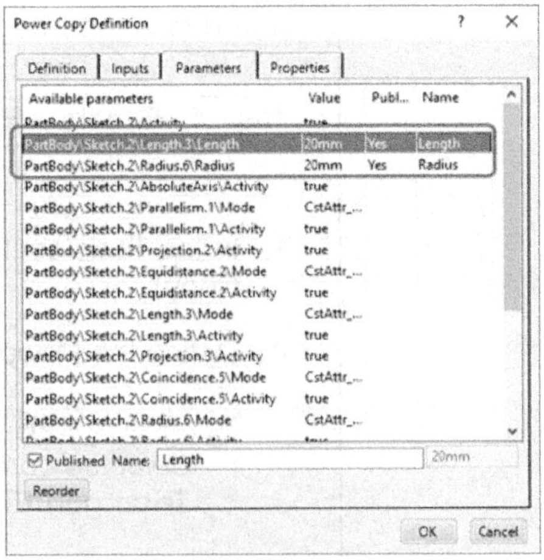

Figure 12–42

5. Click **OK** to complete the **Grip** Power Copy creation. The model displays as shown in Figure 12–43.

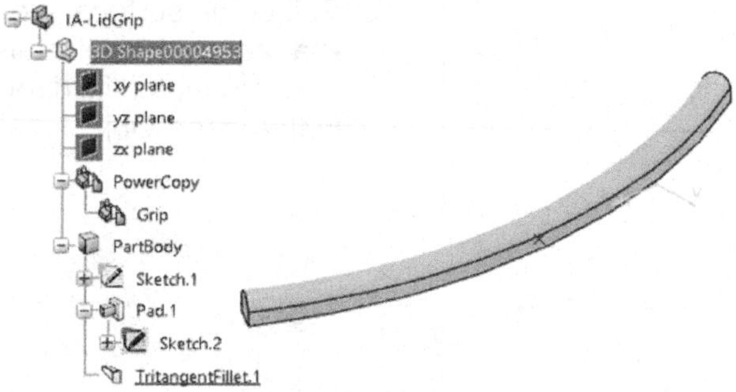

Figure 12–43

Design Considerations

You can publish any parameter of a feature included in a Power Copy. By publishing a parameter, you can change its value at the time of instantiation.

6. Save and close the model.

Task 5 - Instantiate a Power Copy.

1. If not already active, activate **Lid**.
2. In the Tools section of the Action Bar, select (Instantiate From Representation). Search for and select the **LidGrip** model. The Insert Object dialog box opens as shown in Figure 12–44.

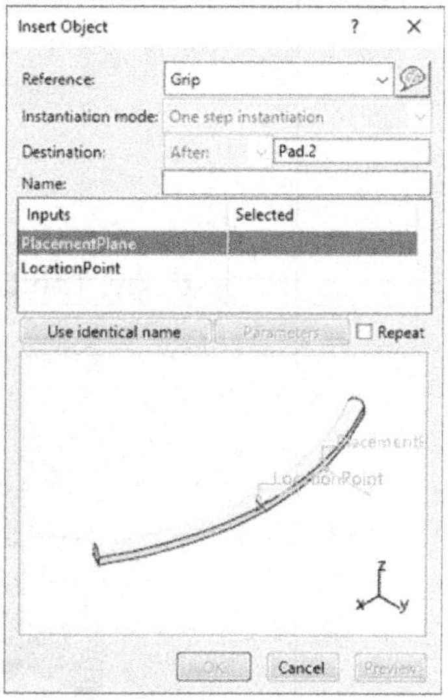

Figure 12–44

3. Select the surface shown in Figure 12–45 as the **PlacementPlane** reference. If necessary, click the green arrow to match its direction with the direction of the red arrow in the Insert Object dialog box.

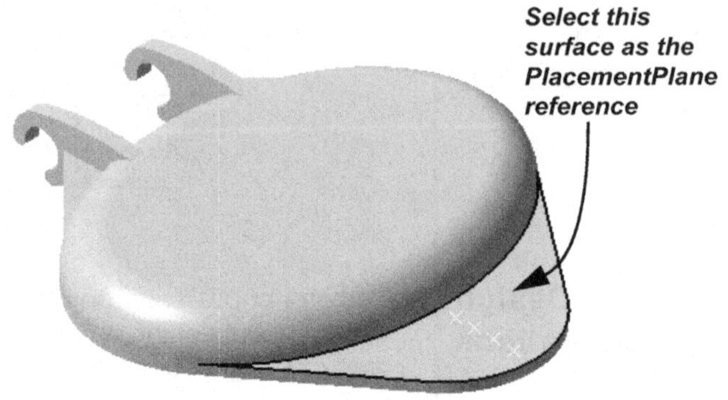

Figure 12–45

4. Select the sketch point shown in Figure 12–46 as the LocationPoint reference.

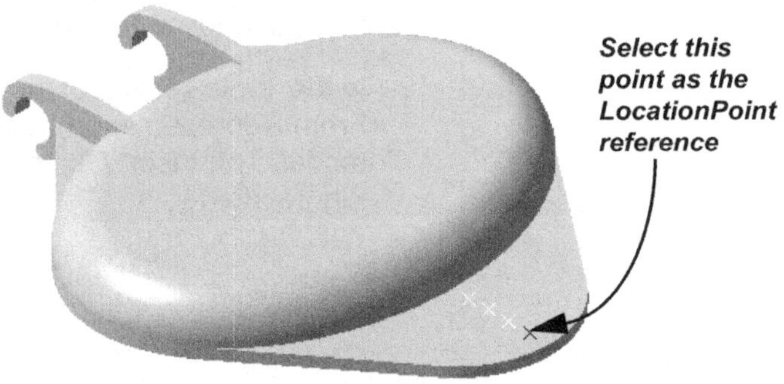

Figure 12–46

5. Click **OK** to complete the instantiation of the **LidGrip** Power Copy. The **Lid** model displays as shown in Figure 12–47.

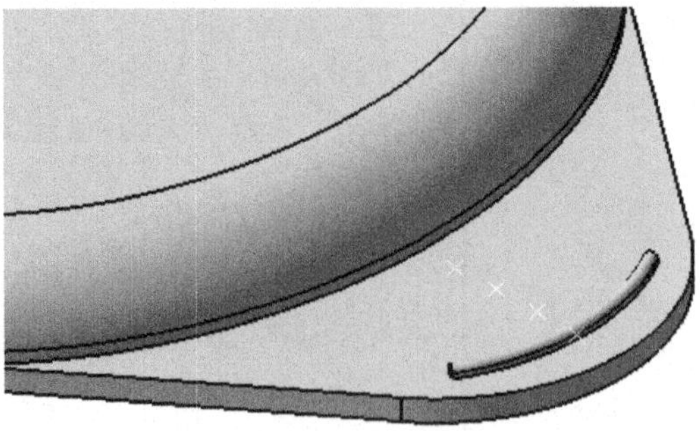

Figure 12–47

Task 6 - Instantiate a Power Copy.

1. Instantiate an instance of the **Grip** Power Copy by selecting  (Instantiate From Representation).

2. Since you are instantiating three instances of the **Grip** Power Copy, activate the **Repeat** option, as shown in Figure 12–48.

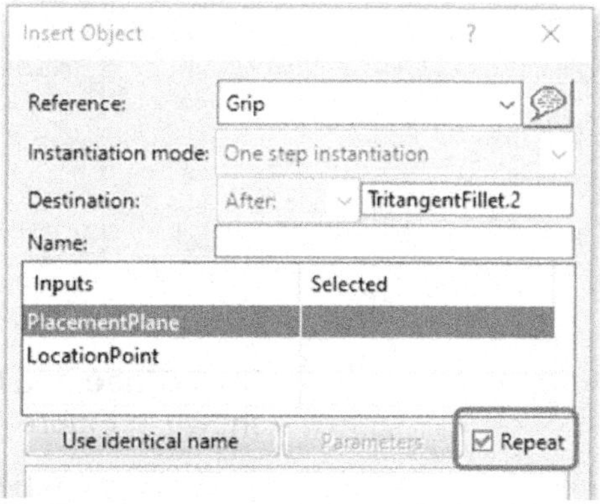

Figure 12–48

3. Use the appropriate references to instantiate the Power Copy, as shown in Figure 12–49.

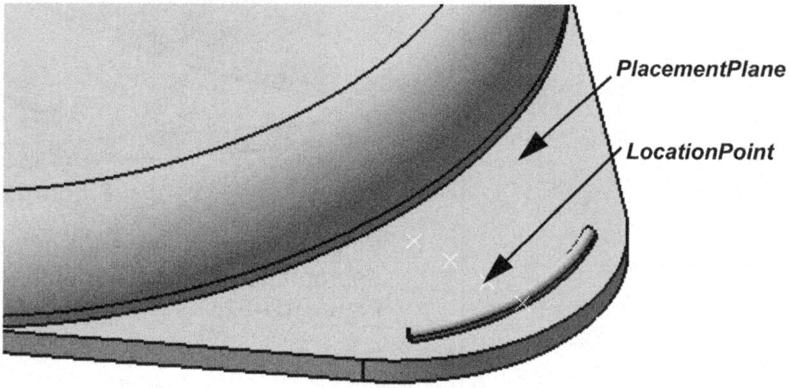

Figure 12–49

4. Click **Parameters**. In the Parameters dialog box, make the following changes, as shown in Figure 12–50:

   • *Length:* **25mm**
   • *Radius:* **30mm**

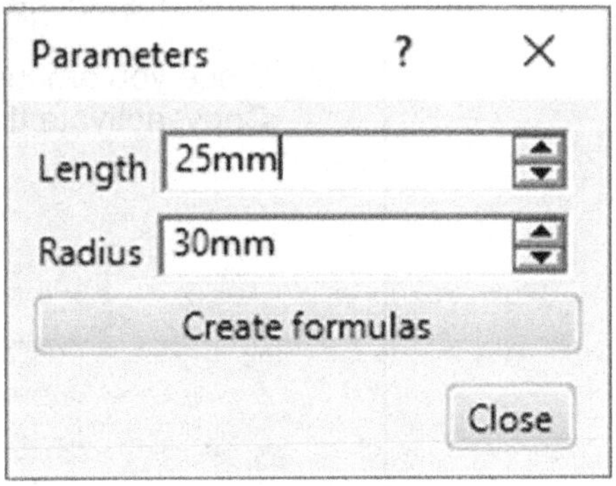

Figure 12–50

5. Click **Close** and **OK**. The **Grip** Power Copy displays as shown in Figure 12–51.

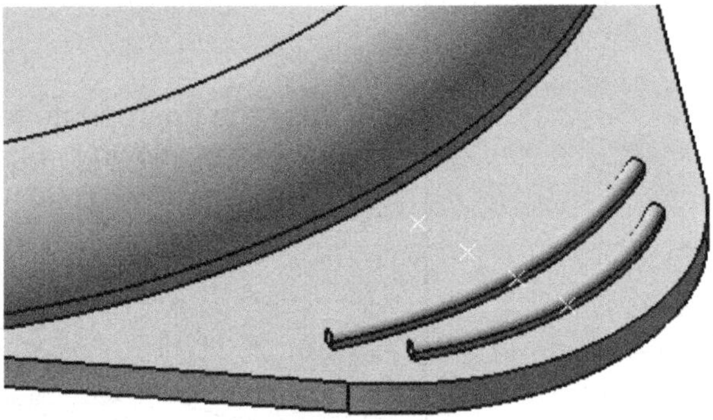

Figure 12–51

6. Place the second instance of the **Grip** Power Copy using the appropriate references and the parameter values shown in Figure 12–52.

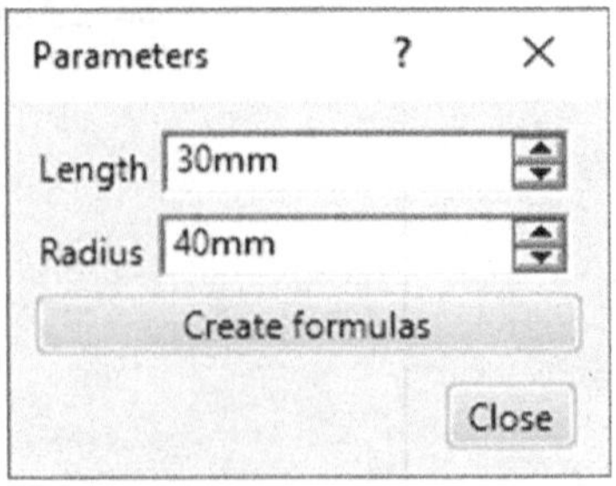

Figure 12–52

7. The second instance of the **Grip** Power Copy displays as shown in Figure 12–53.

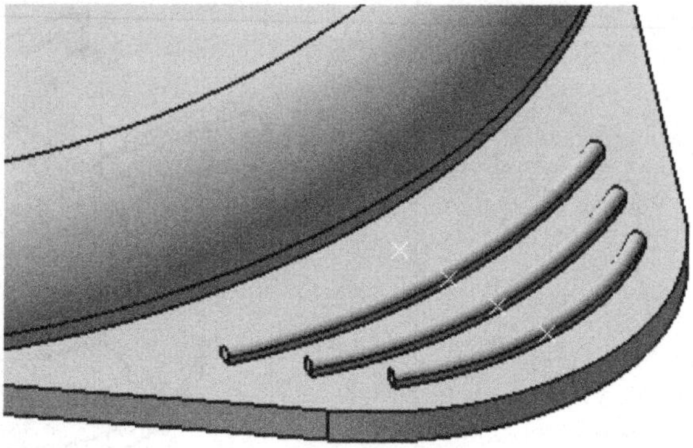

Figure 12–53

8. Instantiate the third instance using the parameter values shown in Figure 12–54.

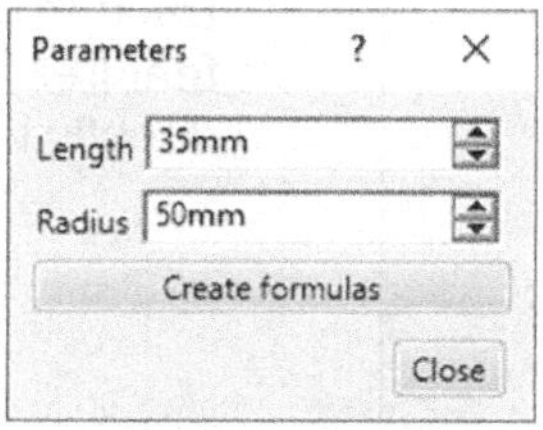

Figure 12–54

The third instance of the **Grip** Power Copy is shown in Figure 12–55.

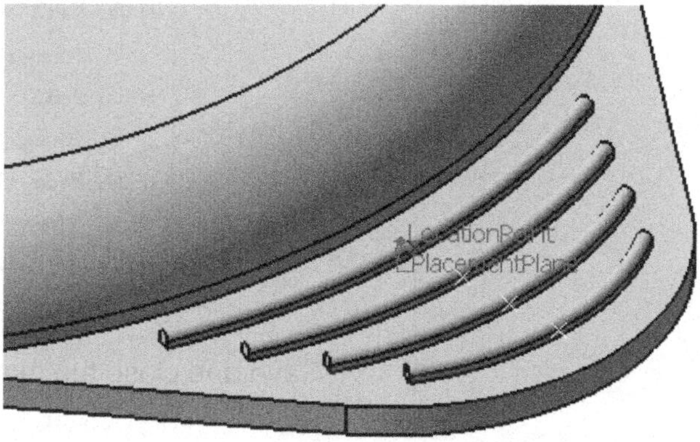

Figure 12–55

9. Click **OK** and **Cancel**. The completed model displays as shown in Figure 12–56.

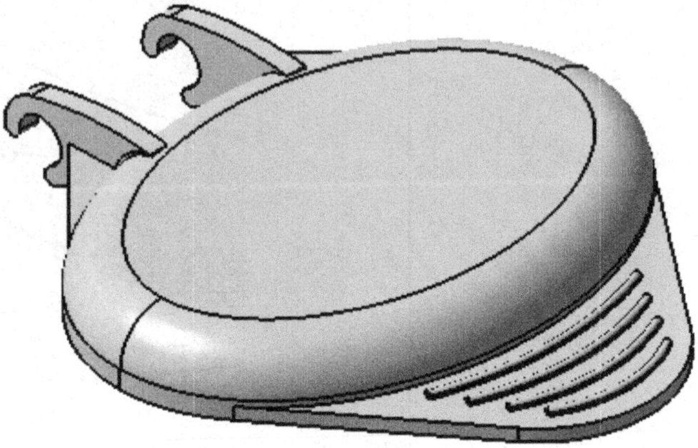

Figure 12–56

10. Expand the specification tree as shown in Figure 12–57. Each Power Copy has recreated a set of Pad and Fillet features. These features behave as if they were created directly in the **Lid** model.

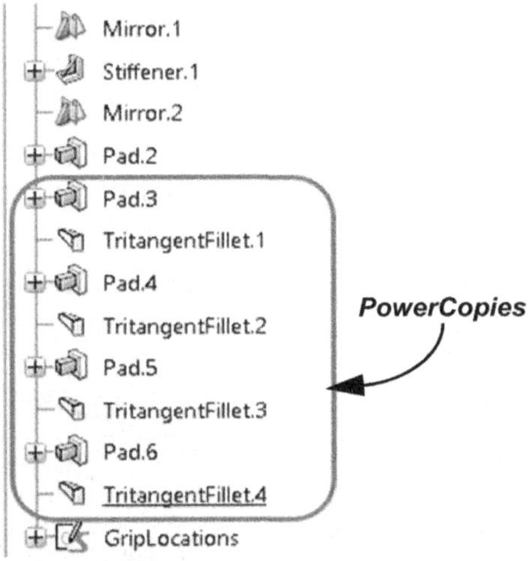

Figure 12–57

11. Save and close the model.

Chapter Review Questions

1. Which of the following is true of Knowledge Templates?.
   a. Features must possess the ability to locate new references.
   b. References must correspond to those used when the geometry was originally created.
   c. Previously-created geometry can be adapted to a new design that is similar in context.
   d. All of the above.
2. A Power Copy copies a selection of features and parameters from the source model into a template that can be applied to target part models.
   a. True
   b. False
3. Creating a Power Copy is the same as using the **Paste** option.
   a. True
   b. False
4. Parameters can be set as variable so they can be changed when placing a Power Copy.
   a. True
   b. False
5. A Power Copy can only be used in the model in which it has been created.
   a. True
   b. False
6. A User Feature adds all of the copied features to the target model.
   a. True
   b. False

Answers: 1d, 2a, 3b, 4a, 5b, 6b

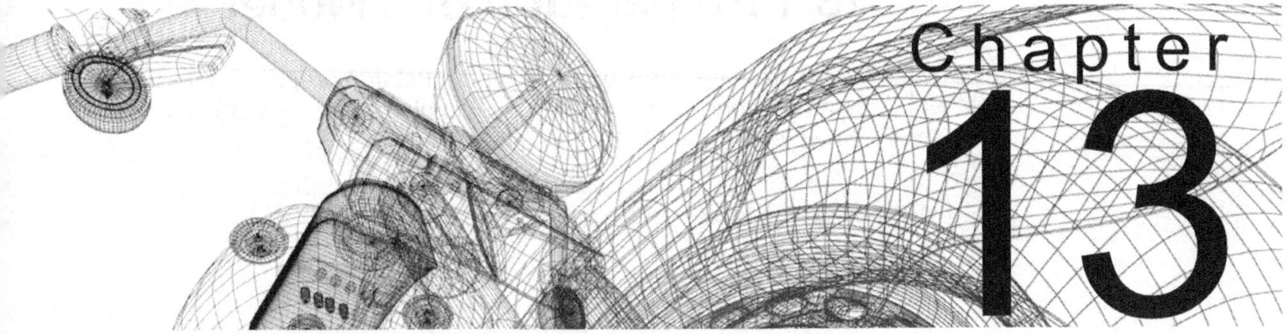

Chapter 13

Part Design Tables

You can use part design tables to create multiple versions of a part using a single file. A part design table uses model parameters to create a variety of design configurations for a specific model. A part design table is very useful for creating a series of models that have a similar geometric shape, but come in a variety of sizes.

Learning Objectives in This Chapter

- Prepare a model for use with design tables.
- Learn to rename parameters and create formulas.
- Create and manipulate design tables.

13.1 Preparation of a Model

When creating a design table, you must first prepare your model by adding parameters to it. An example of a design table is shown in Figure 13–1.

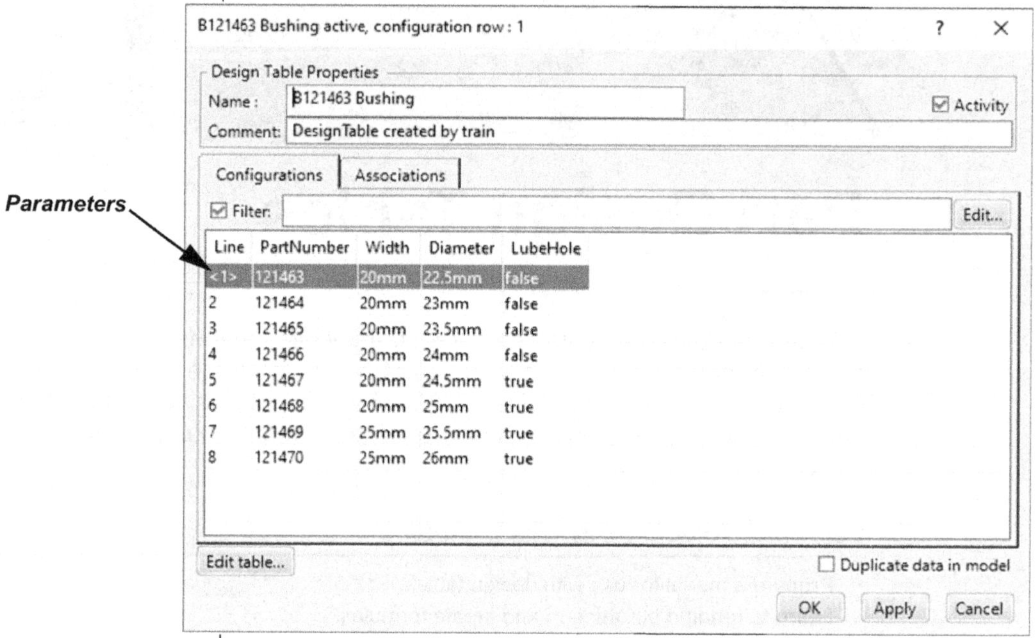

Figure 13–1

You can prepare your model for use in a design table with the following methods:

- Rename parameters
- Create formulas

Rename Parameters

CATIA creates a model parameter for every entity in a model (e.g., dimensions, features, etc.). Even the list of model parameters for a simple model can be difficult to search through. When preparing your model, carefully consider which model parameters to use in the table. Use descriptive names to rename these parameters. Renamed parameters are easier to locate when you create the table and are helpful to users who are unfamiliar with the model.

To rename parameters, click *fx* (Formula) and select the part in the display. The Formulas dialog box opens and the part dimensions display on the model, as shown in Figure 13–2.

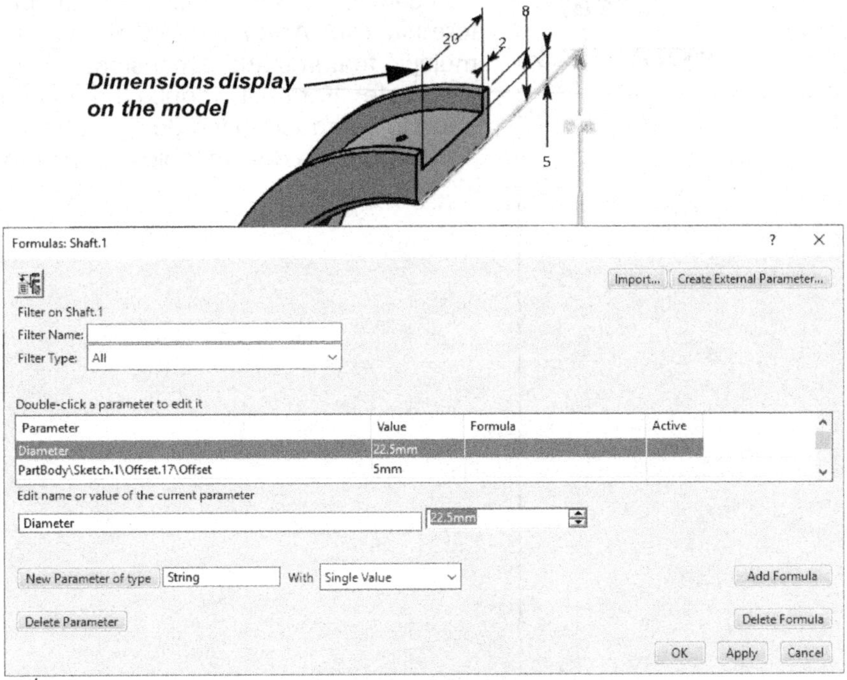

Figure 13–2

Rename the parameters using the Formulas dialog box.

The dialog box used to select parameters for a design table is shown in Figure 13–3. The graphic on the left lists all of the parameters in the model, which you can display by selecting **All** in the Filter Type drop-down list. The graphic on the right shows only the parameters that have been renamed for use in the design table. You can see these parameters by selecting **Renamed parameters** in the Filter Type drop-down list.

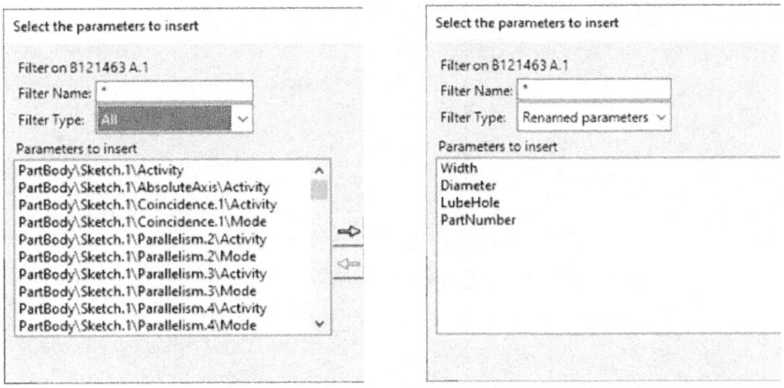

Filter Type = All   *Filter Type = Renamed parameters*

Figure 13–3

Create Formulas

You can use formulas to simplify the design table. To create a formula, click **Add Formula**. You can use formulas to control multiple features and dimensions using a single model parameter. Formulas reduce the number of parameters that need to be added to the design table to drive the design intent. As a result, the design table is easier to understand and modify.

13.2 Creation of a Part Design Table

Once you finish setting up your model, you can create the design table. Part design tables are useful for creating a series of models that have a similar geometric shape, but come in a variety of sizes.

For example, the bolt shown in Figure 13–4 comes in a number of different sizes. Rather than recreate the bolt using separate part files, you can create a design table of the bolt. You can then use the design table to create multiple versions of the bolt using a single part.

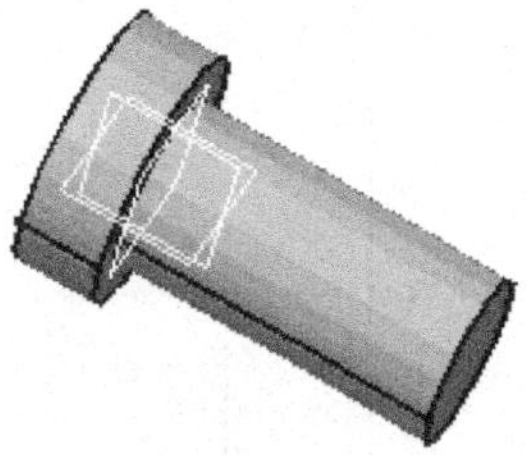

Figure 13–4

General Steps

Use the following general steps to create a part design table:

1. Start the creation of the design table.
2. Specify a creation method and enter the parameters.
3. Define the parameter values.
4. Retrieve a configuration.

Step 1 - Start the creation of the design table.

Click  (Design Table) in Tools section of the Action Bar. The Creation of a Design Table dialog box opens as shown in Figure 13–5.

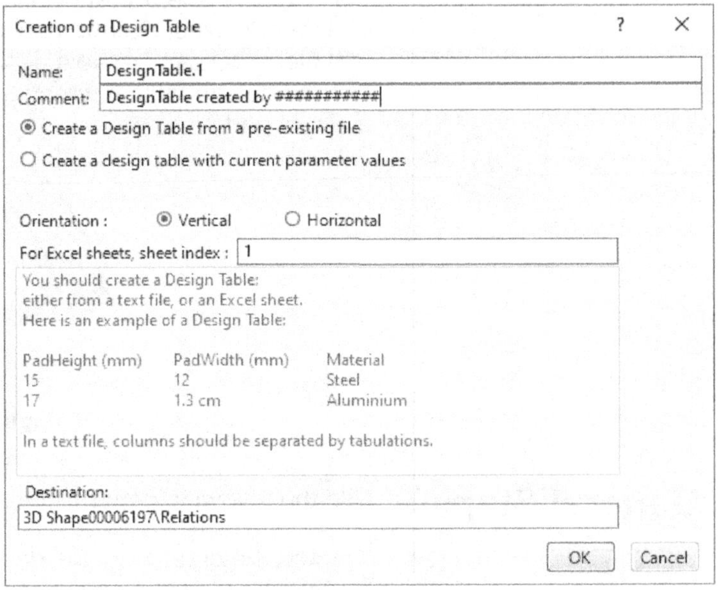

Figure 13–5

Enter a name and descriptive comment for the design table.

Step 2 - Specify a creation method and enter the parameters.

In the Creation of a Design Table dialog box, select one of the following creation methods for the design table:

- Create a design table from an existing file.
- Create a design table with current parameters.

Create a Design Table From a Pre-Existing File

This method uses data from an existing design table to configure the model. Select this option if configurations of your design table are similar to one already created, or the configurations for your design table have been specified in an external file, such as an Excel spreadsheet.

How To: Create a Design Table from an Existing File

1. Select **Create a design table from a pre-existing file** and click **OK**.
2. The Search an object or Import a file dialog box opens. Use the search field to search and select from the existing database or select *Import a file* to upload your own Excel spreadsheet.
3. If importing an Excel spreadsheet the 3DEXPERIENCE will create a new Engineering Document as a container to hold the Excel spreadsheet. Fill out any relevant text data as shown in Figure 13–6 and select **OK**.

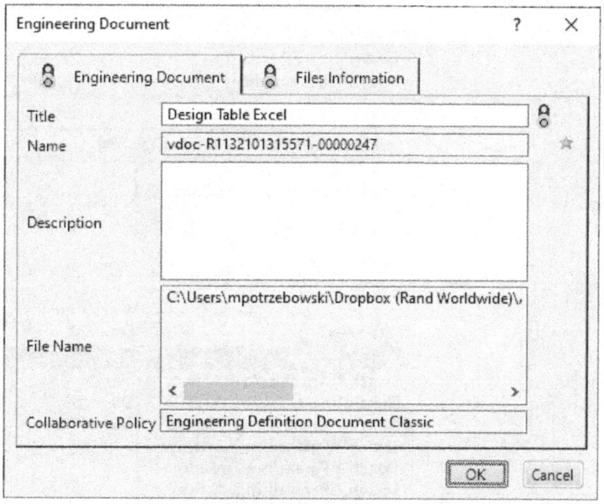

Figure 13–6

4. Once the document is imported and selected, select  (Accept All) in the Search an object or Import a file window.

5. The Automatic associations dialog box opens as shown in Figure 13–7. Click **Yes** to automatically create the association or **No** to manually create the association.

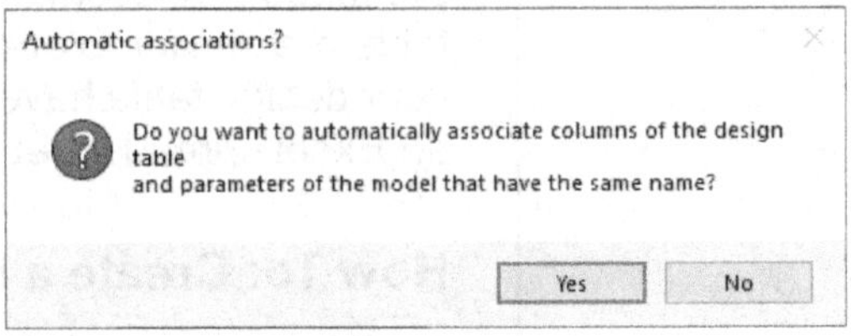

Figure 13–7

The Excel file is linked to the part file. This link is managed by the 3DEXPERIENCE as is any other linked document in CATIA.

Associating Parameters

When a parameter is associated with a column heading, the column controls the value of the parameter for a given configuration.

Select the *Associations* tab to display a list of unassociated column headings, as shown in Figure 13–8.

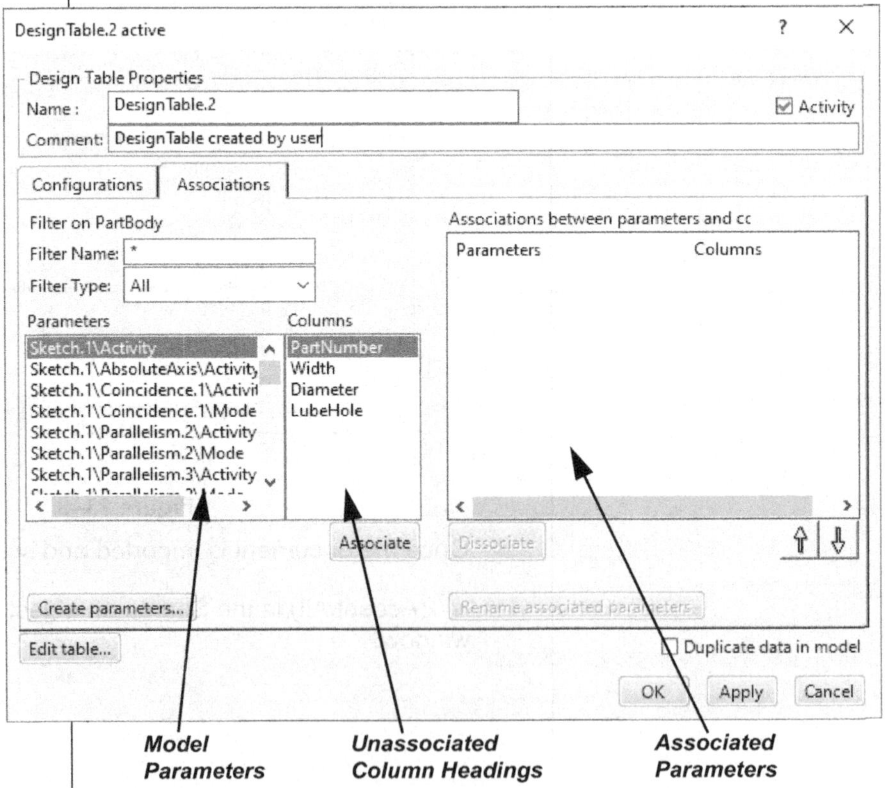

Figure 13–8

Before you complete the design table, you must create an association between any unassociated heading and a model parameter. Select an unassociated column heading in the *Columns* field and a parameter in the *Parameter* field and click **Associate**. The parameter and heading are added to the *Associated Parameters* field on the right in the dialog box.

If a parameter for the column heading does not exist, it can be created using **Create parameters**. The message box shown in Figure 13–9 opens. You can use it to add a new parameter to the model.

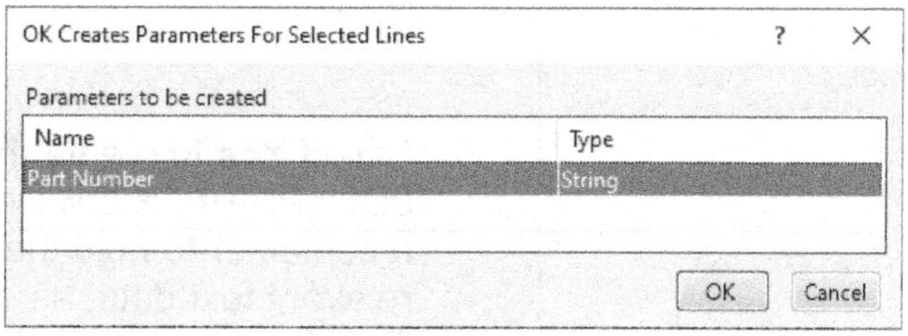

Figure 13–9

Create a Design Table with Current Parameters

This method creates a new Excel spreadsheet for the design table.

How To: Create a Design Table with Current Parameter Values

1. Select **Create a design table with current parameter values** and click **OK**.
2. In the Select parameters to insert dialog box, select the parameters to insert into the design table shown in Figure 13–10. In the Filter Type drop-down list, select **Renamed parameters** to list the parameters you renamed for use in the design table.

Although a model can have multiple design tables, parameters can only be added to one design table per model.

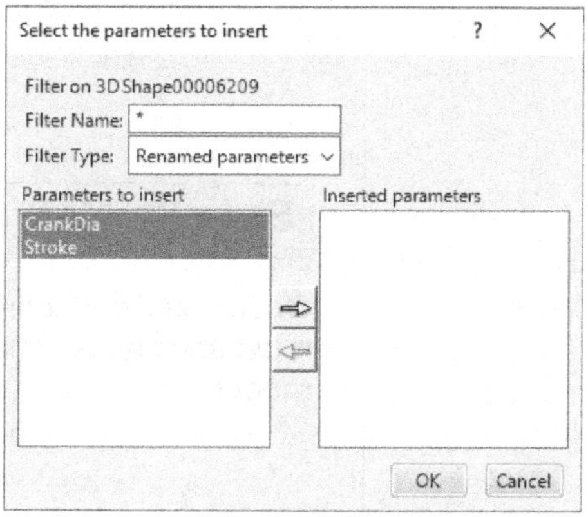

Figure 13–10

3. Click to insert the parameters and click **OK**.
4. A File extension window appears giving you the option to pick the type of document to create. Select **Yes** to create an Excel spreadsheet, or select **No** if you want to create a Text document instead, as shown in Figure 13–11.

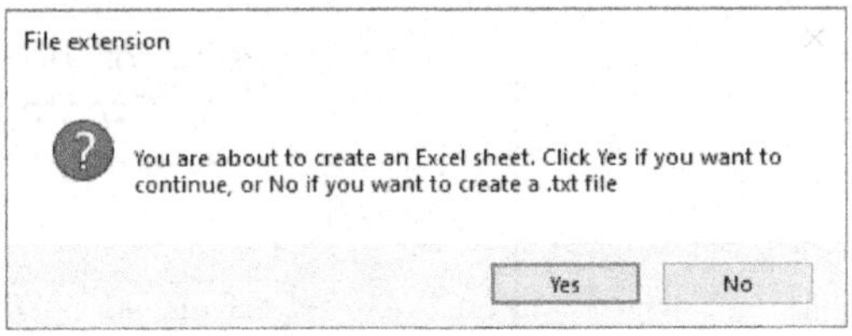

Figure 13–11

5. Select **Yes** to create the Excel Spreadsheet. 3DEXPERIENCE will create a new Engineering Document as a container to hold the Excel spreadsheet. Fill out any relevant text data, as shown in Figure 13–12, and select **OK**. The document will be saved into the 3DEXPERIENCE database.

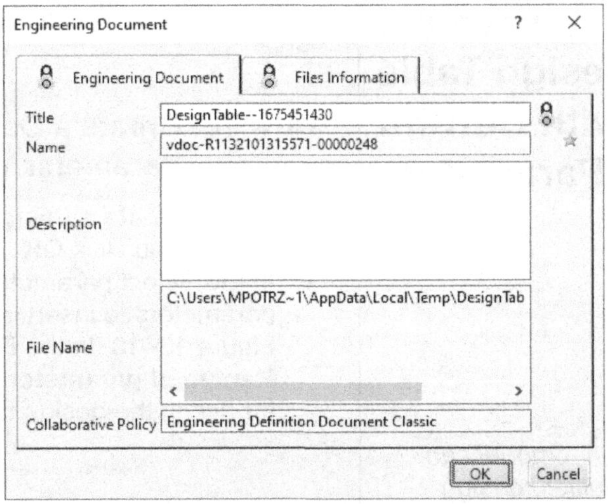

Figure 13–12

Step 3 - Define the parameter values.

Once you have selected the parameters for the design table, you must specify parameter values for each configuration of the model.

How To: Specify Parameter Values

1. Click **Edit table**. The design table opens in Excel.
2. Enter parameter values for each configuration of the model, as shown in Figure 13–13.

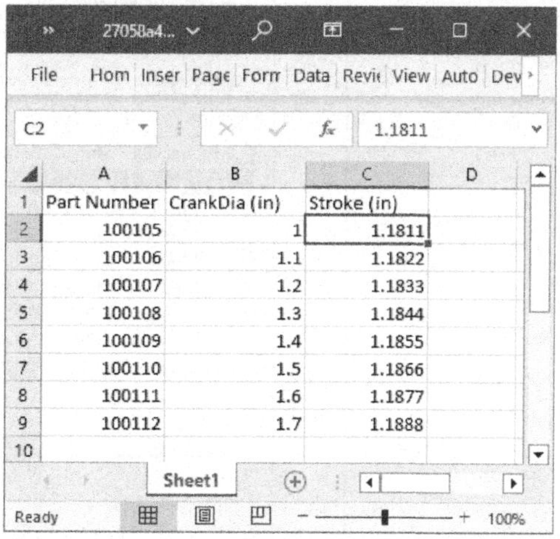

Figure 13–13

3. Save the spreadsheet and close Excel. The Knowledge Report dialog box opens, confirming that the design table has been synchronized, as shown in Figure 13–14.

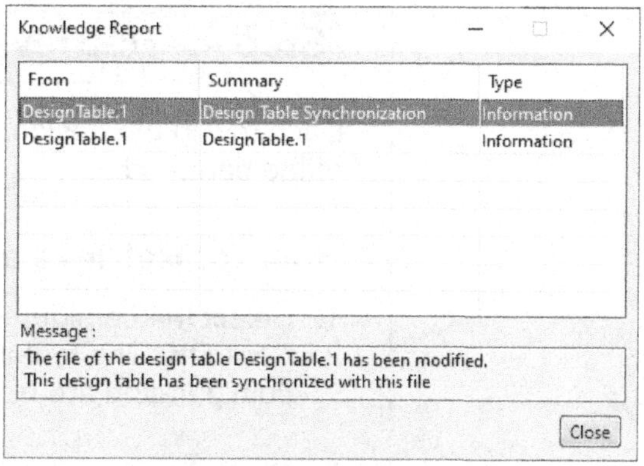

Figure 13–14

4. Close the Knowledge Report dialog box.

5. The DesignTable dialog box updates with the new information, as shown in Figure 13–15.

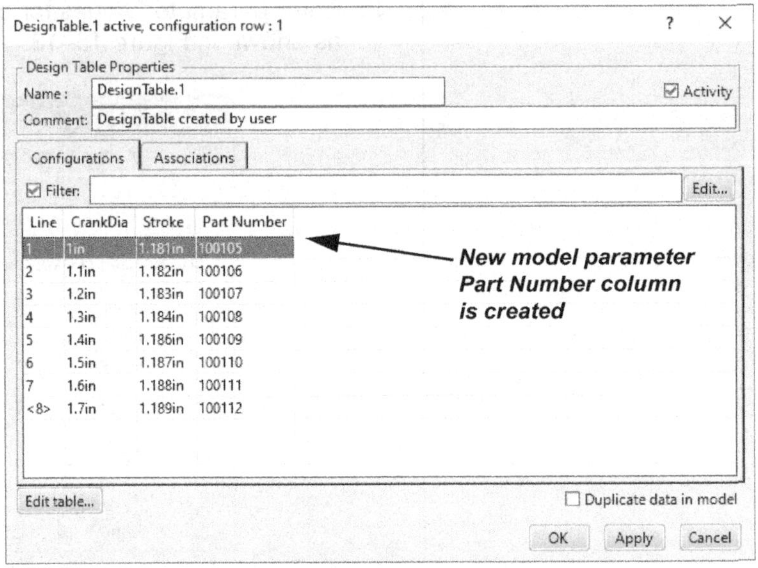

Figure 13–15

If any new columns were added to the spreadsheet while editing, they must be associated with model parameters before they display in the DesignTable dialog box.

Step 4 - Retrieve a configuration.

Each row in the design table represents a different configuration of the part model.

How To: Retrieve a Configuration into CATIA

1. Select the configuration from the design table.
2. Click **OK**. The features affected by the change in configuration are highlighted in red.
3. Click  to update the model with the new configuration.

Practice 13a Parameter Setup

Practice Objectives

- Rename model parameters for use in design tables.
- Establish formulas to control feature deactivation.

In this practice, you will create a design table using formulas and renamed parameters.

Task 1 - Open the part.

1. Import and open **B121463_Bushing.3dxml**. When importing, type your initials followed by the dash symbol into the *Duplication string* field. The model displays as shown in Figure 13–16.

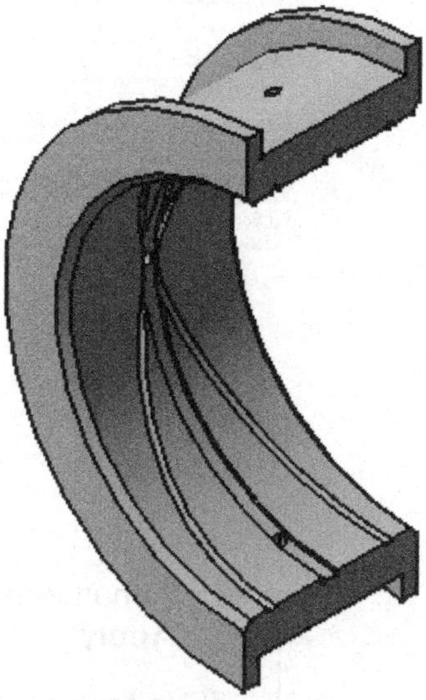

Figure 13–16

Task 2 - Rename parameters for use in the design table.

1. Click  (Formula) and select the part in the display. The Formulas dialog box opens and the PartBody dimensions display on the model.

2. In the model, select the D45 dimension and rename its parameter as **Diameter**, as shown in Figure 13–17.

3. Click **Apply** to complete the change.

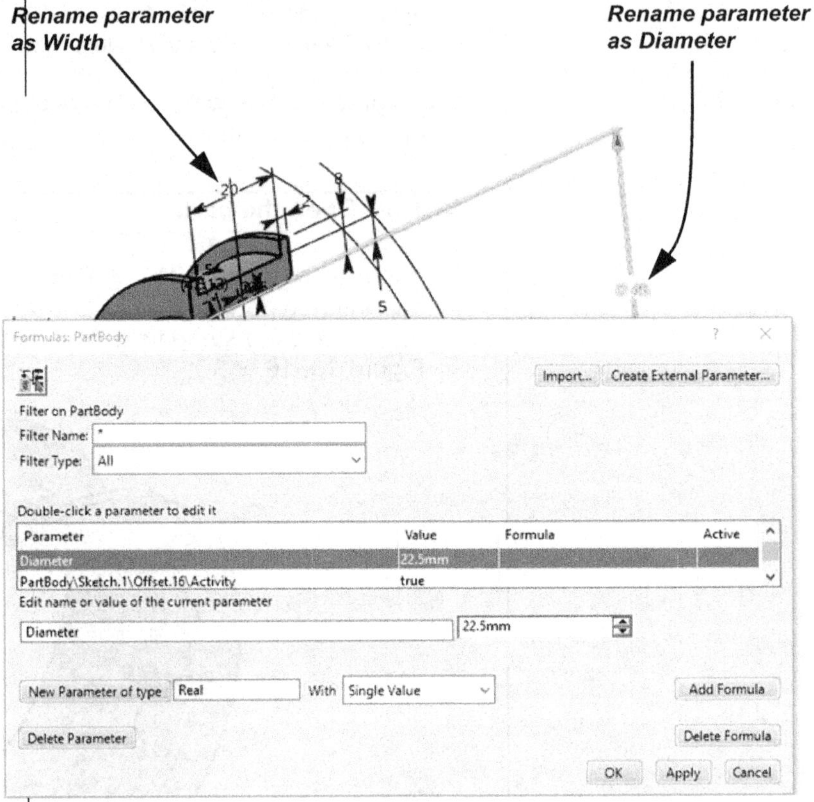

Figure 13–17

4. Rename the 20 dimension parameter as **Width** and click **Apply**.

5. In the specification tree, select the **LubeHole** feature.

6. In the Formulas dialog box, scroll down to the end of the parameters list to locate the default system parameter **PartBody\LubeHole\Activity**, as shown in Figure 13–18. Ensure that you select the last Activity parameter.

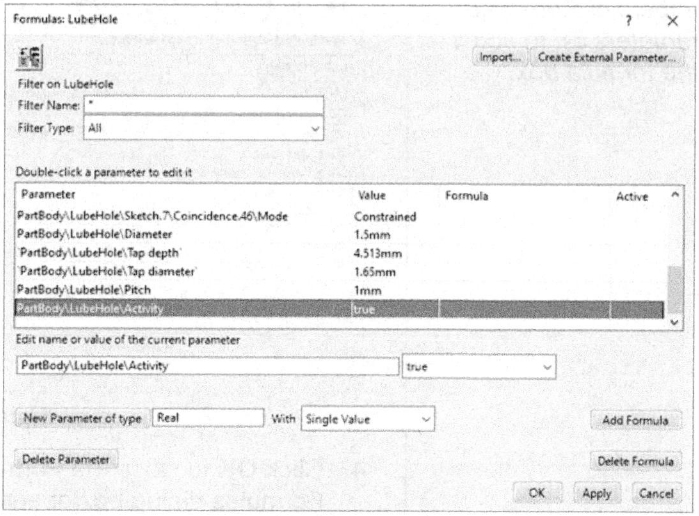

Figure 13–18

7. Rename this parameter as **LubeHole**.

Task 3 - Create a formula.

In this task, you will create a simple formula that controls the Lube Hole Pattern using the Lube Hole feature. This ensures that when the Lube Hole feature is deactivated, the pattern is also deactivated.

1. In the specification tree, select the **Lube Hole Pattern**.
2. In the Formulas dialog box, select **PartBody\LubeHolePattern\Activity** and click **Add Formula**.

3. Set the value of *PartBody\Lube Hole Pattern\Activity* equal to the **LubeHole** parameter, as shown in Figure 13–19.

*Double-click on **LubeHole** from the Members of Renamed parameters list to add it to the formula box.*

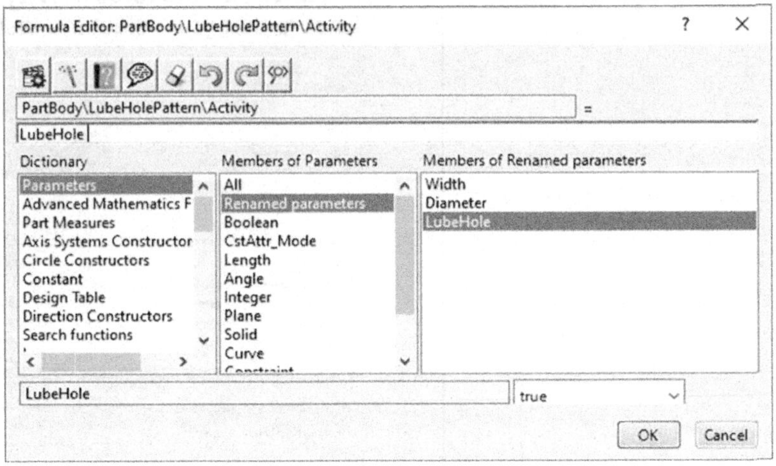

Figure 13–19

4. Click **OK** to close the Formula Editor dialog box. The Formulas dialog box opens as shown in Figure 13–20.

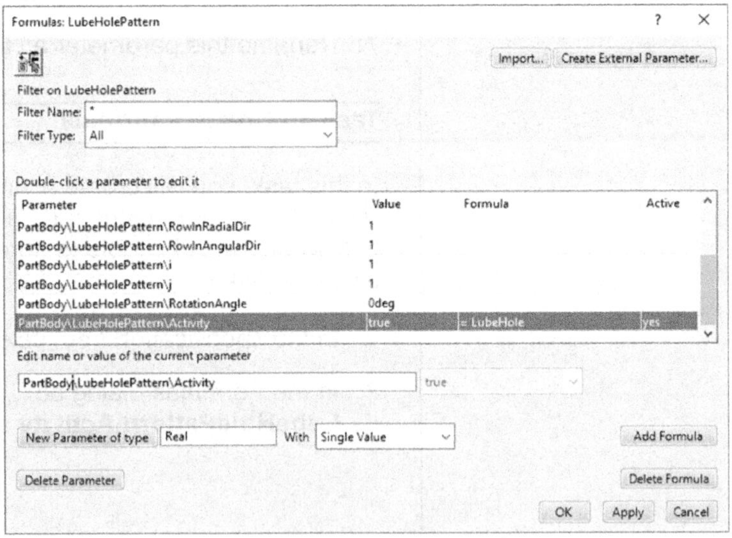

Figure 13–20

5. Click **OK** to close the Formulas dialog box.

Task 4 - Test the formula.

1. Deactivate the **Lube Hole** feature.

2. Clear the **Deactivate aggregated elements** option. The Deactivate dialog box opens as shown in Figure 13–21.

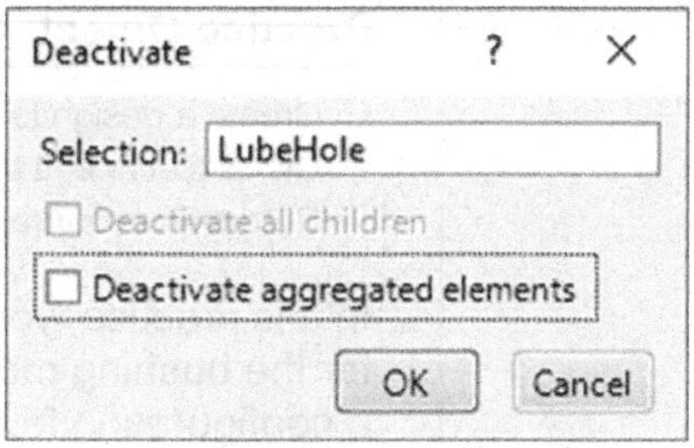

Figure 13–21

3. Click **OK**.

4. Although the children and aggregated elements are not deactivated, no pattern instances display on the model. The formula ensures that the pattern instances are all deactivated when the Lead feature is deactivated. The model displays as shown in Figure 13–22.

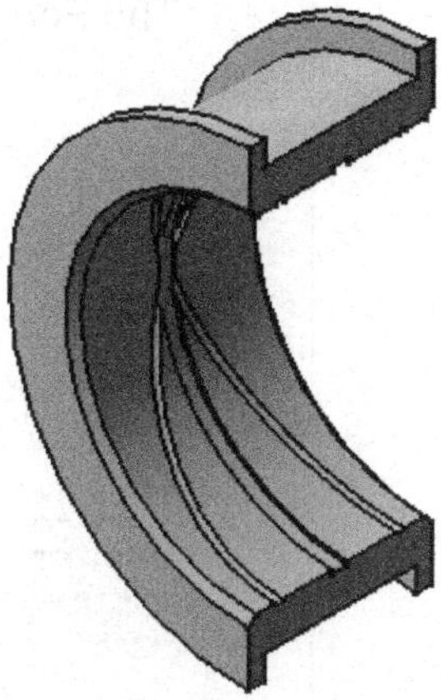

Figure 13–22

5. Activate the Lube Hole feature and save the model. This model is used in the next practice.

Practice 13b Design Table I

Practice Objectives

- Create a design table.
- Use Excel to edit the design table.
- Retrieve configurations of the design table.

In this practice, you will create a number of design configurations for the bushing model using a design table. You will then retrieve a configuration from the design table into the model.

Task 1 - Create a parameter.

1. Ensure that the **B121463_Bushing** model is open. If you did not complete the last practice, open **B121463_Bushing.3dxml** from the *Completed* directory instead.

2. In the Tools section of the Action Bar, click (Formula). The Formulas dialog box opens, as shown in Figure 13–23.

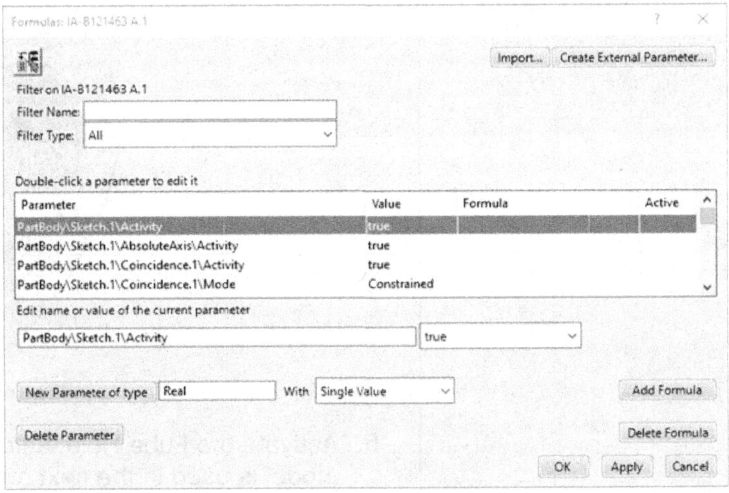

Figure 13–23

3. In the *New Parameter of type* field, double-click **String** and click **New Parameter of type** button, as shown in Figure 13–24.

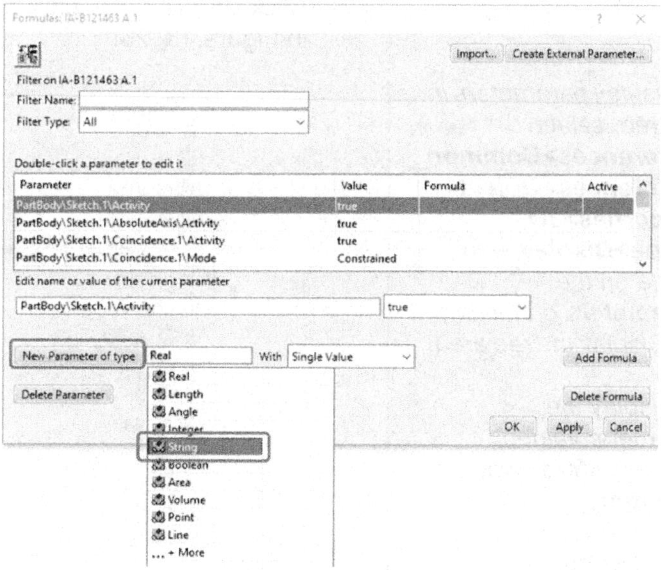

Figure 13–24

4. Rename the newly created parameter to **PartNumber** and modify its value to **121463**, as shown in Figure 13–25.

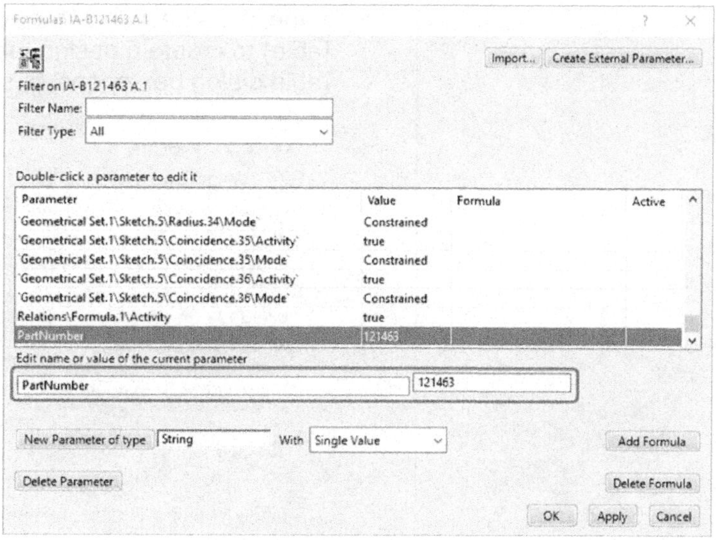

Figure 13–25

*To display parameters in the tree, select **Preferences>Common Preferences>Object Properties>3D Shape>Display**, and toggle on the **Parameters** option in the Display In Tree area.*

*To display the parameter values, select **Preferences> Common Preferences> Parameters, Measures, and Units>Parameters & Relations**, and toggle on the **Display values** option.*

5. Click **OK**. The new parameter is created in the tree, as shown in Figure 13–26.

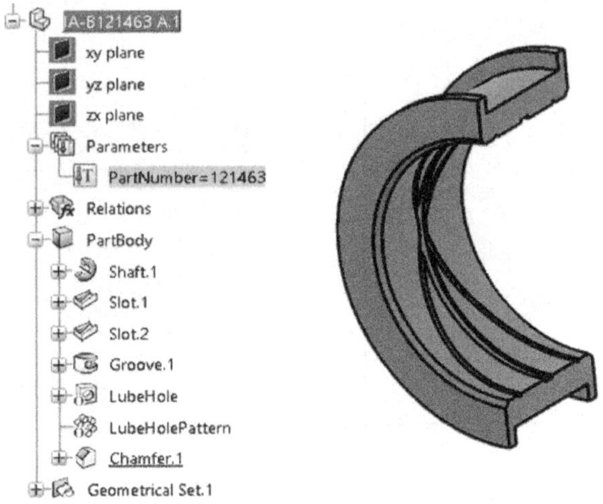

Figure 13–26

Task 2 - Create a design table for the B121463 Bushing.

1. In the Tools section of the Action Bar, click  (Design Table) to create a design table. The Creation of a Design Table dialog box opens as shown in Figure 13–27.

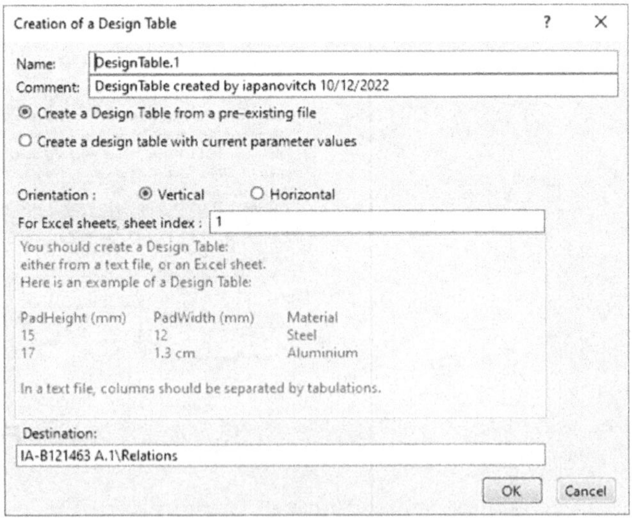

Figure 13–27

2. Select **Create a design table with current parameter values**.

3. In the *Name* field, enter **B121463 Bushing**.
4. Click **OK**. The Select parameters to insert dialog box opens as shown in Figure 13–28.

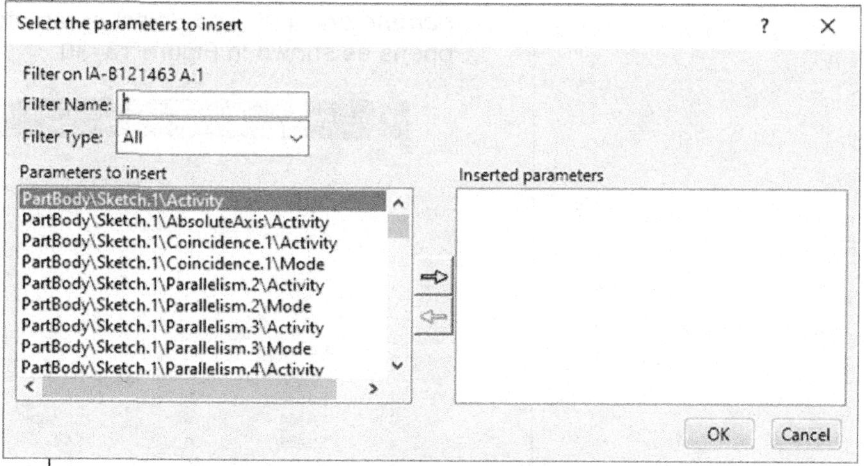

Figure 13–28

5. In the Filter Type drop-down list, select **Renamed parameters** as shown in Figure 13–29.

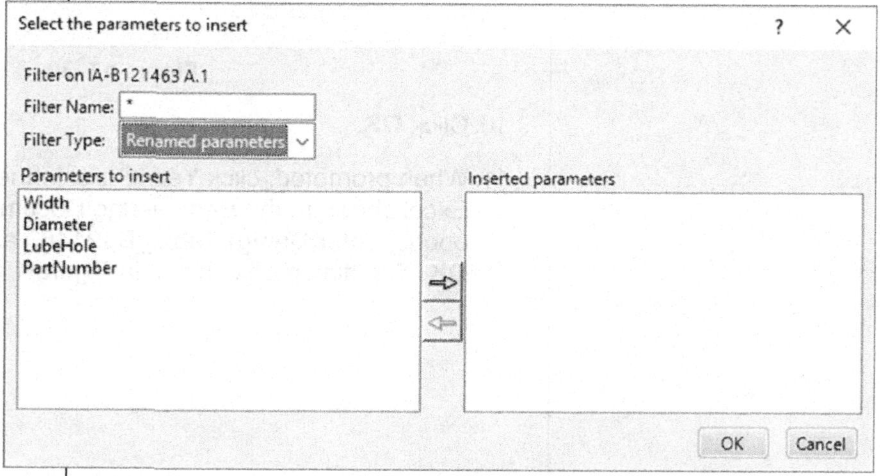

Figure 13–29

6. Select **PartNumber** in the *Parameters to insert* field.
7. Click  to add this parameter to the *Inserted parameters* field.

8. Use <Ctrl> to select **Width**, **Diameter**, and **LubeHole** in the *Parameters to insert* field.

9. Click to add these parameters to the *Inserted parameters* field. The Select parameters to insert dialog box opens as shown in Figure 13–30.

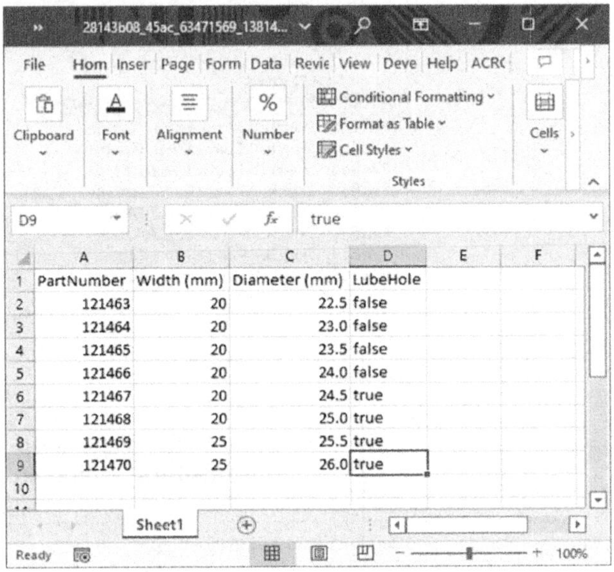

	A	B	C	D
1	PartNumber	Width (mm)	Diameter (mm)	LubeHole
2	121463	20	22.5	false
3	121464	20	23.0	false
4	121465	20	23.5	false
5	121466	20	24.0	false
6	121467	20	24.5	true
7	121468	20	25.0	true
8	121469	25	25.5	true
9	121470	25	26.0	true

Figure 13–30

10. Click **OK**.

11. When prompted, click **Yes** to create the design table as an Excel sheet. In the Engineering Document dialog box that opens, enter **DesignTable_B121463** as the name and click **OK**. The dialog box shown in Figure 13–31 opens.

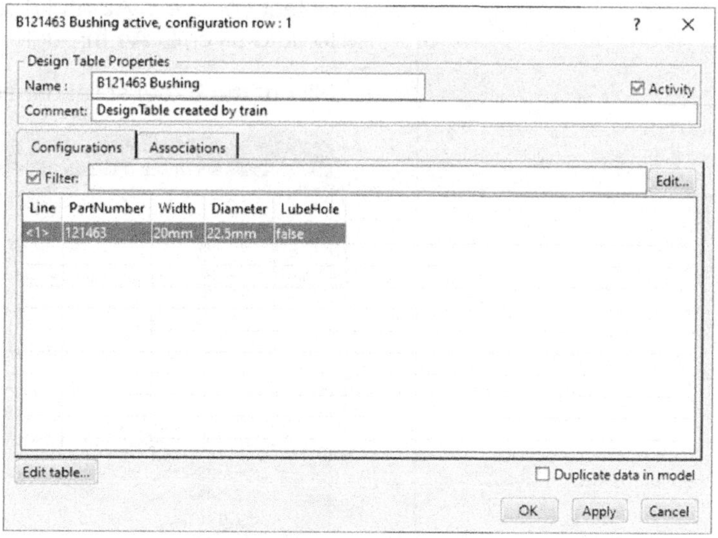

Figure 13–31

Task 3 - Edit the design table using Excel.

1. To open the table in Excel, click **Edit table**. Note that your version of Excel might look slightly different.
2. In cell *A3*, enter **B121464**, as shown in Figure 13–32.

Select this handle and drag the cell down to A9 to enter the remaining data

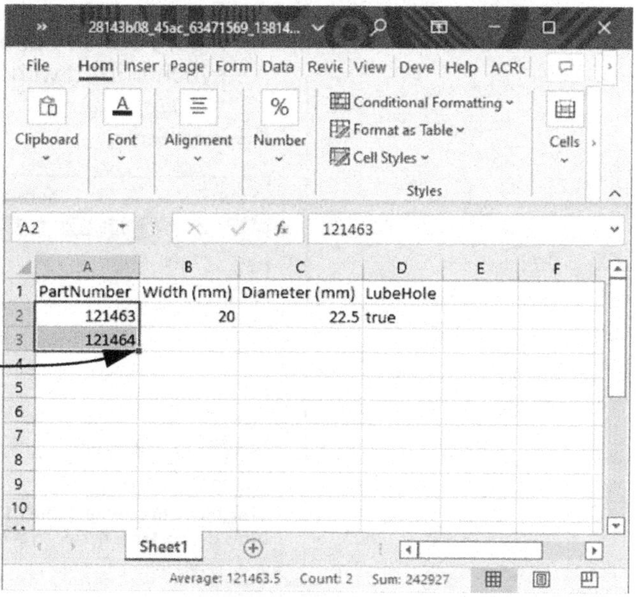

Figure 13–32

3. Select both cells A2 and A3. Drag the cell handle down to A9 to auto-fill cells A4 through A9.

4. Fill out the Excel spreadsheet, as shown in Figure 13–33.

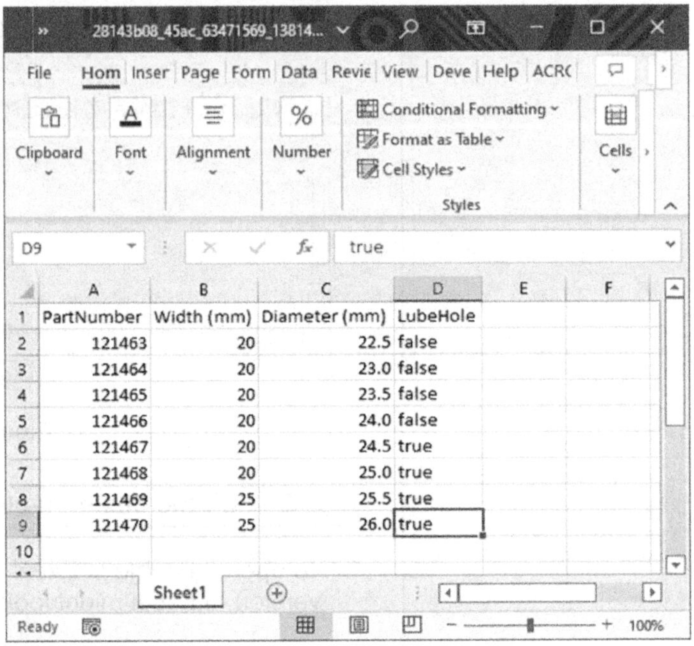

Figure 13–33

5. Save and close the spreadsheet. The dialog box shown in Figure 13–34 opens. The design table has been synchronized with the part model.

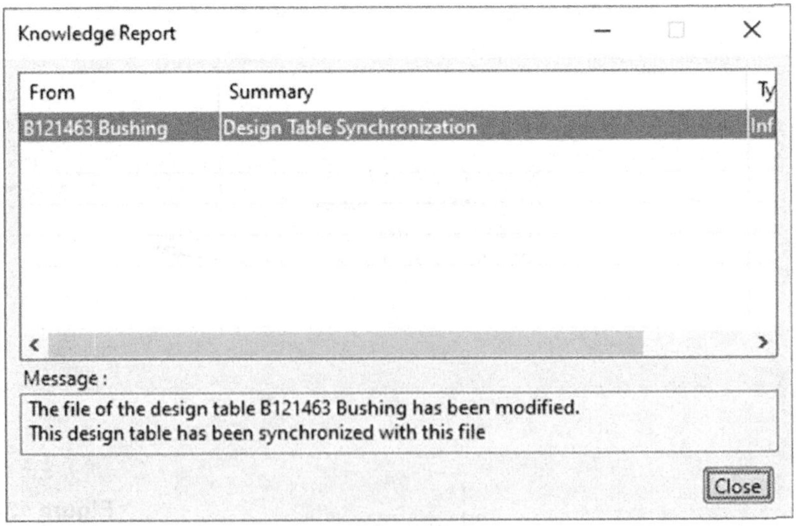

Figure 13–34

6. Click **Close**. The design table opens as shown in Figure 13–35.

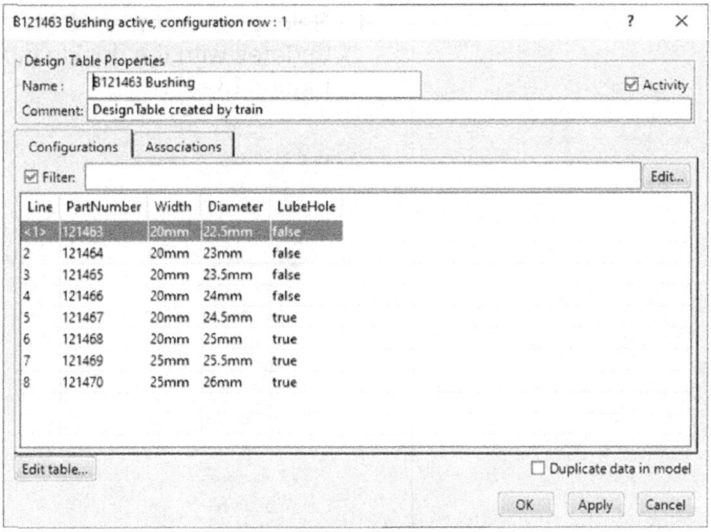

Figure 13–35

Task 4 - Retrieve the configurations of the design table.

1. Click **OK** to close the design table.
2. The model and specification tree display as shown in Figure 13–36. Note that the LubeHole and LubeHolePattern features are deactivated.

*To display the design table in the specification tree, relations must be shown. To do this, select **Preferences>Common Preferences>Object Properties>3D Shape>Display**, and toggle on the **Relations** option in the Display In Tree area.*

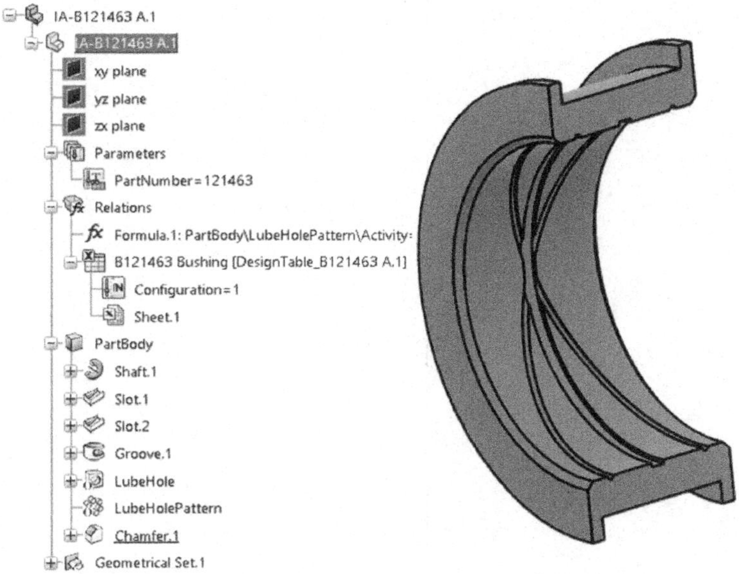

Figure 13–36

3. In the specification tree, under **Relations**, double-click on **B121463 Bushing** to open the design table.

4. Select part number **121470** (line 8) and click **OK**. The model updates with the design table values for **121470**, as shown in Figure 13–37.

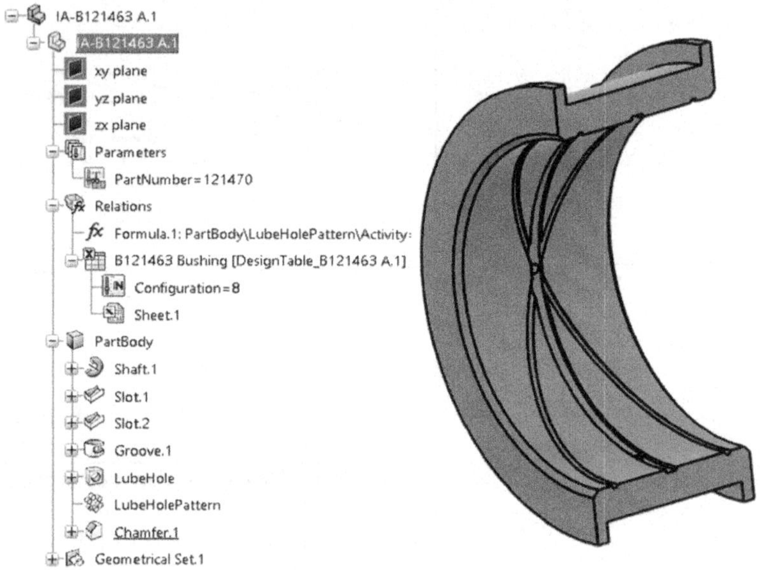

Figure 13–37

5. Save the model and close the window.

Practice 13c (Optional) Design Table II

Practice Objective

- Create a design table without instructions.

In this practice, you will create a number of design configurations for the **L-Bracket** model using a design table without instructions.

Task 1 - Create a design table for the L-Bracket.

In this task, you will create a design table for the **L-Bracket** model.

1. Import and open **L-Bracket.3dxml**. The model display as shown in Figure 13–38.

Figure 13–38

The following parameters have already been renamed, as shown in Figure 13–39.

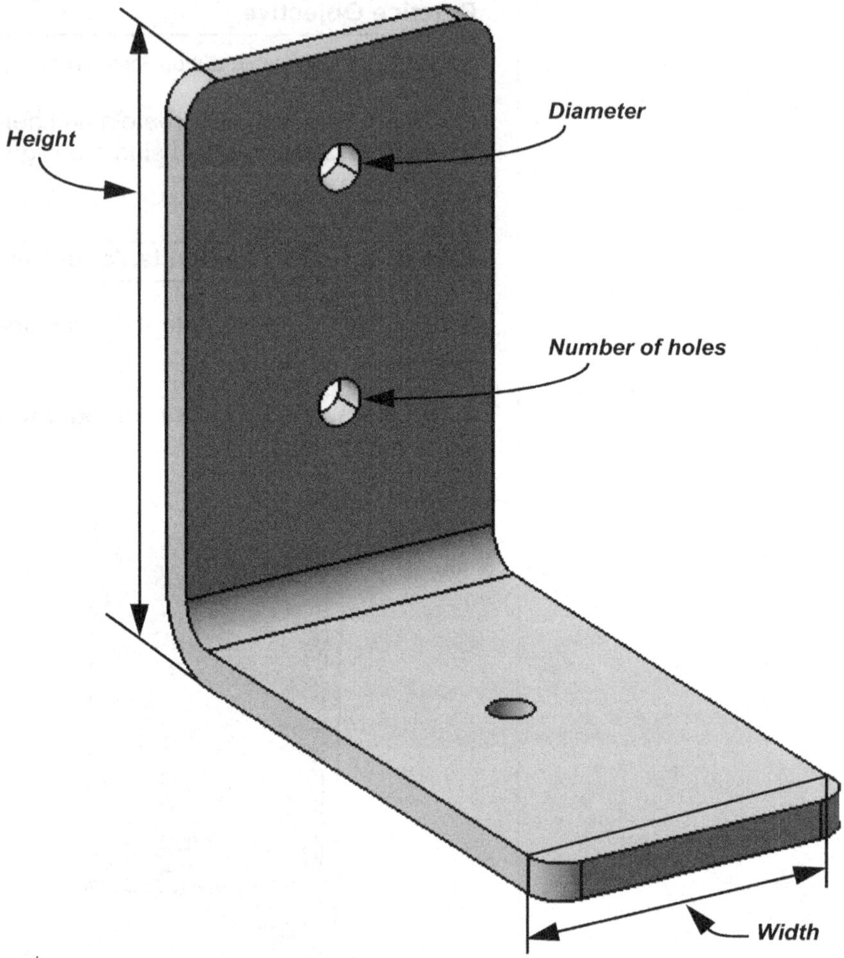

Figure 13–39

During the creation of the part, some of the formulas are assigned to control the positions of **Hole.1** and **Hole.2**. The other formulas are used to make the diameter of **Hole.2** equal to the diameter of **Hole.1**.

2. Create a design table for 9 different configurations of the **L-Bracket**. The values are listed in the table shown in Figure 13–40 below, with the initial values in the first row.

	A	B	C	D	E
1	PartNumber	Height (mm)	Width (mm)	Diameter (mm)	`Number-of holes`
2	B145	125	75	10	2
3	B146	135	75	10	2
4	B147	145	75	10	2
5	B148	155	75	10	2
6	B149	175	75	10	3
7	B150	185	100	15	3
8	B151	195	100	15	3
9	B152	240	100	15	4
10	B153	260	100	15	4

Figure 13–40

3. Open various instances to verify that the design table is functioning correctly.

4. Save the model and close the window.

Chapter Review Questions

1. You can prepare a model for use in a design table by renaming parameters or creating formulas.
   a. True
   b. False
2. CATIA creates a model parameter for every entity in a model, including dimensions and features.
   a. True
   b. False
3. How do formulas simplify a design table?
   a. Formulas can control multiple features and dimensions with a single parameter.
   b. Formulas reduce the number of parameters that need to be added to the design table to drive the design intent.
   c. Formulas make the design table easier to understand and modify.
   d. All of the above.
4. Part design tables are useful for creating a series of models that have a similar geometric shape, but come in a variety of sizes.
   a. True
   b. False
5. Design tables are unique to each design and cannot be stored in external files for reuse.
   a. True
   b. False

Answers: 1a, 2a, 3d, 4a, 5b

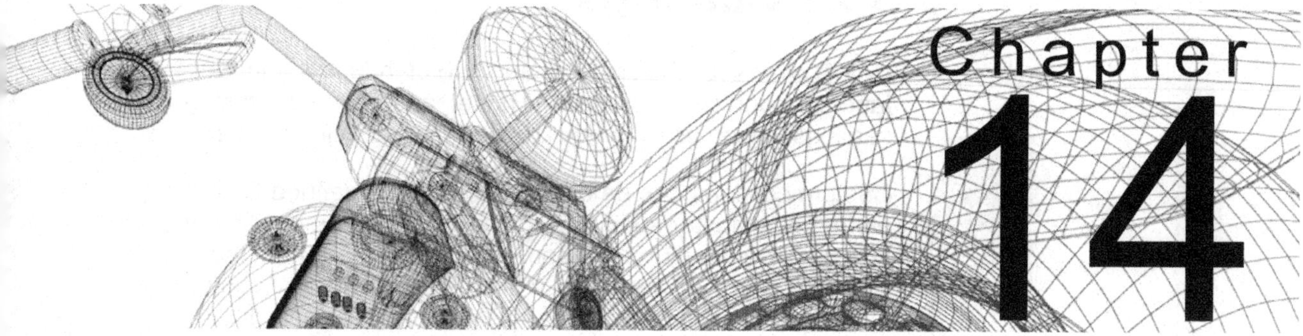

Catalogs

You can use catalogs to browse through standardized parts, or to create custom libraries for company-specific parts. This chapter focuses on creating and working with custom catalogs.

Learning Objectives in This Chapter

- Understand the use of custom catalogs.
- Create custom catalogs.
- Learn how to insert a Power Copy into a catalog.
- Create Component Family catalogs.

14.1 Catalogs

CATIA allows for the creation and use of industry-standard fasteners and common parts. These parts can then be stored in catalogs, which provide quick access to predefined parts.

Custom catalogs can be defined to store predefined CATIA elements, industry-specific parts, and company-specific parts. You can use structured custom catalogs to store and find common parts. This increases consistency and efficiency. Catalogs can also contain many CATIA elements, including:

- Power Copies
- Geometrical Sets
- Sketches
- 2D elements
- User Features
- Part Bodies
- Parameters
- Design tables

14.2 Creation of a Catalog

You can use CATIA to create your own part catalogs based on company-specific requirements.

General Steps

Use the following general steps to create a catalog:

1. Open the Catalog Editor app.
2. Add a new chapter.
3. Add a existing object.
4. Copy a chapter from another catalog, if required.

Step 1 - Open the Catalog Editor app.

Select  (New)>**New Content.** In the New Content box, select **Catalog**, as shown in Figure 14–1.

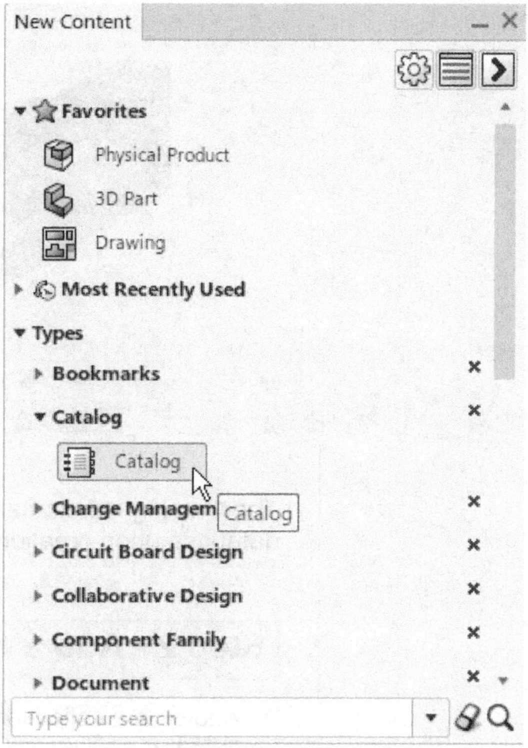

Figure 14–1

A new catalog window is displayed allowing for the *Name* of the catalog to be customized as shown in Figure 14–2. Select **OK** once the name has been entered.

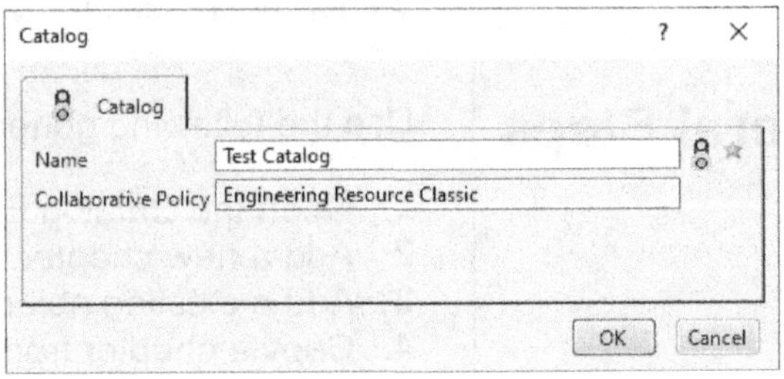

Figure 14–2

The new catalog opens in the *Design IP Classification* app as shown in Figure 14–3.

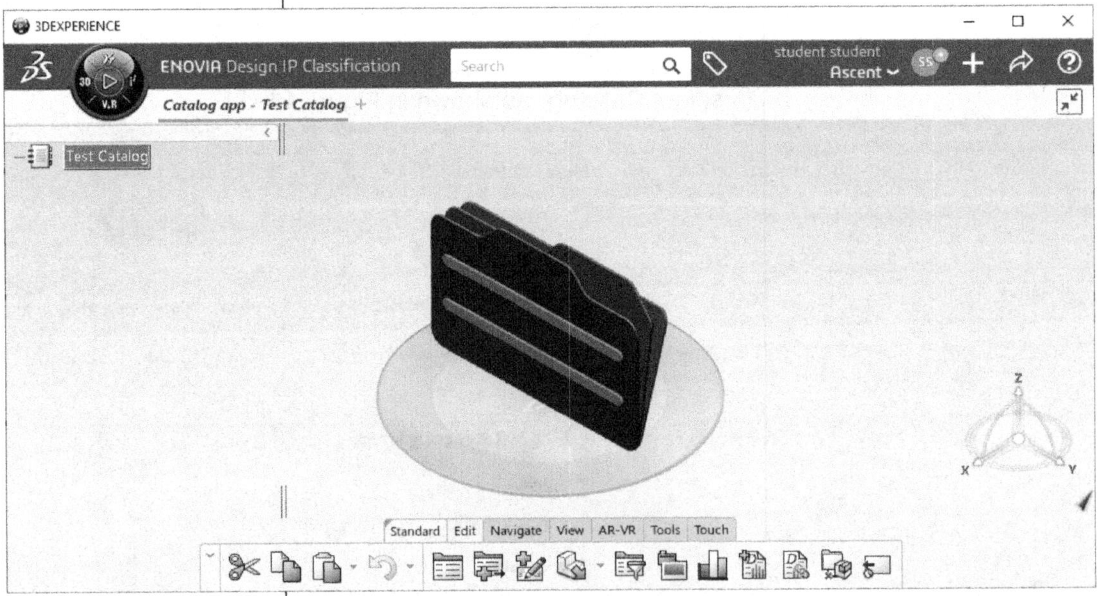

Figure 14–3

The Catalog is automatically saved into the 3DEXPERIENCE database upon creation.

Step 2 - Add a new chapter.

A chapter is a collection of related chapters and/or families of parts in the catalog.

How To: Add a Chapter

1. Click  (New Chapter) from the Edit section of the Action Bar.
2. Select the location in the Catalog tree that you want the new chapter to be located. If this is the first chapter then select the Catalog itself. Subsequent chapters can be nested into other chapters by selecting them. The Chapter Definition dialog box opens as shown in Figure 14–4.

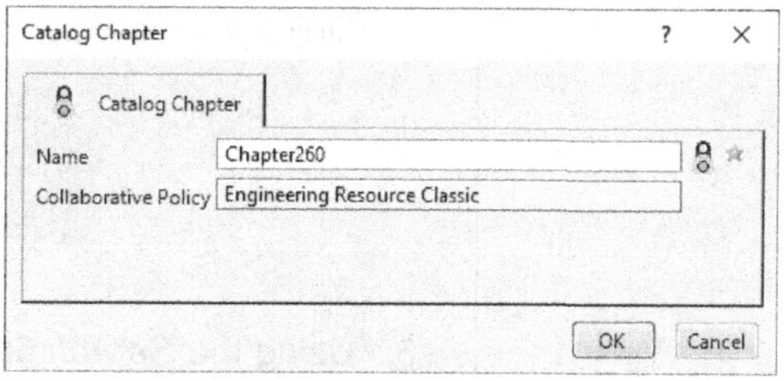

Figure 14–4

3. Enter the name of the chapter and click **OK**. The catalog opens with the new chapter in the tree, as shown in Figure 14–5.

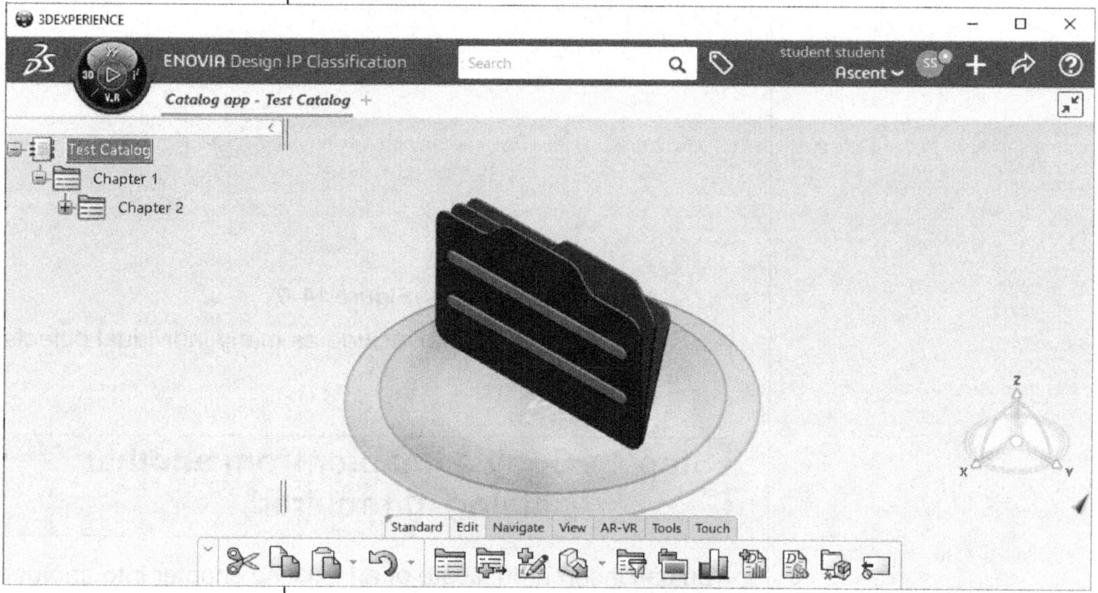

Figure 14–5

To rename a chapter, right-click on the chapter and select **Properties**.

Step 3 - Add a existing object.

An existing object can be place into a chapter of related components that are added into and accessed from the catalog.

How To: Insert an Existing Object

1. Select the chapter to which you want to add the object.
2. Click  (Insert Existing Object). The Selector Search an Object window opens as shown in Figure 14–6.

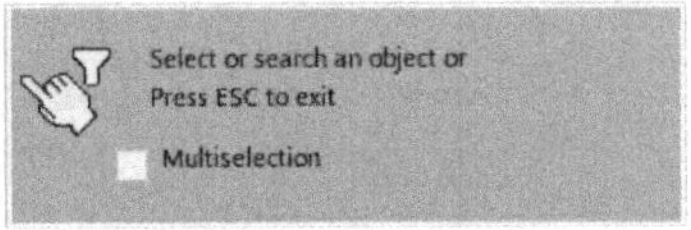

Figure 14–6

3. Using the *Search* field to search and select the object that you wish to insert into the chapter, as shown in Figure 14–7.

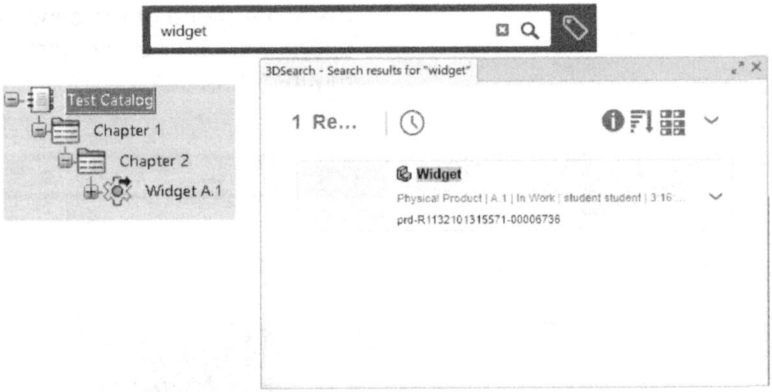

Figure 14–7

4. Repeat Steps 1 to 3 to include as many individual objects as needed.

Step 4 - Copy a chapter from another catalog, if required.

You can insert a duplicate of an existing chapter into another chapter or catalog so that you can access a variety of catalog structures and objects from within a single, top-level catalog.

How To: Create a New Chapter From

1. Open the target catalog of which the chapter will be placed into.
2. Select the target chapter of which the duplicate chapter will be created in.
3. Click  (New Chapter From) from the Edit section of the Action Bar. The Select or search an object window opens. Using the *Search* field, search and select the chapter that you want to duplicate to from the source catalog. The *Copy of (Original Name)* displays under the target chapter. For example, a copy of the Power Copies chapter of another catalog is added beneath **Chapter.2**, as shown in Figure 14–8.

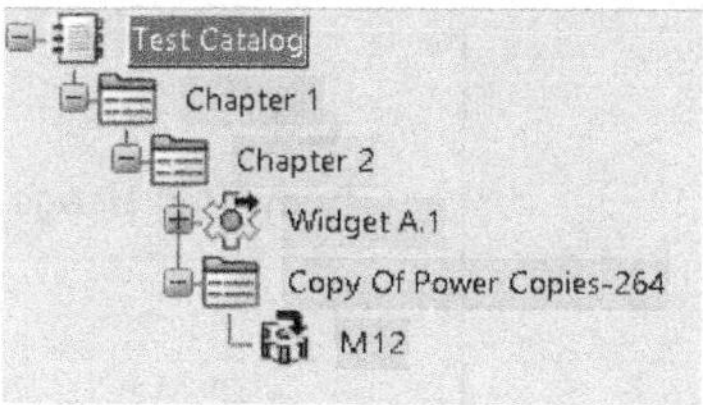

Figure 14–8

Other catalog creation options are described as follows:

Option	Description
 (Persistent Query)	Inserts a persistent query into a selected chapter so a filter can be easily accessible and used to customize catalog results.
 (Item: Feature)	Used to insert features such as 2D components, 2D sketches, and power copies into a chapter of a catalog.
 (Manage Keywords)	Adds, modifies, and removes keywords to chapters so you can find those chapters through a search. Keyword types including integer, string, boolean, angle, etc.
 (Filter)	Allows for the creation, opening, and saving of Catalog Filters that can then be applied to a large catalog to find specific types of objects based on specific keyword criteria.

(Attach New Document)	Attach a new document to a catalog chapter by uploading a local file.
Attach Existing Document	Attach a document that already exists in the 3DEXPERIENCE database into a catalog chapter.
(Manage Thumbnails)	Allows the user to Add/Replace a thumbnail to be displayed for the selected object.
(View Part Usage)	Displays part usage of part family items.
(Remove Item)	Removes selected item from Chapter or General Class.
(Replace by/Insert Latest Revision)	Replaces selected item with the latest revision.

14.3 Cataloging a Power Copy

You can insert a Power Copy, 2D Components, or 2D sketches into a catalog using the Item: Feature tool. While Item: Feature can be used for a variety of different objects, this example will focus on power copies. Start by creating and/or opening the power copy within its own tab. Ensure that the power copy has been saved. Leave this tab open as shown in Figure 14–9.

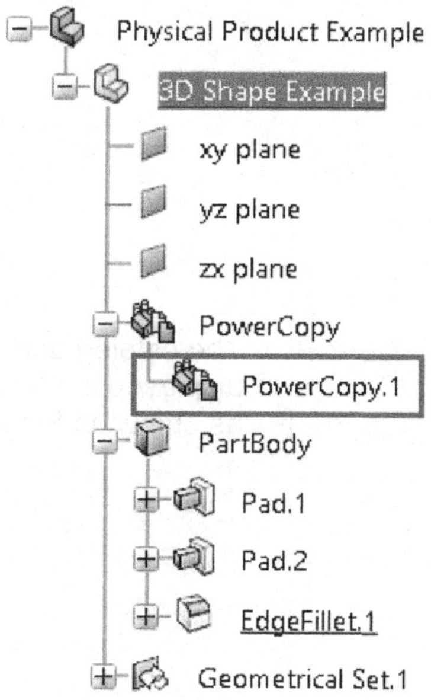

Figure 14–9

Using another tab, have the desired catalog open within the Design IP Classification app. Select the chapter or class that the power copy will be placed into as shown in Figure 14–10.

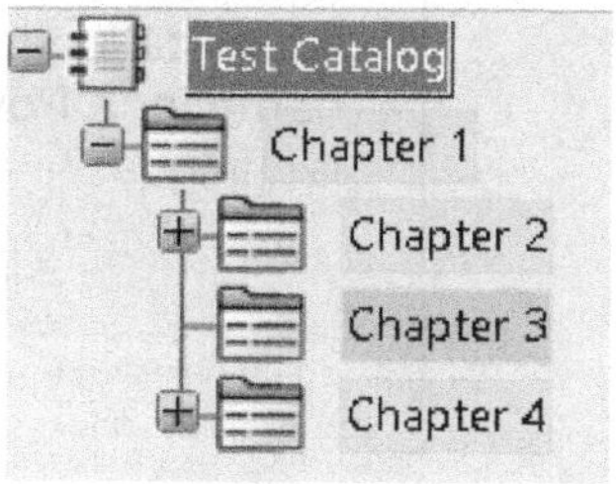

Figure 14–10

Select  (Item: Feature) from the Edit section of the Action Bar. A prompt will appear asking for the user to select the target feature to be inserted. Activate the tab with the power copy in it. Select on the power copy from within the specification tree, as shown in Figure 14–11.

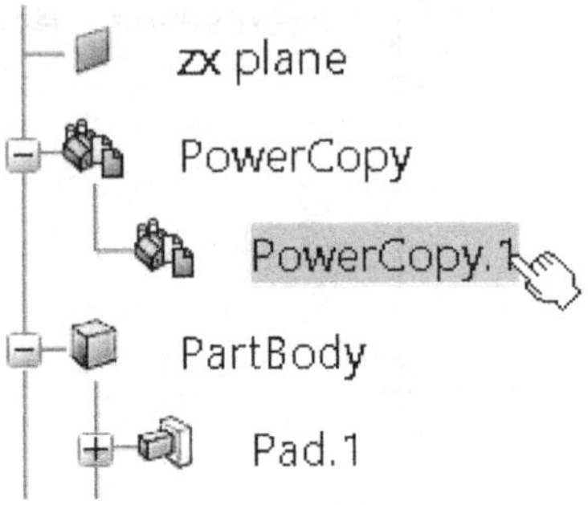

Figure 14–11

The catalog updates with the newly inserted power copy displayed in both the specification tree and on the display plater, as shown in Figure 14–12.

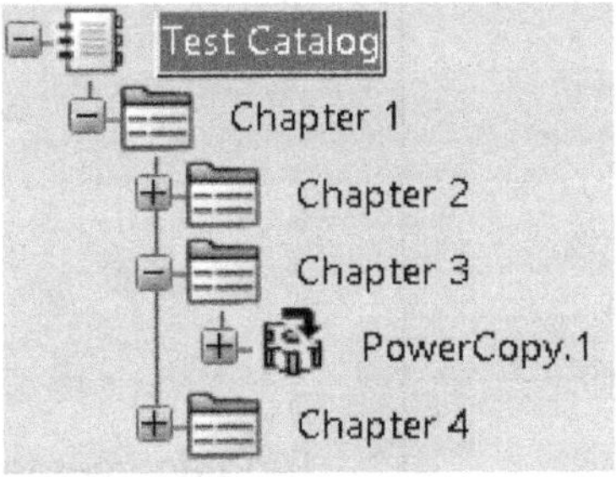

Figure 14–12

If you want to change the name of a chapter within the catalog, right-click on the chapter and select **Properties** from the specification tree. Enter the new name in the *Name* field. The name for a Power Copy can be changed using the same technique.

Instantiate a Power Copy from the Catalog

A Power Copy is instantiated into a document similar to other cataloged features.

How To: Instantiate a Power Copy from a Catalog

1. Click  (Catalog Browser).
2. If this is the first time Catalog Browser is being used then the Select or Search an object window will appear. Select on an already open catalog, or use the search field to located and select on the desired catalog.
3. If a catalog has been chosen in the past, then it will appear in its own window, as shown in Figure 14–13.

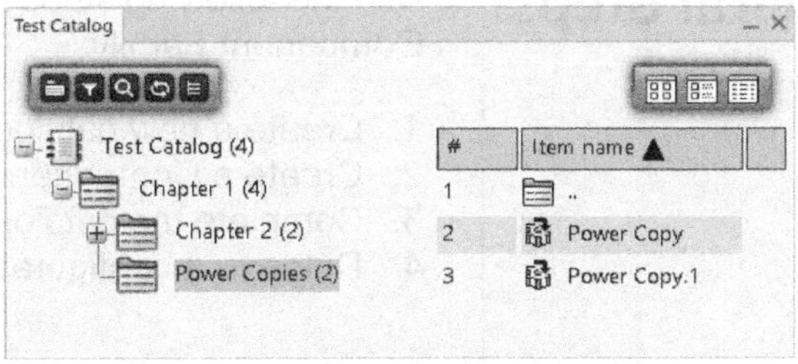

Figure 14–13

4. If the wrong catalog is displayed, click  (Open a catalog) in the upper right corner. This will open a Choose a Catalog or Chapter window as shown in Figure 14–14.

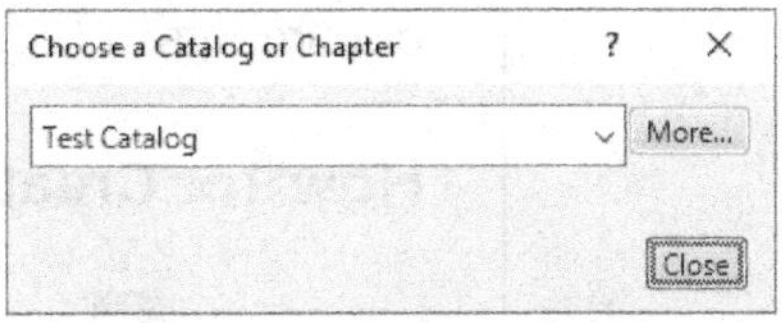

Figure 14–14

5. Click the drop-down arrow to pick from previously loaded catalogs, or select **More...** to search the database for a catalog that has never been loaded.
6. Once a catalog has been chosen, the catalog can be navigated by expanding the  icons to the right of the Chapters. Once the desired chapter has been located, double-click on it to display its associated Power Copies.
7. Double-click on the required Power Copy to open the Insert Object dialog box.
8. Place the Power Copy using the method described earlier.

14.4 Creating a Component Family

Once you create the design table, you can add it to a Component Family where different configurations of the part or assembly can be managed. This allows for the generation of multiple objects, validation of the different values within the design table for each instance, and control of revisions and thumbnails associated with each configuration. When finished, you can retrieve the different configurations as separate part files by placing them into a catalog.

General Steps

Use the following steps to add a design table to a catalog using a Component Family:

1. Create a new catalog.
2. Create a Component Family.
3. Complete the catalog and save the file.
4. Retrieve a configuration.

Step 1 - Create a new catalog.

You can add a part design table to a new catalog or an existing one. It is recommended that you become familiar with any existing catalog document structure before creating new catalog documents.

How To: Create a New Catalog

1. Select  (Add)>**New Content**.
2. In the New Content window, expand *Types* and *Catalog* categories, then select **Catalog**.
3. The Catalog window will appear. Enter the desired name into the *Name* field and select **OK**.
4. Select  (New Chapter) and select the Catalog name in the specification tree. A Catalog Chapter window will appear. Enter the desired name into the *Name* field and then select **OK**. The catalog will update as shown in Figure 14–15.

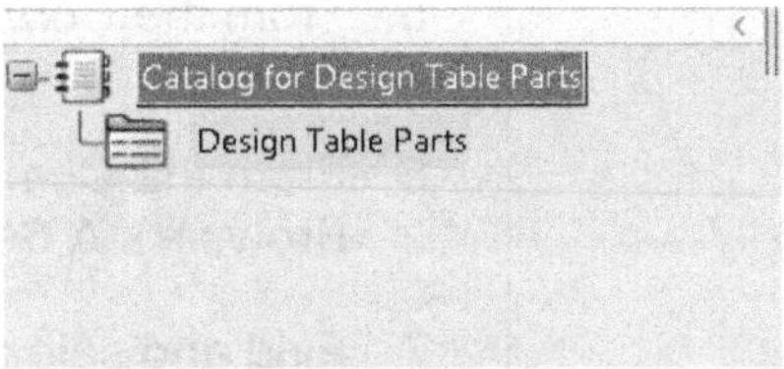

Figure 14–15

Step 2 - Create a Component Family.

1. Select (Add)>New Content.
2. In the New Content window, expand *Types* and *Component Family* categories, then select **Component Family**.
3. The Component Family window will appear. Enter the desired name into the *Name* field and then select the *Component Family Model* tab as shown in Figure 14–16.

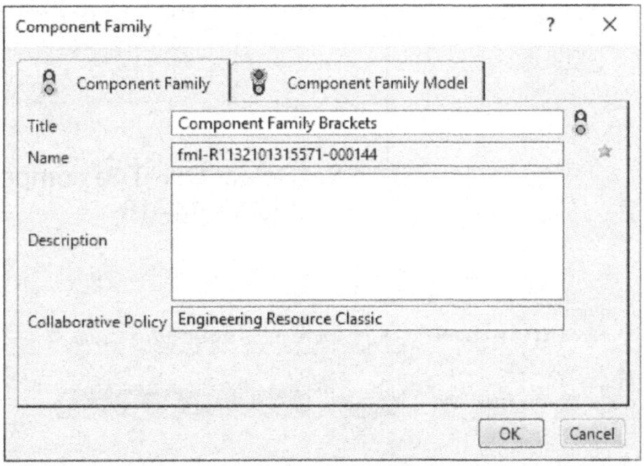

Figure 14–16

4. When creating a component family, there are two different family types to chose from: Standard and Design.

   Standard: Dictates that all items are created by the same generic model iteration. A new revision of the generic model must be created with every change to the component family. Best used for standard components that rarely change.

   Design: Allows for an easier way to manage a component family. This type allows the generic model and table to go through regular changes including new item definition or the changing of geometry.

5. From the *Component Family Model* tab, select **Design Family.**

6. From the *Component Family Model* tab, select (Folder Browser). A Select or Search an object window will appear.

7. Find and select on the part file that contains the design table. This can be done by using the *Search* field or selecting on the name of the part directly if it is already open. The component family window will update as shown in Figure 14–17.

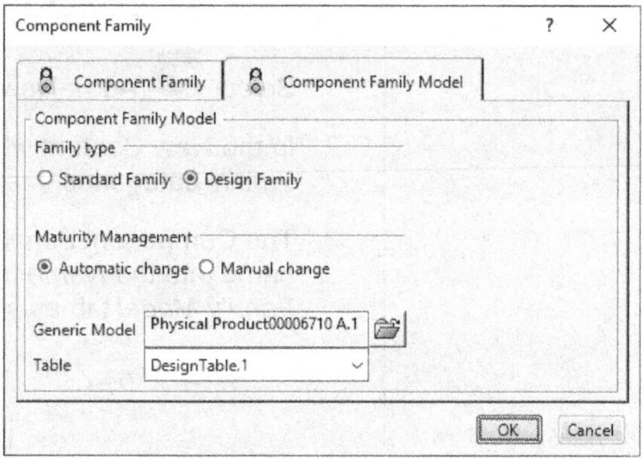

Figure 14–17

8. Select **OK**. The component family will be created as shown in Figure 14–18.

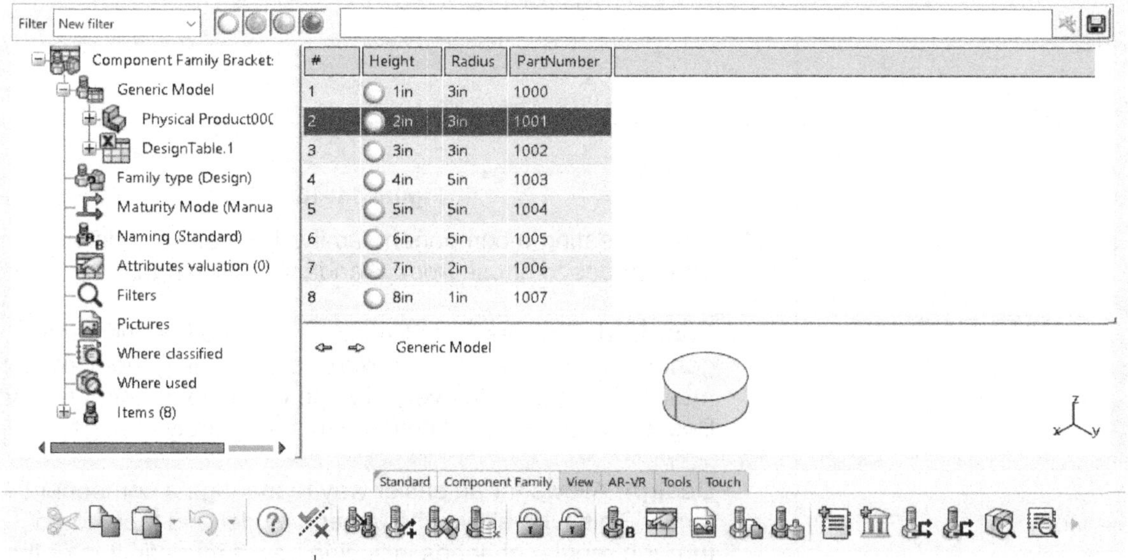

Figure 14–18

9. Save the component family.

Step 3 - Complete the catalog and save the file.

Once you finish adding a part to the component family, you should test and resolve each configuration. Start by holding <Shift>, and select the top and bottom listed items. This should select all of the items in the list, as shown in Figure 14–19.

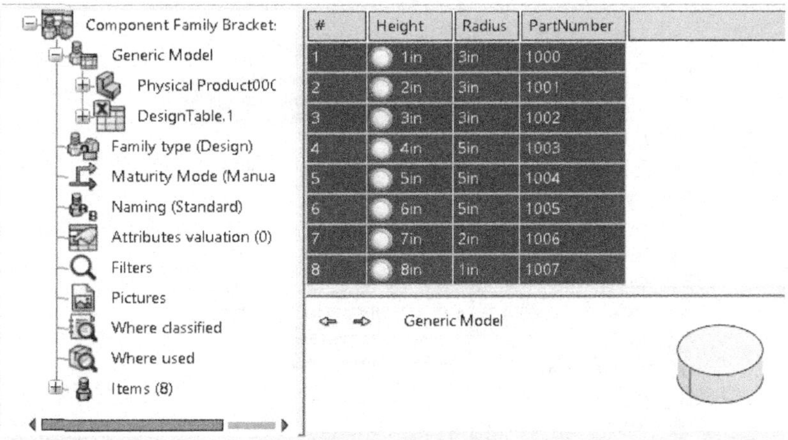

Figure 14–19

Select  (Test and Resolve Family Items). A Test and Resolve Family Items window will appear, as shown in Figure 14–20.

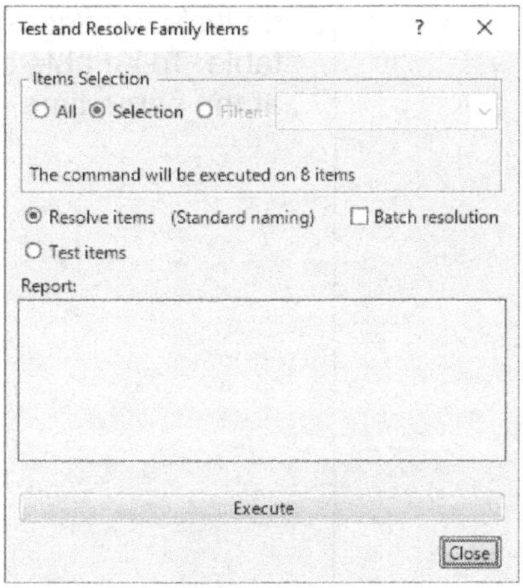

Figure 14–20

Ensure *Item Selection* is set to **Selection** and then select **Execute**. A *Component family items resolution* progression window will appear. Allow for this window to complete its process. When finished, select **Close**.

Resolving enables you to verify that the design table does not contain any errors and that each configuration produces a usable model. Errors are then indicated by stop light system where represents an error and indicates a successful resolve, as shown in Figure 14–21.

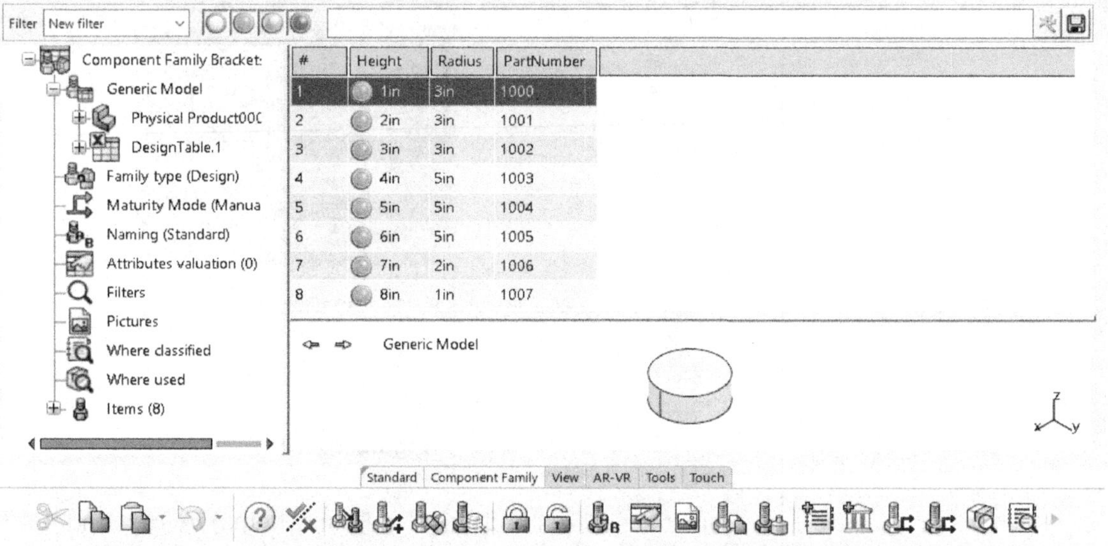

Figure 14–21

At this point, the component family has successfully created multiple configurations of the generic part based on the design table. To be able to use these various configurations in a product at the same time, they will need to be place into a catalog.

Select (Manage Component Family Catalogs) from the Component Family section of the Action Bar. The Catalog management window appears as shown in Figure 14–22.

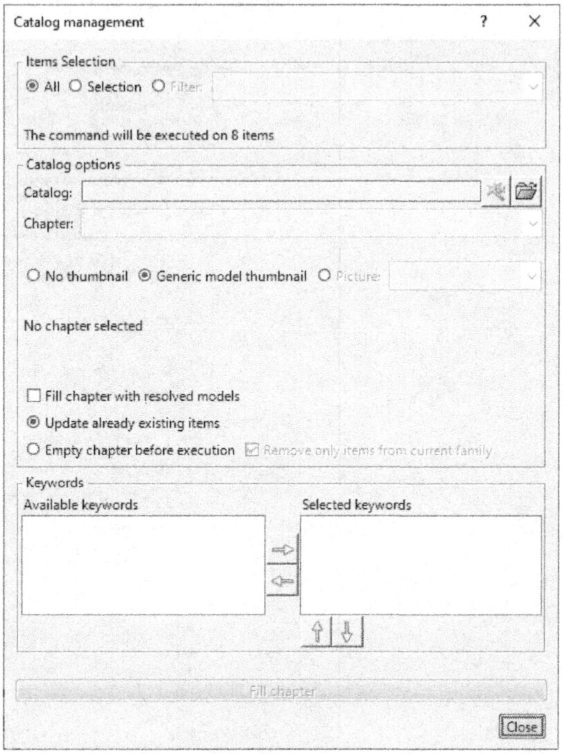

Figure 14–22

Select the (Browser) command to the right of the *Catalog* field, then locate and select the Catalog you created earlier. Once selected, ensure that the desired Chapter is chosen from the drop-down menu as the destination of the components, as shown in Figure 14–23.

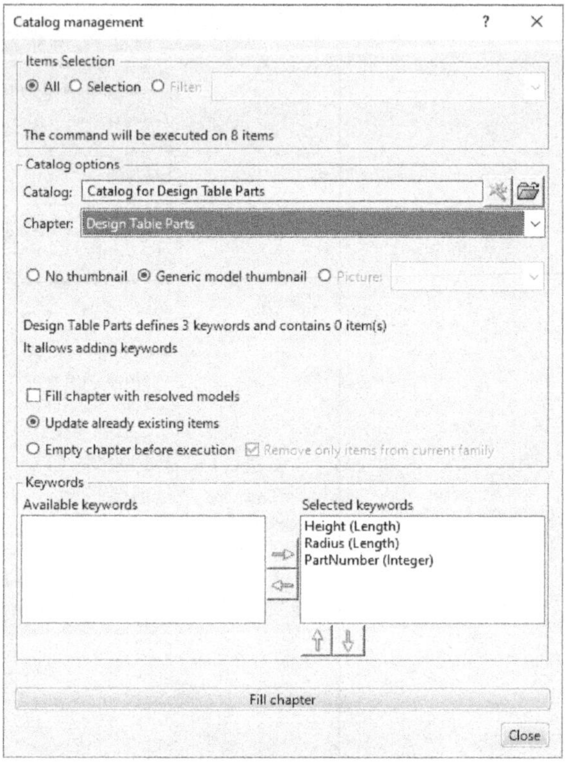

Figure 14–23

With *Items Selection* set to **All** and **Update already existing items** chosen, select the **Fill Chapter** button. A progression window appears while the Individual parts are placed into the catalog.

Step 4 - Retrieve a configuration.

You can now retrieve configurations of the part model using the Catalog Browser.

How To: Retrieve a Part Configuration

1. Open or create the 3D Part or Physical Product to which you want to retrieve the part configuration.
2. Click (Catalog Browser) to open the Catalog Browser.
3. If the wrong catalog is loaded, select (Open a Catalog) and the Choose a Catalog or Chapter window appears.
4. Expand the Current drop-down list and select the catalog containing the part family. If the catalog is not available, click **More...**to search and select the desired catalog.
5. Browse through the catalog tree to locate the required configuration. Double-click on **Chapters** to show the list of items found within. Use filters as needed to reduce the amount of data to search through.
6. Click (Filter the selected chapter) to open the Filter Assistant window, as shown in Figure 14–24.

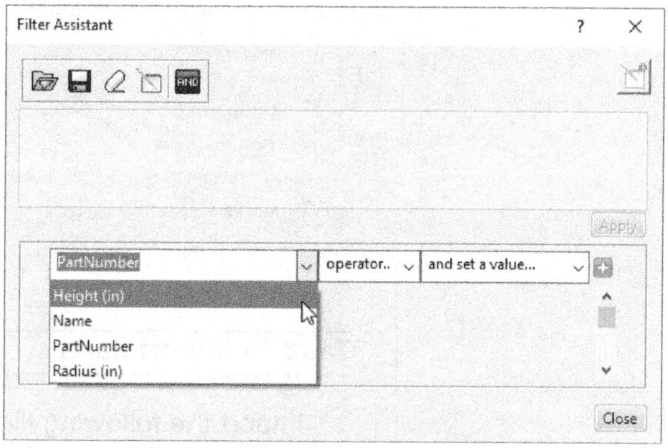

Figure 14–24

For example, to display parameters with a value larger than **0.5** for the **Height** parameter and a **3** for the **Radius** parameter, select **Height>0.5** and **Radius = 3** in the *Filter* fields.

7. Once you locate the required configuration, double-click on the configuration in the Catalog window to select it, then select the Physical Product into which it will be placed. The model is then dropped into the assembly.

Practice 14a Catalogs

Practice Objectives

- Create a catalog.
- Add elements to a catalog.
- Link from one catalog to another.

In this practice, you will create the structure for a catalog. The parts are added to the catalog. Finally, you will generate a new catalog and create a link from the first catalog to the new one. The completed catalogs display as shown in Figure 14–25.

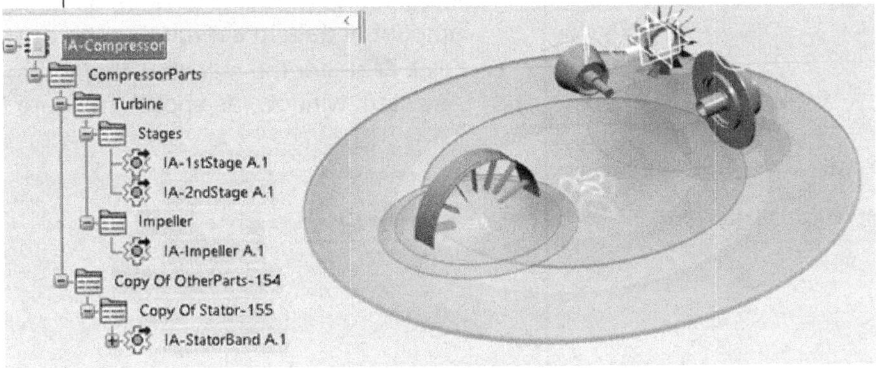

Figure 14–25

Task 1 - Import parts.

1. Import the following files from the *Turbine* directory: **1stStage_2.3dxml**, **2ndStage.3dxml**, **Impeller.3dxml**, and **StatorBand.3dxml**. When importing, type your initials followed by the dash symbol into the *Duplication string* field.
2. Close all the windows for the imported parts.

Task 2 - Create a new catalog.

1. In the Top Bar, click  (Add)>**New Content**.
2. In the New Content dialog box, expand the *Types* section and select **Catalog**.
3. Enter the name for the new catalog as **<*YourInitials*>-Compressor** and click **OK**.

4. In the specification tree, select the root object and click  (New Chapter) in the Action Bar. The Catalog Chapter dialog box opens as shown in Figure 14–26.

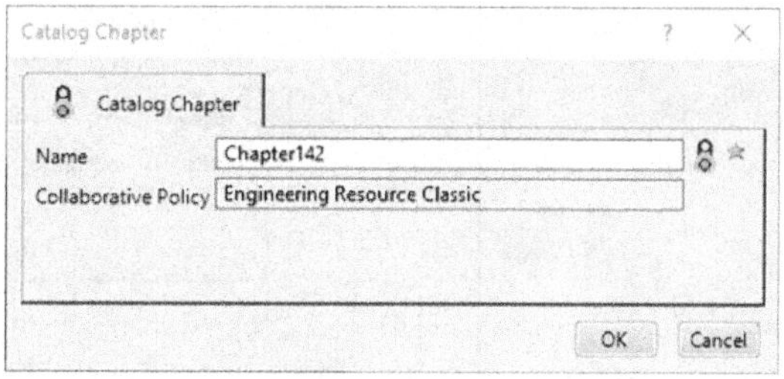

Figure 14–26

5. In the *Name* field, enter **CompressorParts**.

6. Click **OK**. The **Compressor** catalog displays as shown in Figure 14–27.

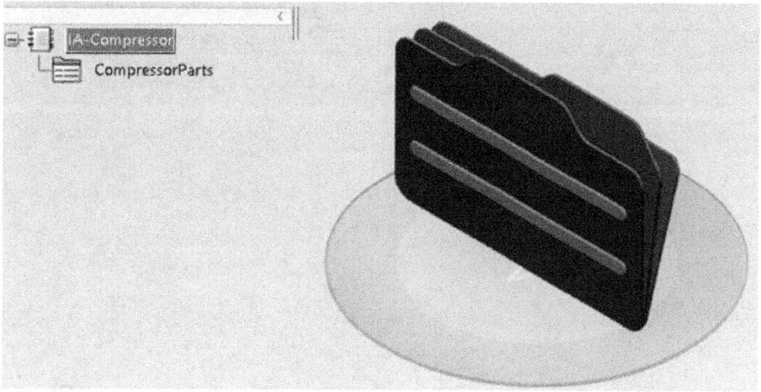

Figure 14–27

Task 3 - Add a chapter.

1. Select the **CompressorParts** chapter in the tree.

2. Click (New Chapter). The Catalog Chapter dialog box opens as shown in Figure 14–28.

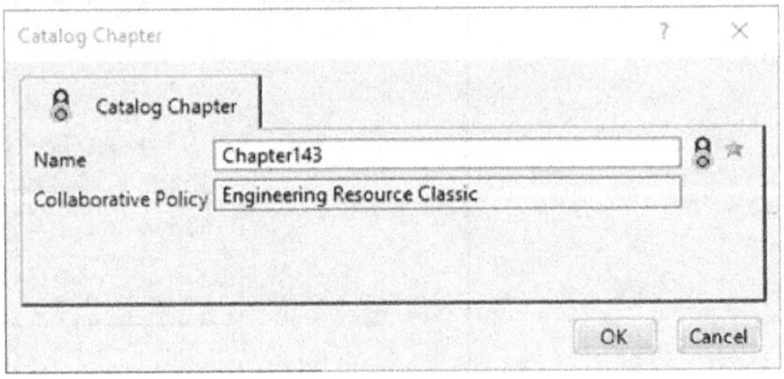

Figure 14–28

3. In the *Name* field, enter **Turbine**.
4. Click **OK**. The catalog displays as shown in Figure 14–29.

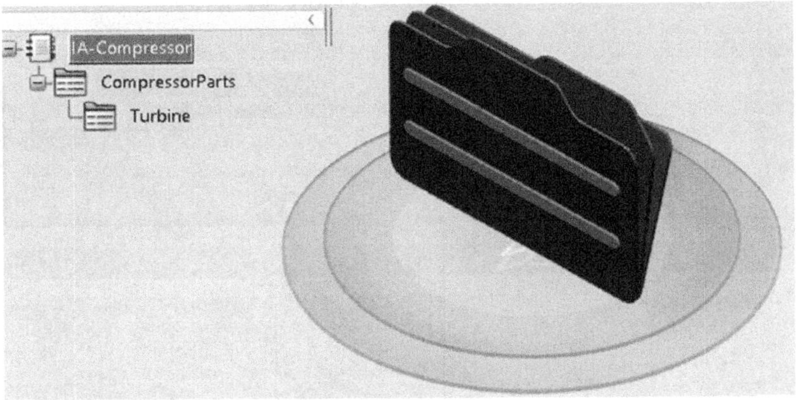

Figure 14–29

Task 4 - Add sub-chapters to a chapter.

1. Select the **Turbine** chapter in the tree.
2. Click (New Chapter). The Catalog Chapter dialog box opens as shown in Figure 14–30.

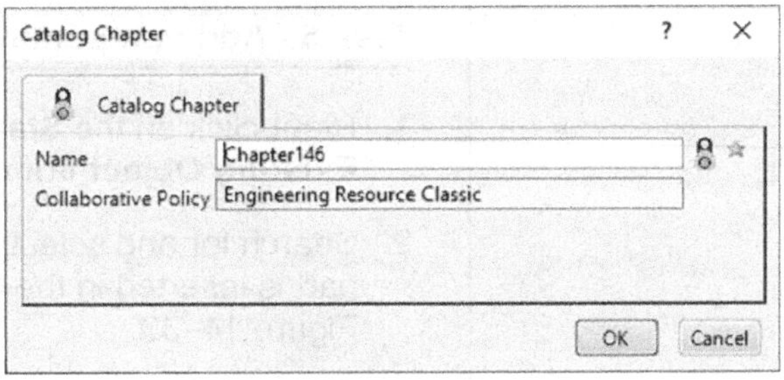

Figure 14–30

3. In the *Name* field, enter **Stages**.
4. Click **OK**. The catalog displays as shown in Figure 14–31.

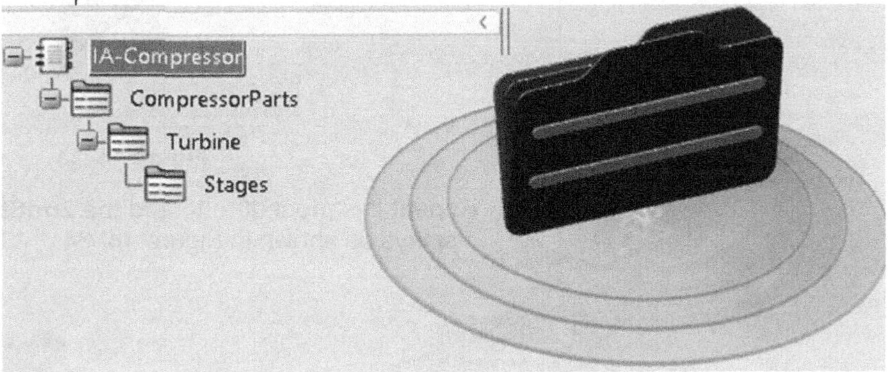

Figure 14–31

5. Add another sub-chapter to the **Turbine** chapter. Change the name to **Impeller**. The *Compressor* catalog displays as shown in Figure 14–32.

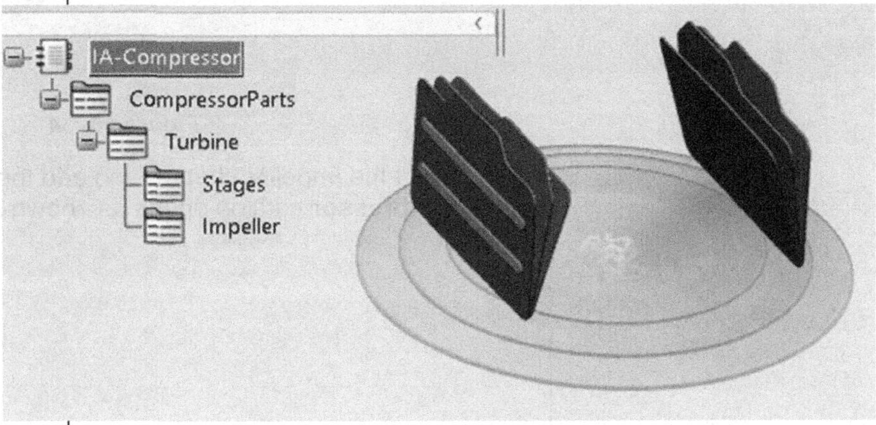

Figure 14–32

Task 5 - Add components to a family.

1. Right-click on the **Stages** chapter and select **Insert>Insert Existing Object** from the contextual menu.
2. Search for and select the **1stStage** part in the database. The part is inserted in the **Stages** chapter, as shown in Figure 14–33.

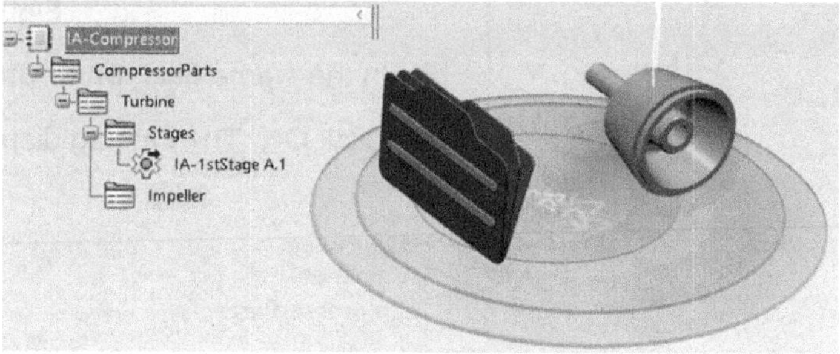

Figure 14–33

3. Repeat this procedure to add the **2ndStage**. The catalog displays as shown in Figure 14–34.

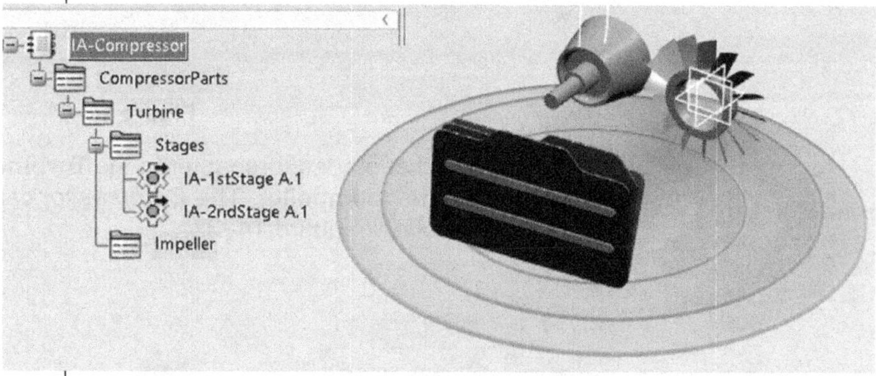

Figure 14–34

4. Select the Impeller chapter and add the **Impeller**. The **Compressor** catalog opens as shown in Figure 14–35.

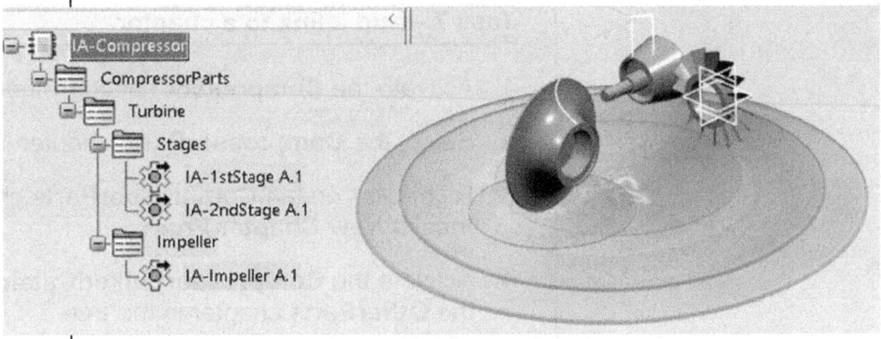

Figure 14–35

Task 6 - Create a new catalog.

1. Create a new catalog named **<*YourInitials*>-Compressor LinkedCatalog**.
2. Create a top-level chapter named **CompressorParts**.
3. Create a new chapter named **OtherParts** beneath the **CompressorParts** chapter.
4. Create a new chapter named **Stator** beneath the **OtherParts** chapter.
5. Add the **StatorBand** part to the Stator chapter. Once complete, the catalog displays as shown in Figure 14–36.

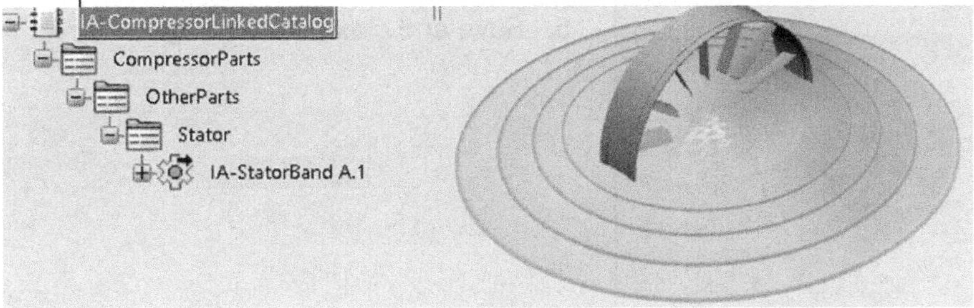

Figure 14–36

6. Keep **CompressorLinkedCatalog** open, because this catalog will be linked to the **Compressor** catalog.

Task 7 - Add a link to a chapter.

1. Activate the **Compressor** catalog window.
2. Select the **CompressorParts** chapter in the tree.
3. Right-click on the **CompressorParts** chapter and select **Insert>New Chapter From**.
4. Activate the **CompressorLinkedCatalog** window and select the **OtherParts** chapter in the tree.

   The chapter is copied in the **Compressor** catalog, as shown in Figure 14–37. Note that the prefix *Copy Of* indicates that it is a chapter linked to a chapter in another catalog.

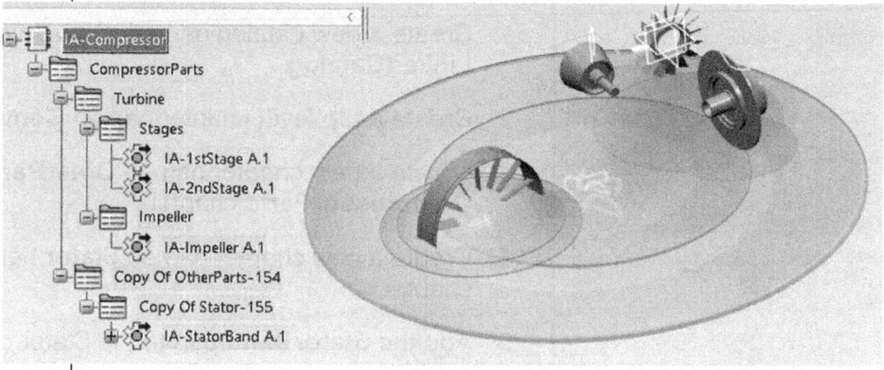

Figure 14–37

5. Save and close the catalogs.

Practice 14b Power Copy in Catalogs

Practice Objectives

- Add a Power Copy to a catalog.
- Insert the Power Copy into a model using the catalog.

In this practice, you will add two instances of the **M12 Boss Power Copy** to the model from an existing catalog. The completed model displays as shown in Figure 14–38.

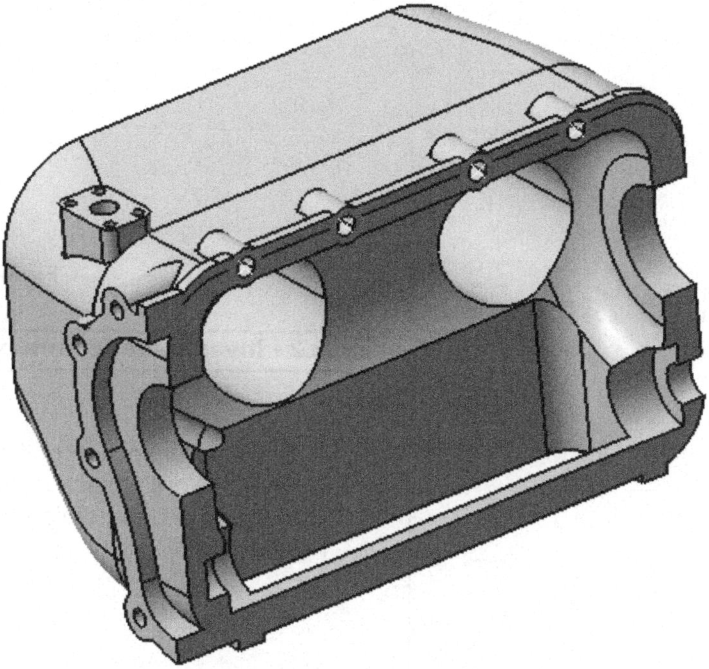

Figure 14–38

Task 1 - Open the part and investigate feature history.

1. Import and open the **M12-BossPC.3dxml** model. When importing, type your initials followed by the dash symbol into the *Duplication string* field. The model displays as shown in Figure 14–39.

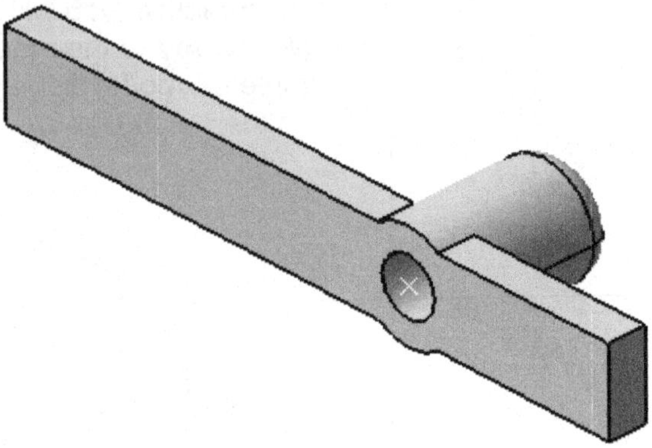

Figure 14–39

Task 2 - Investigate feature order.

1. In the Review section of the Action Bar, select (Scan or Define In Work Object). Expand the drop-down list and select **Update**. The Scan dialog box displays as shown in Figure 14–40.

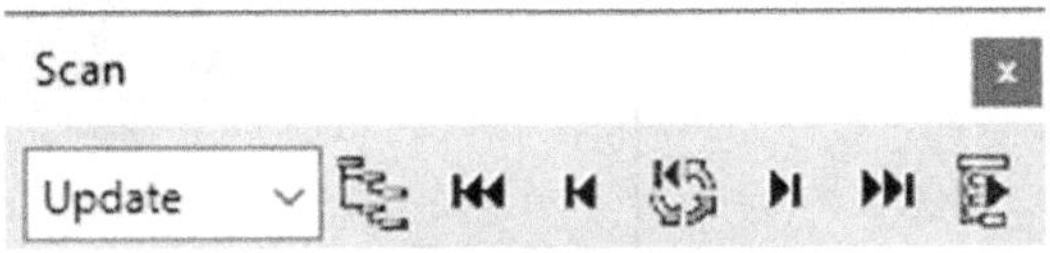

Figure 14–40

2. Click and replay the creation of the model by clicking . Note the feature order and possible references that have been generated. Note that **Point.1** was created before the boss (**Pad.2**).

3. Click to scan to the last feature and close the Scan dialog box.

Design Considerations

Point.1 was updated before **Pad.2**. All references for the boss are to **Point.1**, as shown in Figure 14–41. You should use a face and a point as references when locating circular PowerCopies. This technique uses the minimum amount of references, requires less constraining, and is less confusing than selecting several references.

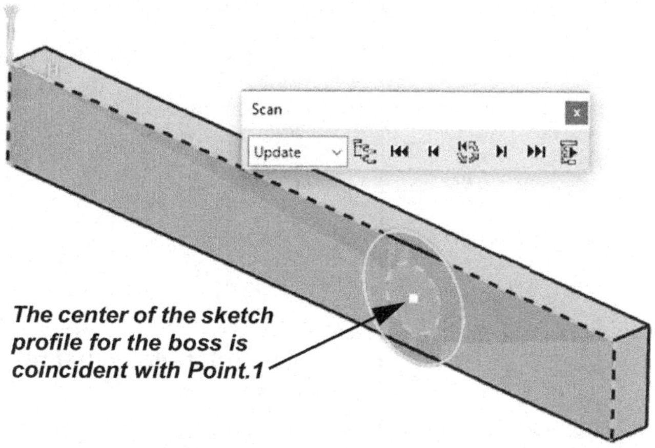

Figure 14–41

Task 3 - Investigate references of a Power Copy.

1. In the specification tree, double-click on the **M12 Boss** PowerCopy. The Power Copy Definition dialog box opens as shown in Figure 14–42.

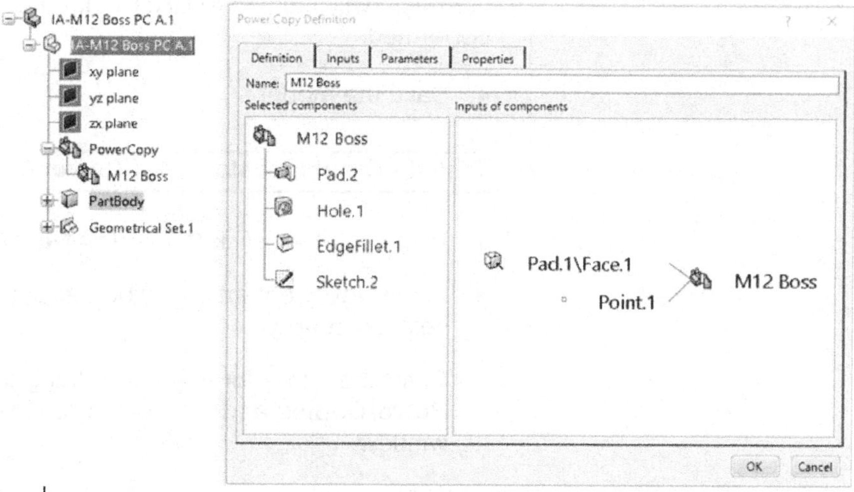

Figure 14–42

2. Select the *Inputs* tab. It lists the references required to place the Power Copy into a model, as shown in Figure 14–43.

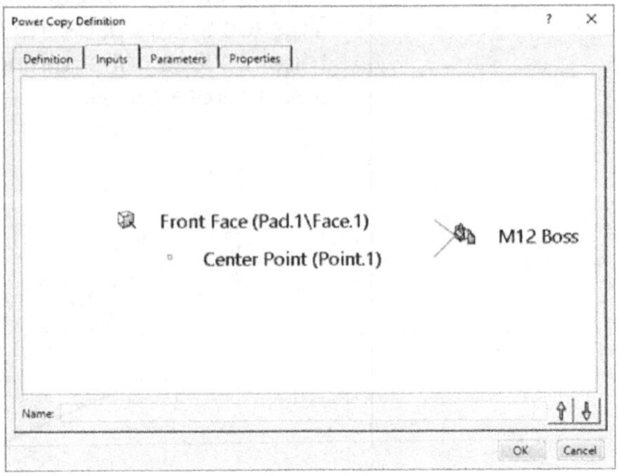

Figure 14–43

The references that are required to place the Power Copy are:

- A face
- A reference point

3. Close the Power Copy Definition dialog box.

Design Considerations

In the next task, you will insert the Power Copy into a catalog. You must always ensure that all changes to a document are saved before you insert a Power Copy into a catalog. Although no changes have been made to the document, the **Scan** operation will indicate to CATIA that a **Save** needs to be performed.

4. Save the model.

Task 4 - Create a catalog for Power Copies.

1. In the Top Bar, click  (Add)**>New Content**.
2. In the New Content dialog box, expand the *Types* section and select **Catalog**.
3. Enter the name for the new catalog as **<*YourInitials*>-PowerCopies** and click **OK**. The catalog opens in a new window.

4. In the catalog's specification tree, select the root object and click  (New Chapter) in the Action Bar. In the Catalog Chapter dialog box that opens, enter **PCs** for the *Name* and click **OK**. The catalog tree displays as shown in Figure 14–44.

Figure 14–44

5. Right-click on the **PCs** chapter and select **Insert>Item: Feature** from the contextual menu.

6. Activate the **M12 Boss PC** part window and select the **M12 Boss** power copy in the tree.

7. The power copy is inserted into the catalog, as shown in Figure 14–45.

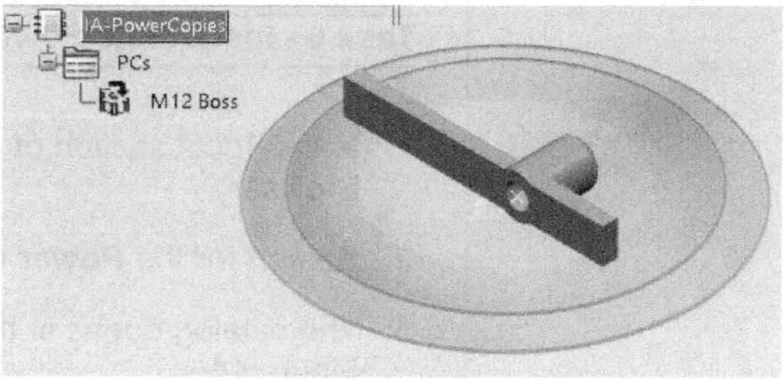

Figure 14–45

8. Close the **M12-BossPC** part window.

9. Close the PowerCopies catalog window.

Task 5 - Open a part file.

1. Import and open **BlockLeft8c.3dxml**. When importing, type your initials followed by the dash symbol into the *Duplication string* field. The part displays as shown in Figure 14–46.

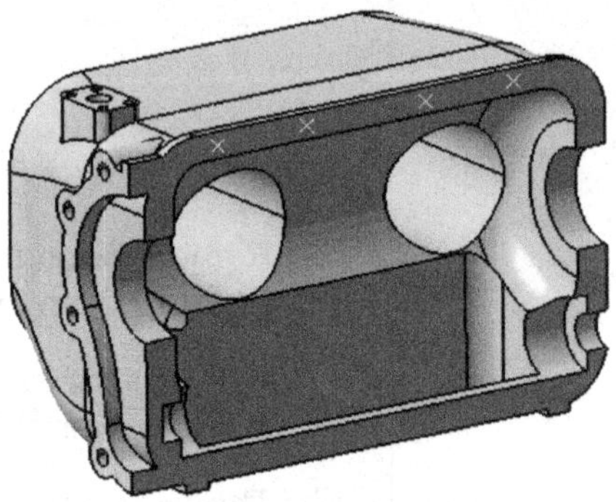

Figure 14–46

Task 6 - Instantiate Power Copy features from the catalog.

1. In the Tools section of the Action Bar, click (Catalog Browser).
2. Search for the **Power Copies** catalog.
3. The catalog opens in the auxiliary window, as shown in Figure 14–47.

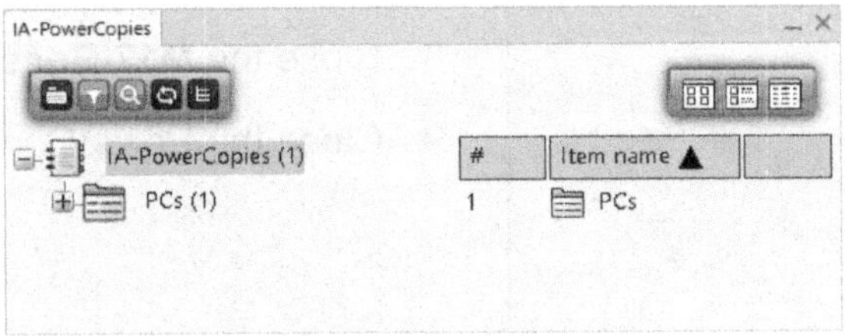

Figure 14–47

4. Double-click the **PCs** chapter to navigate to the M12 Boss power copy, as shown in Figure 14–48.

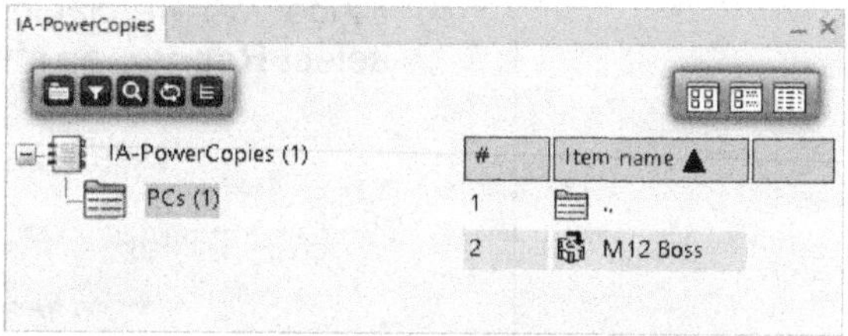

Figure 14–48

5. Double-click the **M12 Boss** object in the catalog. The Insert Object dialog box opens, as shown in Figure 14–49.

6. Select the references shown in Figure 14–49 to locate the Power Copy.

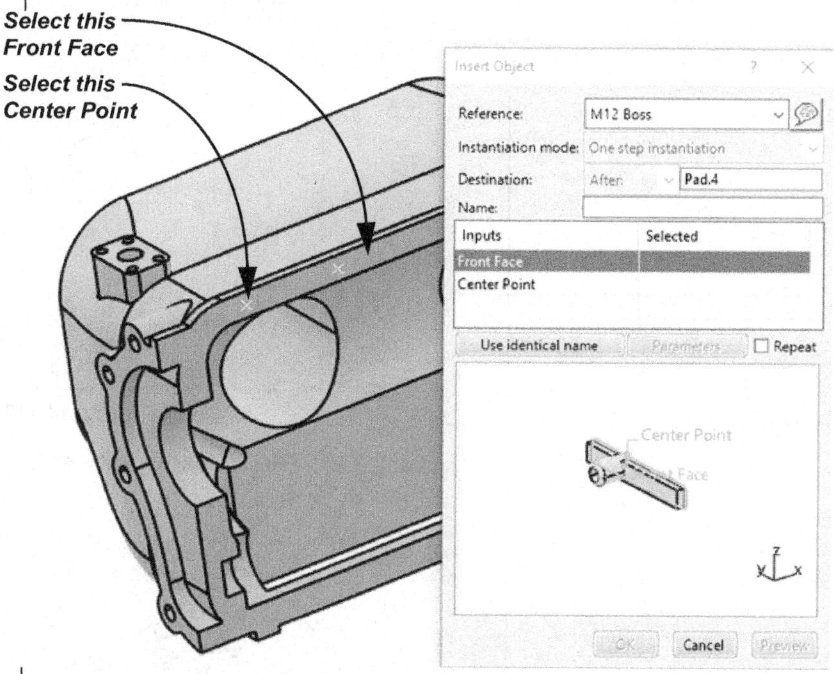

Figure 14–49

7. Click **Preview** to ensure that the placement of the Power Copy is correct.

8. Since you are placing three more instances of the boss, select **Repeat**, as shown in Figure 14–50.

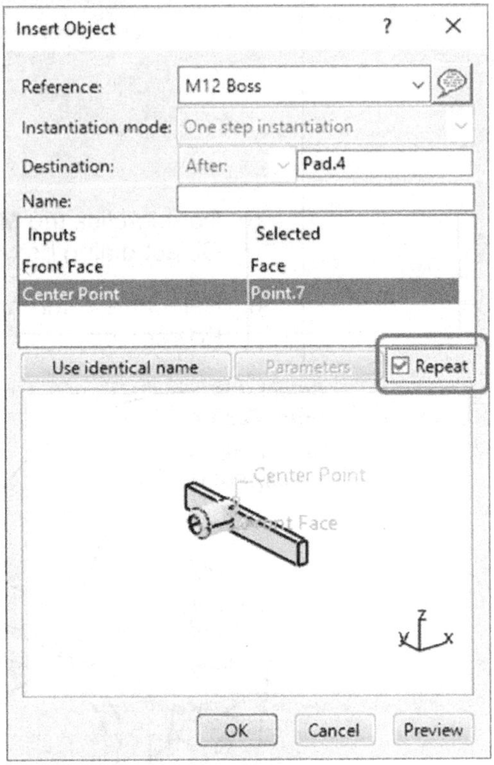

Figure 14–50

9. Click **OK**. The Power Copy displays as shown in Figure 14–51.

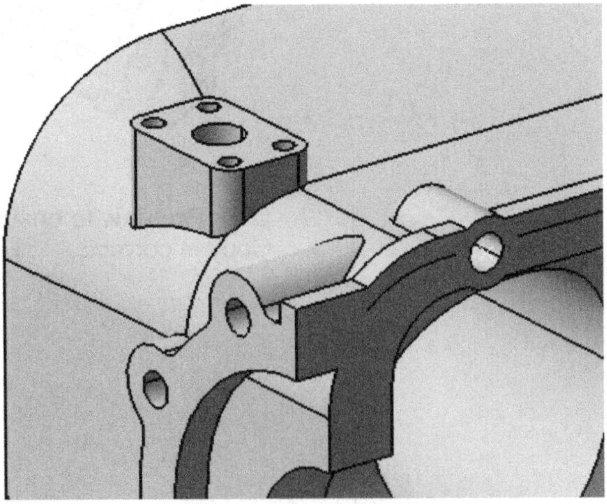

Figure 14–51

10. Note that the Insert Object dialog box stays active and that the **Front Face** is already listed as an input from the previous boss.

11. In the Insert Object dialog box, activate **Center Point** and select the reference point to place the next boss, as shown in Figure 14–52.

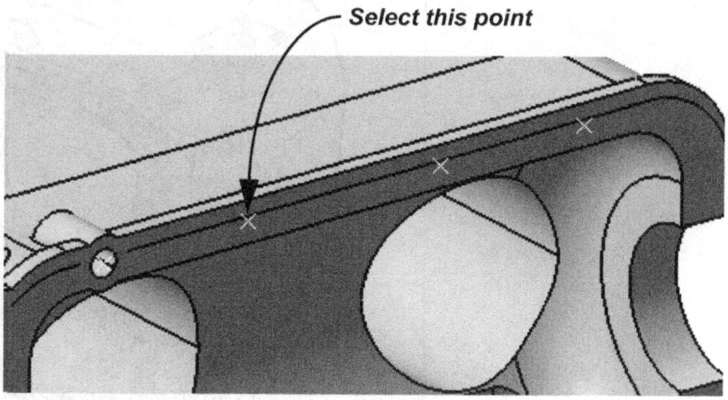

Figure 14–52

12. Click **Preview** to ensure that the placement of the Power Copy is correct.

13. Click **OK**. Select the next point, as shown in Figure 14–53.

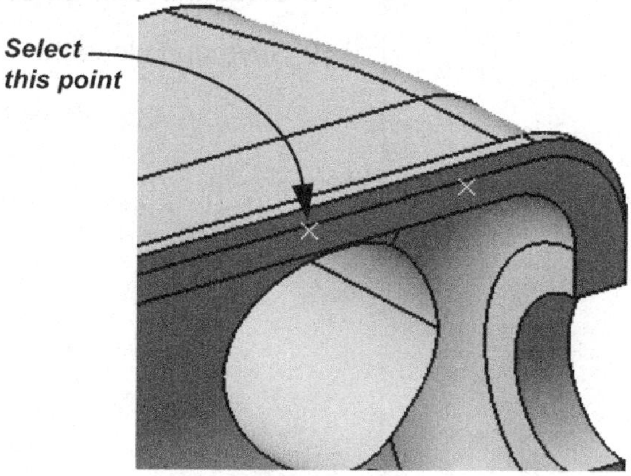

Figure 14–53

14. Click **Preview** to ensure that the placement of the Power Copy is correct.

15. Click **OK**.

16. In the Insert Object dialog box, clear the **Repeat** option.

17. Place the final boss, as shown in Figure 14–54.

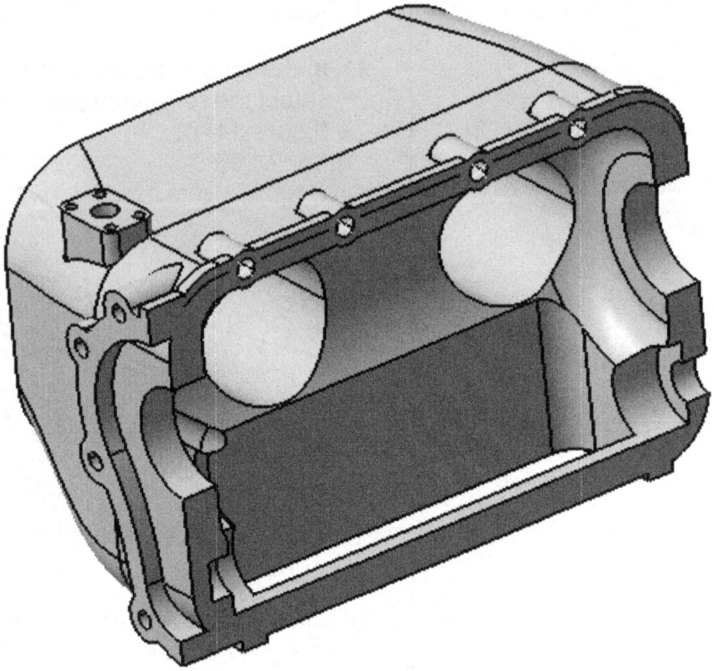

Figure 14–54

18. Close the Catalog Browser.

19. Save and close the model.

Practice 14c Using a Catalog

Practice Objectives

- Open a file from a catalog.
- Insert the Power Copies into a model using a catalog.

In this practice, you will create an engine block using a catalog. You will open the start file from a catalog that is a template file. Then, you will insert all of the required sketches and solid features using a catalog. The completed model displays as shown in Figure 14–55.

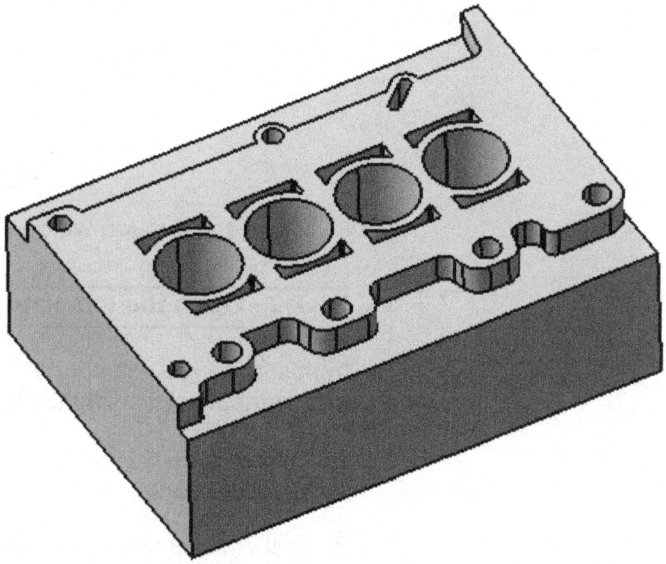

Figure 14–55

Task 1 - Import a catalog.

1. Import the **Engine_block-JY.3dxml** file. When importing, type your initials followed by the dash symbol into the *Duplication string* field.

2. Expand the tree. The imported catalog contains two chapters, as shown in Figure 14–56. The **PowerCopy** chapter contains three power copies: **Engine-pad**, **Pockets**, and **logo**. The **Coordinates** chapter contains the Coordinates template part.

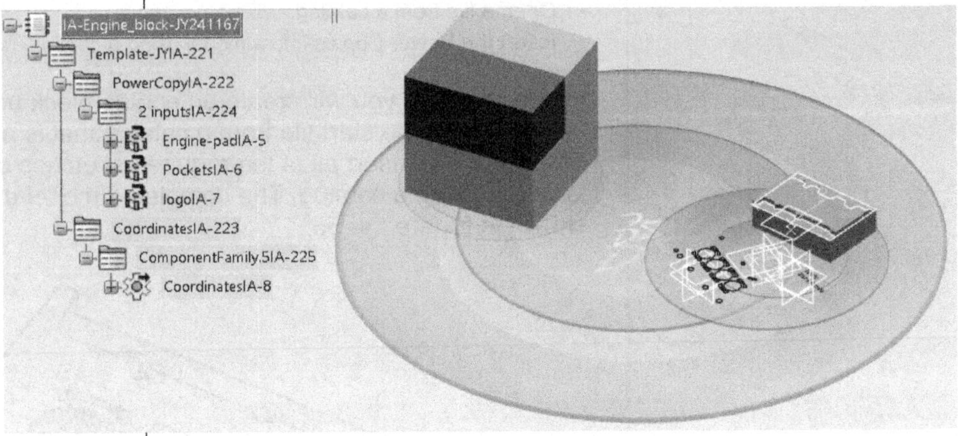

Figure 14–56

3. Close the catalog window.

Task 2 - Open the template file from a catalog.

In this task, you will open the template file that has all of the geometrical sets, using the Catalog Browser.

1. Create a new Physical Product, named ***<YourInitials>*-EngineBlock**.

2. In the Tools section of the Action Bar, click (Catalog Browser). The last used catalog (Power Copies, Practice 14b) opens, as shown in Figure 14–57.

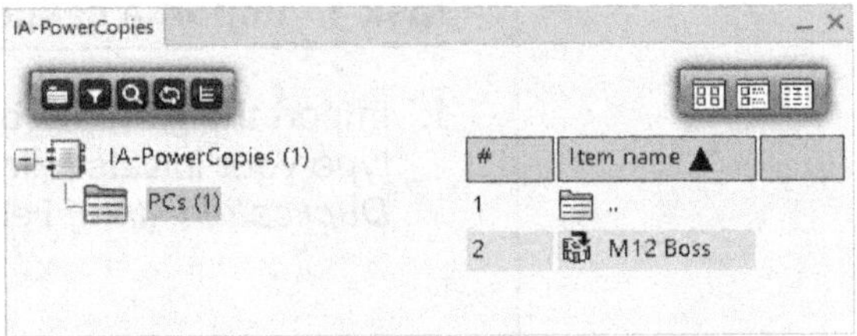

Figure 14–57

3. In the Catalog Browser dialog box, select (Open a catalog). The Choose a Catalog or Chapter dialog box opens, as shown in Figure 14–58.

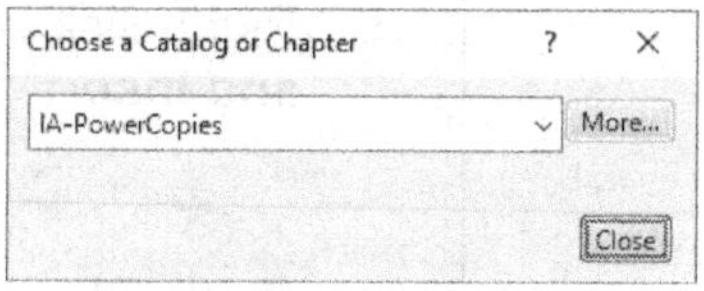

Figure 14–58

4. Click **More** and search for the **Engine_block-JY** catalog. Once the search completes, select the catalog in the search results. The Catalog Browser dialog box now displays the **Engine_block-JY** catalog, as shown in Figure 14–59.

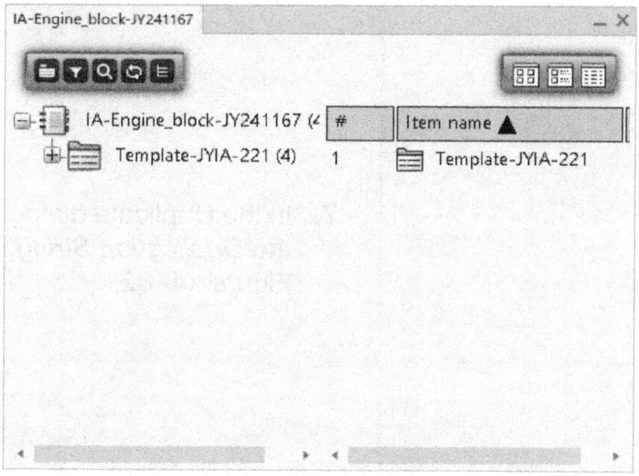

Figure 14–59

5. Expand the catalog's chapters and navigate to the Coordinates, as shown in Figure 14–60.

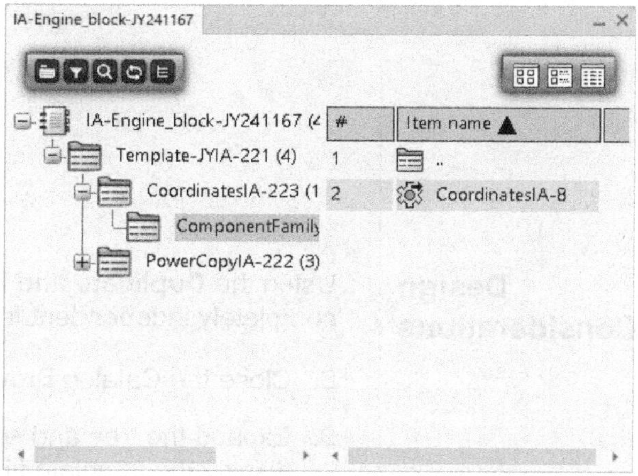

Figure 14–60

6. Right-click on **Coordinates** and select **Use Item>Duplicate and Insert**, as shown in Figure 14–61.

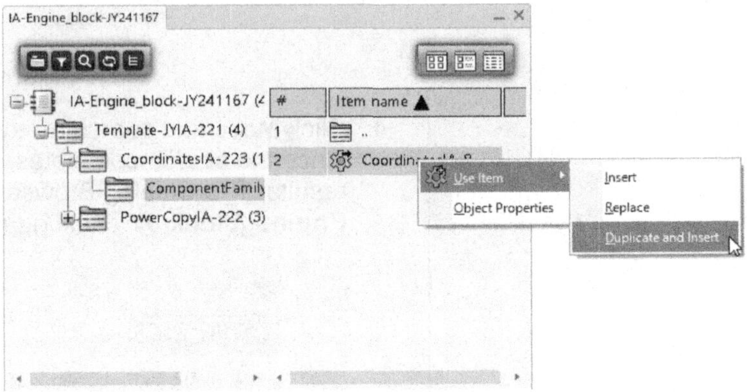

Figure 14–61

7. In the Duplicate dialog box that opens, enter **EBtemplate_** as the *Duplication String*, and click **OK**, as shown in Figure 14–62.

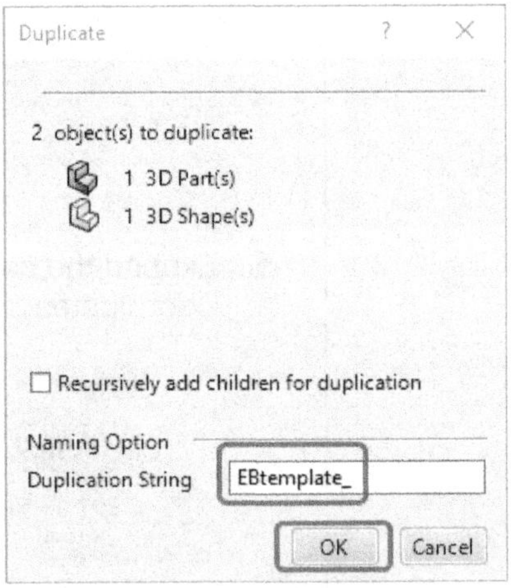

Figure 14–62

Design Considerations

Using the **Duplicate and Insert** option makes the new part completely independent from the catalog part.

8. Close the Catalog Browser dialog box.

9. Expand the tree and set the display to the Isometric View to display the template file, as shown in Figure 14–63.

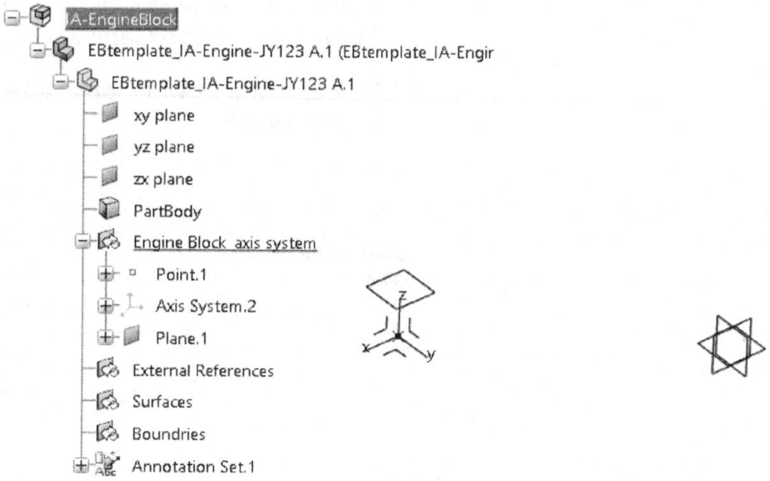

Figure 14–63

Task 3 - Insert the power copies from a catalog.

In this task, you will insert all of the required geometry using a catalog.

1. Double-click the 3D Shape level in the tree to activate, and define the PartBody to be the work object.
2. Click (Catalog Browser) to open the Catalog Browser. Note that it opens the **Engine_block-JY** catalog, since it was the catalog used in Task 2.
3. Navigate to the **2 inputs** sub-chapter in the **PowerCopy** chapter, as shown in Figure 14–64.

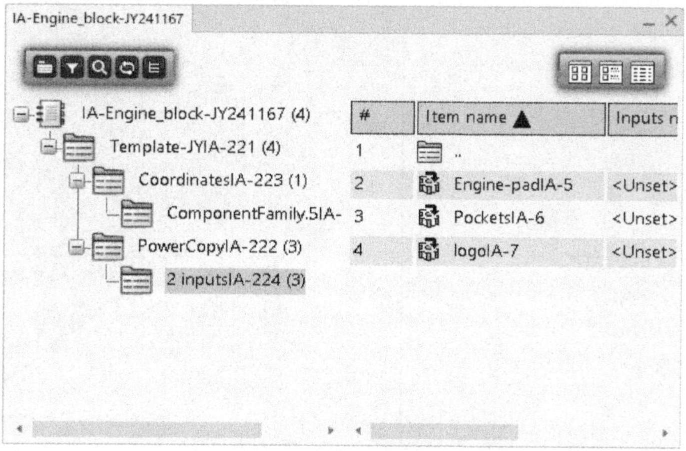

Figure 14–64

4. To instantiate the Power Copy, double-click on the **Engine-pad** in the Catalog Browser.

5. To locate the Power Copy, select the references shown in Figure 14–65.

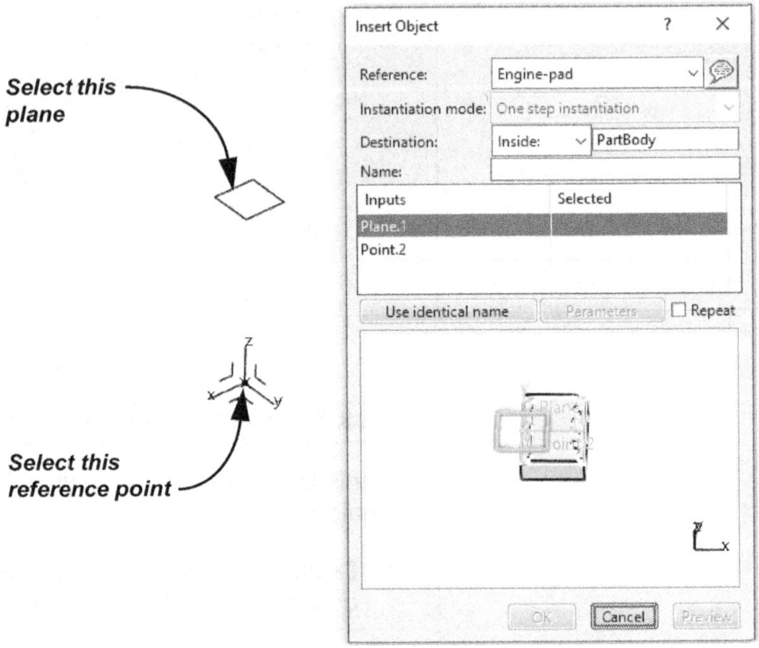

Figure 14–65

6. Click **Preview**. The preview displays as shown in Figure 14–66. Ensure that the placement of the Power Copy is correct.

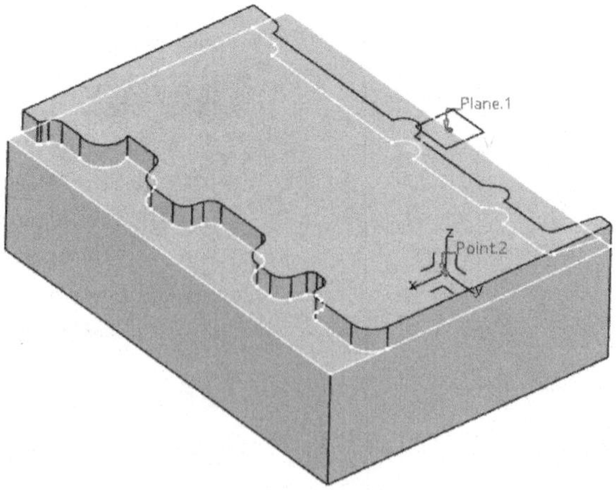

Figure 14–66

7. Click **OK**. Do not close the Catalog Browser.
8. Hide **Plane.1**, **Sketch.1**, and **Sketch.2**.
9. Define the **PartBody** to be the work object.
10. Double-click on the **Pockets** Power Copy in the Catalog Browser dialog box.
11. Note the warning message that displays on the screen, as shown in Figure 14–67, indicating that the Power Copy has three formulas that cannot be copied under the **PartBody**. These elements will be inserted in the **Relations** branch in the specification tree.

Warning : The destination PartBody can be chosen as destination of insertion of this template reference .
However these following elements will be inserted directly under another location:
Formula.1
Formula.2
Formula.3

Figure 14–67

12. To locate the Power Copy, select the references shown in Figure 14–68.

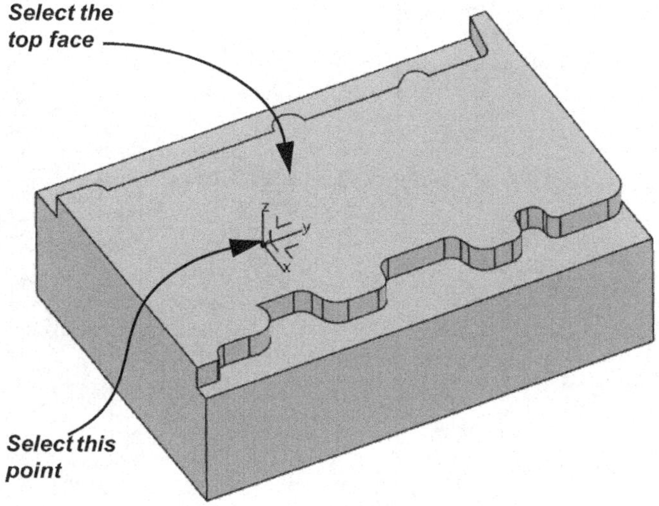

Figure 14–68

13. Click **OK**.
14. Close the Catalog Browser.

15. Hide **Point.1** and **Axis System**. The model displays as shown in Figure 14–69.

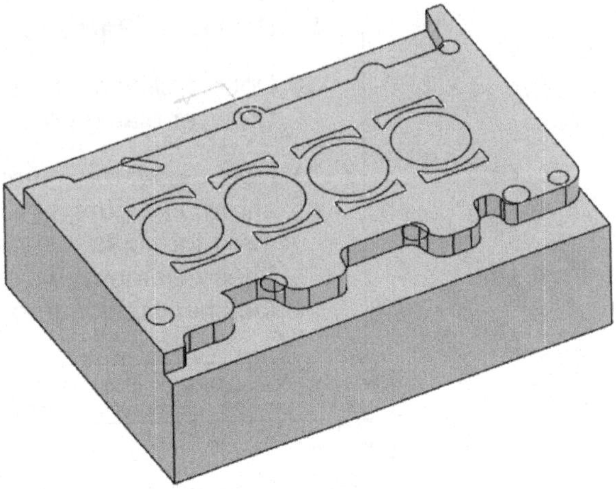

Figure 14–69

16. Using **Sketch.3**, create a Pocket with an **80mm** depth. The model displays as shown in Figure 14–70.

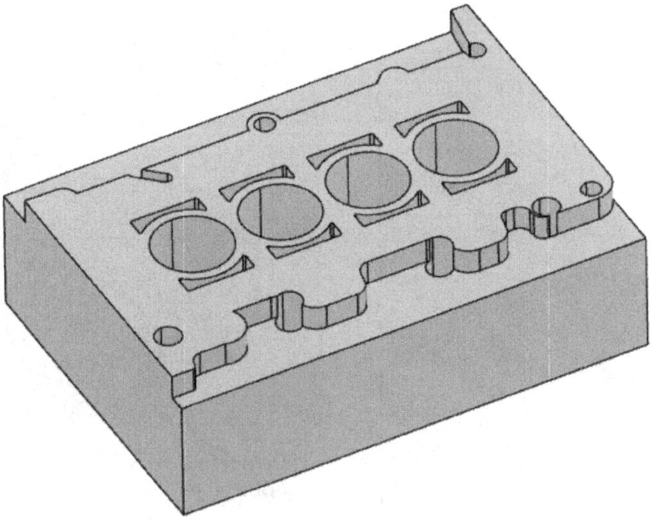

Figure 14–70

17. Save and close the model.

Practice 14d (Optional) Stator Band

Practice Objectives

- Create a Design Table.
- Add the Design Table to a catalog.

In this practice, you will create and add a design table to a new catalog. Begin this practice if time permits.

Task 1 - Open the part.

1. Search the database and open **<*YourInitials*>-StatorBand** model. The model displays as shown in Figure 14–71.

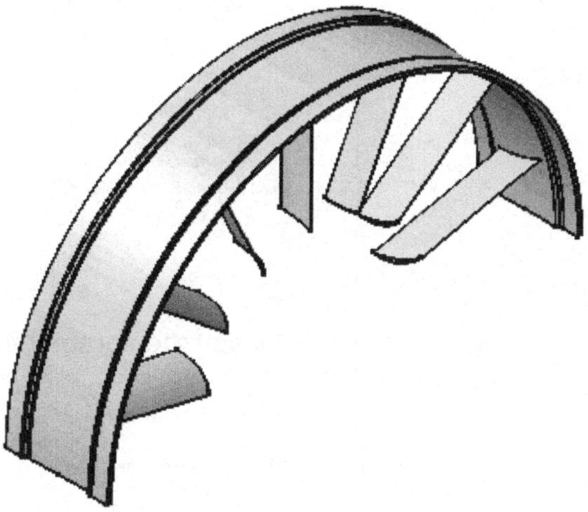

Figure 14–71

Task 2 - Create a design table.

1. Create a design table. Fill in the dialog box as shown in Figure 14–72.

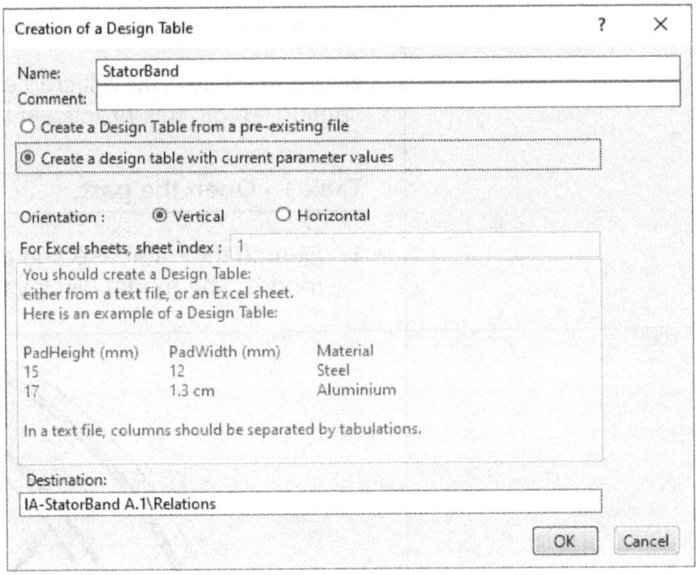

Figure 14–72

2. Insert the parameters shown in Figure 14–73.

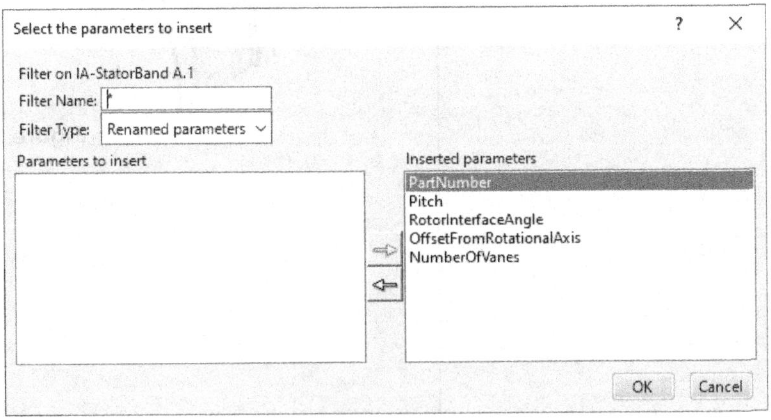

Figure 14–73

3. For the name of the Excel spreadsheet, enter **StatorBand**.

4. Click **Edit table**.

5. Add values to the Excel spreadsheet, as shown in Figure 14–74.

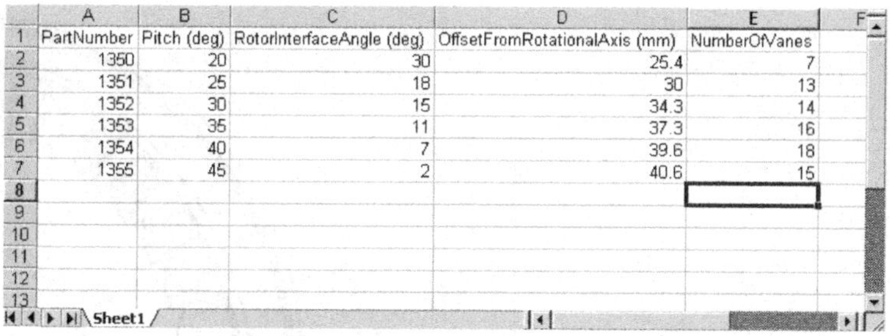

PartNumber	Pitch (deg)	RotorInterfaceAngle (deg)	OffsetFromRotationalAxis (mm)	NumberOfVanes
1350	20	30	25.4	7
1351	25	18	30	13
1352	30	15	34.3	14
1353	35	11	37.3	16
1354	40	7	39.6	18
1355	45	2	40.6	15

Figure 14–74

6. Save and close the spreadsheet. Close any messages that display in Knowledge dialog boxes. The design table dialog box updates as shown in Figure 14–75.

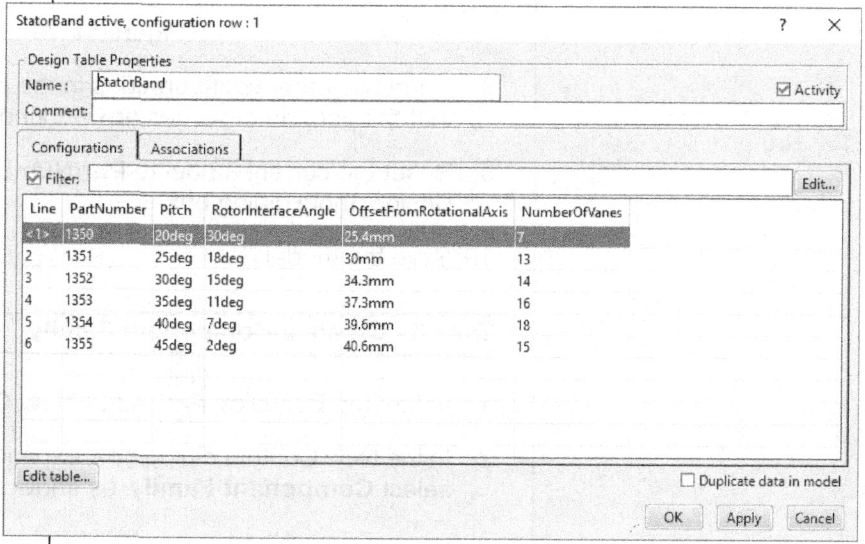

Line	PartNumber	Pitch	RotorInterfaceAngle	OffsetFromRotationalAxis	NumberOfVanes
<1>	1350	20deg	30deg	25.4mm	7
2	1351	25deg	18deg	30mm	13
3	1352	30deg	15deg	34.3mm	14
4	1353	35deg	11deg	37.3mm	16
5	1354	40deg	7deg	39.6mm	18
6	1355	45deg	2deg	40.6mm	15

Figure 14–75

7. Select the configuration with **PartNumber 1355** and click **Apply**. The model displays as shown in Figure 14–76.

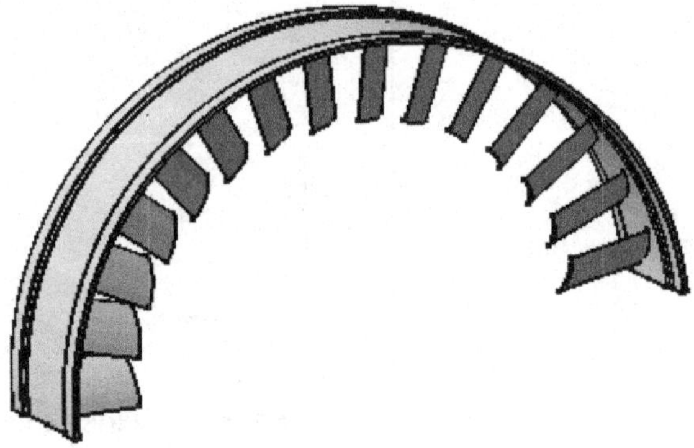

Figure 14–76

8. Open two other configurations in the part window to ensure that the parameter values are working correctly.
9. Reset the current model to **PartNumber 1350** and close the Design Table dialog box.
10. Save the model.

Task 3 - Create a Component Family

1. In the Top Bar, click (Add)>**New Content**.
2. In the New Content dialog box, expand the *Types* section and select **Component Family**, as shown in Figure 14–77.

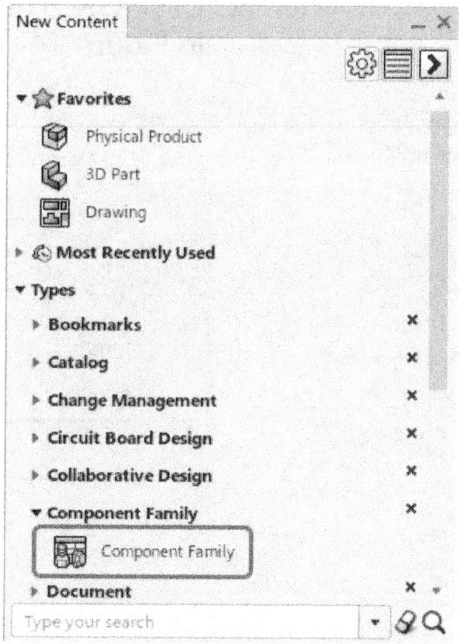

Figure 14–77

3. Enter **StatorBandFamily** as the *Title*.

4. In the *Component Family Model* tab, select **Design Family** option, as shown in Figure 14–78.

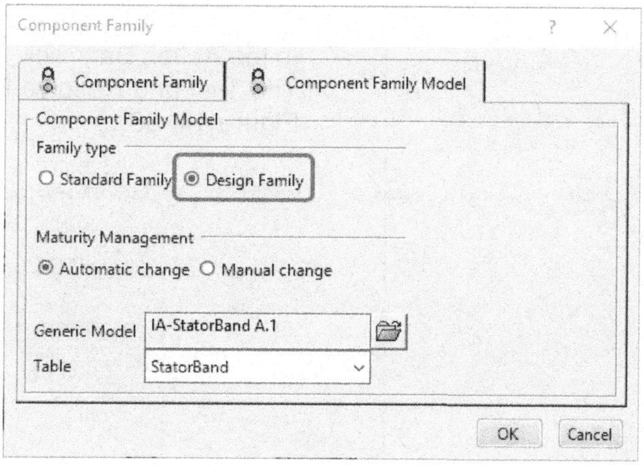

Figure 14–78

5. Click **OK**. The Component Family window opens, as shown in Figure 14–79.

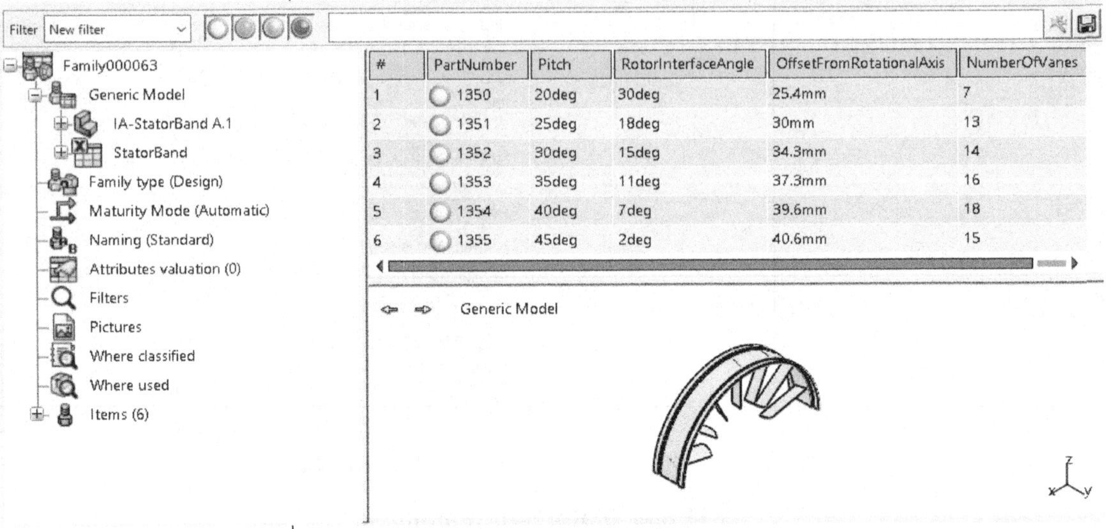

Figure 14–79

6. Save the Component Family.

7. In the Action Bar, click  (Test and Resolve Family Items). The Test and Resolve Family Items opens, as shown in Figure 14–80.

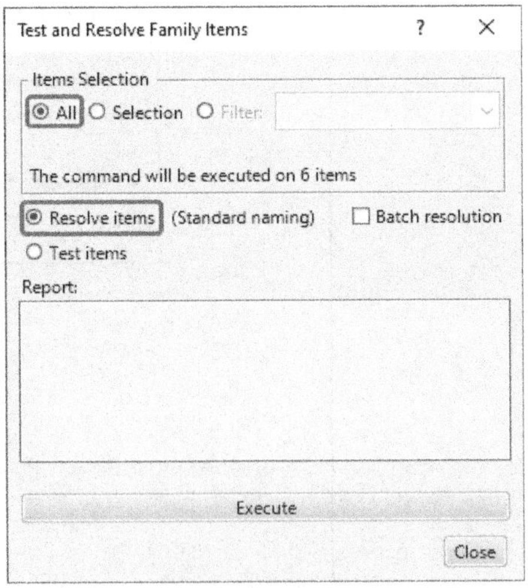

Figure 14–80

8. Select **All** and **Resolve** options, as shown in Figure 14–80, and click **Execute**. Each design table configuration is now generated as a separate part.

9. Close the Test and Resolve Family Items dialog box. The Component Family window displays, as shown in Figure 14–81.

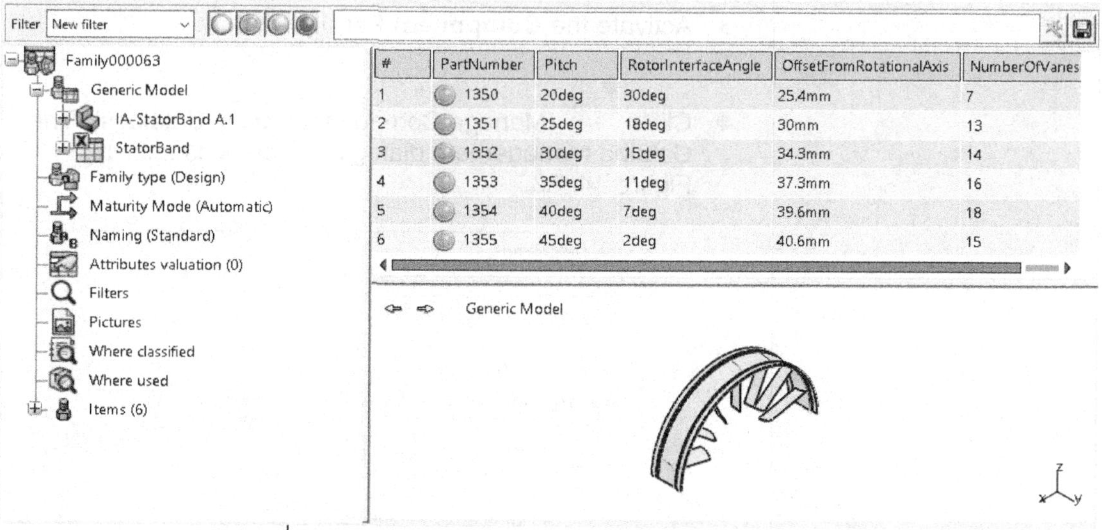

Figure 14–81

10. Use arrow icons in the bottom section of the window to preview the generated parts, as shown in Figure 14–82.

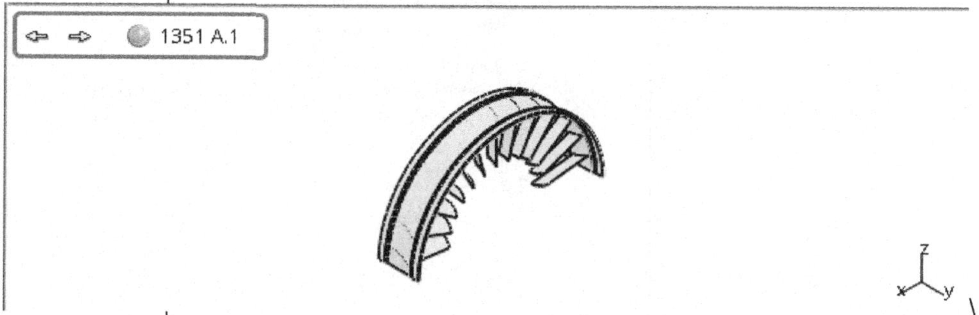

Figure 14–82

Task 4 - Add a component family to a catalog.

1. Import **TurbineComplete.3dxml** from the catalog directory. The catalog opens in a separate window.
2. In the catalog tree, right-click the **Turbine** chapter and insert a new sub-chapter titled **StatorBand**.
3. Activate the **Component Family** window.
4. Click  (Manage Component Family Catalogs). The Catalog management dialog box opens as shown in Figure 14–83.

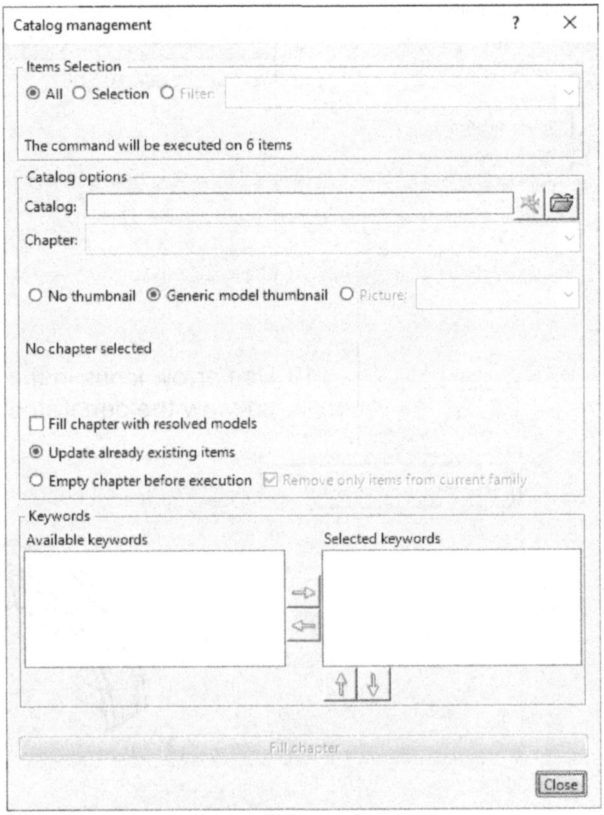

Figure 14–83

5. Click the  icon, activate the catalog window, and select the root object in the tree.
6. In the **Chapter** drop-down list, select the **StatorBand** chapter, as shown in Figure 14–84.

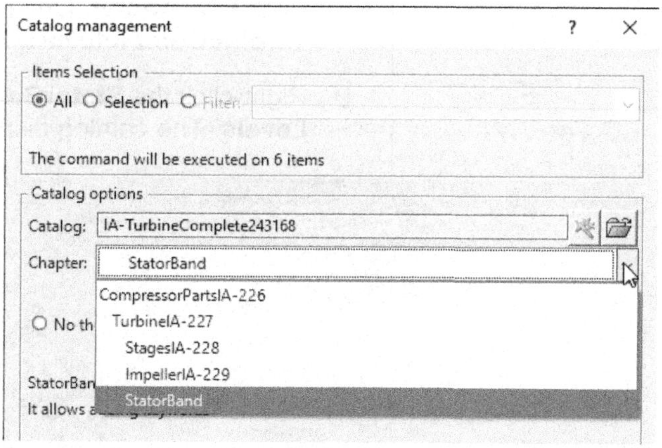

Figure 14–84

7. Add **PartNumber** and remove **Pitch**, **RotorInterfaceAngle**, **OffsetFromRotationalAxis**, and **NumberOfVanes** in the **Selected keywords** list. The Catalog management dialog box displays as shown in Figure 14–85.

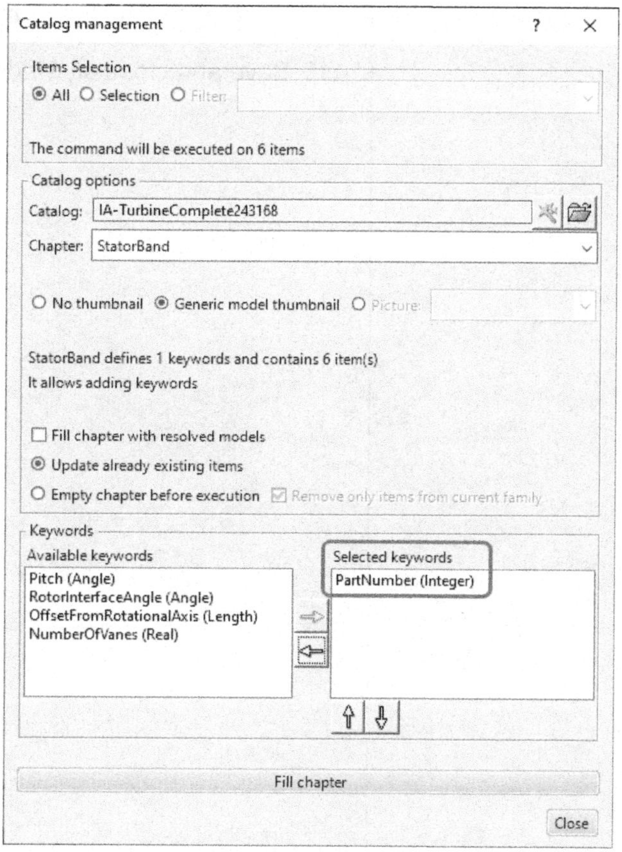

Figure 14–85

8. Click **Fill chapter**. Once the chapter is filled, activate the **TurbineComplete** catalog window.

9. Right-click the **StatorBand** chapter and select **Expand All Levels**. The catalog displays as shown in Figure 14–86.

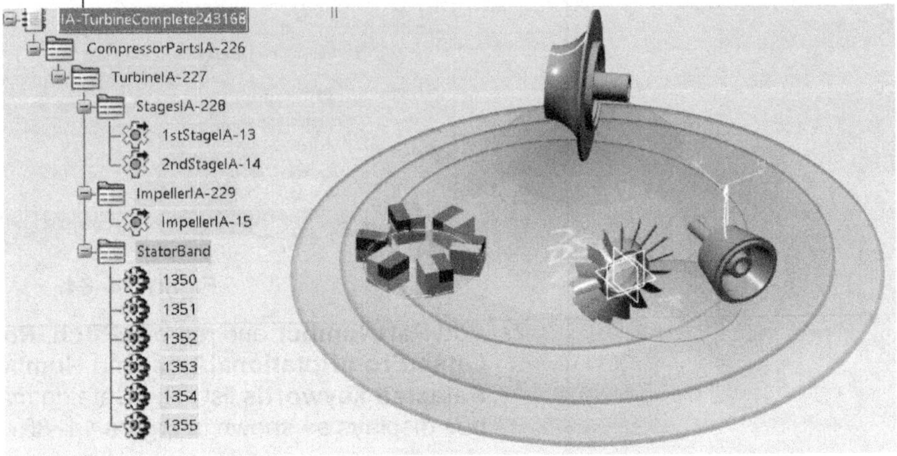

Figure 14–86

10. Save and close all windows.

Chapter Review Questions

1. Which of the following CATIA elements can be included in custom catalogs?
   a. Part Bodies
   b. Power Copies
   c. Sketches
   d. Parameters
   e. All of the above.
2. A chapter is a collection of families of parts in a catalog.
   a. True
   b. False
3. You should resolve each configuration of a part family in a catalog to verify that the design table does not contain any errors and that each configuration produces a usable model.
   a. True
   b. False

Answers: 2e, 4a, 5a

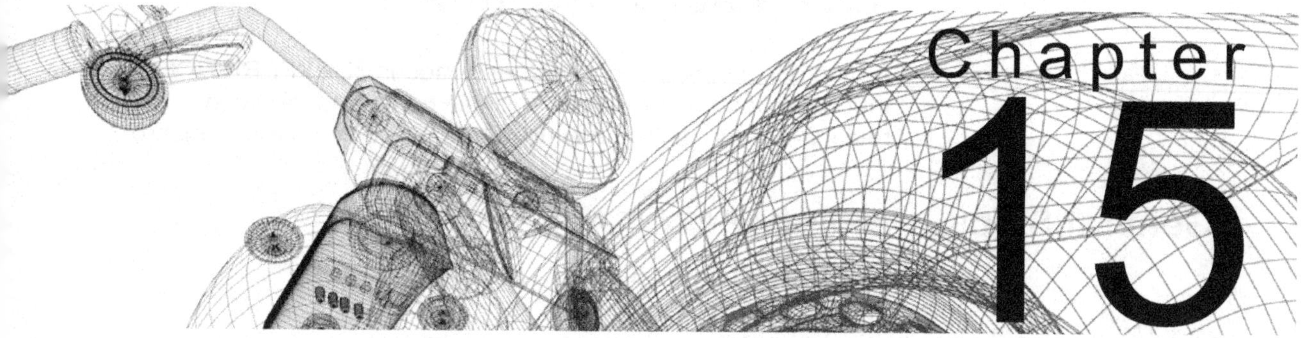

Chapter 15

Introduction to Automation

This chapter introduces tools in 3DEXPERIENCE that you can use to automate the performance of redundant tasks. These tools speed up modeling in 3DEXPERIENCE by recognizing groups of features and operations as a single object, such as a macro or a selection set. This chapter also introduces techniques to search for features in the specification tree.

Learning Objectives in This Chapter

- Learn how to use Macros to help automate your work.
- Understand how visual basic programs are structured.
- Explore the Visual Basic programming interface.

15.1 Macro Creation

A macro is a series of actions performed in 3DEXPERIENCE that have been recorded into a single command. You can replace a string of regularly used menu selections with a macro.

General Steps

Use the following general steps to create a macro:

1. Record the macro.
2. Run the macro.

Step 1 - Record the macro.

The information in a macro is captured using a Visual Basic script. This script can be stored in a macro library in the PLM database. Once the script is stored in a macro library, you can access the macro at any time.

To create a new macro, either select (Start Recording), or enter **c:Start Recording** in the Command Prompt. The Record macro dialog box opens as shown in Figure 15–1.

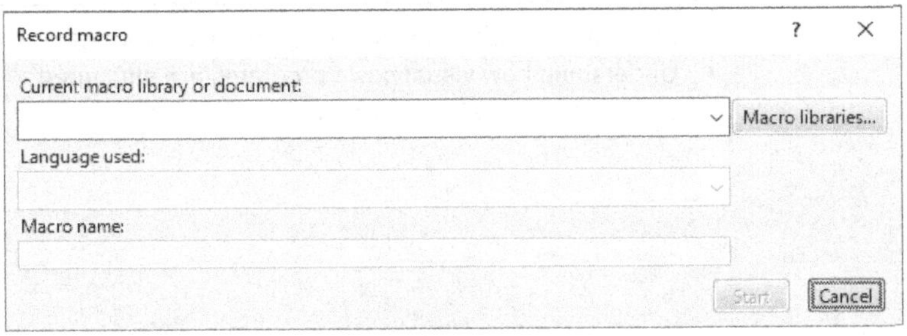

Figure 15–1

1. Click **Macro libraries** and either create a new macro library or select an existing macro library in which to store the recorded macro.
2. Select the programming language. If a **PLM Directory** is used as the macro library, the language choices are either **MS VBScript** or **CATScript**. If a **PLM VBA project** is used as the macro library, the **MS VBA** language must be used. If **PLM VSTA** project is used as the library, then the choices are either **C#** or **VB.Net**.
3. Enter an appropriate macro name. For example, a macro used to create hole features can be named **holes.catvbs**.
4. Click **Start**. Each menu selection and keyboard entry you make is now recorded into the macro. To stop recording the macro, click (Stop Recording).

Some menus cannot be recorded.

Step 2 - Run the macro

1. Select or press <Alt>+<F8>. The Macros dialog box opens as shown in Figure 15–2.

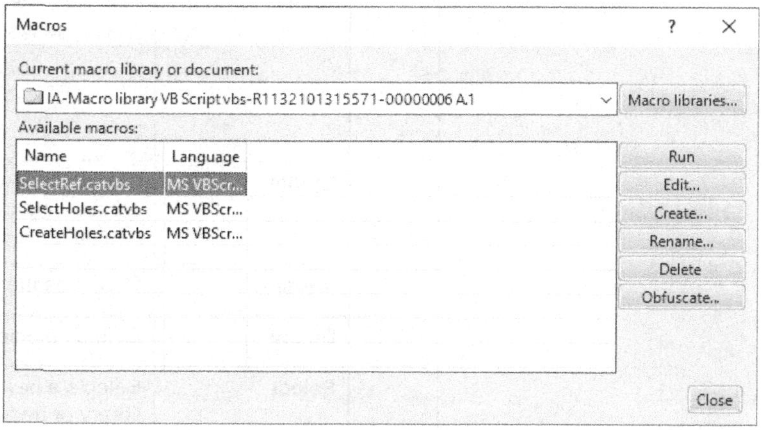

Figure 15–2

2. Select the macro to be run and click **Run**. The options for the Macros dialog box are described as follows:

Option	Description
Current macro library or document	Lists the locations in which the macros are stored. If a macro library is not listed in the drop-down list, browse to it by clicking **Macro libraries**.
Available macros	Lists macros stored under the current macro location. Actions can be performed on a macro by selecting it from the list and clicking one of the following buttons:
Run	Runs the selected macro.
Edit	Edits the selected macro. The Visual Basic script displays in a Macros Editor. 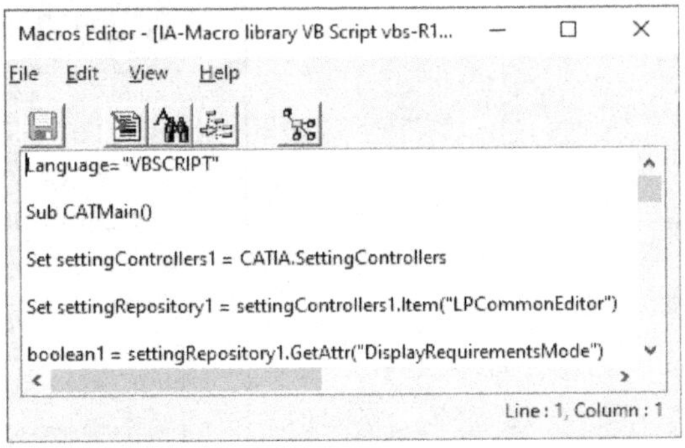
Create	Creates a new macro. When using this method to create a macro, the macro must be scripted manually.
Rename	Renames the selected macro script.
Delete	Deletes the selected macro.
Select	Selects a new macro to add to the current macro library or document.
Obfuscate	Encrypts the selected macro so that it cannot be edited. You are prompted to save the encrypted macro with a new name.

Macro Commands

An alternative way to access a macro is to add the macro to the Action Bar in the 3DEXPERIENCE interface, or specify a keyboard entry or sequence for the macro. To perform either of these tasks, open the Customize dialog box by right-clicking in the Top Bar and selecting **Display>Customize**. Select the *Commands* tab. In the Categories list, select **Macros** as shown in Figure 15–3.Select a macro from the list, and assign an icon, a User Alias, or Accelerator keys.

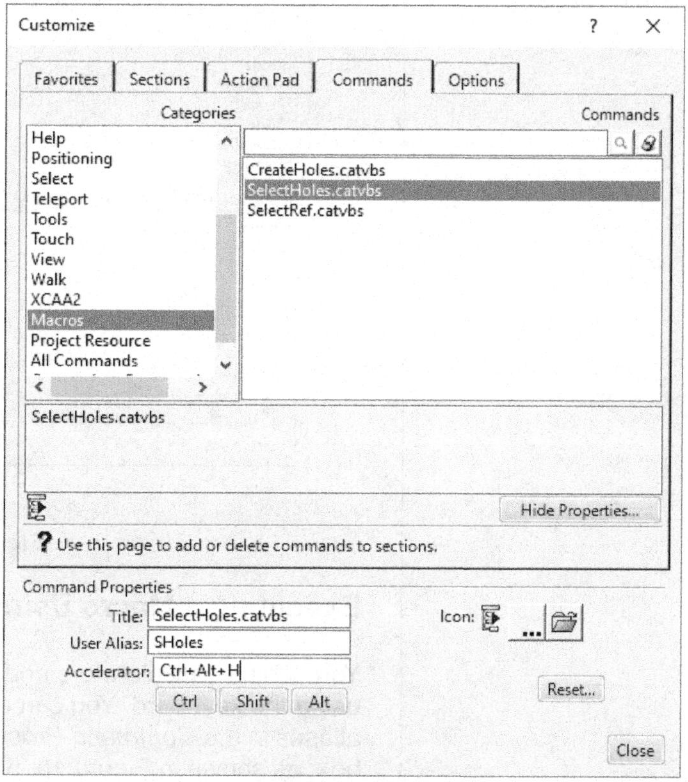

Figure 15–3

Executing a Macro from an Action Bar

Add a macro to the Action Bar by selecting an Action Bar's section in the *Sections* tab, and clicking **Add commands**, as shown in Figure 15–4.

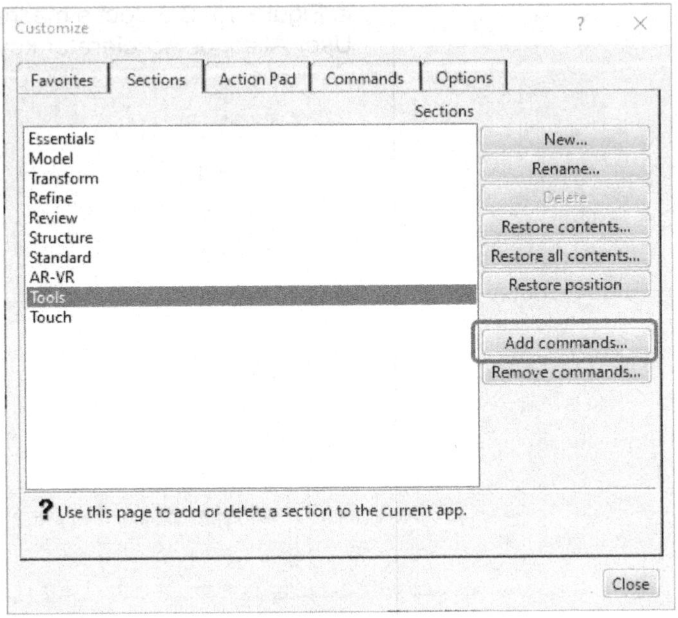

Figure 15–4

Executing a Macro Using the Keyboard

You can use accelerators and user aliases to execute a macro using the keyboard. You can create accelerators and user aliases in the *Command Properties* area in the Customize dialog box, as shown in Figure 15–5.

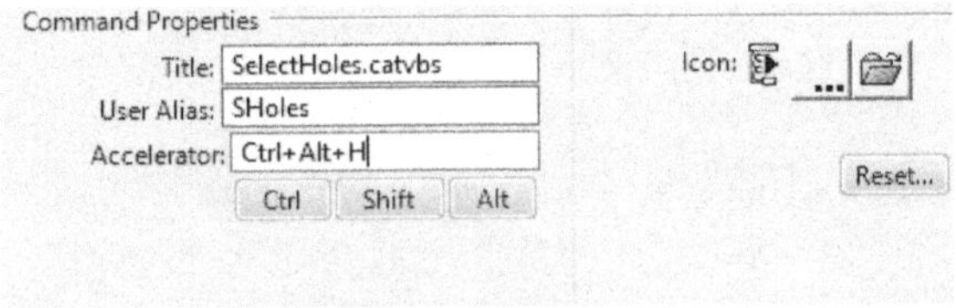

Figure 15–5

A user alias can be used to execute a macro by entering it into the command line. The alias must be preceded by **c:** as shown in Figure 15–6.

Figure 15–6

The accelerator is a keyboard shortcut used to execute the macro. Add the key sequence using the buttons below the *Accelerator* field. The key sequence specified must be unique and not used by any other command. You must press the keys simultaneously when executing an accelerator.

Macro Libraries

To make macros available through the PLM database, you must create a macro library. The library indicates a location on the PLMDatabase in which the macro Visual Basic scripts are stored.

How To: Create a New Macro Library

1. Select  or press <Alt>+<F8>.
2. In the Macros dialog box, click **Macro libraries**.
3. In the Macro libraries dialog box, in the Library type drop-down list, select the appropriate type (PLM Directories, or PLM VBA projects, or PLM VSTA projects), as shown in Figure 15–7.

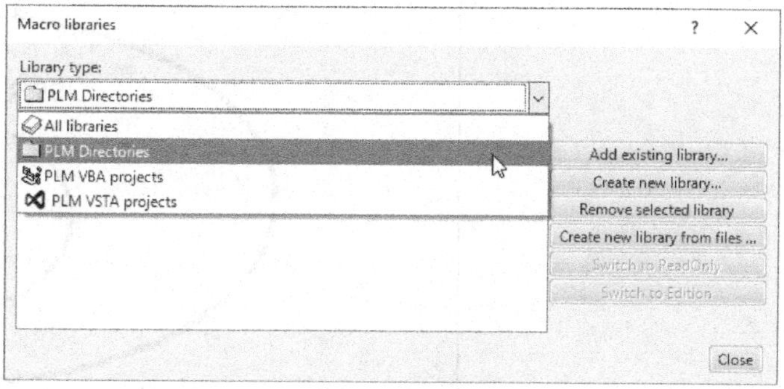

Figure 15–7

4. Click **Create new library** and enter the library title.

15.2 Visual Basic (VB) and VBA

Visual Basic is a programming language used for rapid application development. It was designed to be easy enough to develop so that non-programmers could use it.

VBA (Visual Basic for Applications) is a subset of Visual Basic. VBA is included in many applications, such as 3DEXPERIENCE, Word, and Excel. It provides a programming environment in which you can create, edit, and run your own programs.

VBScript (Visual Basic Script) is a subset of VBA. It can call and use 3DEXPERIENCE objects. While the program is running, it calls the required objects, the functions of the objects, and the properties of the objects.

How Does It Work?

All programs are built in two sections: the interface and the code, as shown in Figure 15–8. To ease the use of the program, interfaces are provided between the user and the program. In this way, you do not need to enter most of the commands to use the program. Instead, you activate the commands using a keyboard and mouse, or by entering the required input.

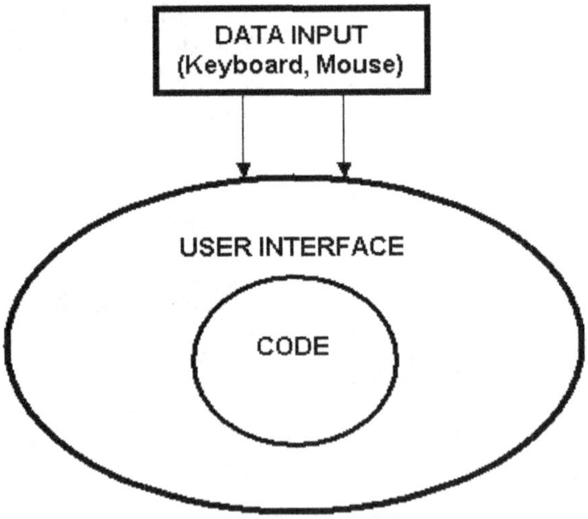

Figure 15–8

You do not see the code while using the program. The code is running in the background, and can interact with other applications, as shown in Figure 15–9.

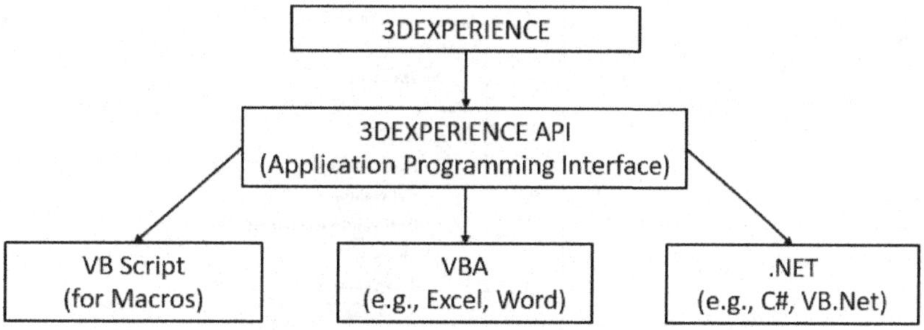

Figure 15–9

Object-Oriented Programming

Object-oriented programming uses objects. An object has its own properties and functions. An object's properties include color or name, and its function determines what it can do. Objects can have more than one function. Objects in 3DEXPERIENCE include line, point, sketch, and pad.

All of the 3DEXPERIENCE objects come from a single base object called **CATIA**. The CATIA object can be categorized in 2 main collections: **Editors** and **Windows**.

Editors

The **Editors** collection stores the data content that is used in the program. The content types for 3DEXPERIENCE can be:

- 3D Shape
- 3D Part
- Physical Product
- Drawing
- Etc.

The Object Model for 3DShape taken from the Dassault help documentation is shown in Figure 15–10.

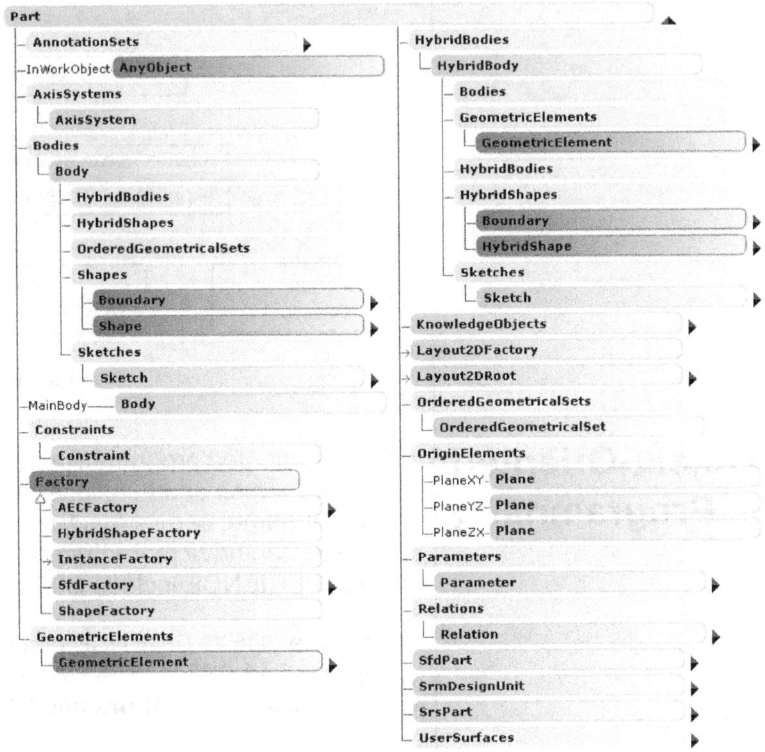

Figure 15–10

The relationship between the items in the 3D Shape object diagram and the specification tree is shown in Figure 15–11.

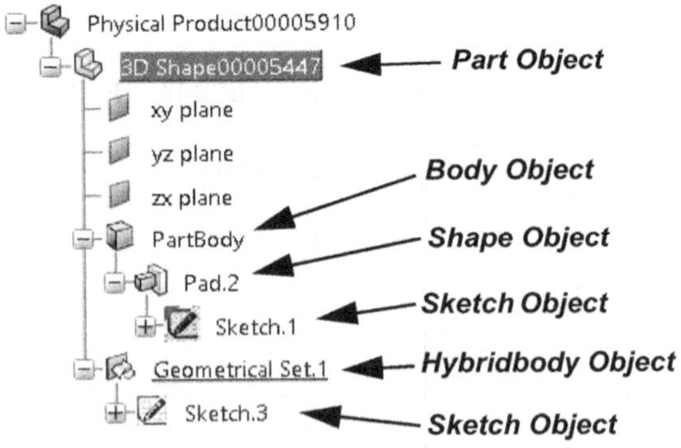

Figure 15–11

Windows

The Windows collection contains information about how the data is viewed.

Developing New Code

Instead of writing all of the code from scratch, you can use other methods to develop code. One way is to take an existing program and begin building from its code, adding and modifying for the required functionality. Another method is to record a macro and build from the code that the macro has generated.

Before recording a macro, make sure a macro library is already created. These can be:

- PLM Directory
- PLM VBA Project
- PLM VSTA Project

Recording macros is a fast way to start your program. It enables you to have a better understanding of how the structure is working. While recording macros, use the following tips:

- Check the *Preferences* when recording.
- Complete the feature before stopping recording.
- Investigate each macro after it is recorded.
- Record only the required actions.
- Do not use **Undo** when recording a macro.
- Do not switch between apps while recording a macro.

VBA Editor

The VBA Editor is the environment in which you can see and build your own programs. To open the VBA Editor, either select  or press <Alt>+<F11>.

The Microsoft Visual Basic window opens as shown in Figure 15–12.

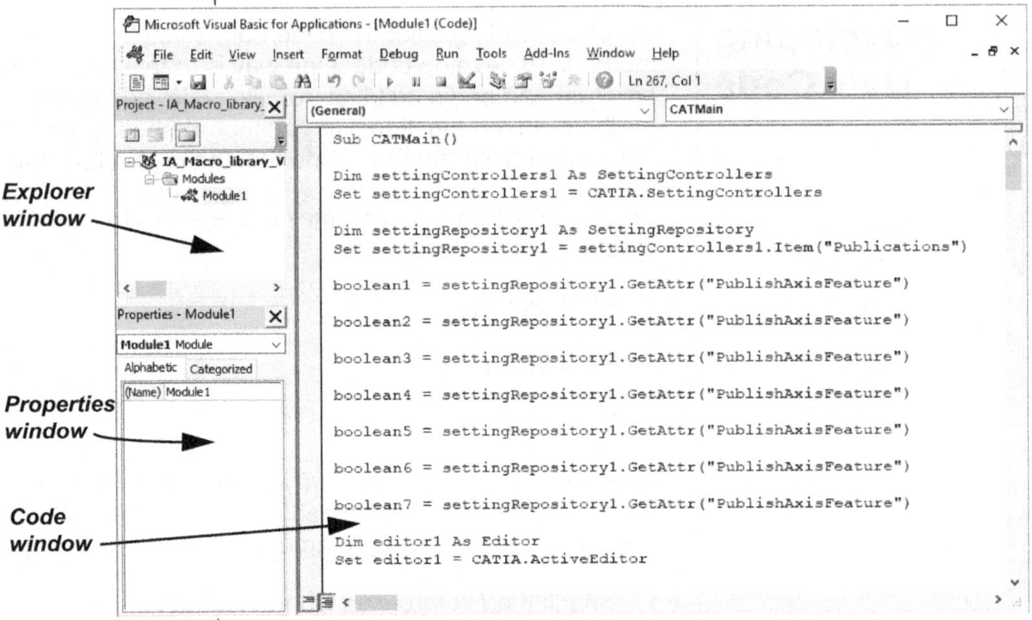

Figure 15–12

There are three main windows that are commonly used during program compilation. The windows are described as follows:

Windows	Description
Explorer window	Displays all of the stored projects.
Properties window	Displays the properties of an active object.
Code window	The window in which you write the code.

Object Browser

Object Browser is a search tool that indicates where the object is located and how it should be used. To open the Object Browser window, select **View>Object Browser**, or click (Object Browser) in the Standard toolbar. Figure 15–13 shows a keyword search in the Object Browser for **pad**. In the *Member* area, find the function that makes the most sense (e.g., **AddNewPad**).

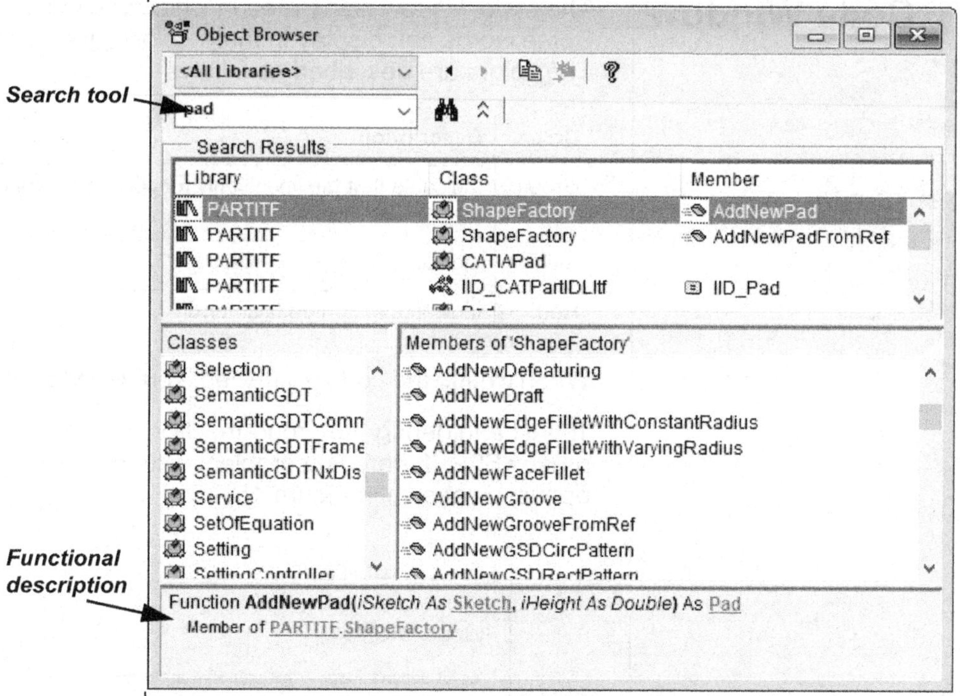

Figure 15–13

The *Class* area indicates which function belongs to which object. The bottom of the window describes how to use the function. This part is the Syntax portion of the object browser. In Figure 15–13, this part indicates that, when calling the **AddNewPad** function, you need to use the ShapeFactory object, and you have to provide two parameters: one sketch object and one number (double precision value), which is the height of the Pad.

Underlined words (as shown in Figure 15–14) are the keywords that you can select to display more information about that object.

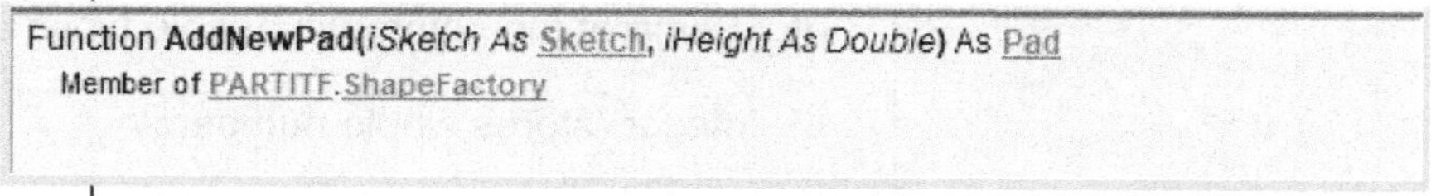

Figure 15–14

Code Window

The code window is the area in which you write the program. Some words can display in three colors: green, blue, and red. The colors are described as follows:

Color	Description
Green	Indicates that the line is only for comment. The comments begin with an apostrophe.
Blue	Indicates reserved words.
Red	Indicates that there is an error.

When writing the code is finished, you need to test your program.

To test and debug the program, click (Run Sub/UserForm) or press <F5>. If there is a problem with the code, an error box opens, as shown in Figure 15–15.

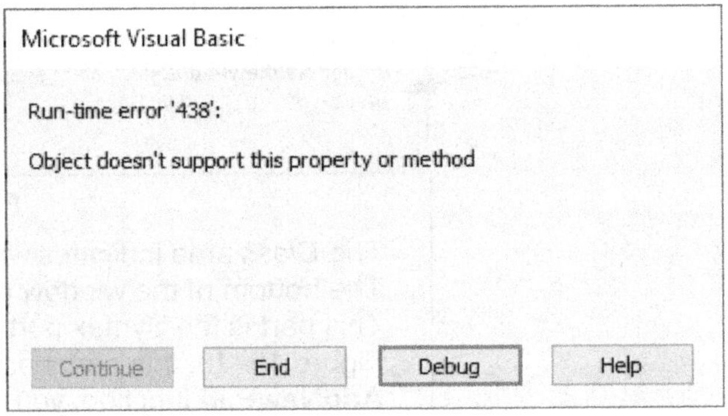

Figure 15–15

It is suggested that you run the program several times during the testing. This makes it easier to identify and solve the problems.

Variables

Variables are the data that is used by the program. Different variable types hold different kinds of data, such as numbers, text, etc. Some of the common variable types are:

- Integer (stores whole numbers)
- Double (stores decimal numbers)
- String (stores text)
- Boolean (its value can be either **True** or **False**)
- Date

Every variable must be named and the data type for the variable also must be specified. To declare a variable, use the following statement:

Dim *VariableName* as **VariableType**

Every program starts with **Sub<*Subroutine_Name*>** command, and ends with **End Sub** command. You write the program between these lines.

Sub *MyNewSub*

Type the code here....

.....

End Sub

A simple example of subroutine is shown in Figure 15–16.

```
Sub Compute_Total

Dim Total As Integer

Total = 5 + 5

MsgBox Total

End Sub
```

Figure 15–16

The second line declares the variable name (**Total**) and the type (**Integer**). The third line adds 5 to 5 and stores the result in the variable (**Total**).

The fourth line displays the result which is stored in the **Total** variable.

Practice 15a Selection Automation

Practice Objectives

- Record and run a macro.
- Search the model for features.

In this practice, you will use a variety of tools to automate feature selections in 3DEXPERIENCE.

Task 1 - Open the part.

1. Import and open **B12255Bushing.3dxml**. When importing, type your initials followed by the dash symbol into the *Duplication string* field. The model displays as shown in Figure 15–17.

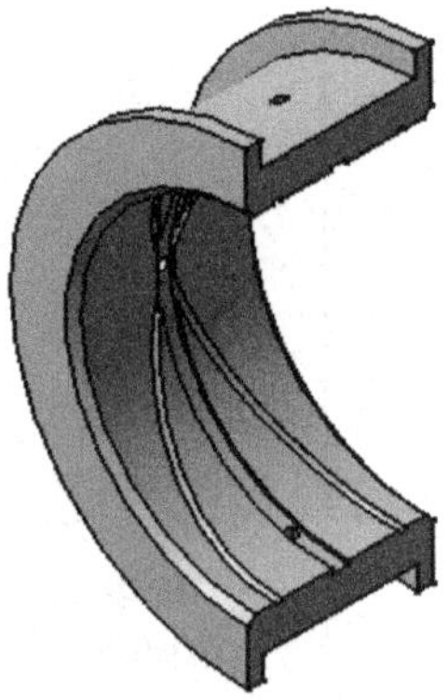

Figure 15–17

Task 2 - Search for features in the model.

In this task, you will perform a search for features by name.

1. Press <Ctrl>+<F>. The Find dialog box opens.

2. In the *Name* field, enter ***plane*** and click (Find). The system highlights all of the plane features in the specification tree.

3. Before you can operate on the located features, you must select them. Click **Select**.

4. In the specification tree, right-click on the zx plane and show the selected features. All planes in the model display, as shown in Figure 15–18.

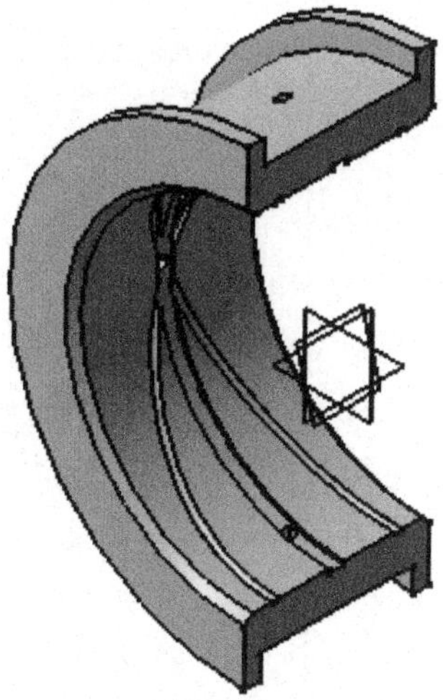

Figure 15–18

5. Click **Select** and hide the plane features.

Task 3 - Perform an advanced search.

In this task, you will perform advanced searches for multiple feature types. The search is saved as a favorite to be reused later.

1. In the Find dialog box, select the *Advanced* tab.
2. In the App drop-down list, select **Part Design**.
3. In the Type drop-down list, select **Plane** and click **Or**. The query is added to the *Composed query* field, as shown in Figure 15–19.

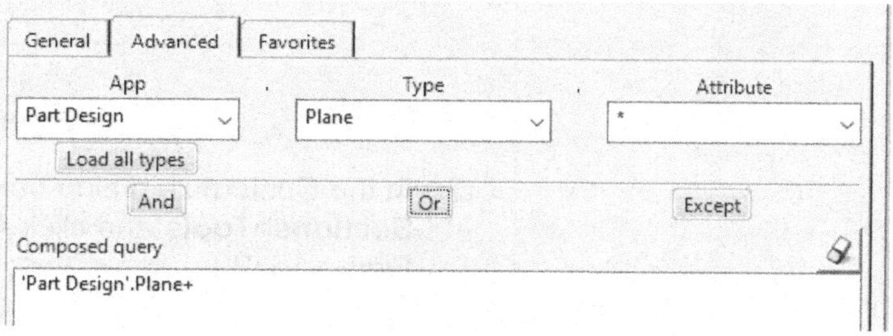

Figure 15–19

4. In the Type drop-down list, select **Point** and click **Or**.

5. Similarly, add queries for **Line** and **Curve** types. The Find dialog box opens as shown in Figure 15–20.

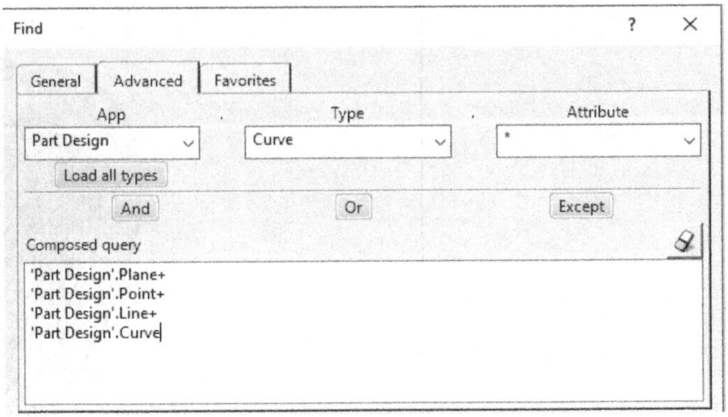

Figure 15–20

6. Click (Find). All of the reference elements in the model are highlighted.

7. Click (Add to favorites) and name the query as **RefElements**.

8. Close the Find dialog box.

Task 4 - Add macro commands to Action Bar.

1. Right-click in the Top Bar and select **Display>Customize**, as shown in Figure 15–21.

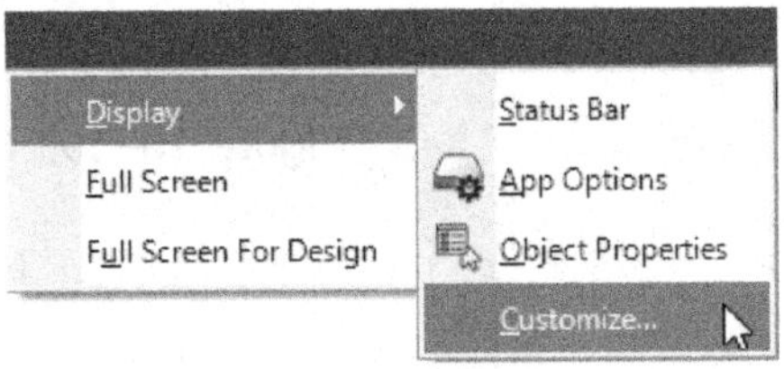

Figure 15–21

2. In the Customize dialog box that opens, select **Sections>Tools** and click **Add commands**, as shown in Figure 15–22.

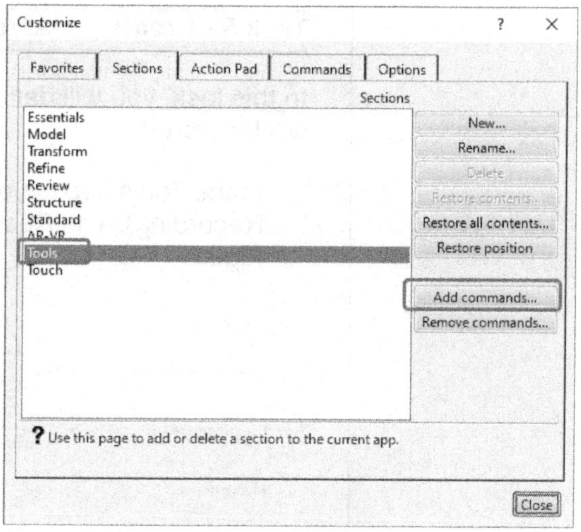

Figure 15–22

3. Add the following commands: **Macros**, **Start Recording**, and **Stop Recording**, as shown in Figure 15–23.

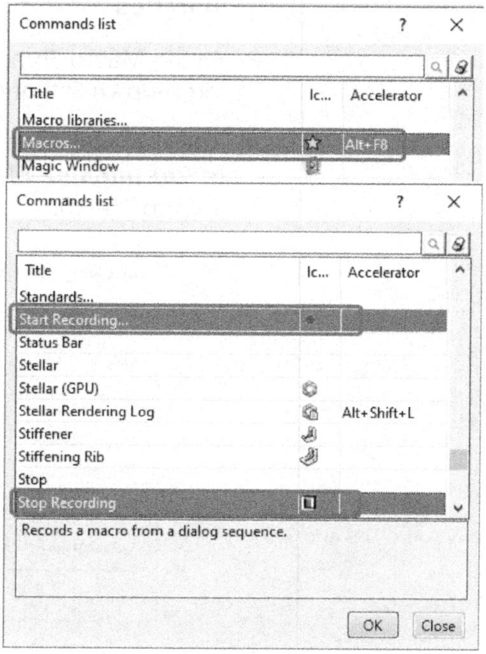

Figure 15–23

4. Close the Customize dialog box.

Task 5 - Create a macro library directory.

In this task, you will define a PLM directory in which the macros will be stored.

1. In the Tools section of the Action Bar, select (Start Recording). The Record macro dialog box opens as shown in Figure 15–24.

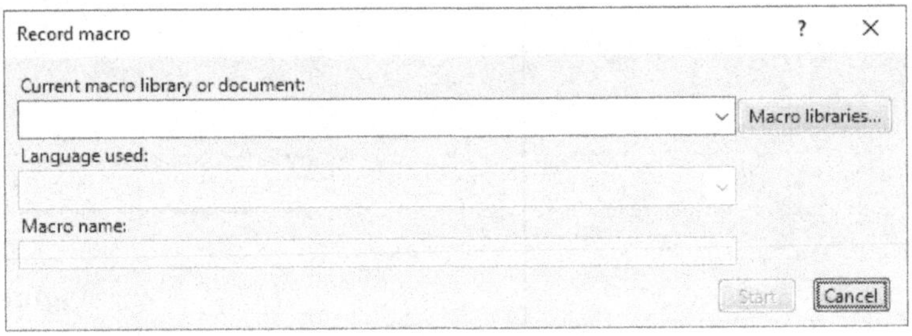

Figure 15–24

2. To create a new location to store macros, click **Macro libraries**.

3. In the Macro libraries dialog box, expand the Library type drop-down list, and select **Directories**.

4. Click **Create new library** and enter the title ***<YourInitials>-Macro library VB Script***, as shown in Figure 15–25.

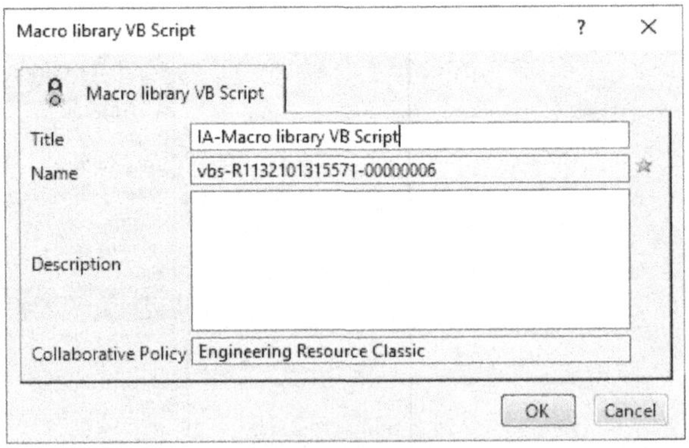

Figure 15–25

5. Click **OK** and **Close**. Keep the Record macro dialog box open.

Task 6 - Record a macro.

In this task, you will create a macro that will search for all of the reference elements in the model using the favorite search that you just created.

1. In the Record macro dialog box, configure the macro with the following options:
    - *Language Used:* Accept the default option
    - *Macro name:* **SelectRef.catvbs**
2. Click **Start**. The Record macro dialog box closes, and the  (Stop macro recording) icon displays in the Action Bar, which can be used to end the macro recording session. All of the icon selections that you make will be recorded in the macro.
3. Press <Ctrl>+<F>.
4. Select the *Favorites* tab.
5. Highlight **RefElements** and click .
6. Click  (Stop macro recording) to end macro recording. The macro is automatically saved to the macro library you specified in Task 5.
7. Close the Find dialog box.

Task 7 - Add the macro to Action Bar.

In this task, you will create an Action Bar button to run the macro you just created.

1. Right-click in the Top Bar and select **Display>Customize**. The Customize dialog box opens.
2. Select the *Commands* tab.

3. In the *Categories* column, select the **Macros** entry. The macro you just created displays in the *Commands* field, as shown in Figure 15–26.

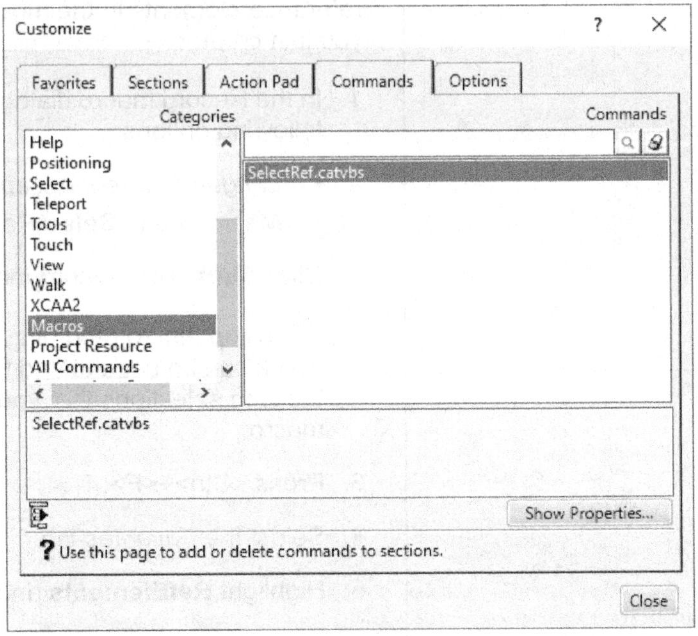

Figure 15–26

4. With **SelectRef.catvbs** selected, click **Show Properties**.

5. Click ... to change the icon for the macro.

You might need to advance a few pages of icons before finding the one shown. If you cannot find it, use any icon.

6. Click ▶ as the new icon and close the Icons Browser.

7. Switch to the *Sections* tab. Highlight the **Tools** entry in the list and click **Add commands**, as shown in Figure 15–27.

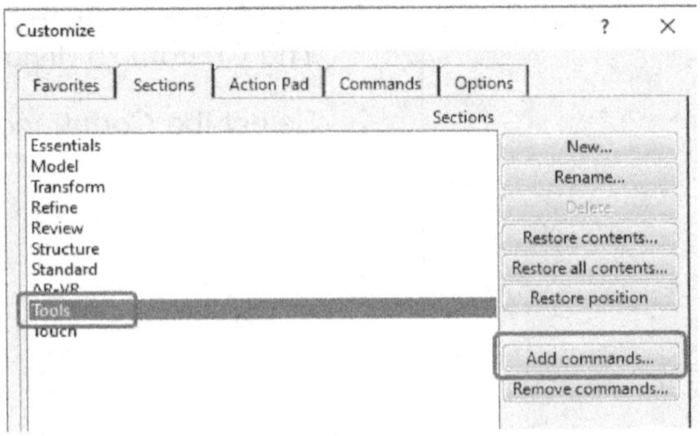

Figure 15–27

8. In the *Commands* list, select **SelectRef.catvbs** and click **OK**, as shown in Figure 15–28.

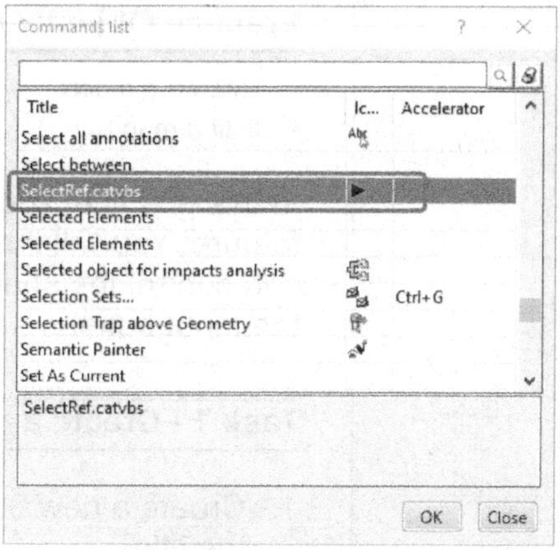

Figure 15–28

9. Close the Customize dialog box.

10. Test the macro by clicking  in the Action Bar to ensure that it selects the required elements. This macro can now be used as a selection tool to show and hide all reference elements in your models.

11. Save the model and close the window.

Practice 15b Editing a Macro

Practice Objectives

- Record a macro.
- Edit a macro.

In this practice, you will record a macro that will create a Pad feature. You will then modify the macro to add input boxes. You can control the shape of the Pad feature by entering values in the input boxes.

Task 1 - Create a new part.

1. Create a new 3D Part. Enter ***<YourInitials>*-PadMacro** as the title.

Task 2 - Create a new VB project.

In this task, you will create a new VB project. When you save the macro in a project, you can open it in the VB Editor.

1. In the Tools section of the Action Bar, select (Macros).
2. To create a new library to store macros, click **Macro libraries**.
3. In the Library Type drop-down list, select **PLM VBA projects**, as shown in Figure 15–29.

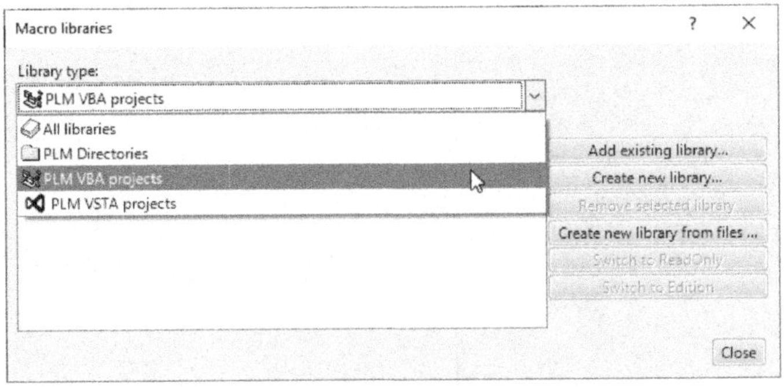

Figure 15–29

4. Click **Create new library** and enter the title **<*YourInitials*>-Macro library VB Script**, as shown in Figure 15–30.

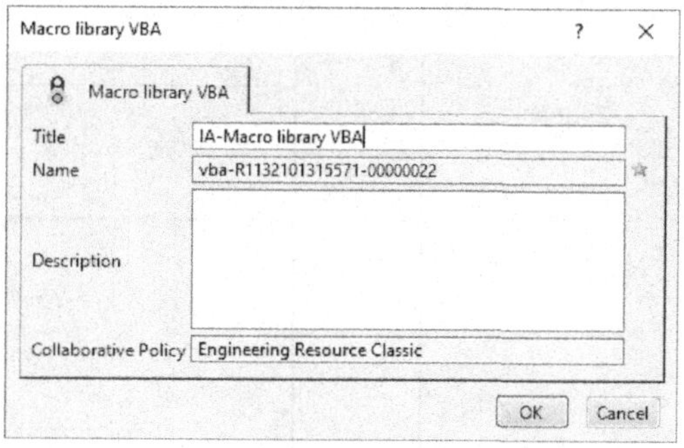

Figure 15–30

5. Click **OK**.

6. Click **Close** twice.

Task 3 - Record a macro.

In this task, you will record a Pad creation.

1. Select (Start Recording). The Record macro dialog box opens as shown in Figure 15–31.

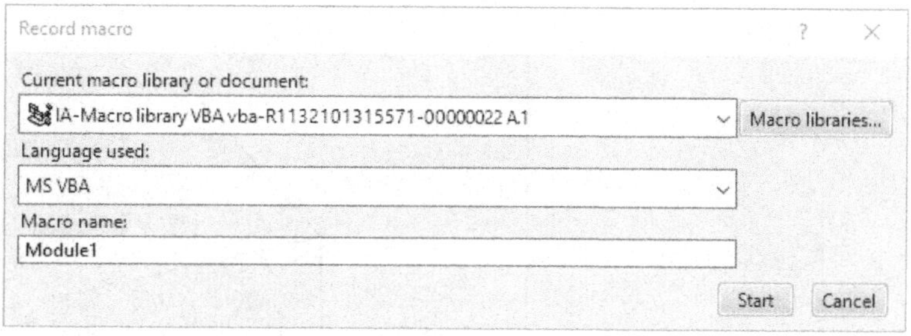

Figure 15–31

2. Click **Start**. The macro recording starts. Do not make any unnecessary selections during the creation of the macro.

3. Create a sketch on the xy plane and draw a rectangular profile with two dimensional constraints, as shown in Figure 15–32. The dimensional values do not need to match the figure. Do not modify the values.

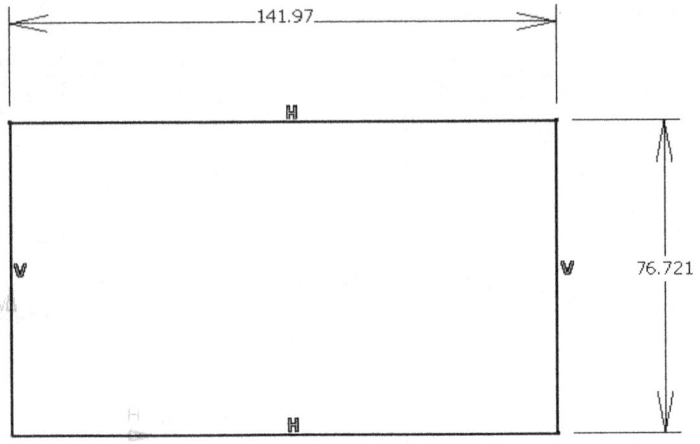

Figure 15–32

4. Exit from the Sketcher app.

5. Create a Pad feature that has a **20mm** height with the rectangular profile, as shown in Figure 15–33.

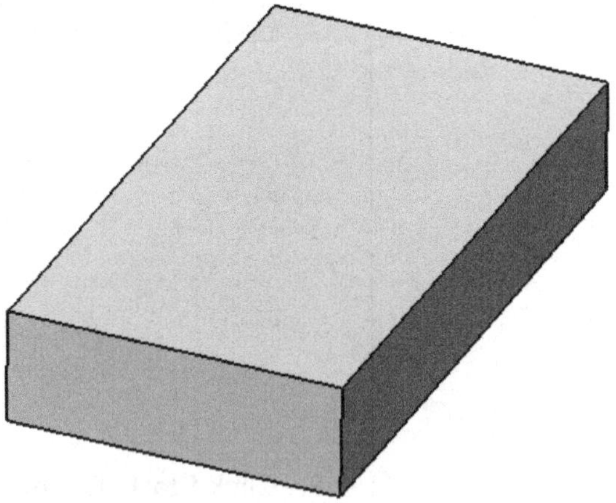

Figure 15–33

6. To end macro recording, click ■. The macro is automatically saved to the VB project you created in Task 2.

Task 4 - Edit a macro.

In this task, you will modify a previously created macro. If the recorded macro is run as is, it will create the same Pad. To create a Pad with different dimensions, you will modify the macro accordingly.

1. Select (Macros). The Macros dialog box opens as shown in Figure 15–34.

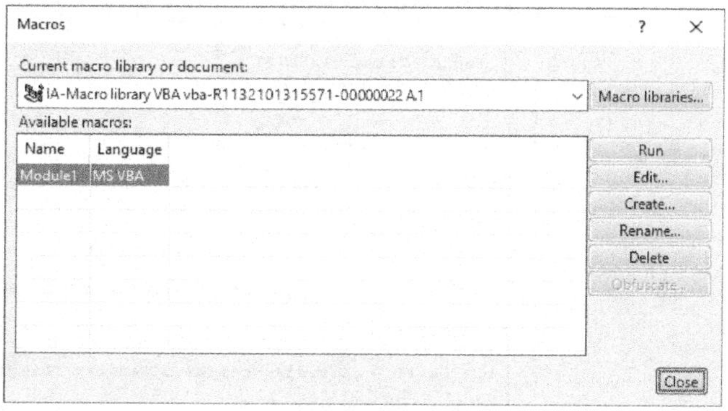

Figure 15–34

2. Click **Edit**. The Visual Basic Editor opens as shown in Figure 15–35.

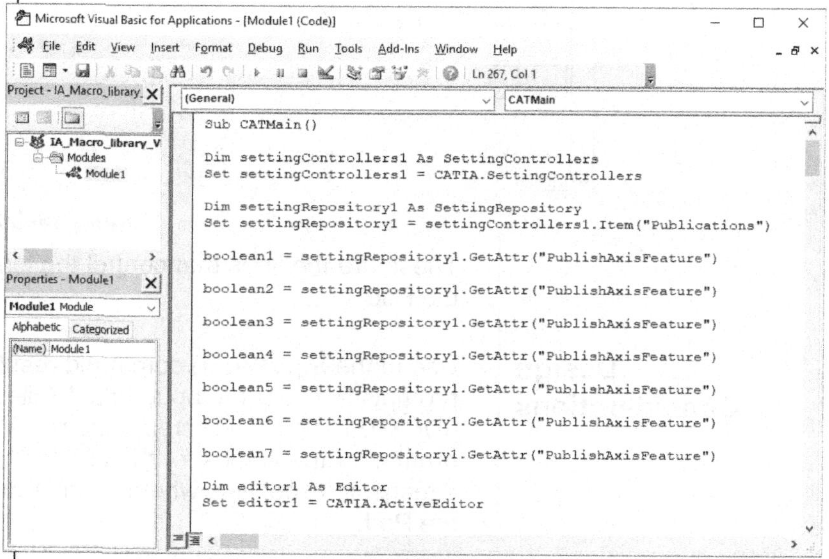

Figure 15–35

3. Scroll-down to the end of the code in the Code window and find the lines shown in Figure 15–36.

```
Set length1 = constraint5.Dimension

length1.Value = 141.97

Dim reference11 As Reference
Set reference11 = part1.CreateReferenceFromObject(line2D4)

Dim constraint6 As Constraint
Set constraint6 = constraints1.AddMonoEltCst(catCstTypeLength, reference11)

constraint6.Mode = catCstModeDrivingDimension

Dim length2 As Length
Set length2 = constraint6.Dimension

length2.Value = 76.721

sketch1.CloseEdition

part1.InWorkObject = body1

boolean9 = settingRepository1.GetAttr("PublishAxisFeature")

Dim settingRepository2 As SettingRepository
Set settingRepository2 = settingControllers1.Item("LPCommonEditor")

boolean10 = settingRepository2.GetAttr("LowLightMode")

part1.Update

boolean11 = settingRepository2.GetAttr("DisplayRequirementsMode")

boolean12 = settingRepository1.GetAttr("PublishAxisFeature")

boolean13 = settingRepository1.GetAttr("PublishAxisFeature")

boolean14 = settingRepository1.GetAttr("PublishAxisFeature")

part1.InWorkObject = body1

Dim shapeFactory1 As ShapeFactory
Set shapeFactory1 = part1.ShapeFactory

Dim pad1 As Pad
Set pad1 = shapeFactory1.AddNewPad(sketch1, 20#)

boolean15 = settingRepository1.GetAttr("PublishAxisFeature")

boolean16 = settingRepository1.GetAttr("PublishAxisFeature")
```

Figure 15–36

These are the lines that control the length, width, and height of the Pad.

Design Considerations

Use of the **InputBox()** command results in a dialog box that prompts the user for input data. While the macro is running, 3DEXPERIENCE will create the rectangular shape and then prompt for the values for the profile. The creation order of the dimensions specifies whether line 1 drives the width or length of the Pad.

4. Modify the first line as shown in Figure 15–37.

```
length1.Value = InputBox("Enter the Width")
```

Figure 15–37

5. Modify the second line as shown in Figure 15–38.

```
length2.Value = InputBox("Enter the Length")
```

Figure 15–38

6. Add the two lines shown in Figure 15–40 above the third line.

Design Considerations

The Pad feature is created using the **sketch1** and **20#** values. To control the height of the Pad, you must declare a new variable using the double type. The double variable type can store decimal numbers. The height variable is equal to the entered value in the input box. If you replace the **20** value with the height variable, you can control the height of the Pad by entering a value during the creation of the Pad feature.

Add these two lines

```
Dim height As Double
height = InputBox("Enter the Height")

Dim pad1 As Pad
Set pad1 = shapeFactory1.AddNewPad(sketch1, height)
```

Delete 20#, then type height here

Figure 15–39

Task 5 - Run the macro.

In this task, you will run the macro that you just modified.

1. Switch to the model window.

2. Delete the Pad and the Sketch from the model.

3. Select  (Macros) and run the macro. The CATIA dialog box opens as shown in Figure 15–40.

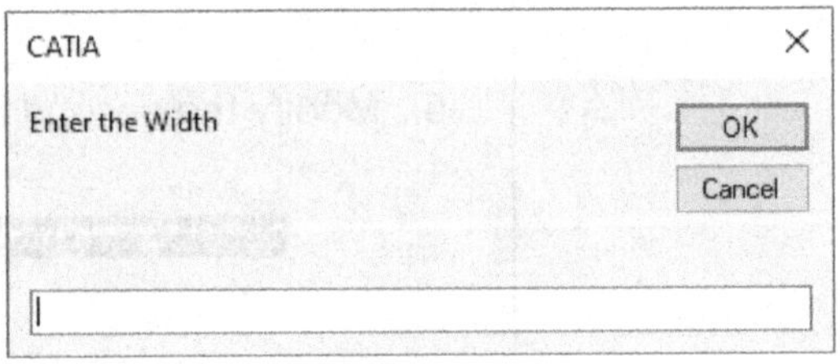

Figure 15–40

4. Enter **50** in the dialog box. The CATIA dialog box opens as shown in Figure 15–41.

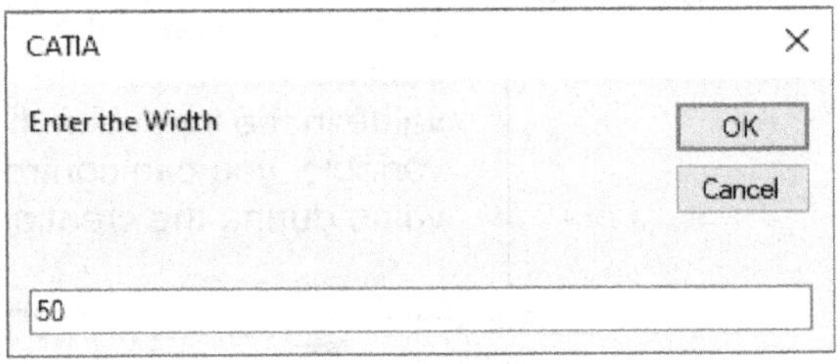

Figure 15–41

5. Click **OK**.

6. Enter **100** for the **Length** in the next dialog box. The CATIA dialog box opens as shown in Figure 15–42.

Figure 15–42

7. Click **OK**.

8. Enter **150** in the dialog box for the **Height** and click **OK**. The model displays as shown in Figure 15–43.

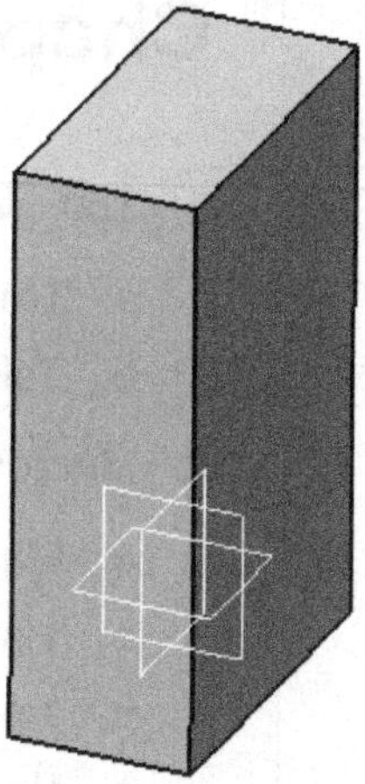

Figure 15–43

9. Close the VB Editor.
10. Close the part without saving.

Chapter Review Questions

1. You can use Macros to record a series of actions in CATIA.
   a. True
   b. False
2. Macros are recorded using _____
   a. Macro script.
   b. Visual Basic script.
   c. Java Script.
   d. None of the above.
3. By default, a new macro is created ______
   a. In a macro library.
   b. Local to the current model.
   c. In a directory on the local network.
   d. In a directory on your hard drive.
4. You can use keyboard accelerators to define keyboard shortcuts to run your macros.
   a. True
   b. False
5. A running VBScript calls:
   a. Required objects.
   b. Functions of the objects.
   c. Properties of the objects.
   d. All of the above.
6. The three main parts of the Microsoft Visual Basic editor window are:
   a. Object Browser, Parameters, and Script windows.
   b. File, Attributes, and Program windows.
   c. Explorer, Properties, and Code window.
   d. None of the above.

7. Words displayed in green in the code window area indicate:
   a. Reserved words.
   b. Errors.
   c. Warnings
   d. Comments
8. Variables can take the form of:
   a. Double
   b. String
   c. Boolean
   d. All of the above.

Answers: 1a, 2b, 3a, 4a, 5d, 6c, 7d, 8d

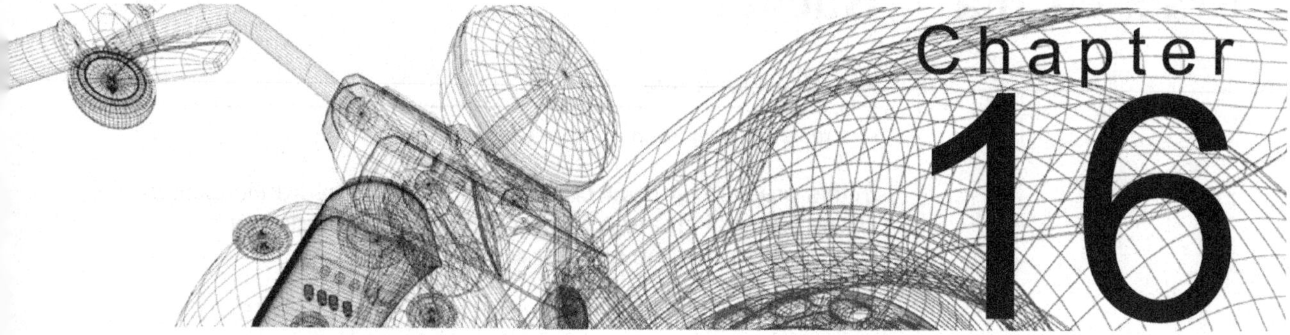

Chapter 16

Projects

In this chapter, you will create three different projects with minimal instructions.

Practice 16a Bucket

Practice Objective

- Create a model using a design table.

In this practice, you will create a bucket for a hydraulic excavator cover. You will create a design table to create different configurations of the bucket, without instructions.

The completed model displays as shown in Figure 16–1.

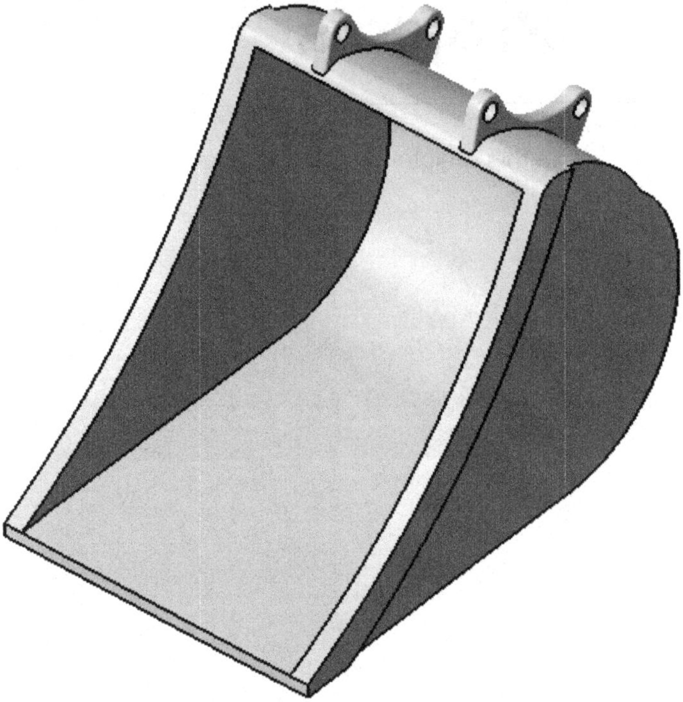

Figure 16–1

Task 1 - Create a new part.

1. Create a new 3D Part.
2. Create the model using Figure 16–2, Figure 16–3, Figure 16–4, and Figure 16–5.

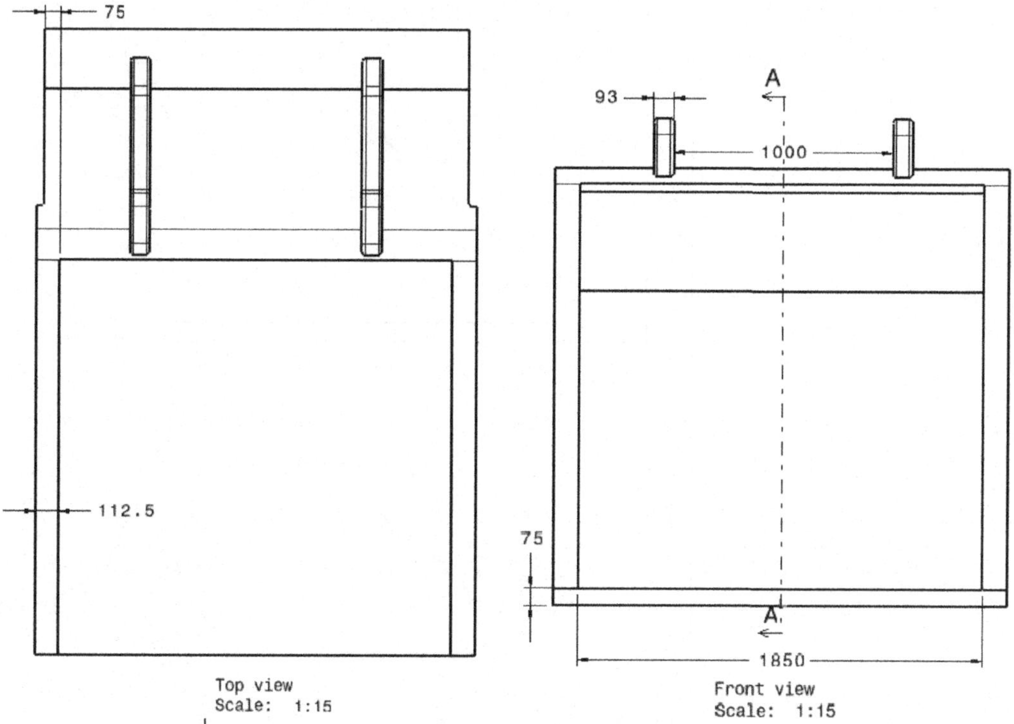

Figure 16–2

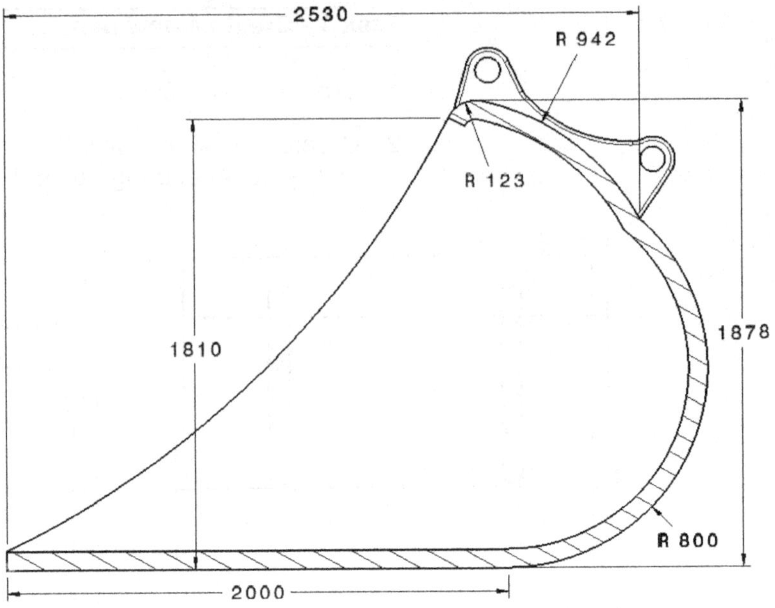

Section view A-A
Scale: 1:15

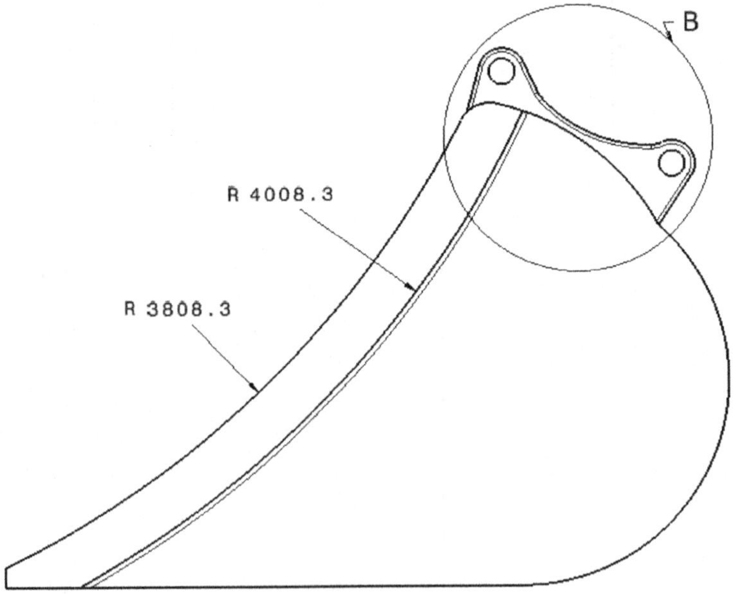

Right view
Scale: 1:15

Figure 16–3

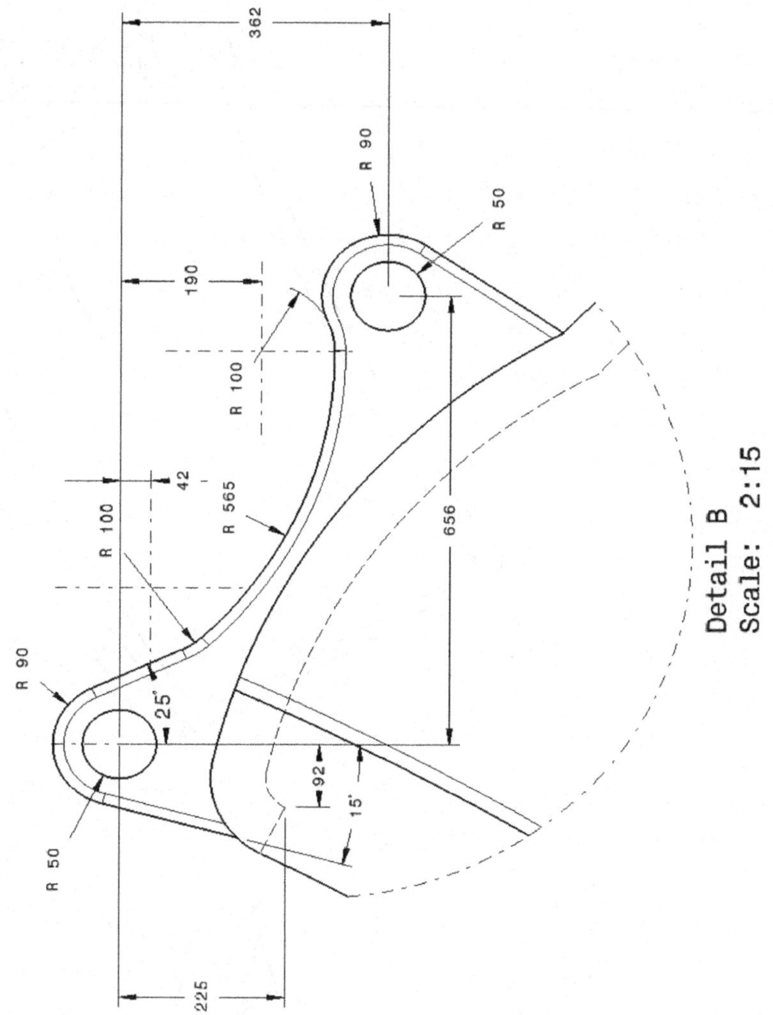
362
R 90
R 50
190
R 100
42
R 565
R 100
656
R 90
25°
92
15°
R 50
225
Detail B
Scale: 2:15

Figure 16–4

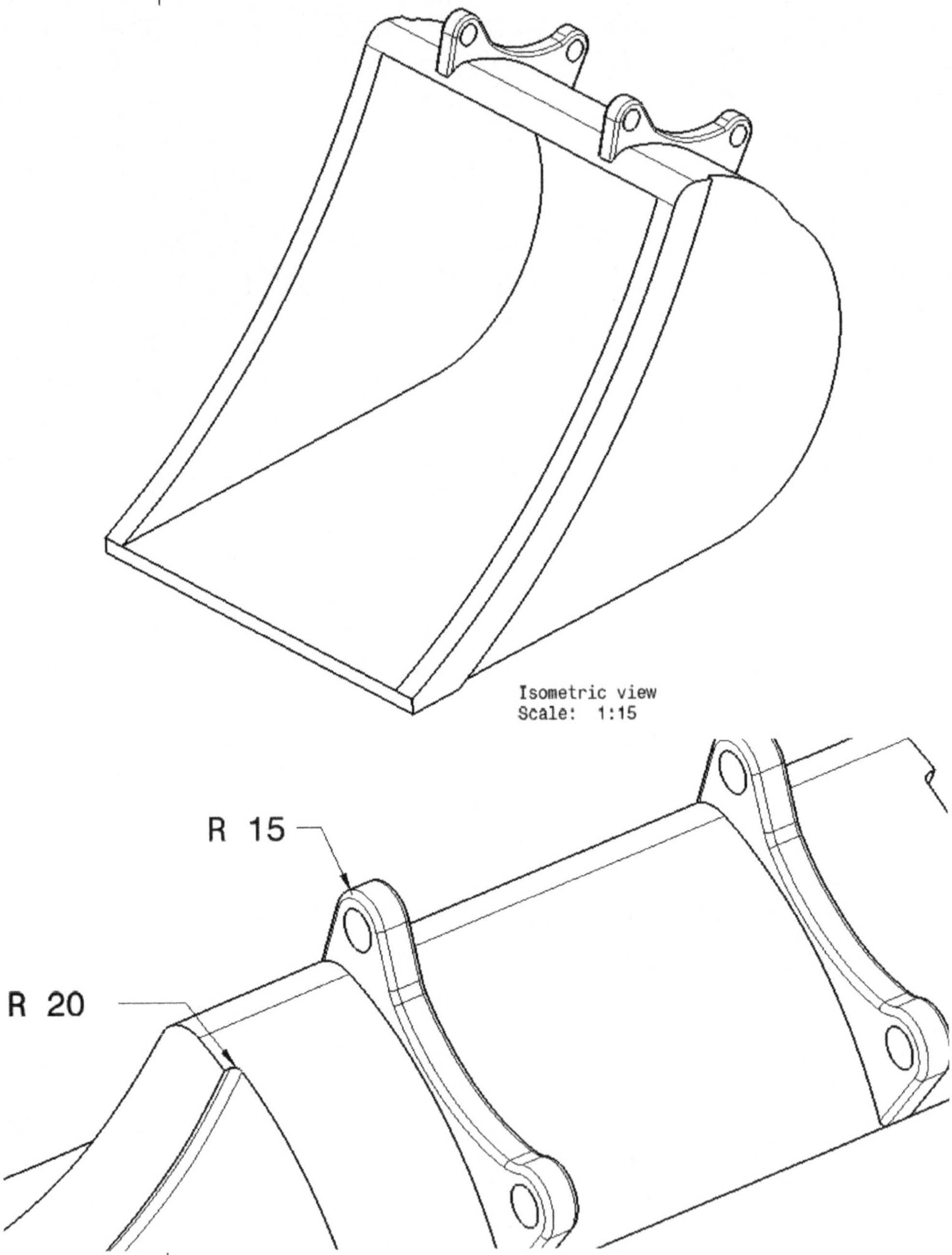

Figure 16–5

Task 2 - Create the design table.

1. Create the design table, as shown in Figure 16–6.

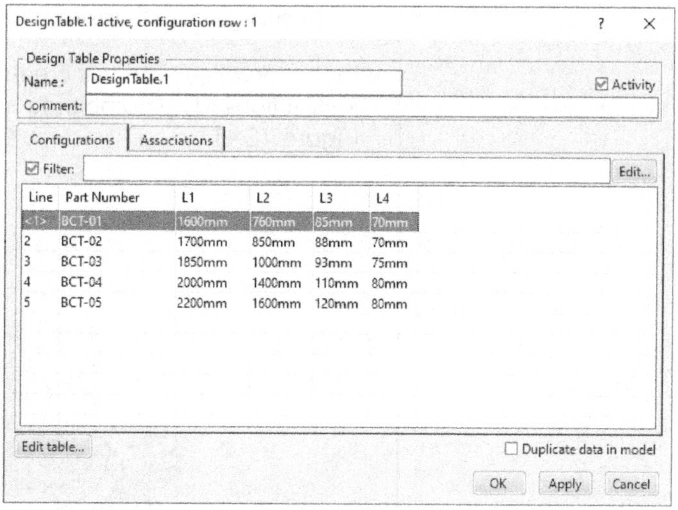

Line	Part Number	L1	L2	L3	L4
<1>	BCT-01	1600mm	760mm	85mm	70mm
2	BCT-02	1700mm	850mm	88mm	70mm
3	BCT-03	1850mm	1000mm	93mm	75mm
4	BCT-04	2000mm	1400mm	110mm	80mm
5	BCT-05	2200mm	1600mm	120mm	80mm

Figure 16–6

The parameters are shown in Figure 16–7.

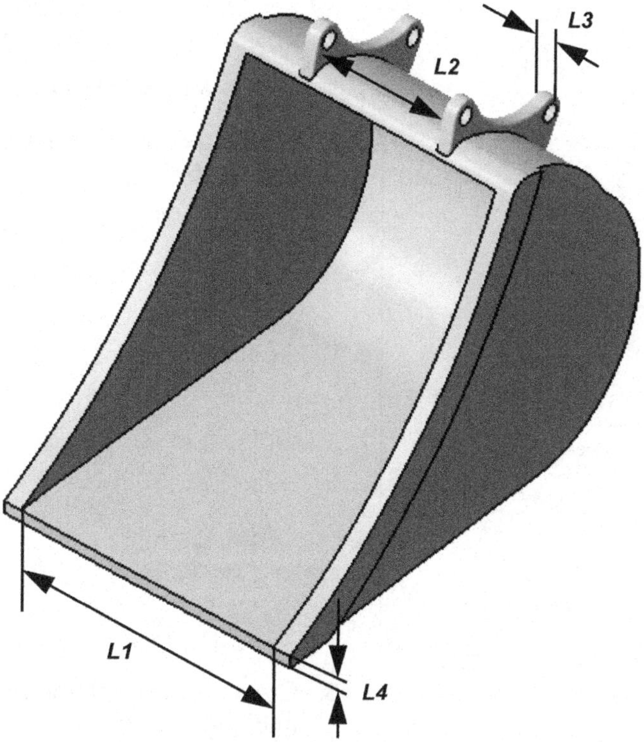

Figure 16–7

Practice 16b Housing Cover

Practice Objective

- Create a model with limited instruction.

In this practice, you will create a housing cover with minimal instructions. The completed model displays as shown in Figure 16–8.

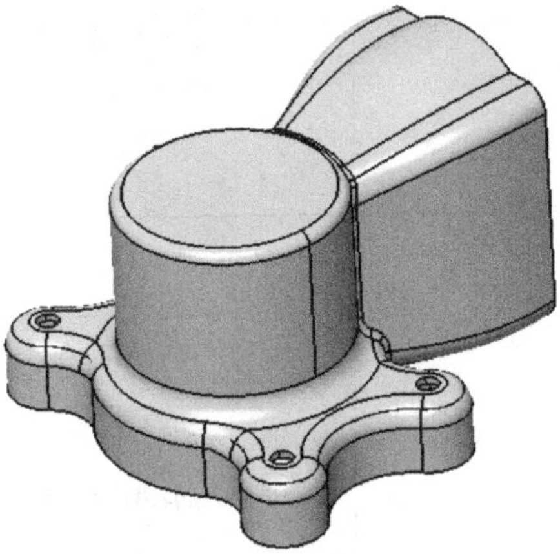

Figure 16–8

1. Create a new 3D Part.

2. Create a circular profile on the xy plane, as shown in Figure 16–9.

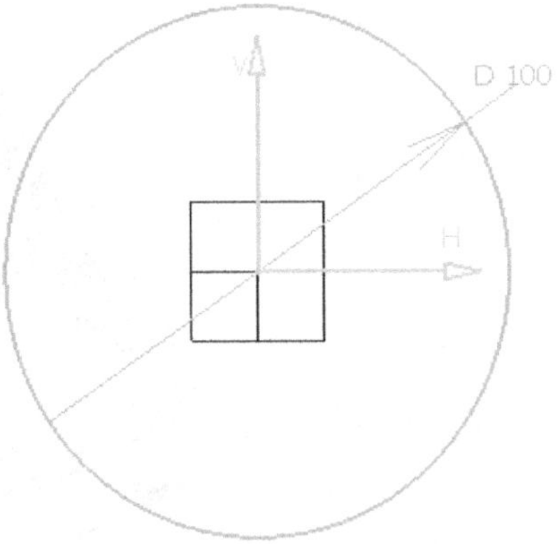

Figure 16–9

3. Create a Pad with the profile that you just created, as shown in Figure 16–10.

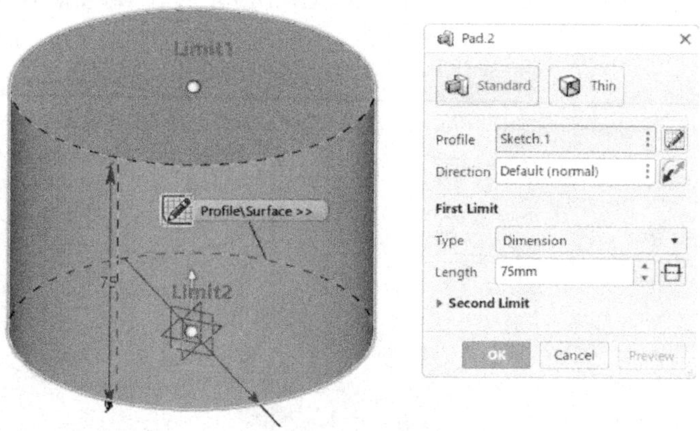

Figure 16–10

4. On the xy plane, create the sketch shown in Figure 16–11.

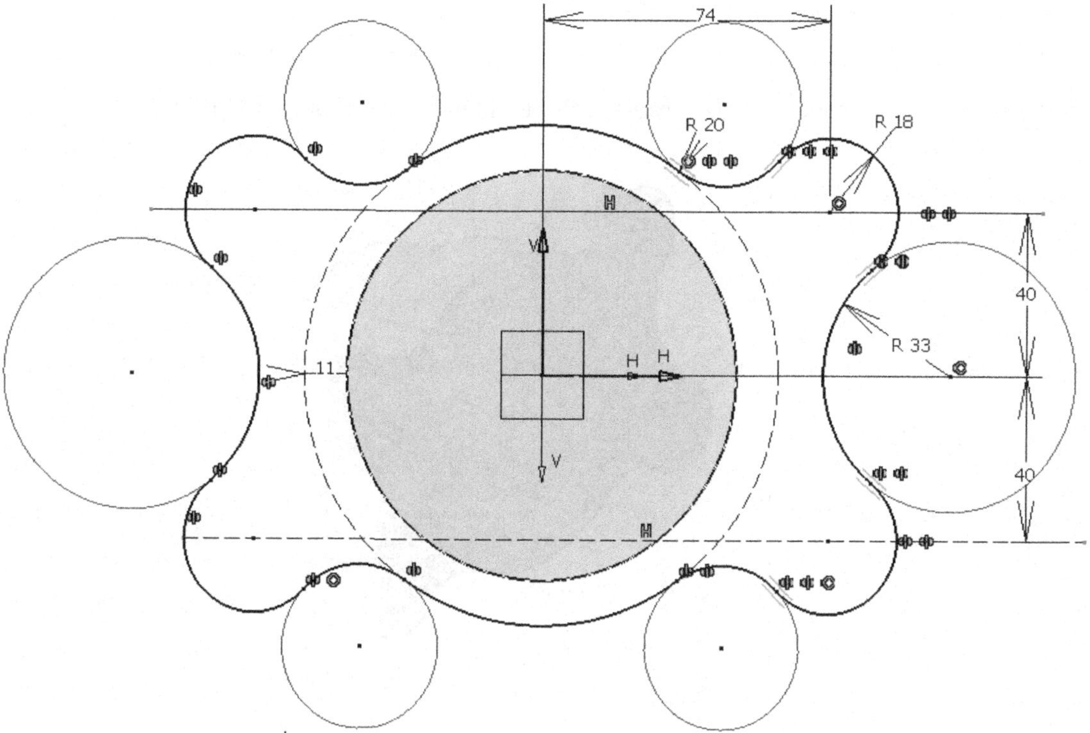

Figure 16–11

5. Create a Pad, as shown in Figure 16–12.

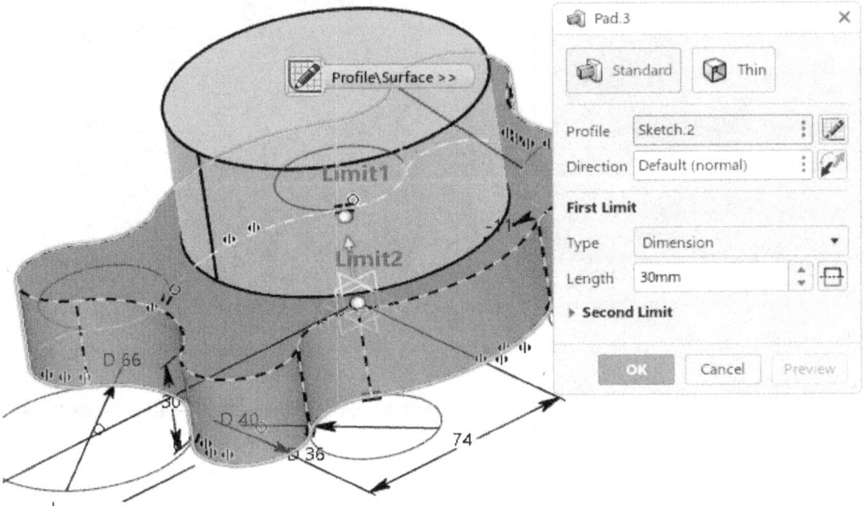

Figure 16–12

6. Create a Shell, as shown in Figure 16–13.

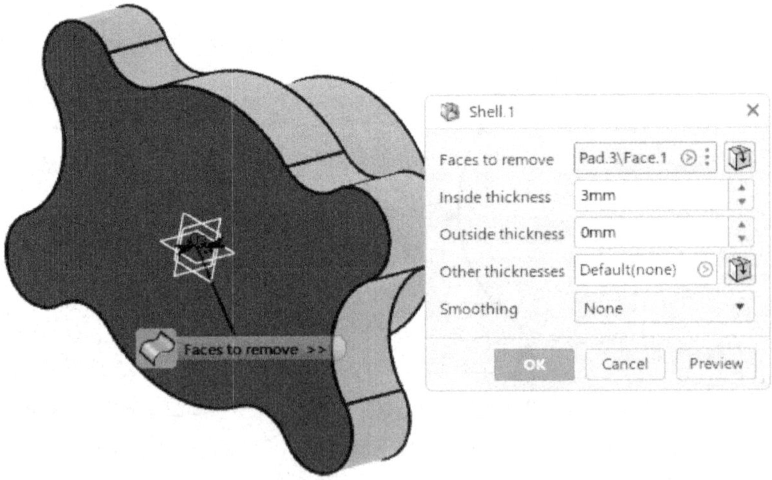

Figure 16–13

7. Create four Holes with a diameter of 10mm, as shown in Figure 16–14.

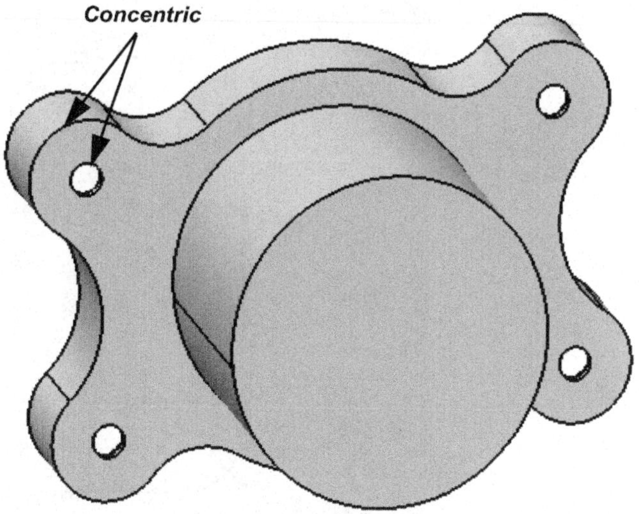

Figure 16–14

8. Create three reference planes, as shown in Figure 16–15.

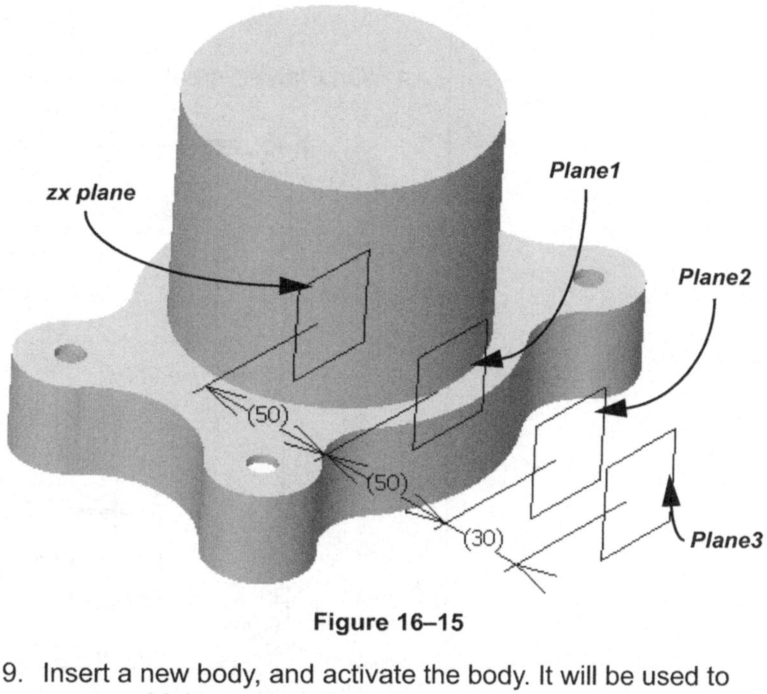

Figure 16–15

9. Insert a new body, and activate the body. It will be used to create a Multi-sections Solid feature.

10. On the zx plane, create the profile shown in Figure 16–16.

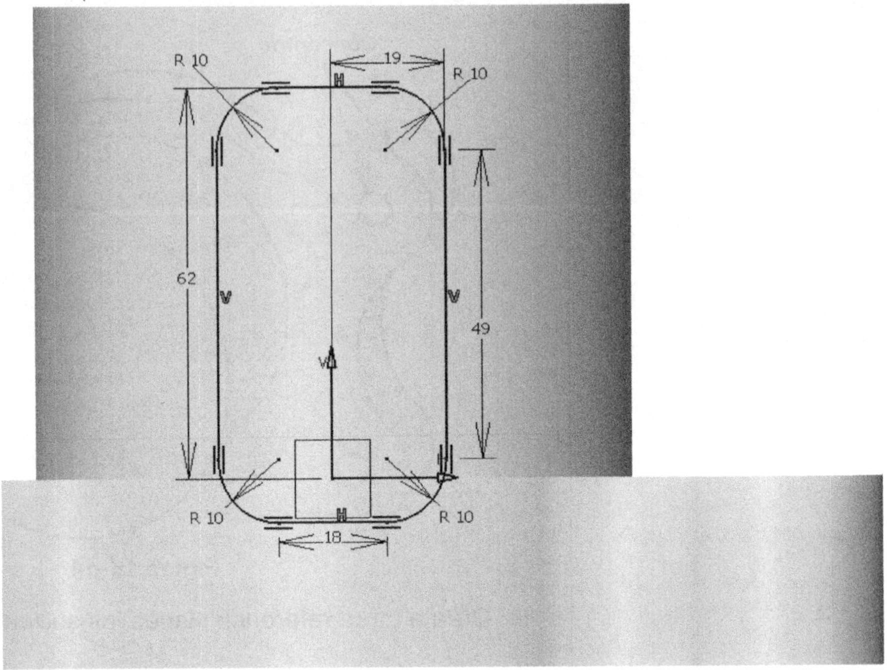

Figure 16–16

11. On Plane1, create the profile shown in Figure 16–17.

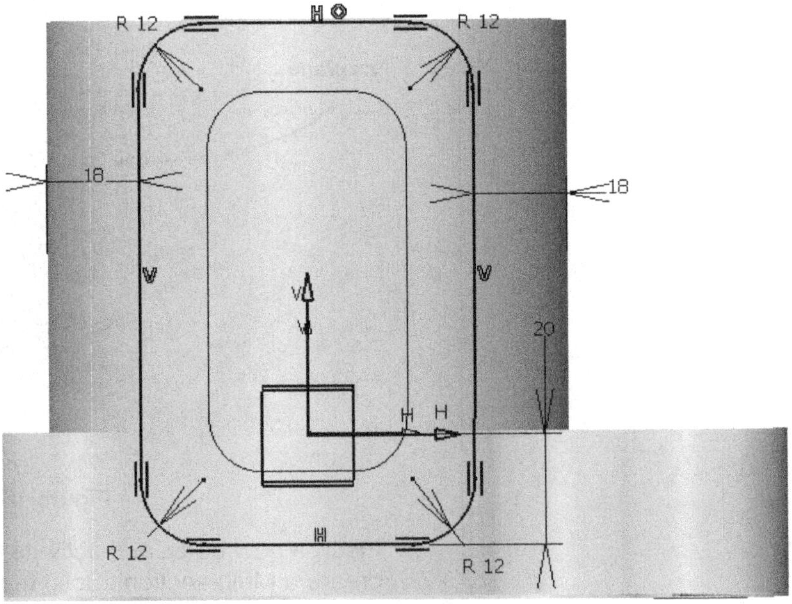

Figure 16–17

12. On Plane2, create the profile shown in Figure 16–18.

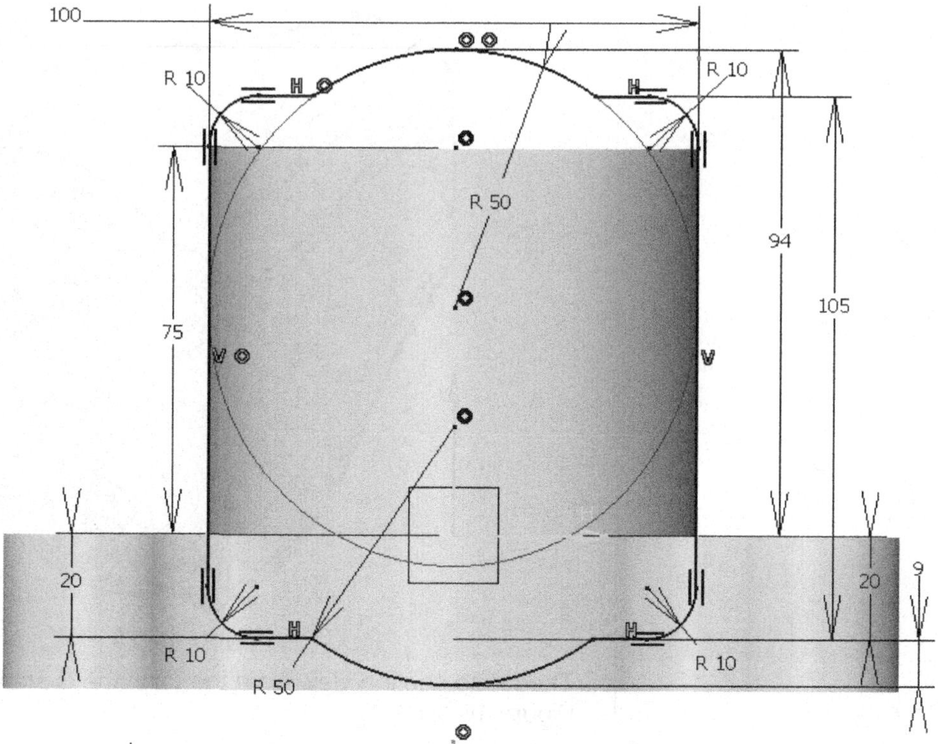

Figure 16–18

13. Copy and paste the last profile you created onto Plane3. The profiles display, as shown in Figure 16–19.

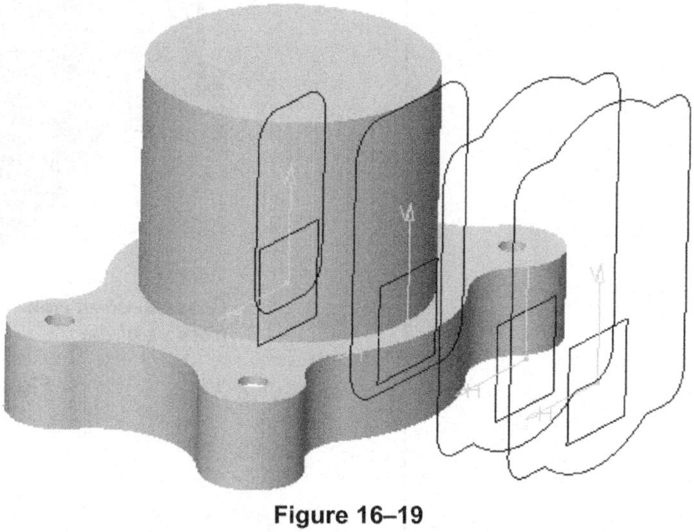

Figure 16–19

14. Create a Multi-sections Solid, as shown in Figure 16–20.

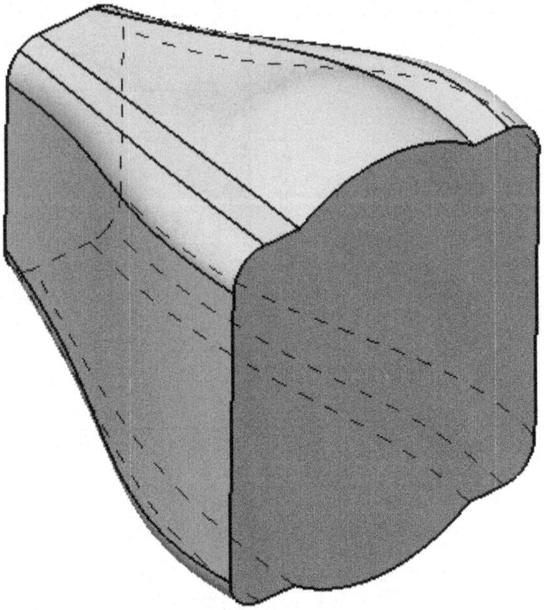

Figure 16–20

The cross-section view from the yz plane is shown in Figure 16–21.

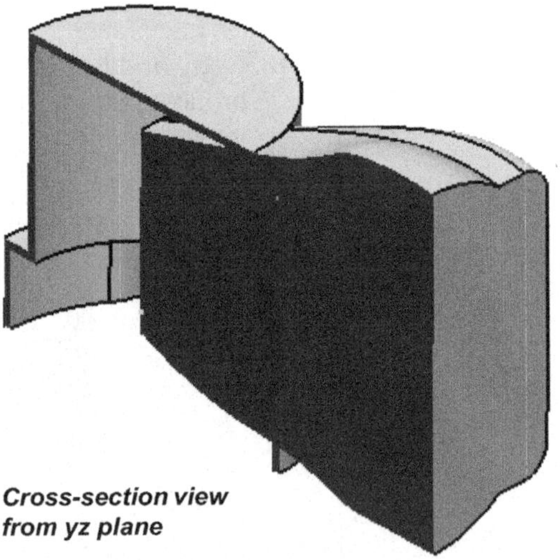

Figure 16–21

15. Insert a new body and activate the body, as shown in Figure 16–22. It will be used to create a Removed Multi-sections Solid feature.

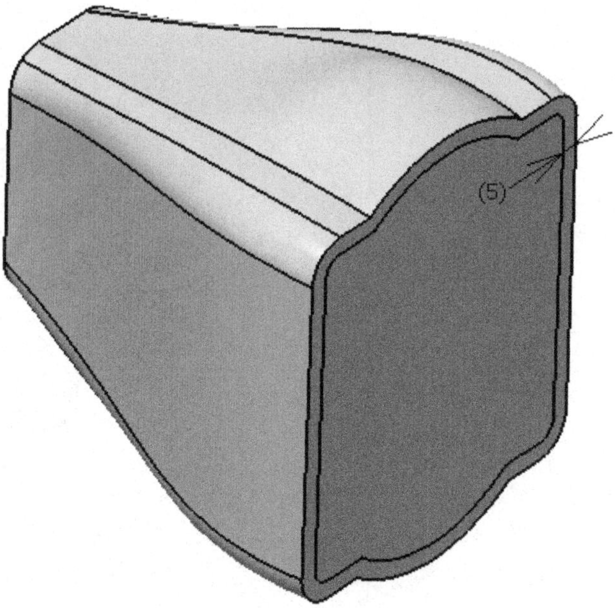

Figure 16–22

16. Use the correct Boolean operations to get the results shown in Figure 16–23, Figure 16–24, Figure 16–25, and Figure 16–26.

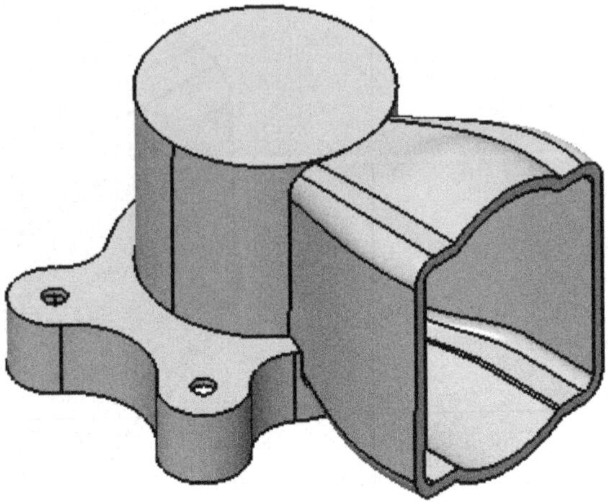

Figure 16–23

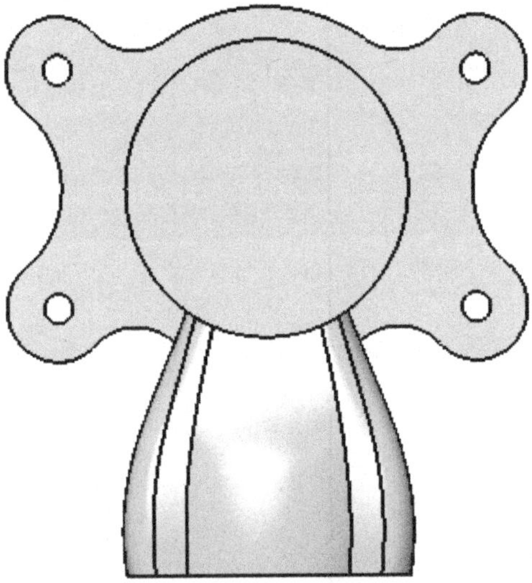

Figure 16–24

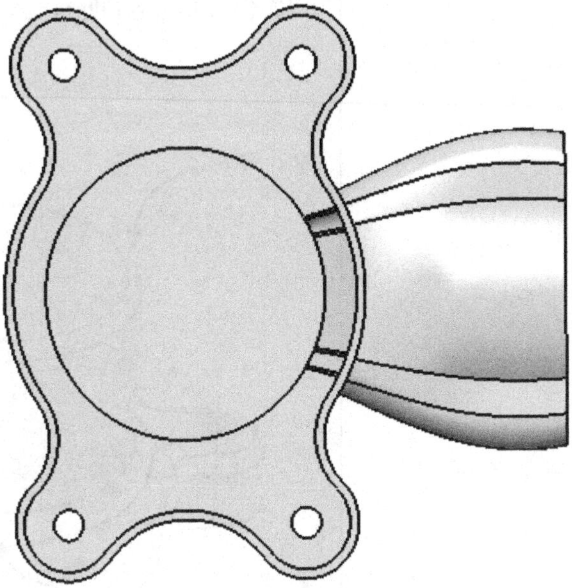

Figure 16–25

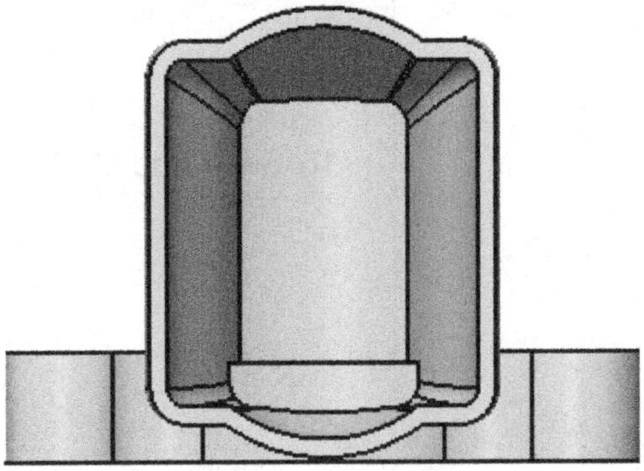

Figure 16–26

17. Create the Fillets, as shown in Figure 16–27.

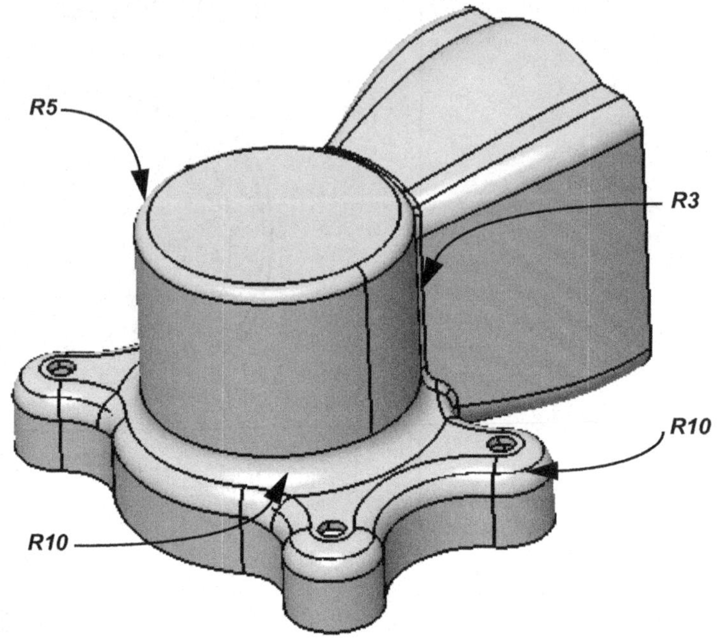

Figure 16–27

18. Save and close the model.

Practice 16c Landing Gear

Practice Objective

- Create a model with limited instruction.

In this practice, you will create a landing gear with given figures. The completed model displays as shown in Figure 16–28.

Figure 16–28

1. Create a new 3D Part.
2. Create the model using Figure 16–29, Figure 16–30, Figure 16–31, Figure 16–32, and Figure 16–33.

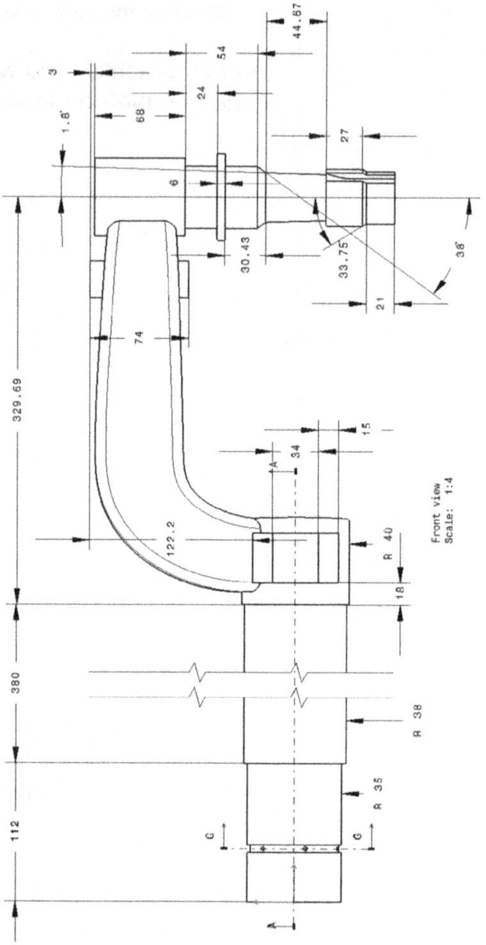

Figure 16–29

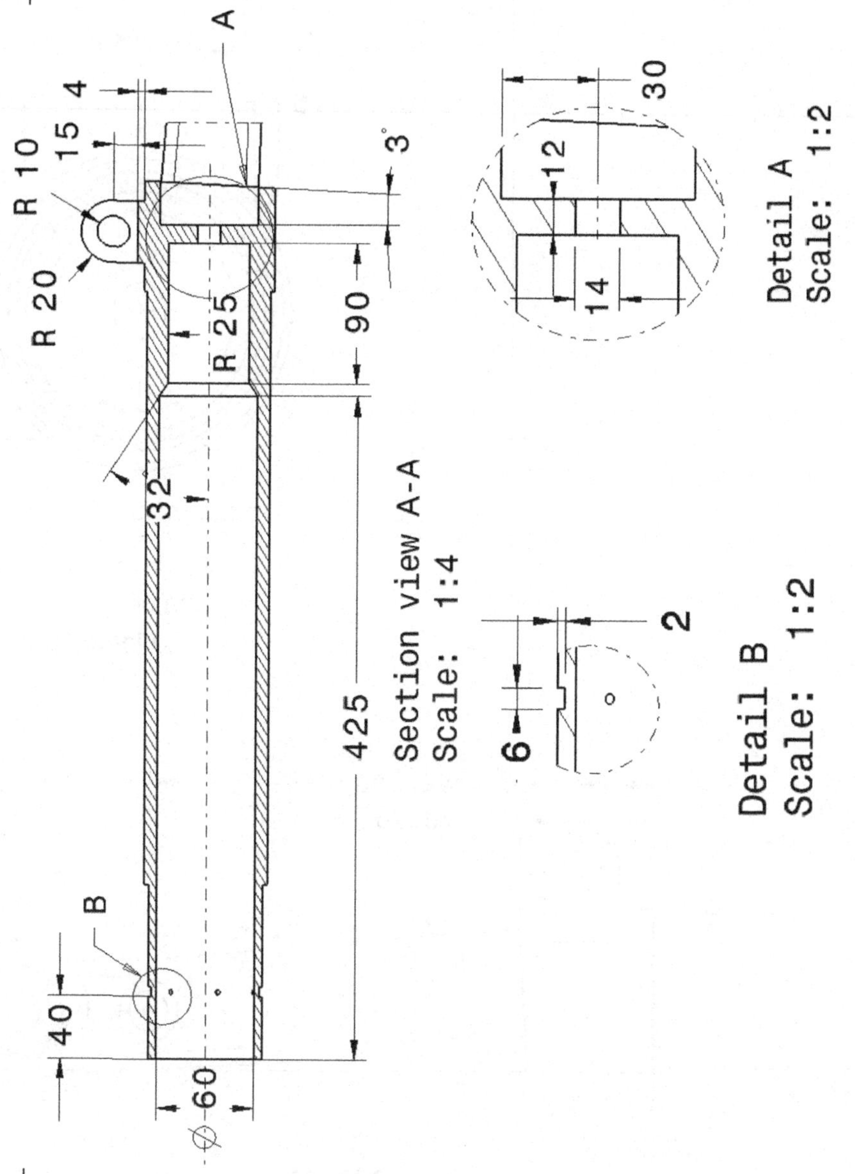
A
4
15
R 10
R 20
3°
R 25
90
32
425
Section view A-A
Scale: 1:4
30
12
14
Detail A
Scale: 1:2
2
6
Detail B
Scale: 1:2
B
40
Ø60

Figure 16–30

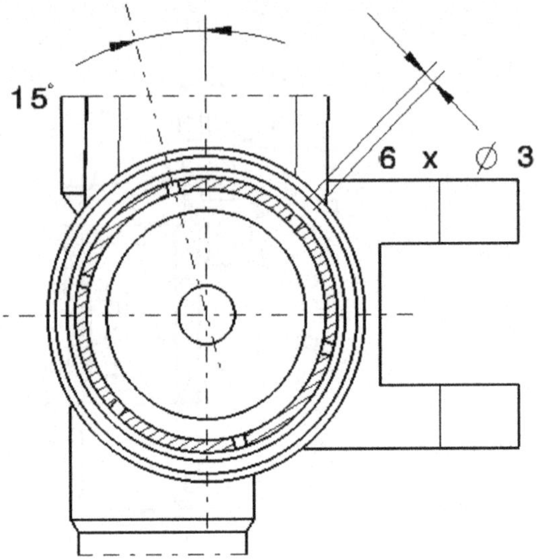

Section view G-G
Scale: 1:2

Figure 16–31

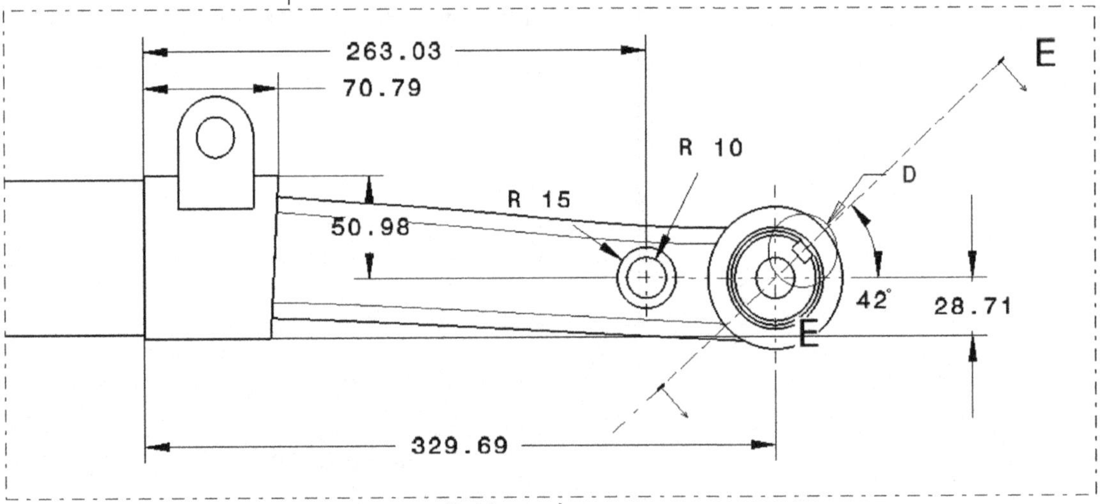

Bottom view
Scale: 1:4

Figure 16–32

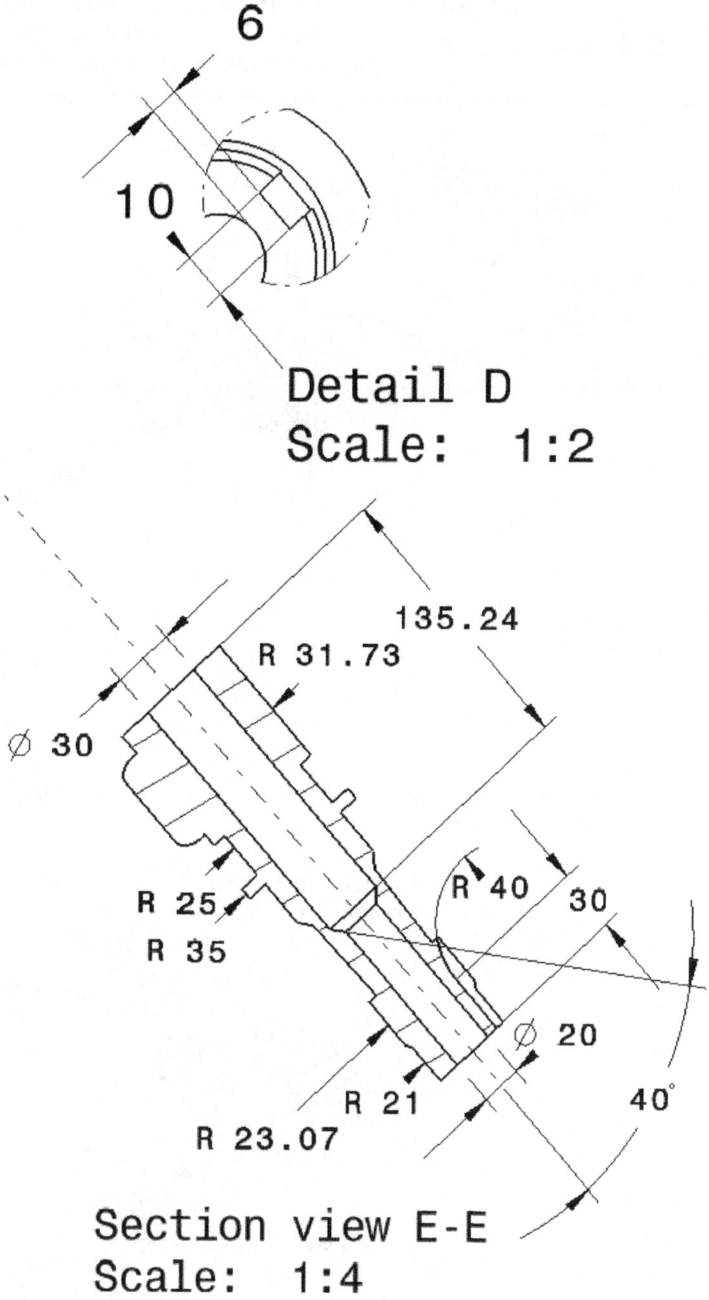
6
10
Detail D
Scale: 1:2
135.24
R 31.73
∅ 30
R 25
R 35
R 40
30
∅ 20
R 21
R 23.07
40°
Section view E-E
Scale: 1:4

Figure 16–33

Design Considerations

The information required to build the Multi-section Solid is shown in Figure 16–34, Figure 16–35, Figure 16–36, Figure 16–37, Figure 16–38, and Figure 16–39.

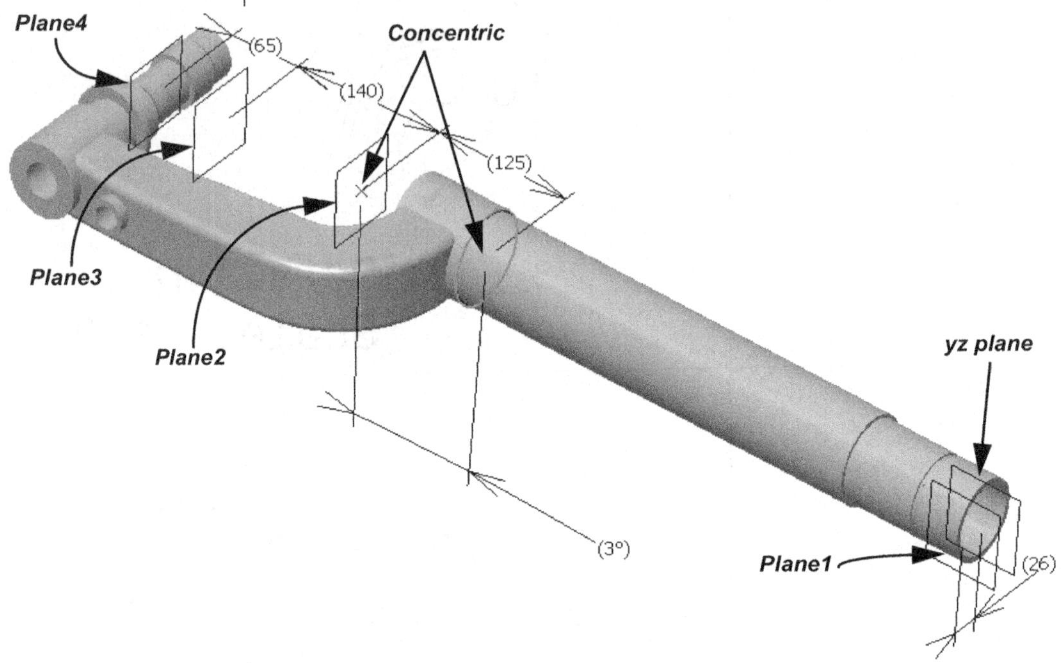

Figure 16–34

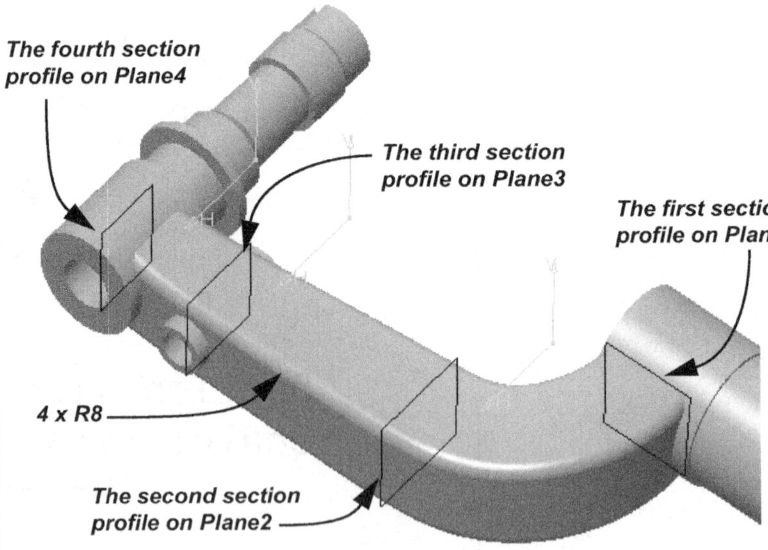

Figure 16–35

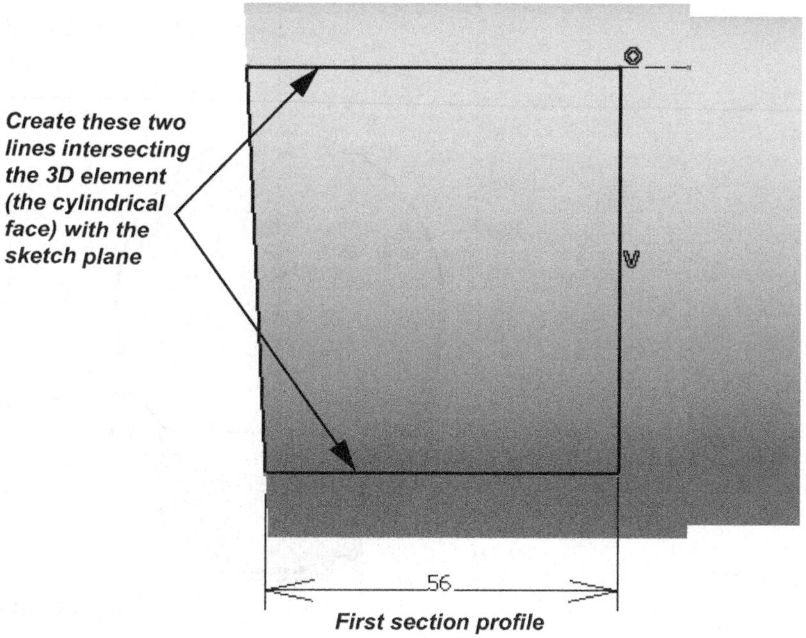

Figure 16–36

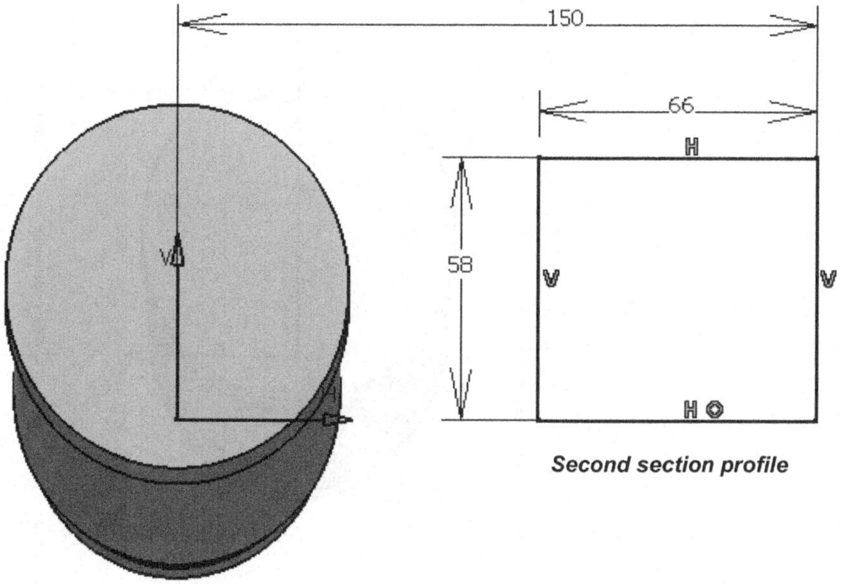

Figure 16–37

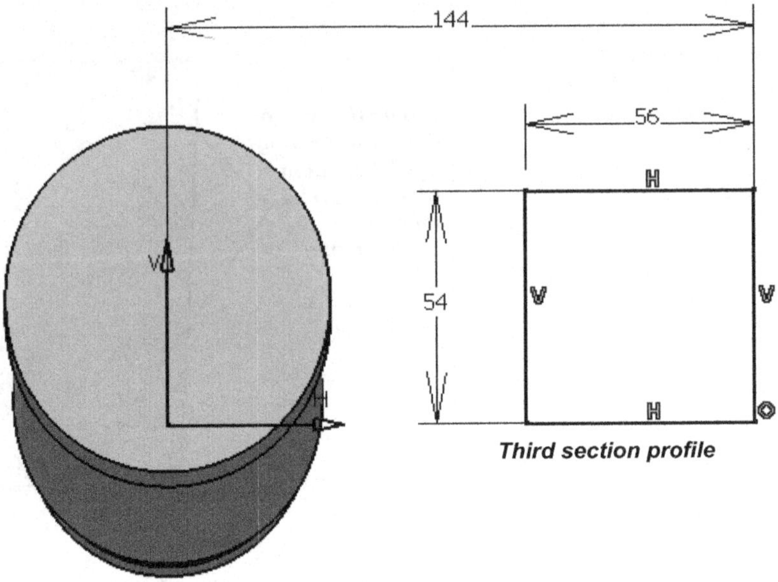

Figure 16–38

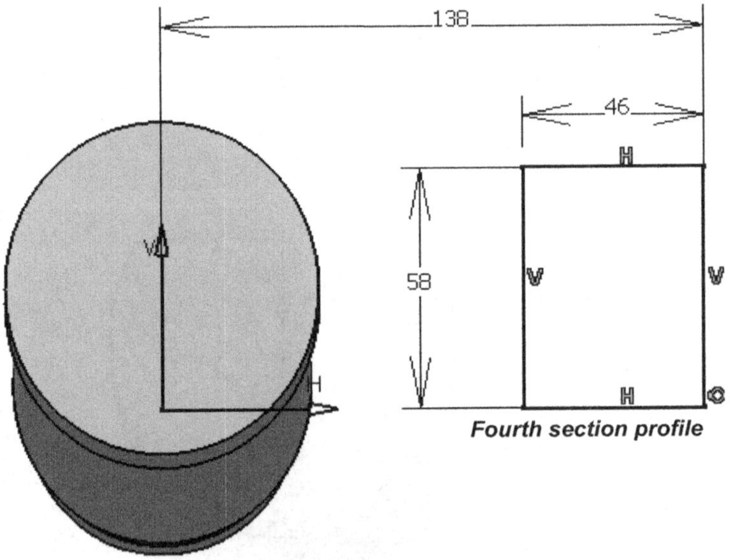

Figure 16–39

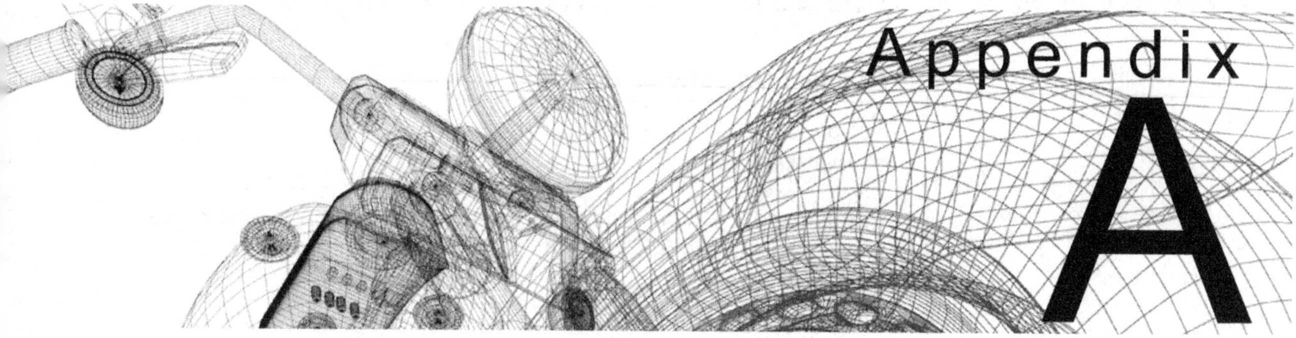

Appendix A

Additional Practices

This appendix contains additional practices that can be done if time permits.

Practice A1 Reusing Existing Designs

Practice Objectives

- Copy and Paste As Result.
- Investigate Links.

In this practice, you will reuse the existing design of **2ndStage** shown on the left in Figure A–1 to create a new design, as shown on the right.

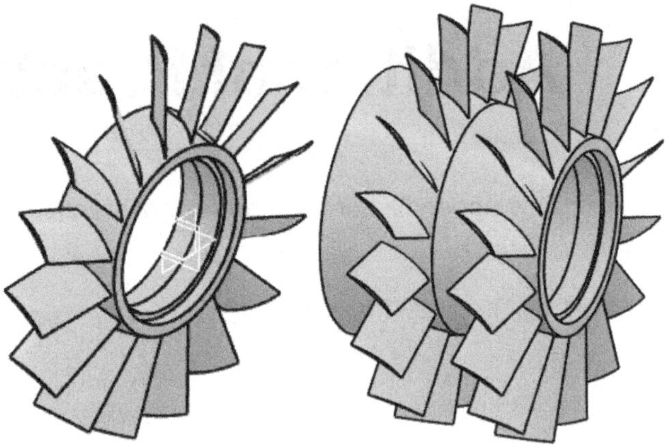

Figure A–1

Task 1 - Open the part.

1. Import and open the part named **2ndStage.3dxml** from the *Turbine* directory. The body displays as shown in Figure A–2.

Figure A–2

2. Set the units to millimeters.

Task 2 - Duplicate the model with a different name.

1. Select  **>Save (expand)>Save with Options**.The Save with Options window will appear as shown in Figure A–3.

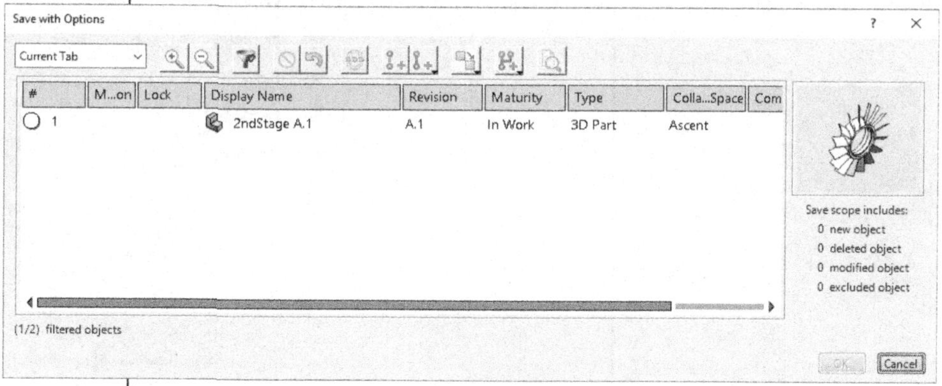

Figure A–3

2. Select **2ndStage** in the list, then select  (Save as New). The Save as New window will open as shown in Figure A–4.

Figure A–4

3. For the new name, enter **3rdand** into the *Duplication string* field. This duplicates the part but with the name **3rdand2ndStage**.

4. Select **OK** twice. The part that is currently open becomes **3rdand2ndStage**.

Task 3 - Copy and paste a part from a different body.

1. Select the *2ndStage A.1(Explore)* tab.

2. Right-click on **2ndStage A.1** in the specification tree and select **Open**.

3. In the specification tree, right-click on the **2ndStage** body and select **Copy**, as shown in Figure A–5.

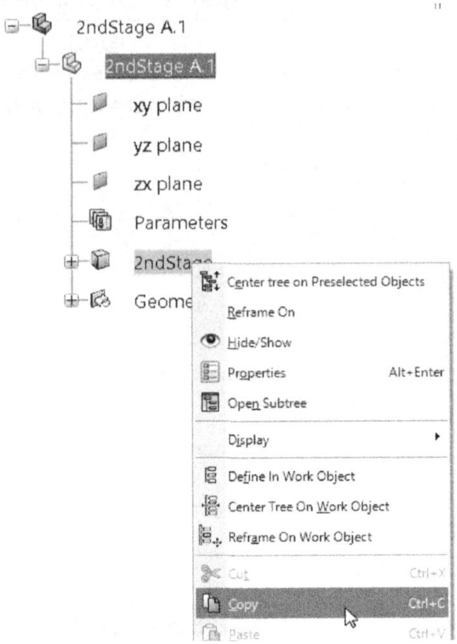

Figure A–5

4. Activate the *3rdand2ndStage* tab.

5. In the specification tree, right-click on the **3rdand2ndStage** title and select **Paste Special**. The Paste Special dialog box opens as shown in Figure A–6.

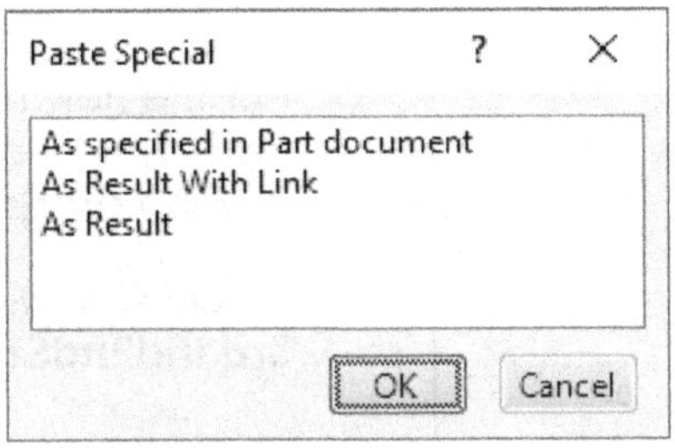

Figure A–6

6. Select **As Result With Link** and click **OK**. A new body named **2ndStage** has been added to the element list in the specification tree.

Task 4 - Rename elements in the specification tree.

1. Change the name of the first **2ndStage** body to **3rdStage**. The specification tree displays as shown in Figure A–7. Note the **Solid.1** element and its associated icon and status symbol.

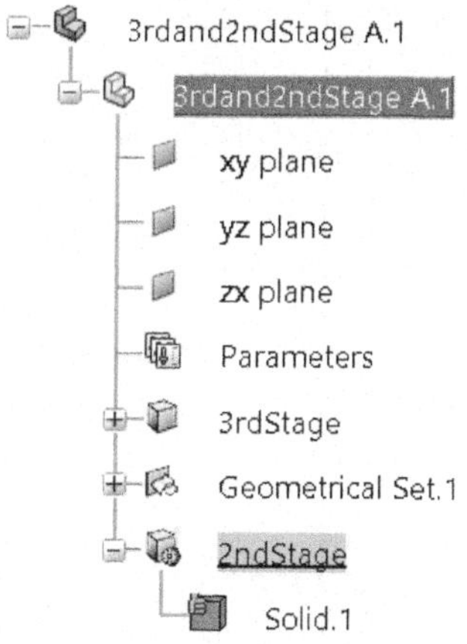

Figure A–7

Task 5 - Move the 2ndStage body.

1. If not already active, activate the **3rdStage** 3D shape by double-clicking on it in the specification tree. It will turn blue when active, as shown in Figure A–8.

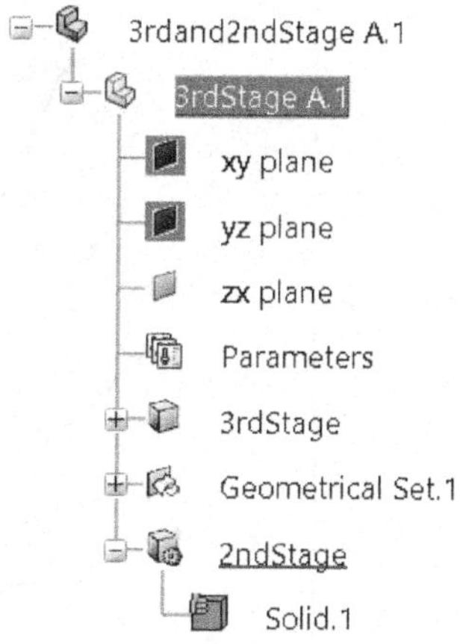

Figure A–8

2. Drag the robot onto the body so that the axis of the robot is oriented, as shown in Figure A–9.

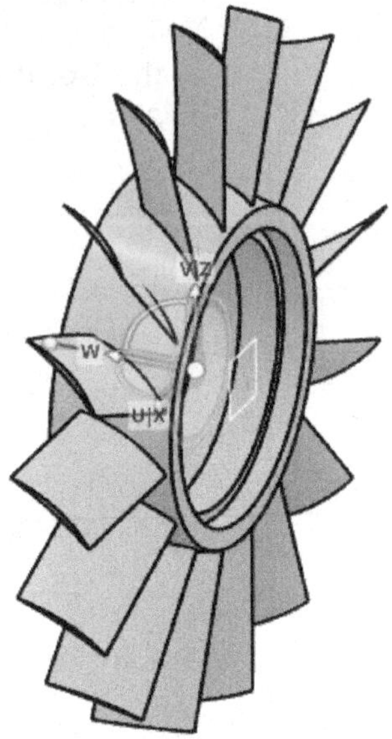

Figure A–9

3. In the specification tree, select **2ndStage** and drag the axis of the robot to the location shown in Figure A–10.

Figure A–10

Task 6 - Explore external links.

1. In the specification tree, select **2ndStage** and select  (Links and Relations) from the Tools section of the Action Bar. The Edit Links and Relations dialog box opens as shown in Figure A–11.

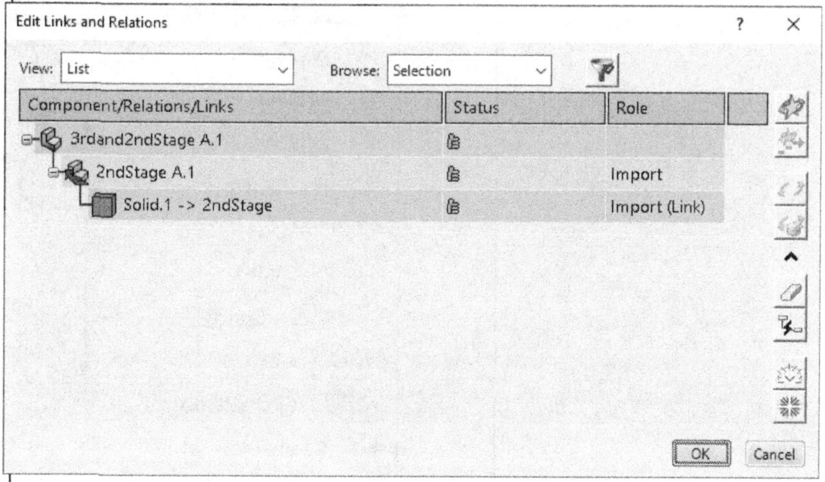

Figure A–11

Note that the red arrow in the *Component/Relations/Links* column shows that 2ndStage impacts the 3rdand2ndStage part. Also notice that the status of Solid.1 is Synchronized.

2. Click **OK**.

Task 7 - Modify the 3rdstage body.

1. Edit **Sketch.1**, which is located under **Shaft.1** of **3rdStage**. The sketch and specification tree display as shown in Figure A–12.

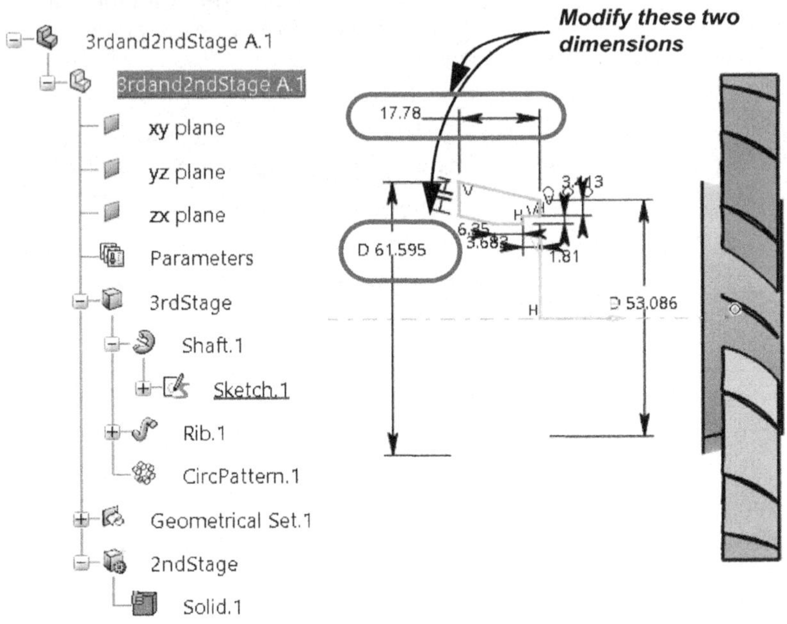

Figure A–12

2. Change the *17.78* value to **29.5**.
3. Change the *61.595* value to **71.2**.
4. Erase the four dimensions shown in Figure A–13.

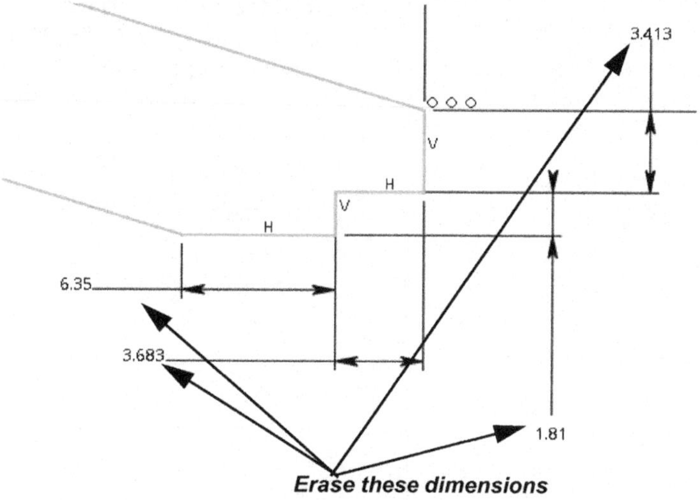

Figure A–13

5. Erase the two sketched lines shown in Figure A–14.

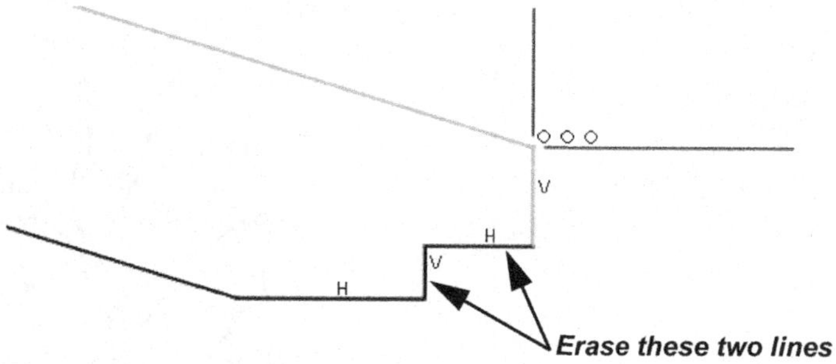

Figure A–14

6. Trim the remaining two lines together and dimension as shown in Figure A–15. Ensure that the sketch is fully constrained (green).

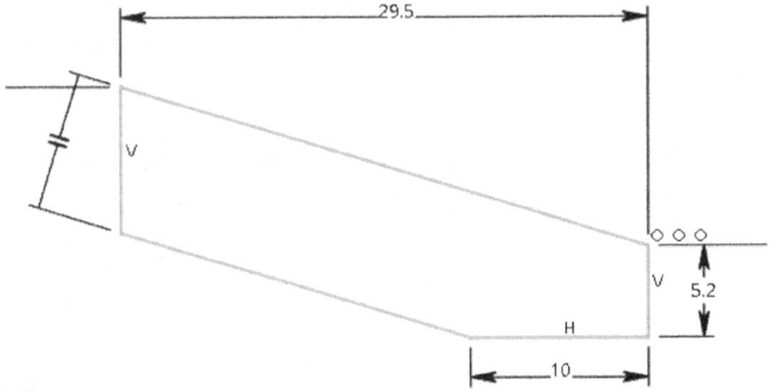

Figure A–15

7. Exit the Sketcher app. The **3rdStage** body displays as shown in Figure A–16.

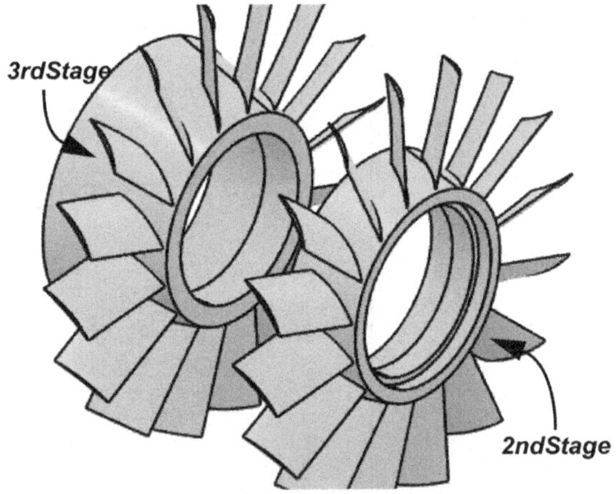

Figure A–16

Task 8 - Modify the pointed document.

1. Activate the *2ndStage* part tab.

2. Modify the *17.78* value of **Shaft.1** to **28.5**, as shown in Figure A–17.

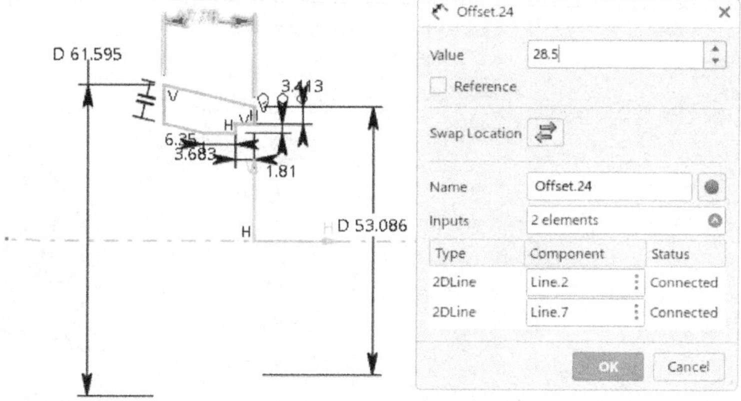

Figure A–17

The body displays as shown in Figure A–18.

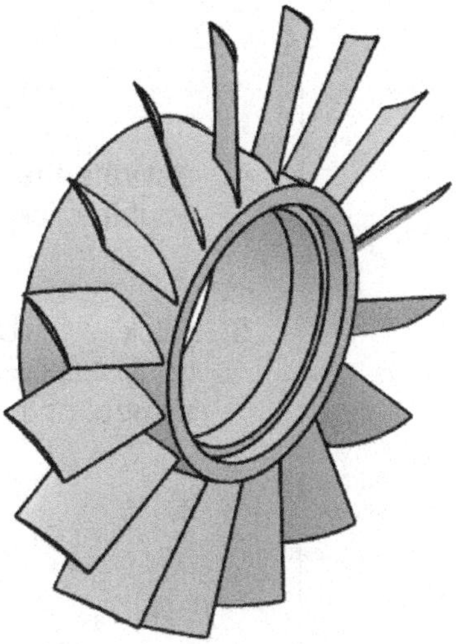

Figure A–18

3. Activate the *3rdand2ndStage* part tab. Note that the system recognizes that changes have been made to a linked document. In the specification tree, expand **2ndStage** and note the status symbol of the **Solid.1** element, as shown in Figure A–19.

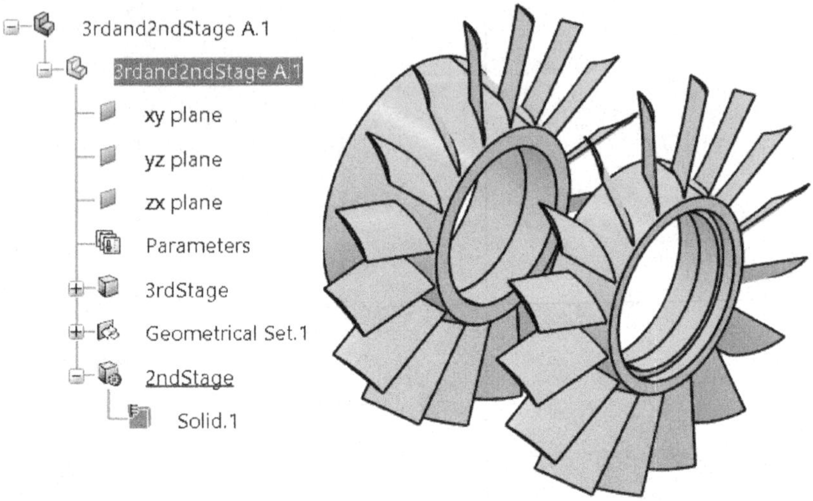

Figure A–19

4. Activate the 3D Part level of the specification tree by double-clicking on **3rdand2ndStage** at the top of the tree.

5. Click (Update) to update the geometry. The updated body displays as shown in Figure A–20. Note the status symbol of the Solid.1 element.

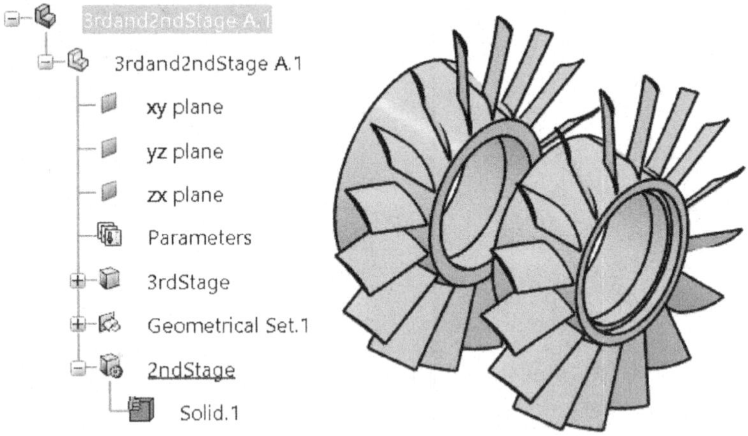

Figure A–20

Task 9 - Create a measurement of the large diameter of 3rdStage.

1. Activate the 3D Shape level of the part called **3rdand2ndStage** by double-clicking on it. It will turn blue as shown in Figure A–21.

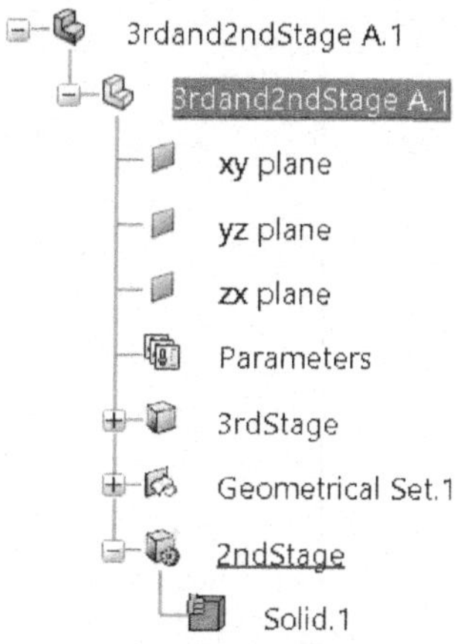

Figure A–21

2. Click  (Measure Item) from the Tools section of the Action Bar to create a measure element.

3. Select the round edge of the **2ndStage**, as shown in Figure A–22. Then place the measurement to the right of the model. Some of the information being displayed will likely be different.

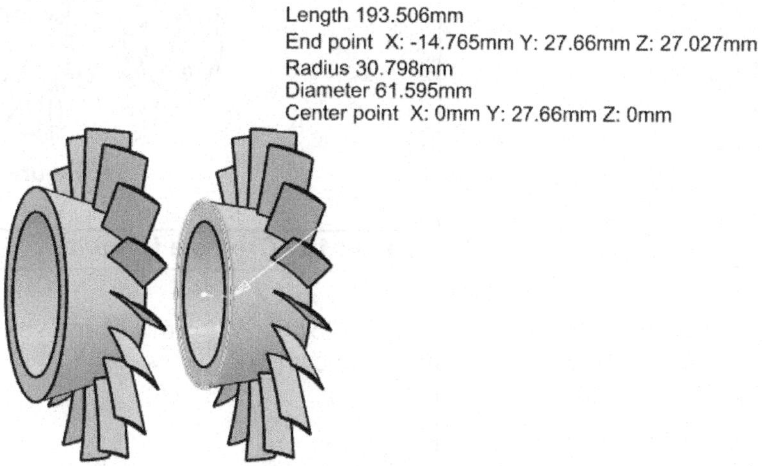

Figure A–22

4. Click on the *Customize* tab and ensure that only the **Diameter** option is selected under the *3D* and *Tab* columns, as shown in Figure A–23.

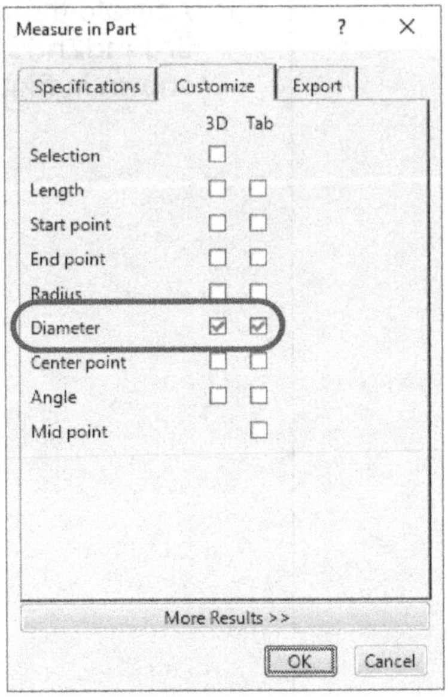

Figure A–23

5. Select the *Specifications* tab. Ensure that the **Keep Measure** option is selected and click **OK** to close the Measure Item dialog box. The model will display as shown in Figure A–24.

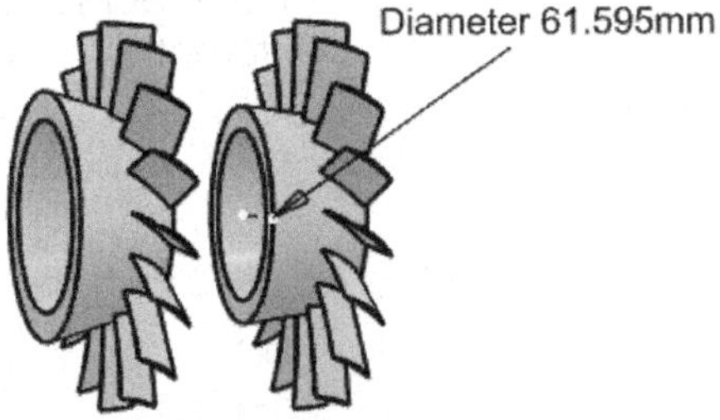

Figure A–24

Task 10 - Create a formula.

1. Click *fx* (Formula) and select the **3rdStage** geometry, as shown in Figure A–25.

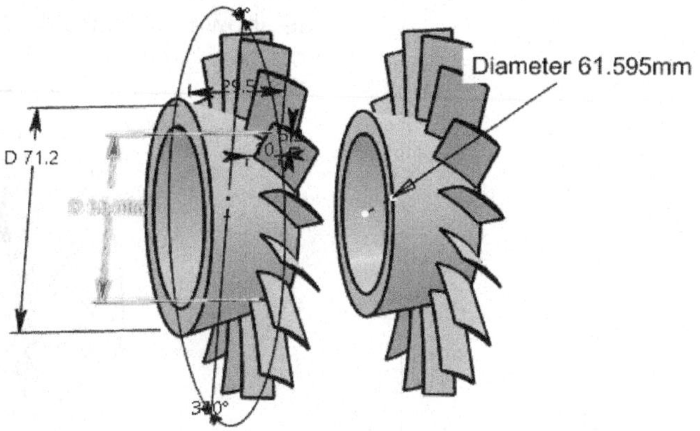

Figure A–25

2. Select the **53.086** dimension so that the parameter is highlighted in the Formulas dialog box. This will be a diameter parameter (named radius by CATIA) with a value of **26.543**.

3. Click **Add Formula** and equate the 53.086 dimension by half the Measure result, as shown in Figure A–26.

To display the radius measurement, select the body. Ensure that you select the Radius parameter.

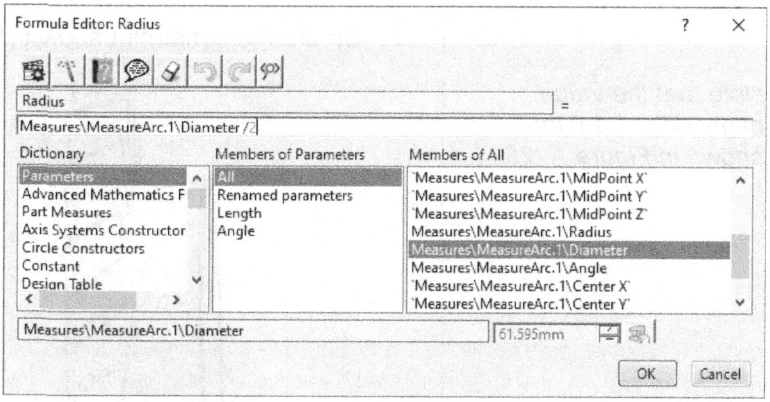

Figure A–26

4. Click **OK** twice to complete the formula. The body is updated, as shown in Figure A–27.

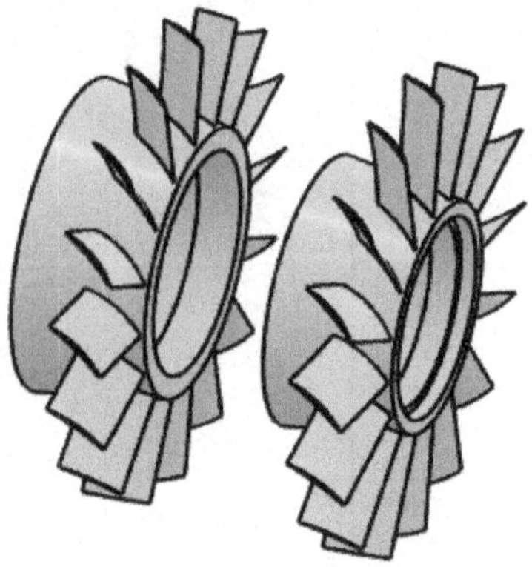

Figure A–27

Task 11 - Create a 3D constraint.

1. In the Transform section of the Action Bar, click  (Constraints).
2. Create the constraint shown in Figure A–28.

Note that the value might differ from that shown in Figure A–28.

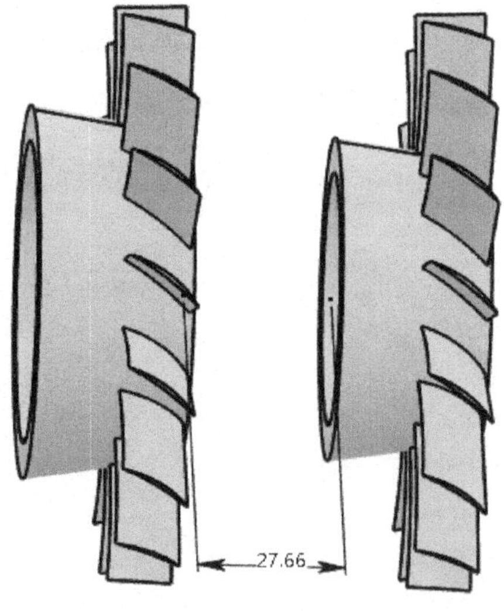

Figure A–28

Include units with the entered value.

3. Set the constraint value to **0mm** with a formula, as shown in Figure A–29.

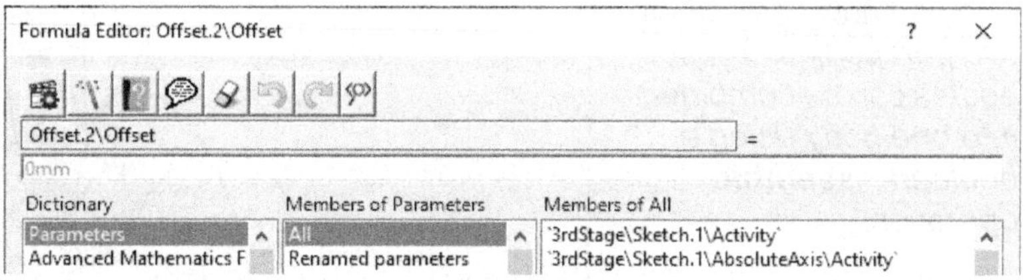

Figure A–29

4. To display the 3D constraint in the specification tree, select **Me>Common Preferences>Object Properties>3D Shape>Display**. In the dialog box, locate the *Display In Tree* section and select **Constraints**. The specification tree displays as shown in Figure A–30.

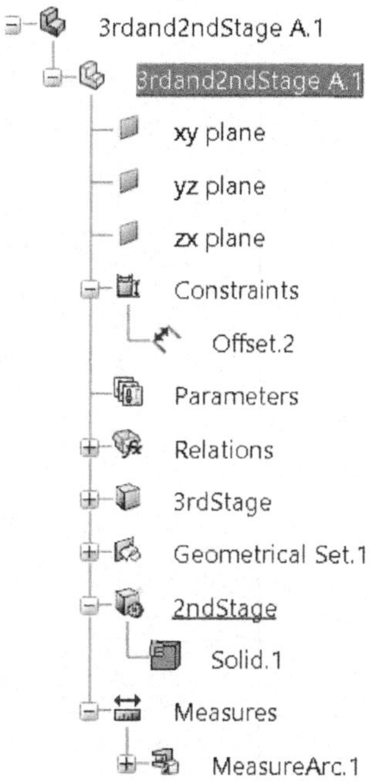

Figure A–30

*The part now consists of two part bodies. These bodies can be combined into one body using a boolean **Assemble** operation.*

5. Hide the constraint. The body displays as shown in Figure A–31.

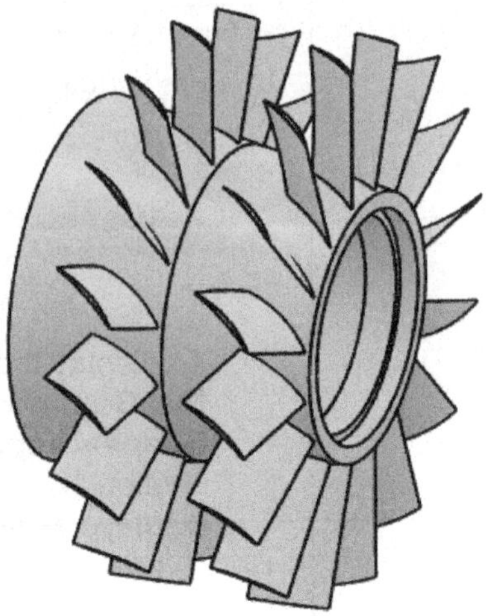

Figure A–31

6. Save the model.

Practice A2

Managing Links

Practice Objectives

- Update a Document.
- Synchronize a Pointed Document.
- Break the Link.

In this practice, you will modify a linked document using the option in the Links dialog box. The completed body displays as shown in Figure A–32.

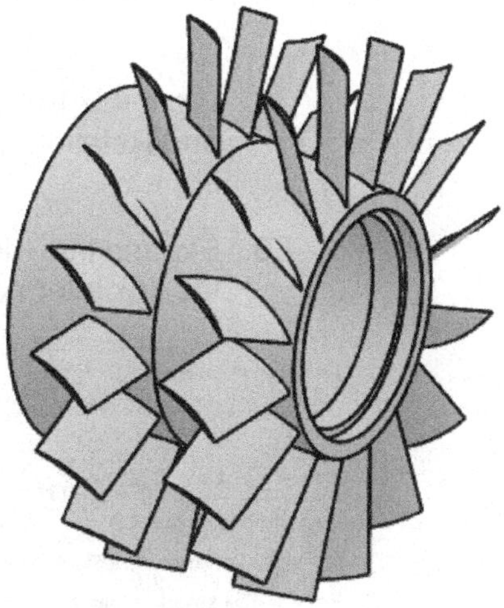

Figure A–32

Task 1 - Open the models.

1. If you are starting this exercise after completing the **Reusing Existing Design** practice, ensure that both the **2ndStage** and **3rdand2ndStarg** parts are still open if they have been closed. Search the database and open both parts in separate tabs. If they are already open, you may skip the rest of this task and start Task 2.

2. If you did not complete the previous practice **Reusing Existing Design**, import and open both **2ndStage_Completed.3dxml** and **3rdand2ndStage_ Completed.3dxml** from the *Completed* directory instead. Once open, the tabs displayed should look like Figure A–33.

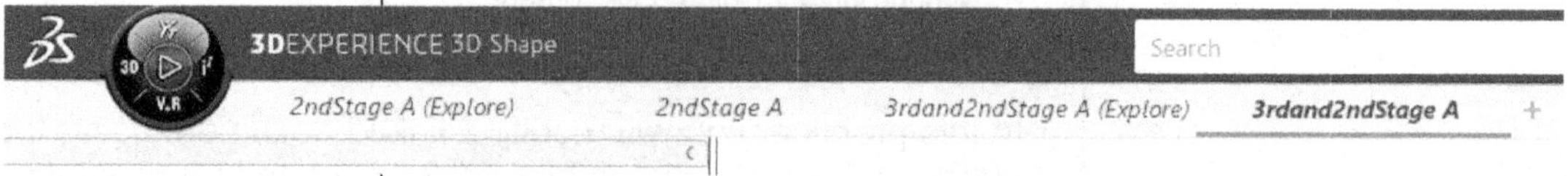

Figure A–33

3. Select the *3rdand2ndStage* tab if not already displayed.

4. From the Tools section of the Action Bar, select  (Links and Relations). The Edit Links and Relations window will appear.

5. Expand the + icon to the left of **3rdand2ndStage** so that all of the link information is displayed as shown in Figure A–34.

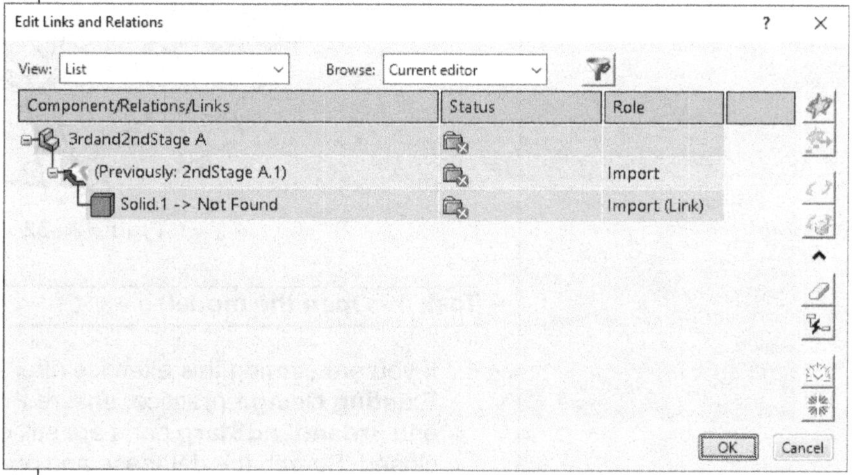

Figure A–34

6. The status indicates that the link exists but is broken because the file can't be found in the database. Select the link in the list to the pointed part (previously called 2ndStage A.1), as shown in Figure A–35.

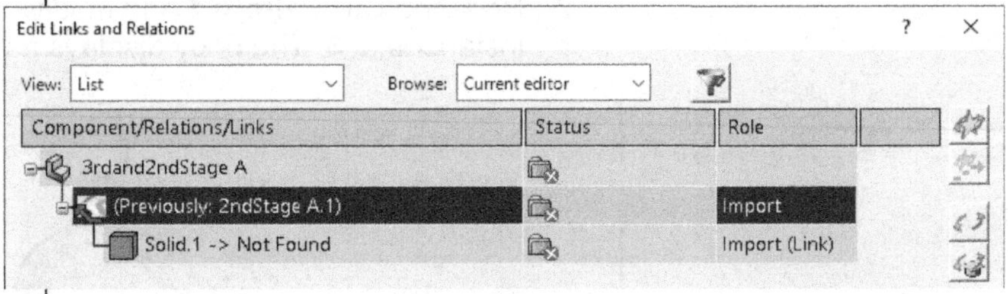

Figure A–35

7. On the right side of the window, select (Manual Reconnection). The Select or Search an object window will appear.

8. At the top of the screen, select the *2ndStage* tab to display the part.

9. In the specification tree, select the title **2ndStage**, as shown in Figure A–36. This will reestablish the link between the two part models.

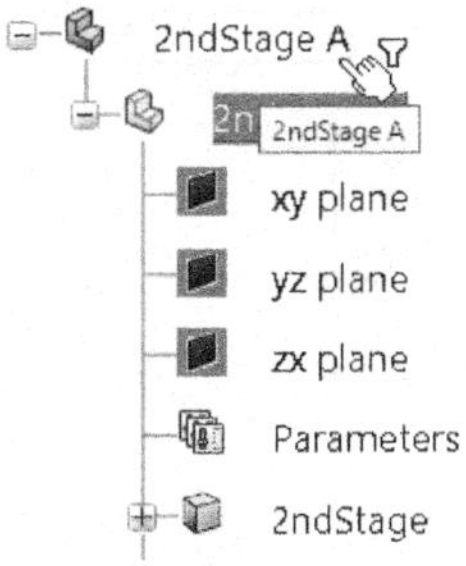

Figure A–36

10. Select **OK** to close the *Edit Links and Relations* window.

11. Leave the parts open for the next task.

Task 2 - Modify the pointed document.

1. Select the *2ndStage* tab to display the part.

2. Redefine **CircPattern.1** and modify the number of pattern instances to **3**. The body displays as shown in Figure A–37.

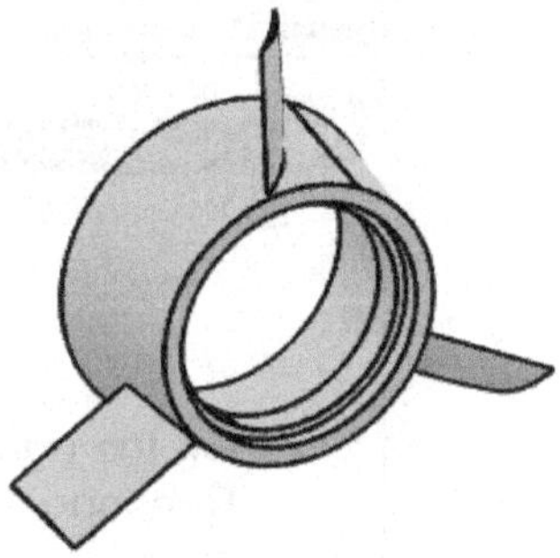

Figure A–37

3. Save the part and close the window.

4. Select the *3rdand2ndStage* tab to display the **3rdand2ndStage** model. The body displays as shown in Figure A–38. Note the status symbol of the **Solid.1** element.

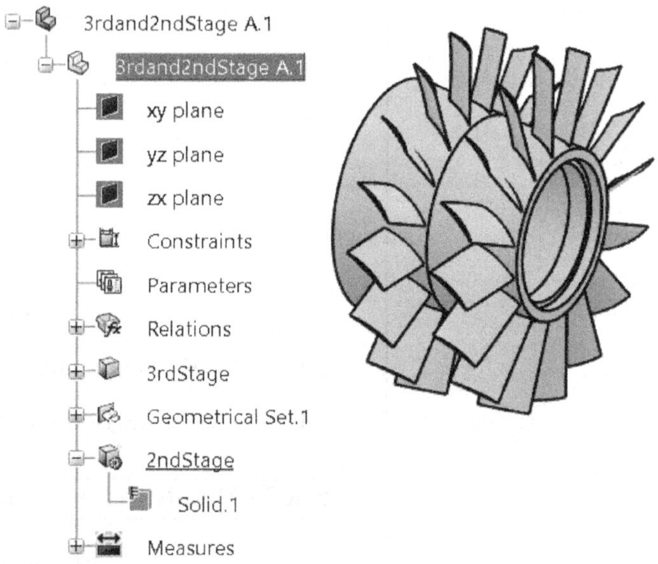

Figure A–38

Task 3 - Synchronize documents.

1. Select (Links and Relations) from the Tools section of the Action Bar.

2. Expand the + icons to the left of the listed items to see the link relationships and note that the Status is (Not Synchronized), as shown in Figure A–39.

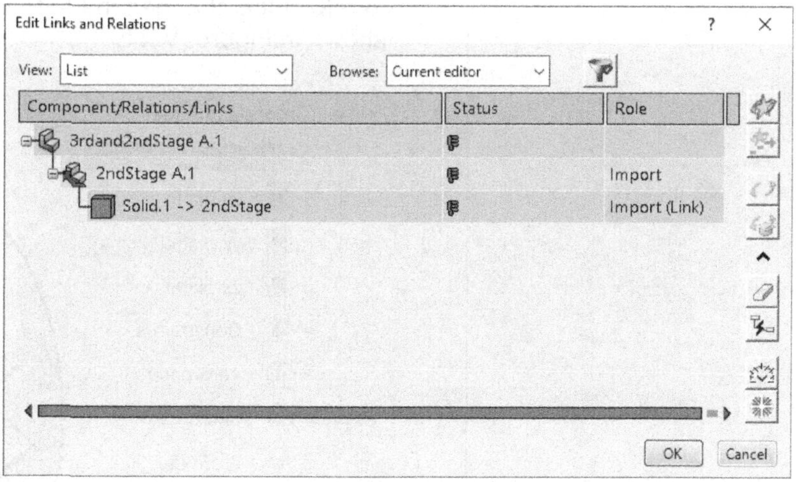

Figure A–39

3. Click (Synchronizes Link). The system synchronizes the link of the pointed document information into session and recognizes that changes have been made.

4. The status symbol of the **Solid.1** element indicates that the element needs to be updated, as shown in Figure A–40.

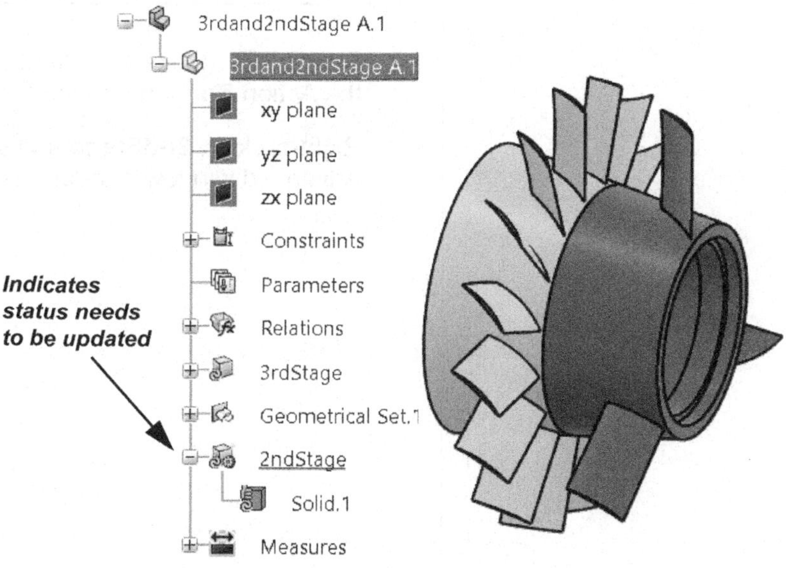

Figure A–40

5. Select **OK** to close the Edit Links and Relations window.

6. Click (Update) to update the body. The body is updated to reflect the changes made to the pointed document, as shown in Figure A–41.

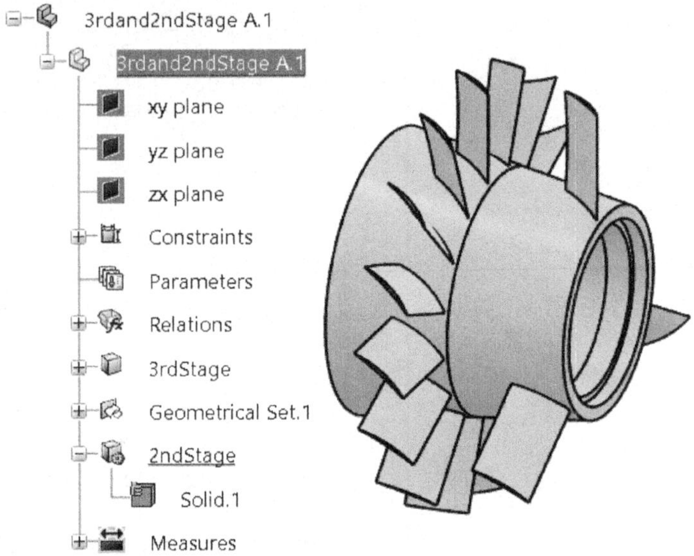

Figure A–41

Task 4 - Open and modify pointed document.

1. Select (Links and Relations) from the Tools section of the Action Bar and expand the links.

2. Right-click on **2ndStage** and select **Open**. The Open Advanced window appears as shown in Figure A–42.

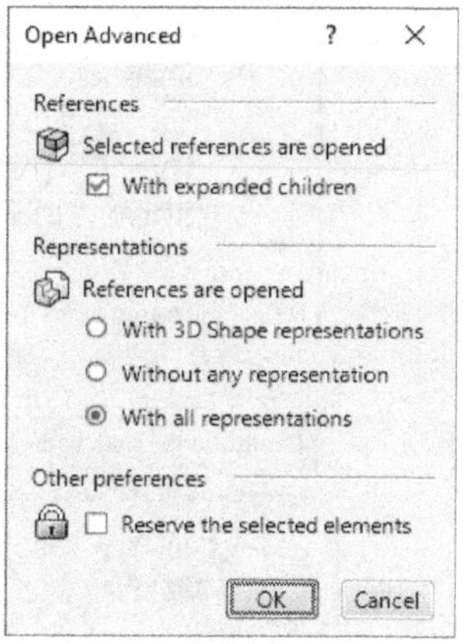

Figure A–42

3. Ensure the same options are selected as displayed in Figure A–42, then select **OK**. The **2ndStage** model displays.

4. Modify the circular pattern to **20** instances.

5. Activate the *3rdand2ndStag* tab. The model displays as shown in Figure A–43.

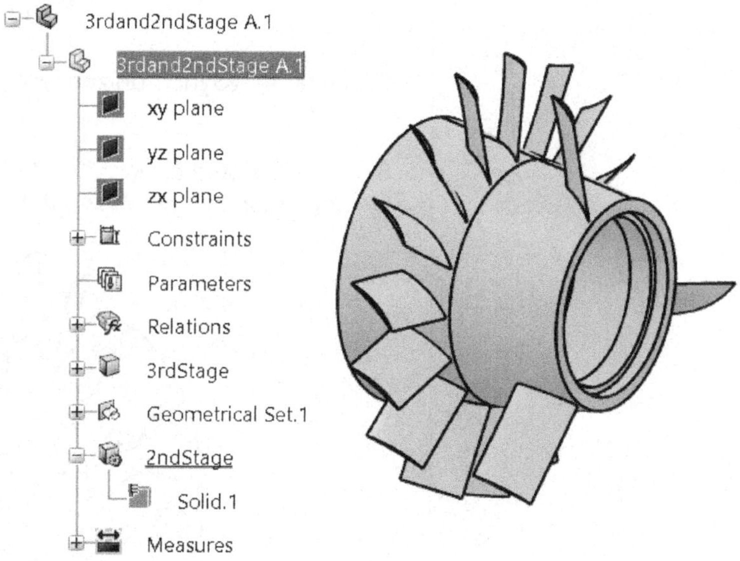

Figure A–43

6. Select (Links and Relations) and expand the links. Note the (Not synchronized) status in the *Status* column, as shown in Figure A–44.

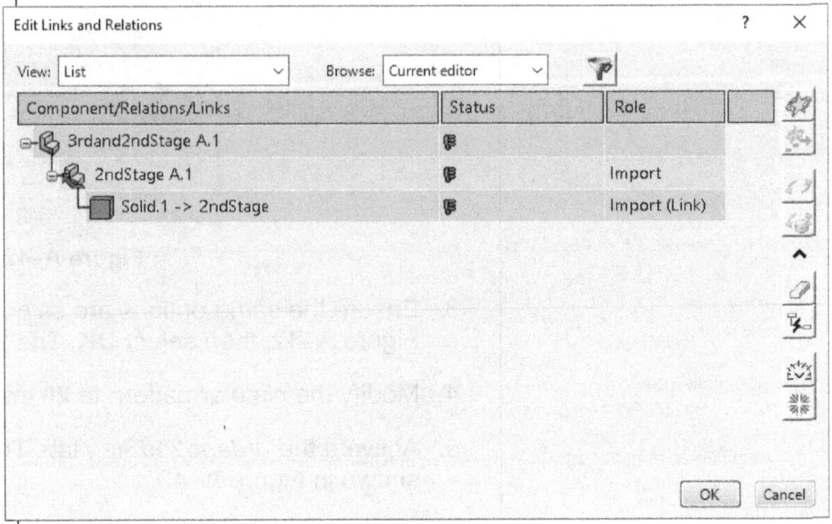

Figure A–44

7. Click (Synchronizes Link).

8. Click **OK** and click (Update) to update the body. The body displays as shown in Figure A–45.

Figure A–45

Task 5 - Break the external link.

1. Select (Links and Relations).

2. Click (Isolates Link), as shown in Figure A–46. Once isolated, the reference will be removed from the Edit Links and Relations window.

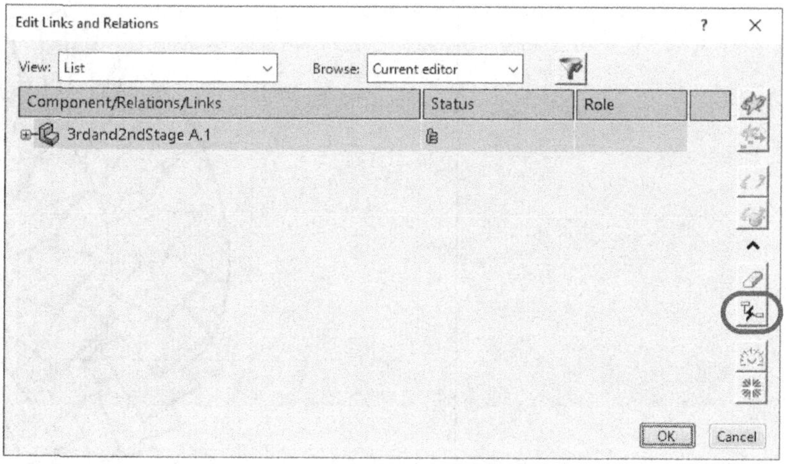

Figure A–46

3. Click **OK**. Note the status symbol of the **Solid.1** element, as shown in Figure A–47.

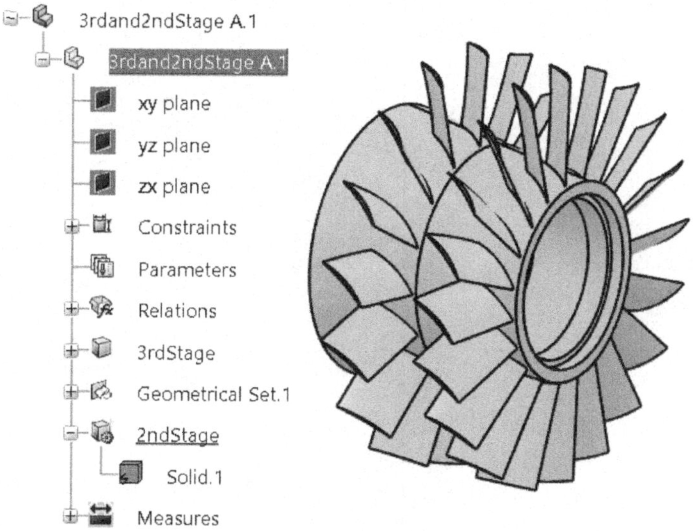

Figure A–47

4. Save the part.
5. Activate the *2ndStage* tab and modify the circular pattern to **16** instances.
6. Save the part and close the window.
7. Modify **CircPattern.1** of **2nd3rdStage** to **22** instances. The body displays as shown in Figure A–48.

Figure A–48

8. Save the model and close the window.

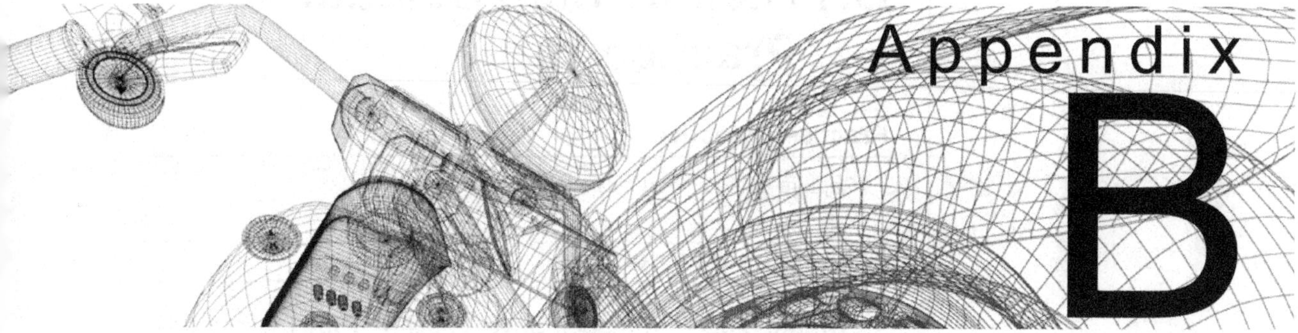

Appendix B

Advanced Practice Solution

This appendix provides a detailed solution to Practice 1a: Capturing Design Intent.

B.1 Step by Step Solution for Practice 1a

Practice Objective

- Capture design intent in Sketcher.

Task 1 - Create a new part.

1. Create a 3D Part model. Save it as **###_Pipe1** where ### represents your initials. The best selection for a Base feature is a Rib using the **Thick Profile** option.

Task 2 - Sketch a center curve.

1. Create the following sketch on the yz plane, as shown in Figure B–1.

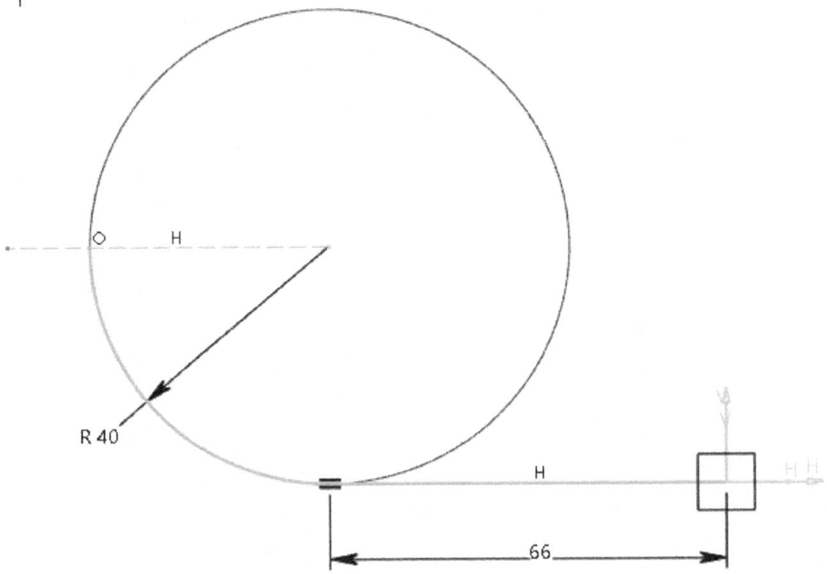

Figure B–1

Task 3 - Sketch a profile.

1. Create the following sketch on the zx plane, as shown in Figure B–2.

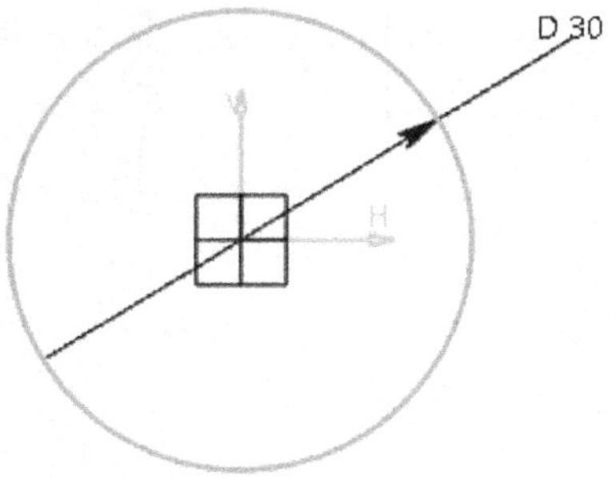

Figure B–2

Task 4 - Create a Rib feature.

1. Create a Rib feature, as shown in Figure B–3.

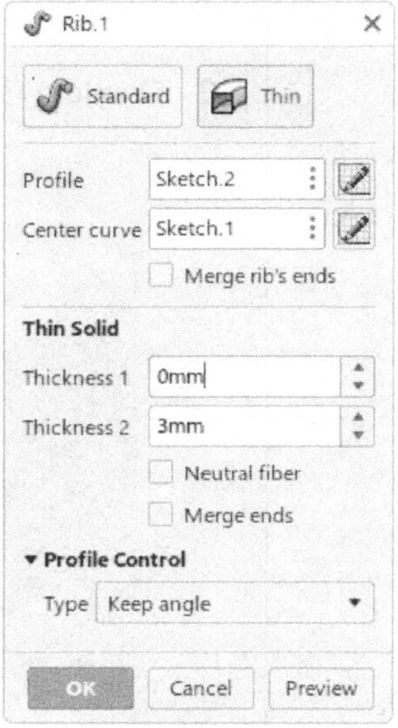

Figure B–3

Task 5 - Create a Pad for the holed flange.

1. Create the sketch shown in Figure B–4.

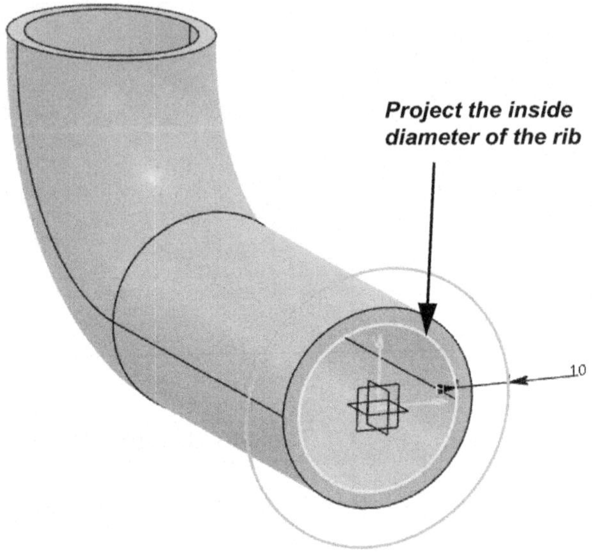

Figure B–4

2. Create a Pad feature, as shown in Figure B–5.

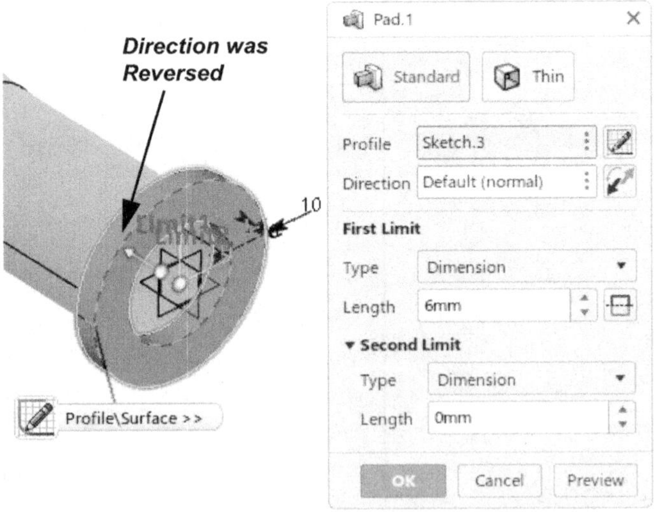

Figure B–5

Task 6 - Create a Pad for the grooved flange.

1. Create the sketch shown in Figure B–6.

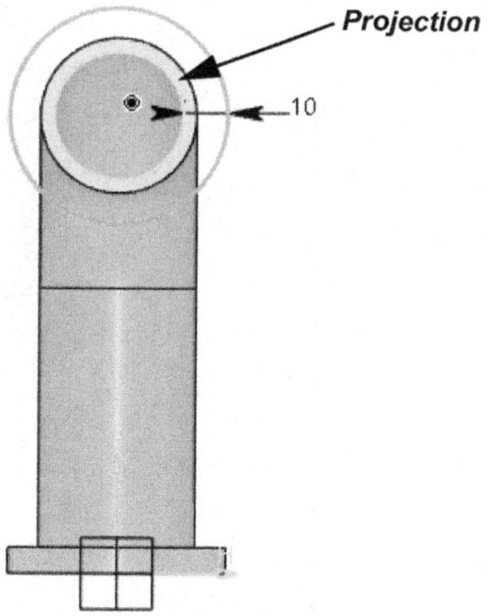

Figure B–6

2. Create the Pad shown in Figure B–7.

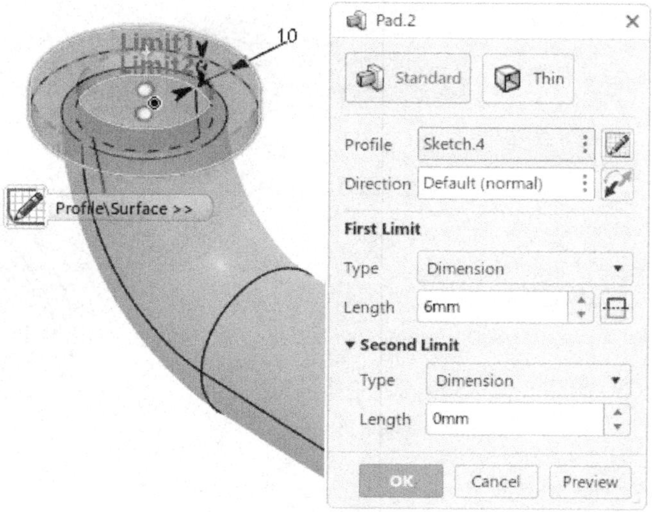

Figure B–7

Task 7 - Create a Pad for the pipe segment.

1. Create the sketch shown in Figure B–8.

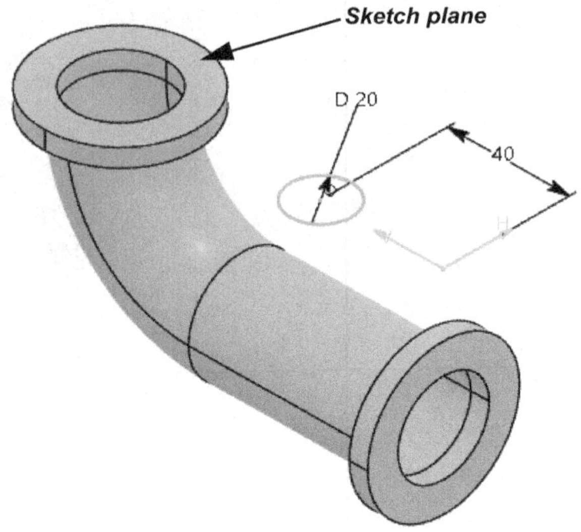

Figure B–8

2. Create the Pad feature shown in Figure B–9.

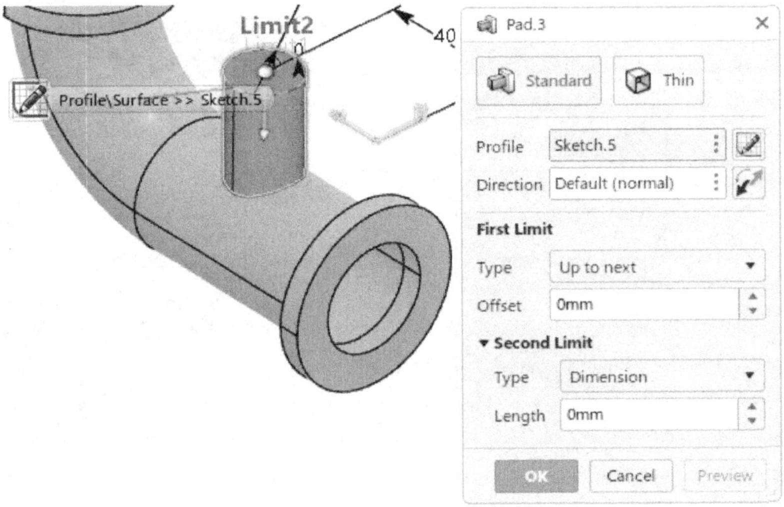

Figure B–9

Task 8 - Create a Pocket feature.

1. Create the sketch shown in Figure B–10.

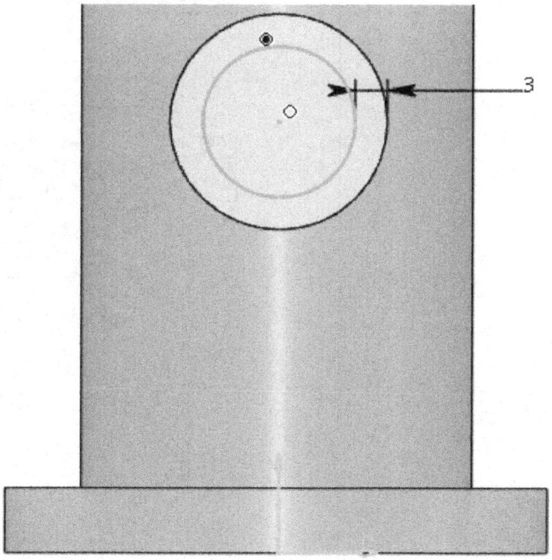

Figure B–10

2. Create the Pocket feature, as shown in Figure B–11.

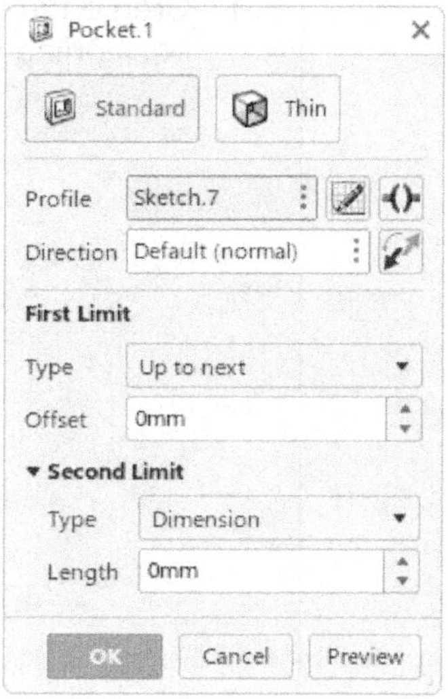

Figure B–11

Task 9 - Create a Groove feature.

1. Create the appropriate sketch and Groove feature shown in Figure B–12.

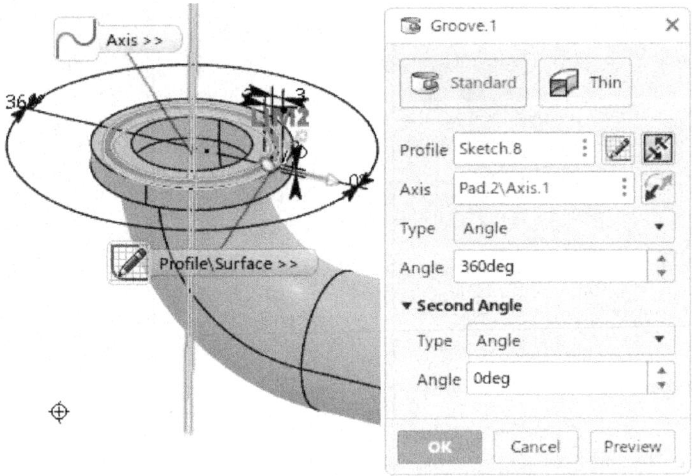

Figure B–12

Task 10 - Create a Hole feature.

1. Create the Hole feature shown in Figure B–13. The positioning sketch is shown in Figure B–14.

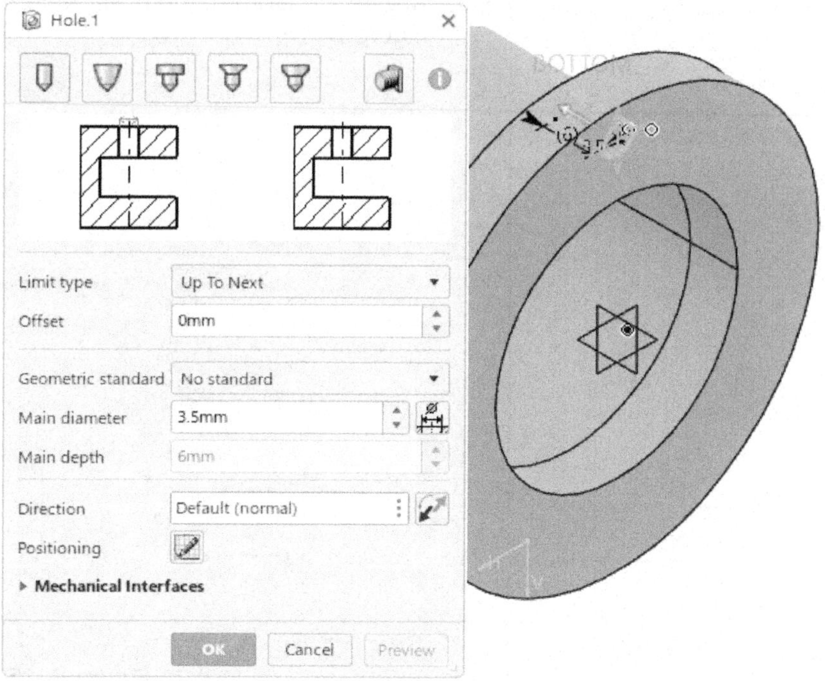

Figure B–13

2. Use the positioning sketch shown in Figure B–14 for the Hole feature.

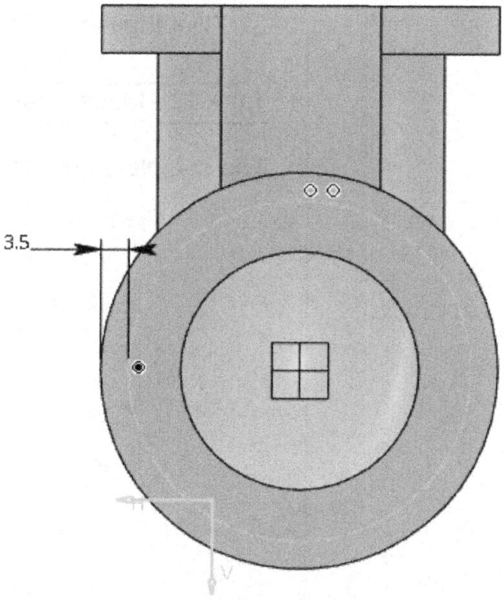

Figure B–14

3. Create a pattern of the Hole feature, as shown in Figure B–15.

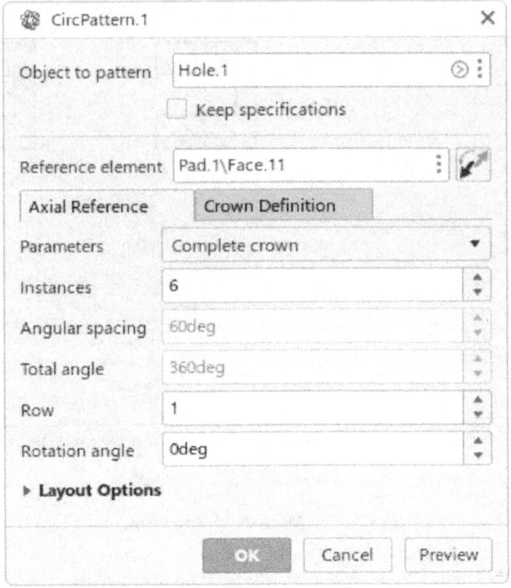

Figure B–15

Task 11 - Create dress-up features.

1. Create the appropriate chamfer.
2. Fillet the model using a single Fillet feature.

Task 12 - Make changes to the inside pipe diameter.

The completed model displays as shown in Figure B–16.

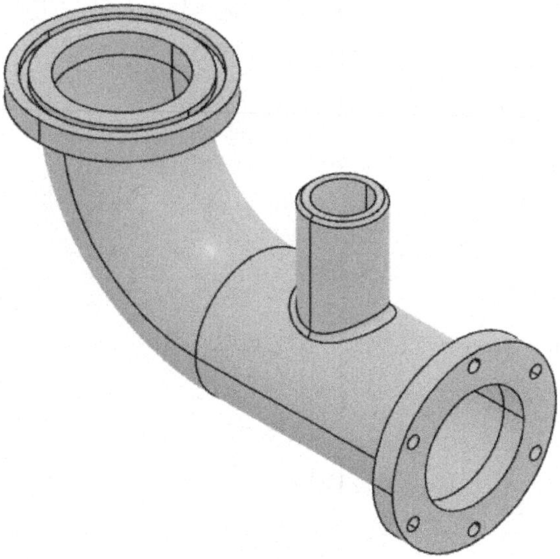

Figure B–16

1. Make dimensional changes to the inside diameter of the pipe to ensure that design requirements have been captured. The pipe displays as shown in Figure B–17.

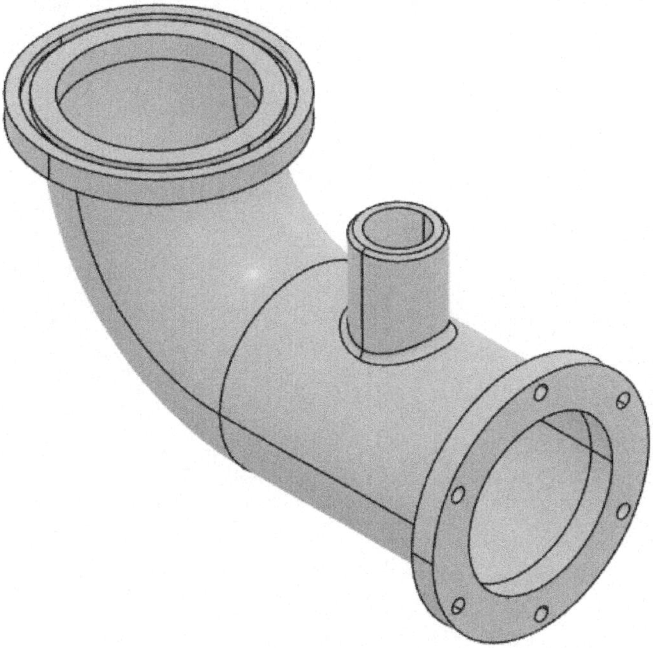

Figure B–17

2. Save the model and close the model.

Made in the USA
Las Vegas, NV
04 May 2026

46375062R00413